Nicaragua

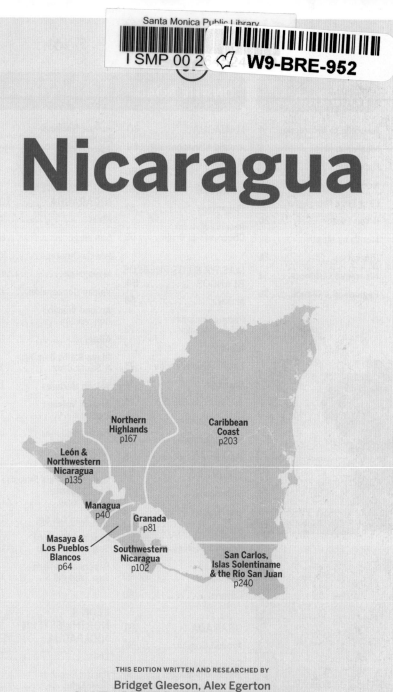

Northern
Highlands
p167

Caribbean
Coast
p203

León &
Northwestern
Nicaragua
p135

Managua
p40

Granada
p81

Masaya &
Los Pueblos
Blancos
p64

Southwestern
Nicaragua
p102

San Carlos,
Islas Solentiname
& the Río San Juan
p240

THIS EDITION WRITTEN AND RESEARCHED BY

Bridget Gleeson, Alex Egerton

Contents

GUIZIOU FRANCK/HEMISPICTURE.COM/GETTY IMAGES ©

EL CASTILLO, RÍO SAN JUAN
PAGE 253

KRYSIA CAMPOS/GETTY IMAGES ©

GRANADA PAGE 81

Contents

Welcome to Nicaragua

Affable Nicaragua embraces travelers with offerings of volcanic landscapes, colonial architecture, sensational beaches and pristine forests that range from breathtaking to downright incredible.

Beaches

Whether it's dipping your toes into the crystalline Caribbean or paddling out to the crashing waves of the pounding Pacific, Nicaragua's beaches always deliver the goods. The big barrels of Rivas are revered in surfing circles while the clear waters of the Corn Islands are superb for snorkeling. More sedentary beach bums can choose between accessible slices of sand lined with fine restaurants and happening bars, or natural affairs backed by a wall of rainforest. Even the best beaches in the country are refreshingly free of development, so you can experience them as nature intended.

Outdoor Adventures

Looking for the ultimate rush? Nicaragua's diverse geography, intense energy and 'anything goes' attitude is perfect for outdoor adventures. Get ready to check a whole gamut of new experiences off your list including surfing down an active volcano, diving into underwater caves, canoeing through alligator-infested wetlands, swimming across sea channels between tiny islands, and landing a 90-plus-kg tarpon beneath a Spanish fortress. Nicaragua's great outdoors are relatively untamed – at many key attractions, there are no signs and few crowds – making this so-called 'land of lakes and volcanoes' a fantastic place for an independent adventure.

Colonial Splendor

Nicaragua's colonial splendor comes in two distinct, but equally appealing, flavors. The elegant streetscapes of Granada, Nicaragua's best-preserved colonial town, have been entrancing travelers for centuries with their architectural grace. The town boasts a meticulously restored cathedral, well-groomed plaza and perfectly maintained mansions that shelter lush internal courtyards. Far less polished, working-class León offers a different colonial experience, where 300-year-old houses are interspersed with revolutionary murals, and architectural masterpieces house corner stores. It's a vibrant city that, while proud of its heritage, is too busy to feel like a museum.

Getting Off the Beaten Track

Few destinations have such beauty as Nicaragua, yet remain undeveloped. Drop off the tourist trail and into a world of majestic mountains, cooperative farms, wetlands thronged with wildlife and empty jungle-clad beaches. Rent a 4WD vehicle, if you're up for it – it's the best way to access some of the less-traveled corners of the country, provided you have a good map – and forge onward to discover remote indigenous communities, overgrown pre-Columbian ruins and untouched rainforests. No matter how far you go, you'll always find friendly locals willing to share their culture with strangers.

Why I Love Nicaragua

By Bridget Gleeson, Writer

I didn't get to know Nicaragua by traveling through its landscape. I hardly saw any of the country when I first came here – I was a volunteer at a non-profit organization in Granada. But I learned some things about Nicaraguan culture and the way people are; I learned to love Nicaraguan food and I started reading about the nation's complicated history. All of that has served me well during my travels here. I don't see Nicaragua as a destination to check off a list, but as a thoroughly unique and beautiful place – and one that's increasingly welcoming to travelers.

For more about our writers, see page 320

Nicaragua

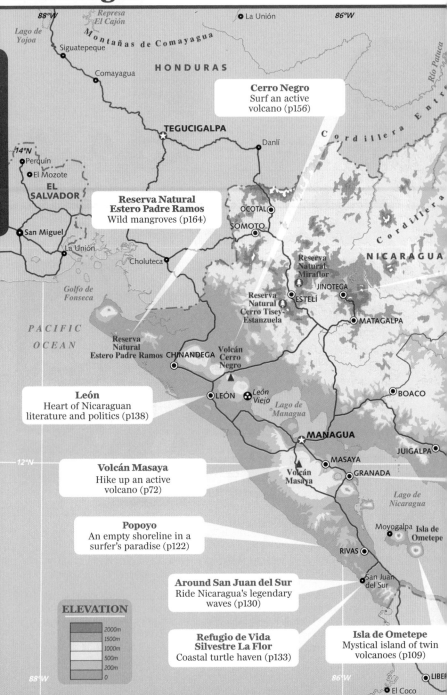

Cerro Negro
Surf an active
volcano (p156)

**Reserva Natural
Estero Padre Ramos**
Wild mangroves (p164)

León
Heart of Nicaraguan
literature and politics (p138)

Volcán Masaya
Hike up an active
volcano (p72)

Popoyo
An empty shoreline in a
surfer's paradise (p122)

Around San Juan del Sur
Ride Nicaragua's legendary
waves (p130)

**Refugio de Vida
Silvestre La Flor**
Coastal turtle haven (p133)

Isla de Ometepe
Mystical island of twin
volcanoes (p109)

ELEVATION

2000m
1500m
1000m
500m
200m
0

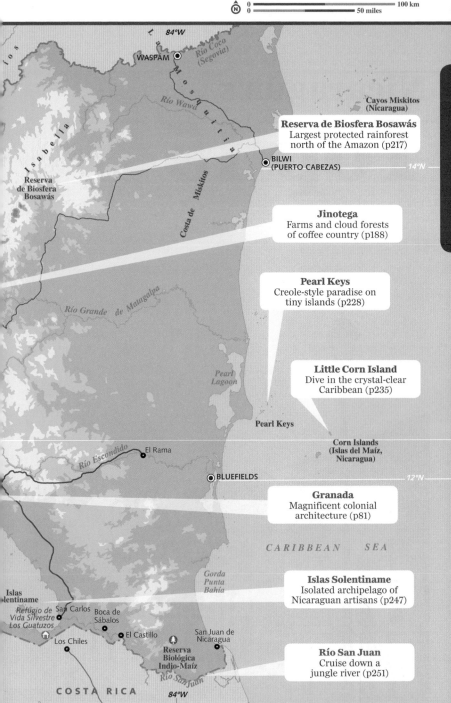

0   100 km
0   50 miles

84°W

WASPAM

Río Coco (Segovia)

Río Wawa

Cayos Miskitos (Nicaragua)

Reserva de Biosfera Bosawás
Largest protected rainforest
north of the Amazon (p217)

BILWI
(PUERTO CABEZAS)   14°N

Reserva
de Biosfera
Bosawás

Costa de Miskitos

Jinotega
Farms and cloud forests
of coffee country (p188)

Río Grande de Matagalpa

Pearl Keys
Creole-style paradise on
tiny islands (p228)

Little Corn Island
Dive in the crystal-clear
Caribbean (p235)

Pearl
Lagoon

Pearl Keys

Corn Islands
(Islas del Maíz,
Nicaragua)

Río Escondido   El Rama

BLUEFIELDS   12°N

Granada
Magnificent colonial
architecture (p81)

CARIBBEAN   SEA

Gorda
Punta
Bahía

Islas Solentiname
Isolated archipelago of
Nicaraguan artisans (p247)

Islas
Solentiname

Refugio de
Vida Silvestre   San Carlos   Boca de
Los Guatuzos   Sábalos

Los Chiles   El Castillo   San Juan de
Nicaragua

Reserva
Biológica
Indio-Maíz

Río San Juan
Cruise down a
jungle river (p251)

Río San Juan

COSTA RICA

84°W

Tortuguero

Nicaragua's
Top 15

1

Granada

1 Granada (p81) is a town of immense and palpable magnetism. At the heart of the city's charms are the picture-perfect cobblestone streets, polychromatic colonial homes and churches, and a lilting air that brings the city's spirited past into present-day focus. Most trips here begin and end on foot, and simply dawdling from gallery to restaurant to colonial church can take up the better part of a day. From there, it's off to explore the myriad wild areas, islands, volcanoes and artisan villages nearby. Catedral de Granada (p84)

Little Corn Island

2 With no cars and no noise, just white-sand beaches and secluded coves mixing with the crystal-clear Caribbean, Little Corn Island (p235) is the premier place to take a break from the big city. There is plenty to keep you occupied during the day, including diving with hammerhead sharks or through underground caves, kitesurfing the stiff breeze or scrambling over jungle-covered headlands, and there's just enough to do at night. Add some great food to the mix and it's no surprise that many find it so hard to leave. Spotted eagle rays

JANE SWEENEY/GETTY IMAGES ©

MARTIN STRMISKA/GETTY IMAGES ©

León

3 A royal city with revolutionary undercurrents, León (p138) both enchants and baffles the legions of backpackers and adventure seekers who gravitate here. You'll find an artsy, slightly edgy vibe originally fueled by the Sandinista revolution and now by the university and a 120-horsepower party scene. Come sunrise, you can spend a day exploring the cathedral (below), museums and downtown area, before heading further afield to honey-blonde beaches, volcanoes, brokeback cowboy towns and open-faced experiences with some of the friendliest people you'll find anywhere on earth.

Isla de Ometepe

4 Lago de Nicaragua's beloved centerpiece, Isla de Ometepe (p109) has it all. Twin volcanoes, lush hillsides cut by walking tracks, archaeological remains, zip lines, monkeys and birdlife, waterfalls, lapping waves at your doorstep, and a laidback island vibe that keeps travelers in the now as they kayak, bike and climb their way through this lost paradise found again. At the heart of the island's charms are cool hostels, camping areas and peaced-out traveler scenes, Ometepe is big enough for all kinds. Volcán Concepción (p114)

Pearl Keys

5 As you approach the dozen tiny islands ringed by snow-white sand and brilliant Caribbean waters that make up the Pearl Keys (p228), you will enter the realms of the ultimate shipwreck fantasy. Fortunately, you'll be marooned with a capable Creole guide who will cook a spectacular seafood meal and source ice-cold beers from a mysterious supply, leaving you more time to swim, snorkel, spot sea turtles, or just lie back in your hammock and take in the idyllic panoramic views.

Río San Juan

6 Once favored by pirates and prospectors as a path to riches, today the Río San Juan (p251) is exalted by nature lovers. All along the river, scores of birds nest on branches overhanging its slow surging waters, while its lower reaches are dominated by the Reserva Biológica Indio-Maíz, an almost impenetrable jungle that shelters jaguars and troupes of noisy monkeys. The only human-made attraction along the river's entire length is the grand Spanish fort over the rapids at El Castillo. Top right: Howler monkey

Coffee Country

7 A visit to Nicaragua's coffee zone is about more than just sipping plenty of joe: it's about getting out and seeing where it all comes from. Hike among the bushes shaded by ethereal cloud forest around Jinotega (p188) and pick ripe cherries alongside your hosts in a community farming cooperative near Matagalpa. And why stop there when you can follow the beans to the roasting plant and then learn to identify flavors in a cupping session. After this, you'll savor your morning cup in a whole new way.

Turtles at La Flor

8 Head to Nicaragua's southern Pacific coast between July and January to witness sea turtles by the thousands come ashore to lay their eggs at Refugio de Vida Silvestre La Flor (p133). There's a decent beach here as well, but the highlight is a night tour (generally from nearby San Juan del Sur) where, if you're lucky, you'll see a leatherback or olive ridley mama come to shore to lay her eggs to end one of nature's most inspiring and remarkable journeys.

Islas Solentiname

9 The Islas Solentiname (p247) are straight out of a fairy tale. You simply must visit in order to experience the magic of this remote jungle-covered archipelago where a community of exceptionally talented artists live and work among the wild animals that are their inspiration. It's a place where an enlightened priest inspired a village to construct a handsome church alive with the sounds of nature, and shooting stars illuminate the speckled night sky. Even having been there, you still find it hard to believe it's real. Nuestra Señora de Solentiname (p247)

The Remote Beaches of Popoyo

10 It's a bumpy ride from Rivas to the remote beaches of Popoyo (p122), famous for their surf breaks. The reward: huge, rolling waves, laid-back surf lodges, sandy shores strewn with vibrant pink shells, looming rock formations and miles of empty shoreline where you can walk for an hour without seeing another person. New surf lodges and guesthouses are opening left and right in this rapidly developing region, but for the moment, these beaches still feel wild. Bring your board, or a good book.

Volcano Boarding on Cerro Negro

11 What goes up must come down. But why walk when you can strap on a custom-built volcano board and rip-roar your way down a slope of fine volcanic ash? That's the genesis of volcano surfing. And one of the best spots on the planet to dig this new adrenaline sport is atop 700-plus-meter Volcán Cerro Negro (p156) in northwestern Nicaragua's Reserva Natural Pilas-El Hoyo. Tour operators in León will even provide you with cool jumpsuits before your dusty-bottomed descent.

PAUL KENNEDY/GETTY IMAGES ©

Wildlife-Watching

12 From the colorful parakeets flying over busy Managua to ubiquitous iguanas scratching across your hotel roof, exotic wildlife is everywhere in Nicaragua. Dedicate some energy to the pursuit and you'll discover some truly phenomenal natural spectacles. Head into the rugged rainforest-covered mountains of the Bosawás (p217) to spot three types of monkeys, toucans and tapirs, while reptile fans will not want to miss getting close to the alligators of Los Guatuzos. Wherever you go, keep your binoculars handy – a wild encounter is never far away.

Reserva Natural Estero Padre Ramos

13 The Reserva Natural Estero Padre Ramos (p164) is a vast nature reserve located in the far northwestern corner of Nicaragua. The largest remaining mangrove forest in Central America, the reserve is home to ocelots, alligators and a universe's worth of birds. While this is a wild corner of Nicaragua, basic tourist services will get you into the spider-webbing mangrove forest, to the surf beaches where sea turtles lay their eggs, and into local communities.

Surfing Near San Juan del Sur

14 Nicaragua sparked into international surf stardom on the wake of tanned-and-toned surfer dudes and dudettes. The surfing scene north and south of regional hub San Juan del Sur (p124) remains cool, reefed-out, soulful and downright brilliant. The stars of the scene are the long rideable waves that cater for surfers of all abilities, but the relaxed surf camps, beach parties and cool breezes add to the vibe, ensuring a great beach vacation for everybody in your crew (even the boogie boarders). Surfer on Playa Maderas (p131)

14

Volcán Masaya & Laguna de Apoyo

15 Hovering above the artisan villages of Nicaragua's Central Plateau, the smoldering Volcán Masaya (p72) and its surrounding national park are a singular highlight not to be missed. This is one of the region's most active volcanoes, and it's pretty exciting just to see the sulfurous columns of gas billow toward the sky as you relish the million-dollar views. Short treks take you to lava caves and butterfly gardens. Afterward, cool off with a dip in gorgeous Laguna de Apoyo (p99), a nearby crater lake.

CHRISTIAN HEEB/GETTY IMAGES ©

15

Need to Know

For more information, see Survival Guide (p289)

Currency
Córdoba (C$)

Language
Spanish

Visas
Generally not required for stays up to three months.

Money
ATMs are widespread in most midsize towns in Nicaragua; stock up on cash in córdobas before heading to rural areas. Credit cards are widely accepted in larger towns but rarely in rural areas. US dollars widely accepted, but for smaller items using córdobas is easier.

Cell Phones
Many travelers buy a phone upon arrival – prices start at around US$15. You can also buy a SIM card (around US$3.50) and insert it into any unlocked GSM phone. Electronic top-ups are available at *pulperías* (corner stores) and gas stations.

Time
Central Standard Time (GMT/UTC minus six hours)

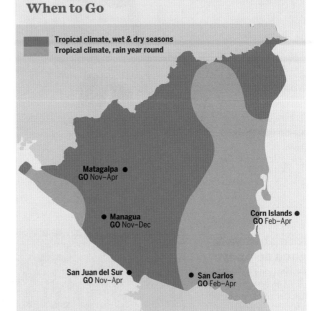

When to Go

■ Tropical climate, wet & dry seasons
■ Tropical climate, rain year round

Matagalpa
GO Nov–Apr

Managua
GO Nov–Dec

Corn Islands
GO Feb–Apr

San Juan del Sur
GO Nov–Apr

San Carlos
GO Feb–Apr

High Season (Dec–Apr)

➡ Prices increase by up to 25% in popular tourist spots.

➡ Make reservations in advance for beachside accommodations.

➡ Hot, sunny and dry conditions in most parts of the country.

Shoulder (Nov)

➡ Rains ease throughout the Pacific but the Caribbean coast is still wet.

➡ Cool weather and green countryside make for the best trekking.

➡ Coffee harvesting energizes the northern region.

Low Season (May–Oct)

➡ Heavy rains make some roads in rural areas difficult to pass and mountain hiking trails slippery.

➡ The biggest swell on the Pacific side pulls a crowd to the best breaks.

➡ Advanced reservations are generally not necessary.

Useful Websites

Lonely Planet (www.lonely planet.com/nicaragua) A comprehensive online overview of the country for travelers.

Vianica.com (www.vianica.com/traveling) Log on to this interactive map and click on your route to find Nicaraguan road conditions, travel-time estimates and more.

Intur (www.visitanicaragua.com/ingles) The official government website is in English and Spanish, with lots of cheerful, vague information and an awesome photo gallery.

Important Numbers

Nicaragua country code	☏505
International access code	☏00
Fire	☏115 from cell phones ☏911
Police	☏118
Ambulance	☏128

Exchange Rates

Australia	A$1	C$19.80
Canada	C$1	C$20.05
Costa Rica	₡100	C$5.23
Euro	€1	C$30.39
Japan	¥100	C$23.12
New Zealand	NZ$1	C$18.12
UK	UK£1	C$39.94
US	US$1	C$28.04

For current exchange rates, see www.xe.com.

Daily Costs

Budget: Less than US$35

➡ Dorm bed: US$9–15

➡ Typical meal: US$4

➡ Museum admission: US$2

➡ Local bus: US$0.15–1

Midrange: US$35–80

➡ Double bed in a midrange hotel: US$20–45

➡ Restaurant meal: US$10–12

➡ Adventure tour: US$25–30

➡ Short taxi ride: US$2–3

Top end: More than US$80

➡ Double bed in a luxury hotel: US$80–120

➡ Gourmet meal: US$18–22

➡ Car hire: US$40–60

➡ Internal flight: US$100–120

Opening Hours

Opening hours vary wildly in Nicaragua as there are many informal and family-run establishments. General office hours are from 9am to 5pm. Some offices and shops close for lunch from noon to 2pm. Government departments usually close earlier and also take a meal break.

Comedores (cheap eateries) usually open for breakfast and lunch while more formal restaurants serve lunch and dinner.

Banks 8:30am–4:30pm Monday to Friday, to noon Saturday

Comedores 6am–4pm

Government Offices 8am–noon & 1–4pm Monday to Friday, 8am–noon Saturday

Museums 9am–noon & 2–5pm

Restaurants noon–10pm

Bars noon–midnight

Clubs 9pm–3am

Shops 9am–6pm Monday to Saturday

Arriving in Managua

Managua International Airport (Managua) Official taxis inside the airport meet all incoming flights and charge around US$20 to most local destinations. During the day, more economical licensed collective taxis wait outside the domestic terminal. It's possible to flag down a cheaper taxi out on the highway but it's not recommended for security reasons. If you're heading out of Managua, it's possible to prearrange a pickup with a private shuttle service.

Urban buses head into town from the highway across the road from the terminal, but are rife with pickpockets and are not a convenient option if you have baggage.

Getting Around

Transport in Nicaragua is functional rather than comfortable, and probably more chaotic than you are used to.

Flights Domestic flights are moderately priced and the fastest way to get you where you're going; however, they only serve more far-off destinations. Often delayed, but rarely canceled.

Car Renting a car enables travel at your own pace and access to off-the-beaten-track destinations. There is not much traffic on the roads and driving in Nicaragua is fairly stress-free (once you learn how to handle the traffic cops).

Buses Nicaragua's old-school buses are slow and uncomfortable but will get you anywhere for next to nothing. There are more comfortable, but far from luxurious, coach services to some long-distance destinations.

PLAN YOUR TRIP NEED TO KNOW

For much more on **getting around**, see p299

First Time Nicaragua

For more information, see Survival Guide (p289)

Checklist

➡ Make sure your passport is valid for at least six months from your entry date

➡ Check latest visa requirements online

➡ Arrange travel insurance with medical evacuation cover

➡ Inform your debit/credit-card issuer that you are traveling to Central America

➡ Organize vaccinations against hepatitis A and typhoid, and consult your doctor about malaria prophylactics

What to Pack

➡ Sturdy walking shoes

➡ Comfortable sports sandals

➡ Insect repellent containing DEET

➡ An emergency supply of US dollars in small bills

➡ A two-pronged electrical adapter

➡ A lightweight raincoat capable of resisting tropical downpours

➡ Contact lens solution and other personal toiletries

Top Tips for Your Trip

➡ Always go for a window seat in public transport: the landscapes are absolutely breathtaking.

➡ Take some Spanish classes. Nicaraguans are outgoing and friendly but few have foreign-language skills.

➡ Hire local guides wherever possible; they're cheap and you'll learn about the attraction you're visiting and about the culture.

➡ Forget about keeping a tight schedule in Nicaragua. Allow extra days in your trip, especially if you're traveling by public transport.

➡ Take advantage of the hearty Nicaraguan-style breakfast served at most hotels (either complimentary or for a low price) – it will get you through a good part of the day.

➡ When in doubt about getting into a taxi, just ask your hostel or hotel to call you one – and agree on a price before getting in.

What to Wear

The heat in Nicaragua can be oppressive, so you'll probably spend most of your time in lightweight T-shirts and shorts or cotton trousers. If you're heading to the northern highlands, you'll probably make use of a pullover for the cool evenings.

Note that in general, men in Nicaragua don't wear shorts unless practicing sports. Go for a jeans and short-sleeved shirt or polo shirt if you are going out with locals.

On the beach women going topless is almost never acceptable, and in rural areas bikinis may draw unwanted attention; consider swimming in shorts and a T-shirt like the locals.

Sleeping

➡ **Hospedajes** These cheap guesthouses are often family-run and are sometimes the only option in smaller towns.

➡ **Hotels** Larger, more polished and less personal; they offer facilities including reception and often a restaurant.

➡ **Hostels** Travelers' hostels with dormitories and common areas are found in the main tourist areas.

➡ **Ecolodges** Usually at the higher end of the market, these offer comfortable rooms surrounded by nature.

Dangers & Annoyances

Despite the fact that Nicaragua has one of the lowest crime rates in Central America, as a 'wealthy' foreigner you will probably be considered a potential target by scam artists and thieves.

➡ Pay extra attention to personal safety in Managua, the Caribbean region, around remote southern beaches and in undeveloped nature reserves.

➡ In larger cities, ask your hotel to call a trusted taxi.

➡ Backcountry hikers should note there may be unexploded ordinance in very remote areas, especially around the Honduran border. If in doubt, take a local guide.

Bargaining

All-out haggling is not really part of Nicaraguan culture. However, a bit of bargaining over a hotel room is considered acceptable, and negotiating the price in markets or with roadside vendors is the norm.

Tipping

Tipping is not widespread in Nicaragua except with guides and at restaurants.

➡ **Guides** Tipping guides is recommended as this often makes up the lion's share of their salary.

➡ **Restaurants** A tip of around 10% is expected for table service. Some high-end restaurants automatically add this to the bill. Small and/or rural eateries may not include the tip, so leave behind a few coins.

LANGUAGE

Even in major tourist destinations, very few Nicaraguans speak English. Learning a few basic phrases in Spanish will make your travels much more rewarding, especially if you're traveling to remote rural destinations. Hiring an interpreter to accompany you around town or on longer trips is affordable – ask at your hotel.

On the Caribbean coast English speakers will have no problem communicating with Creole residents, once you're used to the accent and grammar.

Etiquette

➡ **Greetings** A firm handshake for men and a peck on the cheek for women.

➡ **Titles** When addressing Nicaraguans add *don* (for men) or *doña* (for women) before their given name.

➡ **Drinking** If you are sharing a bottle of rum, use the supplied shot glass to measure your drink; don't pour freely from the bottle.

If You Like

Beaches

The Pacific has the waves, the Caribbean has the reefs.

Little Corn Island Brilliant turquoise waters meet snow-white sand in secluded coves on this enchanted isle. (p235)

Playa El Coco A spectacular stretch of sparkling sand framed by imposing forest-covered headlands. (p133)

Pearl Keys Live out your shipwreck fantasies beneath the coconut palms on this group of tiny, idyllic Caribbean islands. (p228)

El Ostional Charming fishing village with a sweeping brown-sand beach. (p134)

Playa Aserradores Long, smooth stretch of sand with a powerful, hollow beach break. (p163)

Popoyo Famous surf breaks and miles of practically untouched shoreline make Popoyo a current hot spot. (p122)

Volcanoes

Volcán Masaya Watch parakeets return to nest among clouds of sulfuric gases above visible pools of lava. (p72)

Volcán Maderas Hike up through cloud forest to reach a chilly jade-green crater lake. (p118)

Volcán Momotombo Perched regally at the top of Lake Managua, its perfect cone is a symbol of Nicaragua. (p155)

Volcán Cosigüina Climb the remnants of what was Central America's biggest volcano to look out over three countries. (p165)

Volcán Mombacho Accessible cloud forest with great hiking and even better birdwatching. (p97)

Colonial Towns

Granada Charge your batteries. Nicaragua's wonderfully preserved colonial showpiece lays on the charm from the moment you get off the bus. (p81)

León Energetic and unpretentious, this gregarious city has stunning colonial streetscapes, awe-inspiring churches and cosmopolitan eateries. (p138)

Ciudad Antigua Boasting a remarkable Moorish-influenced 17th-century church, this is one of Nicaragua's oldest towns. (p184)

San Rafael del Norte Surrounded by peaks, this charming small town is centered around the light-filled Templo Parroquial San Rafael Arcángel. (p187)

Coffee

Matagalpa and Jinotega departments have the pedigree but Estelí and little-visited Nueva Segovia also produce some outstanding beans.

La Bastilla Ecolodge Hike through immense shade-grown coffee plantations before improving your cupping skills at the laboratory. (p192)

San Ramón Try your hand picking coffee beans at local farms then visit a community roasting plant. (p197)

Selva Negra Follow the coffee from bush to cup or just sit by the mist-covered lake and enjoy a freshly brewed mug. (p199)

Área Protegida Miraflor Combine your coffee tour with a spot of birdwatching or a visit to waterfalls surrounded by cloud forest. (p175)

Wildlife

Refugio de Vida Silvestre La Flor Watching thousands of marine turtles laying their eggs on this beach is one of Latin America's superlative nature experiences. (p133)

Refugio Bartola Don rubber boots and head out into the jungle to spot three kinds of monkeys, fluorescent frogs and maybe even a tapir. (p256)

Refugio de Vida Silvestre Los Guatuzos Perfectly preserved wetlands with fantastic bird-watching during the day and action-packed crocodile-spotting at night. (p251)

Islas Solentiname Bring binoculars to spot some of the thousands of migratory birds nesting in this remote archi-pelago. (p247)

Reserva Natural Macizos de Peñas Blancas Clinging to magnificent mountain peaks, this jungle is home to pumas, jaguars and ocelots. (p200)

Reserva Natural Isla Juan Venado Take a nighttime turtle tour during laying season – July through January – at this barrier island. (p161)

Outdoor Adventure

Volcano Boarding Volcán Cerro Negro is one of the few places on the planet to tick this deranged adventure sport off your list. (p146)

Kayaking & Canoeing Paddle through the mangroves of Padre Ramos, down the mighty Río San Juan or around majestic Isla de Ometepe. (p164)

Tubing Float with the current down the narrow **Cañón de Somoto**. (p180)

Diving Head to the Corn Islands for cave and reef dives in crystal-clear Caribbean waters. (p230)

Surfing Base yourself in San Juan del Sur, a vibrant beach town surrounded by top-class breaks. (p124)

Canopy Tour Thirsting for adven-ture in the capital? Try a canopy tour high above Managua's Tiscapa Lagoon. (p48)

Top: Catedral de Granada (p84)
Bottom: Iguana Beach (p236), Little Corn Island

Month by Month

January

Perfect beach weather in the Pacific region with almost nonstop sunshine, but it's the peak season so expect bigger crowds and more expensive accommodations.

☆ Baseball Finals

Stadiums get packed for the finals of the Liga Nacional de Béisbol Nicaraguense (Nicaraguan National Baseball League; www.lnbp.com.ni). Catch games at the Estadio Denis Martínez in Managua. (p55)

February

Crowds thin out but it's still all sunshine, making this one of the best times to plan a beach break. Can be uncomfortably hot in cities.

☆ International Poetry Festival

Top Spanish-language wordsmiths from around the globe gather for this festival (www.festivalpoesia nicaragua.com) in Granada, with regular readings and low-key fringe events.

March

The heat wave continues with soaring temperatures and dry conditions. Whether it falls in March or April, Easter is big business: prices spike, accommodations sell out and beaches are packed.

☆ San Lázaro

Head to Masaya on the weekend before Palm Sunday for this religious festival that involves getting dressed up in bizarre costumes – even local dogs get in on the act.

☆ Semana Santa

Easter is a major event all over the country but nowhere does it quite like León, where the traditional fireworks and parades are accompanied by sawdust mosaics and a sandcastle competition.

April

More sunshine, this time accompanied by big surf in the Pacific and calm seas throughout the Caribbean. After Easter, crowds drop dramatically.

☆ Surf's Up!

The combination of big swells along the Pacific and bright sunshine brings optimal conditions (and big crowds) to many of Nicaragua's best surf breaks, including the acclaimed Popoyo.

May

Low season is underway with sunshine still sticking around, but by the end of the month the skies open, marking the beginning of the wet season.

☆ Maypole

Bluefields celebrates fertility with a series of neighborhood block parties. It culminates in a bright and boisterous carnival on the last Saturday of the month. During the closing Tululu, the entire town takes a midnight romp through the streets accompanied by a brass band.

June

Heavy rains drench the entire country. This brings significantly cooler temperatures, but turns some rural roads into impassable pools of mud.

San Juan de Bautista

The normally serene flower-growing town of Catarina is transformed by this wild festival in honor of San Juan Bautista, featuring dancing, ceremonial fights and music.

July

Rains continue unabated throughout the country. Most hiking trails are now muddy but waterfalls are at their spectacular best.

Aniversario de la Revolución

Dress in red and black, and head to the plaza in Managua to celebrate the revolution alongside hard-drinking Sandinista supporters from across Nicaragua. Or check out the bohemian fringe event in nearby San Antonio, with fewer speeches and more music.

August

Rains generally ease a little in the Pacific with most days enjoying stretches of sunshine. Meanwhile, the Caribbean experiences one of its wettest months.

Santo Domingo de Guzmán

Managua's biggest religious procession sees believers covering themselves in pitch-black motor oil to accompany a tiny statue of the saint in his journey from the hills of Santo Domingo into the heart of the capital.

Crab Soup

Great Corn Island celebrates the end of slavery with a parade, concerts, plenty of beer, and free bowls of crab soup and ginger bread for all in attendance.

Fiestas de Agosto

Halfway through sultry August, Granada breaks into a festive weeklong celebration to honor the Assumption of Mary. Expect religious processions – the most important one happens on August 15 – equestrian parades, food stands, fireworks and live music in the parks, and revelry by the lakefront.

September

The height of hurricane season in the Caribbean may disrupt travel plans, although when there are no storms the weather is generally bright and there are great deals on accommodations.

October

Rains return throughout the Pacific with frequent heavy downpours in the afternoons. Traveler numbers reach their lowest point.

Turtle-Watching

Refugio de Vida Silvestre La Flor is the backdrop for one of nature's most amazing spectacles when olive ridley turtles arrive en masse (sometimes up to 3000 in one night) to lay their eggs on the sandy shores.

Noche de Agüizotes

This spooky festival in Masaya brings to life characters from horror stories of the colonial period with elaborate costumes. Keep an eye out for the headless priest.

November

Things get moving again following the easing of the rain. Travelers spread out throughout the country and the festival season warms up with a number of important events.

Garifuna Week

Nicaragua's Garifuna community celebrates their rich cultural heritage with drums, dancing and gastronomy in the remote community of Orinoco on the shores of Laguna de Perlas. The closing concert features Garifuna artists from throughout Central America.

December

The end of the rains in the Pacific region sees the high season begin in earnest and beaches becoming busy.

La Purísima

Celebrated on the eve of the Immaculate Concepcíon, La Purísima (and La Gritería) sees hordes of children going door-to-door singing songs to the Virgin Mary and receiving candies. It's celebrated throughout the country but León gets into it with unrivaled vigor.

Plan Your Trip
Itineraries

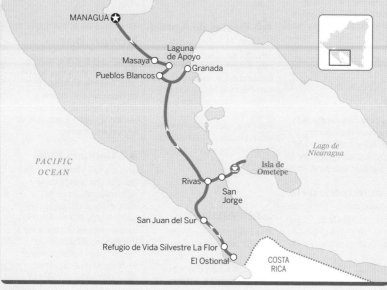

MARTIN PUIG/GETTY IMAGES ©

MANAGUA ★

Laguna de Apoyo

Masaya

Pueblos Blancos

Granada

Lago de Nicaragua

PACIFIC OCEAN

Isla de Ometepe

Rivas

San Jorge

San Juan del Sur

Refugio de Vida Silvestre La Flor

El Ostional

COSTA RICA

Stunning Southwest

If you have limited time in Nicaragua, a trip through the southwest is big on awesome and small on hours in the bus. The region is a condensed wonderland of barreling surf, volcanoes, crater lakes, colonial towns and artisan villages that includes many of Nicaragua's must-see highlights.

Fly into **Managua** and take in the view across town from Sandino's silhouette on the Loma de Tiscapa before heading south and descending into the lush crater at **Laguna de Apoyo** for the night. Spend the next day swimming in the rich sulfurous waters or spotting birds and howler monkeys in the forest, before enjoying the spectacular night sky.

The following morning, visit the artisan workshops of the nearby **Pueblos Blancos**, including the pottery cooperative at San Juan de Oriente.

Then head 30 minutes down the road for some colonial splendor in charismatic **Granada**. Spend three nights taking in the wonderful streetscapes, visiting the museums and churches, and dining in the fine restaurants. While you're here take a

Laguna de Apoyo (p99)

kayaking day trip through the islets just offshore, and hike among the cloud forest atop Volcán Mombacho.

Next head down the highway via **Rivas** to **San Jorge**. From here take the ferry to the out-of-this world **Isla de Ometepe** with its twin volcanoes and endless outdoor activities. Spend a night among the howler monkeys at Reserva Charco Verde and another at the base of Volcán Maderas, from where you can hike to the emerald-green crater lake surrounded by cloud forest.

Next head across the isthmus to the surfing capital of **San Juan del Sur**,

where you'll spend three days lazing on the splendid surrounding beaches or surfing some of the excellent breaks in the area. If you can drag yourself off the beach, take a day trip to the charming fishing village of **El Ostional** or, if you're lucky, to watch sea turtles arrive en masse at **Refugio de Vida Silvestre La Flor**. In the evenings, work your way though the happening beachfront bars and restaurants.

On your way back to Managua, stop at **Masaya** to shop for souvenirs and gifts in the excellent Mercado de Artesanías (National Artisans Market) and visit the hammock workshops.

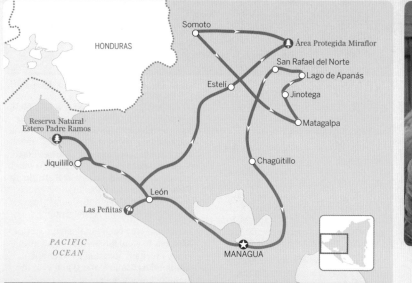

Northern Loop

3 WEEKS

Rich in nature and revolutionary culture, northern Nicaragua is equally rugged and refined. In one trip you'll go from sipping organic coffee at the source to surfing an active volcano. Charge your batteries: you'll want to take plenty of pictures or no one will believe you when you get home.

Upon arrival skip through **Managua** and head for the crumbling colonial beauty of **León** to give Nicaragua the fantastic introduction it deserves. Spend three days exploring this endearing city on foot, visiting fascinating museums, spacious mansions and glorious churches. If you're feeling energetic, hike one of the nearby volcanoes or surf the slopes of Cerro Negro.

From León, head west to the beach at **Las Peñitas** and find a spot in a sand-floor beachside bar for the spectacular sunset. In the morning make an early start to travel north to **Jiquilillo**. Spend a couple of days soaking up the ambience in this pretty fishing village and paddling through the mangroves of the nearby **Reserva Natural Estero Padre Ramos**.

Then travel across the Maribios volcanic chain and into the mountains to **Estelí**, where you can visit cigar factories and check out revolutionary murals. After a couple of days head into the mountains in the **Área Protegida Miraflor** for two days of horseback riding, wildlife spotting and farm-culture immersion.

Move on to **Somoto** and to Monumento Nacional Cañon de Somoto to swim, jump and rappel your way through the canyon.

Next morning travel to **Matagalpa** for a few caffeine-fueled days picking coffee beans and hiking on local plantations. Continue climbing higher into the mountains, stopping at the gorgeous Selva Negra coffee estate, before arriving in **Jinotega**, gateway to the cloud forests of Reserva Natural Cerro Datanlí–El Diablo. Spend a day in town to climb Cerro la Cruz and then spend a couple of days hiking in the reserve.

Give your muscles a break with a boat cruise on **Lago de Apanás** before continuing on to **San Rafael del Norte**. Here you can visit one of Nicaragua's most magnificent churches or fly through the pine forest on a zip line. On your way back to Managua call in at **Chagüitillo** to view the pre-Columbian petroglyphs.

Top: Río Coco (p213), Monumento Nacional Cañon de Somoto
Bottom: Making tortillas, Jinotega (p188)

2 WEEKS
Cruising the Río San Juan

The southeast corner of Nicaragua is an unparalleled playground for nature lovers of all dispositions. It boasts both comfortable eco-retreats and more strenuous adventures among lush wetlands and towering rainforests that are filled with fascinating ruins, colorful reptiles and first-class birdlife.

From **Managua** fly or bus it to **San Carlos** or pick up the ferry in Granada or Ometepe. Spend a morning checking out the old Spanish fort and waterfront before taking the afternoon boat to the enchanted archipelago of the **Islas Solentiname**. Spend a night each on Isla San Fernando and Isla Mancarrón, following jungle trails to in situ petroglyphs, swimming in the clear waters and visiting local artist workshops.

From Mancarrón, charter a boat to the **Río Papaturro** in the **Refugio de Vida Silvestre Los Guatuzos**, stopping to spot the amazing birdlife at some of the smaller islands on the way. Hike through the thick monkey-inhabited forest or kayak in the wetlands before heading out on an alligator safari in the evening.

Next take the public boat back to San Carlos. Pick up a riverboat down the Río San Juan to **Boca de Sábalos**, a small river town surrounded by steamy jungle. Among the many excursions on offer here is a tour to a local cacao plantation and chocolate factory. Or simply relax on your hotel balcony and spot aquatic birds on the banks of the majestic river.

After two nights in Sábalos, continue downstream to **El Castillo**, where an imposing Spanish fort looms over the rapids. Spend two days here riding horses through the rolling green hills and feasting on giant river shrimp.

If you have a day to spare, detour north on a day trip to **Refugio Bartola** biological station, with a network of trails through towering old-growth forest and kayaks to paddle up the narrow jungle-clad Río Bartola to crystal-clear swimming holes.

Otherwise, continue the journey by picking up a riverboat heading downriver to **San Juan de Nicaragua**, where the Río San Juan pours into the Caribbean Sea. Give yourself three days to explore the ruins of Greytown, spot manatees in hidden lagoons and head up the Río Indio into the heart of the Reserva Biológica Indio–Maíz..

Top: El Castillo (p253), Río San Juan
Bottom: Pineapple vendor, Managua (p40)

Off the Beaten Track: Nicaragua

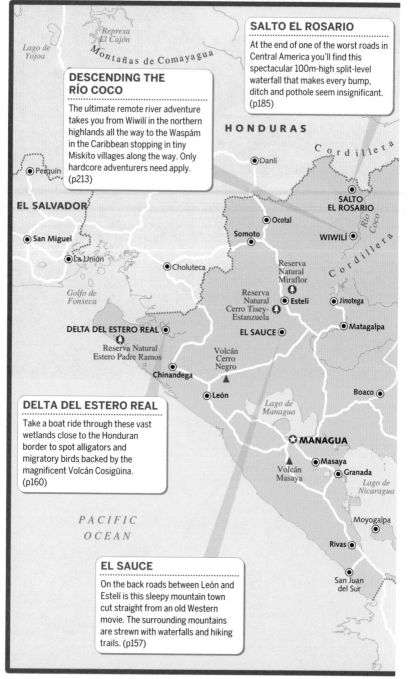

SALTO EL ROSARIO

At the end of one of the worst roads in Central America you'll find this spectacular 100m-high split-level waterfall that makes every bump, ditch and pothole seem insignificant. (p185)

DESCENDING THE RÍO COCO

The ultimate remote river adventure takes you from Wiwilí in the northern highlands all the way to the Waspám in the Caribbean stopping in tiny Miskito villages along the way. Only hardcore adventurers need apply. (p213)

HONDURAS

DELTA DEL ESTERO REAL

Take a boat ride through these vast wetlands close to the Honduran border to spot alligators and migratory birds backed by the magnificent Volcán Cosigüina. (p160)

EL SAUCE

On the back roads between León and Estelí is this sleepy mountain town cut straight from an old Western movie. The surrounding mountains are strewn with waterfalls and hiking trails. (p157)

MISKITO KEYS

Spend the night with welcoming Miskito lobster fishers in their stilted wooden houses that jut out of the turquoise Caribbean Sea among rocky outcrops and coral reefs some 50km offshore. (p210)

Waspám

Río Coco (Segovia)

Río Wawa

MISKITO KEYS

Bilwi (Puerto Cabezas)

RESERVA NATURAL CERRO MUSÚN

Accessed from the town of Río Blanco on the Managua–Siuna Hwy, this ruggedly beautiful mountain reserve has almost a dozen peaks over 1400m and as many dramatic waterfalls. (p284)

Reserva de Biosfera Bosawás

NICARAGUA

Río Grande de Matagalpa

RÍO BLANCO

CORN RIVER

This Creole community accessed by boat charter from San Juan de Nicaragua is the gateway to superb wildlife-watching in this seldom-visited part of the Reserva Biológica Indio-Maíz. (p225)

MONKEY POINT

A perilous ride through the open seas in a small boat keeps the best beaches on the Caribbean mainland completely empty and undeveloped. (p225)

Pearl Keys

Juigalpa

Río Escondido

El Rama

Bluefields

Corn Islands (Islas del Maíz, Nicaragua)

MAKENGE

Deep in the Indio-Maíz, the indigenous Rama community of Makenge is surrounded by the class of jungle you've probably only seen in wildlife documentaries. (p258)

Isla de Ometepe

MONKEY POINT

Gorda Punta Bahía

CARIBBEAN SEA

Islas Solentiname

San Carlos Boca de Sábalos

CORN RIVER

Refugio de Vida Silvestre Los Guatuzos

Los Chiles El Castillo

MAKENGE

San Juan de Nicaragua

Reserva Biológica Indio-Maíz

Río San Juan

COSTA RICA

Liberia

50 km
30 miles

Plan Your Trip

Nicaragua Outdoors

Pristine, largely unpopulated and with an increasing degree of environmental protection, Nicaragua is wide open for authentic wilderness adventure without the corporate sheen. Whether it's sand-boarding down active volcanoes or a leisurely hike through orchid-scented cloud forests, in Nicaragua you are never far from a spectacular nature experience.

Best Outdoor Experiences

Best Wildlife-Watching
Reserva Biológica Indio-Maíz, Refugio de Vida Silvestre La Flor, Reserva de Biosfera Bosawás and Refugio de Vida Silvestre Los Guatuzos

Best Volcano Climbs
Volcán Cosigüina, Volcán Maderas and Volcán Telica

Best Cloud-Forest Trek
Reserva Natural Macizos de Peñas Blancas

Best Surf Spots
Playas Popoyo, Gigante and Aserradores

Best Extreme Sports
Volcano boarding Cerro Negro, abseiling in Monumento Nacional Cañon de Somoto (p180)

Best Diving & Snorkeling
Great Corn Island, Little Corn Island and Pearl Keys

Best Fishing
Río San Juan, San Juan del Sur and Río Escondido

Diving & Snorkeling

With 1040km of coastline, most of it untainted and underdeveloped, it's no wonder that people are interested in getting all wet.

You can dive Nicaragua's Laguna de Apoyo, cruising past underwater fumaroles and saying hello to fish not found elsewhere in the world. But the best place in the country to dive – especially if you like cave dives – are the Corn Islands, where hammerhead sharks and 40 species of coral await.

The reefs surrounding the islands are also great for snorkeling, especially around Sally Peachie on the big island, and Otto Beach on the *islita*. For more outstanding snorkeling, head to the spectacular Pearl Keys, where you can swim among marine turtles and then rest on wonderful white-sand beaches.

Make it Happen

Serious snorkeling enthusiasts will want to bring their own mask, snorkel and fins as rental jobs vary greatly in quality and are not widely available apart from on the Corn Islands.

The following dive shops are PADI certified and offer both courses and leisure dives: Dive Little Corn (p237), Dolphin Dive (p237) and Neptune Watersports (p124).

Hiking

Thanks to an unlikely environmental consciousness (the Nicaraguan government found time to protect dozens of wilderness areas during the turbulent 1980s) and the war, which probably did more to save the rainforests than Unesco did in most countries, there's a lot of fairly pristine forest out there to see.

Some of the most interesting and easily accessible are at Área Protegida Miraflor, Reserva Natural Macizos de Peñas Blancas and Reserva Natural Cerro Datanlí–El Diablo.

The climbs with the real cachet, however, are any of the dozens of volcanoes, including the Maribios chain, Volcán Cosigüina and the volcanoes of Isla Ometepe. And if you're into dominating nature, consider the full-day climb to the peak of Cerro Mogotón (2106m), Nicaragua's highest mountain.

Make it Happen

Guides are usually recommended (and sometimes compulsory) for hikes in all but the best developed natural parks and reserves, particularly for the volcanoes. Even on easy hikes, guides can almost always find things you never would. In smaller towns, ask about guides at the *alcaldía* (mayor's office), usually right on the Parque Central (central park).

Base yourself in the hiking havens of Estelí, Matagalpa or Jinotega to explore the mountains of the north. For volcanoes, the best access is from León.

There are a number of companies offering organized hikes. We recommend Quetzaltrekkers (p146), Tree Huggers (p171) and Matagalpa Tours (p195).

Surfing

The center of Nicaraguan surfing remains San Juan del Sur, with a wave of surf camps and strongholds spreading northward to the holy grail of Nica wave-riding, Popoyo, past flawless beach breaks, scary-fun lava point breaks and lots of barrels when conditions are right. Playa Gigante has the greatest concentration of surf camps, where all-inclusive means room, meals and boat rides out to the best waves in the area every day. North of Popoyo, despite some excellent surfing, services are thin; surfing on the Caribbean coast is possible, but there's no infrastructure and not much information available.

The best breaks often require boats to get to, not just because they're offshore, but because housing developments along the coast block land access. To make up for it, southern Nicaragua is caressed by an almost constant offshore wind, perhaps caused by the presence of Lago de Nicaragua and Lago de Managua.

HIKING GEAR CHECKLIST

Trekking for leisure is not particularly popular among Nicaraguans and quality gear is hard to find on the ground. If you plan on getting of the beaten track, make sure to bring the following:

➡ **Comfortable footwear** Consider both leather hiking boots for long days in the mountains and comfortable, sturdy sports sandals for treks involving river crossings.

➡ **Water purification tablets**

➡ **Lightweight sleeping bag** Believe it or not, it does actually get cold in mountainous regions of Nicaragua.

➡ **Hammock** Indispensable for long boat rides or taking a break in the jungle high above the creepy crawlies of the forest floor.

➡ **Tent** If you find one in Nicaragua, it's likely to be bulky and barely waterproof, so bring a lightweight hiking model from home.

BEST SURF BREAKS

Here are some favorite waves, which we've listed northeast to southwest. All of these beaches are on the Pacific coast. For a comprehensive list of the best breaks pick up a map (US$8) from Surf Maps (www.surfmaps.com).

Playa Aserradores Just northeast of Chinandega, the beach is also called Boom-wavos for the powerful, hollow beach break making all that noise. There's another left five minutes offshore and plenty more waves around.

El Corinto This is one of the best waves in the country, beyond Playa Paso Caballos, but it goes almost unsurfed because it's only accessible by boat. Easier to get to is the river-mouth break with left-breaking peaks.

Poneloya and Las Peñitas Only decent surfing, but the easiest access on Nicaragua's north Pacific, just 20km from León.

Puerto Sandino The stretch from Puerto Sandino to El Velero has a half-dozen reef and rocky-bottomed beach breaks, including one spectacular left.

Playa Huehuete Now is that golden time, between when the road is paved and when the gated communities go up: check out the point, beach and river-mouth break now!

Playa Popoyo This collection of sandy-floored surf lodges may be Nicaragua's next bona fide surf town, with at least four named waves: Popoyo, a right and left point break; aggressive Bus Stop; fast and rocky-floored Cobra; and the best wave in the region, Emergencias, with a left for longboards and hollow right for short boards.

Playa Gigante Accessing another handful of named waves, most of them a boat ride away, it's no wonder that surf lodges are springing up all over this beautiful beach.

Playa Maderas Sometimes called Los Playones, this excellent surf spot with easy access from San Juan del Sur has a slow wave with two rights and two lefts that's perfect for beginners.

Make it Happen

Nicaragua has great waves year-round. March to November is considered the best time to surf, with the biggest waves usually in March, April and October (consistently 1m to 2m, frequently 3m to 4m). November to March is the dry season, with smaller waves (averaging under 2m) but better weather – the best time for beginners.

Water temperatures average around mid-20°C (mid-70°F) year-round, but from December to April an upwelling offshore means that the temperature can drop; consider bringing a long-sleeve wetsuit top.

You can buy, sell and rent boards in San Juan del Sur and Popoyo, but it's generally better to bring your own board (consider selling it when you leave).

Numerous surfing outfits offer everything from one-on-one instruction to week-long all-inclusive surf packages. Listings are provided in the closest city to the waves.

Swimming

From sunny Pacific beaches to cool crater lakes, and lots of rivers and waterfalls, you'll always find places to put your bathing suit to work.

There are eight major crater lakes, with excellent swimming at Laguna de Apoyo, surrounded by lodging options, or undeveloped Laguna de Asososca, near León.

Isla de Ometepe has some excellent swimming opportunities, including the remarkable natural sand jetty at Punta Jesús María and the mineral-rich waters of La Presa Ojo de Agua.

The best beach swims are at some of the stunning coves around San Juan del Sur and in the crystal-clear waters of the Caribbean around the Pearl Keys and the Corn Islands.

Green-and-rufous kingfisher

Wildlife

Nicaragua is home to an impressive array of tropical ecosystems, each offering their own outstanding wildlife-spotting opportunities.

The best spots to see big animals are in the tropical rainforests of the Reserva Bíologica Indio-Maíz and the Reserva de Biosfera Bosawás. One of the rarest ecosystems in the world is the cloud forest, a cool, misty tropical rainforest above 1200m, offering opportunities for seeing wildlife and flora, most famously colorful quetzals and orchids. The easiest to see is at Volcán Mombacho, with easy access from Granada.

Nicaragua's Pacific coast is a haven for literally hundreds of thousands of nesting turtles each year, and some of their nesting sites are surprisingly accessible. In the San Juan del Sur area, you're within easy reach of Refugio de Vida Silvestre La Flor and Refugio de Vida Silvestre Río Escalante Chacocente. There's more turtle action further north at Reserva Natural Volcán Cosigüina.

Birders will also be drawn to Nicaragua's sweet-water wetlands and jungle-lined rivers, which offer outstanding birding opportunities.

BEST BIRDING SPOTS

➡ **Islas Solentiname** Tiny islands with Nicaragua's highest concentration of birdlife including tiger herons and flocks of roseate spoonbills.

➡ **Boca de Sábalos** Pick your spot along the river and observe a fantastic array of waterfowl and rainforest species without moving a muscle.

➡ **Área Protegida Miraflor** Accessible cloud forest boasting quetzals and toucans.

➡ **Refugio de Vida Silvestre Los Guatuzos** Immense wetlands home to around 400 bird species.

Regions at a Glance

Stretching from the sizzling Pacific with its colonial treasures, smoking volcanoes and superb surf beaches, to the crystalline Caribbean with its indigenous communities and islands that groove to an altogether different tune, Nicaragua's geographical diversity is topped only by the range of cultures living within its boundaries.

The country is crowned in the north by spectacular mountain ranges covered in a patchwork of small farms, coffee plantations and cloud forest that offer great hiking and birdwatching opportunities. In the south you'll find the largest freshwater lake in Central America, with more outdoor activities than you could dream of cramming into your itinerary, wetlands brimming with birdlife and the virgin rainforests of the magnificent Río San Juan.

Managua

History
Nightlife
Culture

Revolutionary Roads

Key moments in Nicaragua's tumultuous modern history played out here. Take a stroll down the National Assembly Pedestrian Walk for an overview, ending up at the eerie abandoned cathedral, a reminder of the devastating 1978 earthquake.

Up All Night

This town knows how to party. And while you'll definitely want to keep your senses about you, a diesel-charged night in the rocking lounges and dance halls along Carretera a Masaya is a rite of passage.

Culture Capital

This is the cultural fulcrum of a nation. The university offers great independent learning opportunities, and there are museums and cultural houses, street artists and underground poets.

p40

Masaya & Los Pueblos Blancos

Shopping
Culture
Outdoors

Artisan Headquarters

Masaya has the best crafts market in Nicaragua. Beyond its technicolor stalls, you'll find unique artisan workshops in the compact little villages throughout this region.

Local Encounters

This is a great place for broad-faced encounters with locals. Volunteer or learn Spanish and you'll experience the place on a whole new level.

Volcanoes & Craters

Volcán Masaya offers great hiking trips, never-ending vistas and the all-too-real chance of being blown to smithereens in a pyroclastic burst of light. Southward, you'll come across the unrelenting beauty of Laguna de Apoyo.

p64

Granada

History
Eating
Walking

A Storied Past

Granada's history is as complex as it gets. This fleeting imprint is evidenced on nearly every corner. You'll see it in the city's architecture, its festivals, art and living culture.

Culinary Variety

The city's vibrant restaurant scene will keep foodies busy for several hours each day. There's fusion, mind-blowing local steaks and experimental spots that cater to travelers of all palates.

Outdoor Exploration

A city of movement, age-old grace and continued evolution, Granada is the place to walk till you drop. If that fails, head out by launch to explore a mythical island archipelago with monkey islands, fortresses and birds.

p81

South-western Nicaragua

Surf
Beauty
Wilderness

Famous Breaks

Not many places have surf as good as this. After you hit dawn patrol at legendary spots such as Playas Hermosa and Maderas, you can chill out in your beachfront hammock paradise.

Enchanted Island

Isla de Ometepe is a paradise lost. Find petroglyphs, climb volcanoes, kayak to lost coves and chill out in cool travelers' enclaves on the edge of the wild.

Untamed Beauty

There are lost beaches, tough-and-ready inland towns and unique windows into rural Nicaragua life, wildlife preserves where turtles arrive by the thousands and birds of paradise caw madly from the forest canopy.

p102

León & North-western Nicaragua

History
Volcanoes
Outdoors

Liberal Hotbed

León is where the revolution was televised, and to this day, you can feel the intense strands of rhetoric flowing from this intellectual powerhouse. The partying isn't bad.

Dramatic Geography

The fire theme continues down below and up above in the large nature preserves that encircle massive volcanoes. Come sunset, the sun lights up the Pacific night.

Uncharted Territory

Head north to get further from the tourist track and closer to the wild. Volcanoes that seldom see a climber, waves that rarely embrace a rider and estuaries whose fingers only see a human wake once in a blue moon.

p135

Northern Highlands

Nature
Adventure
Coffee

Birdwatching

Nature lovers will have no shortage of opportunities to spot nesting quetzals, toucans and boisterous howler monkeys among the region's swaths of precious cloud forest.

Treks & Hikes

Whether it's a mountainous trek to a hidden waterfall or tubing through an ancient canyon, the northern region offers unlimited opportunity for off-the-beaten path adventure.

A Gourmet Cup

The shade-grown plantations of northern Nicaragua produce classic gourmet coffees. Get into the fields and see where it comes from, or go one step better and pick some beans yourself.

p167

Caribbean Coast

Beaches
Food
Culture

Island Paradise

Romantic tropical islands with turquoise fringed white-sand beaches shaded by coconut palms anyone? You may find such idyllic beauty elsewhere, but it won't be as empty or undeveloped as here.

Bread & Fish

The Caribbean coast has delicious seafood, most famously in its signature dish 'rundown'. But *costeño* (coastal) cooking goes way beyond fresh lobster, so grab a glass of seaweed punch and follow your nose to the wonderful unsigned bakeries.

Vibrant Music Scene

Big on culture, the Caribbean coast's Maypole rhythms and Miskito pop provide the soundtrack for performances by Nicaragua's best dancers.

p203

San Carlos, Islas Solentiname & the Río San Juan

Wildlife
Outdoors
Art

Boater's Delight

The Río San Juan department is the ultimate boating playground, with kayak and canoe adventures, or alligator-spotting motorboat safaris.

Through the Binoculars

Southeastern Nicaragua offers outstanding birdwatching. The remote Islas Solentinames are a haven for migratory waterbirds; the Río San Juan, home to a grand variety of aquatic and rainforest species.

Indigenous Art Forms

A visit to the isolated island workshops and studios offers fascinating insights into the Primitivist paintings and bright balsa carvings from the Islas Solentiname.

p240

On the Road

Northern Highlands
p167

Caribbean Coast
p203

León & Northwestern Nicaragua
p135

Managua
p40

Granada
p81

Masaya & Los Pueblos Blancos
p64

Southwestern Nicaragua
p102

San Carlos, Islas Solentiname & the Río San Juan
p240

Managua

POP 2,223,375 / ELEV 90M

Best Places to Eat

➜ Doña Pilar (p52)
➜ Cocina Doña Haydee (p53)
➜ La Casa de Los Nogueras (p54)
➜ La Terraza Peruana (p53)

Best Places to Sleep

➜ La Posada del Arcangel (p50)
➜ La Bicicleta Hostal (p52)
➜ Hotel Contempo (p52)

Why Go?

Simply put, Managua is a shambles. It is chaotic and broken, poetic and mesmerizing, all at the same time.

And while most travelers are now skipping the city altogether – instead arranging quick airport transfers from nearby Granada – stay a day or two and you will see that big, bad Managua ain't so bad after all, and that this truly is the heartstring that holds the nation's culture and commerce together.

Aside from diving into the whir of a magnificent beehive of honking horns, sprawling markets, garbage and rancor, this low-rise city with improbable trees, remarkable street art and spirited monuments also gives you easy access to nearby lagoons, the nature reserve of Chocoyero-El Brujo, a smattering of fun beaches like Pochomil, and the hot springs at El Trapiche.

When to Go

➜ September through April is the best time of year for birdwatching. It's also good for turtle tours at nearby beaches and wild encounters in the lagoons and natural attractions just outside the city.

➜ December through April are the dry months. Visiting at this time makes plying the city's streets easier, market days drier and chance encounters just a little more pleasant. Hotels can be a bit pricey now and during Semana Santa, so book ahead.

➜ The best festivals happen around the Day of the Revolution on July 19 or the Festival of Santo Domingo, during the first 10 days in August.

History

A fishing encampment as early as 6000 years ago, Managua has been an important trading center for at least two millennia. When Spanish chronicler Fernández de Oviedo arrived in 1528, he estimated Managua's population at around 40,000; most of these original inhabitants fled to the Sierritas, the small mountains just south, shortly after the Spanish arrived. The small town, without even a hospital or school until the 1750s, didn't really achieve any prominence until 1852, when the seemingly endless civil war between Granada and León was resolved by placing the capital here.

The clever compromise might have worked out better had a geologist been at hand: Managua sits atop a network of fault lines that have shaped its history ever since. The late 1800s were rocked by quakes that destroyed the new capital's infrastructure, with churches and banks crumbling as the ground flowed beneath their feet. In 1931 the epicenter was the stadium – dozens were killed during a big game. In 1968 a single powerful jolt right beneath what's now Metrocentro mall destroyed an entire neighborhood.

And on the evening of December 23, 1972, a series of powerful tremors rocked the city, culminating in a 6.2 quake that killed 11,000 people and destroyed 53,000 homes. The blatant siphoning of international relief funds by President Somoza touched off the Sandinista-led revolution, which was followed by the Contra War, and the city center, including the beautiful old cathedral, was never rebuilt. Rather, it was replaced by a crazy maze of unnamed streets, shacks that turned to shanties that turned to homes

Managua Highlights

1 Parque Histórico Nacional Loma de Tiscapa (p44) Taking in views over the city while standing in Sandino's shadow on a volcano's rim.

2 Malecón (p42) Strolling along the newly revamped waterfront and stopping for a bite at a traditional Nicaraguan eatery.

3 Plaza de la Revolución (p43) Marveling at the crumbling colonial grandeur.

4 Huellas de Acahualinca (p47) Following in the footsteps of Managua's early inhabitants.

5 Antigua Catedral (p42) Taking in the eerie sight of the once grand, hollowed-out shell of a cathedral.

6 National Assembly Pedestrian Walk (p43) Brushing up on modern Nicaraguan history while you stroll.

7 La Casa de los Mejía Godoy (p54) Catching live folk music while knocking back a few cocktails.

MANAGUA IN...

One Day

If you wake up in Barrio Martha Quezada, you can just walk to the top of **Loma de Tiscapa** (p44) and the unmissable silhouette of Sandino. Then grab a cab (negotiate your fare first!) to **Huellas de Acahualinca** (p47) for some ancient history. Heading back to Managua's historic center, visit the **Antigua Catedral** (p42) before strolling the lakeshore **Malecón** (p42), then enjoy a mellow evening of live music at **La Casa de los Mejía Godoy** (p54).

Three Days

The next morning, take the **Tiscapa Canopy Tour** (p48), then after lunch grab a little down time in one of Managua's leafy **parks** before dinner. After your evening meal, catch some theater at **Teatro Nacional Rubén Darío** (p54).

Day three is for shopping: grab souvenirs at **Mercado Roberto Huembes** (p55) or resupply for the hinterlands at markets and malls. After lunch in exclusive Altamira, stop by the **Catedral Metropolitana** (p46). Finish the evening with a local crowd and alfresco drinks at **El Grillito** (p54).

and later buildings. There have been some efforts to resurrect the old city center – the restoration of the waterfront Malecón is certainly a promising development – but most new construction now happens on the outskirts of the city center.

◎ Sights

Managua's sights are few and, with the exception of the often deserted Área Monumental, far between. Taxis are a cheap and worthwhile investment in Managua's muggy climate.

◉ Plaza de la Revolución & El Malecón

This quiet collection of pre-earthquake and post-revolutionary monuments, parks, museums and government offices was once the pulsing heart of Managua; the Malecón (pier), a pleasant stroll from the Plaza de la Revolución, once overlooked a living lake lined with restaurants and festivities. But after the 1972 earthquake and two decades of war and privation, the center was all but abandoned.

Slowly – little by little, as they say in Nicaragua – it is being resuscitated. Government buildings have been rebuilt and trees replanted, and ramshackle restaurants once again host cheerful after-church crowds on the lakefront. At the time of writing, the Malecón was just re-emerging as a family-friendly destination, complete with new restaurants and activities for kids.

★ Antigua Catedral   CATHEDRAL

(Map p46; 14 Av Sureste) The hollow shell of Managua's Old Cathedral remains the city's most poignant metaphor, shattered by the 1972 earthquake – and, despite promises, never restored. Though still beautiful and serene, attended by stone angels and dappled in golden light, it is empty and off-limits: the cathedral without a heart, in the city without a center.

Malecón   WATERFRONT

(Map p46) The *malecón* (pier) has been perked up by the newly renovated Puerto Salvador Allende tourist complex at its base. Still, it can be a bit depressing on off days, especially if you're pondering how we could let Lago de Managua (also known as Lake Xolotlán) become one of the most polluted bodies of water in Central America (foreign governments are helping to clean up the lake). The area has always drawn local families on weekends.

Puerto Salvador Allende   PORT

(Map p46; Malecón; �#) Thanks to a recent (and much-needed) overhaul to Managua's previously barren port area, this breezy lakefront complex is now a destination for tourists and locals alike. With around 20 dining venues – ranging from casual food stands to more elegant restaurants – plus playgrounds for children and pathways for strolling, it's a good bet in the afternoon or evening, especially around sunset when the views over the lake are particularly lovely.

Plaza de la Revolución
PARK

(Map p46) Inaugurated in 1899 by national hero and original anti-American General José Santos Zelaya, this open plaza has been the scene of countless protests, parades, romances and more. On the northeast of the plaza rests the tomb of Sandinista commander Carlos Fonseca.

Palacio de la Cultura y Biblioteca Nacional
HISTORIC BUILDING

(Map p46) The 1930s-era Palacio de la Cultura (Palace of Culture) housed the National Congress until 1994. The historic building now houses the national museum and library.

Museo Nacional
MUSEUM

(Map p46; Palacio de la Cultura y Biblioteca Nacional; admission US$2; ⊙8am-6pm Mon-Fri, to noon Sat) Inside the Palacio de la Cultura y Biblioteca Nacional is the national museum. The timeline starts only 500 million years ago, as Nicaragua is one of the newest places on earth, and takes visitors through the formation of the lakes and volcanoes – not to mention gold mines – before getting to pre-Columbian statuary and one of the best pottery collections in the country, all well signed and explained.

Other exhibits whiz through the Spanish-colonial period before landing in the Sandino and Sandinista eras. Above the main staircase is a mural of revolutionary movements in the Americas by Mexican artist Arnold Belkin, and there's also a room tracing 500 years of art (most from the 1970s). Admission includes a 30-minute guided tour in Spanish.

Teatro Nacional Rubén Darío
BUILDING

(Map p46; ☎2222-7426; www.tnrubendario.gob.ni) Toward the lake is this oblong theater, a 'temple to Nicaraguan art and culture.' Performance times and ticket costs vary; see the website for program details.

Parque de la Paz
PARK

(Map p46) Managua's Peace Park, with its signature lighthouse, is a lasting symbol of the challenges and hopes facing a poor nation emerging from war. The park was inaugurated in 1990 by then President Violeta Barrios de Chamorro. The concept was beautiful: they interred machine guns, pistols and even a tank in concrete – symbolically burying Nicaragua's bellicose past. Since then, the reflection pool has been drained, brass plaques were stolen and even the generators got pinched. Major restorations are planned.

This park is notorious for muggings – visit in the middle of the day, without valuables and in a group. Try asking a guard to walk with you.

Monumento a Rubén Darío
MONUMENT

(Map p46; Av Bolívar) On the lake side of Plaza de la Revolución, this monument was refurbished after the original 1933 statue fell into graffitied disrepair. A group of artists did a guerrilla installation, veiling the city's shame from public view and demanding poetic justice. In 1998 the cash-strapped government bowed to public opinion and, with Texaco Oil's help, restored the likeness of Nicaragua's favorite son.

Tomb of Carlos Fonseca
MONUMENT

(Map p46; Plaza de la Revolución) The tomb of Carlos Fonseca, founder of the Frente Sandinista de Liberación Naciona (FSLN).

Estatua al Soldado
MONUMENT

(Map p46) The monument to Nicaraguan soldiers dates from 1909.

Estatua de Montoya
STATUE

(Map p44) A statue dedicated to national hero Ramón Montoya, a Nicaraguan soldier who died (at the age of 14) in 1907.

Casa del Obrero
LANDMARK

(Map p44; Av Monumental & Calle Colón) A downtown landmark originally dedicated to the Nicaraguan worker.

Monumento al Trabajador Nicaragüense
MONUMENT

(Map p46; Parque Central, 2c S, 1c E) A monument to Nicaraguan workers.

◉ Barrio Martha Quezada & Around

Since the days of the *internacionalistas* (idealistic visitors who came during the revolutionary years in the 1980s), Barrio Martha Quezada has been the city's budget-travel headquarters. It has easy access to Plaza Inter (a shopping center) and most international buses. It's better to take a cab here at night.

National Assembly Pedestrian Walk
AREA, PUBLIC ART

(Map p44; Av Central) East of the National Assembly along Av Central is a pedestrian walk with open-air exhibits on Nicaragua's

Barrio Martha Quezada

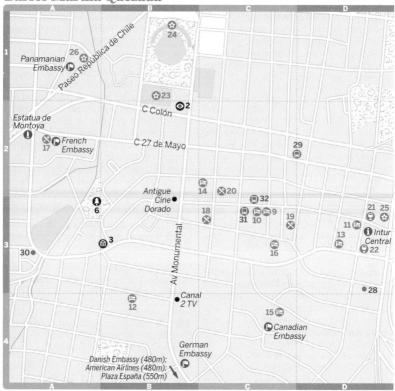

history, featuring everything from historic photos of Sandino to evocative pictures of pre-earthquake Managua. It's a great path to take if you're walking from Barrio Martha Quezada to the lakefront, especially if you're interested in Nicaragua's political and literary histories.

**Parque Histórico Nacional
Loma de Tiscapa** PARK
(Map p44) Home to what's easily Managua's most recognizable landmark, Sandino's somber silhouette, this national historic park was once the site of the Casa Presidencial, where Sandino and his men were executed in 1934; what looks like a dilapidated parking structure was for decades one of Nicaragua's most notorious prisons.

You can see Sandino, hastily erected by the departing FSLN (Sandinista National Liberation Front) government after its electoral loss in 1990, from almost anywhere in town; begin your ascent at the Crowne

Plaza. You'll pass Monumento Roosevelt (p46), constructed in 1939, with lovely lake views (today it's a memorial to those killed in the revolution).

The top of Loma de Tiscapa is actually the lip of Volcán Tiscapa's beautiful little crater lake, with incredible views of the city, both cathedrals and Volcán Momotombo, plus Canopy Tiscapa (p48), a small but fun 1.2km, three-platform, 25-minute tour. Keep in mind that, despite a vigorous cleanup campaign, the lake is polluted with untreated sewage.

Parque El Carmén PARK
(Map p44; Antiguo Cine Dorado, 2c O; ☉dawn-dusk) A couple of blocks from Martha Quezada's concrete jungle, this surprisingly pretty park is a little slice of suburbia, with kids riding bikes, a playground, and a kiosk selling snacks and cold drinks. The park is surrounded by some fairly opulent

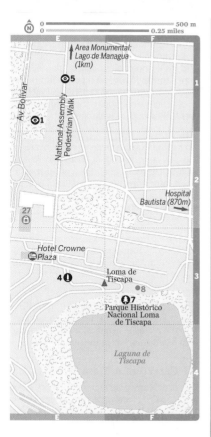

homes, including that of President Ortega – if your taxi driver doesn't know it, tell him *'donde vive Daniel'* (where Daniel lives).

Códice Espacio Cultural   GALLERY
(Map p48; www.galeriacodice.com; Hotel Colón, 1c S, 2½c E; ⊙ hours vary) **FREE** The best place to catch really cutting-edge contemporary art in Managua. Check the website for exhibition information.

Arboretum Nacional   GARDENS
(National Arboretum; Map p44; admission US$0.30; ⊙ 8am-5pm Mon-Fri) These modest gardens, inconveniently located halfway between Barrio Martha Quezada and the Plaza Monumental on Av Bolívar (well, it's convenient if you're making the hot 40-minute walk between them), features more than 200 species of plants, divided into Nicaragua's five major life zones. Of these only the dry tropical forest and central lowlands look happy. Your fee includes

a guided tour, where you'll see a *madriño,* the national tree, and *sacuanjoche,* the national flower.

UCA   UNIVERSITY
(Universidad Centro America; Map p48; www. uca.edu.ni; Rotonda Rubén Darío, 500m O) Founded in 1960 as a Jesuit school, this is one of

Área Monumental

Área Monumental

Nicaragua's premier universities, with a curriculum heavy on science and alternative technologies, Che Guevara sculptures, and vegetarian eateries out front. It's worth a wander – in particular the **Centro Historia**

Militar (free admission), with relics from Sandino to the Sandinistas.

Monumento Roosevelt   MONUMENT
(Map p44) Acsending Loma de Tiscapa from Crowne Plaza, you'll pass Monumento Roosevelt, constructed in 1939 and offering lovely lake views. Today it's a memorial to those killed in the revolution.

UNAN   UNIVERSITY
(Universidad Nacional Autónoma de Nicaragua; Map p48; www.unan.edu.ni; Enitel Villa Fontana, 500m O) The Managua branch of Nicaragua's oldest university (the original is in León, the former capital) was founded in 1958 and has more than 24,000 students.

Epikentro Gallery   GALLERY
(Map p44; www.epikentrogallery.com; Canal 2, 2c N, 2c O; ⊙10am-4pm Mon-Fri) **FREE** Straddling the divide between fine and contemporary art.

Parque Las Palmas   PARK
(Estatua de Montoya, 3c O, 50m N; ⊙dawn-dusk) A cute and shady little neighborhood park with the requisite benches, snack kiosks and even a laid-back bar in the middle.

◎ Carretera a Masaya

Catedral Metropolitana   CATHEDRAL
(Map p48; www.catedralmga.blogspot.com; ⊙9am-7pm) Just north of the Metrocentro mall is an unforgettable Managua landmark that's practically new (the doors opened in 1993). It's an architectural marvel that leaves most visitors, well, scratching their heads. It's not a mosque, really: the 63 cupolas (or breasts, or eggs; speculation continues) symbolize Nicaragua's 63 Catholic churches, and also provide structural support during earthquakes – a good thing, since it sits astride a fault line.

The interior is cool, heartfelt and unspectacular, although the shrine on the northwest side is nice. Of the US$45 million used to construct the cathedral, US$3.5 million was donated by avid pro-Lifer Tom Monaghan, owner of Domino's Pizza.

Parque Japonés   PARK
(Map p48; Star City, 2c E; ⊙dawn-dusk) **FREE** This not-particularly-Japanese park, nestled in the back blocks of the Metrocentro area, is a great place for a bit of time out. There are plenty of trees, some walking tracks and a couple of kids' playgrounds.

Pharaoh's Casino LANDMARK
(Map p48; Carretera Masaya Km 4½) A landmark locals use to give directions in the neighborhood.

La Vicky LANDMARK
(Map p48) The grocery store called 'La Vicky' doesn't stand here anymore, but locals still use it as a point of reference when giving directions.

◉ Northwest of the Centre

Huellas de Acahualinca ARCHAEOLOGICAL SITE
(☑2266-5774; admission US$4; ⊘9am-4pm) Discovered by miners in 1874, these fossilized tracks record the passage of perhaps 10 people – men, women and children – as well as of birds, raccoons and deer across the muddy shores of Lago de Managua some 6000 years ago. Despite early speculation that they were running from a volcanic eruption, forensics specialists have determined that these folks were in no hurry – and, interestingly, were fairly tall, between 145cm and 160cm.

The excavation was undertaken by the Carnegie Foundation in 1941 and 1942, and unearthed 14 layers, or 4m, of earth. They found some later Chorotega ceramics (about 2m down) and other intriguing artifacts, though there's no money to take it further. There is, however, a nifty onsite museum, with human skulls, a fossilized bison track and lots of ceramics; your fee includes a Spanish-language tour of the whole shebang (it's an extra US$1 if you want to take photos). Don't skip this one; it's an international treasure.

The best way to get here is by taxi (US$2 to US$4 per person).

At the time of research this site was closed indefinitely due to damage from heavy rains.

🎓 Courses

La Academia Nicaragüense de la Danza COURSE
(Map p48; ☑2277-5557; UCA, 50m N, Av Universitaria) Offers a huge range of dance classes (salsa, merengue, reggaetón, folk, ballet, flamenco and bellydancing, to name a few).

Alianza Francesa COURSE
(Map p48; ☑2267-2811; www.alianzafrancesa.org.ni; Planes de Altamira, de la Embajada de México ½c N) Offers classes in painting, drawing, French, German and Portuguese, along with occasional art exhibits and poetry readings.

Viva Spanish School LANGUAGE COURSE
(Map p48; ☑2270-2339; www.vivaspanish-school.com; Metrocentro 5c E, Del Edificio Banco Produzcamos, 2c S; lessons per hr US$10) Coming highly recommended by long-term volunteers and NGO workers, classes here start at US$175 for a 20-hour week. Homestays can be arranged for an additional US$140 per week.

DANGERS, SCAMS & STAYING SAFE

Express kidnappings – where a taxi driver holds the passenger hostage by knifepoint and then takes them to ATMs around town until their bank is depleted – are reported in Managua, as well as in Granada, Masaya, San Juan del Sur and San Jorge. Here are a few top tips to stay safe.

Take radio taxis with a bubble on top. There are thousands of illegal cabs in Managua. The ones with the bubble on the roof and/or red plates are considered safer. There should be a name tag with the driver's information on the dashboard. These are registered with a company, and can be ordered by phone.

Ask your hotel to call you a cab. There are reports of people being kidnapped after a friendly stranger on the street helped them hail a cab.

Take cabs after dark. In the downtown area, you should take cabs after the sun sets. Around Carretera a Masaya, you should take them after 10pm. As a general rule, if you see women and kids walking around, you are probably safe to walk there. Don't risk even a short two-block walk at night.

Agree on a price before getting in. Also be sure to ask if you will be going as a *colectivo* (collective that stops to pick up other passengers) or *privado* (private).

Make sure the cab takes you where you want to go. Often cabbies will say a certain hotel is closed just to take you to a spot where they get a commission.

Carretera a Masaya

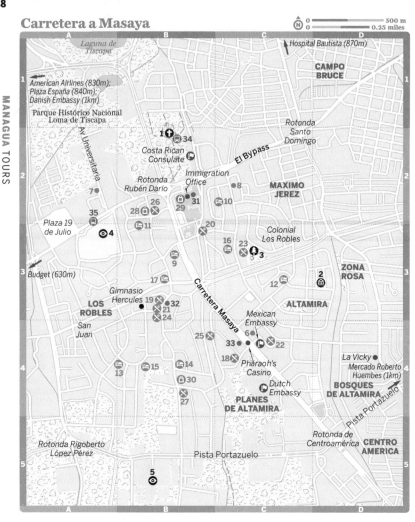

△ 0 ——————— 500 m
Ⓝ 0 ——————— 0.25 miles

Laguna de Tiscapa

Hospital Bautista (870m)

CAMPO BRUCE

American Airlines (830m);
Plaza España (840m);
Danish Embassy (1km)

Parque Histórico Nacional
Loma de Tiscapa

Rotonda Santo Domingo

Costa Rican
Consulate

Av. Universitaria

El Bypass

Rotonda
Rubén Darío

Immigration Office

MAXIMO JEREZ

Plaza 19
de Julio

Colonial
Los Robles

Budget (630m)

ZONA ROSA

Gimnasio
Hercules

LOS ROBLES

San Juan

Carretera Masaya

ALTAMIRA

Mexican
Embassy

La Vicky
Mercado Roberto
Huembes (1km)

Pharaoh's
Casino

Dutch
Embassy

BOSQUES
DE ALTAMIRA

Pista Portazuelo

PLANES
DE ALTAMIRA

Rotonda Rigoberto
López Pérez

Rotonda de
Centroamérica

CENTRO
AMERICA

Pista Portazuelo

👉 Tours

Green Pathways   ADVENTURE TOUR
(Map p140; 📞7877-2940; www.greenpathways.com; del Semaforos de Club Terraza 1c E, ½c N, Managua) 🖉 Socially conscientious operator with a focus on rural tourism.

Canopy Tiscapa   CANOPY TOUR
(Map p44; 📞8872-2555; canopytiscapa@yahoo.com; Lomo de Tiscapa; per person US$17.25; ⊙9am-5pm Tue-Sun) Take to the canopy above the Tiscapa lagoon. Find it at Lomo de Tiscapa (p44).

Puerto Salvador Allende   BOAT TOUR
(Map p46; 📞2222-2745; www.epn.com.ni) This relatively modern port complex is a nice place for a walk by the lake; when the weather's good, you can arrange a boat ride on the lake. There are a few restaurants here, but they're overpriced.

🎉 Festivals & Events

In addition to enthusiastic celebrations of national events, Managua has its own grand parties.

Carretera a Masaya

Carnaval Alegría por la Vida STREET CARNIVAL
(☻ early Mar) The 'Joy for Life' festival is Managua's version of Carnaval, featuring a lively parade of costumed performers, live music, food, dancing and the crowning of a festival queen. There's a different theme each year.

Day of the Revolution NATIONAL HOLIDAY
(☻ Jul 19) You'll understand why people still love President Daniel Ortega when you see the master work a crowd of 100,000 red-and-black-flag-waving faithful during the Día de la Revolución (Day of the Revolution).

Festival of Santo Domingo de Guzman RELIGIOUS
(☻ Aug 1-10) Managua's *fiestas patronales* (patron saint parties) feature a carnival, sporting events, *hípicos* (horse parades) and a procession of *diablitos,* which takes Santo Domingo to his country shrine at the Sierritas de Managua, followed by music and fireworks.

La Purísima RELIGIOUS
(☻ end Nov–mid Dec) The Feast of the Immaculate Conception is celebrated throughout Nicaragua, with festivities culminating on December 8. In Managua, the celebration is particularly colorful, with massive altars to the Virgin Mary set up along the blocks of Av Bolívar leading to the lake. After dark, the avenue turns into a huge street party with food stands and live music.

🛏 Sleeping

Most budget travelers stay in Barrio Martha Quezada, which has about 10 square blocks of fairly strollable streets, and adjacent Bolonia (though note that crime is an issue, especially after dark) – due to easy access to the Tica bus station, the neighborhood is popular with foreigners passing through.

Other options include chain hotels along the Carretera a Masaya and nearby smaller guesthouses on the suburban-feeling side streets; this area is closer to the UCA bus terminal, with frequent connections to León and Granada.

🛏 Barrio Martha Quezada & Around

Better known to *taxistas* as 'Tica bus,' the international bus terminal upon which the barrio (district) is centered, Martha Quezada's been hosting shoestringers for a generation. Just to the south, the leafier, more upscale residential neighborhood of

ESCAPE THE CHAOS IN MANAGUA'S GREEN SPACES

Tired of honking horns, screeching hawkers, pollution and litter? Take an afternoon breather in one of Managua's green areas. For your safety, only visit park areas during the day.

Pop into Parque Japonés (p46), Parque El Carmén (p44) or Parque Las Palmas (p46).

Bolonia has a handful of relaxed boutique hotels. Directions here are usually given from Canal Dos (Canal 2 TV Building).

Pandora Hostel HOSTEL **$**
(Map p44; ☎7524-5303; www.pandorahostel.com; Tica Bus, 1c S, 1c E; dm/d US$12/30; ❄📶) Clean, friendly, and around the corner from the Tica Bus terminal, this brand-new hostel is a great choice for an affordable overnight. There's a bar onsite, and the hostel can arrange an airport shuttle if you ask ahead.

Casa Vanegas HOTEL **$**
(Map p44; ☎2222-4043; casavanegas1@hotmail.com; Tica Bus, 1c O; s/d from US$15/22; 📶) Clean and secure, this friendly family-run spot, just steps from Tica Bus, is convenient if you have an early bus to catch. Casa Vanegas offers decent-sized, unexciting rooms around a small patio plus hammocks, a spacious lounge area and laundry facilities.

Hostal Dulce Sueño HOTEL **$**
(Map p44; ☎2228-4195; www.hostaldulcesueno.com; Tica Bus, 70m E; s/d from US$12/18; 📶) This simple guesthouse has spotless, no-frills rooms, and a central patio with a TV and a shared kitchen. It's a few steps from the Tica Bus terminal, but this block is reputedly quite dangerous at night.

La Posada del Arcangel GUESTHOUSE **$$$**
(Map p44; ☎2254-5212; www.hotellaposadadelarcangel.com; Canal 10 de TV, 100m O, 150m S; d from US$55; ❄📶) Easily one of the most charming places to stay in Managua, this colonial-style inn has a quirky art collection, a leafy garden and guest rooms with hand-carved wooden furnishings and inviting tiled bathrooms. The included breakfast is excellent, too.

Hotel Europeo HOTEL **$$$**
(Map p44; ☎2268-2130; www.hoteleuropeo.com.ni; Canal 2, 75m O; d/tr incl breakfast from US$63/73; P❄@📶🏊) 🍃 A favorite pick in central Managua, the Europeo offers clean, business-style rooms, a pleasant thatched-roof restaurant out back, large gardens and swimming pool. But the real kicker is that all profits from the hotel go to benefit the Dianova Nicaragua Foundation. It's located on a side street off busy Av Monumental, making it relatively safe to walk to at night.

Hotel Casa Real HOTEL **$$$**
(Map p48; ☎2278-3838; www.hotelcasarealmanagua.com; Hotel Seminole Plaza, 3c N, ½cO; s/d from US$60/75; ❄📶) On a residential street a short walk from the busy UCA bus terminal, this hotel is located inside a large house with surprisingly spacious and modern guest rooms. It's within easy walking distance of Metrocentro, too.

Hotel El Conquistador HOTEL **$$$**
(Map p44; ☎2222-4789; www.elconquistadornicaragua.com; del Banco BDF de Plaza Inter, 1c abajo; d from US$58; P❄📶) One of the few hotels with any real style in the area, the Conquistador masks itself as a business hotel, but the granny quilts and wrought-iron bedstands reveal a homespun bed-and-breakfast at heart. Rooms are big and comfortable.

Hotel Mansión Teodolinda HOTEL **$$$**
(Map p44; ☎2228-1050; www.teodolinda.com.ni; Intur, 1c S, 1c O; s/d from US$60/70; P❄@📶🏊) The word *mansión* is a bit misleading: there's nothing palatial about this hotel. The main draw at the Teodolinda is the outdoor pool and the breakfast spread. Guest rooms are bland but fairly spacious, and nightlife and restaurants are within a block's walk.

Hotel Crowne Plaza HOTEL **$$$**
(Map p44; ☎2228-3530; www.ihg.com/crowneplaza; Plaza Inter, 1c S; r from US$90; ❄📶🏊) The latest upscale franchise to inhabit the landmark neo-Aztec pyramid by the mall, the Crowne Plaza offers what you'd expect: comfortable and somewhat bland modern rooms, plus an outdoor pool and a big buffet breakfast. Book a room with a view of the lake – the higher the floor, the better.

Hotel y Apartamento Los Cisneros HOTEL **$$$**
(Map p44; ☎2222-3235; www.hotelloscisneros.com; Tica Bus, 1c N, 1½ O; d/tr from US$55/70,

3-/5-person apt from US$45/95; (P ✳ @ 📶) A great deal with colorful rooms, Los Cisneros is filled with artwork and plants. The apartments are basically just big rooms with a kitchenette, but they're upstairs and you get your own balcony and hammock.

🛏 Centro Comercial & Carretera a Masaya

Although this cluster of upscale neighborhoods includes Metrocentro mall and Managua's busiest intersection, walking around these shady side streets is rather nice, plus it's convenient to the country's best hotels and discos. (But of course you'll have to pay for such convenience.)

Managua Backpackers Inn HOSTEL $
(Map p48; 📞2267-0006; www.managuahostel.com; Monte de Los Olivos, 1c N (lago), 1c O y ½c N, Casa #56, Carretera a Masaya; dm/d from US$10/32; P ✳ @ 📶 ≋) In the quiet suburb of Los Robles, this shoestring hostel is minutes away from the Metrocentro mall and endless nightlife and restaurant options. Rooms are basic but breezy, open and comfortable. And all the hostel amenities are here – common room with DVD player, good-sized pool, well-stocked kitchen and plenty of tourist info.

SANDINO: PROPHET OF THE SEGOVIAS

Born in 1895 to a wealthy Niquinohomo landowner, Gregorio Sandino, and an indigenous servant girl, Margarita Calderón, Augusto César Sandino was always painfully aware of class differences. He spent his childhood in poverty until his mother abandoned him and the Sandinos unenthusiastically took him in.

The family eventually entrusted him with overseeing the farm, but after he almost killed the son of a prominent local Conservative politician in a gun duel, Sandino had to flee the country. He traveled and worked in Guatemala, Honduras and Mexico, discovering yoga, communism and Seventh Day Adventism along the way – even becoming a Freemason. For seven years he primed himself for a higher path, and when the statute of limitations ran out on his attempted murder charges, he returned to Nicaragua, which was by then embroiled in civil war.

Sandino offered his services to the Liberal forces, who refused to arm the untried newcomer. A group of prostitutes loaned Sandino the money instead, and he began a tireless guerrilla campaign, attracting mostly *campesino* (farmer) and indigenous followers.

In 1927 more than 2000 US Marines arrived with a treaty and orders to enforce it. 'All my men surrender,' said the Liberal commander during the formalities, tired of war and now hopelessly outgunned. 'Except one.'

On July 15, 1927, Sandino attacked the marines in Ocotal; the US responded with aerial bombing. Sandino retreated to the mountains and began a six-year, low-intensity war with US occupiers and the Guardia Nacional. Throughout the early 1930s Sandino's ragged army collected a series of hit-and-run victories. He declared himself the incarnation of Caesar, saying that a horrific Managua earthquake was proof of his divinity, and delivering his *Manifesto of Light and Truth,* which revealed that Nicaragua would be the final staging ground in the battle between good and evil. Things had gone way beyond ridding Nicaragua of US imperialism.

By 1933, despite Sandino's position as the de facto president of a large chunk of Nicaragua, the writing was on the wall: international support was gone and popular moderate Juan B Sacasa had just been elected president.

In exchange for peace, Sacasa gave Sandino 36,000 sq km of homestead near Jinotega, which he and his followers operated as a commune, and Sandino seemed to settle down. But the US military, which had to pull out due to domestic pressures, suspected he still had a secret cache of weapons.

As an insurance policy, the US began providing substantial military support to Anastazio Somoza García, a former water company official married to a niece of President Sacasa. He was among the guests at an official dinner party celebrating the big peace treaty with Sandino's forces on February 20, 1934.

After dinner, as they left the presidential palace, Sandino and his supporters were abducted and shot by Somoza's men. Their bodies were never found.

La Bicicleta Hostal
HOSTEL **$$**

(Map p48; ☑2225-2557; www.labicicletahostal.com; Restaurante La Marsellaise, 2½c abajo; dm/d US$18/42; ❋☎) At this cool and sustainably built new hostel, dorms and guest rooms are named after bicycles – try the Tándem for two people, or the Triciclo if you're traveling in a group of three. There's a lovely garden area with hammocks for relaxing, plus free wi-fi and an open kitchen for guest use.

Hotel Brandt's
HOTEL **$$**

(Map p48; ☑2277-1884; www.hotelbrandt.com; Los Robles de San Juan, Zona Hippos, 1c S, 1c O; r US$84; ❋☎) This reasonably priced hotel in the relatively upscale Los Robles neighborhood has clean, modern, airy rooms that sleep up to four people. It's not a charming B&B, but it's a reliable favorite for business travelers passing through, and the buffet breakfast is above par. It's tucked away a few blocks behind the Metrocentro shopping mall.

Hotel Contempo
BOUTIQUE HOTEL **$$$**

(☑2264-9160; www.hotelcontempo.com; Carretera a Masaya Km 11, 400m O, Residencial las Praderas; r US$99-151; P❋@☎≋) This modern boutique hotel is one of the finest in all of Managua. We wish it were a little more centrally located, but the large, ultramodern rooms with flat-screens, MP3 docks, funky architecture and cool attention to detail are delightful. The gardens and pool area are equally impressive, as are the contemporary restaurant and top-notch service.

Hotel Los Pinos
HOTEL **$$$**

(Map p48; ☑2270-0761; www.hotellospinos.com.ni; Reparto San Juan, Calle San Juan 314, Gimnasio Hercules, 1c S, ½c E; d from US$67; P❋@☎≋) This popular hotel is located in a good neighborhood; rooms are modern and spacious with minimalist decoration, facing a cheerful garden and patio area dominated by a large swimming pool.

Hotel Colón
HOTEL **$$$**

(Map p48; ☑2278-2490; www.hcolon.net; edificio BAC, 2c E; s/d US$60/70; P❋@☎) This neo-colonial option offers easy access to nearby nightlife in the Zona Rosa. The pastel building and common areas are quite cheery, while the rooms are modern and spacious (but could use a renovation).

Hotel Los Robles
HOTEL **$$$**

(Map p48; ☑2267-3008; www.hotellosrobles.com; Restaurante La Marsellaise, 30m S; d from US$102; ❋☎≋) This Spanish-colonial-style hotel is one of Managua's rare gems, with an attractively landscaped courtyard, centered on a burbling marble fountain, antique-style wooden furnishings, and modern in-room amenities. The pleasant neighborhood adds to the appeal.

Hilton Princess Managua Hotel
HOTEL **$$$**

(Map p48; ☑2255-5777; www.hilton.com; Carretera a Masaya Km 4.5; r from US$99; ☎≋) An outdoor swimming pool and 24-hour fitness center are welcome perks at this Hilton branch across the busy highway from the Metrocentro shopping mall.

Seminole Plaza Hotel
BUSINESS HOTEL **$$$**

(Map p48; ☑2270-0061; www.seminoleplaza.com; Bancentro Carretera a Masaya, 1c O, 1c S; d from US$92; P⊖❋@☎≋) Business class with a quirky baroque touch: gilded accents, flawless concierge service, surprisingly modern rooms (with '70s-style bathrooms) and an old-school shoeshine stand. There's a free airport shuttle service (arguably half the reason to stay here) and a swimming pool.

Camino Real
BUSINESS HOTEL **$$$**

(☑2255-5888; www.caminoreal.com.ni; Carretera Norte Km 9.5; r US$110; P❋@☎) Got an early flight? The Camino Real is just seconds from the airport.

✖ Eating

Go budget in Barrio Martha Quezada or upscale on Carretera a Masaya. When in doubt, head to a shopping mall food court, like the great one at Plaza Inter.

✖ Barrio Martha Quezada & Around

This area caters to businesspeople and backpackers, so prices are good. For a bit of variety, try the food court at Plaza Inter.

Doña Pilar
NICARAGUAN **$**

(Map p44; Tica Bus, 1c O, ½c N; dishes US$3-6; ⊙6-9pm Mon-Sat) Doña Pilar's been here for years, and this popular evening *fritanga* (sidewalk grill) is a neighborhood institution, both for her juicy, crispy barbecue chicken and the range of ever-so-slightly greasy tacos and enchiladas. It's a great introduction to typical Nicaraguan cuisine, with huge side servings of *gallo pinto* (rice and beans), chopped pickled cabbage and plantain chips.

Ananda VEGETARIAN $
(Map p44; frente Estatua de Montoya; mains US$2-5; ⊙8am-3pm Mon-Sat; 🥗) Enjoy freshly prepared vegetarian plates and a wide range of *licuados* (fruit and veggie juices and smoothies) on this spacious patio overlooking lush gardens. There's a lunch buffet from 11am to 3pm.

Cafetín Mirna NICARAGUAN $
(Map p44; Tica Bus, 1c O, 1c S; mains US$2-6; ⊙8am-5pm Mon-Sat) Come here for a big breakfast with fluffy pancakes, fabulous fresh juices and a good lunch buffet, too – it's a local tradition.

Cafetín Tonalli BAKERY $
(Map p44; Tica Bus, 2c E, ½c S; dishes US$2-6; ⊙8am-2pm Mon-Sat) If you're jonesing for some *pan integral* (wholewheat bread), this simple bakery and cafe, run by a women's co-op, is the place to be. The fresh-baked treats are also good to grab for a long bus ride out of town (it's conveniently located to the Tica Bus terminal).

🍴 Centro Commercial & Carretera a Masaya

Metrocentro (p55) and Galerias Santo Domingo (p55) malls both have large food courts (the latter is a bit more upscale). There are good restaurants along the Carretera a Masaya, but you'll probably need your own car (or a specific plan for your taxi driver) to access them.

Cocina Doña Haydee NICARAGUAN $$
(Map p48; www.lacocina.com.ni; Carretera a Masaya Km 4.5; mains US$5-10; ⊙breakfast, lunch & dinner) This traditional Nicaraguan eatery spot does classic dishes, well presented and carefully prepared, from *gallo pinto* and *guiso de chilote* (cheese soup with baby corn) to steak with all the trimmings. There are takeaway locations in the food court at Plaza Inter and Metrocentro shopping malls, too.

La Terraza Peruana PERUVIAN $$
(Map p48; www.aterrazaperuana.com; de la Pastelería Sampson, 100m al lago; mains US$5-12; ⊙noon-11pm Tue-Sun) A casual but refined Peruvian restaurant set on a cool front balcony overlooking a leafy side street, La Terraza has a huge menu that takes you from coastal to high Andean cuisine. With advance notice you can order such Peruvian classics as *cuy*

(roasted guinea pig). Don't miss a cocktail from the pisco list.

El Garabato Café y Antojitos NICARAGUAN $$
(Map p48; Seminole Plaza, 2½c S; mains US$6-10; ⊙7pm-late) An artsy sort of place (for this side of town, anyway), serving up carefully prepared versions of traditional Nica dishes like *vigorón* (steamed yucca and pork rinds), *nacatamales* (banana-leaf wrapped bundles of cornmeal, meat, vegetables and herbs) and *repocheta* (cheese-stuffed tortillas).

Pan e Vino ITALIAN $$
(Map p48; 🖉2278-4442; www.paneevino.online.com.ni; Enitel Villa Fontana, 200m N; mains US$7-14; ⊙noon-3pm & 6-11pm Mon-Sat) Getting the thumbs up from Italian expats, this stylish yet unpretentious place does good-sized pasta plates and crunchy-crusted pizzas. It has a small but decent selection of Italian, Spanish and Chilean wines to linger over. Check the website: they'll happily deliver food to your hotel.

El Muelle SEAFOOD $$
(Map p48; www.elmuellerestaurante.com; Hotel Intercontinental Metrocentro, ½c E; mains US$6-14; ⊙11:30am-11:30pm Mon-Sat, to 7:30pm Sun) Set behind a line of trees on a busy street, El Muelle ('The Dock') is a well-established seafood institution specializing in fresh fish, ceviche and garlic shrimp. Locals say they have the best *tostones* (green plantains, sliced and fried) around.

La Casa del Café CAFE $$
(Map p48; www.casadelcafe.com.ni; Lacmiel, 1c E, ½c S, Altamira; sandwiches US$6; ⊙8am-7pm) One of the main locations of Nicaragua's popular coffee chain. Grab a table on the spacious and airy upstairs balcony and you'll find it hard to leave. All the standard and gourmet coffee options are available (including a very satisfying frozen *mochaccino*), plus a range of pastries and sandwiches and a couple of breakfast options.

La Hora del Taco MEXICAN $$
(Map p48; 🖉2270-6712; Monte de los Olivos, 1c N; mains US$4.50-9; ⊙noon-midnight) This sprawling Mexican bar and restaurant has a wide-ranging menu that includes standards like nachos and fajitas, plus a few southern Mexican favorites like *cochinita pibil* (suckling pig).

Restaurante Don Pez SEAFOOD $$
(Rotonda Bello Horizonte, 1c E; dishes US$6-11; ◑noon-3pm & 6-11pm Mon-Fri) The best seafood restaurant in the area, the Don also grills a pretty mean steak. It's hard to pass up the surf-and-turf platter (fish, shrimp and beef).

La Casa de Los Nogueras EUROPEAN $$$
(Map p48; www.lacasadelosnogueras.com; Av Principal Los Robles 17; mains US$14-25; ◑noon-3pm & 7pm-late Mon-Sat) One of the most elegant restaurants in town, this cozy European bistro has delightful art, a wonderful garden out back for alfresco eating and top-notch but overly formal service. Note, if you're planning on swinging by after a volcano hike: no shorts allowed.

Marea Alta SEAFOOD $$$
(Map p48; ☏2278-2459; www.mareaalta.net; Seminole Plaza, 1c S; meals US$6-18, set lunch US$8.50; ◑11:30am-3pm & 6-11pm) One of the more highly respected seafood restaurants in town – we recommend the lobster risotto. With an enviable corner location in the middle of the bar district, people-watching opportunities here are endless. There are a few other branches around town.

La Marseillaise FRENCH $$$
(Map p48; ☏2277-0224; www.lamarseillaise-nicaragua.com; Seminole Plaza, 4c S; mains US$12-20; ◑noon-3pm & 6-11pm Mon-Sat) The gold standard in Nicaraguan fine dining has tastefully art-bedecked walls, outstanding wine pairings and authentic French cuisine. Make reservations.

🍸 Drinking & Nightlife

There are bars all over town. Some of the better ones can be found in Barrio Martha Quezada, around the Metrocentro mall and at the Rotonda Bello Horizonte. Take a cab home!

DISCOS OF BELLO HORIZONTE

Dubbed 'the heart of Nicaribeña,' Bello Horizonte is home to the largest concentration of Caribbean-descended Nicaraguans in Managua. Clubs out here have a predictably Atlantic-coast flavor, with a heavier reggae, soca and *punta* (a traditional Garifuna dance involving much hip movement) influence than their counterparts down south.

El Grillito BAR
(Map p44; Intur, ½c N; ◑noon-late) There are a few little outdoor bars like this in the area, but this one consistently gets a good crowd. A range of snacks and more substantial meals (mains US$3 to US$6) are on the menu and the music volume is conversation-friendly. There's a second location a block south.

Reef Bar Lounge & Grill LOUNGE
(Galeria Santo Domingo; ◑6pm-3am Wed-Sat) This popular bar and lounge in the emerging *zona viva*, the nightlife zone behind the Santo Domingo mall, is a favorite pre-dance spot for scenesters.

Tabú GAY
(Map p44; Intur, 100m S; ◑9pm-late Wed-Sat) One of the few gay bars with any longevity in town, Tabu's dance floor gets going on weekends (cover charge varies by night). At the time of writing, it was in the process of expanding into the space next door.

☆ Entertainment

There are dozens of venues around town that occasionally have live music, folkloric dance, alternative theater, poetry readings and other cultural offerings. Thursday editions of *La Prensa* and *El Nuevo Diario* have good listings. You can also take a walk through the UCA (p45) to see what's on.

La Casa de los Mejía Godoy LIVE MUSIC
(Map p44; ☏2222-6110; www.losmejiagodoy.com; frente Hotel Crowne Plaza; cover charge from US$10) Living legends Carlos and Luis Enrique Mejía Godoy, whose folk-music explorations into the heart of Nicaraguan culture have become church hymns and revolutionary standards since they first started laying down riffs in the 1960s, have moved from their original intimate venue to larger premises, complete with a restaurant and bar (open 8am to 4:30pm Monday to Tuesday, and to 1am Wednesday to Saturday). Make reservations if you're planning on seeing the Godoy Brothers play.

Teatro Nacional Rubén Darío THEATER
(Map p46; ☏2266-3630; www.tnrubendario.gob.ni; Área Monumental) One of the few Managua buildings to have survived the 1972 earthquake, this groovy theater often has big-name international offerings on the main stage. It's worth trying to catch some experimental jazz or performance art in the smaller Sala Experimental Pilar Aguirre.

Ruta Maya   LIVE MUSIC
(Map p44; ☎2268-0698; www.rutamaya.com.
ni; Estadio Nacional, 1½c O; cover US$1-5) Look
around for flyers (or check the website) for
happenings at this thatch-roofed venue. You
get everything from Bee Gees cover bands
to Caribbean *palo de mayo* (Afro-Caribbean
dance music) to *son nicaragüense* (traditional Nicaraguan folk music). Barbecued
meat is the specialty on the menu, and dinner shows are worth booking ahead for.

**Estadio Denis
Martínez**   SPECTATOR SPORT, BASEBALL
(Map p44) The national baseball stadium is
absolutely packed between mid-November
and early April, when Nicaragua's four professional teams, including the Managua
Bóers, compete in the national champion-
ships. Get stats, schedules and more at the
Liga de Beisbol Profesional (www.lnbp.
com.ni) website.

Estadio Cranshaw   SPECTATOR SPORT, FOOTBALL
(Map p44) Reflecting football's secondary status in Nicaragua, Estadio Cranshaw
is a more humble affair that squats in the
shadows of its big brother, just to the south.
There has long been talk of constructing a
larger stadium, near UNAN; the **Nicaraguan Football Association** (www.fenifut.org.
ni) will have the latest information.

INCH   PERFORMING ARTS
(Instituto Nicaragüense de Cultura Hispanica;
☎2276-0733; nichispanica@gmail.com; Av del
Campo 40-42, Las Colinas; ☉9am-3pm Mon-Fri)
In the very ritzy hill suburb of Las Colinas
to the south of town, this center hosts some
of the city's best cultural events, including
cinema, theater, art and photography exhibitions, concerts and art-themed workshops.

**La Sala de Teatro
Justo Rufino Garay**   THEATER
(☎2266-3714; www.rufinos.org; Estatua de Montoya, 3c O, 20m N; tickets US$5-8) Fans of alter-
native theater should check out the program
at this small, not-for-profit theater space,
which specializes in experimental, contemporary works – often with a political bent.
Plays are generally staged on Friday and Saturday nights.

Cinema Plaza Inter   CINEMA
(Map p44; www.plazaintermall.com.ni; Plaza
Inter; tickets US$3-4) At Plaza Inter, close to
Barrio Martha Quezada. Mostly mainstream
Hollywood films are screened with subtitles.

CATCHING A FILM

**La Sala de Teatro Justo Rufino
Garay** shows artsy movies. Nearly
every shopping center or mall has a
cinema; most show mainstream Hollywood movies.

Metrocentro Cinemark   CINEMA
(Map p48; Metrocentro Mall; tickets US$2.50)
This bigger-is-better mall has six screens
and shows blockbuster movies.

🔒 Shopping

Boutiques are clustered in Altamira. Artisans sell their work all around town, especially on weekends.

Plaza Inter   MALL
(Map p44; www.plazaintermall.com.ni; ☉11am-
9pm) Adjacent to Barrio Martha Quezada,
it's convenient, with a cinema (with subti-
tled movies), lots of discount shops, a couple
of department stores and a solid food court
that's bustling with Nicaraguan families at
mealtimes.

Mercado Roberto Huembes   HANDICRAFTS
This is more than just the southbound bus
terminal: it has the best selection of souvenirs in Managua, from all over the country.
It's also one of the most dangerous places to
wander around, so see if you can get a local
guide or friend to take you.

Librería Hispamer   BOOKS
(Map p48; www.hispamer.com.ni; UCA, 1c E, 1c N;
☉9am-7pm Mon-Fri, to 5pm Sat) This bookstore
on the edge of the UCA campus has a good
selection of Nicaraguan and Latin American
literature, history and poetry.

Metrocentro   MALL
(Map p48; www.metrocentro.com; ☉8am-9pm)
Upscale mall with restaurants, cinemas and
a good food court.

Plaza España   MALL
(☉8am-7pm Mon-Fri, to 2pm Sat) A shopping
mall with the usual offerings.

Galerías Santo Domingo   MALL
(www.galerias.com.ni; Carretera a Masaya Km 8;
☉10am-8pm) See and be seen at the discos,
eateries and shops of Managua's most upscale mall.

MANAGUA'S BOOKSTORES

Managua has a great selection of bookstores – which is OK if you can read Spanish. (There are better selections of English-language books in San Juan del Sur and Granada, if you're heading there next.) UCA and UNAN both have excellent libraries.

Simplemente Madera   ARTS & CRAFTS
(Map p48; www.simplementamadera.com; Enitel Villa Fontana, 200m N) Simplemente Madera ('Simply Wood') makes gorgeous bespoke furniture out of Nicaraguan wood.

ⓘ Orientation

The Panamericana (Pan-American Hwy) enters Managua from the southwest, via Jinotepe, as Carretera Sur, and exits to the northeast, past the airport toward Matagalpa and El Rama, as Carretera Norte. Running southeast from Metrocentro and Rotonda Rubén Darío is Carretera a Masaya, along which Managua's swankiest discos, restaurants and malls can be found. Heading west are Carretera Nueva and Carretera Vieja (New and Old Hwys) to León. Managua has hundreds of neighborhoods stretched between these highways, and not even the kamikaze *taxistas* (taxi drivers) know them all.

Área Monumental, on the lakefront site of Managua's pre-1972 downtown, is home to the Museo Nacional, Casa Presidencial (Presidential Palace) and Teatro Rubén Darío. It's connected by Av Bolívar, a major thoroughfare, to the Plaza Inter shopping mall, Loma de Tiscapa and Barrio Martha Quezada, which has most services for budget travelers. To the southwest are Barrio Bolonia, with midrange accommodations, and Plaza España, next to Rotonda El Güegüense, with banks, travel agencies and airline offices.

To the southeast is Managua's modern commercial center, a 2km strip of Carretera a Masaya extending southeast from Metrocentro mall and Rotonda Rubén Darío through the cluster of glittering restaurants and bars known as Zona Rosa, as well as swanky Los Robles and Altamira, two of Managua's most exclusive neighborhoods. West of Rotonda Rubén Darío is Universidad Centro America (UCA), with left-wing bookstores and microbuses to most major regional cities, including Granada and Masaya.

Rotonda Bello Horizonte, located east of the Área Monumental, is a nightlife district with a few budget lodging options.

ⓘ Information

DANGERS & ANNOYANCES

Managua has a bad reputation for being a dangerous city, and with fairly good reason. But by using common sense and general caution, you can avoid problems.

➡ Don't flash expensive items. Keep your phone in your pocket or bag.

➡ Look at the map before venturing out on a walk.

➡ Make ATM transactions during daylight hours.

➡ Ask your hotel or hostel to call you a taxi instead of hailing one in the street.

➡ Carry only as much money as you'll need for the day.

➡ If you find yourself surrounded by abandoned houses and businesses, turn around and go back the way you came.

EMERGENCY

Ambulance (Cruz Roja) ☑128
Fire ☑115 (emergency), ☑2222-6406
Police ☑118 (emergency), ☑2249-5714

GAY & LESBIAN TRAVELERS

The gay and lesbian scene is hidden, but you can find it. There are a few gay clubs in Managua, which is a few more than you'll find anywhere else in the country. Hotel, bar and other local tips are available by navigating to the Nicaragua section at www.purpleroofs.com.

IMMIGRATION OFFICES

Migración (Dirección de Migración y Extranjería; ☑2244-3989; www.migob.gob.ni/dgme; Semaf Tenderí, 200m N) The main office is located near the Ciudad Jardín area, but there's a much more convenient **branch office** (Map p48; no phone; www.migracion.gob.ni; Metrocentro; ⊙10am-6pm Mon-Fri, to 1pm Sat & Sun) in the Metrocentro shopping mall.

INTERNET ACCESS

Internet access is fast and plentiful, averaging US$1 per minute at cafes all over town. Wi-fi can be found in most hotels and, increasingly, at cafes and restaurants.

LAUNDRY

Laundry services are sadly lacking here, but most hotels offer laundry (in cheaper places, by hand, so allow time to dry). If your hotel doesn't do laundry, try the one next door.

MEDICAL SERVICES

Managua has scores of pharmacies – some open 24 hours (just knock) – and the nation's best hospitals.

> ### ❶ NAVIGATING MANAGUA
>
> As in other Nicaraguan cities and towns, only Managua's major roads are named. Large buildings, *rotondas* (traffic circles) and traffic lights serve as de facto points of reference, and locations are described in terms of their direction and distance, usually in *cuadras* (blocks) from these points. Many of these reference points no longer exist, and thus addresses may begin with something like *'de donde fue Sandy's'* ('from where Sandy's used to be').
>
> In Managua, a special system is used for the cardinal points, whereby *al lago* (to the lake) means 'north' while *a la montaña* (to the mountains) means 'south.' *Arriba* (up) is 'east' toward the sunrise, while *abajo* (down) is 'west' and toward the sunset. Thus one might hear: *'del antiguo Cine Dorado, una cuadra al lago y dos cuadras arriba'* ('from the old Cine Dorado, one block toward the lake and two blocks up'), meaning one block north and two blocks east.
>
> Confused? You get used to it (and you may be consoled to know that the rest of the country uses the same system, except with the cardinal points named). Listings in this section give the 'address' in Spanish – but we use the cardinal points, N *(norte)*, S *(sur)*, E *(este)* and O *(oeste)*, and 'c' for *cuadra* – so you can ask locals for help or just let the cab driver figure it out.

Hospital Alemán-Nicaragüense (☎2249-3368; Carretera Norte, Km 6) Has some German-speaking staff and modern equipment.

Hospital Bautista (☎2264-9020; www.hospitalbautistanicaragua.com; Casa Ricardo Morales Avíles, 2c S, 1½c E, Barrio Largaespada) Your best bet, with some English-speaking staff.

Hospital Metropolitano Vivian Pellas (☎2255-6900; www.metropolitano.com.ni; Carretera a Masaya Km 9.75) State of the art facility.

MONEY

Managua has scores of banks and ATMs, most on the Visa/Plus system. BAC, with machines at Metrocentro mall, Managua International Airport and Plaza España, accepts MasterCard/Cirrus debit cards and gives US dollars and *córdobas*. Any bank can change US dollars.

POST

Palacio de Correos (Map p46; Plaza de la Revolución, 2c O) The main post office (inside the former Enitel building) has poste restante services (mail is held for up to 45 days).

TELEPHONE

You can purchase a chip to make your cell phone function on local networks, or make phone calls from your hotel. Call centers and internet cafes are also fairly plentiful downtown.

TOURIST INFORMATION

Ineter (Nicaragua Institute for Territorial Studies; ☎2249-3890; www.ineter.gob.ni; frente Dirección de Migración y Extranjeria, Managua) Has the best selection of detailed maps in the country. Many are out of print, but bring a flash drive and they'll upload the files.

Intur Central (Nicaraguan Institute of Tourism; Map p44; ☎2254-5191; www.visitanicaragua.com/ingles; Crowne Plaza, 1c S, 1c O; ◷8am-5pm Mon-Fri) The flagship office of Nicaragua's official tourist-info organization has heaps of flyers. There's another office in the international terminal at the airport.

Marena Central (Ministry of the Environment & Natural Resources; ☎2263-2830; www.marena.gob.ni; Carretera Norte Km 12.5) Bring ID to the inconveniently located headquarters (out past the airport) to access maps, flyers and management plans for most of Nicaragua's 82 protected areas.

TRAVELERS WITH DISABILITIES

Travelers with disabilities will find the modern hotels and restaurants along the Carretera a Masaya much more comfortable than the offerings closer to the historic center.

❶ Getting There & Away

AIR

Managua International Airport (MGA; www.eaai.com.ni; Carretera Norte, Km 13) is a small, manageable airport located about 30 to 45 minutes from most hotels. **Intur** (airport; ◷8am-10pm) has an office inside the international terminal, next to the luggage belt in the arrivals area, where English-speaking staff can recommend hotels, confirm flights and share flyers.

The smaller, more chaotic domestic terminal is adjacent to the main building. The following airlines fly from Managua:

American Airlines (☎2255-9095; www. aa.com; Plaza España, 3c S) Daily flights to Miami.

Delta Airlines (Map p48; ☎2254-8130; www.delta.com; Seminole Plaza, 3½c S) Daily flights to Atlanta.

La Costeña (p300) The domestic carrier has regular service to Bluefields, the Corn Islands, Las Minas, Puerto Cabezas and Waspán.

BUS

Managua is the main transportation hub for the country, with several major national bus and van terminals, plus a handful of international bus lines (most grouped in Barrio Martha Quezada).

International Buses

Tica Bus (p299) is located in a terminal in the heart of Barrio Martha Quezada.

Costa Rica (US$29 to US$46, 10 hours, four daily) Goes to San José.

Guatemala (US$63 to US$80, 30 hours, two daily) To Guatemala City.

Honduras (US$25, seven hours, one daily) To Tegucigalpa.

Panama City (US$74 to US$110, 34 hours, six daily) To Panama City via San José.

San Salvador (US$40 to US$57, 11 hours, two daily)

Transnica (p299) has offices over on the other side of the *laguna*.

Costa Rica (US$29, nine hours, four per day) To San José. There's a luxury bus (US$38) that leaves daily at 1pm.

Honduras (US$30, 10 hours, one daily) For Tegucigalpa.

Transporte del Sol (p299) has two daily buses leaving for San Salvador (US$50) and two for Guatemala City (US$78).

Central Line (Map p44; ☎2254-5431; www. transportescentralline.com; Calle 27 de Mayo, 4½c O, Esso) offers one daily bus to San José, Costa Rica (US$29, eight hours), with stops in Granada and Rivas.

National Buses & Minivans

Buses leave from three main places: **Mercado Roberto Huembes** for Granada, Masaya and southwest Nicaragua; **Mercado Israel Lewites**, commonly known as Bóer, for León and the northern Pacific; and **Mercado Mayoreo** for the Caribbean coast and the northern highlands. Some also leave from the Mercado Oriental, mainly to rural destinations not covered here.

It's faster, more comfortable and a bit more expensive to take **minivans from UCA** (Map p48; pronounced 'ooka') or *expreso* (express) versus *ordinario* (regular) service.

NATIONAL BUS SERVICES FROM MANAGUA

DESTINATION	COST (US$)	DURATION	DEPARTURES	FREQUENCY	LEAVES FROM
Boaco	2.20	3	4am-6:30pm	every 15min	Mayoreo
Carazo (serving Diriamba & Jinotepe)	1.40	1	4:30am-6:20pm	every 20min	Bóer
Chinandega/El Viejo	2.70	3	5am-6pm	every 30min	Bóer
Chinandega minibus	3	2	4am-6pm	when full	Bóer
Estelí	3	2	5:45am-5:45pm	hourly	Mayoreo
Granada	0.75	1	4am-6pm	every 15min	Huembes
Granada minibus	1.25	1	6am-8pm	when full	UCA
Jinotega	3.50	4	4am-5:30pm	hourly	Mayoreo
Jinotepe minibus	1.15	1	5am-8pm	when full	UCA
Juigalpa	2	4	3:15am-10pm	every 20min	Mayoreo
La Paz Centro	1.60	1½	6:15am-8pm	every 30min	Bóer
León expreso (via New Hwy & La Paz Centro)	1.85	1½	10am-6:30pm	every 2hr	Bóer
León ordinario (via Old Hwy)	1.50	2	5am-7pm	every 20min	Bóer
León minibus	2.75	1½	4am-6pm	when full	Bóer
León minibus	2.75	1½	5am-9:15pm	when full	UCA

Shuttle Buses

With frequent, inexpensive public minibuses running to León, Granada and other popular destinations, Managua's shuttle-bus scene is not huge. The biggest draws here are safety and the direct airport departure, meaning you don't have to cab into town to catch an onward bus. **Paxeos** (☎2552-8291; www.paxeos.com) serves Granada (US$40), León (US$70) and many other destinations (prices quoted are for up to three people). **Adelante Express** (☎8850-6070; www.adelanteexpress.com) offers similar services.

CAR & MOTORCYCLE

Driving in Managua is a fool's errand – take a cab. Once you get out of the city, it's easy enough.

Alamo (Map p44; ☎2277-1117; www.alamonicaragua.com; Hospital Militar, 100m E)

Avis (Map p48; ☎Airport 2233-3011; www.avis.com; Metrocentro Intercontinental)

Budget (☎2278-9504; www.budget.com.ni; Holiday Inn, Pista Juan Pablo II)

Easy Rent-a-car (Map p48; ☎2270-0654; www.easyrentacar.com.ni; Carretera a Masaya, Km 7.5)

Hertz (p301)

Lugo (p301)

ⓘ Getting Around

TO/FROM THE AIRPORT

The airport is 11km from town and has its special, more expensive taxis (US$20 to US$25 to most destinations in Managua), which are private – unlike many taxis in Managua, they don't stop to pick up additional passengers along the route. You might also arrange pick up with your hotel for a more competitive price.

BUS

Local buses are frequent and crowded. They're also known for their professional pickpockets, but stay alert and you'll be fine. Routes run every 10 minutes from 4:45am to 6pm, then every 15 minutes until 10pm. Buses do not generally stop en route – look for the nearest bus shelter. The fare is US$0.25. Useful routes:

No 101 Linda Vista to Mercado Mayoreo, via Rotonda Bello Horizonte.

No 109 Plaza de la República to Mercado Roberto Huembes, stopping en route at Plaza Inter.

No 110 Mercado Israel Lewites (Bóer) to Mercado Mayoreo, via UCA, Metrocentro, Rotonda de Centroamérica, Mercado Roberto Huembes and Mercado Iván Montenegro.

No 116 Estatua de Montoya, Plaza Inter, Mercado Oriental and Rotonda Bello Horizonte.

MANAGUA GETTING AROUND

DESTINATION	COST (US$)	DURATION	DEPARTURES	FREQUENCY	LEAVES FROM
Masatepe minibus	1.10	1	6:30am-6:30pm	every 20min	Huembes
Masaya	0.50	1	5:30am-9pm	every 30min	Huembes
Masaya minibus	0.90	½	6am-9pm	when full	UCA
Matagalpa	2.25	2¾	3am-6pm	hourly	Mayoreo
Mateare	0.30	40min	5:50am-6:30pm	every 2hr	Bóer
Naindame	1	1½	11am-3:30pm	every 20min	Huembes
Ocotal	4.25	3½	5am-5pm	hourly	Mayoreo
Pochomil/Masachapa	1.30-1.60	2	6am-7pm	every 20min	Bóer
Río Blanco	5	4	9:15am-12:15pm	hourly	Mayoreo
Rivas expreso	3.25	1½	4am-6pm	every 30min	Huembes
Rivas ordinario	2	2	4am-6pm	every 30min	Huembes
San Carlos	7.50	9	5am-6pm	6 daily	Mayoreo
San Juan del Sur	3.25	2½	5am-6pm	2 daily	Huembes
San Marcos minibus	1	1	4am-6pm	when full	Huembes
Somoto	4	4	5am-6pm	8 daily	Mayoreo
Ticuantepe minibus	0.40	40min	4am-6pm	when full	Huembes

No 118 From Parque Las Piedrecitas, heads down Carretera Sur, then east, passing by Mercado Israel Lewites (Bóer), Rotonda El Güegüense (Plaza España), Plaza Inter and Mercado Oriental on its way to Mercado Mayoreo.

No 119 From Linda Vista to Mercado Roberto Huembes, with stops at Rotonda El Güegüense and UCA.

CAR & MOTORCYCLE

Driving in Managua is not recommended at night – even if you have a rental car, consider getting a taxi, and make sure your car is in a guarded lot. Night drivers should keep their windows rolled up and stay alert.

TAXI

➟ Most taxis in Managua are *colectivos,* which pick up passengers as they go. There are also more expensive private taxis based at the airport, shopping malls, Mercado Roberto Huembes and other places. These are safer, but regular taxis also always congregate close by.

➟ Licensed taxis have red plates and the driver's ID above the dash; if yours doesn't, you're in a pirate taxi. This is probably OK, but don't go to the ATM, and beware of scams no matter what kind of taxi you're in.

➟ At night, take only licensed taxis – there has been an increase in reports of taxi drivers robbing passengers after dark.

AROUND MANAGUA

Managua might not be a city you'd like to linger in for long, but there are a few more attractive destinations within easy reach of the capital. The beach towns of Masachapa and Pochomil are laid-back getaways on the Pacific coast, while nearby Montelimar has an all-inclusive resort that brings a steady stream of beachgoers on a well-beaten path from the airport. Elsewhere, just south of the city, Reserva Natural Chocoyero-El Brujo is a green miniparadise famed for its waterfalls and lively parakeet population.

Masachapa & Pochomil

The twin towns of Masachapa and Pochomil are so close together that they might as well be one. You arrive in Masachapa, a small fishing village with a handful of bars, hotels and restaurants on the beach. Some will rent surfboards and arrange boating excursions.

🏃 Activities

There's great surfing – a left-point break just north of Montelimar, and a hollow right reef break to the south; beach-break Quizala is closer to Masachapa. South of Pochomil there are scores of smallish, predictable peaks, perfect to learn on.

There's a surprisingly clean river between Masachapa and Pochomil that makes for a fun dip.

🛏 Sleeping & Eating

The better hotels are on the beach, but there are several others located along the road to Pochomil. To get there, cross the river to the south of Mesachapa, heading east along a dirt road from the gas station.

There are a few casual places to grab a bite along the beach, and most hotels have their own restaurants. It's also advisable to bring some supplies from Managua or Granada.

Casa del Titito   HOTEL $$
(☑ 8484-7724; www.casadeltitito.com; San Rafael del Sur, Pochomil; d US$60; 🛜 🌊) Right on the beach and featuring an outdoor pool, this easygoing hotel is a good budget pick with a complimentary Nicaraguan breakfast. French, English and Spanish are spoken.

Hotel Altamar   HOTEL $$
(☑ 8692-7971; Centro Turístico Pochomil, terminal de buses 1c E; d US$45; P 🌸) One of the best deals in Pochomil, Altamar has good ocean views and small, spotless rooms. There's a decent restaurant onsite, too.

Casa Larocque   HOTEL $$
(☑ 995-5970; www.casalarocque.com; Vistamar 100m E , Pochomil; d US$75; 🛜 🌊) This friendly little hotel has spacious, clean guest rooms, a lovely pool area, relaxing outdoor lounge space and a great onsite restaurant. No wonder it's such a hit with travelers.

Hotel Vistamar Resort   RESORT $$$
(☑ 2265-8099; www.vistamarhotel.com; Playa de Pochomil; d incl all meals from US$132; P 🌸 🛜 🌊) This is one of the prettiest hotels on this stretch of coast; accommodations are in two-story wooden bungalows and upstairs rooms have lovely views. Three swimming pools, an onsite day spa and a gorgeous stretch of white-sand beach seal the deal. Check here for turtle tours or volunteer ops with its turtle-release program.

Around Managua

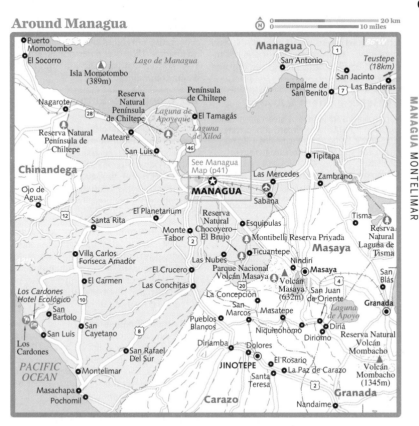

🛈 Getting There & Away

Buses arrive first at Masachapa – if you're planning on staying here, get off at the *empalme* (T intersection).

Buses run from Pochomil and Masachapa to Managua's Mercado Israel Lewites (US$1.30 to US$1.60, two hours) roughly every 30 minutes from 8am to 6pm.

Montelimar

You'll be going the all-inclusive route if you stay around Montelimar. What's the draw? Amazing beaches, some decent surf breaks and a resort bigger than a city.

🛏 Sleeping

There's a big resort and a smaller hotel here; otherwise, head to Pochomil and Masachapa for a wider range of options.

Los Cardones Hotel Ecológico   LODGE $$$
(☑ 8364-5925; www.loscardones.com; Carretera Montelimar Km 49 15km O, Finca Del Mar Beach Community; per person bungalow/cabaña without bathroom US$115/99, incl meals) 🌱 North of Montelimar, this rustic ecolodge has great food and some of the best surfing in Nicaragua, just steps from your hammock. The owners offer fishing, snorkeling and horseback riding, and sea turtles lay their eggs on the beach. The whole operation is not only low-impact (solar energy, composting) but also family-friendly, with surf breaks for kids under 12.

The hotel arranges transportation from the airport for a cost of US$60 one-way for one or two people, or US$80 for three to five people.

**Barceló Montelimar
Beach Resort**   RESORT $$$
(☑ 2264-9310; www.barcelomontelimarbeach.com; Carretera a Masachapa Km 65; r from US$330 all

inclusive; P ⊖ ✳ @ ✉) Formerly the Somozas' summer home, this resort has plenty on offer: spacious rooms and bungalows, several huge pools, tennis courts, discos and restaurants. Prices include all meals, beer, rum and many activities.

❶ Getting There & Away

Many travelers arrive here by prearranged transportation from Managua airport, or by driving themselves. Some accommodations will offer private transportation from Managua airport for a fee.

If you're taking public transportation, get a bus from Managua to Pochomil and Masachapa (US$1.30 to US$1.60, two hours), then a taxi to your hotel.

Ticuantepe

Just 19km from Managua, Ticuantepe is a refreshing escape from the sweltering city, with temperatures ranging from 22°C to 28°C (71°F to 82°F). It's on the western rim of the Complejo Ventarrón Volcanic (Ventarrón Volcanic Complex), across from Nindirí and Masaya.

Occupied for at least 2500 years by the Matagalpa nation, Ticuantepe is today the service center for an enormous and productive agricultural region, colloquially known as the Valle de las Piñas (Valley of Pineapples).

◉ Sights & Activities

Pared de las Serpientes ARCHAEOLOGICAL SITE
One of the most important petroglyphs in the region, the tantalizingly entitled Wall of Snakes has more than 25 beautifully preserved serpent-related drawings, and is within easy walking distance of town. Unfortunately, it's on private property (ask Cantur, downtown, about guides).

Museo Arqueológico Municipal Raúl Rojas MUSEUM
(⊙ hours vary, usually 9am-4pm Mon-Sat) FREE
The closest thing to a tourist attraction in town, this is next to the *alcaldía* (mayor's office), with more than 50 stone and ceramic pieces dug up in the immediate era, plus an impressive mural of Ticuantepe c AD 1200. If it's closed, you may be able to gain entry by stopping in and asking at the mayor's office.

El Ventarrón HIKING
(☑ 8380-6694; La Sabanita) This small outdoor cooperative runs hikes and horseback-riding excursions (US$30 per person) in Masaya Volcano National Park and the rural La Sabanita community.

🍴 Sleeping & Eating

There aren't many hotels around here, just one resort. Most travelers stay in Managua and visit Ticuantepe on a day trip.

There are several good places to eat around Ticuantepe – you could even plan a day trip around dining at one of the local restaurants. Some feature live music and outdoor swimming pools that are great for kids.

La Nueva Borgoña NICARAGUAN $
(☑ 2279-5552; Km 201/2 Carretera a la Concha, Ticuantepe; mains US$3-8; ⊙ 9am-9pm) Traditional Nicaraguan food, mountain views, kid-friendly amenities and live music on weekends make this family-friendly restaurant a great roadside stop.

Restaurante Campestre Las Pitahayas NICARAGUAN $$
(Carretera a Ticuantepe, Km 18; mains US$3-8; ⊙ 11am-10pm) On the road into town, serving good steaks and *comida típica* (regional specialties) under a huge thatched roof beside a fantastic swimming pool.

❶ Getting There & Away

Microbuses to Managua (Mercado Roberto Huembes; US$0.40 to US$0.50, 40 minutes) leave from Parque Central when full (about every 20 to 30 minutes). You can catch a taxi or *moto* (motorcycle) to the area reserves.

Reserva Natural Chocoyero-El Brujo

This deep, Y-shaped valley 23km south of Managua has a small, 184-hectare natural reserve that was originally created to safeguard almost one-third of Managua's water supply. El Brujo (The Wizard) is a waterfall that seems to disappear underground, separated by a 400m cliff from El Chocoyero (Place of Parakeets), the less immediately impressive cascade.

The reserve is great for hiking. Pineapples, coffee and bananas all grow here, and there's good birdwatching: look for the park's namesake *chocoyo* (green parakeet) around the reserve's waterfalls. Show up at around 3pm and you'll see bands of the parakeets come screaming home for their evening gossip.

Start at the interpretive center, with displays about the park's five parakeet species, then follow the two trails leading to the waterfalls, both of which could take all afternoon, if you're slow. Once at the reserve, ask staff about hiking guides or special tours, like the nighttime bat tour or a birdwatching hike.

You can camp here – at what's surely one of the most comfortable public campsites in Nicaragua – for US$5 per two-person tent.

🛈 Getting There & Away

The reserve is 7km away from where the Managua–La Concepción bus drops you off, so it's much easier to get a cab in Ticuantepe (about US$10). If you're driving from Managua, after going 14km on the main road, turn west to Ticuantepe and La Concepción; at Km 21.5 a dirt road goes to the entrance.

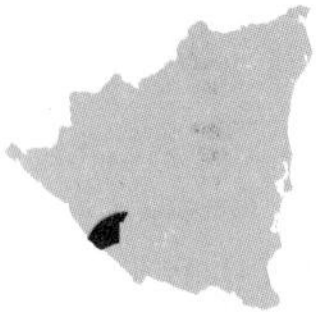

Masaya & Los Pueblos Blancos

Why Go?

Nicaragua's *meseta central* (central plateau) offers a picturesque patchwork of lagoons, steamy volcanic peaks and sleepy colonial villages. Not many people stay here for more than a short day-trip from nearby Granada, leaving plenty of room for exploration and singular encounters with the region's remarkable natural, cultural and artistic imprint.

While trawling Masaya's well-stocked artisan market is obligatory, real fans of the craftsmanship on display should get out to the Pueblos Blancos, where each town or village has its own specialty, from decorative pottery to handcrafted wooden furniture.

Towering over all of this is mighty Volcán Masaya, where hiking trails take you to lava-filled craters and bat-infested caves, and parakeets nest in the crater walls.

Sloping down from the *meseta* are the Carazo towns – pleasant stopovers on the way to a wild and remote stretch of coast.

Best Places to Eat

➡ Mondongo Veracruz (p76)

➡ Hotel El Casino (p80)

➡ La Casona (p79)

Best Places to Sleep

➡ Centro Ecoturístico Flor de Pochote (p76)

➡ La Mariposa Spanish School & Eco Hotel (p79)

➡ Hotel Mi Bohio (p77)

➡ Myrinamar B&B Hotel (p80)

When to Go

➡ Thursday evenings rock in Masaya with the Jueves de Verbena (p67). Stay the evening to sample local food, watch folkloric dances, and stroll through the large crafts market and museum.

➡ December through August is the dry season. Coming around this time makes hiking around Volcán Masaya all the better. Come early in the season for green everywhere.

➡ Sunday is the traditional market day throughout the region. It adds a brimming energy you won't feel other days of the week. There's also a good chance you'll find yourself smack-dab in the middle of a religious or cultural festival.

Masaya & Los Pueblos Blancos Highlights

1 Mercado de Artesanías (p66) Shopping till you drop at the country's most famous handicraft market.

2 San Juan de Oriente (p75) Watching history in action as the potters of these workshops continue the centuries-old craft of ceramics production.

3 Catarina (p74) Peering into the magnificent Laguna de Apoyo from this spectacular lookout.

4 Volcán Masaya (p72) Driving to the 'gates of hell,' then taking a full-moon hike up the tempestuous mountain.

5 La Boquita (p80) Pioneering virgin waves in this lost beach town.

6 Masatepe (p76) Sampling regional specialties – from traditional sweets to *mondongo* (tripe stew) – in hole-in-the-wall shops and eateries.

History

A thriving population center long before the arrival of the Spanish, Masaya and the network of small towns that surround it show signs of Chorotega habitation for at least the last 3000 years. While Masaya is without doubt the modern-day regional center, in pre-Columbian times the tiny town of Diriá was the Chorotega capital, a place where 28 chieftains would meet every seven years to elect a new leader.

Artesanías (handicrafts), the region's claim to fame, has a long tradition, too – as far back as 1548 the Spanish required Masaya to provide hammocks and shoes to the colonizers as a tribute.

Masaya gained official status as a town in 1819, predating Nicaraguan independence by only two years. The delay was most likely due to the fierce fighting spirit of the locals – their opposition to the Spanish in 1529, to William Walker in 1856, to US Marines in 1912 and to the Guardia Nacional throughout the revolution is legendary.

These last skirmishes took a particular toll on the region, none more so than in 1977, when the Masaya suburb of Monimbó rose up against Somoza's forces. During the struggle much of the town's colonial architecture was destroyed. As if that weren't enough, a massive earthquake in 2000 badly damaged the majority of the remaining historical buildings, many of which today still await funding in order to be properly restored.

ⓘ Getting There & Away

Masaya is the regional transportation hub, with regular buses to Managua and Granada, as well as throughout the Pueblos Blancos and Carazo towns. Jinotepe is the western transportation center. Roads are excellent throughout the region, with the exception of beach access, and minivans run regularly between villages.

One of the best reasons to travel this region is the opportunity to ride in a *moto,* a tiny, three-wheeled taxi that uses a motorcycle (or ride-on mower) engine and maxes out at about 40km/h, going downhill. They're everywhere.

MASAYA

Coming from Granada, Masaya may seem a bit down at heel. This is a very workaday little town, unexceptional but for two things – a wonderful, crumbling *malecón*

(waterfront walkway) and the famous artisan market, Mercado de Artesanías de Masaya, where you can stock up for every birthday, Christmas and anniversary for the rest of your life without buying two of the same thing. Nicaraguan tourists, by the way, always make sure their visit coincides with one of Masaya's many spectacular festivals, and there are cultural exhibitions and dances every Thursday evening.

Masaya is 29km southeast of Managua and 16km northwest of Granada. The city sits at the edge of Laguna de Masaya, beyond which rises Volcán Masaya, which can be visited on day trips from here or Granada.

◎ Sights

★ Mercado de Artesanías de Masaya
MARKET

(Mercado Viejo; cnr Calle San Miguel & Av El Progreso; ⊙9am-6pm) Showcasing the highest-quality crafts in the country, this historic marketplace, a black-basalt Gothic structure with a Spanish-fortress motif that includes turrets, towers and over-sized gates, dates from 1888. It's one-stop shopping for Nicaraguan crafts of all kinds and is a popular stop on organized tours. Not to be confused with the section of artisan products inside the Mercado Municipal Ernesto Fernández.

Despite a major fire in 1966, this building was used as a regular market until 1978, when Somoza's Guardia Nacional all but leveled it.

Fortaleza De Coyotepe
FORT

(US$0.70; ⊙8am-5pm) Built in 1893 atop Cerro de los Coyotes, this fortress saw the last stand of Benjamín Zeledón, the 1912 hero of resistance to US intervention. The marines managed to take the fortress – as witnessed by a young man named Sandino, who vowed his revenge. In the end, it was the Guardia Nacional's last stronghold, overrun during the Sandinistas' 1979 offensive.

It's worth the climb just for the view: Laguna de Masaya, Lago de Managua, Volcán Mombacho and, if it's clear, Volcán Momotombo, rising red and black above Managua. Your entrance fee includes a Spanish-language tour of the underground prison, detailing each atrocity.

Hop in a Managua-bound bus (US$0.40) or taxi (US$1) to get here. Taxis may charge extra to take you up the steep hill. Otherwise it's a sweaty half-hour hike.

CHURCHES & PLAZAS

There are 12 major barrios (neighborhoods) in Masaya, all of which were once separate communities with their own churches, plazas and identities: Monimbó, San Jerónimo, Santa Teresa, Villa Bosco Monge, Aserrio, Santa Susana, Las Malvinas, El Palomar, La Ceibita, Cerro Fortaleza de Coyotepe, Sylvio Renazco and Cerro la Barranca.

At the center of it all is the 1750 **Parroquia de la Asunción** (☺ hours vary), an attractive but scarred late-baroque beauty that the Spanish government has offered to help repair. It watches over the Parque Central, formally known as **Parque 17 de Octubre**, in honor of the 1977 fire fight that pitted local residents against Somoza's Guardia Nacional.

Monimbó is Masaya's most famous neighborhood, its ancient center now marked by the 1935 **Iglesia San Sebastián** (cnr Av Real de Monimbó & Calle Las Cuatro Esquinas). Perhaps more important, **Iglesia María Magdalena** (Av Magdalena), sort of the sister church to San Sebastián, is where many of Monimbó's most important festivals begin or end.

Although **Iglesia San Juan** (cnr Av El Tope & Calle Central) is usually closed to the public, check out the surrounding neighborhood strung between La Asunción and the lake, with more than a dozen hammock workshops and factories. Other churches worth seeing include the more modern **Iglesia San Miguel de Masaya** (Calle San Miguel, Mercado Nuevo, 1c E), whose resident San Miguel Arcángel makes the rounds during the procession of St Jerome, and the 1848 **Iglesia San Juan**, which is small, simple and much nicer inside than out.

Parroquia El Calvario (Calle El Calvario, Parque Central, 7c E) is a squat colonial structure with no spire, most remarkable for the extra-gory statues of Jesus and the thieves being crucified, right at the entrance. Those are original – the rest had to be remodeled after the earthquake of 2000.

Among the major buildings worst hit by the earthquake, which also destroyed about 80 homes, was 1928 **Iglesia de San Jerónimo** (p69), the spiritual heart of Masaya and one of the most recognizable silhouettes on the skyline.

Antigua Estación del Ferrocarril de Masaya   MONUMENT
(Av Zelaya) Masaya's elegant former train station, built in 1926 on the north side of the city, is a local landmark. In 2013, the city announced plans to convert it into a cultural center, but at time of writing the project was still underway.

Malecón & Laguna de Masaya   WATERFRONT
(waterfront) Seven blocks west of the Parque Central is an inspiring view in a region famed for them: the view across Laguna de Masaya to the smoking Santiago crater. The attractive, if crumbling, *malecón* was constructed in 1944, when you could still swim, drink or fish in the impressive lagoon. There's a humble collection of restaurant-bars down by the water.

Museo del Folclore   MUSEUM
(Folklore Museum; Mercado de Artesanías; US$2; ☺ 8am-5pm Fri-Wed, to 7pm Thu) A small museum inside the Mercado de Artesanías complex, the Museo del Folclore focuses on dance, local myths and the cultural traditions of Masaya.

Museo y Galería de Héroes y Mártires   MUSEUM
(Av San Jerónimo, Parque Central, 1½c N; ☺ 8am-noon & 1-5pm Mon-Fri) **FREE** Inside the *alcaldía* (mayor's office), this museum honors Masayans who gave their lives during the revolution. There are walls of photos and interesting displays of bomb-building materials and weapons, as well as personal effects including musical instruments and a few Chorotegan funeral urns.

✯ Festivals & Events

Jueves de Verbena   CULTURAL
(US$0.40; ☺ 7:30pm Thu) Once a week this festival has food, music and ballet *folklórico* at the Mercado de Artesanías; most Granada tour outfits offer this as a weekly add-on to their regular Masaya trips.

Masaya

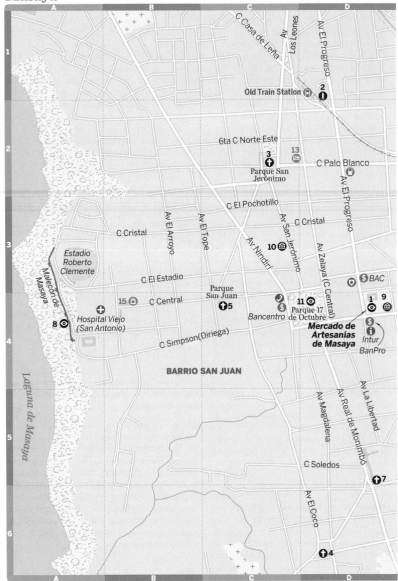

La Virgen de la Asunción RELIGIOUS
(⊙ Mar 16) Better known as the Virgin of the Burning Finger or the Festival of the Cross. The town's top Virgin is taken to the lake for a blessing of the waters and a good look at the slender protrusion of lava that threat-ened the town during the 1772 eruption – until she stopped it.

San Lázaro RELIGIOUS
(⊙ week before Palm Sunday) One of Nicaragua's more unusual religious festivals pays

Masaya

◎ **Top Sights**
1 Mercado de Artesanías de Masaya ... D4

◎ **Sights**
2 Antigua Estación del Ferrocarril de
 Masaya D1
3 Iglesia de San Jerónimo C2
4 Iglesia María Magdalena D6
5 Iglesia San Juan C4
6 Iglesia San Miguel de Masaya E4
7 Iglesia San Sebastián D5
8 Malecón & Laguna de Masaya A4
9 Museo del Folclore D4
10 Museo y Galería de Héroes y
 Martires C3
11 Parroquia de La Asunción D4
12 Parroquia El Calvario F2

◎ **Sleeping**
13 Hotel Maderas Inn C2
14 Hotel Monimbó E5

◎ **Shopping**
15 Hammock Factories B4
16 Mercado Municipal Ernesto
 Fernández F4

Jesús del Rescate   RELIGIOUS
(۞ Apr 3) Scores of *carretas* (ox carts) begin
their journey from Masaya to San Jorge.

Día de la Virgen de la Asunción   RELIGIOUS
(۞ Aug 15) The patron saint María Magdelena is hoisted atop the shoulders of revelers
for her annual tour of Monimbó; fireworks
are involved, as usual.

San Jerónimo   RELIGIOUS
(۞ Sep 30) Officially it's eight days of festivities. The patron saint (in the guise of a
bearded *campesino* named 'Tata Chombó,'
or 'Doctor of the Poor') is taken from the
Iglesia de San Jerónimo (cnr Av San Jerónimo & Calle Palo Blanco) altar and carried
around Masaya during traditional dance
performances. A mock battle ends with
peacemaking ceremonies to commemorate
the September peace treaties of 1856, 1912
and 1979.

Fireworks, marimbas, parades, drag
queens and more make this a fiesta to remember.

Noche de Agüizotes   CULTURAL
(last Fri in Oct) Not to be confused with Hal-
loween or Day of the Dead, this spooky festival features legends come to life and ghosts
of the dead, plus the costumed living parad-
ing through the streets.

homage to San Lázaro, a folk saint who
bestows blessings upon dogs. Locals dress
their pets to the nines; festivities includes a
procession of costumed canines.

El Toro Venado CULTURAL
(⊙ last Sun of Oct, 3rd Sun of Nov) This dance involves a mythical creature that is half bull, half deer (read: half Spanish, half indigenous), whose mission is to make fun of the rest of the fair.

Baile de los Diablitos CULTURAL
(⊙ last Sun of Nov) Little devils dance in honor of Mephistopheles and San Jerónimo.

🛏 Sleeping

There aren't any great hotels here – it's better to sleep in nearby Granada. Most lodging is clustered about four blocks north of Parroquia de la Asunción, along Av Zelaya (also called Calle Central).

Hotel Monimbó HOTEL $$
(✆ 2522-6867; Iglesia San Sebastián, 1c E, 1½c N; s/d US$25/35; 🅿 ✳ @ 🛜) You'll trade off convenience for comfort at this friendly and family-run six-room hotel. It's located in the neighborhood of Monimbó, south of the center, but the rooms are surprisingly nice and spacious.

Hotel Maderas Inn HOTEL $$
(✆ 2522-5825; www.hotelmaderasinn.com; Calle Central, Cuerpo de Bomberos, 2c S; d with fan/air-con US$20/45; ✳ 🛜) This family-run inn is simple and a bit smoky, but there are firm mattresses and service is fairly friendly. Ask for a room upstairs.

🍴 Eating & Drinking

Inexpensive *comedores* (basic eateries) cling to the outside of the Mercado Municipal Ernesto Fernández, just outside the bus terminal. *Vigorón* (mashed yucca topped with coleslaw and pork rinds), fruit salad and *gallo pinto* (blended rice and beans) can be had for around US$1; a sit-down meal with a drink costs around US$2 to US$3. There are also snack stalls on the Parque 17 de Octubre and in the Mercado de Artesanías.

Discos are clustered around the entrance to the *malecón* – go for a walk and see which thumping beat suits you best.

🛍 Shopping

Masaya's major claim to fame is shopping – savvy buyers come here to find great deals on Nicaragua's finest handicrafts. Tours and taxi drivers will drop you off at Masaya's main crafts market, Mercado de Artesanías (p66).

MASAYA & MESETA ARTS & CRAFTS

Masaya itself has been famous since the days before the arrival of the Spanish for its excellent craftsmanship, including leather, woodcrafts and so much more. Intur (p71) has an excellent map of town showing where the various workshops are – you're welcome to drop in, have a look around and, of course, buy something.

Top Buys

Hammocks (US$10 to US$20 for the simple ones, US$25 to US$50 for the nice ones) Bulky but beautiful, Nicaragua's signature craft is made right here in Masaya.

Naive paintings and balsawood carvings (US$8 to US$200) Glowing colors and tropical subjects are a window on the exotic Islas Solentiname.

Black ceramics (US$3 to US$20) Typical of Matagalpa and Jinotega; smooth, heavy ceramics are specially fired for a deep black sheen.

Natural fiber weavings (US$3 to US$10) Whether it's the light, flexible *jipijapa* hats of Camoapa, the elaborately patterned reed mats from Masatepe, or even the woven palm-leaf crickets (US$0.25) that every enterprising eight year old in Nicaragua has on offer, you'll find it here.

Carved jícara shells (US$1 to US$5) You've probably seen the shiny green seeds hanging from the rangy-looking trees, one of the first plants ever domesticated – not for food, but for the shell. Carvings on durable cups and bowls range from simple to stunning, and are priced accordingly.

Soapstone sculptures (US$20 to US$50) They don't take up much space, but these sensually smooth *marmolina* (soapstone) sculptures from San Juan de Limay will weigh you down.

Public buses drop you off in the massive bus lot behind the huge, chaotic Mercado Municipal Ernesto Fernández, a more typical market with unrefrigerated meat counters, colorful vegetable stands, toiletries and a wide selection of somewhat lower-quality handicrafts, cigars, handmade shoes and fun souvenirs at discount prices crammed under the hot, busy tents. Pay attention, watch your backpack and wallet, and have fun.

Can't stop shopping? There are handicrafts workshops all over town. **Hammock factories** (☺ hours vary) congregate in Barrio San Juan, between La Asunción and the lagoon, while wood and leather workshops are hidden throughout Monimbó.

Mercado Municipal Ernesto Fernández   MARKET
(Mercado Nuevo; Calle San Miguel) This is the 'regular' marketplace – i.e. not the Mercado de Artesanías, which brings many travelers to town – though the *mercado municipal* also has a small and worthwhile section dedicated to artisanal goods. Colorful and chaotic, it's a hub of transport, and the first sight you'll see when you climb down from the bus.

ℹ Orientation

The Mercado Municipal (Mercado Nuevo) and main bus station are about six blocks to the east of Parroquia de la Asunción, past the Mercado de Artesanías.

The neighborhood north of La Asunción contains most of Masaya's restaurants and hotels, as well as famed Iglesia de San Jerónimo.

Continue for about 1km and you'll reach the old train station and the main road to Managua.

The entrance to Fortaleza de Coyotepe is 2km to the north, and Parque Nacional Volcán Masaya is about 7km further.

ℹ Information

INTERNET ACCESS
You'll find a few internet cafes near the markets.

MEDICAL SERVICES
Hospital Hilario Sanchez Vásquez (☎ 2522-2778; Calle San Miguel) This hospital has emergency-room services.
Hospital Viejo (San Antonio) (Calle Central)

MONEY
BAC (cnr Calle La Reforma & Av El Progreso)
Bancentro (Av Nindiri)
BanPro (cnr Calle San Miguel & Av El Progreso)

POLICE
Police Station (Calle La Reforma)

TELEPHONE
Enitel (Calle Central, frente Parque 17 de Octubre) For international calls.

TOURIST INFORMATION
Intur (☎ 2522-7615; www.visitanicaragua.com/ingles; Av El Progreso, Mercado de Artesanías, ½c S) This well-funded office has maps and information.

ℹ Getting There & Away

BUS
Minivans to Managua's Universidad Centro America (US$0.90, 30 minutes) leave the park in front of Iglesia de San Miguel (when full). Other buses (US$0.50) and minivans arrive and depart from the **bus station** at the eastern side of the Mercado Municipal.

MASAYA & LOS PUEBLOS BLANCOS ORIENTATION

BUS SERVICES FROM MASAYA

DESTINATION	COST (US$)	DURATION (HR)	DEPARTURES (DAILY)
Carazo (San Marcos, Diriamba & Jinotepe)	0.30-0.50	1¼	5am-6pm, every 30min
Catarina, Diriomo & Diriá	0.30-0.50	40min	6am-5pm, every 20min
Catarina, San Juan de Oriente, Niquinohomo, Masatepe & San Marcos	0.50	1¼	5am-6pm, every 30min
Granada	0.50	40min	5am-6pm, every 30min
Laguna de Apoyo entrance	0.40	20min	5am-5pm, at least hourly
Managua	0.50	1	5am-5pm, every 20min
Matagalpa	3	3	5:30am & 6am
Ticuantepe	0.60	45min	6am-5pm, every 20min

Note that buses don't leave on a regular schedule that you'd want to plan your whole day around (so treat any schedule as a guideline), but they do come and go all day.

❶ Getting Around

Central Masaya is walkable, if confusing to navigate. Taxis charge around US$0.80 for a ride across town.

Parque Nacional Volcán Masaya

The Spaniards said this was the gate to hell, and put the Bobadilla cross (named for the priest who planted it) atop a now sadly inaccessible cliff. Volcán Masaya is the most heavily venting volcano in Nicaragua, and in a more litigious nation there is no way you'd be allowed to drive up to the lip of a volcanic cone as volatile as the Santiago crater. In 2001, an eruption hurled heated rocks 500m into the air, damaging cars and narrowly missing people. At the time of writing, the park was closed until further notice due to dangerous volcanic activity. But if it's open, you should definitely go if you can.

◎ Sights

Nicaragua's largest national park is built around Volcán Masaya and its system of calderas and craters – including the enormous and ancient crater called El Ventarrón, with a barely perceptible rim that runs from Ticuantepe to Masatepe – and around the Laguna de Masaya.

Try to arrive in the afternoon, when the crater's thousands of *chocoyos* (parakeets) return to their nests in the crater walls, apparently unharmed by the billowing toxic gases. There's always lava bubbling at the bottom (you probably won't see it, though), and a column of sulfurous gases rising above.

★Parque Nacional
Volcán Masaya   VOLCANO
(☑2528-1444; Carretera a Masaya Km 23; US$4; ☺9am-4:45pm) Described by the Spaniards as the gates of hell, the craters that comprise Volcán Masaya National Park are the most easily accessible active volcanoes in the country. The two volcanoes at the park, Masaya and Nindirí, together comprise five craters. Of these, Cráter Santiago is still quite active, often smoking and steaming. From the summit of Volcán Masaya (632m), the easternmost volcano, you'll get a wonderful view of the surrounding countryside, including the Laguna de Masaya and town of Masaya.

The park has several marked hiking trails, many of which require a guide (prices vary). These include the lava tunnels of Tzinancanostoc and El Comalito, a small, steam-emitting volcanic cone.

Don't miss the Plaza de Oviedo, a clearing by the crater's rim named after the 16th-century Spanish monk who, suspecting that the bubbling lava was gold, descended to the crater with a bag and small shovel – and came back alive. Here, the smell of sulfur is strong, and it's easy to imagine Lucifer lurking in the depths below.

The park entrance is just 6km from Masaya on the Managua highway. You can get there on any Managua-bound bus from either Masaya or Granada. They'll give you a map and guide.

🏃 Activities

A few outfitters in Granada offer a night tour (US$28 to US$35 per person, four hours) that involves walking through lava tubes and watching what seems to be millions of bats flying in and out of caves. Round-trip transportation is included with those packages, but if you're already at the volcano, you can also join a shorter night tour (US$10) that runs from the visitors' center.

If you can't come at night, a day tour is an option. Most tour outfits in Granada come here as part of a Masaya day trip (around US$15 to US$20 per person), which includes the markets and Catarina overlook, though time at the volcano itself is fairly limited.

Have more time to spend? Explore the park's 20km of hiking trails. Shorter, mostly accessible treks require guides (US$0.70 to US$2 per person), which you pay for with your admission (tips are additional). Sendero Los Coyotes (1.5km) meanders through lava-strewn fields and dry tropical forest; Sendero El Comalito (2km) takes you to a smaller cone surrounded by fumaroles; and Sendero Las Cuevas (1.5km to 6km, depending on which paths you take) lets you explore the very cool lava tunnels of Tzinancanostoc, with bats.

There are also longer hikes (5km to 6km) to lookout points and large rocks that don't require guides (although you could certainly arrange them). If you speak Spanish, have a wander around the attractive museum (free admission) at the visitor center, with impressive natural-history displays and beautiful murals, and a butterfly garden.

The park entrance is 7km north of Masaya. You pay for your entry (US$4) and guided hikes at the entrance gate, and you'll receive a handy brochure with a map and useful information in Spanish and English. It's 5km of paved road to the crater and Plaza de Oviedo. Park officials limit your time here to just five minutes.

🛏 Sleeping & Eating

There's no camping at the park. Most travelers stay in nearby Granada or Masaya.

You can pick up water and basic snacks at the visitors' center, but you should bring your own food. If you're on an organized tour with one of the Granada outfitters, some food or drink is usually included.

❶ Getting There & Away

Many travelers come here on organized tours with transportation included.

Any Managua-bound bus from Masaya or Granada can drop you at the entrance, but it's a steep, hot climb to the crater; hitching is definitely possible, if you're up for it. Alternatively, consider taking a round-trip taxi from Masaya (around US$10) or Granada (around US$15 to US$20), including an hour's wait at the top.

Nindirí

Only 3km north of Masaya, the much more adorable town of Nindirí may have been even more important than Monimbó during the Chorotega era – at least if you're judging by the wealth of archaeological treasures that have been found here. Pre-Columbian artifacts, from urns to masks, tell the story of an ancient indigenous culture that once lived here: check them out at the tiny Museo Arqueológico Tendirí (p73). If the museum is closed, check out the 1529 Catholic church, which has been left in adobe simplicity by subsequent renovations. It's home to Cristo del Volcán, credited with stopping a lava flow from destroying the town during the 1772 eruption that opened the Santiago crater.

◉ Sights

Museo Arqueológico Tendirí   MUSEUM
(☑ 8954-0570; www.manfut.org/museos/nindiri. html; Parque Central, 1c N; US$0.40; ⊙8:30am-noon Mon-Fri, by reservation only Sat & Sun) Vast quantities of priceless ceramics, ancient sculptures and colonial-era artifacts (3000 in all) have been crammed into this cheerfully dilapidated corner building.

🏃 Activities

Adventurous souls can take the short hike to see Cascadas Cailagua and some petroglyphs. Start at the cemetery close to the Nindirí empalme (junction); take the road through the cemetery until you get to the three green crosses; make a right and follow the trail through the gap in the fence and across the field. The waterfall would be more attractive without the litter (and raw sewage), but check out the wall of petroglyphs nearby.

✗ Eating

There are a few traditional Nicaraguan eateries in town. Look for set lunch menus, good value if you're passing through on a day trip.

❶ Getting There & Away

Frequent local buses and colectivos ply the 3km route between Nindirí and Masaya, from where you can catch a bus to Granada, Managua, and a range of other destinations.

LOS PUEBLOS BLANCOS

Originally built from the chalky, pale volcanic tuff upon which this pastoral scene is spread, this series of rural communities, often called the White Villages or Pueblos Blancos, once shimmered a blinding white amid the pale-green patchwork of pasture and jungle.

Today the centuries-old buildings have been painted and the shady roads are paved. Most days the roads between the villages are lined with stands selling vividly painted artesanías. Each town has its specialty: handcrafted ceramics or homemade sweets, wooden furniture or freshly cut flowers; the region is also famous for its curanderos (folk healers). The villages are most often visited as a day trip from Granada, but take the time to explore more and the inner

MASAYA & LOS PUEBLOS BLANCOS NINDIRÍ

workings of life in rural Nicaragua may reveal itself.

Though most visitors pass through Los Pueblos Blancos on road trips, sleeping in nearby Granada or Masaya, there are a few good places to stay in the region – mostly in the ecolodge category, tucked away in rural areas outside the towns.

There are traditional Nicaraguan eateries, basic food kiosks and *fritangas* (grills) scattered throughout the towns. Masatepe is considered the culinary capital of Los Pueblos Blancos: if you're planning a day trip, schedule your lunchtime stop there.

ℹ️ Getting There & Away

Los Pueblos Blancos are generally a road-tripper's destination, but it's relatively easy to visit some of the more popular towns – Catarina, Diriomo, Masatepe – by boarding public buses or vans from Masaya, Granada, or Managua.

Catarina

At the crossroads of Los Pueblos Blancos, Catarina is known for its spectacular *mirador* (viewpoint) over Lago de Nicaragua and Laguna de Apoyo, and for its *viveros* (nurseries) that supply ornamental plants for households across Nicaragua.

Diriomo may be the regional capital of witchcraft, but there's a similar tradition here – along with San Juan de Oriente, Catarina is locally known as a 'bewitched village.'

It's easy to visit Catarina, as almost any regional tour from Masaya or Granada includes a quick stop at the lookout over the Laguna de Apoyo.

⊙ Sights

Mirador   VIEWPOINT
(Viewpoint; entrance per pedestrian or car US$0.80) Catarina's real claim to fame offers views across the startling blue waters of Laguna de Apoyo to Granada and Lago de Nicaragua all the way to Ometepe. Today lined with inexpensive restaurants and souvenir shops connected by windy walkways, this spot is rumored to have been youthful Augusto C Sandino's favorite place to meditate – appropriately so, for this is also the **gravesite of Benjamín Zeledón**, whose burial Sandino witnessed. There's a half-hour trail to the water, with excellent views.

🛏️ Sleeping

There are a couple of places to stay in town, but they're not great: you're better off staying in Granada or Masaya.

🍴 Eating & Drinking

You'll find casual eating options, and a few midrange restaurants with views, around the *mirador* complex.

If you want to party *meseta*-style, there are a couple of discos up at the *mirador*. Otherwise, head to Granada for nightlife.

FESTIVALS & EVENTS OF THE MESETA

With a pantheon of saints and virgins celebrated with an almost pagan vigor, the Masaya *meseta* claims some of the most colorful fiestas in the country. Here's some top events.

San Silvestre Papa (Catarina; Dec 31-Jan 1) A New Year's parade famous for its bouquets of flowers.

Virgen de la Candelaria (Diriomo; ⊘ Feb 2-8) Wake up early – the fireworks will help – to see the Virgin off on her annual trip to nearby Los Jirones.

Domingo de Trinidad (Masatepe; ⊘ mid-May–mid-Jun) Forty days after Semana Santa, this is the biggest *hípica* (horse parade) in Nicaragua; festivities peak on May 23.

San Pedro (Diriá; Jun 17–mid-Jul) Diriá celebrates its patron saint with some dances celebrating Cacique Diriangén, and with others involving dried bull penises.

San Juan Bautista (Catarina; ⊘ Jun 24) Coincidentally falling on the summer solstice, this wild festival features dances, ceremonial fights and music.

Santa Ana (Niquinohomo; ⊘ Jul 26) Folk dances, fireworks and parades make this one of the country's biggest celebrations for this popular saint.

Santa Catalina de Alejandría (Catarina; ⊘ Nov 25-26) Folk dances and a parade.

Los Faroles NICARAGUAN **$$**

(Centro Turístico Mirador de Catarina; dishes US$5–
8) Make your way up to the *mirador,* where
the best restaurants – including Los Faroles
– are scattered around the parking lot, some
with excellent views.

❶ Getting There & Away

There are microbuses for destinations through-
out the *meseta,* while buses run regularly
between the *mirador* and destinations including
the following:

Granada (US$0.60, 30 minutes, 6am to 6pm,
at least hourly)

Managua (US$0.70, 50 minutes, 6am to 6pm,
half-hourly) Arrives/departs Mercado Roberto
Huembes.

Masaya (US$0.50, 30 minutes, 6am to 6pm,
half-hourly)

San Juan de Oriente

This attractive colonial town – known to
some as the sister 'bewitched village' of
Catarina – is famous for its artisan tradi-
tions. San Juan de Oriente, indeed, has
been in the pottery business since before
the Spanish conquest. While production of
inexpensive and functional pottery for lo-
cal consumption is still important, most of
the shops lining the hilly cobblestone roads
are selling decorative pieces (vases, wind
chimes, wall hangings, that sort of thing)
that probably wouldn't fare too well in your
backpack.

The town's most famous workshop, **Co-
operativa Quetzalcóatl**, is found at the
entrance to town, but there are dozens of
places where you can find your masterpiece,
and even probably watch the artisans at
work.

✖ Eating

There are basic food options in town, but for
more of a dining experience, head to nearby
Masatepe.

❶ Getting There & Away

Buses leave more or less hourly for Granada
(US$0.50, one hour) from San Juan de Oriente's
Parque Central, or you can make your way out
onto the highway and flag down any passing bus
making the Granada–Rivas run.

Diriá & Diriomo

Diriomo, home to a number of so-called
'witch doctors,' has long been known as the
Witch Capital of the Meseta. Most healers
work out of their homes, which are unsigned.
Ask at the *alcaldía* (mayor's office). It's also
famous for its *cajetas* (rich, fruit-flavored
sweets), its *chicha bruja* (an alcoholic corn
beverage) and even stiffer *calavera del gato*
('skull of the cat' – drink at your own risk).

Diriá, a twin town across the road,
boasts **Mirador el Boquete**, the mellower,
less-touristed overlook of Laguna de Apoyo,
where views include a few eateries that get
packed with families on weekends. From
the lookout, there's a steep, half-hour trail
to the bottom, where a muddy little beach
offers access to the bright-blue water for
swimming.

◉ Sights

**Iglesia Nuestra Señora
de Candelaria** CHURCH
(Diriomo; ⊙hours vary) This unassuming
church – the perfect centerpiece for this
witchy town – has rather Gothic stone walls
and an extra-interesting collection of saints.
It marks the spot where Cacique Diriangén,
chief of the Dirian peoples at the time of the
Spanish conquest, first met conquistador
Gil González Dávila on April 17, 1523. Unlike
at Nicarao, Diriangén didn't trust the new-
comers and opted to ignore their three-day
deadline to become a Christian. Diriangén
attacked, which in retrospect was the best
course of action.

Today, both Diriá and Diromo – as well
as Diriamba in Carazo – are named for the
indomitable *cacique* (chief).

◻ Sleeping & Eating

There's no lodging here. Head to Masaya
or Granada for hotels. For food, your best
options are the handful of bar-restaurants
(dishes US$4 to US$7) near Diriá's *mirador*.

❶ Getting There & Away

Buses leave almost hourly from Diriomo for Mer-
cado Huembes in Managua (US$0.80) and every
40 minutes for Masaya (US$0.50). If you're in a
rush (or heading south), make your way out onto
the highway and flag down any passing bus.

To get to the *mirador* (viewpoint), take any
Niquinohomo-bound bus (US$0.50, every 30
minutes), which will stop in the city center. It's a
2km walk or a quick taxi ride to the lookout.

Niquinohomo

This quiet, 16th-century Spanish-colonial village is the birthplace of General Augusto César Sandino, who did indeed appreciate the fact that its name is Náhuatl for 'Valley of the Warriors.' Sandino's childhood home, located just steps away from the quiet Parque Central, has been turned into a basic museum with some simple exhibits. Anyone in town can point you toward the building. Nearby, the town's church, **Iglesia Santa Ana**, is one of Nicaragua's oldest.

Sights

Biblioteca Augusto C Sandino   MUSEUM
(by donation; ⊘ 9am-noon & 1:30-5pm Mon-Sat) This simple corner building was the childhood home of revolutionary leader Augusto C Sandino. Now it's a library and small museum, but opening hours are erratic.

Sleeping & Eating

There aren't any hotels here save for a rural homestay or two. Head to Granada for a full range of hotel options. There are a few simple places to eat here, most lining the highway on the way into town.

Getting There & Away

Most travelers drive here. Niquinohomo is located 10km south of Masaya via highway 11B.

Buses make the trip to Granada (US$0.70, 40 minutes), stopping in Catarina on the way.

Masatepe

Photogenic and fabulous, this growing colonial town has a wonderfully well-kept downtown, great regional food, better views of the volcano than Masaya, and a marvelous guesthouse in the countryside, too.

There's not a whole lot to do, although Masatepe's old train station has been reincarnated as one of the better artisan markets in the country.

Towering over Masatepe's attractive central plaza, **Iglesia San Juan Bautista** is home to El Cristo Negro de La Santísima Trinidad, whose feast days mean a month of parties between mid-May and mid-June, and features nationally famous folkloric dances like La Nueva Milpa, Racimo de Sacuanjoche and Masatepetl. The sweeping adobe makes a fine colonial centerpiece, but it's the views from its gates, of fuming Volcán Masaya, that add depth to your prayers.

Sleeping

Centro Ecoturístico Flor de Pochote   ECOLODGE $$
(☑ 8885-7576; www.flordepochote.com; Masatepe; dm/cabins US$10/40; P) This beautiful ecolodge lies within the Reserva Natural Laguna de Apoyo, perched right on the crater rim. Cabins scattered around the 10-hectare *finca* (farm) are made from natural materials. There are lots of activities onsite, from **birdwatching** to biking; the owners also make wine. It's a 4km downhill walk or a short taxi ride from town. Reservations required.

Walking trails crisscross the property, where scores of bird species, including falcons, vultures and hummingbirds, can be seen.

Eating

Around Masatepe, you'll find casual sweet shops, competing restaurants serving the hearty *mondongo* tripe stew, and hole-in-the-wall eateries specializing in local specialites like *tamagus*, which are like a *nacatamale* (banana-leaf-wrapped bundle of cornmeal, meat, vegetables and herbs), but made with sticky rice instead of cornmeal.

Mondongo Veracruz   NICARAGUAN $
(iglesia, 3c N; dishes US$2-6) Masatepe is perhaps best known for delicious, steaming bowls of *mondongo* (tripe soup marinated with bitter oranges and fresh herbs, then simmered with garden vegetables for hours). This is one of the the best places in town to sample the stew (with a traditional side of Flor de Caña Rum), though several other eateries serve good versions, too.

Dulcería Chepita   NICARAGUAN $
(Antiguo Estación Ferrocarril, ½c O; sweets US$1-3; ⊘ 10am-5pm Mon-Fri) A favorite sweets shop, and a good place to sample traditional Nicaraguan *cajetas*.

Shopping

Mercado de Artesanía   HANDICRAFTS
(Artisan Markets; entrance to town; ⊘ 9am-6pm) While Masatepe's famous furniture market features items that probably won't make it home in your backpack, the town's hallmark cane-woven rocking chairs and brightly colored cabinets are still worth checking out.

ⓘ Getting There & Away

Buses leave the Parque Central half-hourly for Masaya (US$0.50) and Mercado Huembes in Managua (US$1.50, one hour), while minivans make the run to Jinotepe (US$0.60, 15 minutes) when full.

CARAZO

This department, blessed with beautiful mountains reaching 870m (bring a sweater) and wide, sandy beaches (bring your swimsuit) – the two are separated by only 35 steep kilometers – is central in Nicaraguan history and myth. It's not only where the first Nicaraguan coffee was sown but also where the nation's most famous burlesque, *El Güegüense,* was anonymously penned in the late 17th century. The comedy, which pits Nicaraguan ingenuity against Spanish power, always gets a laugh. It was written (and is still performed) in Náhuatl, Spanish and Mayangna.

There are plenty of nondescript places to stay in the region, as well as a few standouts, including one in Diriamba and a few on the beach in La Boquita and Casares.

The region is known for coffee. If you're road-tripping through the area, plan to stop in Jinotepe or Diriamba for lunch.

ⓘ Getting There & Away

Many travelers explore this region by car, but there's also regular bus and minivan service between the larger towns and the beach.

Diriamba

Diriamba is considered the birthplace of coffee production in Nicaragua; it was already a bustling settlement when the Spanish arrived. Today, it has a pleasant central plaza and interesting European-style architecture that dates back to the coffee boom in the late 19th and early 20th centuries.

◎ Sights & Activities

Museo Ecológico Trópico Seco   MUSEUM
(☑ 8422-2129; Hotel Mi Bohio, 1c S; US$2; ⊙ 8am-noon & 2-4pm Mon-Fri) Nicaragua's first natural history museum (sort of), this museum offers informative, if low-budget, displays that focus primarily on the ecosystem of the Río Grande de Corazo and turtles of the Refugio de Vida Silvestre Río Escalante Chacocente.

FIESTA DE TORO GUACO

Carazo's four major towns celebrate the interesting, ancient ritual of **Fiesta de Toro Guaco** (⊙ Jan). La Concepción brings out her patron saint, the Black Virgin of Montserrat, to meet Santiago, patron of Jinotepe, the old Nicarao capital; San Sebastián emerges from Diriamba, Jinotepe's ancient Chorotegan rival; and San Marcos appears from the university town of the same name.

Four times throughout the year – the saints' feast days – the saints pay ceremonial visits to each other, an event livened up with striking costumes and masks displayed in dances, mock battles and plays that satirize their Spanish invaders. The biggest bash is on April 24 to 25, in San Marcos.

Gaia Estate   BIRDWATCHING, ECOTOUR
(☑ 8681-5356; www.gaiaestate.com) Birdwatching and coffee tours are conveniently rolled into one at Gaia Estate, an lush, 90-acre organic coffee farm. Over 150 species of birds live here, and forested trails lead past 60 species of trees. Contact the farm for information and tour prices.

🛏 Sleeping

There are several ecolodges just outside of town, and a popular hotel in Diriamba itself.

Hotel Mi Bohio   HOTEL $$
(☑ 2534-3300; www.hotelmibohio.com; costado este Policía Nacional; d from US$45; ❀ 🛜) Your best bet in town, this colonial-style hotel has a pretty central garden and a **restaurant** (open to the public) serving good food and cocktails. There's a spa and fitness center on-site, and the rooms are clean and cheery. (And in case you were wondering, *bohio* is Cuban slang for a small house.)

Ecolodge Carazo   LODGE $$
(☑ 2534-2948; www.ecolodgecarazo.com; Carretera a Managua, salida del pueblo; s US$25, d or tr US$50; 🛜) This lodge located on a verdant coffee farm – located about 1km outside of town, on the way to Managua – has beautiful gardens; simple, cabin-style rooms; and a laid-back atmosphere.

✗ Eating & Drinking

There are a few good places to grab a bite in town, including the restaurant at Hotel Mi Bohio and several simple Nicaraguan eateries clustered close to the market.

Diriamba isn't a nightlife destination per se, but there's plenty of drinking going on at bar-restaurants in the center.

ⓘ Getting There & Away

Jinotepe is the main transportation hub, and you can get a Jinotepe microbus (US$0.40, 15 minutes) any time at the market in front of the clock tower. A few buses and microbuses do leave from this station, including the following services.

La Boquita (microbus; US$0.80, 45 minutes, 6am to 6pm, half-hourly)

La Boquita/Casares (US$0.40 to US$0.80, 1½ hours, 5am to 5pm, hourly)

Managua (US$1.40, 1¼ hours, 5am to 6pm, roughly every 30 minutes)

Jinotepe

Historically separated from its eternal rival by the Río Grande de Carazo (which is, predictably, too polluted for swimming, but worth a wander if you're here), proud Jinotepe is the capital of Carazo. It's famous in Nicaragua for its neoclassical architecture and its locally produced ice cream.

The Spanish colonial–style city is centered on the impressive church, **La Iglesia Parroquial de Santiago**, which has pretty stained glass, and the perpetually bustling **Parque Los Chocoyitos**.

🛏 Sleeping

There aren't many sleeping options here, save for a popular missions house that doubles as a hotel.

Casa Mateo HOTEL $$$
(☎ 2532-3284; www.casamateomissionshouse.vpweb.com; BDF, 1½c O; s/d from US$30/50; ❄ @) The friendliest hotel in town is technically a missions house – i.e. it regularly hosts groups of missionaries – but you can also check in for the night. Rooms are generally spacious and clean, with balconies overlooking a quiet pedestrian walkway. The restaurant downstairs serves up a decent meal.

✗ Eating

Look for shops selling the famously flavorful *helado jinotepino*, or locally produced ice cream. The Parque Central is packed with food stands and *fritangas* (grills) all day long, and there are a few traditional Nicaraguan eateries scattered around the center. A block away is an enormous **Super Palí**, which is the best grocery store in the region.

Cafe París CAFE $
(costado sur de BanPro; snacks US$1-4; ⊙10am-9:30pm Mon-Fri, 8am-10pm Sat & Sun) This brand-new, Parisian-inspired cafe specializes in coffee drinks and freshly baked pastries.

Buen Provecho INTERNATIONAL $
(Plaza Güegüense; dishes US$3-6; ⊙7am-10pm Mon-Fri) Right around the corner from Casa Mateo, this basic eatery serves up typical Nica dishes.

Pizzeria Colisseo PIZZA $$
(BanPro, ½c S; pizzas US$6-9; ⊙noon-2:30pm & 6-10pm Tue-Fri, noon-10pm Sat & Sun) The locals call this brick-oven-baked pizza the best in Nicaragua (a bold claim, to be sure). The pizzeria serves beer and wine – it's one of the more stylish places to eat in town.

ⓘ Information

Intur (☎ 8412-0298; carazo@intur.gob.ni; frente Palí) Conveniently located inside a tiny arts-and-crafts market, it can recommend hotels and offer information for all of Carazo.

BAC (frente Parque Central) Has a Visa/Plus ATM.

ⓘ Getting There & Away

Jinotepe is a transportation hub, and the big, confusing bus station is just north of the Parque Central, on the Panamericana (Pan-American Hwy).

San Marcos

San Marcos is known for a few things: it sits on the site of what's thought to be the oldest human settlement in Nicaragua, and it's the hometown of Anastasio Somoza García, the nation's original dictator.

Today, it has a pronounced and festive student presence thanks to Keiser University – Latin American Campus.

San Marcos' *fiestas patronales* (April 24 to 25) are some of the most impressive in the country.

⊙ Sights

**Keiser University –
Latin American Campus** SCHOOL
(www.avemaria.edu.ni) San Marcos has a pronounced and festive student presence thanks to this educational institution. Previously known as Ave Maria University, the school was taken over as a branch campus of Florida's Keiser University in 2013. Today, it's the only US university in Central America that offers four-year degrees in fields such as biology, international relations, and politics. There are sometimes cultural events and activities happening on campus.

⌂ Sleeping

There are a few good hotels and guesthouses in town. Outside of town, there's La Mariposa, a Spanish school and eco-hotel that's popular with travelers.

Hotel Casablanca HOTEL **$$**
(✆2535-2717; www.casablancanica.com; BanCentro, 1c S; r from US$40; ✳) A decent option in the town's center, this hotel has big, cool rooms – but it's a bit pricey for what you get.

**La Mariposa Spanish
School & Eco Hotel** LODGE **$$$**
(✆8669-9455; www.mariposaspanishschool.com; El Cruce, 50m E, San Juan de la Concepción; per week per person including classes, accommodations & activities US$480; @) ✎ Just out of San Marcos, on the road to Ticuantepe, is one of Nicaragua's prettiest Spanish schools. Set out in the rolling hillside at the base of Volcán Masaya, this wonderful school-hotel minimizes impact through the use of solar electricity, water recycling and reforestation. The setting is lush; afternoon activities include hikes and horseback rides.

During the high season, one-week minimum stays are mandatory, and include accommodation in comfy rooms with lovely views.

**Hotel Boutique
Hacienda San Pedro** HOTEL **$$$**
(✆2535-2859; iglesia católica, 350m N ; d US$60; ✳🛜🛋) A short walk from the main plaza, this colorfully painted, hacienda-style hotel features plenty of beautifully landscaped outdoor space, not to mention a swimming pool. There's also a good restaurant here that's open to the public.

✗ Eating & Drinking

There are food kiosks on the main plaza, and *fritangas* that set up near the Parque Central in the evening. San Marcos also has a few sit-down places.

Thanks to the university presence here, you'll find a few bars scattered around town; some get lively on weekends.

Cafetería Paladar NICARAGUAN **$**
(Parque Central; dishes US$2-4) A basic *comedor* at the corner of the Parque Central, with a *fritanga* that sets up at dusk.

★**La Casona Coffee Shop** NICARAGUAN **$$**
(www.lacasonacoffeeshop.com; Enitel, 1c N; dishes US$4-8; ◷11am-9pm) With a lively atmosphere, patio seating and an espresso machine that staff know how to use, La Casona this is the best cafe (and restaurant) in town. The menu features burgers, sandwiches, salads and desserts. You can also buy locally grown coffee beans to take with you.

ⓘ Getting There & Away

San Marcos lies at the border of the Masaya and Carazo departments, and you may have to changes buses or minivans here to get between them. Minibuses leave (when full) from the Parque Central to Managua (US$1 to US$1.30, one hour), Jinotepe (US$0.40, 20 minutes), Masaya (US$0.70, 45 minutes) and other destinations all day long.

Reserva Ecológica La Maquina

Take a break from dodging potholes at this excellent, respected private reserve about halfway between Diriamba and the beaches. It's a fine place for a swim and a picnic.

⊙ Sights

**Reserva Ecológica
La Maquina** NATURE RESERVE
(✆8887-9141; www.manfut.org/carazo/maquina.html; Carretera a La Boquita Km 58.5; US$2; ◷daylight hours Tue-Sun) Take a dip in the pools beneath spectacular waterfalls at this lovely nature reserve, then explore the hiking trails that traverse the 154-hectare property – mainly primary dry tropical forest with a few bonus waterfalls and big trees, including huge strangler figs.

🛏 Sleeping & Eating

You can camp here (from US$3 per person). Otherwise, come on a day trip and sleep in Diriamba or La Boquita.

There's a basic restaurant (meals US$3 to US$6) at the reserve, but you'll be happier bringing your own food and water for a memorable picnic near the waterfalls.

ℹ Getting There & Away

Many travelers drive here, but you can also catch a bus running between the beaches and Diriamba (US$0.30, 20 minutes), which pass near the entrance every 40 minutes or so during daylight hours.

La Boquita

At this low-key beach village, most tourists are day-trippers from the *meseta* towns. Passing through the big, concrete archway means you've entered the Centro Turístico La Boquita (p80), with beach-friendly services and places to buy food and drinks.

La Boquita is more of a swimming than a surfing beach, but if swells are big, waves can get a nice peak; some restaurants rent boards.

◉ Sights

Centro Turístico La Boquita   OUTDOORS
(car entry US$1.25) This waterfront complex offers amenities for beachgoers, from bars and restaurants to public restrooms.

🛏 Sleeping & Eating

There are a handful of basic hotels here, and one that's very good. The seafood in the dozen or so seaside restaurants is excellent; they all serve variations on the same thing. Fish and shrimp dishes run US$6 to US$15. If you're feeling extravagant, look for the shrimp-stuffed lobster (US$18).

Myrinamar B&B Hotel   HOTEL **$$$**
(☑ 8421-8306; www.myrinamar.com; del empalme Casares–La Boquita, 1km hacia La Boquita; d/5-

person apt from US$70/90; 🛜) A refreshing standout in a coastal area with few good hotels, the lovely Myrinamar perches on a cliff above the beach; there's a private walkway leading down to the sand. The hotel has airy guest rooms with sea views – a few have kitchenettes – and breakfast is served outside. There's also a cocktail bar and bicycle rental.

ℹ Getting There & Away

Many travelers drive here, but you can also catch a bus (US$0.40, 1½ hours, 5am to 5pm, hourly) or taxi (expect to pay from US$10 one-way) from nearby Diriamba.

Casares

Casares is a fishing village that sits on a rocky beach. There's not much to do here except relax, swim in the surf and watch the local fishers carrying in their daily catch from colorfully painted wooden boats.

🛏 Sleeping & Eating

Casares is known for seafood; there are a few simple places to eat near the beach, and a more elegant dining room at Hotel El Casino.

Hotel El Casino   HOTEL **$$**
(☑ 2532-8002;   www.hotelcasinocasares.com; beachfront; d with fan/air-con US$35/45; ❋🛜) You can hear waves crashing from your bed at Hotel Casino, the most modern building on this stretch of coast. There are good sea views from the top-front rooms, and the dining room even has a touch of elegance (a bit out of step with the fish markets right outside).

ℹ Getting There & Away

Many travelers drive here. Buses from Diriamba (US$0.80, 1½ hours, 5am to 5pm, hourly) stop at the *empalme* (junction) above the beach. For Hotel El Casino, head straight downhill toward the water.

Granada

POP 123,000 / ELEV 40M

Best Places to Eat

➡ The Garden Café (p92)

➡ El Tercer Ojo (p93)

➡ El Pizzaiol (p93)

➡ Café de los Sueños (p93)

Best Places to Sleep

➡ Hotel Gran Francia (p91)

➡ Hotel Con Corazón (p91)

➡ Hotel Los Patios (p92)

➡ Mansión de Chocolate (p92)

➡ San Simian Eco Lodge (p100)

Why Go?

Granada drips with photogenic elegance, a picture postcard at every turn. It's no wonder many travelers use the city as a base, spending at least a day bopping along cobblestone roads from church to church in the city center, then venturing out into the countryside for trips to nearby attractions.

Just out of town, half-day adventures take you to an evocative archipelago waterworld at Las Isletas and fun beaches at the Península de Asese. Volcán Mombacho has walking trails and a butterfly sanctuary, not to mention a few hot springs dotted around its foothills. The Laguna de Apoyo is another must-see: its clear turquoise waters and laid-back waterfront lodges offer a splendid natural respite.

Culturally curious travelers might consider a trip to community-tourism operations in nearby villages such as Nicaragua Libre, or out to Parque Nacional Archipiélago Zapatera, home to one of the most impressive collections of petroglyphs and statues in the country.

When to Go

➡ November 28 to December 7 is the celebration of La Inmaculada Concepción, or La Purísima as it is known in Nicaragua. It is celebrated throughout the country, but is especially vibrant in Granada, with parades, dances and, yes, plenty of fireworks.

➡ During February the international poetry festival brings bards and wannabes from across Latin America to celebrate the word and wax poetic. Expect a city of magic surrealism with just a touch of pretension.

➡ The December to May high season brings more people, higher prices and better weather. Book at least a week in advance during these times, especially during Christmas and Easter weeks and during the mid-August festivals.

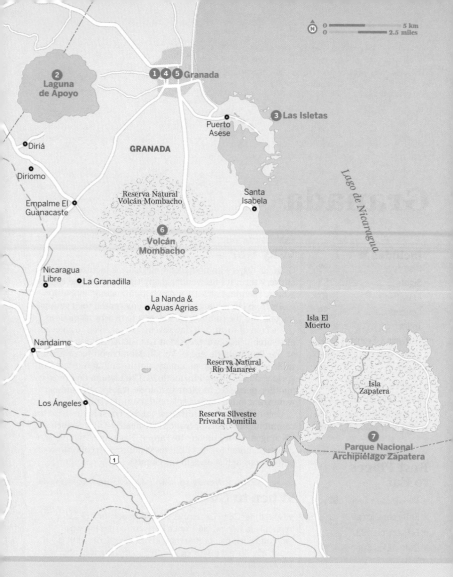

Granada Highlights

1 Iglesia La Merced
(p84) Catching a stunning sunset over the lake from the bell tower.

2 Laguna de Apoyo
(p99) Taking a dip in this gorgeous volcanic lake.

3 Las Isletas (p97)
Cruising the narrow waterways, where luxury holiday mansions

cast shadows on humble fishing shacks.

4 Granada City Tour
(p89) Reliving a more romantic past on a horse-drawn city tour.

5 Granada's Restaurants
(p92) Feasting on some of Nicaragua's most innovative cuisine.

6 Volcán Mombacho
(p97) Hiking below the imposing summit and tasting locally produced coffee.

7 Parque Nacional Archipiélago Zapatera
(p100) Checking out the petroglyphs.

History

Nicknamed 'the Great Sultan,' in honor of its Moorish namesake across the Atlantic, Granada was founded in 1524 by Francisco Fernández de Córdoba, and is one of the oldest cities in the New World. It was constructed as a showcase city, the first chance that the Spanish had to prove they had more to offer than bizarre religions and advanced military technology. The city still retains an almost regal beauty, each architectural masterpiece faithfully resurrected to original specifications after every trial and tribulation.

A trade center almost from its inception, Granada's position on the Lago de Nicaragua became even more important when the Spanish realized that the Río San Juan was navigable from the lake to the sea. This made Granada rich – and vulnerable. Between 1665 and 1670, pirates sacked the city three times.

Undaunted, Granada rebuilt and grew richer and more powerful, a conservative cornerstone of the Central American economy. After independence from Spain, the city challenged the colonial capital and longtime Liberal bastion León for leadership of the new nation.

Tensions erupted into full-blown civil war in the 1850s, when desperate León contracted the services of American mercenary William Walker and his band of 'filibusters.' Walker defeated Granada, declared himself president and launched a conquest of Central America – and failed. Walker was forced into a retreat after a series of embarrassing defeats, and as he fell back to his old capital city, he set it afire and left in its ashes the infamous placard: 'Here was Granada.'

The city rebuilt – again. And while its power has waned, its importance as a tourist center and quick escape from bustling Managua keeps the city of Granada vibrant.

◉ Sights

There's plenty to see in pretty Granada to keep you occupied for a day or two, though you'll likely feel the pull of attractions in the

---

PIRATES OF LAKE NICARAGUA

The sacking of Central America's crown jewel, Granada, was one of the most daring exploits in pirate history, a career coup for dashing up-and-coming buccaneer Henry Morgan and his band of rum-soaked merry men.

It couldn't have been done in a full-sized sailing vessel – if you follow Morgan's path up the Río San Juan you'll see how those rapids would tear a regular ship apart. But this crafty band of quick thinkers appropriated six 12m wooden canoes (after their regular pirate ships were impounded by Spanish authorities) following an equally spectacular sacking of Villahermosa, Mexico. The atypical craft proved more than adequate for further pillaging along the Caribbean coast, which gave the 30-year-old Morgan an idea.

The crew battled the currents of the Río San Juan at night, hiding their canoes during the day. They then made their way across the great lake. The June 1665 attack caught complacent *granadinos* completely off guard: the pirates occupied the city for 16 hours – just like the Pirates of the Caribbean Disney ride, but more violent – then stole all the ammunition, sank all the boats and sailed off to a warm welcome, as heroes and legends in Port Royal, Jamaica. Eat your heart out Jack Sparrow.

Between 1665 and 1670, Granada was sacked three times, even as Morgan took more pirate canoes up the Río Coco, where he made powerful allies of the Miskitos. With their help, pirates sacked Ciudad Antigua and Estelí, where Morgan himself stayed for a while, and founded several of the surrounding towns.

Pirates actually founded more cities in Nicaragua than they ever sacked, including Pueblo Viejo and several surrounding towns in the Segovias, Bilwi, on the Caribbean coast, and most famously Bluefields, named for founder Abraham Blewfeldt, a Dutch pirate who worked the waters from Rhode Island to Panama.

Although the 1697 Treaty of Ryswick guaranteed that England, Spain, France and Holland would respect each other's property in the New World, the pirates continued to try for Granada. In 1769, 17-year-old Rafaela Herrera commanded Spanish forces at El Castillo against pirates trying to sack Granada yet again. She won, signalling the beginning of the end for the pirates of the Caribbean.

immediate surroundings: Las Isletas, Laguna de Apoyo and Volcán Mombacho.

Convento y Museo San Francisco CHURCH

(Map p88; 📞 2552-5535; costado norte de Plaza de Leones, 1 c E; US$2; ⏰ 8am-4pm Mon-Fri, 9am-4pm Sat & Sun) One of the oldest churches in Central America and the most striking building in Granada, Iglesia San Francisco boasts a robin's egg-blue birthday-cake facade and houses both an important convent and one of the best museums in the region. Originally constructed in 1585, it was subsequently burned to the ground by pirates and later William Walker, rebuilt in 1868 and restored in 1989.

The museum is through the small door on the left, where guides (some of whom speak English) are available for tours; tips are appreciated. Museum highlights include top-notch Primitivist art, a scale model of the city and a group of papier-mâché indigenous people cooking, relaxing in hammocks and swinging on *comelazatoaztegams,* a sort of 360-degree see-saw.

Also here: the Zapatera statuary, two solemn regiments of black-basalt statues looming above large men and possessed of 10 times their gravity, carved between AD 800 and 1200, then left behind on the ritual island of Zapatera. Most were discovered in the late 1880s and gathered in Granada in the 1920s.

Casa de los Leones & Fundación Casa de los Tres Mundos BUILDING

(Map p88; Parque Central, 50m N; ⏰ 8am-7pm Mon-Fri, to 6pm Sat & Sun) Founded in 1986 by Ernesto Cardenal, the Fundación Casa de los Tres Mundos moved to elegant 1720 Casa de los Leones in 1992. At the entrance, a board lists special events: poetry readings, classical ballet, folkloric dance and free movies. During regular business hours, your entrance fee buys you a look at a beautiful mansion and a few art displays.

Iglesia La Merced CHURCH

(Map p88; Calle Real & Avenida 14 de Septiembre; bell tower US$1; ⏰ 11am-6pm) Perhaps the most beautiful church in the city, this landmark was built in 1534. Most come here for the spectacular views from the **bell tower** – especially picturesque at sunset.

Originally completed in 1539, it was razed by pirates in 1655 and rebuilt with its current baroque facade between 1781 and 1783. Damaged by William Walker's forces in 1854, it was restored with the current elaborate interior in 1862. Today Catholics come here to see an important image of the Virgen de Fátima.

Catedral de Granada CATHEDRAL

(Map p88; Parque Colón; ⏰ hours vary) The Cathedral of Granada, on the east side of the plaza, was originally built in 1583 but has been destroyed countless times since. This

---

GRANADA IN...

One Day

Hit the **Garden Café** (p92) for breakfast, then duck around the corner to see what's on at the **Fundación Casa de los Tres Mundos**. Check out the art, then head back to **Parque Central**. Take a two-hour tour in a horse-drawn carriage to see the town's main sights. Next head to the lake for a boat tour of **Las Isletas**. Grab a cab back into town and recharge with a coffee overlooking the plaza, then get ready for dinner in the city center. From there, head down Granada's bustling bar strip, **Calle La Calzada**, for drinks and people-watching.

Three Days

Follow the one-day plan. On day two, grab a coffee in town, then head to **Doña Elba Cigars** (p94) to witness the cigar-making process. Back in town, stop for a snack at the outdoor stands on **Parque Central**, then lounge for an hour by the pool at **Mansión de Chocolate** (p92). For dinner, choose from the restaurants on and around **Calle La Calzada**.

On day three, get out of town. Book a tour (or DIY) to hike on **Volcán Mombacho** (p97), where trails and a zipline canopy tour await. Go further afield to the artisan villages around Masaya – the **Pueblos Blancos**, or enjoy a day of swimming at **Laguna de Apoyo**.

STATUARIES OF NICARAGUA

Of all the archaeological sites currently under investigation (and the scores more waiting for funding to be adequately explored), four statuary sites stand out. The figurative pieces found here range from 1m to 4m tall and are probably between 1200 and 1400 years old. The best guess for construction methods is that they were carved using obsidian tools, sanded smooth, then possibly painted. While there are stylistic overlaps, work at each site displays its own distinguishing characteristics.

Chontales Statuary

These finely detailed statues with expressive features are taller and thinner than others. Main sites are in Boaco, Matagalpa and Zalaya. The theory is that they were originally used as building columns. Make up your own mind at Juigalpa's incredible Museo Arqueológico Gregorio Aguilar Barea.

Isla de Ometepe Statuary

The squat, realistic figures at Isla de Ometepe are thought to represent chiefs and other dignitaries. Only a few examples are on display, beside the church in Altagracia. It's thought that there are many more, buried over the years beneath the ashes of Volcán Concepción's eruptions.

Isla Zapatera Statuary

While the best examples from this site are on display at Granada's **Convento y Museo San Francisco** (p84), there are various remaining pieces on the island – mostly at Pensacola, Zonzapote, Punta de las Figuras and Las Cañas. These figures show advanced workmanship and feature human-animal hybrids, probably referring to myths that humankind emerged from beneath the earth.

León Statuary

Including the Isla de Momotombito, this is the least-known of the four. In 1854 there were a reported 50 statues in this collection – today, sadly, most of them have mysteriously disappeared.

GRANADA SIGHTS

most recent version, built in 1915, has four chapels; a dozen stained-glass panels are set into the dome.

★**Museo de Chocolate**　　MUSEUM
(Map p88; ☎2552-4678; www.chocomuseo. com; Calle Atravesada, frente Bancentro; chocolate workshop adult/child US$21/12; ⊙7am-6:30pm; ⊛) FREE Granada's new chocolate museum is excellent if you're traveling with children: the 'beans to bar' chocolate workshop, where participants learn to roast and grind cocoa beans, and mold their very own Nicaraguan chocolate bar, is hands-on fun for all ages. The museum is located at the Mansión de Chocolate hotel (p92), which also has a chocolate-oriented spa and a popular buffet breakfast (US$6), plus a great swimming pool you can use for an extra US$6.

Cementerio de Granada　　CEMETERY
(Map p86; Nandaime s/n) Used between 1876 and 1922, this beautiful cemetery has lots of picturesque mausoleums and tombs, including those of six Nicaraguan presidents. Most people come to see the 1880 neoclassical stone **Capilla de Ánimas** (Chapel of Spirits), a scale model of the French chapel of the same name. Close by is another scale model, this time of Paris' Notre Dame cathedral.

**Antigua Estación
del Ferrocarril**　　LANDMARK
(Old Train Station; Map p86) Nine long blocks north of town along Calle Atravesada you'll find **Parque Sandino**, next to the old train station, now a technical vocational school. It was built in 1882 and operational in 1886; the US Marines remodeled it in 1912. There's lots of playground equipment, some with train themes, and a few well-preserved railroad cars are on display nearby. Out front is the **Parque de los Poetas**, dedicated to Nicaragua's literary giants.

Granada

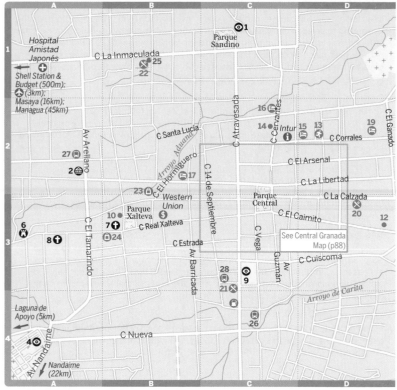

Iglesia de Xalteva
CHURCH

(Map p86; frente Parque Xalteva; ☺10am-6pm) This dilapidated but attractive Iglesia de Xalteva, built in the 19th-century, houses La Virgen de la Asunción.

Fortaleza La Polvora
FORT

(Map p86; Calle Real; donations appreciated; ☺8am-5pm) Originally called the Fortaleza de Armas when it was constructed in 1748, this lavishly turreted Spanish fortress still has the best views in town, over ancient, water-stained church domes all the way to Lago de Nicaragua. You can also check out a roomful of paintings and a couple of artifacts.

Mi Museo
MUSEUM

(Map p88; ☎2552-7614; Calle Atravesada, Cine Karawala, ½ c N; US$5; ☺8am-5pm) **FREE** This museum displays a private collection of ceramics dating from at least 2000 BC to the present. Hundreds of beautifully crafted pieces were chosen with as much an eye for their artistic merit as their archaeological significance.

Centro Turístico
BEACH

(Map p86) **FREE** This lakefront tourist center has restaurants, discos, sandy beaches, kids' play areas, picnic spots, and is the place to go to hire a launch or kayak for a Las Isletas excursion (hire boats at Cabinas Amarillas, 3km south from the park's entrance gate, or through Inuit Kayak). Take cabs to and from here after dark.

Mercado Municipal
MARKET

(Map p86; Calle Atravesada) Head to the overflowing and lively (if not particularly good for souvenir shopping) Mercado Municipal, a neoclassical building constructed in 1892.

La Capilla María Auxiliadora
CHURCH

(Map p86; ☺hours vary) This gorgeous little church is worth a look for its beautiful pastel interior.

N
0 ———————————— 500 m
0 ———————————— 0.25 miles

E   F

Lago de Nicaragua

Cruz Roja

Parque

Río Cacuanatoya

Las Isletas (5km);
Puerto Asese (6.5km)

GRANADA ACTIVITIES

Antigüo Hospital   HISTORIC BUILDING

(Map p86; Av Arellano, Iglesia Xalteva, 1 c O, 1½c N) The city's old hospital is a landmark locals often use when giving directions.

Plaza de la Independencia   SQUARE

(Plaza de los Leones; Map p88) North of Parque Central is Plaza de la Independencia, also known as the 'Plaza de los Leones.' The obelisk is dedicated to the heroes of the 1821 struggle for independence, while the Cruz de Siglo was erected in 1900 to mark the new century.

Capilla del Sagrado Corazón   CHURCH

(Map p86; ⊙ hours vary) The 1626 Iglesia de Guadalupe was originally built as a fort.

🏃 Activities

Aside from enjoying the pleasures of town, many people end up using Granada as a base for day trips to nearby attractions such as Laguna de Apoyo, Volcán Mombacho and the Pueblos Blancos.

Inuit Kayaks   KAYAKING

(Map p86; ☑ 2552-6695; Centro Turístico; US$25-35 per person) Inuit Kayaks runs several guided tours around Las Isletas.

Pure   SPA

(Map p86; ☑ 8481-3264; www.purenica.com; Calle Corrales, Convento San Francisco, 1½ c E; day/weekly/monthly pass US$5/15/29, class & treatment prices vary; ⊙ 7am-9pm, class times vary) Sign up for yoga classes, daily, weekly

Central Granada

Central Granada

◎ Top Sights
1 Museo de Chocolate A1

◎ Sights
2 Casa de los Leones & Fundación
   Casa de los Tres Mundos B1
3 Convento y Museo San Francisco C1
4 Iglesia La Merced A2
5 Mi Museo A1
6 Plaza de la Independencia B1

◎ Activities, Courses & Tours
7 Alianza Francesa de Granada C1
   Amy's Centro de Arte .... (see 39)
8 Erick Tours C2
9 Horse-Drawn Carriage Tour B2
10 Leo Tours Comunitarios C2
11 Nahual Tours D2
12 Spanish Dale! Language School B1
13 Tierra Tour D2

◎ Sleeping
14 Casa del Agua.. C3
15 Hostal El Momento B1
16 Hotel Casa Capricho D1
17 Hotel Casa del Consulado A2
18 Hotel Casa San Martín C2
19 Hotel Gran Francia.................................. B3
20 Hotel La Pérgola...................................... D3
21 Hotel Patio del Malinche D3

22 Hotel Plaza Colón B2
   Mansión de Chocolate .... (see 1)

◎ Eating
23 Café Blue B3
24 Café de las Sonrisas.............................. A2
25 Cafetín El Volcán A3
   Comidas Tipicas y Más .... (see 10)
26 Don Luca's.. D2
27 El Camello.. D3
28 El Pizzaiol... C2
29 El Tercer Ojo... C2
30 El Zaguán... C2
31 Kathy's Waffle House............................. C1
32 La Hacienda C1
33 Taco Stop A1
34 The Garden Café...................................... C2

◎ Drinking & Nightlife
35 Kelly's Bar..C3
36 Nectar C2
37 O'Sheas...D2

◎ Entertainment
38 Imagine C2

◎ Shopping
   Lucho Libro Books .... (see 38)
39 Olé C2
   The Garden Shop .... (see 34)

or monthly gym memberships, or massages (US$26) at this peaceful day spa and gym.

🐾 Courses

Casa Xalteva LANGUAGE COURSE
(Map p86; ✆2552-2993; www.casaxalteva.org; Calle Real Xalteva, Iglesia Xalteva, 25m N; 1 week from US$160; ⊙8am-5pm Mon-Fri) Next to the church of the same name, Casa Xalteva also runs a program providing breakfast and education for street kids.

**Alianza Francesa
de Granada** LANGUAGE COURSE
(Map p88; www.alianzafrancesagranada.org; Calle El Arsenal s/n; prices vary; ⊙9am-9:30pm Mon-Fri) French and Spanish courses, plus French-inspired cultural events.

**Nicaragua Mia
Spanish School** LANGUAGE COURSE
(Map p86; ✆2552-0347; Calle El Caimito, alcaldía, 3½ c E; 1 week all-inclusive US$280 per person) Run by a women's co-op, with a range of teaching methods and years of experience.

**Spanish Dale!
Language School** LANGUAGE COURSE
(Map p88; ✆8866-4581; www.spanishdale.com; Calle Atravesada, frente Bancentro; 1 week per person from US$140; ⊙8am-5pm Mon-Fri) A Spanish-language school inside the Mansión de Chocolate (p92).

Xpress Spanish School LANGUAGE COURSE
(Map p86; ✆2552-8577; www.nicaspanishschool.com; Calle Cervantes, Parque Central, 2½ c N; prices vary) Centrally located, with a young and dynamic staff.

Amy's Centro de Arte ART COURSE
(Map p88; ✆8616-7322; www.nicaragua-art.com; Calle La Calzada, Parque Central, 1 c E; classes from US$6; ⊙class times vary) This friendly art center offers painting and drawing classes.

👆 Tours

Corazón Trips TOUR
(Map p86; ✆2552-8852; www.hotelconcorazon.com; Calle Santa Lucía 141) Located inside the Hotel Con Corazón, this nonprofit tour operator offers well-organized trips including bike tours, cooking classes and trips to Mombacho.

Leo Tours Comunitarios TOUR
(Map p88; ✆8422-7905; leotoursgranada@gmail.com; Calla la Calzada, Parque Central, 1½ c E; ⊙8am-9pm) Enthusiastic locally owned business that offers all the usual options – Las Isletas boat tours (US$15), Mombacho (US$29), and a full-day trip to Masaya (US$39) – as well as some interesting visits to local communities.

Horse-Drawn Carriage Tour TOUR
(Map p88; rides 30min/1hr US$5/10) This classic Granada tour takes a horse-drawn carriage from in front of Parque Central for an hour-long whirl past churches, the cemetery, the *malecón* (waterfront) and more with a Spanish-speaking guide. These guys know how to give a tour, too: this has been a family business since 1868, when carriages were first introduced here and in Masaya.

Tierra Tour TOUR
(Map p88; ✆2552 8723; www.tierratour.com; Calle La Calzada, catedral, 2 c E) A recommended company that offers all the usual, plus camping and day trips to Finca La Calera.

Nahual Tours TOUR
(Map p88; ✆2552-3779; www.nahualtours.com; Calle La Calzada, Parque Central 1 c E; shuttle to Laguna de Apoyo one-way/round-trip US$5/10) Runs daily shuttles to and from the Monkey Hut at Laguna de Apoyo, as well as a standard range of tours and activities.

GRANADA COURSES

GRANADA FOR CHILDREN

Granada's a fairly kid-friendly city: wide footpaths, little traffic, a couple of pedestrian areas, a sizable Parque Central to chase pigeons in, and a good number of highchair-equipped restaurants – some high-end hotels even have portable cribs. And a couple of Granada's must-dos are well suited to junior travelers – it would be a world-weary kid indeed who didn't get a kick out of a ride in a horse-drawn carriage, or a tour of Las Isletas with a mixture of boat rides, swimming, monkeys and island lunches.

The old train station has a decent playground and an old steam engine out front. The Centro Turístico is a couple of kilometers of grassy lakefront with some surprisingly modern play equipment. Or take a Volcán Masaya night tour past glowing red lava before strapping on a helmet and headlamp and descending into a bat cave – the kids will love you forever.

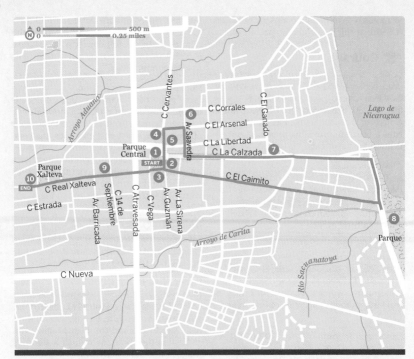

🏃 City Walk
Colonial Explorer

START PARQUE CENTRAL
END IGLESIA DE XALTEVA
LENGTH 4.5KM; THREE HOURS

Begin at the fine **1 Parque Central**, pleasantly shaded by mango and malinche trees. The oft-destroyed **2 Catedral de Granada** (p84) sits on the eastern side of the plaza. This most recent version was built in 1915.

On the park's southeastern corner, the beautifully restored **3 Hotel Gran Francia** (p91) was formerly the home of William Walker. Head north to **4 Plaza de la Independencia** (p87), with its impressive obelisk and Cruz de Siglo.

On the eastern side of this plaza is the Casa de los Leones, named for the carved lions on the portal. Rebuilt as a stately private home in 1920, it currently houses the **5 Fundación Casa de los Tres Mundos** (p84).

Head one block east on Calle El Arsenal to check out the grand facade of **6 Convento y Museo San Francisco** (p84), best captured on film close to sunset. From here,

head south on Calle Cervantes until you get to Calle La Calzada. On your way to the lake, one hot kilometer away, you'll pass **7 Capilla del Sagrado Corazón** (p87), originally built as a fort.

When you get to Lago de Nicaragua, the ferry terminal is on your left, but make a right through the green Spanish fortress for the **8 Centro Turístico** (p86), a lazy lakeside park with restaurants, bars and beaches, and docks where you can catch boats to explore the Las Isletas volcanic lake archipelago.

Grab a cab back to Parque Central, where you can stop for a break on a shady park bench. From here, head west on Calle Real Xalteva, which once connected the Spanish town of Granada to its much older indigenous neighbor, Xalteva. Four blocks west of Parque Central, you'll pass the beautiful **9 Iglesia La Merced** (p84).

The old indigenous neighborhood, now wholly assimilated, is marked by **10 Iglesia de Xalteva** (p86), the attractive 19th-century church that houses La Virgen de la Asunción.

Erick Tours   TOUR
(Map p88; ☑ 8974-5575; www.ericktoursnicara
gua.com; Parque Central 3 c al lago; prices vary) All
the standard tours (Las Isletas, Mombacho,
a one-day trip to Ometepe) plus airport
transfers for US$15 per person.

★★ Festivals & Events

Granada hosts a variety of interesting events
and festivals throughout the year.

International Poetry Festival   CULTURAL
(www.festivalpoesianicaragua.com; ☉ Feb) This
festival brings together wordsmiths from all
around the country and Latin America.

Fiestas de Agosto   RELIGIOUS
(☉ 3rd week August) Granada celebrates the
Assumption of Mary with fireworks, concerts in the park, bullfights (although it's
illegal to kill the bull in Nicaragua), horse
parades and major revelry by the lakefront.

Inmaculada Concepción   RELIGIOUS
(Purísimas; ☉ Nov 28–Dec 7) Neighborhoods
bear elaborate floats through the streets in
honor of Granada's patron saint, the Virgen
Concepción de María. They signal their arrival by blowing on conch shells to drive the
demons away.

🛏 Sleeping

There's a huge range of sleeping options in
Granada, from budget-friendly hostels and
guesthouses to some of the nicest hotels in
this part of Nicaragua.

Hostal El Momento   HOSTEL $
(Map p88; ☑ 2552-7811; www.hostelgranadanic-
aragua.com; Calle del Beso; dm/d US$10/40; @ 🛜)
Catering to the mature backpacker set, this
hip hostel has cool common spaces, iPads
in the lobby and a shared kitchen. Private
rooms are a good bet, some maintaining the
historic character of the building.

Casa del Agua   HOTEL $$
(Map p88; ☑ 8872-4627; www.casadelaguagra-
nada.com; Av Guzmán s/n; d from US$38; @ 🛜 ♒)
Big rooms surround a small pool in a prize
location just off Parque Central. Furnishings
are all new and tastefully selected, and bath-
rooms are big. There's a fully stocked kitch-
en for guest use and and on-site bike rentals.

Hotel El Maltese   HOTEL $$
(Map p86; ☑ 2552-7641; www.nicatour.net; Cen-
tro Turístico entrance; s/d from US$29/43; P ❄)
Right in front of Lake Nicaragua, this simple

spot has heavy wooden ceiling beams and
rustic regional decor. There's a restaurant on-
site, and bikes and canoes for rent, but this
area is seedy at night – consider taking a taxi.

Hotel La Pérgola   HOTEL $$
(Map p88; ☑ 2552-4221; www.lapergola.com.ni;
Calle El Caimito, alcaldía, 3 c E; r from US50;
P ❄ 🛜) This cozy hotel with its little center
courtyard, spacious rooms and big, firm
beds is a decent bet. Note: there's no hot
water.

Hotel El Club   HOTEL $$
(Map p86; ☑ 2552-4245; www.elclub-nicaragua.
com; Calle Libertad de la Piedra Bocona, 1 c O; d
from US$42; ❄ 🛜 ♒) This corner hotel, locat-
ed in a pretty colonial building, can be noisy
at night. But it's decent value, with a small
pool and a nice cocktail bar.

Hotel Casa San Martín   HOTEL $$
(Map p88; ☑ 2552-6185; www.hotelcasasan-
martin.com; Calle La Calzada, Parque Central, 1 c
E; s/d US$43/55; ❄ 🛜) In a reasonably quiet
section of Granada's popular pedestrian
promenade, this guesthouse has understat-
ed charm. Rooms vary, but each is special –
either for spaciousness, views, furnishings
or atmosphere – making this a solid mid-
range bet.

Hotel Gran Francia   HISTORIC HOTEL $$$
(Map p88; ☑ 2552-6000; www.lagranfrancia.com;
Av Guzmán, esq SE del Parque Central; d from
US$100; P ❄ @ 🛜 ♒) Just off the main
plaza, this elegant hotel is set in an opulent
old building. Across the street, the Gran
Francia's restaurant, bar and lounge (set in
William Walker's former home) are equally impressive, and well worth a wander for
those interested to see just how lovingly an
old building can be restored.

Hotel Con Corazón   HOTEL $$$
(Map p86; ☑ 2552-8852; www.hotelconcorazon.
com; Calle Cervantes, Parque Central, 3 c N; s/d/
tr/q US$62/73/94/121; ❄ @ 🛜 ♒) 🍃 An ele-
gant nonprofit hotel that directs earnings
to the development of local educational pro-
grams. The rooms are simple and pleasing,
spacious enough without being luxurious.
The building itself blends modern and tradi-
tional styles to perfection, with much of the
decoration coming from recycled materials
made by local craftspeople. Ask about vol-
unteer ops here.

It has salsa classes on Monday nights that
are open to the public.

Mansión de Chocolate
HOTEL $$$

(Map p88; ☑ 2552-4678; www.mansiondechoco late.com; Calle Atravesada, frente Bancocentro; d from US$104; ❄️🛜🏊) This elegant and expansive Spanish colonial mansion – once a hospital – is now a chocolate-themed hotel with a lovely pool (available for day use, US$6) and a hands-on chocolate museum, the Museo de Chocolate (p85), perfect for families. Guest rooms are spread out; some face courtyards, others are located up quaint wooden staircases. The all-you-can-eat breakfast is open to the public (US$6).

Hotel Casa San Francisco
HISTORIC HOTEL $$$

(Map p86; ☑ 2552-8235; www.hotelcasasanfran cisco.com; Calle Corrales 207, Convento San Francisco, ½ c O; d from US$87; 🅿️❄️@🛜🏊) 🍴 There's plenty of charm in the ivy-covered walls, mosaic tiles, Turkish lamps, cute little balcony sitting areas and stylish decorations in this lovely colonial house turned boutique hotel: it's the passion project of a pair of sisters from California, who each served in the Peace Corps before falling in love with Granada.

Hotel Casa del Consulado
HISTORIC HOTEL $$$

(Map p88; ☑ 2552-2709; www.hotelcasaconsula do.com; Calle el Consulado 105; d US$110; 🅿️❄️@🛜🏊) This elegant boutique hotel in an immaculately preserved *casona* (historic home) is one of the nicer options in town. The large pool in the immaculate central garden is the focus of the cane-roofed patio areas. Guest rooms have high ceilings, cane roofs and massive bathrooms with river-rock showers.

Hotel Los Patios
BOUTIQUE HOTEL $$$

(Map p86; ☑ 2552-0641; www.lospatiosgranada. com; Calle Corrales 525; d from US$115; 🅿️❄️🛜🏊) Contemporary style and colonial charm come together at this five-room boutique hotel. Scandinavian design sensibilities, including low-slung beds, modern fixtures and space-age zen gardens add to the allure.

Hotel Plaza Colón
HISTORIC HOTEL $$$

(Map p88; ☑ 2552-8489; www.hotelplazacolon. com; Parque Central, costado O; d from US$107; 🅿️❄️🛜🏊) 🍴 The last word in plaza-side luxury, this chart-topper contends for the best high-end spot in town. Rooms are large and airy, with serious dark wood and wrought-iron trimmings, and come equipped with all the modern conveniences. It's worth splashing out the extra US$20 to get a room with a deep, wide balcony overlooking the plaza.

Hotel Patio del Malinche
HISTORIC HOTEL $$$

(Map p88; ☑ 2552-2235; www.patiodelmalinche. com; Calle El Caimito, alcaldía, 2½ c E; s/d incl breakfast US$75/94; ❄️🛜🏊) This lovely house has been thoughtfully restored and outfitted with authentic features such as cane inlaid ceilings. There are actually two patios, both comfortably appointed with wicker furniture, the back one featuring a pool and bar area.

Rooms are moderately sized and stylish in a minimalist way.

Hotel Casa Capricho
GUESTHOUSE $$$

(Map p88; ☑ 2552-8422; www.hotelcasacapricho granada.com; Calle El Arsenal 401; d from US$56; 🅿️❄️@🛜🏊) Casa Capricho ('House of Whimsy' in English, more or less) is sort of sprawling and cozy at the same time: rooms are comfortable, with hardwood and wrought-iron furniture, and look out onto small balconies that overlook the dip pool and leafy patio.

🍴 Eating

Granada is full of restaurants serving a wide variety of cuisines, and new options are opening all the time. The city has excellent street food, too. Look for it around Parque Central and Mercado Municipal (p86) in the morning, and just before sunset, at *fritangas* (grills) set up around town. Two supermarkets are convenient stops for self-caterers.

★ The Garden Café
CAFE $

(Map p88; www.gardencafegranada.com; Calle La Libertad, Parque Central, 1 c E; mains US$4-8; ⏱7am-9pm; ❄️🍴) 🍴 This lovely cafe, set on a colonial-style patio around a gorgeous courtyard garden, offers great breakfasts, healthy sandwiches and salads, plus a daily special featuring a traditionally home-cooked Nicaraguan dish (on the day we visited, it was *carne tapada*, stewed beef cooked with carrots, potatoes and chayote.) It also has cocktails, sangria and wine, plus an excellent fair-trade store on-site.

Café de las Sonrisas
NICARAGUAN $

(Map p88; www.tioantonio.org; Iglesia de la Merced, 50m al lago; dishes US$2.50-4; ⏱7am-4pm Mon-Fri, to 3pm Sat) Practice your international communication at this nonprofit cafe run by staff who are hearing impaired. It has a picture-gram menu, sign charts and basic, hearty and wholesome Nicaraguan fare.

Cafe de los Sueños
INTERNATIONAL

(Map p86; ☑ 2552-7272; Calle La Calzada, frente Centro Escolar Carlos A Bravo; dishes US$4-8; ☺ 11am-10:30pm) A few steps from the loudest stretch of Calle la Calzada, this adorable cafe and eatery does good salads, freshly grilled fish, and a few international dishes such as Mexican-style tacos and savory crepes.

Taco Stop
TEX-MEX $

(Map p88; www.tacostopnicaragua.com; Ex-Cine Karawala, Calle Atravesada, Parque Central, 1 c O, ½c N; mains US$3-8; ☺ 10:30am-midnight Sun-Tue, to 3am Wed-Thu, to 5am Fri-Sat; 🛜) Located inside the shell of a vintage movie theater, this fast-food-style *taquería* (taco stall) is casual but stylish. Grab a burrito to go, or sit down for a spicy Mexican stew and cold beer. The tortillas are made in-house; there's even a small salsa bar. Be warned – the salsa verde is made with local jalapeños and has a real kick.

Don Luca's
PIZZA $

(Map p88; Calle La Calzada s/n; pizza US$2.50-4, mains US$5-10; ☺ noon-2pm & 6-10pm Tue-Thu & Sun, to 11pm Fri & Sat) This friendly pizzeria offers outdoor seating – a great vantage for people-watching – and a wide selection of Italian faves.

Café Blue
CAFE $

(Map p88; Calle Vega, Parque Central, 1 c S; dishes US$2-4; 🅿) A refreshingly simple little cafe serving up good American and Nica breakfasts, some spicy huevos rancheros, pancakes and a range of sandwiches under a cane ceiling.

Kathy's Waffle House
BREAKFAST $

(Map p88; www.kathyswafflehouse.com; Calle El Arsenal; dishes US$3-5; ☺ 7am-2pm) Drop into Kathy's, a long-time breakfast institution for tourists and locals alike, for waffles, pancakes, bottomless coffee and great views of Convento San Francisco from the front porch.

Cafetín El Volcán
NICARAGUAN $

(Map p88; Calle 14 de Septiembre, Iglesia de La Merced, 1 c S; quesillos US$0.50-2) You could come for the good-value set lunches (US$3), but pretty much everyone in town agrees that the real draw here are the *quesillos* (grilled corn tortillas stuffed with cheese and topped with pickled onions and cream), some of the tastiest around.

El Tercer Ojo
FUSION $$

(Map p88; ☑ 2552-7774; www.eltercerojonicaragua.com; Calle La Calzada, catedral, 1½ c E; meals US$6-14; ☺ 11am-11pm; 🛜🍽) Hip and lively, with silent movies projected on the wall at night, El Tercer Ojo (The Third Eye) is your go-to for sushi, Indian and Thai food. The expansive menu also features panini and salads, including several vegetarian and gluten-free options. Come for the daily happy hour (5pm to 8pm), or later for live music – check the online schedule.

El Zaguán
STEAK $$

(Map p88; ☑ 2552-2522; Av La Sirena s/n; meals US$7-13; ☺ noon-11pm; 🍷) Scoring consistent props for the best steak in town, this large yet somehow cozy restaurant just behind the cathedral specializes in locally sourced, melt-in-your-mouth steaks, flame-grilled before your eyes. Some solid chicken and fish dishes and a good wine list round out the menu. Make reservations in high season; it's popular with tourists.

El Camello
MIDDLE EASTERN $$

(Map p88; http://.granadarestaurant.wordpress.com; Hotel Gran Francia, 2 c al lago; mains US$6-8; ☺ noon-10pm Wed-Mon) This laid-back eatery takes you on a tour of the Middle East, featuring lamb stews, falafel and hummus.

El Pizzaiol
ITALIAN $$

(Map p88; Calle La Libertad s/n; mains US$7-12.50; ☺ noon-10pm) At this popular Italian trattoria, the food is pretty authentic – with a few regional variations – and the dessert list is to die for. The thin-crust pizza tops the menu, though you will do equally well with the savory pasta and meat dishes.

La Hacienda STEAK $$

(Map p88; Av Saavedra; dishes US$6-9; ⊙noon-midnight Tue-Sun) Good imported steaks and Tex-Mex favorites. The undercover outside seats have a great view of Convento San Francisco across the road.

Comidas Típicas y Más NICARAGUAN $$

(Map p88; Calle La Calzada, iglesia, 1 c E; dishes US$4-6; ⊙6pm-late Thu-Tue) Typical Nicaraguan food on the main pedestrian street. Dishes here cost more than at your local *comedor* (basic eatery), but it has a sweet patio setting and the food is carefully prepared. Try the *indio viejo* (beef stew; US$2.50), *nacatamales* (banana-leaf-wrapped bundles of cornmeal, meat, vegetables and herbs; US$2) or quesadillas (US$2.50).

Supermercado Colonia SUPERMARKET

(Map p86; www.lacolonia.com.ni; Calle La Inmaculada, Esso, 3 c arriba; ⊙8am-9pm) An upscale supermarket where you can stock up on food and drink before leaving town.

Palí SUPERMARKET

(Map p86; Calle Atravesada; ⊙9am-8pm) A grocery store with basic stock, good prices and a tiny bakery, in front of Mercado Municipal.

🍷 Drinking & Nightlife

Granada hops most nights, but Thursday to Saturday is when the real action takes place. Most people start or end the night off at one of the bars along Calle La Calzada, known for outdoor drinking and prime people-watching.

Lakeside Centro Turístico (p86), though it's not what it used to be, is home to a few discos and bars. Always take cabs between the Centro Turístico and central Granada at night.

Nectar LOUNGE

(Map p88; Calle La Calzada, Parque Central, 1½ c E; dishes US$4-6; ⊙11am-11:30pm) A small lounge-bar with a good list of cocktails (come for happy hour) and some cozy sitting areas. In high season it often gets visiting DJs and live bands to liven the place up. Some delicious light meals and snacks make up the small, creative menu.

O'Sheas IRISH PUB

(Map p88; www.osheas-nicaragua.com; Calle La Calzada s/n; ⊙8:30am-2am) One of the most popular pubs along the Calzada pedestrian strip, with friendly service and good pub grub.

Kelly's Bar IRISH PUB

(Map p88; cnr Av La Serena & Calle El Caimito; ⊙6pm-late) Belfast meets Granada in this friendly pub with sidewalk seating, a rear patio, and, of course, sport on the TV.

Inuit Bar BAR

(Map p86; ☑8661-7655; Centro Turístico; ⊙24hr) This lakeside bar is a low-key spot for a beer by the water; you can also arrange tours of Las Isletas through Inuit Kayaks (p87).

⭐ Entertainment

For a city of this size and popularity, there aren't as many cultural offerings as you'd expect in Granada, though live music and film screenings happen on and around Calle La Calzada on weekends.

Imagine LIVE MUSIC

(Map p88; www.imaginerestaurantandbar.com; Calle La Libertad s/n; ⊙5-11pm) Just like John Lennon would have liked it, this chilled-out bar features live music most days of the week.

🛍 Shopping

The Fundación Casa de los Tres Mundos (p84) sells a very good selection of books, magazines and other souvenirs. The fair-trade shop at the Garden Café (p92) is another great option for crafts, coffee, jewelry and clothing made around Nicaragua.

The Garden Shop CRAFTS

(Map p88; www.gardencafegranada.com; Calle La Libertad, Parque Central, 1 c E; ⊙9am-6pm; 🐾) 🌿 A fantastic new addition to the popular Garden Café (p92), this sustainably minded boutique offers crafts, jewelry, clothing and artwork produced through NGOs and fair-trade organizations throughout Nicaragua. Artisans from Chinandega, Diriamba, Granada, Masatepe, Managua and Masaya are all represented here; you can also buy coffee beans and postcards, and there's a good-sized book exchange at the entrance.

Doña Elba Cigars CRAFTS

(Map p86; ☑2552-3217; Calle Real Xalteva, Iglesia Xalteva, ½ c O; ⊙8am-5pm) If you aren't heading to Estelí this trip, stop here for a cognac-cured taste of Nicaragua and a peek at the cigar-manufacturing process. You can even practice rolling a cigar.

Lucha Libro Books BOOKS
(Map p88; www.luchalibrobooks.com; Calle Cervantes; ☉noon-5pm Wed-Mon) Swing in to this friendly store with a good selection of English-language books and maps.

Olé HANDICRAFTS
(Map p88; Calle La Calzada, Parque Central, 1 c E; ☉10am-6pm Wed-Mon) A clothing boutique and handicrafts store specializing in produce from local co-operatives. The emphasis is on rare and unique items not available elsewhere.

Casa El Recodo CRAFTS
(Map p86; www.casaelrecodo.com; Calle Consulado, Parque Central, 4 c O; ☉10am-5:30pm Mon-Sat) The oldest house in Granada has been faithfully restored and converted into a high-end souvenir shop.

ℹ Information

DANGERS & ANNOYANCES
There have been some reports of robberies on the road leading down to the lake and south into the Centro Turístico – take a cab after dark. Many assaults have been reported by tourists who attempt to bicycle to Península de Asese.

EMERGENCY
Ambulance (Cruz Roja) (Map p86; ☑2552-2711)
Police (☑2552-2929)

INTERNET ACCESS
Most hotels, and many restaurants and cafes, have wi-fi. You'll also spot a few internet cafes near the main plaza.

INTERNET RESOURCES
Find It Granada (www.finditgranada.com) A somewhat complete guide to the city's business, restaurants and hotels.
Lonely Planet (www.lonelyplanet.com/nicaragua/granada-and-the-masaya-region/granada) For planning advice, author recommendations, traveler reviews and insider tips.

LAUNDRY
Most hotels and hostels offer laundry services.

MEDICAL SERVICES
Hospital Amistad Japonés (Map p86; ☑2552-2719; Calle La Inmaculada, Esso station, 2km O) The most frequently recommended private hospital is out of town, on the road to Managua.

MONEY
Several banks are within a block of Parque Central.

BAC (Map p88; Calle La Libertad, Parque Central, 1 c O)
BanPro (Map p88; Calle Consulado, Parque Central, 1 c O)
Western Union (Map p86; Calle Real Xalteva) International money transfers.

POST
Post Office (Map p88; Calle Atravesada, BanCentro, ½ c S) Opposite the ex–Cine Karawala, now the home of Taco Stop.

TELEPHONE
Claro (Map p88; Parque Central)

TOURIST INFORMATION
Check at hostels and tour operators for the latest tourist info.
Intur (Map p86; ☑2552-6858; www.visitanicaragua.com/ingles; Calle Corrales) The Granada branch of the national tourist office has up-to-date transportation schedules, a reasonable city map, and lots of information and flyers.

TRAVELERS WITH DISABILITIES
Some tour outfitters and many hotels can accommodate travelers with disabilities, but because Granada's city streets are lined with bumpy cobblestones and old colonial houses, it's best to plan ahead.

ℹ Getting There & Away

BOAT
Traditionally, **twice-weekly ferries** (p95) have left Granada's ferry terminal for Isla de Ometepe. But service was suspended indefinitely at the time of writing due to low water levels on Lago de Nicaragua. Check www.ometepenicaragua.com/ferryboat.php for updates on services.
Puerto Asese (☑2552-2269), about 2km southeast of town, has boats for the Las Isletas and Parque Nacional Archipiélago Zapatera.
Dock for boats to San Carlos & Isla de Ometepe (Map p86) Service is suspended (until further notice). Travelers can check www.ometepenicaragua.com for updates.

BUS
For most international services, you'll need to go to nearby Managua. If you're headed south to Costa Rica, though, you can get on a passing **Transnica** (p299) or **Ticabus** (p299) – check their websites for more information.
Buses to Managua (Map p86)
Buses to Destinations South (Map p86)
Microbuses to Managua (Map p88)
Buses to Masaya (Map p86)

Shuttle Bus

Considering that Managua is a one-hour, one-dollar hop in a minibus (and that León buses leave from the spot where you arrive) and that other destinations are nearly equally accessible, shuttle service is not so popular here. If you have your heart set on shuttle travel, try to get a group together or you may find yourself paying for the entire trip (in either case a taxi may work out way better).

Erick Tours (p91) Airport transfers.

Nahual Tours (p89) Has two daily shuttles to Laguna de Apoyo (one-way/round-trip US$5/10).

ⓘ Getting Around

BICYCLE

While cycling in town might require nerves of steel, there are several mellow rides around town; many tour operators and some hostels rent bikes.

BUS

Granada doesn't have one central bus terminal.

Buses to Managua (p95) (US$0.75, one hour, 4am to 7pm, every 20 to 30 minutes), arriving at Managua's Mercado Roberto Huembes, depart from the lot just north of the old hospital on the western edge of town.

Microbuses to Managua (p95) (US$1.25, one hour, 5am to 7:30pm, every 15 to 30 minutes), arriving at UCA in Managua, leave from the convenient lot just south of the Parque Central on Calle Vega.

Buses to Masaya (p95) (US$0.50, 30 minutes, 5am to 6pm, every 20 to 30 minutes) leave from two blocks west of the Mercado Municipal, around the corner from Palí.

Buses to destinations south (p95) leave from a block south of the market, across from the **Shell petrol station**.

Carazo (US$0.75, 45 minutes, 6am to 5:05pm, every 20 minutes) For San Marcos, Diriamba (with connections to the Carazo beaches) and Jinotepe.

Catarina & San Juan de Oriente (US$0.60, 30 minutes, 6am to 6pm, every 30 to 60 minutes).

Rivas (US$1.25, 1½ hours, 5:45am to 3:10pm, nearly hourly) Early-afternoon buses will allow you to make the last boat to Isla de Ometepe.

CAR & MOTORCYCLE

Nicaragua's (relatively) traffic-free and decent roads around Granada make motorbiking an enjoyable way of getting around, particularly if you're planning a day trip to the Laguna de Apoyo or a tour of the Pueblos Blancos. Ask at tour operators around town.

It's generally cheaper to rent cars in Managua, where your rental is probably parked right now – so be sure to allow a couple of hours for it to arrive. This region has good roads, and many attractions, including the Pueblos Blancos. With some forward planning, you can take cars to Isla de Ometepe.

Budget (Map p86; ☑ 2552-2323; www.budget.com.ni; Calle Inmaculada, Plaza Inmaculada) At the Shell station.

Dollar (Map p88; ☑ 2552-8515; www.dollar.com.ni) At Hotel Plaza Colón.

TAXI

Taxis are plentiful. Always agree on a fare before getting into the taxi, which should be less than US$1 per person if you're getting into a shared taxi anywhere in the city.

It's inexpensive and convenient to take taxis to other destinations, including Masaya and Laguna de Apoyo, keeping in mind that fares vary according to gas prices and your bargaining skills. You can always ask your hotel or hostel to call you a taxi and settle on a price before you're picked up.

AROUND GRANADA

Even on the shortest trip through Granada, you'll understand why Nicaragua's nickname is the 'land of lakes and volcanoes.' Volcán Mombacho and the gorgeous crater lake of Laguna de Apoyo are both within easy proximity of the city, accessible on day trips – either DIY or organized by tour outfitters – from town. Mombacho, active and often shrouded with clouds, is a great destination for quiet hiking and birdwatching. If you have time to spare, spend the night at one of the hotels or hostels on the shores of the lake: an early-morning dip in these clean, clear waters is a rare pleasure. Also in this region you'll find the dormant volcano on the little-visited island of Zapatera on Lago de Nicaragua; it's beautiful but still rather undeveloped for tourists.

While many travelers visit destinations around Granada on day trips from the city, staying overnight on the shores of Laguna de Apoyo is a treat – and there are several good guesthouses, hostels and hotels to choose from.

Bring snacks if you're hiking Volcán Mombacho and bring everything you'll need (including drinking water) if you're heading to Isla Zapatera. Most hotels and hostels around Laguna de Apoyo have restaurants open to the public (most with great views of the lake.)

LAS ISLETAS

An easy morning or afternoon trip from Granada takes you by boat to this miniature archipelago of 365 tiny tropical islands. Along the way you'll spot rare birds, colorful flowers and some interesting indigenous fauna – keep your eye out for osprey, kingfishers, caimans and howler monkeys (along the mainland). The privately owned islands that would make a tremendous evil lair are highlights, as well as lunch at the handful of island hotels and restaurants.

There's even a Spanish fortress. Castillo San Pablo was built in 1784 and has great views of Granada and Volcán Mombacho, plus a fine swimming hole nearby.

Most tours also pass Isla de los Monos (Monkey Island). The spider- and capuchin-monkey residents are friendly (they were brought here by a veterinarian living on a nearby island), but may run off with your picnic lunch.

Formed 10,000 years ago when the very visible Volcán Mombacho exploded into its current ragged silhouette, these islands were once one of the poorest neighborhoods in Granada, and some are still home to impoverished families, who in general have no official property rights. They are being gradually supplanted by the beautiful homes of folks such as the Pellas family (Flor de Caña owners), former president Chamorro, and lots of expats in paradise. Want to join them? There are plenty of 'For Sale' signs and your guide will know all the prices.

Most tour companies run trips to Las Isletas, or do it yourself with Inuit Kayaks (p87), about 1km from the Centro Turístico entrance, an outfitter that runs several guided kayak tours. Touts will offer to hook you up with a boat tour as soon as you enter the Centro Turístico. If you're on your own or in a small group, wait around until a larger group forms (unless you want to pay for the whole boat yourself – around US$20 for a one-hour tour); the boat operators will offer discount seats just to fill their boat up. For the best birdwatching, arrange your trip the day before to leave at dawn. Sunset is also quite nice, but that tour is quicker, with less exploration of the further-afield corners of the island group.

A turnoff to the right, just after Inuit Kayaks (look for the sign saying 'Marina Cocibolca'), takes you to the other side of the Península de Asese to Puerto Asese, where you can hire boats to tour the *isletas* on this side. This is a less popular option, so chances of forming an impromptu group are slimmer. The advantage of a tour here is that there are fewer power lines and other boats, so it's a more tranquil experience, but it involves a fair bit of time in open water.

There are numerous restaurants in the island chain. Ask your boat operator to include a stop at one, where a large meal of locally caught fish will cost around US$7.50.

GRANADA RESERVA NATURAL VOLCÁN MOMBACHO

❶ Getting There & Away

Many travelers drive themselves to Mombacho or Laguna de Apoyo, or visit these destinations on organized tours. Several tour outfitters in Granada, such as **Nahual Tours** (p89), offer shuttle-van service to and from Laguna de Apoyo. It's possible to travel by public bus, though drop-off points aren't particularly convenient: be prepared to walk or hike.

Reserva Natural Volcán Mombacho

It's been a few decades since this 1345m volcano, the defining feature of the Granada skyline, has acted up, but it is still most certainly active and sends up the periodic puff of smoke, just to keep locals on their toes. It's easy to get to the crown of cloud forest, steaming with fumaroles and other bubbling volcanic activity beneath the misty vines and orchids.

◉ Sights

Reserva Natural Volcán Mombacho NATURE RESERVE
(📞 2552-5858; www.mombacho.org; El Guana caste, carretera Granada-Nandaime Km 50; park entrance per car/pedestrian US$20/5, mariposario US$2; ⊙8am-5pm Fri-Sun, by reservation other days for groups of 10 or more) Reserva Natural Volcán Mombacho is managed by the Fundación Cocibolca, which since 1999 has been building trails and running an eco-mobile (think refurbished military jeeps seating 25)

on the 40% grade up to 1100m. Get there early to take the short trail through the **organic coffee farm**, or check out the **mariposario** (butterfly garden) and **orchid garden** (free with entrance), close to the parking lot.

At the top you can find three species of monkey, 168 species of bird and more than 100 types of orchids as part of the jungle canopy that this park is intent on preserving. There is a choice of several trails, including **Sendero del Cráter**, a 1.5km jaunt to the fumaroles, plus great views of Granada and Las Isletas, and **Sendero la Puma**, a steeper 4km trek around the lip of the crater, with even better views. Guides, many of whom speak English, are available at the entrance and cost US$12 to US$22 per group of up to seven. Guides are required for a trek up **Sendero el Tigrillo**, a heart-pumping two-hour tromp up to two overlooks.

The park is open to the public with regular hours on Friday, Saturday, and Sunday. However, groups of 10 or more can make arrangements to visit on other days. Time your arrival to coincide with an eco-mobile departure, at 8:30am, 10am and 1pm.

If you have a 4WD, you can drive up the volcano for an extra US$22 – plus US$5/3 for every adult/child in the car.

There are several attractions in the immediate vicinity, including a pair of interesting rural communities. Inside the reserve but hidden away on a farm, and thus more easily accessible on a separate day trip from Granada, the beautifully maintained, 45°C (113°F) hot springs of **Aguas Termales de Calera** are replete with sulfur, calcium and other minerals quasi-scientifically proven to keep you radiant and healthy. Look for the excursion listed at outfitters in Granada; expect to pay around US$25 per person, including round-trip transportation.

Nicaragua Libre   NATURE RESERVE
(☑2552-0238; www.ucatierrayagua.org; entrada de Monte Verde, 500m SE; guided tour US$3 per person; ☺tours by reservation) This small rural community at the base of Volcán Mombacho is part of the UCA community-tourism project. It offers guided trips through organic coffee farms, horseback rides to San Juan de Oriente and walks to Mombacho. A concerted effort has been made to rescue the art of traditional handicrafts here; look for young artisans selling their work. It's a 1km walk from where the bus drops you on the Granada–Nandaime road, or you can contact UCA's Granada office for more details.

Aguas Agrias –
La Nanda Community   NATURE RESERVE
(☑8439-9658; www.ucatierrayagua.org/aguas-agrias; Carretera Granada-Nandaime, entrada a Monte Verde 12km E; guided tours US$3 to US$5; ☺tours by reservation) This rural community, located just south of Mombacho volcano, is an off-the-beaten-path destination where local guides lead two-hour hikes through a traditional plantation. The unusual volcanic landscape, dotted with a series of refreshing lagoons – some of which you can swim in – makes for an interesting excursion. The community is run by the Union of Cooperative Agriculturalists 'UCA Tierra y Agua.'

Lunch is available on-site for US$4.50. Transport here is tricky – contact UCA for details. If you're driving yourself from Granada, turn left at the entrance to Monte Verde and follow the first road for 12 km.

Activities

Aguas Termales de Calera   SPRING
(☑2222-4208) **FREE** Tucked away on Finca Calera, inside the reserve and right by the lake, these hot springs 45°C (113°F) are rich with sulfur, calcium and other beautifying minerals. Due to the location, it's best to visit on a day trip from Granada. Outfitters offer the excursion for around US$25 per person, including round-trip transportation.

Sleeping & Eating

Most visitors come to the park on a day trip and sleep in nearby Granada. But there are a couple of lodges and guesthouses in the area. You can also camp in the park for US$20 per tent.

The park's visitor center has a cafeteria serving drinks and snacks. It's wise to bring supplies from Granada.

Albergue Rural
Nicaragua Libre   GUESTHOUSE
(☑8965-7017; www.ucatierrayagua.org; entrada de Monte Verde, 500m SE, El Coyolar; d US$20) The peaceful and pleasantly rustic guesthouse at Nicaragua Libre is a good place to base yourself for excursions in the area. Simple guest rooms have exposed brick walls, beds draped with mosquito nets, and patios strung with hammocks.

La Granadilla   LODGE $
(☑2552-0238; www.ucatierrayagua.org/la-grana-dilla; lodging per person US$5-8, meals US$3-5) A bit further down the road from Nicaragua

Libre, La Granadilla (a member of the UCA project) offers rustic accommodations and meals. Electricity is iffy, but you're only 20 minutes from the entrance to Volcán Mombacho. You can arrange guided hikes up the mountain, visits to farms in the area, ox-cart rides and bicycle tours.

🛈 Getting There & Away

Public transportation is inconvenient: most visitors drive themselves here or come on an organized tour from Granada.

You can also take any Nandaime bus from Granada and ask to be let off at the entrance. From here, you'll walk two steep kilometers (stay left where the road splits) to the spot where the eco-mobiles pick up passengers for the uphill drive.

Reserva Natural Laguna de Apoyo

A vision in sapphire set into a lush forest crater, this 200m-deep, 200-centuries-old crater lake is said to be the country's cleanest and deepest. The warm undersea fumaroles feed the healing and slightly salty waters, howler monkeys bark overhead every morning, and there's a cool air that make this a favorite respite for peace-seeking travelers.

While technically considered a natural reserve, this wild area has plenty of hotels dotting the lake's shore and limited environmental protection from the various agencies that claim jurisdiction. Tread lightly.

Some visitors are content with just taking in the view from the crater's edge in Catarina or Diriá. But it's well worth making your way to the bottom for one of the finest swims you'll ever enjoy. A tiny town lies at the bottom of the paved road into the crater, accessible via an often unsigned turnoff about 15km north of Granada, along the Carretera a Masaya.

🏃 Activities

There's a free **beach** at the bottom of the road; look for the trail just to the right of the T intersection. Otherwise, pay for a day pass at one of the hotels for access to their beaches, docks and kayaks (US$5 to US$7). Scuba-diving classes are available through Hotel SelvAzul (p99).

Peace Project DIVING
(☎8266-8404; www.thepeaceprojectnicaragua.org; de Los Ranchos, 100m N, Catarina) This sustainably minded outfitter and community organization offers introductory courses and excursions for certified divers, plus lodging and volunteer opportunities.

Scuba Diving at SelvAzul DIVING
(☎8631-1890; www.hotelselvazul.com; triángulo, 500m N; 1 tank dive US$40, introductory course US$60) Located in the Hotel SelvAzul, this PADI operation also has certification courses.

Apoyo Spanish School LANGUAGE COURSE
(☎8882-3992; www.gaianicaragua.org; triángulo, 1km N; classes from US$7 per hour) Located at the Estación Biológica, this language school claims to be the longest-running in Nicaragua. Certainly the location is tough to beat.

🍽 Sleeping & Eating

You can easily visit Laguna de Apoyo as a day trip from Granada, but it's wonderful to wake up here, and there are several good places to stay – including a number of rental houses that are ideal if you're staying for more than a night or two. Check online, and shop around, as there were new properties opening at the time of writing.

There's a basic store 50m north of the T intersection. Most hotels also have restaurants, but it's also a good idea to bring some of your own snacks from Granada.

Monkey Hut HOSTEL $
(☎8887-3546; www.themonkeyhut.net; triángulo, 450m N; dm/d/cabin US$14/39/59; P 🛜) This popular waterfront property (US$6 day use for nonguests) features a small beach on the edge of the lake, terraced lounge and picnic areas, a dock with plenty of kayaks, a cocktail bar and cafe, and a pizzeria. Overnight guests also have access to a kitchen and outdoor grills; choose between dorms, private rooms or a freestanding cabin.

Hostel Paradiso HOSTEL $
(☎2520-2878; www.hostelparadiso.com; triángulo, 300m E; dm US$10, s/d without bathroom US$15/25, d/tr US$32/40; P ✳ @ 🛜) A great pick for budget travelers, this lakefront hostel has a large terrace, private dock, kayaks, and shared kitchen, plus a good restaurant and bar. Day passes cost US$7 per person. The hostel runs a shuttle to and from Granada for US$3 each way; check the website for details.

CasAromansse   B&B $$
(2520-2837; www.casaromansse.co; triángulo, 1.5km E; d from US$50;) This sweet five-room B&B and yoga retreat offers down-to-earth lakeside accommodations – rooms have beds draped with mosquito nets, and some feature water views – and excellent French-influenced Nicaraguan food. Check the website for more on yoga workshops and classes.

La Orquídea   GUESTHOUSE $$
(8872-1866; www.laorquideanicaragua.com; triángulo, 1.8km N; d US$60;) If you need to rent a whole house for four people, then this is the place to stay. You get your own living room, gorgeous, spacious rooms – there are just two bedrooms – with big windows leading out onto balconies with excellent lagoon views. The water's a short walk down the hill.

San Simian Eco Lodge   LODGE $$$
(8850-8101; www.sansimian.com; Norome, 1km S; s/d from US$40/50;) This Swiss-owned lodge has beautiful little cabins that blend into the hillside. Most have stone-walled, alfresco bathrooms, and all have plenty of air and light, and mosquito nets over the beds. You can access the beach and kayaks if you come for the day (US$5 per person). A daily shuttle from Granada (US$11 including day pass) is available on request.

Posada Ecológica la Abuela   CABIN $$$
(8880-0368; www.posadaecologicalaabuela.com.ni; triángulo, 2km NE; bungalow for 2/4 US$75/120;) On a steep hillside leading down to the water, these cute little cabins are comfortable enough to make you feel at home, complete with coffeemakers and fridges. These are some of the nicest grounds along the lake: the restaurant and dock offer spectacular lake views.

Apoyo Resort   RESORT $$$
(2520-2085; www.apoyoresort.com; triángulo 1km S; apt US$100, 1-bedroom villa US$135;) Running up the hill from the lakeside road, this recently revamped resort has spacious apartments and villas – many with kitchens – that are ideal for families. There's also a swimming pool and a good restaurant, The Grill.

❶ Information

Estación Biológica (8882-3992; www.gaia nicaragua.org; triángulo 1km N) This ecological research station hosts scientists studying the region's endemic fish population. The center also runs seminars, arranges volunteer opportunities, and hosts overnight guests, making it a helpful resource for travelers.

❶ Getting There & Away

Many hotels and hostels on the lake offer daily shuttle transportation to and from Laguna de Apoyo from Granada (from US$3 one way), including options for day visitors and overnight guests. Check for details and times on the websites of the **Monkey Hut** (p99) and **Hostel Paradiso** (p99), or walk around Granada and see what's on offer.

Outside the posted shuttle times, you could also arrange a taxi from Granada (US$12 to US$15), Masaya (US$10 to US$12), or Managua (US$30 to US$40) to the door of your hotel or destination in Laguna de Apoyo.

Both of these options are generally preferable to taking public transportation. Laguna de Apoyo is close to Granada and Masaya, but most buses don't go close to the hotels; they usually drop passengers off near the crater rim. The half-hour, 2km descent isn't a bad walk, but going uphill again is hard work, especially on a hot day.

The main entrance is from a road off the Carretera a Masaya at Km 37.5. Buses run every half-hour between Masaya and the crater rim (US$0.50, 6am to 6pm). Only three buses, which read 'La Laguna,' descend all the way to the waterfront (US$0.70, 5:30am, 10:30am and 3:30pm).

Often directions given are from El Triángulo – the T intersection where the road splits once it hits the waterfront, either heading to the right (south) or left (north).

Parque Nacional Archipiélago Zapatera

Isla Zapatera, a dormant volcano rising to 629m from the shallow waters of Lago de Nicaragua, is an ancient ceremonial island of the Chorotega, and male counterpart to more buxom Isla de Ometepe, whose smoking cone can be seen after you take the three-hour hike to the top. The 45-sq-km island and surrounding archipelago of 13 islands are part of Parque Nacional Archipiélago Zapatera, designated to protect not only the remaining swaths of virgin tropical dry and wet forest, but also the unparalleled collection of petroglyphs and statues left here between 500 and 1500 years ago.

A handful of archaeologists have worked these sites, including Ephraim Squier, who shipped several of the 15 statues he discovered here in 1849 to the US, where they are displayed at the Smithsonian Museum, and Swedish scientist Carl Bollivius, who discovered more statues, many of which are displayed at Granada's Convento y Museo San Francisco.

Perhaps the most impressive expanse of petroglyphs is carved into a 95m by 25m expanse of bedrock at the center of Isla El Muerto, where many statues have also been found. Several of the other islands also have petroglyphs and potential archaeological sites.

About 500 people live here quasi-legally, fishing and subsistence farming and hoping that no one puts pressure on Marena (Ministry of the Environment and Natural Resources) to do anything about it. Fortunately for them, the government isn't doing much of anything with these islands, which also means that infrastructure is basic and access is inconvenient.

Tours (US$30 per person) are run by the Isla Zapatera Community. Visit the website (http://zapatera.blogspot.com) for more information.

🛏 Sleeping & Eating

Basic lodgings (dorm US$7) are available at a rural lodge run by farmers in the Sonzapote community. Visit the website of the Isla Zapatera Community (http://zapatera.blogspot.com) for the latest details. You can also camp on the island.

There is no potable water on the island, nor any place to buy supplies. Bring your own food from Granada. There are basic meals (US$3 to US$7) available at the Sonzapote community's rural lodge.

❶ Getting There & Away

The island is located about 30 to 90 minutes by boat (depending on weather) from the Asese port of Granada, but there is currently no public transportation to the island. Isla Zapatera Community (www.zapatera.blogspot.com) may arrange transportation from Puerto Asese, or you can hire a private boat from there for around US$80 round-trip. Stop at a travel agency in Granada for more information. The same agencies offer day-long tours from Granada for around US$85 per person.

GRANADA PARQUE NACIONAL ARCHIPIÉLAGO ZAPATERA

Southwestern Nicaragua

Best Places to Eat

➡ Café Campestre (p119)

➡ G&G Gourmet (p129)

➡ Party Wave Gigante (p122)

➡ Barrio Café (p128)

Best Places to Sleep

➡ Playa Hermosa Ecolodge (p133)

➡ Hotel Popoyo (p123)

➡ La Posada Azul (p128)

➡ Morgan's Rock (p132)

Why Go?

Packed with attractions, the southwest offers up some of Nicaragua's hallmark vistas and adventures. Surfers have been hitting this coastline for years, drawn by perfect, uncrowded waves and chilled-back surfing encampments. Most start their trip through the region in San Juan del Sur, where you'll find better accommodations, high-octane parties and a solid selection of restaurants catering to international appetites. Beyond this are spirited fishing villages, sea-turtle nesting grounds and tough-and-true inland towns.

No trip to the southwest would be complete without a few days on Isla de Ometepe. The island itself is shaped like an infinity symbol, with bookend volcanoes dominating either side of a secluded universe where you'll discover waterfalls, wildlife, lost coves and enchanted forests. There's kayaking, swimming, hiking and biking, and many travelers extend their stay as they dive into paradise, lost in the quiet spots and friendly traveler encampments that define this island escape.

When to Go

➡ November through May is the dry season. It means less verdant foliage, slightly longer days, plenty of adventure opportunities and remarkable sunsets over the curving Pacific Ocean.

➡ April to December is surf season, when you get big barrels and double-overhead exposure. Book ahead for surf camps during this time. Beginners may want to consider other times of the year to avoid the wave traffic.

➡ September to October is the peak season for sea turtle arrivals at Refugio de Vida Silvestre La Flor. If your timing is right you could see over 3000 turtles arrive on the same day!

History

Although first inhabited by the little-known Kiribisis peoples, it's the Chorotega who really left their mark on this region, most famously with the stone monoliths that are today on display beside the church in Altagracia. The Chorotega were soon overrun by the Nicarao, however, and it was Cacique Nicarao who met Spanish conquistador Gil González on the shores of Lago de Nicaragua in 1523. The Cruz de España marks the spot where the chief famously traded over 18,000 gold pesos for a few items of the Spaniard's clothing – a trade which some say set the tone for Nica–Euro commerce for centuries to come.

With time, this narrow strip of earth became the only land crossing for the gold-rushers traveling from New York to California. Talk continues today of a 'dry canal' railroad that would carry goods between the Pacific and Lago de Nicaragua, to continue on by boat.

Rivas was the site of some stunning defeats for filibuster William Walker, whose later plans to attack San Juan del Sur were thwarted by the British in 1858. Once the railroads connected the USA's East and West Coasts, gold prospectors gave up on this route and the region slipped back into its former torpor. This was briefly disturbed in the 1979 revolution, as spirited resistance to Somoza troops turned the hills behind San Juan del Sur into bloody battlegrounds. The Isla de Ometepe was spared from such scenes and the horrors of the Contra War – possibly one reason that the island's nickname, 'the oasis of peace,' has stuck.

🛈 Getting There & Away

Rivas is the regional travel hub, and its enormous, chaotic bus lot connects the region to Granada, Masaya and the rest of the country. It's usually easier to take *colectivo* taxis to San Jorge, where the main ferry terminal to Isla de Ometepe is located. You can also get to Ometepe via ferry from Granada.

Regular buses and shuttles serve the beach towns around San Juan del Sur, though you'll likely need to arrange a taxi (or brave a bumpy ride on one of a few daily chicken buses) to access the comparatively remote beaches around Popoyo.

Rivas

Rivas has its fans – people say it's au and lively, with some wonderful bu downtown. Maybe. But with the beaches, the lake and Isla de Ometepe beckoning, few travelers pause here long enough to find out.

Rivas' strategic position on the only sliver of land between the Pacific and Atlantic Oceans made it an important spot back in the colonial days. Now, with all the development on the southwestern beaches and Ometepe, it is once again an important trading and transport hub.

◉ Sights

Museo de Antropología e Historia MUSEUM (☑ 2563 3708; mercado, 1c S, 1c E; US$1; ☺ 9am-noon Mon-Sat) If you have just two hours in town, this is the place to go. Inside you'll find some moth-eaten taxidermy, a wall of myths and legends and, best of all, a well-signed (in both English and Spanish) collection of pre-Columbian artifacts, many of them recently discovered by the Santa Isabela Archaeological Project.

This Canadian-Nicaraguan team is excavating what it believes to be Cacique Nicarao's ancient capital of Quauhcapolca, just north of San Jorge. The site was occupied between AD 1000 and 1250, and the 400,000 artifacts they have uncovered there include tools, blow guns, jewelry, funeral jars and cookware, as well as a fertility-goddess complex and representations of the Aztec deity Quetzalcoatl.

The building itself, **Hacienda Ursula**, is an 18th-century architectural treasure and the site of William Walker's decisive defeat. After his troops, limping home following an embarrassing rout by the Costa Rican military, took control of the hacienda, schoolteacher Emmanuel Mongalo y Rubio set the fortress on fire. Most of Walker's men were shot or captured as they fled the burning building.

🛏 Sleeping

Most people heading for Ometepe choose to stay in San Jorge to be close by for the first ferry, or head southward to nearby San Juan del Sur for more attractive accommodations options.

South-western Nicaragua Highlights

1 Isla de Ometepe (p109) Climbing a volcano, kayaking the wetlands or swimming in a lagoon...or all three.

2 Refugio de Vida Silvestre La Flor (p133) Welcoming the thousands of endangered olive ridley and leatherback turtles that lay their eggs at this wildlife refuge.

3 Playa Popoyo (p122) Enjoying sun, sand, and solitude on wild and far-flung beaches dotted with dramatic rock formations.

4 Playa Maderas (p131) Riding giant waves and working on your tan at the world-class beach enclaves along this stretch of coast.

5 San Juan del Sur (p129) Watching a sunset and saying goodbye to the day at a chilled-out beachside bar.

6 El Ostional (p134) Escaping the crowds on idyllic and near-empty sands near the border of Costa Rica.

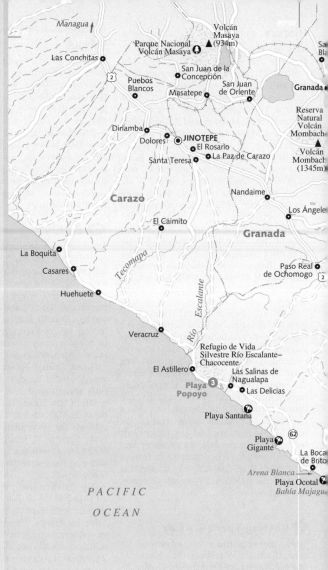

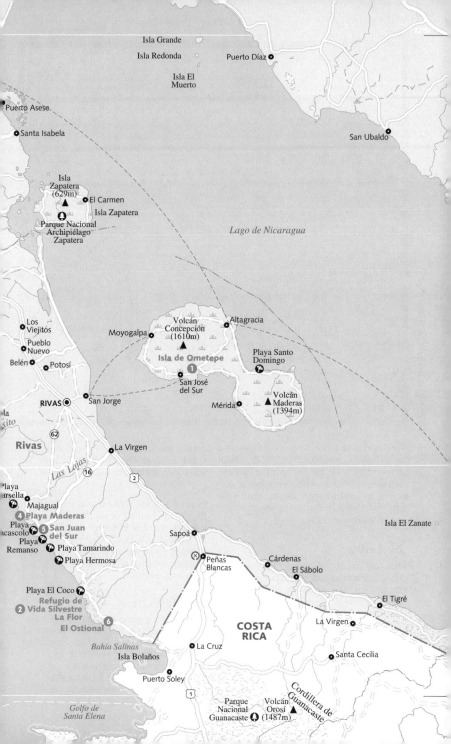

Isla Grande

Isla Redonda

Puerto Díaz

Isla El
Muerto

Puerto Asese

Santa Isabela

San Ubaldo

Isla
Zapatera
(629m)

El Carmen

Isla Zapatera

Parque Nacional
Archipiélago
Zapatera

Lago de Nicaragua

Los
Viejitós

Moyogalpa

Volcán
Concepción
(1610m)

Altagracia

Pueblo
Nuevo

Belén

Potosí

Isla de Ometepe
❶

Playa Santo
Domingo

San José
del Sur

RIVAS

San Jorge

Mérida

Volcán
Maderas
(1394m)

Rivas

62

La Virgen

Las Lajas

16

2

Playa
Marsella

Majagual

❹ **Playa Maderas**

Playa
Macascolo

❺ **San Juan
del Sur**

Sapoá

Isla El Zanate

Playa
Remanso

Playa Tamarindo

Playa Hermosa

Peñas
Blancas

Cárdenas

El Sábolo

Playa El Coco

**Refugio de
❷ Vida Silvestre
La Flor**

❻

El Ostional

El Tigré

La Virgen

**COSTA
RICA**

Santa Cecilia

Bahía Salinas

La Cruz

Isla Bolaños

Puerto Soley

1

*Cordillera de
Guanacaste*

*Golfo de
Santa Elena*

Parque
Nacional
Guanacaste

Volcán
Orosí ❹ (1487m)

Rivas

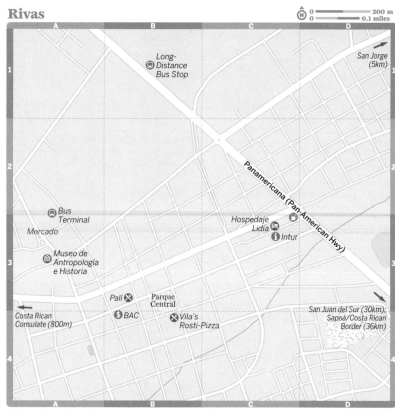

0 — 200 m
0 — 0.1 miles

Long-Distance Bus Stop (B1)

San Jorge (5km) (D1)

Panamericana (Pan-American Hwy)

Bus Terminal (A2-3)

Mercado (A3)

Hospedaje Lidia (C2-3)

Intur (C3)

Museo de Antropología e Historia (A3)

Palí (B3-4)

Parque Central (B3-4)

BAC (B4)

Vila's Rosti-Pizza (B4)

Costa Rican Consulate (800m) (A4)

San Juan del Sur (30km); Sapoá/Costa Rican Border (36km) (D4)

Hospedaje Lidia   GUESTHOUSE **$**
(☑ 2563-3477; Texaco, ½c O; d US$25, without
bathroom US$10/18; 🛜) The location isn't too
desirable, but this no-frills, family-run operation offers decent budget lodging, with well-
scrubbed rooms and a better-than-average
room-to-bathroom ratio.

✗ Eating

Rivas has plenty of cheap eats, with the
very cheapest clinging to the outside of the
chaotic *mercado* (market). There's also a
big supermarket where you can stock up
on basics before heading to Ometepe or the
beaches.

Vila's Rosti-Pizza   PARRILLA **$$**
(costado sur, Parque Central; dishes US$5-10;
⊙10am-midnight) This centrally located
eatery is one of the better dining picks
in town. Come for steaks, burgers and

people-watching from the front tables: the
entire town crosses the Parque Central at
least once during the course of a meal.

Palí   SUPERMARKET
(www.walmart.com; Parque Central, 1½c O; ⊙8am-
10pm) This branch of the Walmart-owned
supermarket chain doesn't necessarily of-
fer a great selection, but it's a good place
to stock up on basics and snacks if you're
heading to more remote areas in the sur-
rounding region.

ℹ Information

Rivas has the biggest *mercado*, best grocery
selection and the widest choice of banks and
businesses in southwestern Nicaragua. Stock
up here before heading elsewhere.

BAC (frente Hotel Cacique Nicarao)

Costa Rican Consulate (☑ 2563-5353;
ichaves@rree.go.cr; frente hospital, Rivas)

Intur (☑ 2563-4914; rivas@intur.gob.ni; Texaco, ½c O; ☺ 9am-6pm Mon-Fri) Offering a decent selection of flyers on Rivas, San Juan del Sur and Ometepe.

❶ Getting There & Away

BUS

Rivas is a transport hub. The **bus terminal** (☑ 8669-0330) is adjacent to the *mercado*. You can catch more luxurious long-distance buses (most headed to and from Managua, not Granada) at the **long-distance bus stop** (Pan-American Hwy) just north of the exit to San Jorge. If you're headed south to Costa Rica, catch a **Transnica** (☑ 2563-5397; www.transnica.com) bus or **Ticabus** (☑ 8877-1407; www.ticabus.com) on its way to San José (US$29 to US$40) from Managua.

TAXI

Colectivos (shared taxis or minibuses) run regularly to San Jorge (US$0.70) and San Juan del Sur (US$2). Private taxi drivers also wait around the bus terminal, waiting to scoop up travelers who need a ride to the Tola beaches or San Juan del Sur. They'll quote a wide range of prices, depending on exactly where you're going (and whether you're toting a surfboard,) but it shouldn't cost more than US$20 to San Juan del Sur, or more than US$35 per carload to the Tola beaches. It's best to hook up with other travelers here to share the cost.

Around Rivas itself, pedicabs are cheap and fun for shorter trips; the usual cost is US$1 to US$2 to any destination in town.

Regular taxis (holding up to four passengers) charge about US$5 to US$6 for a ride between the Rivas bus terminal and the San Jorge ferry terminal.

San Jorge

Just 15 minutes from the bustle of Rivas are the beaches of San Jorge, lined with inexpensive seafood restaurants and casual bars – not to mention the country's best views of Isla de Ometepe. It gets packed during Semana Santa, and on sunny summer weekends, with revelers from all over the region.

International tourists, however, tend to just roll through en route to the island, stopping at the ferry terminal just long enough to wonder if those delicious breezes might be worth enjoying a moment more.

◉ Sights

The breezy, volcano-gray beach, Playa San Jorge, stretches 20m into the water during high season, when gentle waves lap the coast and families congregate around their cars parked right on the sand. During rainy season (June to November), lake levels rise and reduce the beach to a slender strand, and many of the restaurants keep limited hours.

Cruz de España   MONUMENT
Ask your taxi driver to point out this monument, suspended from a gleaming half-arch above the traffic, which marks the spot where conquistador Gil González Dávila and Cacique Nicarao first met on October 12, 1523. Brightly colored statues of both men flank the monument.

Nuestra Señor de Rescate   CHURCH
The most striking church in town has been repainted a brilliant purple with a mix that uses *huevos de amor* (fertilized chicken eggs) donated by parishioners. It's a national

SOUTHWESTERN NICARAGUA SAN JORGE

BUS SERVICES FROM RIVAS

DESTINATION	COST (US$)	DURATION (HR)	FREQUENCY
Granada	1.25	1½	hourly, departs through early evening
Managua	2	2½	4:30am-6pm, every 30min
Salinas & Tola beaches	2	1½	6-8 daily
San Jorge	0.30	20min	every 30min
San Juan del Sur*	1	45min	almost hourly
Southern beaches (San Juan del Sur, Playa el Coco, La Flor and El Ostional)	2.50	2-3	4 daily

* A few buses per day offer onward service to El Ostional.

BORDER CROSSING: TO PEÑAS BLANCAS, COSTA RICA

Whether you've booked an international bus from Rivas or Managua or are taking a local bus and crossing on your own, the busy border crossing between Sapoá (Nicaragua) and Peñas Blancas (Costa Rica) is fairly easy to navigate. Depending on the season, however, there could be long lines, and many travelers find the process somewhat confusing. Bring cash and be prepared to stand around. If you're on a Ticabus or Transnica bus, the process will be largely managed for you.

The 1km-long, enclosed border is relatively simple, although the sudden (and strategic) crush of 'helpers' can be intimidating. Pedicabs (US$1 to US$3) not only roll you through, they also protect you from the masses. Banks on either side exchange local currency for US dollars, while money changers (called *coyotes* for a reason) exchange all three currencies freely but may try to rip you off; look for folks wearing identification badges. Exchange as little money as possible here, and figure out in advance about how much you're supposed to get back.

On the Nicaraguan side, get your passport stamped at a window in the large, poorly marked cement building just east of the main road. It costs US$12 to US$13 to enter Nicaragua. You can buy snacks and drinks in the immigration and customs areas on the Nicaraguan side; bathrooms are a short stroll away (just ask for directions). It's free to enter Costa Rica, but note that there's a new US$8 exit fee when you leave. Costa Rica's immigration building has a restaurant, clean restrooms and a bank with an ATM. Everyone entering Costa Rica technically needs a ticket for leaving the country, but it's rarely asked for. If it's your unlucky day, Transportes Deldu and Transnica, both located right outside, sell tickets from San José to Managua.

Don't plan on spending the night on either side: Sapoá has no real lodging, other than a few dodgy, unsigned guesthouses, and Peñas Blancas has none at all. Although the border is open 6am to 10pm Monday to Saturday, and until 8pm Sunday, buses run only between 6am and 6pm – after which taxis triple their fares.

Buses from the border run at least hourly to Rivas (US$1, 45 minutes) between 6am and 5:30pm, where you can make connections throughout Nicaragua. *Taxistas* (taxi drivers) may tell you that Nicaraguan buses aren't running, or are unsafe, but that is incorrect.

Transportes Deldu buses leave from Peñas Blancas to San José (US$10, six hours) about nine times per day, with more departures during peak travel times. There are also regular departures to Liberia in Costa Rica (US$3, 1½ hours).

It's always, of course, faster and easier to take a taxi, which may be prohibitively expensive on the Costa Rican side (US$50 to Liberia), but much more reasonable from Sapoá to Rivas (from US$12), San Jorge (from US$15), San Juan del Sur (from US$20) and Granada (around US$50). Find other tourists to share your taxi while you are still inside the border zone, and bargain hard.

historic landmark, and the destination of an annual caravan of some 150 *carretas* (wooden ox carts) from Masaya each year. They arrive April 23, the anniversary of San Jorge's miraculous appearance on the coast of Lago de Nicaragua. The ensuing **fiestas patronales** include parades, rodeos and several ceremonial dances.

🛏 Sleeping & Eating

There are several simple and affordable hotels near the ferry terminal. You can camp at the beach for free, though it would only be appealing during dry season.

The restaurants lining the beach are convenient if you're waiting on your ferry. There are also a couple of places to grab a bite to eat (or a cold beer) within the ferry terminal complex itself.

Hotel Hamacas HOTEL $$
(☎2563-0048; www.hotelhamacas.com; ferry terminal, 100m O, 25m S; s/d with fan US$25/30, with air-con US$35/40; [P][❄][🛜][🏊]) Cute little brick rooms painted in cheerful colors make this hacienda-style hotel the most atmospheric offering in town. Rooms surround a leafy courtyard area, with the requisite hammocks strung up around the porch areas.

Hotel Dalinky HOTEL $$$
(☎8912-1205; www.hoteldalinky.com; ferry terminal, 200m O; d from US$50; [P][❄][🛜][🏊]) Gleaming

tiled rooms a stone's throw from the ferry entrance make this a top pick. Upstairs there's a balcony with island views.

ⓘ Orientation

San Jorge's center is separated from the waterfront by a featureless 1km walk past a faux-Spanish fortress on the main road. Most travelers spend their time in or around the ferry terminal, where there are several restaurants and bars.

ⓘ Getting There & Away

The road from Rivas to San Jorge ends at the ferry terminal, where there's guarded parking (US$3) for your car and a regular boat service to Isla de Ometepe. Eighteen boats make the trip from San Jorge to Isla de Ometepe (US$1.50 to US$3, one hour) each day between 7am and 5:45pm. Most are ferries headed to Moyogalpa, though some are smaller boats that go to San José del Sur – these are best avoided on windy days if you're prone to seasickness. There's no need to reserve ahead. Passengers simply board and pay on the boat. If you're trying to put your car onto a ferry, though you might have to kill some time: there's often a short waiting list.

Buses leave for Rivas (US$0.25) almost hourly from the ferry terminal, passing by the Parque Central.

Taxis charge about US$5 to US$6 for a ride between the Rivas bus terminal and the San Jorge ferry terminal.

ISLA DE OMETEPE

Ometepe never fails to impress. Its twin volcanic peaks, rising up out of Lago de Nicaragua, have captured the imagination of everyone from precolonial Aztecs (who thought they'd found the promised land) to Mark Twain – not to mention the relatively few travelers who make it out here. The island's fertile volcanic soil, clean waters, wide beaches, wildlife population, archaeological sites and dramatic profile are quickly propelling it up traveler tick lists.

More than 1700 petroglyphs have been found on Ometepe, making this a DIY-ers fantasy island.

Sleeping options on the island range from extremely basic hostels to high-end, eco-friendly lodges with swimming pools and first-rate restaurants. Plan ahead.

Almost everything grown on Ometepe is organically farmed, simply because fertilizers are unnecessary in the rich volcanic soil and pesticides prohibitively expensive. Its

rice and beans are considered the country's best, and the papayas are certainly among the largest. This is good news for travelers – even at the most basic hostel restaurants, the food is pretty good. You'll find more interesting options at the better hotels and lodges.

🏃 Activities

Many of the island's tourist attractions are hard to find or even a bit dangerous – take that active volcano, for example. Sometimes it's just worth hiring a guide.

Hiking

The island's two volcanoes can be ascended from Moyogalpa or Altagracia for Volcán Concepción (p114), and Fincas Magdalena, El Porvenir and Hacienda Mérida for Volcán Maderas (p118). The uphill slog to Cascada San Ramón (p120), more a walk than a hike, also makes for an excellent day trip.

Relatively less challenging hikes abound, including to the halfway point up Maderas on the Finca Magdalena trail, and El Floral, a five- to seven-hour round-trip to a viewpoint about 1000m up Concepción.

Swimming

Swimming off Ometepe's beaches is excellent. Keep in mind that Lago de Nicaragua rises dramatically in the rainy season (and, if the rains are particularly heavy, the couple of months afterwards), shrinking the beaches to thin strands. By the end of the dry season in April, however, some 20m of gray volcanic sand may stretch out to the water.

The most popular beaches are Playa Santo Domingo, Playa Balcón and the other beaches around Charco Verde and Punta Jesús María. If you're just looking for a dip, the mineral-rich rock pools at Ojo de Agua (p118) make a fine day trip.

Kayaking

Kayaking is also big on the island, with Isla del Congo, Isla de Quiste and the Río Istiam (p118) being the most popular destinations. Most hotels near these places rent kayaks.

Cycling

Cycling is a fun way to get around (and, with the sketchy bus service, sometimes the only way). Bikes can be rented in Moyogalpa, Altagracia, Playa Santo Domingo and most hotels.

Horseback Riding

Horseback riding is another popular local transportation choice here. Any tour

Isla de Ometepe

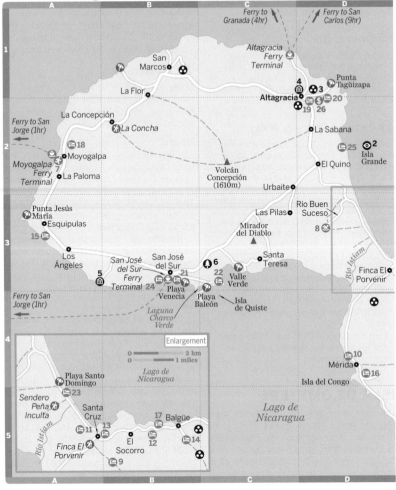

operator or hotel can set you up with a ride. Prices are generally US$4 to US$6 per hour, with guides US$10 to US$20 per group.

Volunteering

Volunteering options abound – check around at the hostels. A growing number of farms on the island are signing up to the **Fincas Verdes agro-tourism program** (www.fincasverdes.com), offering farmstays, horseback-riding expeditions and tours of farm facilities explaining traditional, often organic farming techniques.

👉 Tours

The majority of tour operators are based in Moyogalpa. Just about any hotel on the island can organize horseback riding and tours. Guides are not really necessary for San Ramón waterfall, Ojo de Agua or Reserva Charco Verde, although it's always easier to have someone else arrange transportation. Air-conditioned minivan tours of the island are much easier – but also more expensive, and potentially less fun – than doing the scenic figure-eight on a public Bluebird school bus (US$2 to US$4).

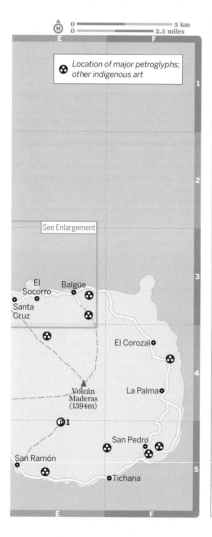

0 — 5 km
0 — 2.5 miles

Location of major petroglyphs; other indigenous art

See Enlargement

El Socorro   Balgüe
Santa Cruz

El Corozal

Volcán Maderas (1394m)   La Palma

1

San Pedro

San Ramón

Tichana

SOUTHWESTERN NICARAGUA ISLA DE OMETEPE

After various tourists got lost and died climbing volcanoes solo, it's now illegal to climb the volcanoes without a guide. Guides are available at or near the major trailheads in Altagracia, Moyogalpa, Balgüe and Mérida. Another place where it's worth having a guide along is on a kayak cruise of the Río Istiam – they know where all the animals are, and can call up a caiman for you.

❶ Orientation

Isla de Ometepe's 78km main road runs in a rough barbell shape, circling each volcano and running along the northern shore of the isthmus between

them. The Concepción side of the island is more developed, and the major port towns of Moyogalpa and Altagracia are connected by a paved road.

Moyogalpa is the major town on the island: you'll find the majority of services for tourists here. Altagracia is the only other real population center and is a smaller, much more laid-back and less-touristed spot. This said, there's not much reason to come here, except to check out the statues and museums, or catch a boat to Granada or San Carlos.

Playa Santo Domingo is the most popular lodging spot on the isthmus; the road splits upon arriving on the less-developed Volcán Maderas side of the island, going right to Mérida and the

San Ramón waterfall, left to Balgüe and Finca Magdelena.

ⓘ Getting There & Away

The most convenient way to get to Isla de Ometepe is the 17km boat ride from San Jorge to **Moyogalpa** or **San José del Sur**. There are 18 departures per day (US$1.50 to US$3, one hour) between 7am and 5:45pm. Most are ferries headed to Moyogalpa, though some smaller boats go to San José del Sur instead. Between November and February winds can make the sea rough, particularly in the afternoon; consider taking the ferry.

Ferries also run from **Altagracia** to Granada and San Carlos, although at time of writing these services have been suspended until further notice. (Updates will be posted on the bottom of the Ferry Schedules page on www.ometepe nicaragua.com.) If service is running again and you're thinking about doing the Granada–Altagracia run one way only, it's best to leave from Granada – you travel in the day, get some views and arrive late afternoon. Leaving Altagracia for Granada you travel at night and arrive in the early hours of the morning.

Most boats can transport bikes and other equipment without a problem. If you're loading your car onto the ferry, you might have to wait, depending on availability; otherwise, no reservations are required. Passengers pay on the boat.

ⓘ Getting Around

The southern loop between Moyogalpa and Altagracia, the island's two major towns, is a beautifully paved road. The conditions of all other roads varies. The island is bigger than it looks

GETTING YOUR WHEELS ONTO OMETEPE

Taking a car to Ometepe involves a bit of forward planning, some runaround and cash. Since rental cars on the island are expensive and public transport isn't always convenient, it may just be worth the hassle. Four-wheel drives are best for the spiky volcanic roads.

To do it, get an early start on one of the early ferries from San Jorge to Moyogalpa (or call ahead – it doesn't hurt to try to get on a waiting list the day before.) Otherwise, be prepared to wait your turn if it's busy – only a small number of cars fit on each ferry – and come with cash to pay the port tax, 'car tax' and ferry transit fee, around US$20 to US$25 each way. Passengers buy separate tickets.

and very few destinations are really walkable. The lack of traffic makes hitching a problem (although any passing pickup will almost certainly give you a ride) – but you'll also be happy if you have your own rental car or motorbike.

BUS

There's only one main road on the island; this simplifies things. Take a good look at a map before boarding any buses, though, and consult the latest bus schedules at www.ometepenic aragua.com. Bus service is solid (fares US$0.25 to US$1, depending on how far you're going), but the terrible roads in the southern part of the island take their toll on buses and schedules change frequently. Between Moyogalpa and Altagracia there are hourly buses; fewer run on Sunday. All buses from Moyogalpa to the Maderas side of the island stop in Altagracia about one hour later, then head down the isthmus past Playa Santo Domingo.

At Santa Cruz, buses go right (south) to Mérida and San Ramón, and left (east) to Balgüe, perhaps continuing to La Palma. Buses do not serve the southeastern portion of the island, between San Ramón and La Palma, at all.

CAR & MOTORCYCLE

Moyogalpa is the place to rent cars and motorbikes; you'll also find places to rent motorbikes (around US$25 per day) on the other side of the island, around Playa Santo Domingo.

Car rentals are trickier. There aren't a lot of cars available, and one can run you as much as US$100 a day. If you want to drive a car around Ometepe, you're probably better off bringing one from the mainland.

TAXI

Taxis are rare and expensive, and they're all minivans, jeeps or pickups with 4WD. They meet all ferries, but otherwise you should have your hotel make arrangements with a driver at least a few hours in advance.

From Moyogalpa, expect to pay at least US$20 to Altagracia, US$20 to Playa Santo Domingo, US$25 to Balgüe, US$30 to Mérida and US$45 to San Ramón, though your drivers might quote you higher prices – and on an island as remote as this, you won't have a lot of options other than to pay what they request.

Moyogalpa

Moyogalpa is home to the ferry terminal for hourly boats from the mainland, and, as such, the nerve center for Ometepe's nascent tourist industry. There are several hotels and restaurants here, and many of the island's tour companies; it's also base camp for the climb up Volcán Concepción. But it's not exactly an island paradise you'll want to linger in: you're only passing through.

🏃 Activities

Moyogalpa itself doesn't have much in the way of sightseeing, but it's an access point to major attractions on the island – the most obvious being the trek up Volcán Concepción. People based in Moyogalpa quite often take a bus or bike ride out to Punta Jesús María, which makes a good day trip.

There are numerous tour guides operating on the main road between the ferry dock and the main plaza.

Fundación Entre Volcanes   VOLUNTEERING
(☑ 2569-4118; www.fundacionentrevolcanes.org; frente Enitel) A locally founded grassroots NGO involved in education, health, nutrition and environmental projects on the island. It accepts volunteers with an intermediate level of Spanish and a two-month minimum commitment.

🎊 Festivals & Events

Fiestas Patronales   RELIGIOUS
(☉ Jul 23-26) Moyogalpa's *fiestas patronales*, honoring the patron saint Santa Ana, are famous for the Baile de las Inditas, a celebration of both Spanish and indigenous culture. The festival includes a procession to Punta Jesús María, where there are fireworks and drinking by the lake.

🛏 Sleeping

The most atmospheric sleeping options are elsewhere, but there are a few perfectly good hotels in town. The ones on the block closest to the port are not the best – they're loud at night and standards for cleanliness aren't very high, though they'll work in a pinch. Keep walking uphill and the options get better.

Hospedaje Soma   GUESTHOUSE **$$**
(☑ 2569-4310; www.hospedajesoma.com; frente al Instituto J.R. Smith; d US$10, r with/without bathroom US$35/25, 2-person cabins with air-con/fan US$60/50; ☞) Book ahead if you're hoping to score a room at this relaxed but professionally run guesthouse, set a 10-minute walk from the ferry dock. Choose between a dorm, private room or cabin, all scattered around a large and beautiful tropical garden. The owners are helpful with planning excursions around the island.

Cornerhouse B&B   B&B **$$**
(www.thecornerhouseometepe.com; muelle, 1c O; s/d/tr US$25/35/45; ☞) There are just four rooms at this sweet B&B, a block uphill from the port – and they're available only on a first-come, first-serve basis (no reservations), so you'll have to try your luck when you get off the boat. Breakfast at the lovely Cornerhouse cafe downstairs is included in the price.

Hotel Casa Moreno   HOTEL **$$**
(☑ 8357-7349; muelle, 2c E, 3c S; dm/d from US$7/20; ☞) This pretty yellow corner hotel, located about a five-minute walk from the port, has plenty of outdoor space where you can swing in a hammock or relax in a rocking chair. It almost makes up for the less-than-genial service. Fan-cooled rooms are average but clean.

🍴 Eating & Drinking

Moyogalpa has a few good places to eat within a few blocks of the ferry dock. There's a bit of a nightlife scene at the laid-back bars near the ferry dock, though nothing too crazy (this is a small town on a remote island, after all).

Cornerhouse   CAFE
(www.thecornerhouseometepe.com; muelle, 1c E; mains US$3-7; ☉7am-5pm Mon-Fri, to 3pm Sat; ☞☑) Easily the most stylish eating venue on this corner of the island. Breakfast is served all day at this rustic-chic cafe just uphill from the port; the menu features eggs Benedict with roasted tomatoes and fresh basil. There are also gourmet sandwiches and salads, including a great one with papaya and toasted almonds, and wi-fi. It's part of the Cornerhouse B&B.

Los Ranchitos   INTERNATIONAL **$**
(muelle, 2c E, ½c S; mains US$4-6; ☉7am-9:30pm) One of the better-looking restaurants in town, with open walls, thatched roofs and a pressed-dirt floor. The menu's your fairly standard range of meat, chicken and seafood, with some good pizza and pasta options thrown in.

❶ Orientation

The ferry terminal is at the bottom of Moyogalpa's main street; almost all services are within one block of this street. Buses and taxis stop at the dock after 8:30am; before 8:30am they leave from the Catholic church at the top of the street. Go left for the dirt road to La Flor and San Marcos, right for the paved road to Charco Verde, Playa Santo Domingo and Volcán Maderas.

ℹ Information

Hospital (☑ 2569-4247; Parque Central, 3c S) Offers basic emergency services. For anything serious it's best to get off the island, to Rivas at least.

BanPro Credit (muelle, 3c E) Accepts Visa. Not always operational.

ℹ Getting There & Away

BOAT

Boats leave San Jorge for Moyogalpa fifteen times each day between 7am and 5:45pm. Fares are around US$2 to US$3 per person, depending on the boat. Consult the ferry schedule at www.ome tepenicaragua.com for the latest departure times.

BUS

Bus departures are more frequent here than anywhere else on the island. In theory, there's a bus from Moyogalpa to Altagracia every hour.

But timetables change rapidly – if you're going out for the day, ask your driver what time the last bus returns. Bear in mind that all buses pass Altagracia, where they stop for half an hour, and that it can take three hours (on a good day) to get from Moyogalpa to San Ramón. Bus services:

Altagracia (US$0.80, one hour, 5:30am to 6:45pm, hourly)

Balgüe (US$1.20, two hours, two daily)

Mérida (US$1.40, 2½ hours, three daily)

San Ramón (US$1.10, three hours, daily at 9:30am)

Volcán Concepción

This massive (and active) volcano is an Ometepe landmark. The 10- to 12-hour hike up loose volcanic stone to the summit of this looming peak can be tough, so be in good physical condition and bring water, snacks and real hiking shoes. Most hikes leave from either Moyogalpa or Altagracia. Remember that there's no shade above the tree line, it's even steeper than it looks, and it can get windy and cold at the top, particularly if it's cloudy out.

There are three main trails to the top: **La Concha** and **La Flor** (the most popular trail), both close to Moyogalpa, and **La Sabana**, a short distance from Altagracia. It's almost always cloudy at the top, which means your chances of seeing the fuming craters and awesome views over the lake and across Central America's volcanic spine are slim, even during dry season.

Guided treks up the volcano cost around US$25 to US$40 per person; tours leave from both Altagracia and Moyogalpa.

ℹ Getting There & Away

It's only recommended to ascend the volcano with a guide, which can be arranged at any hotel on the island – the excursion is also offered by various outdoor outfitters and guide associations in Moyogalpa and Altagracia. Tours include transportation to trailheads.

Around Volcán Concepción

This has been the more populous side of the island (despite the looming, active volcano overhead) since the Chorotega arrived, and remains so today. You can see its main attraction, Volcán Concepción (at 1610m, Nicaragua's second-highest volcano) from a great distance away.

Esquipulas

This little town, south of Moyogalpa on the road that circles the island, is unremarkable except for a few attractions nearby. There's the turnoff for **Punta Jesús María**, a naturally formed sand spit and lookout point on the lake. A little further along the road, on the other side of town, is the turnoff to the farmstay and restaurant at Finca Samaria (p115). And beyond that, about halfway between Esquipulas and San José del Sur, there's the turnoff to the island's best museums, Museos El Ceibo.

◉ Sights

Museos El Ceibo MUSEUM
(☑ 8874-8706; www.museoselceibo.com; one/both museums US$5/8; ⊙ 8am-5pm) An excellent pair of museums. The **Museo Numinásti-co** (Coin Museum) documents the troubled history of the Nicaraguan economy through its coins and banknotes. Across the road, the **Museo Precolombino** (Pre-Columbian Museum) displays an excellent collection of more than a thousand pieces of ceramics, metates, funeral urns and jewelry, all collected from around the island. The museums are located 2km down a shady lane off the main road, about halfway between Esquipulas and San José del Sur.

VOLCÁN CONCEPCIÓN'S EXPLOSIVE MOOD SWINGS

Volcán Concepción is Central America's most symmetrical and arguably loveliest volcano, not to mention one of its most active and dangerous. Concepción roared back to life the same year that Krakatoa blew, in 1883, after centuries of hosting gentle cloud forests around its now gray and smoking craters.

The fiery flow seems cyclical. In 1921 ash gave way to glowing red, and the following year lava and boulders were tossed out, with explosions heard in Granada. In 1944 ash falls as far as Rivas were just a warning; six months later lava flows consumed hectares of crops. In 1957 tongues of flame 15m high leapt from the summit following months of ashy exhalation. President Somoza sent boats to evacuate the island – not one person left, but not one person died. And although no lava burst forth, ash inaugurated another two years of activity between 1983 and 1985.

In late 2005, in its first tantrum since the revolution, Concepción showered ash over Rivas, and guides were excitedly explaining that it 'smelled like lava' at the top. Volcano treks were cut short and everybody looked up a lot more than usual, but in the end there was no grand spectacle. In the 2007, 2009 and 2012 explosions there was more rumbling, smoke and ash, but again, no real drama. That said, you can bet that we haven't heard the last from this fiery cone just yet.

🛏 Sleeping & Eating

The restaurant at Finca Samaria is a solid bet if you're looking to stop along this stretch of road. Otherwise, there's a range of options in nearby Moyogalpa.

Finca Samaria　　　　　　　LODGE **$**
(☑ 8824-2210; Cementerio Esquipulas, 30m al lago; dm/d US$9/23; 🛜) A beautiful and eco-friendly farmstay option not far from Moyogalpa. Rooms are fairly basic, but the farm is lovely, with hammocks galore in the shady garden, which backs onto a tree-lined beach with some of the best sunset views on the island. There's a great vegan-friendly **restaurant** on-site that's open to the public; the family also rents bikes and horses.

🛈 Getting There & Away

Buses from Moyogalpa pass through Esquipulas (10 minutes, US$0.40) many times each day.

San José del Sur

This sizable workaday village is an arrival point for boats from San Jorge. There are a few places to stay here, most located on the gray-sand beaches near the ferry dock, but you won't feel the need to stick around long.

🛏 Sleeping

Playa Santa Martha Hostal　　　CABIN **$$**
(☑ 2569-4733; d from US$28; 🛜) This cabin complex down on the waterfront is convenient if you're catching the ferry. They're basic, but still a good deal, particularly if you can get one that fronts onto the beach.

🛈 Getting There & Away

Lanchas (motorboats) for the 40-minute trip to San Jorge depart from the dock (just off the main road in the center of town) at 7:20am and 3:20pm; they leave San Jorge for San José del Sur at 9:30am and 5pm. Buses meet the *lanchas* at the dock.

Charco Verde & Isla de Quiste

On the southern side of Concepción lies a lush, less windblown clutch of beaches, centered on Reserva Charco Verde. The fine green Laguna Charco Verde is accessible from a short hiking trail that begins at Hotel Charco Verde.

Not only is this a lovely spot for swimming, hiking and wildlife-watching, but it's also the home of Chico Largo, a tall, thin and ancient witch who often appears swimming or fishing in the lagoon. His primary duty is to protect the tomb and solid-gold throne of Cacique Nicarao, buried nearby.

Just offshore, **Isla de Quiste** is within swimming distance of the beach. Any of the area's hotels can arrange boat service and perhaps rental tents, as it's a prime camping, fishing and birding spot.

◎ Sights

Reserva Charco Verde   NATURE RESERVE
(admission US$0.75) Rich with wildlife and fringed with black-sand beaches, this wooded ecological reserve is a quiet spot for hiking, birdwatching or taking a dip in the lake.

🛏 Sleeping & Eating

There are many places to stay on this part of the island; most are fairly rustic. You'll probably eat most or all of your meals at your hotel. It's wise to bring your own snacks and water from town.

Hotel El Tesoro de Pirata   HOTEL **$$**
(✉ 8927-2831; Valle Verde; d with fan/air-con US$25/35; ❋ 🌐 🐾) Two kilometers to the south of Charco Verde is the turnoff to Valle Verde (Green Valley). It's another 2km walk from the bus stop down to this remote hotel with a secluded beach. The rooms aren't anything to write home about, but for the price this is an excellent option on this side of the island.

Hotel Finca Venecia   CABIN **$$**
(✉ 8887-0191; d US$25, cabins with fan/air-con from US$30/50; 🅿 ❋ 🌐) A decent budget bet on this side of the island, this grouping of cabins and basic rooms sits near the beach. The restaurant is hit-or-miss.

Hotel Charco Verde   CABIN **$$$**
(✉ 2560-1271; www.charcoverde.com.ni; Charco Verde; 2-/3-person cabins from US$48/70; ❋ 🌐) This hotel occupies a fabulous beach, and has a growing collection of cabins, all with private patios and some with beach views. There are kayaks and laundry facilities, and a fairly good on-site restaurant.

❶ Getting There & Away

Charco Verde is close to the ferry terminal at San José del Sur, convenient if you're arriving here by boat from Moyogalpa. Otherwise, it's about a 10-minute walk from the main road if you're catching a bus to or from Moyogalpa (US$0.50, 20 minutes, hourly from 5:30am to 6:30pm Monday to Saturday, less frequent on Sundays).

El Quino

Just south of Altagracia, El Quino is more of a landmark than anything: it's an intersection that's used as a point of reference for hotels and natural attractions on this side of the island. From here, you can access many of Ometepe's loveliest stretches of coastline, and access public transportation to either side of the island.

🛏 Sleeping & Eating

There's a great restaurant and bar at San Juan de la Isla. Other hotels and lodges nearby also have good restaurants open to the public.

San Juan de la Isla   LODGE **$$$**
(✉ 8210-6957; www.sanjuandelaisla.com; El Quino, 500m N; r from US$75; ❋ 🌐 🐾) 🌿 This top-end choice is located just north of the village of El Quino. Set on a working farm right on the beach, the hacienda-style hotel has a private beach, remarkable volcano views from the well-tended grounds, and a friendly common area where you can eat dinner or laze out in a hammock.

❶ Getting There & Away

All buses from Moyogalpa that are headed to Playa Santo Domingo and Volcán Maderas stop in Altagracia, just north of El Quino.

Altagracia

With more natural protection from Concepción's occasional lava flow than Moyogalpa, this is the original indigenous capital of Ometepe, and still the island's most important town. For travelers, there's not much to see here, but it can be a convenient base for exploring the surrounding area – and a good place to crash if your boat gets in late from Granada.

◎ Sights

Isla Grande   ISLAND
Close to Altagracia, this island, basically a plantain *finca* (farm) gone feral, is rarely visited despite being a fantastic place for birdwatching. If you're interested, you could certainly arrange a custom trip – ask at your hotel.

Monoliths   ARCHAEOLOGICAL SITE
A place to see some of the finest remaining ancient excavated statues on Ometepe is beside the Altagracia church, close to the Parque Central, where a handful of softly eroding monoliths still stand sentry.

Museo de Ometepe   MUSEUM

(Parque Central, 1c O; US$2; ☺8am-noon & 1-5pm Mon-Fri, 9am-1pm Sat) The village's main attraction is this museum packed with information (in Spanish) about the island. (Though you'll find a much more comprehensive collection at the Museos El Ceibo (p114).) Non-Spanish speakers will still appreciate the amazing scale model of the volcanoes, as well as a few stone sculptures, petroglyphs and lots of pottery thoughtfully displayed as part of a timeline.

🏃 Activities

This is base camp for the other trailhead to Concepción, called La Sabana, which begins about 2km from town. Hotels can arrange guides. The town's Parque Central is the center of the action, and features a sweet relief map of the island.

🎊 Festivals & Events

Fiestas Patronales   RELIGIOUS

(☺Nov 12-18) Altagracia's *fiestas patronales* honor San Diego, whose feast day is coincidentally the same as that of Xolotl, the ancient city's original patron deity. The party's most famous dance, Baile del Zompopo (Dance of the Leafcutter Ant), was clearly choreographed long before the Christians got here.

🛏 Sleeping & Eating

A few basic local hotels offer convenient, if un-exciting, accommodations near the plaza. All the hotels have restaurants, but the cheapest eats are served up at the Parque Central – during the day a couple of kiosks serve snacks, and starting at dusk several *fritanga* (barbecue) set-ups offer roast chicken and *gallo pinto* (rice and beans).

Hotel Central   HOTEL $

(☎2569-4420; www.hotel-central-altagracia-ome tepe.com; iglesia, 2c S; s/d US$10/19, 2-person cabins from US$25; 🌀☀) The best-looking rooms in town are a simple affair but a good deal. Rooms out front are arranged around a garden; the cabins out back are basic but cute, and the hotel restaurant serves good, cheap Nicaraguan food and cold beer.

Hotel Castillo   HOTEL $

(☎2569-4403; www.hotelcastillo-ometepe.blog spot.com; iglesia, 1c S, ½c O; dm/s/d from US$6/8/15; 🌀@☀) Nothing fancy going on here, but it's fairly clean and brightly painted, with a couple of common areas. Spend a few more dollars for air-con (provided it's working.) The restaurant (dishes US$3 to US$5) is good, and serves real coffee. You can arrange tours here, and rent bikes.

ℹ Orientation

Buses stop at the attractive Parque Central. The museum and all services are within three blocks of here. To get to the ferry terminal, look for the big sign pointing away from the plaza, then follow that road for 2.5km to reach the port.

ℹ Information

The small artisan cooperative in the Parque Central can dispense basic tourist information but has no maps and few brochures.

BanPro (iglesia, 2c S)

ℹ Getting There & Away

BOAT

Ferries cross the lake between Granada and San Carlos twice weekly, stopping in Altagracia (unless the weather is really bad) en route. Schedules change frequently – consult the Ferry Schedules page of www.ometepenicaragua.com before making plans. Ferry services include the following:

Altagracia to Granada (US$4.25, four hours, 3pm Tuesday)

Altagracia to San Carlos (US$6, nine hours, 6pm Monday and Thursday) Also serves San Miguelito.

Granada to Altagracia (US$4.25, four hours, 2:30pm Monday, 2pm Thursday)

San Carlos to Altagracia (US$6, nine hours, 2pm Tuesday and Friday)

BUS

Buses heading south from Moyogalpa all pass by here one hour after leaving, before continuing south. Services include the following:

Balgüe (US$1.10, two hours, 11:30am, noon, 4:30pm and 6pm)

Mérida (US$1.25, 2½ hours, 9:30am, 3:30pm and 5:30pm)

Moyogalpa (US$0.75, one hour, 5:30am to 6:45pm, every hour)

San Ramón (US$1.10, three hours, 9:30am and 3:30pm)

Playa Santo Domingo & Santa Cruz

Windswept sandy beaches and many of the island's finest accommodations lie southeast of Altagracia, on the long and lovely lava isthmus that cradles **Playa Santo Domingo**.

Heading south to **Santa Cruz** along the island's main road, the beach gets progressively less crowded. Santa Cruz itself has a few places to eat and sleep, and the views are gorgeous.

🏃 Activities

The main attraction is the **beach**, a 30m to 70m (depending on lake levels) expanse of gray volcanic sand that retreats almost to the sea wall at the height of the rainy season.

You can hire bikes and horses from Hotel Finca Santo Domingo and other local businesses.

Ojo de Agua   SWIMMING
(US$3; ☺dawn-dusk) Take a pleasant stroll through banana plantations to the well-signed, shady swimming hole about 1.5km north of Playa Santo Domingo. The mineral-infused water here bubbles up from 35 small underground springs; with an average temperature of 22°C to 28°C (71°F to 82°F), it makes for a refreshing dip.

Río Istiam   KAYAKING
On the south side of the isthmus, this river shimmers as it snakes through the island's lava valley. The best way to explore the river (which is really a swamp) is by kayak – you're pretty much guaranteed to see turtles, caimans and howler monkeys. Inquire at nearby hotels, like Caballito's Mar (p120), which offers the trip for US$25 per person.

🛏 Sleeping & Eating

There are a few hotels along this coastal stretch, and a couple of excellent places to stay in the town of Santa Cruz. Make reservations well in advance during the high season.

There are good restaurants at hotels that are open to the public. Stock up on snacks and water in one of the larger towns if you're planning on heading out on hikes.

Finca del Sol   LODGE **$$**
(☑8364-6394; www.hotelfincadelsol.com; Santa Cruz; 2-person cabins from US$49; ☎) 🌿 Quiet, eco-friendly cabins with private porches, free bicycle rental, boxed lunches on request, a breakfast made of tropical fruit grown in the garden – and the whole place

powered by solar energy? We think we've found paradise on this corner of the island. You can even walk to the beach from here. It's located in the village of Santa Cruz.

El Encanto   HOTEL **$$**
(☑8867-7128; www.goelencanto.com; Santa Cruz; d/cabin from US$35/70) Set on a banana farm, rooms here are simply but pleasantly decorated, with big, screened windows and clean, modern bathrooms. Hammocks out front of your room have great lake views. The restaurant gets raves for its mix of Nica classics and international food, including curries, wholemeal bread and several vegetarian options.

Hotel Villa Paraíso   CABIN **$$**
(☑2569-4859; www.villaparaiso.com.ni; d/cabin from US$35/75 ; [P][✳][@][☎]) The nicest rooms in Santo Domingo are found at this friendly beachfront hotel. The elegant *cabañas* have air-con, Direct TV and private terraces. The excellent staff will arrange tours and there's a fantastic restaurant.

❶ Getting There & Away

Two daily buses go from Moyogalpa to Balgüe (US$1.20, two hours). A taxi will cost US$20 to US$30 from the Moyogalpa ferry dock.

Volcán Maderas

Volcán Maderas   VOLCANO
Climbing this 1394m volcano is challenging but worthwhile. Guides are required for the seven- to eight-hour round-trip trek (with four to five hours of climbing); at the top, you'll reach a misty cloud forest ending with a steep crater descent to a chilly jade-green lake. There are three trails to the top: the original at **Finca Magdelena** and two slightly longer trails beginning at **Hacienda Mérida** and **Finca El Porvenir**. The Finca Magdelena trail offers the money shot of Volcán Concepción (p114).

Prices depend on where you start, whether you need transportation, and how many are in your group: you'll pay anywhere between US$5 and US$25 per person. Any hotel can help you arrange the excursion, as well as hikes or horseback riding to the area's **petroglyphs**.

Walking (or biking) some or all of the circumference of Maderas (35km) on the rough dirt road makes for a great day trip.

Around Volcán Maderas

This is the lusher, wilder side of the island. It's even less developed than Concepción's side, and petroglyphs are much more common. The star attraction, of course, is the towering Volcán Maderas (1394m), covered with coffee plantations at the bottom and cloud forest at the top.

Most travelers sleep in villages or towns on the island – Santa Cruz is the closest – and ascend the volcano on a day trip.

There are restaurants and services in nearby Santa Cruz, and in the other towns and villages on the island. Bring plenty of food and water for the strenuous hike up Volcán Maderas, and remember that there are no stores or restaurants on the road between San Ramón and La Palma.

Balgüe & Around

The northern slopes of Volcán Maderas are one of the island's hot spots: many of the nicest accommodations and dining options are located here, and it's a lovely area for horseback riding, hiking, or just relaxing.

🛏 Sleeping

There's a high concentration of lovely lodges, hostels, and guesthouses in the area, many with an eco-friendly mission.

Finca Magdalena HOSTEL **$**
(☑8418-5636; www.fincamagdalena.com; hammocks or campsites per person US$4, dm/d US$12/23, cabins US$46; @) ⚑ This Ometepe mainstay on the slopes of Volcán Maderas is a classic backpacking spot. Rooms and dorms on this working coffee *finca* are set in a rickety old wooden farmhouse are due for a revamp, but really – with sweeping views of the lake and Volcán Concepción, lush surroundings, good food – you can probably rough it for a few days.

Note that it's a 1.5km climb to the *finca* from the bus stop.

Hospedaje Así es Mi Tierra GUESTHOUSE **$**
(☑8493-0506; www.mitierraometepe.com; r US$20) At the southern end of town is a sweet little family-run affair offering basic but functional rooms. The best part is a jungle trail that leads down to a pebble beach, complete with an open-air bungalow that's just waiting for you to kick back in a hammock and pop open a *cerveza* (beer).

El Zopilote Finca Ecológica HOSTEL **$**
(☑8961-8742; www.ometepezopilote.com; 200m up trail from road; hammock/dm US$4/7, 2-person cabins from US$16; 🐦) ⚑ A hippie-style hideaway where many people stay longer than they'd planned. This organic farm offers a range of accommodations scattered around a lush hillside on a sizable working farm. Dorms are basic and cabins are rustic (but fun!) – there's a cool common area, a yoga space, and an organic restaurant.

To reach this place on the inland side of the road, follow the trail to the left of the converted school bus/organic market, then 200m right to the clutch of traditionally constructed thatched-roof huts on the grassy hillside. You'll see signs.

Totoco Ecolodge LODGE **$$$**
(☑8358-7718; www.totoco.com.ni; Callejón de la Palmera, 800m arriba, Balgüe; cabins from US$150; 🅿🐦🍽) ⚑ This gorgeous ecolodge features *cabañas* perched high above the beach on a large organic farm that runs on solar power and recycles gray water. It's not on the beach, but there's a beautiful pool with views from here to eternity. The romantic rooms are the best on the island, and the **restaurant**, open to the public, is excellent.

🍴 Eating

Some of the best dining options on the island are at the hotels and lodges in and around Balgüe, all open to the public. There's also a cluster of casual, locally run cafes near the main road, just to the north of town.

Café Campestre INTERNATIONAL **$$**
(☑8571-5930; www.campestreometepe.com; dishes US$3-8; ⏱11:30am-9pm; 🐦🍴) This popular cafe employing local ingredients from the adjacent organic farm has something for everyone: good coffee, freshly baked breads, huge salads and international dishes from hummus platters to Thai curries. There's even kid-friendly amenities and free wi-fi.

ℹ Getting There & Away

Buses leave Balgüe for Altagracia (US$1.10, one hour) six times per day between 5:30am and 4:30pm, continuing to Moyogalpa; check with your hotel or hostel or online at www.ometepenicaragua.com for the latest scheduled times.

Santa Cruz to Mérida & San Ramón

Although more heavily populated than the rest of the southern part of the island, this stretch of road still feels wild and untamed. As with the rest of the island, road conditions are laughable (except in the wet season, when they're no joke) and bus service is patchy at best.

⊙ Sights

Some of Ometepe's must-see attractions are accessed from this part of the island, including the **petroglyphs** at Albergue Ecológico El Porvenir, where a well-marked trail meanders past approximately 20 of these rock carvings.

Cascada San Ramón   WATERFALL
(US$3) This stunning 40m waterfall is one of the jewels of the island. The trail begins at the Estación Biológica de Ometepe; it's a steep, four-hour round-trip on an easy-to-follow trail that's lost some of its charm since lots of trees were cut down. But it's still mossy and beautiful at the top, and fabulous for a dip on a hot day.

🏃 Activities

Being relatively sheltered, this side of the island is perfect for **kayaking**. An obvious destination is **Isla del Congo**, now called **Isla de los Monos** (Monkey Island), home to the descendants of four spider monkeys. Spider monkeys aren't present anywhere else on the island (howler and white face monkeys are), so these creatures are pretty much alone. Don't get too close – these little guys bite. Hacienda Mérida is the closest place to the island that rents kayaks.

The other classic kayaking trip is to the Río Istiam (p118), a swampy inlet that's home to turtles, caimans, the occasional howler monkey and an array of bird life. Caballito's Mar is the closest kayak-rental place to the entrance of the river and it has guides who know where all the wild things are.

🛏 Sleeping & Eating

There are great places to stay on this part of the island, and most are budget-friendly. Your best bet for eating around here are the restaurants at the hotels and hostels. Head to Balgüe for more options.

★ Hacienda Mérida   HOTEL **$$**
(☑ 8868-8973; www.hmerida.com; campsites or hammock per person US$5, dm US$8, r with/without lake view US$35/25; P @) On the south side of Mérida, this is by far the nicest budget option around (with some very nice mid-range rooms thrown in), offering every activity you could possibly want – volcano hikes, kayaking, excellent mountain bikes, sailing, swimming etc. The superstar rooms are upstairs, with awesome lake views and a shared balcony with king-sized hammocks.

Albergue Ecológico El Porvenir   LODGE **$$**
(☑ 8438-4851; www.hotel-elporvenir-isladeometepe.com; s/d from US$11/23; P) At the foot of Volcán Maderas, this sunny lodge and restaurant that has it all – great volcano views and petroglyphs amid attractive gardens, a restaurant serving good-value meals, and simple but spacious guest rooms. You can arrange everything here from horseback riding to guided hikes.

Caballito's Mar   HOSTEL, GUESTHOUSE **$$**
(☑ 8842-6120; www.caballitosmar.com; dm/r/cabin US$8/25/35) About 1km before Mérida, look for a sign to this simple little guesthouse-hostel right on the beach, with great lake views from the waterfront bar-restaurant. Choose between basic dorms, private rooms, or cabins. This is the best place to start **kayak tours** of the Río Istiam (US$25 per person) or DIY trips to nearby Isla del Congo.

❶ Getting There & Away

Buses leave Mérida for Altagracia (US$1.20, 1½ hours) at 4am, 5:45am, 8:30am, 10:15am, and 3:30pm, and San Ramón for Altagracia (US$1.50, 2½ hours) three times per day.

If you're headed to a specific hotel or hostel, consult with them first – they can help you come up with the best plan for the time of day you're arriving so you can avoid getting stranded.

PACIFIC BEACHES

Southwestern Nicaragua's Pacific beaches offer amazing surf, sand and sun. To get to the Tola beaches – El Astillero down to Playa Gigante – you'll need to pass through Rivas and Tola, then head toward the beach. There is only rough 4WD access on the coast between Veracruz and El Astillero. San Juan del Sur serves as the access point for the beaches between Playa Marsella in the north downward to El Ostional.

ℹ️ Getting There & Away

To access the region from elsewhere in Nicaragua, you'll most likely need to pass through the transport hub of Rivas.

Bus services include:

Granada (US$1.25, 1½ hours, hourly with departures through the early evening)

Managua (US$2, 2½ hours, 4:30am to 6pm, every 30 minutes)

Salinas & Tola beaches (US$2, 1½ to two hours, six to eight times daily)

San Jorge (US$0.30, 20 minutes, half-hourly)

San Juan del Sur (US$1, 45 minutes, 6am to 6pm, almost hourly) A few buses per day offer onward service to El Ostional.

For beaches north and south of San Juan del Sur, you catch a beach shuttle from San Juan del Sur. If you're heading south, you can also catch the bus (US$1.50, 20 minutes to one hour, three to four times daily) to Playa Remanso, Playa El Coco, Refugio de Vida Silvestre La Flor and Playa El Ostional.

Tola & the Tola Beaches

Tola ('the land of the Toltecs') is developing into a service town for the big resort communities, but there's not much reason for most travelers to stop here – especially when you're on your way to the rugged and gorgeous nearby coastline.

Once almost inaccessible and totally wild, the Tola beaches are slowly coming into their own. They still retain some of that lost-paradise feel, with top-notch surf and good vibes, but the pace of life is speeding up, thanks to new roads going in and new development dollars. It's the kind of place where you could walk an hour down the sand without running into another human being.

While there are wonderful places to stay here, there are no banks or real grocery stores; internet and cell-phone coverage is patchy at best. Do what you need to do before you hit the trail, then enjoy getting away from it all.

Sleeping options in the region fall into one of a few categories: high-end resorts, surf camps, hostels on the beach or mid-range hotels with restaurants.

Most dining options are attached to hotels or all-inclusive surf camps. If you're self-catering, stock up in Rivas, because there aren't any real supermarkets once you leave town.

ℹ️ Getting There & Away

Many travelers headed to this region drive their own rental cars or arrange transportation with surf camps. Though there are regular buses from Rivas to the general area, they couldn't be called convenient – you'd have to walk (or hope to hitch a ride) several kilometers to your destination from where the buses drop passengers.

If you're up for the hike, buses leave Rivas for Las Salinas several times daily (US$2.50, two to 2½ hours), stopping along the way in the vicinity of all of the beaches listed here. Let your driver know where you're going.

If you don't have a car and you're not on a shoestring budget, just arrange a shared taxi from Rivas' bus terminal. Taxi drivers will approach you; the cost depends on what you negotiate, and how many passengers (and surfboards) are riding along, but you can expect to pay anywhere between US$20 and US$50 for one-way service to Playa Gigante, Rancho Santana, El Astillero, and Playa Popoyo.

Playa Gigante

This glorious crescent of white sand, tucked into wildly forested mountains, was once a traditional fishing village largely inaccessible to travelers. Today, the popular sandy beach break right in front of 'town' gets hollow and fun when conditions are perfect, attracting a steady stream of surfers and sun-seekers.

🏃 Activities

Surf opportunities abound. There's the surf break right in front of town, and an endless tube about 45 minutes north. Special-name waves include **Chiggers** and **Outer Chiggers** (close to a rocky reef), and **Hemorrhoids** – this tube is for serious surfers, as it dumps you right onto gravel.

You'll need to hire a boat to get to most of the breaks, including the point break at Punta Manzanillo, just south (also called Punta Reloj). Ask the driver to take you past the 2m-long 'footprint' left in the rocky headlands.

🛏️ Sleeping

For most of the year, the area's surf camps offer all-inclusive deals providing everything from airport pick-up to meals, drinks and boat rides out to the breaks.

Camino del Gigante HOSTEL **$$**
(☑️ 8712-8888; www.gigantebay.com; beachfront, 300m south of town; dm US$12, d with/without

bathroom US$39/31; 🛜🐾) The location's the draw at this beachfront hostel: forget about the lackluster dorms and lax service, you're here for the ocean views, the mellow communal areas, and access to great surf spots. There's a bar and restaurant, but more importantly, the hostel runs a sunset catamaran cruise that's not to be missed.

Giant's Foot Surf Camp LODGE $$$
(📞 8384-2331; www.giantsfootsurf.com; per week per person from US$1350; 🐾) Set on the southern end of the beach, this laid-back surf camp offers guided trips to 14 local breaks. The camp accommodates ten surfers at a time. Packages include surfing, boat, transfers, three daily meals – even local beer and rum – plus a daily wake-up call with coffee and cereal so you can catch an early wave.

Dale Dagger's Surf Lodge LODGE $$$
(www.nicasurf.com; per week per person from US$1240; 🐾@) Surf legend Dale Dagger's setup is a sweet little oceanfront beach house in the middle of the village. It's got three boats on call, so getting to the break is a snap – in fact, they advertise as the only area outfitter offering unlimited daily boat trips to the surf. Also rents out a couple of independent houses for groups.

✕ Eating

There are a handful of simple restaurants on the beach and on the road leading to it; there are more options here than at many of the other surf villages along the coast. There's a small *pulpería* (general store) on the main drag.

Party Wave Gigante CAFE $
(Pulpería Mena, 50m S; mains US$3-7; ⊘7am-4pm Mon-Fri, 8am-4pm Sat, 8am-2pm Sun; 🛜) This popular little cafe offers breakfast, good coffee, homemade baked goods, burritos, bagels, sandwiches and wraps – and there's even wi-fi.

Blue Sol NICARAGUAN $$
(Camino de Acceso, Playa Gigante; mains US$6) An easygoing (and affordable) bar-restaurant on the road to the beach, this is a good place to be for mojitos with an ocean view at sunset, or a traditional Nica dish like grilled fish with rice, beans and plantains.

Santana

The only way to enjoy some of the prettiest beaches on this stretch of coastline – Las Cinco Playas (the Five Beaches), also known as **Playa Escondida**, **Playa Santana**, **Playa Duna**, **Playa Rosada** and **Playa Los Perros** – is if you're a guest or resident of the plush Rancho Santana resort.

The most famous of these beaches is probably Playa Rosada, with pretty pink sand, great surfing and an odd hydro-geological formation that shoots ocean water several meters into the waves.

🛏 Sleeping

Rancho Santana RESORT $$$
(📞 8882-2885; www.ranchosantana.com; ste from US$249; 🐾🛜🐾) This thriving resort village has it all, almost – clubhouses, rental homes, pools, horses, tennis courts, a helipad and Las Cinco Playas (The Five Beaches), to name a few. In March 2015, the new addition **Inn at Rancho Santana** opened its doors, complete with its own art gallery, cafe and gorgeous guest suites.

ℹ Getting There & Away

All travelers arriving here are staying at Rancho Santana; most arrange shuttle transportation with the resort itself. If you're going it alone, try taking a bus from Rivas to Las Salinas (US$2.50 to US$4, two to three hours, eight times daily), then arranging or hitching a ride – Rancho Santana is about a 20 minute drive south of here.

Playa Popoyo & Around

Home to one of the most storied waves in Nicaragua, the little town of **Las Salinas de Nagualapa**, named for the salt evaporation ponds you'll pass on the way in, is beginning to feel a bit like a beach town. Apart from a few surfers and fishers, this stretch of sand is almost empty, ideal for a long walk at sunset. The large, dramatic rock formations on the beach are fun to explore at low tide.

Most people continue past town to **Playa Guasacate**, where a shallow lagoon and slow river shift through the long, sandy beach. It's often called **Playa Popoyo** in honor of its famed beach break.

🏃 Activities

Playa Popoyo is well known for its right and left point breaks, which break huge and hollow over the outer reef when conditions are right. Other named waves include **Bus Stop**: fast, powerful and unpredictable, it ends in shallow water with a rocky bottom. **Cobra**, nearby, is another fast wave, breaking left on more rocks. **Emergencias**, considered the best wave in the region, has a long, smooth left for longboarders and a short, fast, hollow right for shortboarders.

Many surfers bring their own boards, but you can also rent one for around US$10 from hostels and associated outfitters. If you're staying at a surf camp, equipment is provided. Check www.popoyo.com for surf conditions, beach-house rentals and other area info.

NicaWaves SURFING
(www.nicawaves.com; entrada a Popoyo, 1km S) Rents out boards (US$10/60 per day/week) at a hostel near the entrance to town.

🛏 Sleeping & Eating

There are several excellent places to stay in the area, from surf lodges to beachfront hostels to stylish hotels, and the scene is quickly developing – look for new places opening up. You'll do most of your eating at the hotels' restaurants, almost all of which are very good. Keep in mind that you're far from everything here, so bring any extra snacks or drinks you'd like to have before heading to Tola.

Hotel Magnific Rock HOTEL $
(☑8916-6916; www.magnificrockpopoyo.com; Playa Popoyo; 2-person cabins US$40, 2-person studios from US$70, 4-person apt from US$100; ❄🍴🛜) Built on what truly is a magnificent rock outcropping, this friendly surfer's hotel has amazing views on all side of Popoyo beach. The cabins are simple, but good enough, and the studio doubles have incredible beach views. The restaurant comes highly recommended, too. It's located 1.5km off the main road; look for the signs.

El Club del Surf HOTEL $$
(☑8456-6068; www.clubdelsurf.com; Playa Guasacate; s/d from US$40/54; ❄🛜) Just past Popoyo Beach Hostel, this popular hotel has spotless and spacious rooms, as well as a great pizzeria that's open to the public. You're not quite on the beach – that's about 100m away – but there's good access to the Popoyo break itself, and guests rave about the helpful staff and hearty breakfast.

Popoyo Beach Hostel HOSTEL $$
(☑8722-2999; www.popoyobeachhostel.com; Playa Guasacate; dm/d/tr US$10/25/35; 🛜) This friendly beachfront hostel, located in a converted house, has powerful ceili four-bed dorms, a relaxed beachfront and plenty of hammocks. It's located abc 1km past the turn-off for Playa Guasacate; look for signs. (And a tip if you're asking for directions: locals refer to it as 'Casa Maur.')

Sunset Villas Hostel HOSTEL $$
(☑8464-9428; www.surfsunsetvillas.com; 5km toward beach from Tola road; dm/d US$10/35; 🅿🛜) One of the best budget spots in town, Sunset Villas has dorms and private bungalows with firm beds and mosquito nets. There's a beachfront restaurant and plenty of hammocks. You can book surf lessons here, too (US$25 for two hours.)

Hotel Popoyo HOTEL $$$
(☑8885-3334; www.hotelpopoyo.com; Calle del Toro 29, Playa Guasacate; d/tr from US$50/70, 2-person apt US$100; 🛜🍴) This gem of a hotel hits all the marks: a lovely swimming pool, stylish and spacious guest rooms, a fantastic on-site restaurant and bar (**El Toro**, open to the public) and easy access to a near-empty beach that's a one-minute walk from the front gate. There's also an independent apartment with a fully equipped kitchen and a private ocean-view balcony.

El Astillero

This picture-perfect fishing village fronts a gently scalloped white-sand beach. There's surf north of here (accessible when turtles aren't arriving) and a tourist information office in the center of town.

🛏 Sleeping

Hostal Las Hamacas HOSTEL $$
(☑8810-4144; www.hostalhamacas.com; escuela, 50m S; s/d with fan US$25/30, s/d with air-con US$40/45; ❄🛜🍴) Set on a grassy lot with wide beachfront access, this laid-back guesthouse has peaceful, marine-blue rooms with comfy beds, TV and spacious bathrooms, plus a small swimming pool and – as the name suggests – plenty of hammocks to relax in.

ℹ Getting There & Away

Drive yourself or take a bus. From Managua, you can take a bus to Rivas at Nandaime, then take another bus from the market to El Astillero (at the time of writing, buses departed daily at 9am and 2:30pm). From Rivas, take a bus to Las Salinas (US$2.50 to US$4, two to three hours, eight daily), then connect to El Astillero.

...de Vida Silvestre ...lante-Chacocente

...ent at this remote **wildlife** ...2532-3293; www.marena.gob.ni; ... mass arrival of female turtles (at intervals between July and December), who crawl up onto the sandy shores to lay their eggs. It's an occasion worth planning a trip around, though Chacocente, as it's often called, is also a nice year-round destination, with deserted beaches and good birdwatching.

The refuge protects five species of turtle, as well as 48 sq km of dry tropical forests and mangrove swamps.

Marena (Nicaragua's Ministry of the Environment and Natural Resources) runs a biological station here where you can camp (US$2 per person), stay overnight in hostel-style accommodations (from US$4) or stop for a simple meal (US$3 to US$5).

There's currently no public transportation or regularly offered organized tours to the refuge, but if you have a 4WD you can take a signed, rough track 7km north of town here. Or you could walk along the shore 7km from El Astillero.

San Juan del Sur

Easygoing San Juan del Sur (SJDS) is the hub for exploration of Nicaragua's toned-and-tanned southern Pacific beaches. The town itself, with its clapboard Victorian houses, a towering statue of Christ on a neighboring hillside and a steady influx of young and beautiful international travelers and surfers, is quite fun, with a good range of dining, drinking, shopping and nightlife venues.

And while the once-sleepy fishing village doesn't sit on an amazing stretch of coastline – you need to head just north or south for that – its half-moon, brown-sugar beach is pretty for a sunset stroll. Top it all off with a string of world-class surfing enclaves located within easy distance of town, and you have all the workings to kick off an amazing adventure in paradise.

⊙ Sights

Cristo de la Misericordia   MONUMENT
(Christ of Mercy statue; US$2; ⊙8am-5pm) This 25m statue of Jesus – one of the tallest in the world – overlooks the town from its perch

2km to the north. Take the one-hour hike up to catch a great bird's-eye (or son-of-God's-eye) view of the harbor and ocean.

🏃 Activities

Surfing & Diving

The best surfing is generally from April to December, but waves are less crowded in the low season. There's a **beach break** on bigger swells at the northern end of the beach, but most surfers hire boats or stay at the beaches north and south of town. Casa Oro Hostel (p125) runs a daily shuttle out to Playa Maderas.

Good Times Surf Shop   SURFING
(☑8675-1621; www.goodtimessurfshop.com; entre El Gato Negro y Barrio Café; ⊙7:30am-7pm) Rents gear and organizes shuttles, surf lessons and day trips to nearby breaks.

Barefoot Surf Travel   SURFING
(www.barefootsurftravel.com; 7-day packages from US$950) This well-regarded outfitter, which also runs surf camps in Bali and Ecuador, offers week-long packages in San Juan del Sur that cater to beginners. Packages include accommodations in a private villa, transportation to area beaches, all breakfasts and some additional meals. Check the website for schedules.

Neptune Watersports   DIVING
(☑2568-2752; www.neptunenicadiving.com; mercado, 1c O, 10m N; dives from US$85; ⊙8am-7pm) Enquire here for dives and boat excursions.

Fishing

If you look south, you'll see an enormous peninsula jutting out into the sea, a wall of rock that hems in currents – and the critters that ride them, including sailfish and dorado (best June through October), yellow-fin tuna (April and May) and marlin (August and September). In addition to the pricier professional operations at the surf and dive shops in town, you can always book a trip with local fishers more cheaply.

Hiking

A popular daytime expedition starts at the north of town, heading for the spectacular lookout at the Cristo de la Misericordia statue. Cross the pedestrian bridge north of town and follow the signs up.

Cycling

Several outfitters in town rent bicycles if you want to pedal the dirt roads heading to the northern and southern beaches. You can also take your bike on buses that run between SJDS and El Ostional.

Horseback Riding

Rancho Chilamate   HORSEBACK RIDING
(📋 8849-3470; www.ranchochilamate.com; Escamequita; daytime/sunset ride US$75/79) Excellent horseback riding tours at a beautiful ranch located a 20-minute drive south of San Juan del Sur (round-trip transportation provided.) Daily rides last around three hours and happen at low tide. Riders must be at least 18 years old.

Volunteering

Volunteer opportunities abound here. Some require several months' commitment; check online first. For details about volunteering with the San Juan Del Sur Lending Library and Mobile Library Programs, contact **Hotel Villa Isabella** (📋 2568-2568; www.villaisabellasjds.com; iglesia, ½c E; s/d US$120/150; ❄️✳️🛜❄️).

Comunidad Connect (📋 2568-2731; www.comunidadconnect.org) arranges all-inclusive 'voluntourism' packages (including placement, Spanish-language classes, homestays, transport etc).

Yoga

Zen Yoga   YOGA
(📋 8465-1846; www.zenyoganicaragua.com; frente Parque Central; drop-in class US$10) Get in touch with your inner Zen at this friendly yoga retreat. Consult the online schedule for class times.

🥢 Courses

There are several language schools in town. Check bulletin boards at hostels for cheaper, private Spanish-language instruction and exchange.

APC Spanish School   LANGUAGE COURSE
(📋 8450-8990; www.spanishschoolapcsjds.com; Casa de Cultura, Av del Mar s/n, BDF Bank, 20m S; per person per week from US$120, with lodging from US$195) This fun language-learning operation offers accommodations, tours, a cultural center and volunteer opportunities.

Spanish Corner School   LANGUAGE COURSE
(📋 2568-2142; www.spanishcornerschool.com; Royal Chateau Hotel, 1c N; classes per 1hr/10hr/20hr US$9/80/125; ⊙ 8am-10pm) Spanish lessons with an emphasis on Nicaraguan history and culture.

👉 Tours

Many businesses in town offer a similar range of excursions: surfing lessons, sailing tours, fishing trips and turtle-watching outings, to name a few.

★ Da Flying Frog   ADVENTURE TOUR
(📋 8613-4460; www.daflyingfrog.com; per person US$30; ⊙ 8am-4pm Mon-Sat; 🚐) This popular and professionally run canopy tour is fun for the whole family. With 17 platforms and 2.5km of cables, it's one of the biggest zip lines in Nicaragua. Getting to and from the rural site, outside of town on the road to Playa Maderas (transport provided, if you need it) is a great opportunity for monkey- and birdwatching, too.

🎊 Festivals & Events

Semana Santa   RELIGIOUS
(⊙ Mar or Apr) Holy Week (the week before Easter) is one of the busiest times of the year in San Juan del Sur and the surrounding area. In addition to a full range of religious pageants and processions, the beaches explode with parties and celebrations.

Procession of the Virgin of Carmen   RELIGIOUS
(⊙ Jul 16) The Virgin – patron saint of fishers – is taken aboard a local ship at 2pm, placed on an altar decorated with fishing nets and poles, and sailed around the bay to bless the boats. The celebrations feature seafood and mariachi music.

🛏 Sleeping

San Juan del Sur is one of the few destinations in Nicaragua with pronounced seasonal rates: prices rise dramatically during the high season (December to March) and double for Semana Santa and Christmas. There are bargains during the rainy season.

Casa Oro Hostel   HOSTEL **$$**
(📋 2568-2415; www.casaeloro.com; Av del Cine, Parque Central, 1c O, 50m N; dm/d from US$10/32; ✳️@🛜) This backpacker standby has all the amenities – a great information center, free breakfast, communal kitchen, lounge space, free wi-fi (with complimentary iPads), rooftop bar with ocean views – and good vibes 24/7. Dorm beds and rooms are only available by walk-in: first-come, first-served. Casa Oro also runs the most popular and reliable beach shuttles; check the website for the latest schedules.

San Juan del Sur

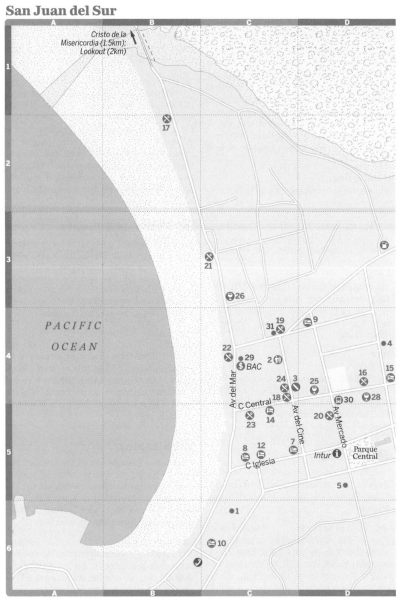

SOUTHWESTERN NICARAGUA SAN JUAN DEL SUR

Rositas Hotel   HOTEL **$$**
(☑ 8326-7733; www.rositashotel.com; mercado, 1½c O; d/tr/q from US$33/39/45) This classic hotel has dated and rather quirky guestrooms, but it's a great deal. The location is just half a block from the beach, and the hotel features a breezy common area on the 2nd level. Choose between a 'quiet' room or one with a nice balcony over the street.

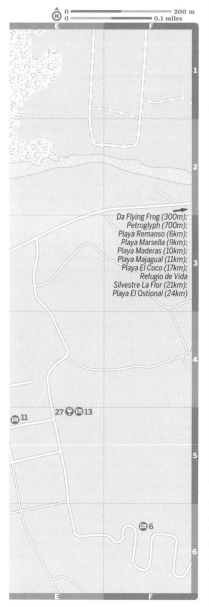

Da Flying Frog (300m);
Petroglyph (700m);
Playa Remanso (6km);
Playa Marsella (9km);
Playa Maderas (10km);
Playa Majagual (11km);
Playa El Coco (17km);
Refugio de Vida
Silvestre La Flor (21km);
Playa El Ostional (24km)

known as Barrio Frente Sur, this quiet hostel with a mellow atmosphere has beautiful views – especially from the rooftop terrace (and the vantage point of a hammock.) Some rooms have ocean views, too. There's also a communal kitchen.

Hotel La Dolce Vita   HOTEL **$$**
(☏ 2568-2649; www.hoteldolcevitasanjuan.com; UNO Station, 1c O; d from US$45; ❋ 🅰) Brightly painted in attractive shades of blue and yellow, this is one of the better-looking hotels in town. Rooms are on the small side but face onto a cheery courtyard that converts into a good Italian restaurant at night.

Buena Onda Backpackers Hostel   HOSTEL
(☏ 8743-2769; www.sanjuandelsurbackpackers. com; Casa de Dragón, 50m a mano izquierda, Barrio Frente Sur; d with/without view US$21/26; 🅰) A few minutes' climb from the center of San Juan del Sur, in the hilltop neighborhood

La Posada Azul
HISTORIC HOTEL **$$$**

(⏰2568-2524; www.laposadazul.com; Av del Parque (Calle Iglesia); d from US$100; ❄🛜🏊) This classy converted Victorian boutique is located just a half-block from the beach. Rooms have vaulted ceilings, tasteful island decorations and whimsical artwork, while the gardens and pool area provide a lush retreat, complete with a *palapa* (open-sided thatched shelter) and honor bar. To top it off, the breakfast, served on a pretty porch, is legendary in San Juan del Sur.

El Coco Azul
HOTEL **$$$**

(⏰2568-2697; www.elcocoazul.com; Av del Parque (Calle Iglesia); d with/without bathroom US$60/50; 🛜) This petite, boutique-style hotel, cheerfully painted in blue and white, is youthful and affordable. The place has plenty to offer: a location just a stone's throw from the beach, inviting common areas and clean, airy guest rooms, each with a private balcony.

Pelican Eyes Resort
RESORT **$$$**

(⏰2563-7000, ext 310; www.pelicaneyesresort.com; d from US$170, villa for 4 US$490 ; ❄🛜🏊) With sweeping bay views and fairly fabulous villas featuring hacienda-style furnishings, kitchens, terraces and satellite TV, this resort is the best in town. It has three pools, bookstores, a spa and two restaurants; the beach is a short stroll away. Even if you're not staying here, you'll want to come up to Pelican Eyes for sunset drinks at La Cascada (p129).

Hotel Victoriano
HISTORIC HOTEL **$$$**

(⏰2568-2005; www.hotelvictoriano.com; Av del Mar; s/d from US$143/154; 🅿❄@🛜🏊) Looking more like something out of a fairy tale than a real building, this wooden classic dates back to 1902 and used to be one of the Somoza family's fabulous weekend getaways. If you've got the cash, splash it on one of the upstairs rooms – the four-poster beds are plush and the small bay windows have priceless views.

Royal Chateau Hotel
HOTEL **$$$**

(⏰2568-2551; www.hotelroyalchateau.com; mercado, 1c E; d from US$75; 🅿❄🛜) The phrase 'royal chateau' gives you the wrong idea – this is more like a motel with a tropical spin – but this place is good value, with bright and spacious modern rooms set around a palm-studded parking area. If your legs can take it, go for a top-floor room – highlighted by naive art – for sweeping bay views.

🍴 Eating

Dining out in San Juan del Sur is a pleasure: you'll find everything from taco shops and traditional Nicaraguan eateries to higher-end seafood restaurants and gourmet pubs.

Asados Juanita
NICARAGUAN **$**

(Av Mercado; mains US$3-5; ⊙6-10pm Mon-Sat) Follow the plumes of smoke to this hugely popular outdoor *fritanga* where you'll choose between steak or chicken, sweet or savory plantains, and *gallo pinto* – eat in, or take away, it's delicious and inexpensive.

El Gato Negro
CAFE **$**

(UNO Station, 2½c O; sandwiches & light meals US$4-7; ⊙7am-3pm; 🛜) 🍴 This hippie-dippy cafe offers the standard range of coffees, juices and fruit plates, plus crepes, bagels and other breakfast-oriented specials. The main draw is the ample lounge space and leafy back patio – both great places to meet other travelers – and the excellent selection of new and used books.

Super Frutto
ICE CREAM **$**

(Hotel Estrella, ½c E; ice cream US$2-3) Arguably the best frozen treat in all of Nicaragua. Super Frutto does terrific Italian-style gelato, all made in-house. Note: in the heat, you're better off avoiding cones.

Taco Stop
TEX-MEX **$**

(www.tacostopnicaragua.com; Av del Cine; mains US$3-7; ⊙8:30am-5:30am) This centrally located branch of Nicaragua's modern taco chain offers tacos, quesadillas, burritos, salads, and soups – you can eat in-house or take it to go. Note the hours: it's almost never closed. There's a rival taco shop on the other end of the same block.

Mesón Español
SPANISH **$$**

(Av del Mar s/n; mains US$6-13; ⊙11am-10:30pm) Four words for you: paella on the beach. One of the more upscale beachfront eateries, this Spanish restaurant also does good tapas and seafood dishes.

Barrio Café
INTERNATIONAL

(www.barriocafesanjuan.com; Av del Cine & Calle Central; dishes US$3-8; ⊙6:30am-10pm) Excellent coffee; gourmet breakfasts; killer ceviche; an all-Nica staff; potent, fruity rum cocktails – what's not to like? This breezy cafe is on a centrally located corner just a block from the beach. There's a nice boutique hotel attached.

G&G Gourmet
INTERNATIONAL $$$

(☑ 7789-7460; www.ggsanjuan.com; mercado, 25m S; mains US$9-13; ⊙ 6:30-10pm Tue-Sat) A step up from most of the offerings in this laid-back beach town, the refined G&G, owned by a Guatemalan-Argentinian couple, offers a short menu of gourmet menu items, including shrimp marinated in passionfruit, seafood risotto, and the excellent pasta *vongole* (homemade pasta with fresh clams, garlic, white wine and cream). The chocolate volcano dessert is locally famous. Make reservations.

Restaurante El Timón
SEAFOOD $$$

(www.eltimonsanjuandelsur.com; beachfront, Av del Mar; dishes US$6-16; ⊙ 8am-late; 🐾) This classic beachfront restaurant, the best of the offerings along this stretch of sand, is the place to go for an upmarket seafood dinner or sunset cocktails. There's folkloric music on Thursday evenings, and good happy-hour specials on food and drink many nights of the week.

Bambu Beach
FUSION $$$

(Av del Mar, Hotel Casa Blanca, 600m N; dishes US$7-12; ⊙ noon-1am; 🐾) Mixing Asian, Italian and Nicaraguan influences, this elegant restaurant has some of the best food in town – and more importantly, it's right on the beach, so you can dine under the palm trees. It's a stroll down the sand from the center of town.

🍷 Drinking & Nightlife

Most of the beachfront restaurants do double-duty as bars and lounges. San Juan del Sur is famous for its party scene, but it's still a surf town, so the atmosphere is pretty laid-back.

San Juan del Sur Cervecería
BEER HALL

(www.sjdsbrewers.com; Av Mercado; ⊙ 11am-2am Wed-Mon) Nicaragua's first craft brewery is – unsurprisingly – a huge hit. Established by American beer enthusiasts, the sleek industrial space is a great place to try the house brews on tap, like the chocolatey 'Pelibuey' porter or the rose-hued 'Jamaica' tart wit. There's live music some nights, brunches on the weekend and a free brewery tour on Sundays at noon.

Howler Bar
BAR

(beachfront; ⊙ 11am-2am) Across from the beach, indoor-outdoor Howler Bar offers a little of everything under an open-air thatched-roof *palapa*: fresh smoothies and Latin American food, live music, cinema nights and cultural events, craft cocktails and late-night dancing. The bartenders are famous for their *micheladas* (cocktails made with beer, lime juice and various spices).

Bar Republika
BAR

(Calle Central; dishes US$3-8; ⊙ 8:30am-late) When you're tired of Toña and rum, this hipster-friendly French-style bar should be your first stop: they do martinis, White Russians and gin and tonics – to name just a few – and offer food specials from tacos and burgers to salads and pitas with hummus. Also open for breakfast.

La Cascada
BAR

(www.pelicaneyesresort.com; Pelican Eyes Resort; ⊙ 7am-10pm) The hilltop bar and restaurant at Pelican Eyes (p128) is a lovely spot for sunset drinks – happy-hour specials often include access to the small but scenic swimming pool. There's live music and entertainment on Wednesday nights and other times, too; check local listings.

🛍 Shopping

In the center of town, you'll find several Nicaraguan surf shops, local design boutiques, and stores and cafes stocking books in English and other languages.

ℹ Information

DANGERS & ANNOYANCES
Don't walk alone on the beach at night. When heading home from the bars, walk in a large group or jump in a cab.

LAUNDRY
Many hostels and hotels offer laundry facilities and/or services.

MONEY
BAC (Hotel Casa Blanca, Av del Mar) One of several banks and ATMs in town.

TELEPHONE
Claro (Av del Mar s/n) Pick up a SIM card for your mobile phone here.

TOURIST INFORMATION
Casa Oro Hostel (p125) Probably the best spot for information on the area, including destinations and transportation.

Intur (☑ 2568-3022; Calle Iglesia, frente Parque Central) Well stocked with brochures and willing (if not always able) to answer questions about the town and surrounds.

❶ Getting There & Away

Several outfitters in San Juan del Sur offer shuttle service to beaches north and south. **Casa Oro Hostel's** (p125) daily shuttles for instance, make the trip to Playa Maderas (round-trip US$5) four times daily, to Playa Hermosa (round-trip US$8) twice daily, and to Playa Remanso (round-trip US$8) once daily. Have a stroll around town to see who's advertising shuttle services to other beaches in the region, including popular destinations like Playas Marsella and Majagual.

BUS

There is regular bus service from the bus stop in front of the market to destinations including the following:

Rivas (US$1, 45 minutes, 6am to 6pm, roughly every 30 to 60 minutes). Here you'll make connections to onward destinations like Granada and Managua.

Southern beaches (US$1.50, 20 minutes to one hour, three to four times daily.) Service to Playa Remanso, Playa El Coco, Refugio de Vida Silvestre La Flor and Playa El Ostional. Departure times change occasionally; stop into a hostel in San Juan del Sur to see or ask about the latest posted times. Bus service to the beaches south of town is regular, but depends on road conditions – if you're here in the wet season, you may find it drastically reduced (or even cancelled).

Shuttle Bus

Several travel agencies and outfitters in town, like **Iskra Travel**, offer shuttle services to Managua, Granada, Masaya, San Jorge (for the ferry to Ometepe), the border of Costa Rica, and other destinations. Book in advance.

Iskra Travel (☑ 2568-2054; www.iskratravel. com; UNO Station, 2½c O; shuttle to San Jorge or Granada US$30, shuttle to Managua US$40; ☺ 9am-6pm) Offers shuttle services to San Jorge (the ferry to Ometepe), Granada, Managua, the border of Costa Rica and other destinations. Prices quoted are for solo travelers; the per-person rates get progressively more affordable if you're traveling with others. Next to El Gato Negro.

CAR & MOTORCYCLE

Alamo (☑ 2277-1117; www.alamonicaragua. com; Av del Mar) rents sedans and 4WD vehicles. You'll probably want the latter, especially if you're heading to the beaches north of town.

TAXI

Taxis congregate close to the market. In theory, each driver has a list of set rates for destinations

outside of town, but you'll hear a small range of prices. Get together with other travelers for the best deal.

Beaches North of San Juan del Sur

The gorgeous beaches north of San Juan del Sur are magnets for surfers and sun-bathers alike. The scene is rapidly developing: yoga retreats and boutique hotels are popping up along the coast, and the breaks can get crowded during high season.

One of the best hotels in Nicaragua is located on Playa Ocatal. There are several good options on Playa Marsella, too, though you can also stay in San Juan del Sur and visit these beaches on day trips.

You'll find dining options at hotels and hostels on the beaches. There aren't many other services here, though, so you'll want to bring your own food and water from San Juan del Sur if you're day-tripping.

❶ Getting There & Away

Most travelers drive their own 4WD vehicles to these beaches or take a shuttle service from San Juan del Sur.

The **Casa Oro** (p125) shuttle (US$5, four daily) drops passengers off at nearby Playa Maderas, a short walk away from Majagual.

Hiring a cab from San Juan del Sur is a third option. Expect to pay anywhere from US$10 to US$30 per carload; you can pre-arrange this with your hotel or hostel, or negotiate with the licensed taxi drivers parked near the market.

Playa Marsella

This beautiful beach lies about 9km north of San Juan del Sur. The water is calm and it makes for a good swimming spot. Although the best surfing is just north, at Playa Maderas (you'll need to go back out to the road; you can't walk around the point), there's a good estuary break right here.

🛏 Sleeping & Eating

There's a small market on Chocolata, the main road, where you can stock up on a few basics.

Hotel Villa Mar HOTEL **$$**
(☑ 8663-0666; www.hostalvillamar.com; Playa Marsella; d from US$38; ❈ ☎) Across the road from the estuary, but close enough to the beach to be rocked to sleep by the sound of crashing waves (ask for a room out front).

Rooms are plain but comfortable, with cool, tile floors. There's a good on-site restaurant and tours on offer, too.

Rancho Marsella NICARAGUAN **$**
(Playa Marsella; dishes US$3-6; ☺8am-8pm) Rancho Marsella serves simple meals and cool drinks on the beachfront. Try the *sopa de mariscos* (seafood stew.)

ℹ Getting There & Away

To get to Playa Marsella, drive yourself (in a 4WD vehicle) or take a shuttle service from San Juan del Sur. Some outfitters may offer a direct shuttle, while others, like the **Casa Oro** (p125) shuttle to Playa Maderas (US$5, four daily) will drop you off near Marsella if you advise the driver. In a pinch, hire a cab from San Juan del Sur.

Playa Maderas

A good-time-vibes backpacker and surfer hangout, this stunning beach – with rocky expanses that offer excellent tide pooling and wide, wonderful sandy stretches for sunbathing – is famed for having one of the best beach breaks in the country.

🏃 Activities

The surf break here, sometimes called **Los Playones**, is a slow wave in fairly deep (2m) water, good for beginners, with two right and two left breaks that get hollow on a rising tide.

If the swell is really big on a low-to-medium tide, there's a faster, intermediate-level reef break between Madera and Majagual called **Panga Drops** – accessible by boat only – that offers an awesome ride before dumping you onto the rocky shallows. It gets choppy and you can be caught in the shore break, so watch the wind. Waves get big, as do the crowds.

Rebelde Surf Schools SURFING
(Playa Maderas) Rents surfboards and offers instruction.

🛏 Sleeping

There's a basic hostel right on the beach, and several higher-end lodges, yoga retreats and foreign-owned rental properties in the immediate vicinity.

Matilda's Hostal HOSTEL **$**
(☑8456-3461; www.hostalmatilda.com; Playa Maderas; dm/s/d from US$10/15/25) A basic but

beloved family-run complex, ▮ surfer huts and basic rooms.

Casa Maderas Ecolodge
(☑8786-4897; www.casamader: Playa Maderas–Marsella, 200ľ US$18/38/42/48; ☜▣) ✔ A budg. both Playa Maderas and Playa Marsella, this lodge-style hostel is set on 3 hectares of lush, jungle-like terraced gardens. Choose between dorm beds draped in mosquito nets or cozy cabins on the hillside. The food's only so-so, and it's not exactly on the beach – it's a ten-minute walk away – but it's fair value.

Buena Vista Surf Club LODGE **$$$**
(☑8863-4180; www.buenavistasurfclub.com; Playa Maderas; rates on request; ☜) ✔ Where the road dips after Parque Maderas, take a right to get to this lovely getaway with spectacular views over the bay. Six treehouse-style *cabañas,* all tucked into the forest, are outfitted with beautiful natural wood, huge mirrors and comfortable beds. Traditional Nicaraguan food is served family-style; yoga and surf lessons are also on the menu.

🍴 Eating

There's a taco shop right on the beach at Playa Maderas, and many nearby hotels have restaurants. But it's also a good idea to bring your own supplies from San Juan del Sur.

Tacos Locos MEXICAN **$$**
(beachfront, Playa Maderas; dishes US$6-14) A breezy taco shop overlooking the beach; it's also a good place to seek shelter from the sun on a hot day.

ℹ Getting There & Away

Many surf shops and hostels in San Juan del Sur – including **Casa Oro** (p125), which goes four times daily – offer shuttles here (one-way/round-trip US$2.50/5.)

Bahía Majagual

This beautiful bay, with its steep, white-sand beach, is perfect for swimming – watch the rip current, though. It has only average surfing; you'll need to walk about ten minutes to get to the big breaks. Note that tourist services are quite limited here.

₋ best bet for getting to Majagual is to ₋ve your own 4WD vehicle or take a shuttle service from San Juan del Sur. Some outfitters may offer a direct shuttle to Majagual, while others, like the **Casa Oro** (p125) shuttle (US$5, four daily) drop passengers off at nearby Playa Maderas, a short walk away from Majagual. If all else fails, hire a cab from San Juan del Sur.

Playa Ocotal

The only way to visit this shady cove beach is by booking a cabin at what may be the very best hotel in all of Nicaragua, the fantastic ecolodge Morgan's Rock.

Beyond Ocotal, on the north side, is the beach called **Arena Blanca**, with some of the clearest water and whitest sand on the Pacific coast. This little inlet is accessible only by rented boat or along a very rough dirt road that runs across very private property – ask permission to cross, or ask around in San Juan del Sur to see about renting a boat.

🛏 Sleeping

⭐ **Morgan's Rock**   LODGE **$$$**
(☏ 2254-7989; www.morgansrock.com; s/d from US$240/396; 🛜🌊) 🅿 With its own idyllic tropical beach and 4000 acres of jungle real estate, this fabulous ecolodge offers a superlative experience. Yes, it's expensive, but you're staying in the poshest dream bungalow ever – gleaming with precious woods and dappled with the forest light – which filters through the parrot- and monkey-filled jungle canopy right into your screened-in porch.

ℹ Getting There & Away

Nearly all travelers here arrange transportation with Morgan's Rock or drive here themselves. Follow the signs to Majagual and turn right after passing a black-and-yellow gate; continue until you get to the beach.

Beaches South of San Juan del Sur

Heading south from San Juan del Sur towards the border of Costa Rica, a string of low-key beach villages offer surf breaks, sea turtle–watching opportunities, and calm waters for snorkeling. There's an interesting wildlife refuge, but you'll also see plenty of monkeys in the trees if you just keep your eyes open while traveling along the hilly forested road. Several segments of *Survivor* were filmed in Playa Hermosa; today, it's a private beach with an admission fee.

Many of the beach towns along this stretch of coastline have simple guesthouses. Most options are found in Playa El Coco and Playa Hermosa.

There are basic beach bars serving drinks and traditional Nica food in many of these beach villages.

ℹ Getting There & Away

Although there is regular bus service between San Juan del Sur and El Ostional (US$1.50, one hour, four daily), you'll need to walk several kilometers from the bus stop to many of the beaches. Playa El Coco, La Flor, and Playa El Ostional are all close to the road. Driving is also a convenient option.

Playa Remanso

The most accessible in a cluster of pretty beaches, this crescent of white sand has decent surfing, interesting caves and good opportunities for swimming and lounging around in tide pools. The smallish beach break is ideal for beginners when it's not so crowded.

ℹ Getting There & Away

Buses stop in Remanso on their way from San Juan del Sur to Playa El Ostional (US$1, 20 minutes, four daily). Outfitters in San Juan del Sur also offer shuttle service (US$5). At the time of writing, **Casa Oro** (p125) was going once daily at 11:30am and returning at 4pm or 6pm.

Playa Tamarindo

Playa Tamarindo is located about a half-hour walk down the beach from Playa Remanso. It's generally less crowded; surfers come with the rising tide to try for a long wave with right and left breaks, which can get hollow coming off the rock wall when swells are under 1m.

ℹ Getting There & Away

Buses roll through Tamarindo on their way from San Juan del Sur to Playa El Ostional (US$1, 25 minutes, four daily). But the beach is a hike from the bus stop; you'll be happier if you drive yourself.

Playa Hermosa

Playa Hermosa is famous for great surfing – there are five breaks on this beach alone – and a cool, lost-in-paradise vibe. It's a privately owned beach, so you'll need to pay an entrance fee of US$10 at Playa Hermosa Ecolodge. Here, at the lodge and surf camp, you can also arrange activities such as horseback riding, sailing, fishing, zip-lining and the like.

Just south of Playa Hermosa (and north of Playa El Coco) are the increasingly popular beaches and surf breaks of **Playa Yankee** and **Playa Escameca**.

🏃 Activities

Playa Hermosa
Surf Camp   SURFING, SNORKELING
(☑ 7667-5436; www.playahermosabeachhotel.com; Playa Hermosa; board rental per day US$10, surfing lessons US$30) The surf camp and shop at Playa Hermosa Ecolodge offers lessons and board rentals. Also available here are horseback riding, snorkeling, fishing and sailing trips (to name just a few).

🛏 Sleeping

Playa Hermosa Ecolodge   LODGE $$$
(☑ 8671-3327; www.playahermosabeachhotel.com; Playa Hermosa; dm US$25, d from US$80; 🖥) This is considered by many the best beach hostel on Nicaragua's south Pacific coast. The open-air, six-bed dorm rooms in this rustic paradise catch the breeze to stay cool at night. Private rooms upstairs have giant mosquito nets. There's a great vibe and surf scene here, with a chilled-out, open-air restaurant. Transfers from San Juan del Sur are included.

❶ Getting There & Away

Playa Hermosa Ecolodge includes transfers to and from San Juan del Sur in the room prices and day-use passes (US$10).

Otherwise, buses stop in Playa Hermosa on their way from San Juan del Sur to Playa El Ostional (US$1.25, 35 minutes, four daily). Some outfitters in San Juan del Sur also offer shuttles to the beach (US$8 to US$10). At the time of writing, **Casa Oro** (p125) shuttles were going twice daily (US$8, at 9:30am and 11am) and returning twice in the afternoon (at 3pm and 4pm.)

Playa El Coco

This is a world-class beach – a spectacular stretch of sparkling sand punctuated by cliffs so pretty that they grace about half of the country's tourist literature. Prices here are steep for the area.

🛏 Sleeping

There are more sleeping options here than anywhere else between San Juan del Sur and the border of Costa Rica. It's also the closest place to sleep near Refugio de Vida Silvestre La Flor.

La Veranera   GUESTHOUSE $$$
(☑ 8328-6260; www.laveranera.net; Calle Playa El Coco; d from US$90, q with shared bathroom US$80; ❄ 🖥 ⛱) This sweet beachfront B&B has just four fan-cooled guest rooms, all with access to a pretty swimming pool. There's a simple on-site bar and restaurant. Though comparatively pricey, the one quad room that sleeps four (with shared bathroom) is a good budget pick. Note that air-conditioning costs US$10 extra per night.

🍴 Eating

The restaurant at Parque Marítimo El Coco, **Puesta del Sol** (www.playaelcoco.com.ni/restaurante; Parque Marítimo El Coco, beachfront; mains US$9-20; ⊗ 7am-late; 🚹), is hit or miss, but offers great sunset views. Bring your own snacks from town, as there aren't lots of services around here.

❶ Getting There & Away

Buses stop in Playa El Coco on their way between San Juan del Sur and Playa El Ostional (US$1.30, 40 minutes, four daily). Some outfitters in San Juan del Sur also offer shuttle service (US$10), usually with a minimum of five passengers required.

Refugio de Vida Silvestre La Flor

One of the principal laying grounds for endangered olive ridley and leatherback turtles, **Refugio de Vida Silvestre La Flor** (☑ ranger station 8419-1014; US$8, campsites per tent US$20) – locally called by its shorter name, 'La Flor' – is situated 20km south of San Juan del Sur. It's easy to visit on a guided tour from San Juan del Sur or from the Playa Hermosa Ecolodge in Playa Hermosa.

Turtles lay their eggs here (usually between 9pm and 2am) between July and January, peaking in September and October. Leatherbacks usually arrive solo, but olive ridleys generally come in flotillas or *arribadas*, when more than 3000 of them pack the beaches at a time. Some people time these arrivals by moon cycles, but no one really knows for sure until the ladies arrive; call the ranger station if you want to be sure.

When there aren't any turtles around, the park still has an attractive, undeveloped beach, a couple of monkeys on-site and a few short trails; there's a decent beach break (right and left) at the northern end. It's off-limits during turtle season.

You can camp at the reserve (US$20 per tent). The closest hotels are in Playa El Coco.

Buses pass near the entrance of the park on their daily trips from San Juan del Sur to Playa El Ostional (US$1.50, 50 minutes, four daily). Advise the driver of your destination, and after you get off the bus, follow the signs to La Flor (it's a bit of a walk).

El Ostional

This fishing village, practically a stone's throw from the Costa Rican border, has an attractive brown-sugar beach that's often totally empty. These calm waters are great for snorkeling and swimming; the beach is a lovely spot to get away from it all while still remaining in easy distance of San Juan del Sur. As the tide rolls in, fisherfolk push their colorful wooden boats out into the surf – a prime photo opportunity.

🛏 Sleeping & Eating

There's not much in the way of services around El Ostional. You'll find two or three small beach bars on the walk between the bus stop and the beach (and at least one is usually open.)

Manta Raya Hospedaje   GUESTHOUSE $$
(☑ 8353-7091; beachfront, north end; s/d/tr US$15/25/35) The rooms here are quite basic – a bed, fan and lamp – but some come with ocean views (and a slight breeze).

❶ Getting There & Away

Buses go to and from San Juan del Sur (US$1.50, one hour, four daily). In El Ostional, the bus stop is located about 600m inland from the beach; just follow the signs to get to the water.

León & Northwestern Nicaragua

Best Places to Eat

➡ Pan y Paz (p149)

➡ Quesillos Guiligüiste (p158)

➡ Cafe La Nicaragüita (p149)

➡ Costa Azul (p163)

Best Places to Sleep

➡ Bomalu (p154)

➡ Surfing Turtle Lodge (p153)

➡ Rancho Tranquilo (p164)

➡ Paz de Luna Bed & Breakfast (p148)

Why Go?

This is Nicaragua at its fieriest and most passionate. The regional capital of León is – and will always be – a hotbed of intellectualism and independence. The city has nourished some of Nicaragua's most important political and artistic moments. Less polished but somehow more profound than its age-old rival Granada, the city is beloved for its grand cathedral, breathtaking art museum, hopping nightlife and spirited revolutionary air.

Just out of León, more than a dozen volcanic peaks wait to be climbed (or surfed). This region has some of the best beach accommodations – and gnarliest surfing – in the country. And the virgin wetlands of the Reserva Natural Isla Juan Venado are not to be missed.

Further afield, you'll find the biggest mangrove forest in Central America, awe-inspiring beauty at Reserva Natural Volcán Cosigüina and unique windows into everyday Nicaraguan life in the little towns along the way.

When to Go

➡ December is good for cooler-than-usual temperatures. This is the hottest part of the country; daytime temperatures are just above 30°C (86°F) almost year-round, spike in sweltering April and dip into the relatively cool mid-20s°C (mid-70s°F) in December.

➡ October and November are the peak months to see nesting turtles at the Reserva Natural Estero Padre Ramos; the whole season lasts between July and December. This is also a good time to think about volunteering as a beach warden or visiting Reserva Natural Isla Juan Venado.

➡ Semana Santa is held in late March to early April – Easter week is a Technicolor dreamscape in León. There are sawdust 'carpets' in colonial suburbs, and a sand-castle competition at a nearby beach.

León & Northwestern Nicaragua Highlights

1 **Maribios chain**
(p155) Climbing a spectacular volcanic peak then enjoying the thrill of sandboarding down its slopes.

2 **Playa Jiquilillo**
(p164) Getting away from it all in a beachside cabin.

3 **Reserva Natural Isla Juan Venado**
(p154) Going for a peaceful swim and watching nesting turtles in action.

4 **La Paz Centro**
(p157) Feasting on savory *quesillos* in the town of their origin.

5 **León** (p138) Mixing with the university crowd and taking in some politically charged street art in this vibrant city.

6 **Las Peñitas**
(p153) Riding a chicken bus to the white sandy beaches of this paradise.

7 **Reserva Natural Estero Padre Ramos**
(p164) Kayaking through Central America's largest mangrove forest.

8 **Volcán Cosigüina** (p165) Soaking those aching bones in Potosí hot springs after climbing this volcano.

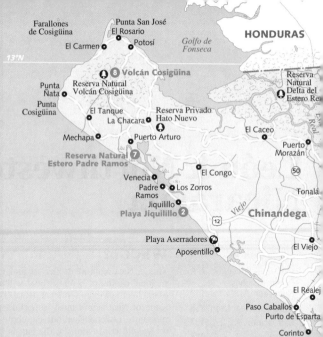

Farallones de Cosigüina
Punta San José
El Rosario
El Carmen
Potosí
Golfo de Fonseca
HONDURAS
13°N

8 **Volcán Cosigüina**
Reserva Natural Volcán Cosigüina
Reserva Natural Delta del Estero Re

Punta Ñata
Punta Cosigüina
El Tanque
La Chacara
Reserva Privado Hato Nuevo
El Caceo
Puerto Morazán

Mechapa
Puerto Arturo
50

7 Reserva Natural Estero Padre Ramos

Venecia
El Congo
Tonalá
Padre Ramos
Los Zorros
Viejo
Jiquilillo
Chinandega
2 Playa Jiquilillo
12

Playa Aserradores **7**
El Viejo
Aposentillo

El Realej
Paso Caballos
Purto de Esparta
Corinto

PACIFIC OCEAN

12°N

N
0   30 km
0   15 miles

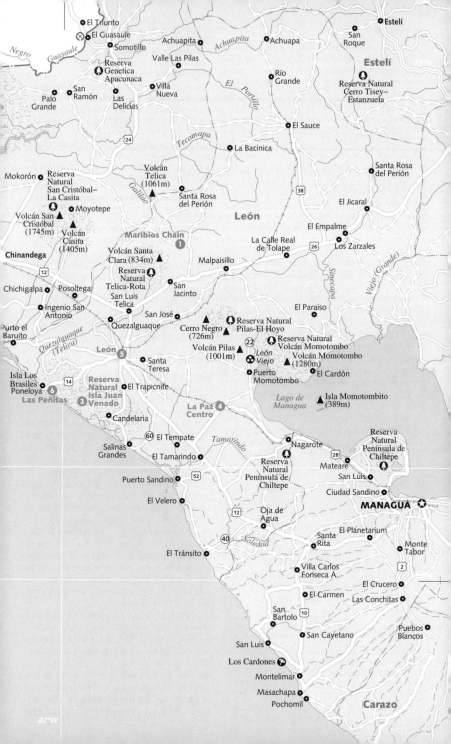

History

The Maribios people were the first inhabitants of what is now León, in the township/suburb of Subtiaba. After a series of volcanic eruptions led to the evacuation of the original city of León (now called León Viejo), this site was chosen. It turned out to be a good choice – Subtiaba provided plenty of indigenous labor, it was far enough from the ocean to prevent the pirate attacks that had plagued Granada, and the volcanoes were distant and dormant enough not to threaten the city.

León has produced various heroes, most famously poet Rubén Darío, but also independence fighter Miguel Larreynaga (look for him on the 10-córdoba note) and Luisa Amanda Espinoza, the first female Frente Sandinista de Liberación Nacional (Sandinista National Liberation Front; FSLN) member to die in combat. A Sandinista stronghold, the city saw some of the toughest battles during the revolution, documented in the city's murals, museums and bullet-pocked walls.

Despite León's status as a religious and academic center (and the fact that it had been the nation's capital for 242 years), it was Chinandega, to the north, that was chosen as the meeting place for the ill-fated Confederation of American States in the 19th century. Chinandega's claim to fame as the 'city of oranges' waned in the 20th century, as cotton became the principal crop. This in turn changed as world cotton prices plummeted and farmers turned to sugarcane and peanuts, the region's main crops to this day.

Corinto – these days Nicaragua's busiest commercial port – has entered the history books in a big way twice: firstly when it was the landing site for William Dampier and a band of French and British pirates in the only recorded pirate attack on León, and secondly when US president Ronald Reagan ordered the illegal mining of the bay, which set in motion a series of machinations that would eventually lead to the Iran-Contra affair.

ⓘ Getting There & Away

Minivans making the short, sweet run from Managua to León leave regularly from the UCA bus lot. Normal buses and minivans also leave from Mercado Israel Lewites – frequently for León, less so for Chinandega.

Both León (92km northwest of Managua) and Chinandega (37km northwest of León) are transportation hubs. Buses to more remote beaches and volcanoes can be inconvenient, with perhaps only one departure per day.

You can rent cars in both León and Chinandega; hire a 4WD in the rainy season if you plan to do much exploring. The roads of the Cosigüina peninsula are some of the country's worst, and beach access can be a muddy mess by October.

If you're heading to El Salvador, contact Ruta del Golfo (p152) or Tierra Tours (p151) in León. Both arrange border crossings across the Gulf of Fonseca via boat and 4WD.

León

Intensely political, buzzing with energy and, at times, drop-dead gorgeous (in a crumbling, colonial kind of way), León is what Managua should be – a city of awe-inspiring churches, fabulous art collections, stunning streetscapes, cosmopolitan eateries, fiery intellectualism, and all-week, walk-everywhere, happening nightlife. Many people fall in love with Granada, but most of them leave their heart in León.

History

Originally located on the slopes of Volcán Momotombo, León was the site of some of the Spanish conquest's cruelest excesses; even other conquistadors suggested that León's punishment was divine retribution. When the mighty volcano reduced León to rubble in 1610, the city was moved to its current location, saint by saint, to sit next to the existing indigenous capital of Subtiaba.

The reprisals did not end there. Eager to win the civil war with Granada – which had, since independence, been contesting the colonial capital's continuing leadership role – in 1853 León invited US mercenary William Walker to the fight. After the Tennessean declared himself president (and Nicaragua a US slave state), he was executed; the nation's capital was moved to Managua, and Granada's Conservatives ran the country for the next three decades.

Finally, in 1956, Anastasio Somoza García (the original dictator) was assassinated at a social event in León by Rigoberto López, a poet. The ruling family never forgot, and when the revolution came, their wrath fell on this city in a hail of bullets and bombs, the scars of which have still not been erased.

León has remained proudly Liberal – even a bit aloof – through it all, a Sandinista stronghold and political power player that has never once doubted its grand destiny.

◎ Sights

León is the most culturally rich of Nicaragua's cities; architecture and history buffs will want to spend a few days exploring.

☉ Central León

⭐**Museo de Arte Fundación Ortiz-Gurdián**   MUSEUM
(Parque Central, 2c W; admission US$0.80; ☉10:30am-6:30pm Tue-Sat, 9am-6pm Sun) Probably the finest museum of contemporary art in all of Central America, the Ortiz-Gurdián Collection has spilled over from its original home in Casa Don Norberto Ramiréz, refurbished in 2000 to its original Creole Civil style, with Arabic tiles and impressive flagstones. The collection includes works by Picasso, Chagall, Miró and a number of noted Nicaraguan artists. Begin surrounded by the luxurious realism of the Renaissance and spare beauty of the colonial period, then wander through romanticism, modernism, postmodernism and actually modern pieces by Cuban, Peruvian and other Latin American schools. Big names make an appearance, but it's the work by Latin American masters – Diego Rivera, Rufino Tamayo, Fernando Botero, Roberto Matta and more – that define the collection.

Catedral de León   CATHEDRAL
(Parque Central; ☉8am-noon & 2-4pm Mon-Sat) Officially known as the Basílica de la Asunción, León's cathedral is the largest in Central America, its expansive design famously (and perhaps apocryphally) approved for construction in much more important Lima, Peru. Leónese leaders originally submitted a more modest but bogus set of plans, but architect Diego José de Porres Esquivel, the Capitan General of Guatemala (also responsible for San Juan Bautista de Subtiaba, La Recolección and La Merced churches, among others), pulled the switcheroo and built this beauty instead.

This is the cathedral's fourth incarnation. The 1610 original was replaced in 1624 with a wood-and-adobe structure that pirate William Dampier burned to the ground in 1685. Another adobe was used until work began on this enormous 'Antigüeño,' Central American baroque-style masterpiece in 1747. Construction, done primarily by indigenous laborers from Subtiaba and Posoltega, went on for more than a hundred years.

The cathedral is a sort of pantheon of Nicaraguan culture. The **tomb of Rubén Darío**, León's favorite son, is on one side of the altar, guarded by a sorrowful lion and the inscription 'Nicaragua is created of vigor and glory, Nicaragua is made

---

THE CITY OF CHURCHES

With more than 16 places to pray, including several more in Barrio Subtiaba, the city tourist board is lobbying to have León officially declared 'The City of Churches.'

The 1639 **Iglesia de San Francisco** (Parque Central, 2c O, ½c N; ☉hours vary) is one of the oldest in the city – a national heritage site with lots of gold, a gorgeous nave and a rather rococo interior. It was abandoned between 1830 and 1881, then refurbished with two elaborate altarpieces for San Antonio and Nuestra Señora de La Merced (Our Lady of Mercy). The attached **Convent San Francisco**, founded in 1639, was badly damaged during the 1979 battle for León. Check out what used to be the convent at Hotel El Convento next door.

Nuestra Señora de Guadalupe (7a Calle SE & Av Central), built in 1743, is León's only church that's oriented north–south; it's historically connected to the city by the 1850 **Puente Guadalupe**, built across the Río Chiquito. And don't let the dumpy, modernist, neoclassic exterior of 1625 **Capilla San Juan de Dios** (cnr 1a Calle SO & 3rd Av SO) fool you – when it's open, the interior is one of the city's prettiest, with lots of precious wood and a very human scale.

For something completely different, swing by ultra-Gothic 1884 **Iglesia Zaragoza** (Parque Central, 4c O, 2c N; ☉hours vary), one of the best spots for film students to stage a vampire flick. They could also use one of the several ruined churches around town, including **Ruinas Veracruz** and **Ruinas Iglesia Santiago** in Barrio Subtiaba, and **Ruinas San Sebastián** (Parque Central 3c S), near La XXI (the 21st Garrison).

León

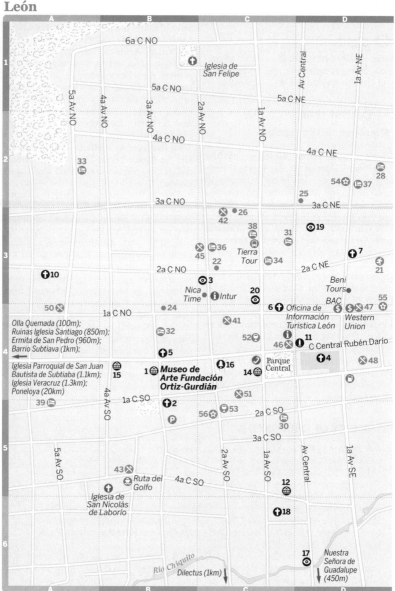

for freedom.' Nearby rest the tombs of lesser-known Leónese poets Alfonso Cortés and Salomón de la Selva, as well as Miguel Larreynaga.

Among the magnificent works of art within are the Stations of the Cross by Antonio Sarria, considered masterpieces, and El Cristo Negro de Pedrarias, possibly the oldest Catholic image in the Americas, brought here in 1528. Marble statues inside are beautifully crafted, most notably the elaborate Inmaculada Concepción de María.

If it's clear, take the **roof tour** (US$0.80), with a spectacular view of the city and smoking volcanoes beyond. The cathedral was having a face-lift at research time but should be completed by the time you read this. Regardless, it will still be open to the public.

Museo Rubén Darío · MUSEUM
(www.rubendario.enriquebolanos.org; cnr Calles Central Rubén Darío & 4a Av SO; admission by donation; ☉8am-noon & 2-5pm Tue-Sat, 8am-noon Sun) Nicaragua's most famous poet, Rubén Darío, lived in this house for the first 14 years of his life – indeed, he started writing poetry right here at age 12. That first poem is on display here, as are various personal effects. Of all the museums and monuments dedicated to the poet that are scattered across his doting homeland, this colonial house seems like the one where you'd be most likely to run into his ghost.

Exhibits are displayed throughout the house, ranging from everyday items that provide a window into well-to-do Nicaraguan life in the late 1800s to handwritten manuscripts of Darío's famous works. His bible, the bed where he died 'an agonizing death' and the fancy duds he wore as the ambassador to Spain are just highlights among the historic bric-a-brac.

Darío's final resting place is in the León cathedral (p139).

Museo de Leyendas y Tradiciones MUSEUM
(☏2315-4678; 4a Calle SO, frente Ruinas San Sebastián; admission US$2; ☉8am-5pm) León's most entertaining and eclectic museum, the Museum of Myths & Traditions, is now housed in **La XXI** (the 21st Garrison). What makes this museum unmissable is the striking contrast of its main subjects: a quirky collection of life-sized papier-mâché figures from Leónese history and legend, handmade by founder Señora Toruña (who is also represented in glorious papier-mâché), and murals graphically depicting methods the Guardia Nacional used to torture prisoners.

You're led from room to room, each dedicated to a different aspect of Leónese folklore, from La Gigantona – the giant woman who represents an original colonist, still ridiculed by a popular ballet *folklórico* – to La Carreta Nagua (Chariot of Death), which picks up the souls of those foolish enough to cross intersections kitty-corner.

And between each rundown of local legends, your Spanish-speaking guide will cheerfully shift gears to describe the gory human-rights abuses – stretching on racks, beatings, water tortures etc – that took place here regularly until June 13, 1979, when Commander Dora María Téllez successfully breached Somoza's defenses and secured La XXI for the Sandinistas, releasing all prisoners. Signage is in English and Spanish.

León

Museo Histórico de la Revolución MUSEUM
(Parque Central; admission US$2; ◎8am-5pm)
León is the heart and soul of liberal Nicaragua. Stop into this museum for an overview of the Nicaraguan revolutionaries who stood up against the Somoza dictatorship, tracing national history from the devastating earthquake of 1972 to the Sandinista overthrow.

Iglesia de la Recolección CHURCH
(1a Av NE, 2a Calle NE; ◎hours vary) Three blocks north of the cathedral, the 1786 Iglesia de La Recolección is considered the city's most beautiful church, a Mexican-style baroque confection of swirling columns and bas-relief medallions that portray the life of Christ. Dyed a deep yellow, accented with cream and age, the lavishly decorated facade may be what makes the cover of all the tourist brochures, but be sure to stop inside and admire the slender mahogany columns and ceiling decorated with harvest motifs.

Iglesia de La Merced CHURCH
(Parque Central, 1c N) Home to León's patron saint, La Virgen de La Merced, this is considered the city's second-most-important church. After Volcán Momotombo erupted and forced the city's evacuation, the Leónese built a new church here in 1615, replaced with the current building in the early 1700s.

Parque Rubén Darío PARK
This quaint park has a **statue** of the poet master and busts of other, lesser Leónese poets, including Alfonso Cortés (1893–1969), Azarias H Pallais (1884–1954) and Salomon de la Selva (1893–1959). They are engraved with a few choice verses.

Museo Entomológico MUSEUM
(☑2311-6586; www.bio-nica.info; cnr 3a Av NE & 2a Calle NE; admission US$1; ⊙9am-noon & 2-4pm Thu-Tue) For a truly comprehensive collection of creepy crawlies, butterflies, scorpions and other critters from all over Central America, drop into this museum. The specialty is *Lucanidae*, a genus of beetles whose males usually display ferocious-looking pincers. Anyone for a mosquito net?

Mausoleo de los Héroes y Mártires MONUMENT
A monument to the local heroes, the eternal flame of the Mausoleum of Heroes and Martyrs rests within a small plaza just north of the Parque Central, surrounded by the city's best murals.

Iglesia El Calvario CHURCH
(Parque Central, 4c E) A hodgepodge of neoclassical and baroque styles, the richly hued El Calvario dates from the 18th century. It's notable, among other attributes, for the symmetry of its design.

El Fortín de Acososco FORT
The Guardia Nacional's last holdout in León, El Fortín can be reached by the 2.5km dirt road that begins on the western side of Guadalupe cemetery, on the southern border of Barrio Subtiaba. The large, squat, gray building was originally constructed in 1889 to take advantage of the great city views. It was abandoned until the 1950s, when the Somozas realized that they needed to keep an eye on León itself. They lost the fort on July 7, 1979. You may need to ask for permission to enter. Muggings are common on this stretch, so go in a group and leave your camera and other valuables at the hotel.

Casa del Obrero LANDMARK
(cnr 2a Calle NO & 2a Av NO) An early-20th-century landmark, the Casa del Obrero (House of the Worker) honors Nicaraguan laborers.

Iglesia San Juan CHURCH
(3a Av SE, 4a Calle NE; ⊙hours vary) Built in the 1850s on the edge of León's downtown.

Iglesia de San Nicolás de Laborío CHURCH
(Parque Central, 3c O, 3c S) Felipe III of Spain ordered this church to be built in 1618.

Iglesia de San Felipe CHURCH
(estadio, 2c S) A 17th-century church that occupies a whole block on the northern edge of downtown.

Puente Martín BRIDGE
Spans the river on the southern edge of downtown.

⊙ Barrio Subtiaba

A regional capital long before León moved in, the *barrio* (district) of Subtiaba takes its name from a local tribe who still count themselves apart from León, and Nicaragua, as a whole. After refugees from León Viejo arrived in 1610, the two separate towns coexisted as equals until 1680. Flexing their rebuilt military muscle, the Spanish forced 12,000 indigenous inhabitants of Subtiaba to become part of León, basically relegating them to slave labor. Tensions simmered for two generations, until a police crackdown in 1725 inspired a revolt. Although the insurrection was violently shut down by the Spaniards, Barrio Subtiaba was able to remain a separate entity until 1902, when it was finally, officially, annexed to the city.

It's a solid 20-minute walk or US$0.80 taxi ride to Subtiaba from the León cathedral, or else you can take one of the covered trucks (US$0.20) plying the streets. Catch a Subtiaba-bound truck at the southwest corner of the Parque Central (in front of Sandinista headquarters) and yell 'Catedral Subtiaba' as they haul you inside, which might be while the truck is still moving. Hang on!

Iglesia Parroquial de
San Juan Bautista de Subtiaba CHURCH
(Calle Real, sobre la Loma del Conejo; ⊙hours vary) The Subtiaba neighborhood is centered on this church, located about 1km west of the León cathedral. It's better known as 'Catedral Subtiaba,' and is the oldest intact church in the city. Built in the 1530s and reconstructed in 1710, its relatively plain beige facade and precious wood interior is largely unadorned; even the struts are there to stabilize the structure during earthquakes.

There are two exceptions: spirals outside, and an extraordinary sun icon mounted to the typical arched timber roof, pay homage to deities far older than the Spanish conquest.

Ermita de San Pedro CHURCH
(Iglesia San Juan Bautista, 2c E, 1c S; ⊙hours vary) This church, two blocks east and one block south of San Juan Bautista, was constructed between 1706 and 1718. It's considered one

of the best examples of primitive baroque style in Nicaragua, meaning that it's almost unadorned – save for three brick crosses inlaid into the adobe.

Iglesia Veracruz   RUIN
(Iglesia Santiago, 3c O) A few blocks west of the Iglesia Santiago are the ruins of this 16th-century church destroyed by a volcanic eruption in 1835. It remains a spiritual center, and as the indigenous counterpoint to La Grítería, on December 7 people gather here for a pre-Columbian festival involving torches and the sun deity on the roof of San Juan Bautista.

UCAN   UNIVERSITY
(Universidad Cristiana Autónima de Nicaragua; www.ucan.edu.ni; Av Central, catedral, 2½c N) Pricey private school worth checking out for a look into León's university scene.

UCC   UNIVERSITY
(Universidad de Ciencias Comerciales; www.ucc.edu.ni; costado oeste de la UNAN, frente a Campus Médico) This university specializes in architecture and tourism-related degrees. Cruising around here makes for a good afternoon.

🏃 Activities

Get Up Stand Up   SURFING
(☑ 5800-2394; www.gsupsurf.com; del Banco Procredit, ½c S; ⊙ 9am-9pm) This cool surf shop – the only one in León – runs daily shuttles to and from Las Peñitas and arranges lessons and gear rental in conjunction with Bigfoot Beach Hostel (p153). The indie brand also designs and prints its own T-shirts. It's a great stop for information if you're considering a surf excursion.

Asociación Mary Barreda   VOLUNTEERING
(☑ 2311-2254; www.mary-barreda.org; Iglesia de La Recolección, ½c E; ⊙ hours vary) Runs a variety of education programs focusing on women's rights, sex education and STD prevention.

📖 Courses

Hostels are the best places to inquire about private Spanish tutors (who charge from around US$7 per hour).

León Spanish School   COURSE
(☑ 8183-7389; www.leonspanishschool.org; La Casa de Cultura, 1a Calle NO, Iglesia de La Merced, 2c O; 20hr course without/with homestay US$150/250) Based in La Casa de Cultura, this is a professional operation with plenty of cultural activities and out-of-town excursions.

🏃 City Walk
Revolutionary & Cultural León

START PARQUE CENTRAL
END MUSEO-ARCHIVO RUBÉN DARÍO
LENGTH 3-5KM; FOUR TO SIX HOURS

Begin at **1 Parque Central**, a fine place for people-watching and enjoying that most Leónese of treats, *raspado* (shaved ice flavored with fruit).

Enjoy your treat in front of the eternal (more or less) flame at **2 Mausoleo de los Héroes y Mártires** (p143) on the northern side of the park, where a phenomenal and heartbreaking mural traces Nicaraguan history from the Spanish conquest to the most recent revolution, complete with smoking volcanoes.

Dominating the plaza is **3 Basílica de la Asunción** (p139), Central America's largest cathedral; take a rooftop tour for views of the Volcáns Maribios.

On the southern side of the cathedral is 1679 **4 Colegio La Asunción**, the first theological college in Nicaragua. It was partially destroyed by fire in 1935 and rebuilt in its current Gothic style. Next door is **5 Palacio Episcopal** (Bishop's Palace), designed by Marcelo Targa and one of the first buildings to display Leónese neoclassical architecture. In this group of buildings is also the **6 Archivo Histórico Dicesano de León**, which holds documents dating back to 1674.

Continuing around the cathedral is the 1680 **7 Colegio de San Ramón**. Revolutionary hero Miguel Larreynaga, who drafted the first Central American constitution, was educated here. The college was rebuilt in 1752, and housed the Universidad Autónoma, Nicaragua's first university, though it's been a high school since 1945.

Head south on 1a Ave SE, then west on 3a Calle SO one block, then south one block on Av Central to **8 La XXI**, an old military garrison that's today home to the truly fabulous **9 Museo de Leyendas y Tradiciones** (p141); check out the mosaic tile work at the entrance. Across the street are the photogenic **10 Ruinas San Sebastián**; the church was bombed almost into oblivion in 1979.

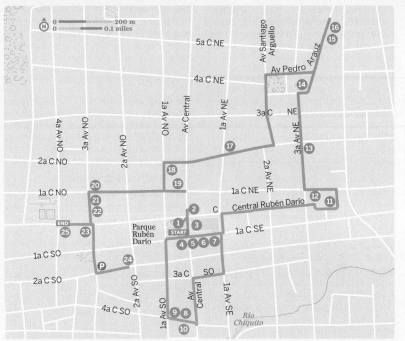

Backtrack up 1a Ave SO and through Mercado Central, then make a right on Calle Central Rubén Darío and continue to the early-18th-century ⑪ **Iglesia El Calvario** (p143), famed for its comic-book-style facade. Close by, ⑫ **Antiguo Reformatorio de Menores** (Old Reform School) is a rare, almost all-original *casa pinariega*–style building. The squat adobe has *tejas* (ceramic half-pipe ceiling tiles), plus classic corner double doors.

Head north on 3a Av NE, stopping in at ⑬ **Museo Entomológico** (p143). Then it's on to somewhat scruffy 1625 ⑭ **Iglesia San Juan de Dios**, rebuilt in 1860 in the modernist neoclassical style. Close by is ⑮ **Mercado San Juan** (p150) and the ⑯ **old train station**, constructed in 1882.

Backtrack two blocks along 4a Av NE to 2a Calle NE and make a right to reach the unmissable 1786 ⑰ **Iglesia de La Recolección** (p142). This ornate masterpiece was described by one critic as 'the most important monument to passion in Nicaragua.'

Two blocks west on 2a Calle NE is the flagship campus of ⑱ **UNAN**, with several beautiful buildings and a collection of cheap restaurants and festive bars.

From the UNAN campus, head south on 1a Av NO for the 1615 ⑲ **Iglesia de La Merced** (p142), another of León's signature churches, then head west on 1a Calle NO, stopping at ⑳ **La Casa de Cultura** (p146), with its excellent art collection (including a portrait of former US president Ronald Reagan that you'll want to photograph), then head south on 3a Av NO.

Tired? Fortify yourself at ㉑ **Hotel El Convento** (p148), which has an amazing collection of colonial-era religious art and a good, if pricey, restaurant. Attached ㉒ **Iglesia de San Francisco** (p139) was badly damaged during the revolution but is slowly being restored to its former glory.

Allow at least two hours to appreciate the best art museum in Central America, ㉓ **Museo de Arte Fundación Ortiz-Guardián** (p139), south of Calle Central Rubén Darío, then head two blocks further south and one block east to see if anything's on later that night at 1885 ㉔ **Teatro Municipal José de la Cruz Mena** (p150). Finally, backtrack to the corner of Calle Central Rubén Darío and 4a Av SO for the poet's home and national museum, ㉕ **Museo-Archivo Rubén Darío** (p141).

La Isla Foundation   COURSE
(☑2315-1261; www.laislafoundation.org; 3a Calle NE, Av Central) Stop by to learn about Spanish, yoga and salsa classes, and volunteer opportunities.

La Casa de Cultura   COURSE
(☑2311-2116; 1a Calle NO, Iglesia de La Merced, 2c O; ⊙10am-6pm Mon-Fri) Ask here about art, dance and music classes.

👉 Tours

Volcano surfing is all the rage around León, which involves riding a 'sandboard' (something like a modified snowboard) or toboggan down black-gravel slopes. Agencies around town offer excursions to Cerro Negro, Volcán Cosigüina and other area volcanoes.

Tierra Tour   ADVENTURE TOUR
(☑2315-4278; www.tierratour.com; Iglesia de La Merced, 1½c N) A well-established operator with locations in both León and Granada. Full- and half-day tours go to the volcanoes (including both trekking and sandboarding excursions) and pretty much anywhere you'd want to go in the region, from León Viejo to Reserva Natural Isla Juan Venado. Also offers daily shuttles to and from Granada, as well as to Antigua and El Salvador.

Tierra Tour also arranges passage on the daily boat across the Gulf of Fonseca to El Salvador.

VOLUNTEERING IN LEÓN
Hostels are a good starting point for information. **Quetzaltrekkers** uses volunteer guides to lead volcano treks.

León is also home to a range of grassroots, Nicaraguan-run NGOs. You'll probably need a higher level of Spanish than if you were volunteering in Granada or San Juan del Sur, but chances are it will be more rewarding work. There are many NGOs at work in and around the city, including the **Asociación Mary Barreda** (p144), which runs a variety of education programs focusing on women's rights, sex education and STD prevention. Intermediate Spanish and a two-month commitment are required.

Quetzaltrekkers   ADVENTURE TOUR
(☑2311-7388; www.leon.quetzaltrekkers.org; Mercantil, ½c O) 🏃 Profits from this outstanding operator go to Las Tias, a charity that helps children from underprivileged areas learn to build their own lives, and other worthy causes; volunteers are very welcome.

Eco-Camp Expeditions   ADVENTURE TOUR
(☑2311-1828; www.ecocampexpeditions.com; Parque Rubén Darío, 2c N, 10m E; ⊙9am-6pm Mon-Sat) A solid operation for camping and other adventure activities outside León.

🎊 Festivals & Events

Every Saturday, from early afternoon till midnight, the Parque Central comes alive for the **Tertulia Leónesa**, inviting everyone outside to eat, drink and dance to music played by local combos. León also plays host to a number of lively annual celebrations.

Semana Santa   RELIGIOUS
(⊙late Mar or early Apr) The Leónese Semana Santa is something special, with Barrio Subtiaba's colorful sawdust 'carpets,' temporary and beautiful images that the funeral procession for Jesus walks over, and a sand-castle competition in Poneloya.

Masacre del 23 Julio 1959   CULTURAL
(⊙Jul 23) One afternoon in 1959, local schoolchildren staged a demonstration against Somoza. As they chanted 'Freedom! Freedom!,' the Guardia Nacional fired into the crowd, killing four students and wounding several others. Those wounded, some in wheelchairs, still lead a parade, right after every single marching band from the area has announced that their generation will not forget.

La Gritería Chiquita   RELIGIOUS
(⊙Aug 14) This celebration began in 1947, as an erupting Cerro Negro threatened to bury the city in ashes. The volcano suddenly halted its activity after an innovative priest, Monseñor Isidro Augusto Oviedo, vowed to initiate a preliminary *gritería* (shouting) – similar to December's but changing the response to *¡La asunción de María!* ('The ascension of Mary!').

Día de la Virgen de Merced   RELIGIOUS
(⊙Sep 24) León's saint's day is solemnly observed, but the preceding day is more festive: revelers don a bull-shaped armature lined with fireworks, then charge at panic-stricken onlookers as the rockets fly.

WORTH A TRIP

LEÓN VIEJO

Buried and lost for over 300 years, this was Nicaragua's first capital – a rough-and-ready settlement that some say was doomed from the start. Founded in 1524, the town was governed by a series of unusually cruel and money-hungry tyrants, whose public spectacles included beheadings and setting wild dogs on captured natives in the central plaza.

All of which gives some weight to the theory that divine intervention played at least a part in the series of earthquakes that shook the town from 1580 to 1609, culminating in the eruption of nearby **Volcán Momotombo** (1280m) that buried the city under ash in 1610.

The Spanish fled, carrying whatever they could with them (including La Virgen de La Merced), and settled in present-day León, and the old city began to fade from memory.

Fast forward to 1967. After years of searching and theorizing, archaeologists from León's UNAN university finally located the old town, unearthing its chapel and central plaza (and the headless remains of Francisco Fernández de Córdoba, founder of both León and Granada, beneath it).

In 2000 it was declared a Unesco World Heritage site – Nicaragua's first – and excavations have continued (funds allowing). This is not Machu Picchu – most walls are about 1m high and you need a fair bit of imagination to see that there was once a city here – but it makes for an interesting day trip, more than anything for the evocative commentary provided by local guides.

Admission includes a Spanish-language guided tour, but detailed signs are also in English. The best time to visit is the second Sunday in November, when La Virgen de La Merced leaves her comfortable new church and, leading a procession of the faithful from La Paz Centro, revisits her first home in the New World.

Almost every tour outfit in León (as well as several in Managua and Granada) arranges visits to León Viejo (US$45 from León), which can be combined with a hike to the top of Cerro Negro (726m) and/or a cool swim in Laguna de Asososca, both nearby. But it's easy to visit on your own. Buses run every 50 minutes between León and La Paz Centro (US$0.80, 45 minutes), meeting buses to Puerto Momotombo (US$0.50), less than 1km from the site. Driving, the turnoff is 3km east of La Paz Centro on the new León–Managua highway. From there it's a 15km drive along a cobblestone road; make the poorly signed right to the ruins when you get into town.

If you continue straight through Puerto Momotombo, however, you'll quickly come to a less-than-appealing beach scene on **Lago de Managua**, where a handful of disposable-looking restaurants and a playground enjoy a truly awesome view of Volcán Momotombo, the hydro-electric plant steaming eerily against its naked red and black slopes, and **Isla Momotombito**.

Carnaval Mitos y Leyendas   CULTURAL
(Nov 1) This fun Halloween-esque fiesta features the papier-mâché crew from the Museo de Leyendas y Tradiciones (p141) on a parade from the cathedral to Barrio Subtiaba.

Día de la Purísima Concepción   RELIGIOUS
(☉ Dec 7) Known simply as 'La Purísima' and observed throughout the country, this lively celebration of Nicaragua's patron saint is the occasion for the *La Gritería* (a shouting ritual that honors the Virgin Mary), enjoyed here with unusual vigor.

🛏 Sleeping

León probably packs in more hotels and hostels per square meter than any other place in the country – it's hard to imagine them all filling up, although it may happen around the Christmas or Easter high season. Still, you'll have better selection if you plan ahead.

Hostal Las Vacaciones   GUESTHOUSE $
(📱 8552-1568; Iglesia La Recolección, 200m E; s/d US$20/25; 🛜) This popular guesthouse is perfectly located and affordably priced, offering hostel-style accommodations and

comfortable private rooms. Amenities include a shared kitchen, bicycle rental and leafy terrace space.

Lazybones Hostel
HOSTEL $

(☎ 2311-3472; www.lazyboneshostelnicaragua.com; 2a Av NO, Parque Rubén Darío, 2½c N; dm US$8, r without/with bathroom US$20/30; P @ ⚡ ☎) This quiet, less party-oriented spot has trim grounds, excellent rooms and dorms, and a laid-back atmosphere. The age-old patio and sitting areas are every bit as lovely as those in some midrange hotels, and the bar, good-sized pool and yummy breakfasts make this a good deal.

Tortuga Booluda
HOSTEL $

(☎ 2311-4653; www.tortugabooluda.com; 1a Calle SO, Catedral, 4½c O; dm/r US$8/24; @ ⚡) More small hotel than hostel, the 'Lazy Turtle' does, however, offer all the hostel amenities, namely a great kitchen, book exchange, free coffee, pool table, some good chill-out areas and a sociable atmosphere. Rooms are simple but stylish, and dorms are spacious enough. Note that you can't reserve dorm beds – they're first-come, first-served.

Vía Vía
HOSTEL $

(☎ 2311-6142; www.viaviacafe.com; del Banco Pro-Credit, ½c S; dm/s/d US$7/19/29; ⚡) The Vía Vía chain of hostels, which stretches from Kathmandu to Buenos Aires, consistently comes up with the goods. This is no exception, offering beautiful, colonial-style rooms with great bathrooms, and spacious six-bed dorms with their own bathrooms. The patio area is lush and there's an atmospheric cafe-bar area out front.

Hotel Real
HOTEL $$

(☎ 2311-2606; www.hotelrealdeleon.net; 2a Calle NE, Iglesia de La Recolección, 1½c E; d US$55; ❄ ⚡) The 'Royal Hotel' has a quaint front sitting area and an old-style *casona* (historic mansion) feel, but with relatively modern rooms bedecked with flat-screen TVs and firm beds. Rooms are big and comfortable, and the rooftop terrace has excellent views of steeple tops and the volcanoes beyond.

Casona Colonial
HISTORIC HOTEL $$

(☎ 2311-3178; www.casonacolonialguest.com; 4a Calle NE, Parque San Juan, ½c O; s/d from US$20/25; ⊝ ❄ ⚡) With more character than many in this price range, the medium-sized rooms here are long on colonial atmosphere without all the costly little extras. Beds are big, with lavish bedheads, and the occasional chip in the paintwork or tear in the wallpaper adds to (rather than detracts from) the charm.

Bigfoot Hostel
HOSTEL $$

(☎ 2315-3863; www.bigfoothostelleon.com; del Banco Procredit, ½c S; dm/d from US$8/26; ❄ ⚡ ☎) With kitchen access, a miniature swimming pool and freshly made mojitos on offer, it wouldn't really matter what the rooms were like, but they're a good deal. There's a good travelers' vibe – staff swear the party shuts down at 10pm – and a sweet little cafe-bar out front.

Hotel El Sueño de Meme
HOTEL $$

(☎ 2311-5462; www.hotelmeme.com; de Museo Archivo Rubén Darío, 350m N; s/d with fan US$19/28, with air-con US$30/35; ❄ ⚡) With its pastel color scheme and cutesy decorations, this one steps firmly outside the quaint colonial box. Rooms are spacious and comfortable, if a little soulless. It's a bit removed from the action in the city center.

Paz de Luna Bed & Breakfast
B&B $$$

(☎ 2311-2581; www.pazdelunabb.com; Iglesia La Recolección, 1½c N; d US$80, s/d with shared bathroom US$29/45) Centrally located, with rooms laid out around a pretty courtyard, popular Paz de Luna has old-fashioned charm — and, thoughtfully, a range of options to suit many budgets. Reserve a spacious room with its own patio, or save your cash and book a smaller room with a shared bathroom. The owners also run the excellent cafe at the entrance.

Hotel Azul
BOUTIQUE HOTEL $$$

(☎ 2315-4519; www.hotelazulleon.com; catedral, 2½c N; s/d US$65/71; ⚡ ☎) Set in a typical colonial house but decorated with a minimalist twist, petite and slightly upscale Hotel Azul has a courtyard swimming pool – beautifully illuminated at night – and a small patio with a nifty daybed that's suspended, hammock-style, from the ceiling. Guest rooms are a little tight, but the place is comfortable.

Hotel El Convento
HISTORIC HOTEL $$$

(☎ 2311-7053; www.elconventonicaragua.com; Iglesia de San Francisco, 20m N; s/d US$95/140; P ❄ ⚡) There's atmosphere galore at this historic hotel on the grounds of one of the city's most notable convents and churches. The centerpiece garden is impressive and you're surrounded by precious artwork.

Guest rooms, with exposed brick walls, are comparatively simple, but comfortable.

Hotel Austria
HOTEL **$$$**
(☏ 2311-1206; www.hotelaustria.com.ni; Catedral, 1c S; d US$85; ❈ ☎) Tucked away on a side street just south of the cathedral, this well-run hotel has somewhat dark rooms set around a leafy central courtyard with a stone fountain. Several good breakfast options are included in the room rate.

Hotel La Perla
HISTORIC HOTEL **$$$**
(☏ 2311-3125; www.laperlaleon.com; 1a Av NO, Iglesia de La Merced, 1½c N; d US$160; P ❈ ☎ ☒) A pearl indeed. Set in one of León's most impressive mansions, the Perla has everything you would expect for the price, done with exquisite taste in a great location. There's a classy onsite restaurant and bar, stately rooms with hardwood furnishings and a decent-sized swimming pool.

Posada Doña Blanca
B&B **$$$**
(☏ 2311-2521; www.posadadonablanca.com; 1a Av NO, Iglesia de La Merced, 1c N; d from US$60; P ❈ @) In a modern Nicaraguan family's home, this downtown oasis is all cool, open spaces with colonial flourishes. Rooms are comfortable, and the family is friendly; the central courtyard is a lovely place to relax on a hot afternoon.

✗ Eating

The best place to eat on the cheap or buy fresh veggies is the Mercado Central, with several inexpensive eateries serving *comidas corrientes* (set meals). After hours, two of the best *fritangas* (grills) in town set up right outside, on the street behind the cathedral, where you can enjoy a huge meal for around US$2. La Unión Supermercado (p149) is a big supermarket option for self-caterers, though La Colonia (p149) is more upscale.

★ Pan y Paz
CAFE **$**
(☏ 8631-2760; www.panypaz.com; esquina de los bancos, 1½c E; mains US$3-6; ◷ 7am-9pm Mon-Sat; ☎) ✔ Run by a European couple, this fabulous French bakery specializes in homemade breads. Grab a table on the breezy interior courtyard and choose from a menu of freshly baked pastries and gourmet salads and sandwiches. Later in the day, try the cheese plate; they even have Argentine wines by the glass. An added bonus: the prices are more than fair.

Paz de Luna Café
CAFE **$**
(☏ 2311-2581; www.pazdelunabb.com; Iglesia La Recolección, 1½c N; mains US$3-6) At this sleek, hipster-friendly coffee shop – think black-and-white tiled floors, a gilded chandelier, fruit crates repurposed as furniture – a wall-sized chalkboard menu spells out the long menu of coffee drinks, breakfasts (both traditionally Nicaraguan and otherwise), crêpes, panini, omelettes, salads and pastas.

Comedor Lucia
NICARAGUAN **$**
(2a Av NE, Bigfoot Hostel, 10m N; mains US$2-4; ◷ 7am-3pm Mon-Sat) In 'Backpacker Alley,' this no-frills Nica joint gets a predictable mix of locals and travelers.

Mercado Central
MARKET **$**
(Parque Central, 2c E; ◷ 6am-5pm) León's central market is surrounded by simple *comedores* (eateries) and food stands.

Supermercado La Colonia
SUPERMARKET **$**
(www.lacolonia.com.ni; La Casa de Cultura, 2c O; ◷ 9am-9pm) A good supermarket for stocking up on supplies; there's also a small *cafetería* offering prepared foods, and a juice bar.

La Unión Supermercado
SUPERMARKET **$**
(1a Calle NE; ◷ 8am-10pm Mon-Sat, to 8pm Sun) La Unión is the largest supermarket in town.

Café La Nicaragüita
INTERNATIONAL **$$**
(Iglesia La Merced, 2c N, ½c O; mains US$4-8; ◷ noon-9pm Thu-Tue) This friendly little restaurant uses fresh and local produce to make a solid range of menu items: sandwiches, salads, burgers, pastas, steaks and fajitas, to name a few, plus a few Nicaraguan small plates (like *tostones*, or fried plantain slices) for good measure. Also on the chalkboard: fresh fruit smoothies and icy rum-based cocktails, from mojitos to daiquiris (US$2).

Taquezal
NICARAGUAN **$$**
(1a Calle SO, Parque Central, ½c O; dishes US$4-7; ◷ 4pm-late) With a grand, high-ceilinged dining room kept cool by a battalion of ceiling fans, this is one of León's most atmospheric eating spots. The food is good and there's a cozy, candlelit rear patio.

CocinArte
VEGETARIAN **$$**
(☏ 8854-6928; www.cocinarterestaurant.com; 4a Calle SO, frente El Laborío; mains US$4-7; ◷ noon-10pm Wed-Mon; ☎) León's vegetarian hot spot. This colorful eatery offers meat-free

versions of dishes from around the world in the elegant but relaxed surrounds of an old colonial house. There are a few meat dishes (cooked in separate pans and served with separate cutlery) to keep the carnivores happy, and a leafy patio; the most popular tables are on the front porch.

El Mediterraneo MEDITERRANEAN **$$**
(✏ 2311-0756; 2a Av NO, Parque Rubén Darío, 2½c N; dishes US$6-13; ⊘6pm-late) Date night? Check out one of the longer-running dining institutions in town. Some say it's not as good as it used to be, but the decor is gorgeous, and carefully prepared seafood, pasta, meats and curries are reliable. There's also a wine list featuring Argentinean and Chilean wines.

El Sesteo NICARAGUAN **$$**
(Calle Central Rubén Darío, frente Parque Central; mains US$5-10; ⊘11am-10pm) You can't beat the location of this landmark cafe, positioned right on the plaza with spectacular people-watching and views of the cathedral. The food is hit-or-miss, but you won't go wrong with a fresh fruit smoothie, a cappuccino or a cold beer.

Al Carbón STEAK **$$$**
(✏ 2311-4761; Iglesia La Merced, 25m O; mains US$5-15; ⊘7am-11pm) León's best steakhouse has a long menu – there's great grilled fish and chicken, too – and a sumptuous patio dining area inside a well-preserved *casona*.

🍷 Drinking & Nightlife

León's university students fuel the party. There are plenty of other places to get your drink on – 1a Calle west of the park is a particularly good area to go bar-hopping. Many hostels have lively bars that attract both travelers and locals.

There are some discos just outside of town on the bypass road, but also a few good dance floors right in the center of town.

Olla Quemada BAR
(Colegio La Salle, 150m O) This hot spot features a line-up of live music, indie films, Latin dance nights and a good mix of locals and travelers all week.

Solera Bar BAR
(2a Av SO, frente Teatro; ⊘5pm-midnight Mon-Sat) Attracting a slightly older crowd, this is a great place to go for a few drinks if you actually want to hear what the other person

is saying. Live music on Tuesday and some Thursdays.

Bohemios Bar-Disco CLUB
(1a Av NO, Parque Central, ½c N; ⊘9pm-3:30am Wed-Sat) In the unsigned orange building in front of the basketball court, this is your classic Latin disco – plenty of rum, reggaetón and *bacchata* (romantic Dominican dance music).

⭐ Entertainment

La Casa de Cultura (p146) often has folk music and other events.

Teatro Municipal
José de la Cruz Mena PERFORMING ARTS
(www.teatrojcmena-nicaragua.com; 2a Av SO, Parque Central, 1c O, 1c S; ⊘hours vary) Check the board in front of this attractive 1885 theater to see what's on here and around town during your visit. It's been impressively restored, and for less than US$3 you may be able to catch anything from Salvadoran rock groups to art films to the national ballet on the very accessible stage. There's also an online schedule.

Alianza Francesa PERFORMING ARTS
(✏ 2311-0126; www.alianzafrancesa.org.ni; 1a Av NE, Iglesia de la Recolección, 1½c N; ⊘8am-noon & 2-5pm Mon-Fri) Often screens art-house movies in French and Spanish and sponsors concerts. Drop in for its monthly program.

Plaza Siglo Nuevo CINEMA
(www.psiglonuevo.com; 1a Calle NE, La Unión, 20m E; tickets US$3) León's cinema shows many big-budget American films.

🛍 Shopping

Mercado San Juan MARKET
A workaday marketplace located on the northeast edge of León's downtown.

ℹ Orientation

León actually has a system of clearly signed and logically numbered *calles* (streets) and *avenidas* (avenues), allowing anyone to pinpoint any address. Unfortunately, no one actually uses it, preferring the old reliable '2½ blocks east of the Shell station' method instead.

Just for kicks, this is how it works: Av Central and Calle Central Rubén Darío intersect at the northeast corner of the Parque Central (central park), forming the city's northeast, northwest, southeast and southwest quadrants. Calles running parallel to Rubén Darío are numbered NE (Calle 1 NE, Calle 2 NE) north of the cathedral, SE to the south. Av 1 SO (*suroeste;* southwest), one block from Av Central, forms the park's western boundary, paralleling Av 2 SO and so on.

Calle Central Rubén Darío is the city's backbone, and runs east from the cathedral to striking Iglesia El Calvario, and west almost 1km to Barrio Subtiaba, continuing another 20km to the Pacific. The majority of tourist services are within a few blocks of the cathedral, with another cluster of museums and churches in Barrio Subtiaba.

ℹ Information

EMERGENCY

Ambulance (Cruz Roja; ☏ 2311-2627)
Fire (☏ 2311-2323)
Police (☏ 2311-3137)

INTERNET ACCESS

Internet cafes are all over town. Nearly every hotel has wi-fi.

LAUNDRY

Clean Express Lavandería (cnr Av Central & 4a Calle NE; ☺7am-7pm) DIY machine wash (US$2) and dry (US$1.25 per 20 minutes) your clothes, or pay a little extra to have it done for you.

MEDICAL SERVICES

Hospital San Vicente (☏ 2311-6990) Out past the main bus terminal, the region's largest hospital is a 1918 neoclassical beauty that attracts architecture buffs as well as sick tourists.

MONEY

Several banks have ATMs that accept Visa/Plus debit cards.

BAC (1a Calle NE, La Unión, 10m E)
BanPro (Bigfoot Hostel, 20m N) ATM is open 24 hours and accepts Visa and MasterCard.
Western Union (1 Calle NE) International cash transfers.

TELEPHONE

Claro (cnr Parque Central & Calle Central Rubén Darío) Sells cell-phone SIM cards.

TOURIST INFORMATION

Check the hostels for information first, then head to the tour agencies. The tourist info offices should be your last line of defense.

Intur (☏ 2311-3382; www.intur.gob.ni; 2a Av NO, Parque Rubén Darío, 1½c N) Helpful (if they're not too busy) staff have lots of flyers and a reasonable city map. For really tricky questions, the hostels are often better informed.

Marena (Ministry of the Environment & Natural Resources; ☏ 2311-3776; www.marena.gob.

ni; frente Shell station; ☺10am-6pm Mon-Fri) Inconveniently located across from the Shell station at the southern entrance to the León bypass road, it administers three volcanic national reserves – Telica-Rota, Pilas-El Hoyo and Momotombo – and nonvolcanic Isla Juan Venado. It offers general information. Your best bet is going directly to the Isla Juan Venado ranger station in Las Peñitas or with a private tour.

Oficina de Información Turistica León (☏ 2311-3528; Av Central, Parque Central, 25m N; ☺ 8:30am-noon & 2-6pm Mon-Fri, 9am-5pm Sat & Sun) A good source for information.

ℹ Getting There & Away

BUS

International Buses

There are several international-bus agencies running through Nicaragua, but the main terminal and booking centers are in Managua. Buses headed south stop first in Managua, with an often lengthy wait between connections – it's better to make your own way there and take the bus from Managua.

Buy bus tickets to Costa Rica and Honduras online, or at **Beni Tours** (☏ 2315-2349; ☺ 9am-6pm Mon-Fri). If you're heading north for Guatemala or El Salvador, area travel agencies can help you book tickets.

Shuttle Buses

Shuttle services are a good (and secure) way to go between León and various key destinations. Many tour operators in town offer trips, most leaving around 8:30am to 9:30am, in air-conditioned vans. Be sure to book ahead. If you're headed to less popular destinations, be aware that most shuttles don't leave without at least four passengers.

Tierra Tour (☏ 2315-4278; www.tierratour. com; 1a Av NO, Iglesia de La Merced, 1½c N) and **Nica Time** (☏ 8404-9638; agencianicatime@gmail.com) go to Granada, Managua and San Juan del Sur. **Gekko Explorer** (☏ 001-305-560-5354; www.gekkotrailsexplorer.com; Procredit Bank, 25m S) goes to Chinandega, plus international destinations like Antigua, Guatemala.

If you're headed to El Salvador, try Gekko Explorer or Tierra Tour. The latter offers a package combining the boat ride from Potosí, Nicaragua to La Union, El Salvador with a night at a beachfront hostel (US$80 per person).

Buses to Beaches

Buses to Poneloya and Las Peñitas (US$0.50, 40 minutes) depart hourly, 6am to 6pm, from El Mercadito in Subtiaba. Day-trippers take note: the last bus returns around 6pm, too.

Another option: Bigfoot Hostel (p148) runs a daily shuttle to Bigfoot Beach Hostel (p153) in Las Peñitas.

BOAT

A convenient (and beautiful) way to get to El Salvador is the shuttle and boat trip organized by **Ruta del Golfo** (☑ 2315-4099; www.ruta-delgolfo.com; Vapues, costado norte, Iglesia El Laborío; border crossing to El Salvador from US$99; ⏱ 9am-6pm); advance booking required. The trip involves a pickup in León and 4WD transfer to Potosí via Chinandega, then a boat trip across the Gulf of Fonseca to La Unión. Travel time is about five hours, with two to three departures weekly, but factor in another couple of hours for the border crossing itself. Tierra Tour (p151) also handles the trip.

CAR & MOTORCYCLE

Petrol Station (Parque Central, 1c E)

❶ Getting Around

The city is strollable, but big enough that you may want to take taxis, particularly at night.

The one-way streets and (relative) lack of traffic make León a good bicycling city. You can rent bikes for around US$5 to US$7 per day from hostels.

Pacific Beaches Near León

The most accessible beaches from León are Poneloya and Las Peñitas, both an easy 20-minute bus ride from Mercadito Subtiaba in León. The road splits at the sea: go right for Poneloya proper, left for more developed Las Peñitas and Reserva Natural Isla Juan Venado.

Several wilder, less accessible beaches further south are a bit more difficult to reach, including Salinas Grandes, with regular bus service from León and its own access to Reserva Natural Isla Juan Venado. A group of three even less explored beaches can be reached from the fractured but passable Carretera Vieja to Managua: Puerto Sandino, El Velero and El Tránsito.

For the widest variety of sleeping options, head to Las Peñitas. There's also a famous hostel, Surfing Turtle Lodge (p153), off the coast of Poneloya. Many visitors also visit these beaches on day trips from León.

Las Peñitas has the highest concentration of restaurants and dining options, most of which are connected to hotels and hostels. It's also wise to bring snacks from nearby León.

NATIONAL BUS SERVICES FROM LEÓN

Most buses leave from León's chaotic **main bus terminal** (☑ 2311-3909; 6a Calle NE, Palí, 1½km E), which has a fun market area nearby (watch your wallet.) If you're heading south, you'll invariably pass through Managua.

DESTINATION	COST (US$)	DURATION (HR)	FREQUENCY (DAILY)
Chinandega (bus)	0.80-1	1½	4:30am-8pm, every 20min
Chinandega (microbus)	1.20	50min	4:30am-8pm, departs when full
Estelí	2.70	2½-3	5:20am-3:30pm, 4 daily
Granada (microbus)	3	2-3	hourly
La Paz Centro	0.75	40min	every 45min
Managua (microbus)	2.75	1¼	4:30am-7pm, departs when full
Managua (Carr Nueva, via La Paz Centro) expreso	1.80	1¼	5am-4pm, almost hourly
Managua (Carr Vieja, via Puerto Sandino) ordinario	1.50	1¾	5am-6:30pm, every 20min
Masaya	2.90	2½	hourly
Matagalpa	3	2½	4:30am-2:45pm, 3 daily
Nagarote	1	1	hourly
Rota (Cerro Negro)	0.75	2¼	5:50am-3:20pm, 3 daily
Salinas Grandes	0.80	2	5:15am-4pm, 4 daily

ℹ️ Getting There & Away

There's regular bus service between León and the beaches; hostels and surf outfitters in the city also run private shuttles that are convenient for travelers.

Poneloya

Although this beach has the famous name – it's highly praised in the *Viva León Jodido* theme song – it's considerably less suited to tourists than its sister beach, Las Peñitas. For many travelers, it's simply the point of departure to the beautiful island of Isla Los Brasiles.

🛏️ Sleeping & Eating

There are a few places to sleep in Poneloya, but by far the most memorable is Surfing Turtle Lodge, across the water on the island of Isla Los Brasiles. If you're looking to stay on the mainland, there's a much better range of options in nearby Las Peñitas.

There are a few casual eateries on or near the beach, though you'll find more places to eat up the coast in Las Peñitas. If you're making the trip to Isla Los Brasiles, note that no off-site food or drink is allowed at Surfing Turtle Lodge (and the restaurant can be hit or miss).

⭐ **Surfing Turtle Lodge**   LODGE **$$**
(☑ 8640-0644; www.surfingturtlelodge.com; Isla Los Brasiles, Poneloya; dm US$10-12, r US$35-45, cabin US$60; 🖤) 🖉 Getting to this Utopian-like island paradise is half the fun. From Chepe's Bar in Poneloya, you catch a small boat (US$1) to the 7-km-long island known as Isla Los Brasiles, then walk 15 minutes (or get a lift in a horse-drawn carriage, on request) to this beachfront hideout. There's good surf right out front, and bonfires at night.

The 2nd-story dorm is one of the coolest spots in all of Central America with a giant view to the ocean. Camping in pre-set-up tents will save a few bucks, or you can go for it with a cabin all of your own. Electricity starts here at 6pm, and there's an onsite restaurant and turtle protection program.

ℹ️ Getting There & Away

Buses (US$0.50) run between Poneloya, Las Peñitas and León (not to the center, but to El Mercadito, a small market on the western edge of town in the neighborhood called Subtiaba)

roughly every 50 to 60 minutes between 4:30am and 6pm. Coming from León, the bus stops in Poneloya first, then goes up the coast to Las Peñitas.

If you're headed to Surfing Turtle Lodge, check the website for information about catching the daily shuttle (US$3 one-way) from León.

Las Peñitas

A wide, sandy stretch of beachfront paradise fronted by a fine collection of hotels and restaurants, Las Peñitas offers the easiest access to the turtles and mangroves of Reserva Natural Isla Juan Venado. There's also good, if not spectacular, surfing here, with smallish regular waves that are perfect for beginners. Several hotels and hostels offer tours into the reserve, plus surf lessons and board rentals.

👉 Tours

Barca de Oro   TOUR
(www.barcadeoro.com; bayfront, across from the bus stop, Las Peñitas) Barca de Oro is a hotel (dm/d US$7/27) and restaurant (7am-10pm) with bay views – but more importantly, for most travelers, it's one-stop shopping for tours and information about Reserva Natural Isla Juan Venado (p154). Stop in to ask about boat tours, bike rentals, nighttime turtle tours and fishing.

🛏️ Sleeping & Eating

Las Peñitas is expanding quickly. At the time of writing, several new hostels, guesthouses and dining options had recently opened. It's is a compact and easygoing place: you can walk everywhere easily.

All of the hotels listed have restaurants. It's also a good idea to bring your own snacks and drinks from León.

Bigfoot Beach Hostel   HOSTEL **$**
(☑ 8410-0409; www.bigfoothostellaspenitas.com; del la Policia, 250m S; dm US$5, d/tr with shared bathroom US$15/20, tents US$3; 🖤🖾) The beachfront sister of the popular Bigfoot Hostel (p148) in León, this youth-oriented spot has a swimming pool, a beach-volleyball court, a bar-restaurant with daily happy hour specials, even tent rental (US$3 per person). The hostel offers surf lessons in conjunction with Get Up Stand Up (p144) in León, and runs a convenient daily shuttle to and from town.

Simple Beach House   GUESTHOUSE **$$**
(☑7658-2009; Las Peñitas; d with ocean view US$53; ☎) The name says it all, almost. Simple Beach House has just three rooms, and while they're indeed simple, the place is so comfortable – and the whole operation so smoothly run – that you'll likely feel more relaxed here than at a fancy resort. It's right on the beach and has a great restaurant.

Bomalu   GUESTHOUSE **$$**
(☑7532-5546; www.bomalunicaragua.com; cruce Peñitas–Poneloya, 900m S; d without bathroom US$20, d with air-con US$38; ☎⊠) This mellow beachhouse-style spot, located right on the sand, has seven affordable guest rooms (most which share a few bathrooms). Guests rave about the outdoor lounge space and the excellent restaurant, which is open to the public and specializes in seafood. The hotel offers transportation to León for US$4 per person.

Lazy Turtle   HOTEL **$$**
(☑8546-7403; www.thelazyturtlehotel.com; d/ste US$35/50) Facing the calm waters of the tidal bay, this relaxed *hotelito* (little hotel) is a hit with travelers. Simple but relatively modern rooms and suites come with drinking water – a nice touch – and the onsite restaurant is well known for its Mexican-inspired cuisine and burgers (including a good veggie burger).

Hotelito Oasis   HOSTEL **$$**
(☑8839-5344; www.oasislaspenitas.com; Las Peñitas; dm/r/bungalow US$8/25/29; ☎) A long-time surfer favorite, the Oasis definitely has that lazy backpacker vibe, helped along by a relaxed beachfront location. Rooms are simple; luckily, they catch some ocean breezes at night. There's an onsite bar and restaurant with a two-for-one happy hour each evening.

Dulce Mareas   PIZZA **$$**
(mains US$3-8; ⊙8am-9pm Wed-Sun) It's known for pizzas baked in a clay brick oven, but this sweet beachfront eatery also does breakfast and lunch – plus coffee, desserts and cold cocktails, all with a view of the water. You can also rent out rooms (d US$40).

❶ Information

Ranger Station (☑in León 2311-3776; Las Peñitas; US$2.50-4)

❶ Getting There & Away

Buses (US$0.50) run between Poneloya, Las Peñitas, and León (not to the center, but to El Mercadito, a small market on the western edge of town in Subtiaba) roughly every 50 to 60 minutes between 4:30am and 6pm. Coming from León, the bus swings through Poneloya first, then heads north to Las Peñitas. The last stop, where the bus turns around and heads back to León, is at the parking lot outside Barca de Oro (p153), but you can also pick it up at a bus stop outside the hotel Playa Roca.

Another option is the daily shuttle between Bigfoot Hostel (p148) in León and Bigfoot Beach Hostel in Las Peñitas. Stop into the hostel in León for the latest prices and availability.

In a pinch, you can also hire a taxi from León for about US$15 one-way.

Reserva Natural Isla Juan Venado

This 18km-long, sandy barrier island (in some places only 300m wide) has swimming holes and lots of wildlife, including nesting turtles and mosquitoes galore. On one side of the uninhabited island (admission US$4.50) you'll find long, wild, sandy beaches facing the Pacific, on the other, red and black mangroves reflected in emerald lagoons.

During the turtle egg-laying season, which runs July through January and peaks in September and October, thousands of olive ridleys, careys and leatherbacks lay their eggs in El Vivero, close to the Las Peñitas entrance. For the best wildlife-watching opportunities, it's best to go at low tide, or at dawn or sunset if you're especially interested in birds. If it's turtles you're here to see, try a nighttime turtle tour (US$25 per person, June to December).

Several hotels and lodges in and around town offer guided boat tours (US$55 for up to four people) of the reserve. You can also go to the reserve yourself if you can negotiate a ride with a local fisher. Another option is to hire a local guide (US$10) and rent a kayak (US$12 per person) – ask at the Las Peñitas ranger station or stop into the hotel-restaurant-tour outfitter Barca de Oro (p153).

Puerto Sandino

This is a hard-working port town with 'Hawaii-sized waves.' There's reliable and rocky-bottomed Poneloya, which is not actually in Poneloya (look for it at Playa Diamante); the most photogenic break is at the mouth of the port but isn't always working. The best wave around, sometimes called Miramar (although it's not actually in Miramar), is about 6km south of Puerto Sandino. At low tide, there's a reliable reef break just south.

🛏 Sleeping & Eating

There aren't many services around here, except for those offered at hotels, so it's smart to bring your own snacks and any supplies you'll need from León.

La Barra Surf Camp LODGE $$$
(✒ in US 1-310-424-3530; www.labarrasurfcamp.com; Puerto Sandino; 5-night package from US$950; 🌐 ☒) This popular and professionally run beachfront surf camp, managed by AST Adventures in California, isn't the kind of place you drop into for a couple of nights – travelers generally book all-inclusive packages that include everything from airport transportation to all meals, bikes, city tours of León etc. There's a large yoga deck and a swimming pool.

Miramar Surfcamp LODGE $$$
(✒ 8945-1785; www.miramarsurfcamp.com; s/d US$50/70, s/d incl meals from US$120/160; 🌐 ☒) For surfers (including beginners), the location of this surf camp – and the friendly staff – are huge draws. But the rooms and meals are basic. Check the website for the full range of packages and offers.

Restaurante Chango NICARAGUAN $$
(✒ 2312-2297; Telcor, 100m E; mains US$4-12; ◷ 11:30am-late) This basic Nicaraguan eatery serves fresh fish, shrimp and – if you're lucky – *rondon*, a slow-cooked seafood stew.

❶ Getting There & Away

Most travelers drive here or arrange transportation through a surf camp. But local buses also leave town for León (US$0.85, 30 to 40 minutes) regularly; confirm departure times with your hotel.

El Tránsito

This little fishing village on the coast between León and Managua sits on a near-perfect crescent bay. The sand is blacker here, due to volcanic residue. The beach could use a good clean-up and there's a strong undertow, but to the south, near the lava flows, there are protected swimming holes that are especially fun for kids.

🛏 Sleeping & Eating

There are a few basic beachfront restaurants here, but it's also a good idea to bring your own snacks.

Solid Surf & Adventure HOTEL $$$
(✒ 5770-6419; www.solidsurfadventure.com; baseball stadium, 100m O, El Tránsito; 7 days all-inclusive US$1095; 🌐) Solid Surf runs all-inclusive surf and yoga camps, some geared to beginners. The rooms are pretty basic, but there's a cool beachfront patio for hanging out and you're miles away from the crowded waves of the southern beaches. Depending on occupancy, dorms and rooms may also be available by the night – contact the owners for more information.

❶ Getting There & Away

Many travelers drive themselves here. Buses to Managua (US$1.20, 1½ hours) leave a few times daily – all at inconvenient early morning hours, at the time of writing – and make the trip back from Managua's Mercado Oriental a few times each afternoon.

Volcanoes Near León

The Maribios chain is the epicenter of one of the most active volcanic regions on earth. The easiest and safest way to visit the volcanoes is on a guided hike or excursion, arranged by many outfitters in León and elsewhere.

If you do decide to go to the volcanoes alone, consult park management first. It's split between two Marena (Ministry of the Environment & Natural Resources) offices: Marena León (p151) manages Reserva Natural Volcán Momotombo, Reserva Natural Telica-Rota and Reserva Natural Pilas-El Hoyo, which includes Cerro Negro; Marena Chinandega (p160) keeps tabs on Reserva Natural San Cristóbal-La Casita and Reserva Natural Volcán Cosigüina.

◎ Sights

Reserva Natural
Volcán Momotombo VOLCANO
(✒ in León 2311-3776; www.marena.gob.ni) The perfect cone of Volcán Momotombo, destroyer of León Viejo and inspiration for its own Rubén Darío poem, rises red and black 1280m above Lago de Managua. It is a symbol of Nicaragua, the country's most beautiful threat, and has furnished at its base itself in miniature – the island of Isla

Momotombito (389m), sometimes called 'The Child.' Most people come to climb Momotombo, a serious eight-hour excursion. It's definitely best to go with a guided tour.

There are several other structures worth seeing in the reserve, including the 4km-diameter, 200m-deep **Caldera Monte Galán**, tiled with five little lagoons (alligators included) that reflect the theoretically extinct **Cerro Montoso** (500m), but you'd need to arrange a custom tour to see them.

Isla Momotombito is accessible from Puerto Momotombo, just around the corner from the ruins of León Viejo, and Mateare, both on the shores of Lago de Managua. The basaltic cone has long been a ceremonial site, and a few petroglyphs and statues are still visible on it. If you're coming from Puerto Momotombo, ask about private boat transportation. Boat operators hang around the handful of lakeshore restaurants, which all serve beer and traditional Nicaraguan food.

Reserva Natural Pilas-El Hoyo   VOLCANO
([✉] in León 2311-3776; www.marena.gob.ni) Most people come to this reserve to see the volcano **Cerro Negro** (726m and growing), one of the youngest volcanoes in the world. It first erupted from a quiet cornfield in 1850, and its pitch-black, loose-gravel cone has been growing in spurts ever since. Other peaks worth seeing include the dormant **Volcán Pilas** (1001m), which last had gas in 1954; and **El Hoyo** (1088m), the park's second-most active peak, which is basically a collapsed crater with fumaroles.

Almost every guide in León offers a guided hike to the top of El Hoyo, a shadeless, two- to three-hour climb into the eye-watering fumes of the yellow-streaked crater. Then your outfitter will offer a faster way down (what's known as volcano surfing). Afterward, relax in the deliciously cool **Laguna de Asososca**, a jungle-wrapped crater lake that's poorly signed and on private property (and thus difficult to visit on your own). If you book a tour climbing Cerro Negro (or are visiting León Viejo, nearby), definitely try to get this as an add-on.

**Reserva Natural
San Cristóbal-La Casita**   VOLCANO
([✉] in Chinandega 2344-2443; www.marena.gob.ni) Eye-catching **Volcán San Cristóbal** (1745m), the tallest volcano in Nicaragua, streams gray smoke from its smooth cone. Achieving the summit of this beauty is a serious hike: six to eight hours up, three hours down. A guide is highly recommended, as access is difficult and dangerous and requires crossing private property. The volcano is very active, with two large eruptions at the end of 2012.

There are several other volcanic structures worth seeing here, including **El Chonco** (715m), an inactive volcanic plug contiguous with San Cristóbal, and nearby **Moyotepe**, a small crater lake at 917m accessible from the Chinandega–Somotillo road.

Reserva Natural Telica-Rota   VOLCANO
([✉] in León 2311-3776; www.marena.gob.ni) This very active, 90.52-sq-km complex peaks at **Volcán Telica** (1061m), the twin craters of which are a mere 30km north of León. Also called the 'Volcano of León,' Telica is active in four- to five-year cycles; the last really big eruption was in 1765. Most eruptions these days involve gases and a few pyroclastic belches. There are several 'extinct' cones around the base, including **Cerro Agüero** (744m), **Loma Los Portillos** (721m) and **Volcán Rota** (832m), which has constant fumaroles.

There are big plans for this park, which is considered a potential ecotourism gold mine due to its easy access from San Jacinto.

🏃 Activities

This area is ground zero for **volcano boarding** – also called volcano surfing – an increasingly popular (and possibly dangerous) adventure sport. Intrepid travelers and locals used to coast down the side of active volcanoes on surfboards, old mattresses, even cardboard boxes. But now there are professional outfitters, custom-made boards and expert boarders hurtling downhill at break-neck speeds. A half-day excursion generally includes transportation, equipment and instruction for around US$35 a person – try Tierra Tour (p146) in León.

🛏 Sleeping & Eating

Many travelers camp on or around the volcanoes as part of organized excursions from León, or else they sleep in León and visit the volcanoes on day trips.

Bring your own water and food into the natural reserves. If you're on an organized trek, it may be provided for you – but it's best to be prepared with some of your own snacks, as there aren't many services once you leave León.

ⓘ Getting There & Away

Drive yourself or arrange transportation with one of the many outfitters in León that offer organized excursions into the park.

San Jacinto

The only town of any size on this stretch of the Ring of Fire, San Jacinto, located 20km northeast of León, is base camp for climbs up **Volcán Telica** (1061m; six to eight hours), **Volcán Rota** (832m; three to five hours) – which has great views of Telica – and **Volcán Santa Clara** (834m; three to five hours).

⊙ Sights

San Jacinto Hot Springs   SPRING
(San Jacinto; admission US$2; ⊙7am-5pm) Sometimes referred to as 'mud fields,' this series of hot springs and mud holes – likely connected to the Telica volcano – is an interesting sight to wander around as boiling hot mud spurts up from the steaming holes. There are no marked trails, so accept the services of the local child **guides** (US$1) who will invariably approach you – they know their way around You'll want to hire one of the local child guides (US$1) to show you around, as there are no marked trails. Organized tours (usually operated out of León) typically stop here.

⏨ Sleeping

San Jacinto is the base for many volcano climbs, but as it's close to León, most travelers sleep in the city.

ⓘ Getting There & Away

Many travelers come here on organized tours with included transportation. Buses go to and from León (US$0.80, 40 minutes) roughly every half-hour between 5am and 5pm.

El Sauce

Once a bustling and important link on the national railway, today scenic El Sauce is just a sleepy mountain town cut straight from an Old West movie. The town bursts into life on the third Sunday in January, when pilgrims from all over Nicaragua, Guatemala and beyond make their way here to pay their respects to **El Señor de Esquipulas** (The Black Christ).

The image, to which all manner of miracles has been attributed, arrived in El Sauce in 1723 from Esquipulas, Guatemala, and refused to move another centimeter upon arriving at this lovely spot. The beautiful, if not flashy, 1828 **Templo de El Sauce** was declared a national sanctuary in 1984, but burned down in 1999. The Black Christ, however, was saved, and all of El Sauce pitched in to rebuild the sanctuary.

✈ Activities

The gateway to the Cordillera Dariense, El Sauce is surrounded by cool green mountains strewn with waterfalls, and several **hiking trails** begin in town. Ask around for directions to the trailhead through the year-round green of the forest to **La Piedra de San Ramón**, which starts about 3km north of town.

⏨ Sleeping & Eating

There are simple Nicaraguan eateries and street-food stands scattered around the center of town.

Hotel Blanco   HOTEL **$**
(☑2319-2403; alcaldía, 1c S, 1c O; s/d with fan US$22/25; 🛜) The best rooms in town are found at this small and friendly hotel. Twelve rooms are set around a central courtyard; all have cable TV, wi-fi and private bathrooms.

ⓘ Getting There & Away

Many travelers pass through El Sauce on road trips in their own rental cars. Buses to León (US$2.75, 2½ hours, six daily) leave from El Sauce's market, downhill from the sanctuary.

La Paz Centro

The traditional Nicaraguan town of La Paz Centro is famous for the production of two things: *tejas* (sunset-colored half-pipe ceramic shingles, characteristic of Spanish colonial architecture) and *quesillos* (a taco-like snack featuring a grilled corn tortilla stuffed with cheese and topped with cream and onions). Most *tejas* are actually sold in Costa Rica, where wealthy homeowners have been buying them to top off their dream homes, but the *quesillo* remains very much a local attraction.

It was supposedly invented here, making the town a stop on many a foodie road trip, though the neighboring town of Nagarote claims the same ownership over the classic Nicaraguan street-food staple.

⌭ Sleeping

There aren't many options in town; most travelers stay in nearby León and visit on a day trip.

✖ Eating

Eating *quesillos* is practically the whole point of coming to La Paz Centro. There are several good places to try the local specialty in town.

Quesillos Guiligüiste　　　NICARAGUAN $
(4ta Av SE; quesillos US$1.50; ☉ hours vary) The original (and still the best, many say) *quesillo* spot in town is found right at the entrance to the city (conveniently close to the bus stop). It's usually open from 10am through to early evening but the hours can vary.

❶ Getting There & Away

Buses leave for León (US$1.20, 45 minutes, 6am to 6pm, hourly) and Managua (US$1.60, one hour, every 45 to 60 minutes). Buses drop off and pick up near the entrance of town.

Chinandega

Sultry Chinandega's never going to end up on anyone's Top 10 list. It isn't that the town's ugly (it's OK) or that there's nothing to do (there's some stuff) – it's because Chinandega is the gateway to some of the most breathtaking spots in the entire northwest. And by the time you get to the region's beaches and natural reserves, you're likely to forget about this little workaday town.

◉ Sights

Parroquia Santa Ana　　　CHURCH
(alcadía; ☉ hours vary) This is Chinandega's most important church, with a splendid Stations of the Cross, lots of gilt and some Russian Orthodox styling that earn this one 'Best Interior in Town.' A richer yellow with white trim, it stands watch over the festive Parque Central, crammed full of play equipment, canoodling teenagers and fast-food stands. There's sometimes ballet *folklórico* and live music in the central kiosk.

Iglesia San Antonio　　　CHURCH
(Parque Central, 2c S, 1c O; ☉ hours vary) This dramatic facade is painted pastel-yellow; inside, find delightful Easter egg–blue and yellow columns and arches.

NAGAROTE & LA PAZ CENTRO: THE QUESILLO CONTROVERSY

The towns of Nagarote and La Paz Centro don't receive much tourist traffic – there just ain't that much to see or do. Sure, **La Paz Centro** has a few monuments and a lovely 1600s adobe church, El Templo Parroquial Santiago, while **Nagarote** has its Mercado de Artesanía across from the bus terminal, fun swims in nearby Río Tamarindo, and a tranquil plaza and cultural center. But really, none of it's enough to hold your attention for very long.

But if you are passing through, you won't want to miss trying Nicaragua's most famous national dish, the *quesillo* (a thick, steaming corn tortilla topped with a pancake of mozzarella-like cheese, then loosely rolled into a cylinder and fitted into a special plastic bag). They cost just US$1 and normally include optional toppings like onion chutney (do it!) or sour cream (think twice!).

Two towns have a legitimate claim as the *cuña* (cradle) of *quesillo* culture: Nagarote, birthplace of innovator and originator Señora Socorro Munguía Madriz; and La Paz Centro, where she came up with the culinary triumph. In 1912, along with the Rueda sisters, she began selling *quesillos* at both the Nagarote and La Paz Centro train stations, further confusing the issue.

As *quesillos* proliferated across the country, this original crew opened what's now an almost pilgrimage-worthy destination, **Quesillos Guiligüiste** (p158; kay-*see*-yos wil-ee-*wee*-stay) – so popular that it has its own freelance car-parking personnel out front. This, of course, is in La Paz Centro. But, as Nagarote natives note, Doña Dalila Lara, another early *quesillo* adherent, moved to Nagarote in the 1970s, where she opened Quesillos Acacia – also pilgrimage worthy, especially if you're still hungry.

Chinandega

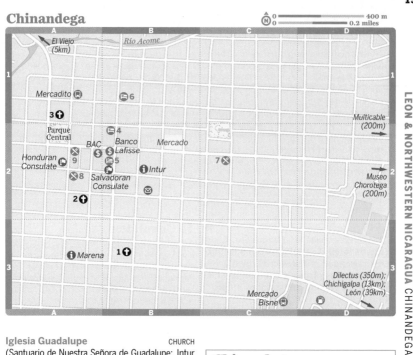

Iglesia Guadalupe
CHURCH

(Santuario de Nuestra Señora de Guadalupe; Intur 3½c S; ⊙hours vary) Chinandega has some seriously striking churches, including the 1878 Iglesia Guadalupe, which despite the radiant – and rather grandiose – colonial-style facade has a simple, precious wood interior with an exceptionally lovely Virgin.

Museo Chorotega
MUSEUM

(☑2341-4291; Multicable, 1c S, Reparto los Ángeles; US$4; ⊙8am-5pm Mon-Fri) Anyone with even a passing interest in archaeology should stop in here, one of the finest museums in the country. The collection focuses on pre-Columbian ceramics and is presented in a logical timeline, from the early inhabitants up until the arrival of the Spanish.

There are about 1500 pieces in the collection, of which about 400 are on display. Of particular interest is the small collection on burial rituals, where the guide will no doubt put forward the theory that the flesh of human sacrifices was sometimes eaten as a religious practice.

🛏 Sleeping

There are a few places to stay here, though you might want to move on – even Mana-

guans complain that Chinandega is hot. Consider paying extra for air-con.

Hotel Plaza Cosigüina
HOTEL **$$**

(☑2341-3636; www.hotelplazacosiguina.com; esquina de los bancos, ½c S; d US$52; P✳@☎) The rather hodgepodge blend of modern, motel-like styling with hip 1960s accents may not win any design awards, but the comfort factor is here – and the location is a winner.

OFF THE BEATEN TRACK

RESERVA NATURAL DELTA DEL ESTERO REAL

There's no tourist infrastructure at all for this enormous **reserve** (☑ Asociación Selva 8884-9156), about 20km – two hours by bus on this terrible road – north of Chinandega in the desperately poor town of Puerto Morazán. But this monumental river delta luxuri- ating along the Honduran border is beautiful, with alligators lounging alongside the lush, mangrove-lined shores, views to Volcán Cosigüina and natural lagoons all aflutter with migratory birds. Unfortunately, it is also threatened: its inaccessibility has emboldened poachers, loggers and dirty shrimping operations.

To visit, head out early for a day trip to Puerto Morazán; several buses leave daily from the Chinandega Mercadito (US$1, two hours), or else you can arrange a taxi ride. Fishing boats holding four, plus your Spanish-speaking guide, cost about US$25 for a four-hour tour of the reserve.

As there's no tourist infrastructure here, you'll have to sleep in Chinandega and bring your own food and water from town.

Hotel San José
HOTEL **$$**

(☑ 2341-2723; esquina de los bancos, 2½c N; s/d US$30/41; ❄️ 🛜) Heavy, dark-wood furniture and an overload of religious-themed deco- ration give this place a somewhat somber feel, but the rooms are spacious enough, with big TVs.

Hotel los Balcones de Chinandega
HOTEL **$$$**

(☑ 2341-8994; www.hotelbalconeschinandega. com; esquina de los bancos, 1c N; d US$52; 🅿️ ❄️ 🛜) This colonial-style hotel is one of the nicer places to stay around here. There are, in fact, balconies, but you may choose to spend your time on the tiny roof terrace instead.

✖ Eating

The best cheap eats set up at dusk in the Par- que Central, which is lined with hamburger stands. There are two great *fritangas* (grills) beside the basketball court just beyond.

Fritanga Las Tejitas
GRILL **$**

(mercado, 2c E; mains US$2-5) A local institu- tion, this *fritanga* gets packed breakfast, lunch and dinner – and mariachis could show up at any time to play some music. It's a solid buffet with a nationwide reputation.

Palí
SUPERMARKET **$**

(frente Parque Central; ⊗ 9am-8pm) A super- market stop for the basics.

La Parrillada
STEAK **$$**

(Palí, 1c S; set lunch US$2.50, mains US$4-8) This locals' favorite is part steakhouse, part piz- zeria, part *fritanga;* if you can't find some- thing you want to eat here, chances are you're not hungry.

❶ Orientation

Chinandega is on a logical Spanish grid, but note that the *alcaldía* (mayor's office) is actually five blocks east of the natural city center at Parroquia Santa Ana. Most of the development here is going on outside the historic city center, with new malls springing up along the highways. Churches keep sporadic hours.

❶ Information

BAC (Parque Central, 1c E, ½c S)
Banco Lafisse (Parque Central, 3c E)
Honduran Consulate (☑ 2341-8974; con- sulhn@cablenet.com.ni; Palí, 20m S; ⊗ 9am- 4pm Mon-Fri)
Intur (☑ 2341-1935; chinandega@intur.gob.ni; mercado, 1c O, ½c S) The local tourist office has a good collection of flyers and handy, information-packed scrapbooks.
Marena (Ministry of the Environment & Natural Resources; ☑ 2344-2443; www.marena.gob. ni; Iglesia Guadelupe, 1½c O; ⊗ 9am-4:30pm Mon-Fri) This office keeps tabs on Reserva Nat- ural San Cristóbal-La Casita, Reserva Natural Volcán Cosigüina and Reserva Natural Estero Padre Ramos, all with reasonable access; and Reserva Natural Delta del Estero Real, where you're on your own. Staff also keep an eye on Reserva Genetica Apacunaca (Apacunaca Genetic Resource Reserve).
Post Office (mercado, 2cE)
Salvadoran Consulate (☑ 2341-2049; esquina de los bancos, ½c S)

❶ Getting There & Away

BUS

Most travelers make their connections through Mercado Bisne, on the south side of the city (it's best to take a cab to and from here, as it's not within easy walking distance of downtown), though some buses leave from the smaller station known as Mercadito.

Bus Services from Mercadito

El Viejo (bus US$0.80, 20 minutes, 5am to 6pm, every 15 minutes, microbus US$0.60, 10 minutes, 5am to 6pm, departs when full)

Playa Jiquilillo & Reserva Natural Estero Padre Ramos (US$1.20, two hours, three to five per day)

Potosí (Reserva Natural Volcán Cosigüina) (US$1.50 to US$1.75, 3½ hours, three daily)

TAXI

Taxis also make the runs to El Viejo (US$3 to US$5) and Corinto (US$6 to US$8).

Around Chinandega

We'll be frank with you: while the larger region has plenty to offer, there's not a whole lot to see around Chinandega. But the region has a claim to fame: the town of Chichigalpa is home to the famous Flor de Caña rum factory, as well as Nicaragua's largest sugar refinery.

Just outside of town is El Viejo, an ancient indigenous capital; further afield, there's the Reserva Natural Delta del Estero Real, a remote birdwatcher's paradise, and wide open spaces on either side of the road leading to Somotillo, the last town on the border between Nicaragua and Honduras.

ⓘ Getting There & Away

There's frequent minibus service between Chinandega and Chichigalpa. If you're headed to El Viejo, take a bus from Chinandega to Potosí and ask the driver to drop you off at the *empalme* (junction).

Most travelers headed to the border of Honduras drive themselves or hire a driver or transportation service.

El Viejo

Just 5km from Chinandega is the ancient indigenous capital of Tezoatega, today called El Viejo, best-known for its Basílica de Nuestra Señora de la Inmaculada Concepción de la Virgen María.

◉ Sights

Basílica de Nuestra Señora de la Inmaculada Concepción de la Virgen María CHURCH
(Costado Este del Parque Central; ⊘ hours vary) This beautiful church is home to Nicaragua's patron saint and mistress of its biggest national religious event, **La Gritería**, when troupes of *festejeros* shout *¿Quién causa tanta alegría?* ('Who causes so much joy?') and receive the response, *¡La concepción de María!* ('The conception of Mary!').

Dedicated pilgrims show up a few days early for the **Lavada de la Plata** (Polishing of the Silver) on December 5 and 6. The work is meditative but fun, with mariachis serenading the faithful.

🛏 Sleeping & Eating

As with most of small-town Nicaragua, the best, most fun eating to be had is at the *fritanga* stands in the Parque Central.

Hotel Fronteras HOTEL **$**
(☑ 2346-2515; d US$20; P ❉) If you need to stay the night near the border, try this family-run hotel. Cash only.

BUS SERVICES FROM CHINANDEGA (MERCADO BISNE)

DESTINATION	COST (US$)	DURATION (HR)	FREQUENCY (DAILY)
Chichigalpa (microbus)	0.30	15min	5am-6pm, departs when full
Corinto (bus)	0.50-0.60	40min	4:30am-6pm, every 15min
Corinto (microbus)	0.75	25min	4:30am-7pm, departs when full
El Guasaule (Honduran border; bus)	1.70	1¾	4am-5pm, every 25min
El Guasaule (Honduran border; microbus)	2	1	4:30am-7pm, departs when full
León (bus)	0.80	1½	4am-7pm, every 15min
León (microbus)	1.20	1	4:30am-7pm, departs when full
Managua (bus)	2.70	3	4am-5:20pm, hourly
Managua (microbus)	3	2	4:30am-7pm, departs when full

ⓘ Getting There & Away

All buses headed north from Chinandega to Potosí or the Cosigüina beaches stop at the El Viejo *empalme* about 20 minutes after leaving Chinandega.

To Chinandega, you can get buses and minivans (US$0.60 to US$0.80, 10 to 20 minutes, every 15 minutes) from in front of the basilica. A taxi to Chinandega costs US$3 to US$5.

Drivers: note that this is the last chance for gas on the peninsula.

Chichigalpa

Chichigalpa, Nicaragua's cutest-named town, is best known as the source of Flor de Caña rum, made in seven beloved shades, from crystal clear to deepest amber. It's also home to Ingenio San Antonio, the country's largest sugar refinery, and cane fields carpet the skirts of Volcán San Cristóbal, which rises from the lowlands just 15km from the city center.

There's no tourist information office here, but the Chichigalpa *alcaldía*, about two blocks from the charming Parque Central, has a Commission of Culture that can arrange guided tours of Flor de Caña (not open to the general public), city tours that take in the ruins of Iglesia El Pueblito, and guided hikes to the top of San Cristóbal via Parque Ecológico Municipal.

◉ Sights

Parque Ecológico Municipal   PARK
This smoking city park, about 10km from town and accessible only by 4WD, preserves 50 *manzanas* of mostly primary forest, including a trailhead to the top of the Volcán San Cristóbal.

⌂ Sleeping

Hotel La Vista   HOTEL $$$
(☎2343-2035; alcaldía, 1c E, 75m N; s/d US$40/60; P❋@) The only hotel in town is nothing to write home about, but rooms are clean – it'll do for an overnight.

ⓘ Information

Alcaldía (☎2343-2456; alchichi@ibw.com.ni)

ⓘ Getting There & Away

Microbuses to Chinandega (US$0.30, 15 minutes) depart from the market when full, 5am to 6pm.

Cosigüina Peninsula Beaches

The Cosigüina peninsula is well on its way to becoming an island, worn away on two sides by brilliant estuaries and fringed with sandy beaches, ranging from the pearl-grays of Jiquilillo to coal-black at Playa Carbón.

These aren't the easiest beaches to visit, but you'll be rewarded with impressive stretches of sand interrupted only by fishing villages, sea turtles and mangrove swamps. The surfing is great but largely unexplored, and hotels are relatively few and far between.

Playa Aserradores is emerging as a popular destination; there are several good places to stay on the beach, and a nice eco-friendly lodge off the road between Potosí and El Viejo.

ⓘ Getting There & Away

Buses and minivans ply the routes between Chinandega and the beaches.

El Corinto

Nicaragua's only deep-water port was originally a much older town, Puerto El Realejo; founded in 1522, it was subsequently attacked by such famous pirates as William Dampier and John Davis. As time passed and sand filled in the estuary, the barrier island of Punto Icaco became the port, where Corinto was founded in 1858.

This was where US president Ronald Reagan mined in 1983, after which Congress passed a law specifically forbidding the use of taxpayer dollars for overthrowing the Nicaraguan government. Thus began the Iran-Contra affair.

Corinto's 19th-century wooden row houses, narrow streets and broad beaches score high on the 'adorability potential' scale, although actual adorability ratings are much lower. It's a bit sad: although some 65% of the nation's imports and exports flow through, very little of the money stays here. Cruise ships arrive throughout the year, but passengers are whisked away to more scenic spots.

◉ Sights

The Parque Central is downright audacious, a concrete confection of fountains and turtles with a very *Jetsons*-esque clock tower. A squat, green Catholic church is the **final resting place of poet Azarías H Pallais**, although most literature ignores him, noting instead that Isla El Cardón, just offshore, inspired Rubén Darío's poem 'A Margarita Debayle.'

Activities

The beaches close to town are dirty, but walk just a few minutes north to find cleaner **Paso Caballos**, with a string of thatched restaurant-bars, a terrible rip current and good **surfing**. Between Corinto and Paso Caballos, a big, hollow left is supposed to be one of the best waves in the country, but it's boat access only. North of Paso Caballos is a river-mouth break and some peaks break left. The protected bay also offers world-class **windsurfing**, if you've brought your own equipment – big swells roll in toward the estuary when the tide changes, good for jumps.

At the waterfront restaurants, ask about arranging a **boat ride** (usually around US$40 for one to three people) to take you on a sightseeing tour of the islands.

Festivals & Events

Fiesta Gastronómica del Mar FOOD
(⊙ first weekend of May) El Corinto gets packed during this annual food festival. It begins with a fishing competition and ends with every chef in the department turning out top-quality seafood dishes for the crowd. Cultural activities, parades, beauty contests and lots of dancing help you work it off.

Sleeping

Hospedaje Luvy GUESTHOUSE $
(⌧ 2342-2637; Parque Central, 1½c N; d without bathroom US$12) This budget hotel is pleasant for a short stay – no frills, but guest rooms are cheap, with clean bathrooms and good fans.

Hotel Central HOTEL $$
(⌧ 2342-2380; frente puerto; d US$40; P ❄) Watch the goings-on in the port from your room at Hotel Central, one of the only sleeping options around with air-conditioning (a major selling point, depending on when you visit).

Eating

Corinto is known for traditional seafood. Simple cafes and ice-cream shops are located around the main plaza. Finer dining options are located on the water, a short walk away.

El Peruano PERUVIAN $
(alcaldía, 1c S; mains US$3-7; ⊙ 10am-late) A simple dining option on the waterfront with open-air seating and fresh fish specials.

Costa Azul NICARAGUAN $$
(⌧ 2342-2888; www.restaurante-costaazul.com; costado, oeste de la alcaldía, 1c S, Puerto de Corinto; dishes US$5-12; ⊙ 11am-9pm) Slightly upscale Costa Azul has breezy patio seating and a great seafood menu featuring various kinds of ceviche, plus freshly caught shrimp and lobster prepared in a variety of ways. You might be tempted to linger here all afternoon.

Restaurante El Espigón NICARAGUAN $$
(⌧ 2340-6248; de la Escuela José Schendel, 3c W, 1c N, Barrio los Pescadores, Puerto de Corinto; mains US$4-9; ⊙ 11am-9pm) *The* place to eat in Corinto. El Espigón specializes in seafood and steaks, and it's located right on the water. On weekends, there's live music. It's also a good choice for cocktails with a view.

❶ Getting There & Away

Buses (US$0.60, 40 minutes) and microbuses (US$0.80, 25 minutes) leave regularly for Chinandega, 19km away, from the bus terminal, just outside of town. If you're arriving in Corinto by bus, you can catch a ride from the terminal to the plaza or port in a pedicab (US$0.60 per person).

Playa Aserradores

This long, smooth stretch of sand has excellent surfing: the main attraction here is a serious wave, best for experienced surfers. There are other activities on offer here, too, from fishing and kayak tours to horseback riding and bicycle rental. It's also a quiet place to just relax by the sea.

Sleeping & Eating

There are a few good sleeping options on the beach – places where you'll be tempted to stay a night or two longer than you planned.

The hotels here have restaurants, but it's also smart to bring your own supplies from larger towns, as there aren't many services here.

Hotel Chancletas
HOTEL $$$

(☑ 8868-5036; www.hotelchancletas.com; Playa Asserradores; dm US$10, tr without/with bathroom US$100/45; P ❄ 🗑) Perched up on a grassy hillside overlooking Aserradores' famous break, this relaxed surfer's spot has nice rooms and a variety of activities on offer. There's surfboard rental, too, and a good restaurant open for breakfast, lunch and dinner.

Marina Puesta del Sol
RESORT $$$

(☑ 8880-0019; www.marinapuestadelsol.com; Playa Aserradores; r from US$190; P ❄ 🗑 🏊) A very upmarket yacht club offering great views of smoking San Cristóbal from the infinity pool – and even better ones from the enormous, fully equipped rooms and suites. There's a lovely private beach, too, and a nice restaurant by the water (open to the public).

❶ Getting There & Away

Many travelers drive here: you'll want a 4WD vehicle for the bumpy ride from the well-signed exit off the Chinandega–Potosí Hwy.

At the time of writing, there was only one daily bus from Chinandega to Aserradores, departing from Chinandega's Mercadito at 12:30pm (US$1, 1½ hours). Hotels offer private transport for around US$90 for one or two people.

Playa Jiquilillo

This endless pale-gray beach frames what you thought existed only in tales that begin 'You should have seen it back when I was first here...' The picture-perfect fishing village fronts a dramatic rocky point, where tide pools reflect the reds and golds of a huge setting sun, Cosigüina's ragged bulk rising hazy and post-apocalyptic to the north.

The region remains largely undeveloped, despite its beauty and accessibility, because a devastating 1992 tsunami completely wiped this village out.

The beach here is lovely – there's no real rip current in the calm cove. Just beyond is a good break, with regular peaks where you can almost always carve out a few turns; bring your own board.

🛌 Sleeping & Eating

There are several good places to stay on this stretch of coastline; the hotels here all have restaurants, but you should bring any necessities from town.

Rancho Tranquilo
HOSTEL $

(☑ 8968-2290; www.ranchotranquilo.wordpress. com; Los Zorros Jiquilillo; dm/s/d US$7/20/22; P) This collection of bungalows and a small dorm on its private stretch of beach is a great budget choice. There's a cool bar and common area, and vegetarian dinners (US$2 to US$4.50) are served family-style. Check online for information on the area's turtle rescue program.

Rancho Esperanza
GUESTHOUSE $$

(☑ 8879-1795; www.rancho-esperanza.com; Jiquilillo; dm US$8, 2-person cabañas without/with bathroom US$25/35) 🌿 This quiet and eco-friendly collection of simple bamboo huts – which are scattered across a grassy field just slightly removed from the beach – offers volunteer opportunities in community projects related to education and environmental issues. There's also a small library of English-language books and a good breakfast (served all day).

Monty's Beach Lodge
LODGE $$$

(☑ 8473-3255; www.montysbeachlodge.com; d per person per week incl meals US$600; @) This upscale hotel/surf camp is pleasantly set right on the waterfront. Rooms are fan-cooled and the beds draped with mosquito nets. Most travelers come here on week-long packages that include all meals, but you can also contact the lodge directly for alternatives.

❶ Getting There & Away

Buses to Chinandega (US$1, 1½ hours) come and go a few times a day. Hotels like Monty's Beach Lodge (US$120 for up to 10 people) also offer direct transportation from Managua's airport; contact the hotels directly for more information.

Reserva Natural Estero Padre Ramos

A few minutes north of Los Zorros is the community of Padre Ramos, one of the small towns inside the federally protected wetlands of Reserva Natural Estero Padre

Ramos. The river delta is part of the largest remaining mangrove forests in Central America, and is key in the proposed **Reserva Biológica Golfo de Fonseca** (Gulf of Fonseca Biological Corridor), a wetlands conservation agreement between Nicaragua, Honduras and El Salvador.

There's not much tourist infrastructure here but hotels in the area offer boat, kayak, and birding tours for around US$10 to US$40 per person. Sea turtles lay their eggs here between July and December, peaking in October and November.

🛏 Sleeping & Eating

There's a resort in nearby Mechapa. Many travelers stay in Playa Jiquilillo, where there are more options.

If you're staying at a hotel around here, you'll be eating most or all of your meals there. Bring supplies from town, because there aren't many services around the reserve.

Redwood Beach Resort LODGE $$$
(☑ 8996-0328; www.redwoodbeachresort.com; 100 Beach Way, Las Cabanas, Mechapa; d US$120; P ❄ 🛜) Across the estuary in Mechapa, this cozy little resort is shaded by coconut trees right on the beach. Accommodations are in charming cabins, each with balconies overlooking the waves. The restaurant is for guests only, though the **Tiki Bar** is open to daytime visitors between 10am and 4pm.

Activities here include kayak tours of the estuary, surfing (beach breaks only), fishing, Cosigüina treks and horseback riding. Access is tricky – there's the three-hour bus ride from Chinandega, or if you call ahead, staff can come pick you up from Jiquilillo or Padre Ramos. Adventurous souls can try to hire a launch here from Playa Jiquilillo.

❶ Getting There & Away

Many travelers to the region drive themselves. Buses to Chinandega (US$1.20, two hours) come and go to Padre Ramos from Chinandega Mercadito three to five times per day. Alternatively, you could take the bus to Mechapa from Chinandega daily, leaving the Mercadito at 2pm, or arrange private shuttle transportation with your hotel or resort.

Reserva Privada Hato Nuevo

Just near the turnoff to Mechapa, this ecolodge (☑ in Chinandega 2341-4245; www.hatonuevo.com; Carretera El Viejo–Potosí Km 177.5; s/d incl breakfast US$40/50) sits on a large private reserve. Rooms in the old farmhouse are a careful blend of rustic charm and modern amenity, and the dining area, bar and gardens are all beautifully designed. It offers trekking, horseback riding and boat tours.

Reserva Natural Volcán Cosigüina

It was once the tallest volcano in Central America, perhaps more than 3000m high, but all that changed on January 20, 1835. In what's considered the Americas' most violent eruption since colonization, this hot-blooded peninsular volcano blew off half its height in a single blast that paved the oceans with pumice, left three countries in stifling darkness for days and scattered ash from Mexico to Colombia. What remains today of Volcán Cosigüina reclines, as if spent, the broad and jagged 872m heart of the peninsula.

Beyond all that lies the **Golfo de Fonseca**, bordered by the largest mangrove stand left in the Americas. In the other direction, around the volcano's back, **Punta Ñata** overlooks cliffs that plunge 250m into the sea; beyond lie the **Farallones del Cosigüina** (also known as the Islotes Cosigüina), a series of volcanic islets. There are many black-sand beaches around here for DIY exploration.

🏃 Activities

It's a very manageable (if blisteringly hot) three-hour climb up one of two trails to the top: **Sendero La Guacamaya**, which starts at the ranger's station near El Rosario; and **Sendero el Jovo**, which descends to more developed Potosí. The rare dry tropical forest, home to one of the continent's last sustainable populations of huge red macaws, as well as pumas, spider monkeys and plenty of *pizotes* (coatis), loses its leaves by January. You can do the trail as a loop, and go on foot or horseback. Many León-based operators run organized tours lasting between two and three days, but you can also go with Cosiguina Tours in Potosí, the central hub for exploring this region. You can also check with Marena (www.marena.gob.ni) for current conditions and travel advice.

Sore muscles? Head to the hot springs. In Potosí, Centro Ecoturistico Potosí (☑2344-2381; www.ecodetur.com; Potosí) offers a soothing soak in some (shaded) hot springs, along with food service.offers hot springs with shade and food service, or else go wild at one of several undeveloped springs that locals will happily point out.

Cosigüina Tours   HIKING, BIRDWATCHING
(☑2344-2381; www.ecodetur.com; entrance to Potosí) This home-grown tour operator offers a variety of tours in the region, including half-day treks to Volcán Cosigüina and birdwatching trips to the neighboring Los Islotes islands. Check the website for a full list of tours and to consult about the latest prices, which are much more affordable if you're traveling with a few other people.

🛏 Sleeping & Eating

There are a few basic eating options around Potosí, but if you're going into the reserve, bring your own supplies from León.

Hotel Brisas del Golfo   HOTEL $$
(☑8774-4356; Frente a la Iglesia Católica, Potosí; dm/s/d from US$9/17/23; 🖥) This friendly hotel has fan-cooled rooms, wi-fi and an onsite restaurant specializing in seafood dishes.

ℹ Getting There & Away

There are three buses daily between Chinandega and Potosí (US$1.50 to US$1.75, 3½ hours) that pick up and drop off close to the reserve's entrance, though many travelers explore this region in their own cars or visit on an organized tour.

Northern Highlands

Best Places to Eat

➡ El Pullaso (p197)

➡ La Vita é Bella (p196)

➡ Rincón Pinareño (p174)

➡ Restaurante Tipiscayán (p174)

➡ La Casa de Don Colocho (p190)

Best Places to Sleep

➡ La Bastilla Ecolodge (p192)

➡ Montebrisa (p196)

➡ Selva Negra (p199)

➡ Hotel Los Altos (p173)

➡ Finca Esperanza Verde (p198)

Why Go?

You've officially escaped Central America's backpacker super-highway and arrived in a place where colorful quetzals nest in misty cloud forests, and where Nicaragua's best coffee and tobacco are cultivated with both capitalist zeal and collective spirit. With a little time and commitment you'll duck into ancient, crumbling cathedrals; get pounded by countless waterfalls; explore recently discovered canyons; and pay tribute to the pirates, colonists, revolutionaries, artists and poets who were inspired by these fertile mountains and mingled with the humble, open-hearted people who've lived here for generations.

On either end of the region are two up-and-coming cities: hardworking Estelí buzzes with students, farmers and cigar moguls, while Matagalpa is slightly hipper – and better funded, thanks to nearly a century of successful coffee cultivation. All around and in between are granite peaks and lush valleys dotted with dozens of small towns and infinite caffeine-fueled adventures.

When to Go

➡ The northern highlands' stunning landscapes are at their best from May to October, when the wet season brings out vibrant shades of green and the many waterfalls are at their best.

➡ If you plan on hiking, consider visiting from November to February, when the weather is fairly dry – yet mild – and the scenery is still lush. This is also the height of the coffee harvest, which affords you the chance to not only drink endless cups of the stuff but to also pick and sort your own beans.

➡ The region's other cash crop, tobacco, is harvested from March to April; cigar fans visiting then can follow the leaves from the fields to the rolling tables.

Northern Highlands Highlights

1 **Reserva Natural Cerro Datanlí–El Diablo** (p191) Picking coffee beans beneath the towering cloud forest.

2 **Cañon de Somoto** (p180) Scrambling, swimming and floating along a magnificent gorge.

3 **Área Protegida Miraflor** (p175) Riding horses through magnificent countryside to swimming holes.

4 **Jalapa** (p186) Soaking in piping-hot thermal waters surrounded by forest.

5 **Estelí** (p170) Visiting the tobacco fields and hand-rolled cigar factories.

6 **Jinotega** (p188) Scrambling up Cerro la Cruz for breathtaking mountain views.

7 **Matagalpa** (p193) Getting over-caffeinated in the Northern Highlands' most urbane city.

8 **Reserva Natural Macizos de Peñas Blancas** (p200) Rappelling down spectacular waterfalls shrouded in old-growth forest.

9 **Lago de Apanás** (p192) Cruising the high-altitude waters with local fisherfolk.

10 **San Ramón** (p197) Exploring cavernous, abandoned gold mines and authentic rural villages.

Champigny

Cordillera
Entre Ríos

Jalapa

Aguas
Calientes

Salto El Rosario

Reserva de
Biosfera Bosawás

Valle
Cangjas

Murra

Ayapal

Jinotega

Río Coco

Plan de Grama

Wiwilí

Wiwilí
de Jinotega

Quilalí

Reserva Natural
Cerro Kilambé

San José
de Bocay

51

57

La Rica

43

Zinica

Las Walices

El Cuá

Pantasma

Reserva Natural
Macizos de
Peñas Blancas

Waslala

5

San Rafael
del Norte

43

Asturias

57

Caratero

Cordillera Isabelía

8

Yaoska

Lago
Asturias

Mancotal

Lago de
Apanás

San Pedro
de Buculmay

5

San Antonio
de Kuskawas

Sisle

9

La Dalia

Río Tuma

Wanawas

Jinotega

1

6

Reserva Natural
Cerro Datanlí–
El Diablo

El Quebracon

Reserva Natural
Cerro El Arenal

El Arenal

El Tuma

Matagalpa

Selva
Negra

5

Monte
Grande

Reserva Natural
Cerro Apante

La Rosa

Garita

Reserva
Genetica
Yacúl

Santa
Elsa

Reserva
Natural
Cerro Musun

3

7

Matagalpa

San
Ramón

Pancasán

Chagüitillo

10

San Pablo

33

21

Sébaco

El Chile

Matiguás

19

Río Grande de Matagalpa

San Dionisio

Muy Muy

9

Pineda

History

Originally home to Náhuatl refugees from the Aztec empire, the northern highlands were off the radar until gold was discovered here in 1850, attracting an influx of Spanish, *mestizos* (persons of mixed ancestry; usually Spanish and indigenous people) and the first wave of German immigrants to Matagalpa. The Europeans married local, planted the region's first coffee bushes, and then sold their berries in Berlin.

When the revolution bloomed in 1977, many of the region's impoverished farmers became armed Sandinistas. Some of the heaviest fighting took place in the mountains in and around Jinotega. When the Frente Sandinista de Liberación Nacional (Sandinista National Liberation Front; FSLN) seized power, they made the area a priority, nationalizing and redistributing much of the highlands' arable land into community farming cooperatives. Some have since been divided up among the cooperative members, but the spirit of collective farming remains strong throughout the region.

ⓘ Getting There & Away

Bus connections in the region are excellent, and both transportation hubs, Estelí and Matagalpa, are around 2½ hours by bus from Mercado Mayoreo in Managua.

Road conditions can go from bad to worse in the back country, especially in the rainy season. Before traversing the dirt roads in a rental car make sure to check road conditions with multiple sources, and consider splurging for the 4WD.

There are two Honduras border crossings: mellow El Espino, close to Somoto; and busy Las Manos, just north of Ocotal.

Estelí

A Sandinista stronghold, a university town, a market center for the thousands of farmers that populate its surrounding hills, Estelí has a multifaceted soul. On weekdays you can wake up with sunrise yoga before Spanish class; on Saturday you can mingle with farmers at the massive produce market, then see them again at midnight, dancing like mad in a *ranchero* bar. And we haven't even mentioned the world-class cigars or the zeal with which a city with socialist roots has taken to slot machines. You don't have to be a Che Guevara devotee to dig this town.

Set on the Pan-American Hwy close to the Honduran border, Estelí was a strategic gateway that saw heavy fighting and helped turn the revolution and, later, the Contra War. It's no surprise then, that Estelí has remained one of the Sandinistas' strongest support bases.

⊙ Sights

Although Estelí's most impressive attractions are in the surrounding mountains, the 1823 **Catedral** has a wonderful facade and is worth a wander. Keep an eye out for the interesting **murals** that crop up about town, many of which were painted by participants in the Funarte children's mural workshop (www.funarte.org.ni).

★ **Galería de Héroes y Mártires** MUSEUM
(☑ 2714-0942, 8419-3519; http://galleryofheroes andmartyrs.blogspot.com; Av 1a NE & Calle Transversal, ½c N; admission by donation; ⊙ 9:30am-4pm Tue-Fri) Be sure to stop by this moving gallery devoted to fallen revolutionaries, with displays of faded photos, clothes and weaponry. Check out the exhibit (with English signage) on Leonel Rugama, the warrior-poet whose last line was his best. When he and Carlos Fonseca were surrounded by 300 Guardia Nacional troops supported by tanks and planes, they were told to surrender. 'Surrender, your mother!' he famously replied. (Which proves that a 'your mama!' retort is always a solid Plan B.)

Opening hours are irregular; if there's no one around swing by later.

🎓 Courses

CENAC Spanish School LANGUAGE COURSE
(☑ 2713-5437; www.spanishschoolcenac.com; Panamericana, btwn Calles 5a SE & 6a SE; per week with/without homestay US$195/120) Professionally run Spanish school with classes for all levels.

Horizonte Nica LANGUAGE COURSE
(☑ 2713-4117; www.escuelahorizonte.edu.ni; Av 2a SE, Calle 9a SE, ½c S; per week with/without homestay US$220/150) This well-established program uses its extensive contacts with local development groups to get students involved in the community.

Ananda Yoga YOGA
(cnr Ave 1a NE & Transversal; per class US$1; ⊙ 6am & 5pm Mon-Fri, 6:40pm Mon-Tue & Thu-Fri) Yoga classes are offered at the Licuados Ananda health-food restaurant, next to the **Casa de Cultura** (☑ 2713-3021; cnr Av 1a NE & Calle Transversal; ⊙ 8am-8pm).

⌖ Tours

★ **Tree Huggers** CULTURAL TOUR
(☑ 8496-7449; http://treehuggers.cafeluzyluna.org; Av 2a NE & Calle 3a NE; ⊙ 8am-8pm) 🥾 This friendly and vibrant tour office is the local specialist for trips to Miraflor and Tisey, but also offers other interesting community tourism trips throughout the region and a great-value cigar tour. Friendly staff dispense a wealth of impartial information for independent travelers. Profits support local social projects.

Cigar Tours

Estelí produces and rolls some of the world's finest tobacco. Seeds are original Cuban stock, as are the curing and rolling techniques you can witness firsthand in the warehouse-like factories. Fumes can get intense, but you'll acclimatize. Tobacco is harvested March through April and *puros* (cigars) are rolled always and forever.

While the tobacco industry is a massive employer in the region and a major contributor to the local economy, conditions for workers vary dramatically. Some factories have airy and spacious rolling areas while others are your classic sweatshop.

Many of the major producers have special tax status and are unable to sell cigars from their factories. It is not possible to send cigars home via the postal service in Nicaragua.

Local tour guide **Leo Flores** (☑ 8415-2428; leoafl@yahoo.es) is well connected in the industry and can gain you access to a wide variety of factories and plantations. You can also organize a tour with Tree Huggers to watch the rolling process at Cuban-owned **Tabacalera Santiago**, which costs US$8 (plus a suggested US$2 donation to the organization's Library Bus), and includes transport and a local guide. The tour offers insights into the entire cigar-making process and visitors are free to talk to the staff as they roll 60 varieties of stogie. Cigars are available for purchase at the end of the tour.

It's also possible to contact some factories and arrange a visit directly. Factory visits are easiest to schedule during the week, when plantation access is more flexible.

Drew Estate CIGAR TOUR
(www.cigarsafari.com; Barrio Oscar Gamez 2) Estelí's most innovative cigar company offers all-inclusive, multiday 'Cigar Safari' tours aimed at serious cigar enthusiasts.

Tabacalera Cubanica CIGAR TOUR
(☑ 2713-2383; Panamericana & Calle 7a SE) This pioneering factory produces Padrón cigars, Nicaragua's most prestigious (and costly) brand.

Plasencia Cigars CIGAR TOUR
(☑ 2713-4074; Escuela Normal, 200m N) Large company that produces over 30 brands of *puros*, including a selection of organic cigars. It's one of the most socially responsible factories.

★ Festivals & Events

Virgen del Carmen RELIGIOUS
(⊙ Jul 16) *Fiestas patronales* (patron saint festival) with fireworks, fiestas and Masses.

Virgen de Rosario RELIGIOUS
(⊙ Oct 7) An annual event since 1521, this was originally celebrated in Villa de San Antonio Pavía de Estelí – too close to the river and those pesky pirates – and moved here with the Virgin in the late 1600s.

⛏ Sleeping

Iguana Hostel HOSTEL $
(☑ 8824-2299; Av Central, Transversal, 75m S; dm/s/d US$7/12.50/14) The cheap and cheerful Iguana has a central location and everything budget travelers need: spacious rooms, a guest kitchen and hammocks in the courtyard. The dorms are particularly good value – they have just a couple of comfortable beds in each.

Hostal Tomabú HOTEL $$
(☑ 2713-3783; www.hostaltomabu.com; costado sur Parque Infantil; s/d US$15/20; ℗ ⊛) Friendly and welcoming, this unpretentious hotel on the south side of the Parque Infantil offers smallish but comfortable rooms – some offering mountain views – with hot water, writing desks and flat-screen TVs.

Hospedaje Luna HOSTEL $$
(☑ 8405-8919, 8441-8466; www.cafeluzyluna.org; cnr Av 2a NE & Calle 3a NE; dm/s/d/tr US$10/20/28/33; ⊛) 🥾 With a central location, spotless rooms, a courtyard common area and a wealth of information on Estelí and the surrounding area, this nonprofit hostel is the budget traveler's favorite. There is a small kitchen for guest use and fast wi-fi throughout. Profits are donated to community projects in Miraflor, which also welcome volunteers.

Estelí

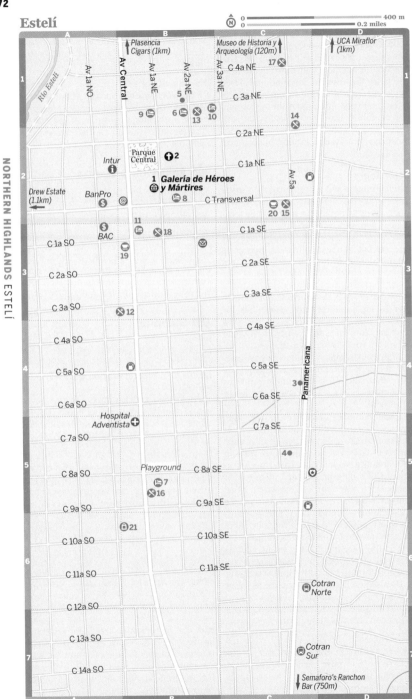

N 0 ———— 400 m
0 ———— 0.2 miles

↑ Plasencia
Cigars (1km)

Museo de Historia y ↑
Arqueología (120m)

↑ UCA Miraflor
(1km)

Av 1a NO
Av Central
Av 1a NE
Av 2a NE
Av 3a NE
C 4a NE
17 ✕

C 3a NE

5 ●
9 🏛 6 🏛 ✕
13 10 🏛

14 ✕

C 2a NE

Intur ℹ
Parque
Central
↑ 2

C 1a NE

Av 5a ●

Drew Estate
(1.1km)

BanPro
$
@

1 **Galería de Héroes
y Mártires**
🏛 8 C Transversal

20 ✕ 15

$
BAC

11
🏛 ✕ 18

C 1a SE

C 1a SO

🏛
19

✉

C 2a SE

C 2a SO

C 3a SE

C 3a SO

✕ 12

C 4a SE

C 4a SO

🏛

C 5a SE

C 5a SO

3 ●
Panamericana

C 6a SE

C 6a SO

Hospital
Adventista ✚

C 7a SE

C 7a SO

4 ●

Playground
🏛 7
✕ 16

C 8a SO

C 8a SE

🏛

C 9a SO

C 9a SE

🏛

🏛 21

C 10a SO

C 10a SE

C 11a SO

C 11a SE

C 12a SO

Cotran
Norte 🏛

C 13a SO

Cotran
Sur 🏛

C 14a SO

↓ Semaforo's Ranchon
Bar (750m)

NORTHERN HIGHLANDS ESTELÍ

Estelí

Hotel Puro Esteli　　　　　　HOTEL **$$**

(☑2713-6404; www.hotelpuroesteli.com; Catedral, 1c N, ½c E; s/d/tr US$18/30/39; ☐) You'll feel the Esteliano tobacco culture in this small, cigar-themed hotel, which has a collection of *puros* for sale in the reception area. The smallish rooms are not flash but are set around a sunny internal garden and feature fast wi-fi and cable TV.

★Hotel Los Altos　　　BOUTIQUE HOTEL **$$$**

(☑2713-5264; hotel_losaltosesteli@hotmail.com; Calle Transversal, Av 1NE, 50m E; s/d/tr US$55/60/70 incl breakfast; ☒☐) In a meticulously restored colonial house right in the center of town, Los Altos manages to be both stylish and unpretentious. The welcoming lobby has a high, wild-cane ceiling, wrought-iron chandeliers and classic Spanish tiles. Rooms are all different but all feature bright tile floors, elegant wooden furniture and spacious work desks. Breakfast is served in the charming internal courtyard.

Hotel Los Arcos　　　　　　HOTEL **$$$**

(☑2713-3830; www.hotelosarcosesteli.com; cnr Av 1a NE & Calle 3a NE; s/d with fan US$45/51, with air-con US$56/63, all incl breakfast; P☒) ✎ Run by a nonprofit organization, Los Arcos remains the best hotel in town, with a dream location one block north of the cathedral, a roof deck with kick-ass mountain and city views, and spotless rooms with soft sheets, Spanish tiles and high ceilings. The rooms at the rear get more natural light.

✘ Eating

El Quesito　　　　　　　NICARAGUAN **$**

(cnr Calle 2a NE & Av 4a NE, Del Asoganor, 1c N; breakfast US$0.70-2.50, mains US$4.50; ⊙6:30am-8pm) Pull up a handmade wooden chair at this rustic corner diner and enjoy homemade yogurt flavored with local fruits, *quesillos* (corn tortillas stuffed with cheese and topped with pickled onions and cream) and *leche agria* (sour milk) – yes, what most of us pour down the sink is a delicacy in Nicaragua! It also prepares excellent, nongreasy Nica breakfasts and good meals.

Buffet Castillo　　　　　　NICARAGUAN **$**

(☑2713-0337; Parque Central, 4c S, ½c O; meals US$2-4; ⊙7am-6pm Mon-Sat) Often packed at lunchtime, this spacious diner offers up restaurant-quality meals, including ribs, fried fish and jalapeño chicken, at a budget price. The original branch across the road is still open if you can't find a seat in the new building.

Repostería Gutiérrez　　　　　　BAKERY **$**

(☑2714-1774; Av Central, btwn Calles 8a SE & 9a SE; pastries US$0.20-1; ⊙7am-8pm) A local institution that sells delicious cookies, cakes, donuts or local pastries stuffed with fruit and cream.

Farmers Market　　　　　　MARKET **$**

(Parque Central; items from US$1; ⊙7am-noon Fri) ✎ Every Friday morning farmers from the surrounding hills come down to Estelí and set up stalls on the north side of the park to sell fresh organic vegetables, cheeses and typical foods.

Café Luz INTERNATIONAL **$$**
(🖉8405-8919; www.cafeluzyluna.org; cnr Av 2a NE
& Calle 3a NE; snacks US$2-4, mains US$6.50-9;
⊗8am-11pm; 🛜🖉) 🥢 Bored of Nica grub?
Pop into this hip coffee house where the bur-
ritos and fajitas have some kick and the or-
ganic salads arrive on your table direct from
the growers in Miraflor. The diverse menu
includes many vegetarian options. It's also
the best place in the center for a social drink
in the evening.

Rincón Pinareño CUBAN **$$**
(🖉2713-4369; Av 1a SE & Calle 1a SE; mains
US$5.50-17, sandwiches from US$3.50; ⊗noon-
10pm) A tasty Cuban diner with a lovely
2nd-floor veranda serving deliciously messy
pressed sandwiches, tasty smoked chicken,
pork chops and ribs. Also a popular spot for
dessert.

Restaurante Tipiscayán NICARAGUAN **$$**
(🖉2713-7303; cnr Calle 4a NE & Av 4a NE; mains
US$3.50-10; ⊗noon-10pm Thu-Tue) The family
of San Juan de Limay soapstone sculptor
Freddy Moreno serves good-quality tradi-
tional fare, including great quesadillas and
Nica-style tacos in an elegant space full of
art. Also serves good coffee and traditional
drinks such as *pinolillo* (a chilled beverage
of maize and cacao).

The sculptures that line the walls are all
for sale and begin as low as US$10 for a min-
iature version.

Pullaso's Ole STEAK **$$$**
(🖉2713-4583; cnr Av 5a SE & Calle Transversal;
dishes US$10-25; ⊗noon-11pm) Named for an
Argentine cut of beef (the *pullaso*), this
sweet, family-owned grill serves beef, pork,
chicken and chorizo on its front porch and
in a quaint dining room crowded with racks
of South American red.

🍷 Drinking & Nightlife

As a university town teeming with students,
and an ag-town surrounded by farmers and
ranchers, Estelí throws a good party. Most
nightlife is out on the Panamericana.

★**Semaforo's Ranchon Bar** BAR
(Panamericana & Hospital, 300m S; ⊗6pm-4am
Thu-Sun) Get down with the good, working
people of Estelí, Tisey and Miraflor at a
proper *ranchero* bar. This indoor/outdoor
club with a *palapa* (thatched) roof and
bandstand brings terrific live music to a
crowd that's here to dance in their boots and

cowboy hats. You will see asses (aged 18 to
60) shimmy and shake.

Cafe Don Luis CAFE
(Av Central & Calle 1 SO; coffee US$0.50-1.60;
⊗7:30am-10pm Mon-Sat, 2-10pm Sun) This corner cafe on the main drag is the preferred
destination for Estelianos to gossip with
friends and watch the comings and goings.
The java is pretty good but the real reason to
visit is for the fascinating window onto local
society. Food is hit-and-miss.

Mocha Nana Café CAFE
(🖉2713-3164; Calle Transversal, Av 4a SE, ½c E;
drinks US$1-2.50; ⊗11am-9pm) Where Estelí
intellectuals gather to sip caffeine, debate
politics and culture, and munch tasty waf-
fles. On Friday evenings there is often live
music by local bands (cover US$2.50).

🛍 Shopping

The must-have souvenir of Estelí is a box of
cigars, best purchased after a cigar tour. The
region is also known for reasonably priced
custom leather: saddles, boots and wallets
are available at the many workshops located
along Av 1a SO.

Calzado Figueroa SHOES
(🖉8946-4341; Av 1a SO & Calle 9a SO, 30m S;
⊗8am-7pm Mon-Sat, to noon Sun) Get in touch
with your inner cowboy with some genuine,
handcrafted, Cuban-heel riding boots (from
US$80 to US$100) at this high-quality leather workshop. Peruse the large selection or
order a tailor-made pair and watch the entire boot-making process.

ℹ Orientation

Atypically, Estelí utilizes a street-numbering
system, and most blocks are clearly signed.
Avenidas run north–south; calles are east–west.
Both ascend in number the further they get from
the city center. Streets and avenues are also
suffixed NE (northeast), SO (southwest) etc,
according to their town quadrant. The intersection of Av Central and Calle Transversal is the
center of the grid; it's steps away from the lovely
Parque Central.

ℹ Information

DANGERS & ANNOYANCES
Police (🖉2713-2615; Panamericana, Calle 8a SE)

INTERNET ACCESS
Estelí@Net (Calle Transversal, Av Central, 20m
O; per hr US$0.50; ⊗8am-8pm) Also offers
international calls.

LAUNDRY

Lavandería Express (☎ 2714-1297; Av 2a SE, Calle 1a SE, 30m S; per pound US$0.80; ☺ 9am-5pm) Economical wash and dry service.

MEDICAL SERVICES

Hospital Adventista (☎ 2713-3827, 8851-5298; Av Central, Calle 6a SO, ½c S; ☺ 24hr) Private clinic with a variety of specialists.

MONEY

BAC (Av 1a NO, Calle Transversal, 50m S) MasterCard/Cirrus/Visa/Plus ATM.
BanPro (cnr Calle Transversal & Av 1a NO) Reliable ATM.

POST

Correos de Nicaragua (Av 2a SE, Calle 1a SE, 20m S; ☺ 8am-4pm Mon-Fri, to noon Sat)

TOURIST INFORMATION

UCA Miraflor (Unión de Cooperativas Agropecuarias de Miraflor; ☎ 2713-2971; www.ucamiraflor.com; Gasolinera Uno Norte, 2c E, ½c N; ☺ 8am-noon & 1-5:30pm Mon-Fri, 8am-3pm Sat) Arranges tours to Área Protegida Miraflor.

Intur (☎ 2713-6799; Plaza Plator, Parque Central, ½c O; ☺ 8am-4pm) Official tourist office with an abundance of regional brochures, but not a lot of expertise.

❶ Getting There & Away

BUS

Estelí has two bus terminals: the blue-collar **Cotran Norte** (☎ 2713-2529) has plenty of slot machines and a soft-rock soundtrack, while **Cotran Sur** (☎ 2713-6162) is more refined. Both are located at the southern end of the city on the Panamericana.

CAR & MOTORCYCLE

Many petrol stations can be found along the length of the Panamericana.

Área Protegida Miraflor

Miraflor is not your average tourist destination. Part nature reserve, part rural farming community, it's challenging to get to and even more difficult to define. There are no big hotels or restaurants here, just a loose

BUSES FROM ESTELÍ (COTRAN NORTE)

DESTINATION	COST (US$)	DURATION (HR)	FREQUENCY (DAILY)
Jalapa	3.50	2¾	4:10am, noon
Jinotega (via Concordia, San Rafael)	1.80	2	5:45am, 8:15am, 9:15am, 2:15pm, 3:45pm, 4:45pm
León (bus)	2.80	2½	3:10pm
León (microbus)	3	2	departs when full around 6am and 1pm
Masaya	3	3	2pm & 3pm
Ocotal	1.80	1½	6am-11am, hourly
San Juan de Limay	1.80	2½	5:30am, 7am, 10am, 12:15pm, 2pm, 3pm
Somoto	1.15	1½	5:30am-6:10pm, hourly
Yalí (via Miraflor)	2	2½	6am, 9:15am, 12:30pm, 3:45pm

BUSES FROM ESTELÍ (COTRAN SUR)

DESTINATION	COST (US$)	DURATION (HR)	FREQUENCY (DAILY)
León	2.80	2½	5am, 5:45am & 6:45am Mon-Sat, 6:45am Sun
Managua (expreso)	3	2½	hourly 4:45-9:45am & 12:15-3:15pm (from 6:45am Sun)
Managua (ordinario)	2.25	3½	3:30am-6pm, half-hourly
Matagalpa (ordinario)	1.25	1¾	5:15am-5:40pm, half-hourly
Tisey	1	1½	6:30am-1:30pm Thu-Tue

collection of like-minded farmers with an interest in tourism and the environment.

Its namesake is a small mountain lake around which the Área Protegida Miraflor (declared a reserve in 1999) unfurls with waterfalls, blooming orchids, coffee plantations, swatches of remnant cloud forest home to hold-out monkey troops, hiking trails and dozens of collective-farming communities that welcome tourists. Yes, nature is glorious here, but the chance to participate in rural Nicaraguan life – making fresh tortillas, milking cows, harvesting coffee, riding horses through the hills with local *caballeros* (horsemen) – is unforgettable.

Advanced reservations are essential to ensure visitor income is distributed evenly among participating farmers and your hosts are prepared for your arrival.

History

Miraflor played an integral role in Nicaragua's revolutionary struggle. When the Contras snuck over the Honduran border with a plan to march into Managua and seize political power, a large contingent came through these mountains, planning to sack nearby Estelí. But the farmers here rose up in resistance and helped turn the Contra War toward the Sandinistas.

Afterward, Ortega nationalized this farmland and gave it back to the people, who organized themselves into *colectivos*. This population may look and act humble, but it has war stories and ambitious, utopian dreams of economic equality burned into its collective brain.

⊙ Sights & Activities

Miraflor has three climate zones (ranging from 800m to 1400m) and is home to over 200 species of orchid and 307 bird species, linked by 20km of trails and rutted roads. The *zona bajo* (low zone), around Coyolito, is a tropical, oak savanna ecosystem; the *zona intermedia* (intermediate zone), which includes Sontule, has some remnant cloud forests and tonnes of orchid varieties; and in the *zona alta* (high zone), you'll find coffee farms, more swatches of cloud forest, and some excellent quetzal and monkey viewing near Cebollal in Los Volcancitos.

Local guides (US$15 for solo travelers, US$20 for groups of two to four) are both inexpensive and a great resource. They know all the best hikes and climbs and can share insights into Miraflor's unique history and local daily life. If you plan on exploring much beyond your homestay, guides become essential – paths are poorly marked and cross private farms where permission must sometimes be negotiated. Horses are also available (around US$15 per day) and are a good choice if you plan on visiting various different communities.

Dedicated coffee tours with tasting sessions (US$70 for up to 10 participants) can be arranged with advance notice. Other specialized tours include orchid hikes (US$35 for up to 10 participants) and birdwatching trips (US$35 to US$50 for up to six participants).

Some landowners charge admission to visit sights or pass through their property, so bring plenty of change.

UCA Miraflor (p175) in Estelí manages the reserve and can help you plan a visit, hook you up with an English-speaking guide and book family homestays. Alternatively, Tree Huggers (p171) provides detailed, impartial advice on planning a trip, and can also make reservations.

Los Volcancitos   WILDLIFE-WATCHING

This destination for wildlife lovers is where you'll find the best remaining patch of vir-

OFF THE BEATEN TRACK

SAN JUAN DE LIMAY

San Juan de Limay's cobblestone and brick streets seemingly appear from the dust 44km west of Estelí to form a precious country town, known for its stone carvers and surrounded by soaring peaks.

Look for the enlightened *gorda* (pudgy lady); she's the town's signature symbol. Most often she's carved from *marmolina* (soapstone), a heavy rock that is mined in nearby Cerro Tipiscayán and carved and sanded in home workshops until it shines.

The best gallery, Taller Casco Dablia (📞8842-5162, 2719-5228; detras del colegio; ⊗8am-6pm), is located behind the school and opposite the town square. The road to Limay branches off the Panamericana north of Estelí, near the community of La Sirena. Buses leave the Cotran Norte in Estelí for Limay (US$2, 2½ hours) six times daily.

gin cloud forest (although deforestation is a serious issue), home to Technicolor quetzals in April and May, as well as troops of spider and howler monkeys. It's most easily accessed from Cebollal.

Walk 45 minutes to the La Rampla bus stop on the Estelí–Yalí road; it's then a further one-hour walk south to the jungle-covered, volcano-shaped mountain (which, despite the name, isn't actually a volcano).

La Perla
CULTURAL TOUR

A fine place to immerse yourself in the collective-farming world of Miraflor, this small village is in the high zone, which means there are hundreds of orchid varieties here. It's also home to a women's farming cooperative. Guests are encouraged to wake up to the smacking rhythm of fresh, handmade tortillas; milk the cow; collect the eggs and work the farm before hiking into the nearby forests. La Perla is also a convenient spot from which to visit the Laguna Miraflor.

Cebollal
HIKING, BIRDWATCHING

The first settlement to cater to tourists, it remains the most popular. You can stay with families or in more comfortable *cabañas* (cabins) and enjoy kilometers of trails that reach up to 1400m, with pockets of cloud forest that draw colorful quetzals to the canopy in May and June.

Coyolito
HIKING, BIRDWATCHING

The lowest settlement (in elevation), Coyolito is the warmest and closest to Estelí. It offers magnificent views, especially from the Mirador La Meseta (admission US$1), and access to several waterfalls that range from trickling to thundering depending upon the season, such as Las Tres Cascadas, a series of cascades and swimming holes. Another is La Chorrera, a towering, 65m-high waterfall once used as an execution site by Somoza's troops; it sometimes dries up completely and is only worth visiting after prolonged rains.

There's also brilliant birdwatching in the forest that lines the river here.

🛏 Sleeping & Eating

There are several choices of accommodations within the reserve, all of which should be booked through UCA Miraflor (p175) or Tree Huggers (p171) in Estelí.

Farmhouse rooms allow the most interaction with local families; *cabañas* have more privacy. Both options are rustic and some

accommodations have pit latrines. Expect to pay around US$28 per person, including three meals.

If creature comforts are important, Finca Neblina del Bosque (☑8701-1460; www.neblinadelbosque.com; Cebollal; cabañas per person incl meals US$30-40), owned by a Nica-German couple, is the most comfortable option in Miraflor (though it has decidedly less rural farming flavor).

Accommodations packages usually include three home-cooked, farm-style meals.

ℹ Getting There & Away

For Coyolito (US$0.70, one hour) and La Pita (US$1, 1¾ hours) buses leave Estelí from the Pulpería Miraflor (near the Uno gas station on the Panamericana north of town) at 5:45am and 1pm daily, returning from La Pita at 7:30am and 2:30pm.

There is one direct bus daily (except Sunday) from Estelí to Cebollal (US$1.50, two hours) via Sontule and La Perla, leaving from the Cotran Norte at 2:15pm and returning from Cebollal at 6:45am.

Alternatively, for Cebollal take the Estelí–Yalí (via Miraflor) bus at 6am, noon or 3:45pm from Cotran Norte to La Rampla (US$1, two hours), from where it's a 1km walk uphill to the beginning of the accommodations. The bus continues onto Puertas Azules, from where it's a 20-minute walk to La Perla and a 1¾-hour walk to Sontule.

It's also possible to walk up the hill from La Pita to Cebollal in around 45 minutes, but it's a steep climb.

Área Protegida Cerro Tisey-Estanzuela

Smaller, drier and less populated but every bit as gorgeous as Área Protegida Miraflor, this *other* protected area, just 10km south of Estelí, has also jumped on the tourism bandwagon. You won't see the same species diversity in Tisey (which is what locals call the region), but those rugged, pine-draped mountains, red-clay bat caves, waterfalls and marvelous vistas that stretch to Lago de Managua – and even El Salvador on clear days – are worth the trip.

It's possible to visit Tisey on a day trip from Estelí; however, the reserve's attractions are spread out all over its 9344 hectares and public transportation is limited, so you'll see more if you spend the night.

⊙ Sights

The main entrance to Tisey is accessed from the dirt road beside Hospital San Juan de Dios in Estelí. In the park's lower elevations, just 5km from Estelí, is the inspiring **Salto Estanzuela** (admission US$1), a gushing 36m waterfall that careens over a bromeliad-studded cliff and breaks into a half-dozen foaming threads that feed a perfect swimming hole. Locals descend in hordes during Semana Santa.

After the falls, the road begins to climb high into the mountains before arriving at the Eco-Posada, where you'll find a handful of Spanish-speaking guides for hire (US$20 to US$25 per day).

A short walk further along the road is the entrance to Alberto Gutiérrez' singular **Galería del Arte el Jalacate** (admission by donation), where you can see his charming murals carved into the cliff-face. About 3km further is the cute hamlet of **La Garnacha**, known for a chapel that housed huddled refugees of a Contra invasion during the war, and a dairy cooperative that produces artisanal, Italian-style goat cheese.

🏃 Activities

The **Mirador de Tisey Trail** (2km), found near the Eco-Posada is absolutely spectacular. After meandering up an oak- and pine-draped hillside, you'll reach a peak with 360-degree views that encompass a dozen volcanoes, including mighty **San Cristóbal**, and the blue outline of a Salvadorian peak.

ASOPASN TOUR
(☑ 8658-1054; garnchaturistica@yahoo.es; Comunidad La Garnacha) This progressive farming cooperative has branched out into tourism and organizes several interesting activities, including organic **agriculture tours** (US$8 per person) and **soapstone-carving classes** (US$8 per person). It also rents horses and organizes guides (US$8 per person) for the rugged five-hour trail to the **Cuevas de Cerro Apaguaji**, three caves at 1580m that are teeming with bats.

🛏 Sleeping & Eating

It's possible to visit Tisey as a day trip from Estelí but if you want to explore the area without being rushed it's worth staying the night. The hamlet of La Garnacha has the widest range of accommodations options.

The one *comedor* (basic eatery) in La Garnacha serves excellent *comida típica*

(regional specialties; dishes US$3 to US$5) made from local ingredients, including organic salads and, of course, cheese.

Eco-Posada LODGE $
(☑ 8658-4086; r per person US$7, cabañas US$18; ℗) This place offers comfortable *cabañas* with flush toilets and front porches slung with hammocks overlooking a small creek lined with flowers and fruit trees, as well as spartan, tin-roofed rooms with shared bathrooms. Cheap meals are available in the attached *comedor*.

Homestay Reynaldo HOMESTAY $$
(☑ 8524-4764; La Garnacha; r per person incl meals US$28) 🍴 For a full cultural immersion, check out this family homestay, in the house of an energetic local farmer, that's surrounded by lovely gardens. Meals are prepared using organic produce fresh from the host's farm.

Cabañas La Garnacha LODGE $$
(☑ 8658-1054; garnchaturistica@yahoo.es; La Garnacha; r per person US$10, cabañas US$25-30) 🍴 These cute *cabañas* with hot water are run by the community and overlook a small lake. There are also cheaper, hotel-style rooms with tiled bathrooms by the entrance. Reserve in advance.

ⓘ Information

There have been many reports of robberies recently on the path to the Salto Estanzuela falls from the main Tisey road; check on the latest in Estelí before setting out. If you decide to go, travel in a group and don't take any valuables.

ⓘ Getting There & Away

Tisey is served by two buses a day (US$1, 1½ hours), which are marked 'La Tejera' and leave from Estelí Cotran Sur at 6:30am and 1:30pm. The buses pass Salto Estanzuela and Eco-Posada before arriving at the La Garnacha turnoff, a 1.5km walk from the community. Buses return to Estelí from the La Garnacha turnoff at 8:30am and 3:30pm. On Wednesday there is no service.

In the dry season, you may be able to charter a taxi from Estelí (about US$50 for five to six hours), but the road is in fairly poor condition and most drivers don't want to rough up their sedans. Alternatively, Tree Huggers (p171) offers round-trip transport in pick-ups for US$60, which is a good option for day-trippers.

Salto Estanzuela is about a 90-minute walk or 40-minute bicycle ride from the Hospital San Juan de Dios in Estelí. Expect to pay around US$15 each way in a taxi.

Condega

Dyed a deep terracotta, scarred proudly by revolution and surrounded by gorgeous, forested hills, Condega translates from the indigenous Náhuatl as 'the place of the potters.' You'll see their wares in a museum and at a famed factory shop on the outskirts, but if terracotta doesn't get you going, then check out the Somoza-era bomber shot down here in 1979 and reassembled on a hilltop. Talk about spoils of war.

◎ Sights

Condega's Parque Central is actually at its extreme southern end, opposite **El Templo Parroquial de Condega**. The church gets packed December 11 and 12 for the **Virgin of Guadalupe festival**. Come a few days later for the **Feria del Patio**, when local women dress up as Mother Nature – in dresses made of corn husks and medicinal plants – and throw a huge party.

Across from the park, the **Museo Arqueológico Julio César Salgado** (Parque Central; admission US$0.30; ⊗8am-4pm Mon-Fri, to noon Sat) is packed with ceramic bowls, studded incense burners, and stone tools dating back to AD 300. A map in the corner marks some 60 unexcavated or partially excavated archaeological sites in the area.

The best new stuff can be found at the Taller de Cerámica Ducualí Grande (see Shopping), a collective of women who sell their fine work all over Nicaragua.

NORTHERN HIGHLANDS CONDEGA

FAIR TRADE & CAFFEINE DREAMS

More fiercely traded than any global commodity other than oil, black coffee makes up half of Nicaragua's exports and is the jittery engine upon which the economy turns. Until 1989 coffee prices were regulated by the International Coffee Organization (ICO), after a drought in Brazil doubled prices several years before. But the USA pulled out of the ICO about the same time that Vietnam and other new producers were beginning to flood the market with beans. By 1999 coffee prices had dropped from a spike of more than US$3 to only US$0.42 per pound, less than it costs to produce.

In Nicaragua, small farmers abandoned their land; of Matagalpa's 25 major haciendas, 20 closed, putting 36,000 people out of work. Some went to Costa Rica or other parts of the country to work; most were stuck here, begging for change by the sides of the road. A union, Rural Workers Association (ATC), formed, and former coffee workers shut down the highway four times until the government fell back on an old Sandinista tactic and agreed to give each family a plot of land, for which they would need to pay half.

Some farmers, with the help of international organizations, began growing organic coffee. It was relatively easy to become certified in Nicaragua, as agriculture has never relied on fertilizers and pesticides (because farmers couldn't afford them). It was expensive, however. No single organization certifies coffee 'organic' or 'fair trade'; Starbucks, for example, has its own certification program. But there are dozens of others, including Rainforest Alliance and Utz Kapeh. A cooperative of 150 farmers pays around US$2500 per year to be certified, which is still a good deal considering how much more the coffee earns.

Despite the fact that fair trade basically asks consumers to voluntarily pay extra (who thought that would work?), it's now the fastest-growing segment of the coffee market. Some 800,000 farmers in 40 countries are working fair-trade plots. In Nicaragua, communities often still work together as Sandinista-style cooperatives, making group decisions and encouraging women to participate.

Just when things were looking up for the nation's coffee growers local crops were devastated by coffee rust disease, with farmers in some areas losing as much as 80% of their crops. The outbreak was not just a disaster for crops but also for the status of organic farming among growers: farmers who use chemical additives lost less to the disease than organic growers. By the time the outbreak reached its height, many formerly organic farmers were dousing their plantations with chemicals in a bid to salvage something.

The diseased bushes have since been uprooted and replaced with more hardy varieties as farmers begin the long journey to restoring their production. But it is going to take consumers willing to pay real premiums on the price of organic beans to convince farmers the chemical-free approach is worth the risk.

Condega's most unique attraction is the riveted twin-engine bomber used by the FAN (Nicaraguan Air Force) to bomb the region. It was shot down on April 7, 1979. Now it sits, tagged with lovers' graffiti, at **Airplane Park**, the local make-out point overlooking mountain mesas. Alongside the aircraft is a faux control tower **mirador** (admission US$0.20), which offers fantastic views of the town, its tiled roofs and palm trees jutting out of a canopy of green. To get to the park, climb the steep dirt trail across the street from the museum.

🍴 Sleeping & Eating

Most accommodations in town are right by the park.

Several cheap and tasty *carne asada* (grilled steak) stalls are located on the northeast corner of the park.

★**Hospedaje Baldovinos**   GUESTHOUSE $
(📞2715-2222; Parque Central; s/d/tr US$9/11/18; 🅿🛜) Set in a lovely colonial house with a vibrant internal courtyard, this family-run *hospedaje* (guesthouse) offers simple, cool brick rooms with tiled bathrooms. It's the most comfortable and atmospheric choice in Condega. The hotel also arranges private transport to local attractions, including the workshops at Ducualí.

🛍 Shopping

Taller de Cerámica Ducualí
Grande   CERAMICS
(📞2715-2418; Restaurante Guanacaste, 1km O; ⊙9am-4pm) This collective of women potters sells their fine work all over Nicaragua. It's located in the community of Ducualí Grande, 3km northwest of town. Any northbound bus will drop you at the intersection on the Panamericana; it's then a 1km walk to the community. In the village, take a left at the basketball court and look for the small sign.

❶ Getting There & Away

Buses depart from Condega's new bus terminal on the Panamericana for the following destinations:

Estelí (US$0.60, 45 minutes, 6am to 7pm, every 20 minutes)

Ocotal (US$1, one hour, 7am to 7pm, every 45 minutes)

Somoto (US$0.80, one hour, 4:15am to 5:45pm, every 45 minutes)

Somoto

Diminutive Somoto has not always been a shoe-in on the itineraries of visitors to northern Nicaragua. In fact, until 2003 this was just another sleepy colonial town in the Honduran shadow, famed for its donkeys and *rosquillas* (crusty cornbread rings). Then two Czech scientists stumbled onto a rift in the rugged, overgrown clay earth outside town and, just 75 million years after these charcoal granite cliffs pierced the earth's surface, Europeans 'discovered' Cañon de Somoto (Somoto Canyon), where the Río Coco is born.

Of course, the locals living nearby have known about it all along and formerly referred to the site as 'La Estrechura' (The Narrows), while it's said that the area's original inhabitants, the Chorotegas, referred to the region as Tepezonate (Mountain of Water).

⊙ Sights

Iglesia Santiago   CHURCH
This wonderfully understated adobe church fronting the shady Parque Central was constructed in 1661, making it one of the oldest places of worship in Nicaragua.

★**Monumento Nacional**
Cañon de Somoto   NATIONAL PARK
(Carrertera Somoto–El Espino Km 229.5; US$2) The Coco (or Wangki), Central America's longest river, runs all the way to the Caribbean, but its first impression may be its most spectacular. Gushing from underground, it has carved solid rock into this 3km-long gorge that drops 160m, and at times is just a hair under 10m wide. Protected as Monumento Nacional Cañon de Somoto, the canyon is an unmissable experience.

There are three routes to explore the canyon. You won't always have comfortable footing, so reef shoes or sandals help a lot, and you'll have more fun if you're fit. Within the canyon proper there is one deep stretch of about 200m where you'll have to swim (tours will always supply life vests).

The full six-hour, 13km circuit will take you to two **bat caves** well above the rim before you **hike** down to the river, boulder-hop, swim through (small) rapids and leap off 8m rocks into deep swimming holes. This version is highly recommended for nature fanatics, as you'll hike through pristine landscapes and get to see the point where the Tapacalí and Comali rivers join at the birthplace of the Río Coco.

The most popular option is the four-hour, 6km classic loop: you head straight to the far entrance of the canyon, from where you'll swim, hike and leap beneath slate-rock faces and jagged peaks until you reach the exit.

For those who are adverse to exercise, there is also a three-hour 'lite' tour where you are paddled up the gorge a short distance in a small boat and then can splash around in the canyon mouth or float around in an inflatable tube.

Following a couple of incidents, local guides (US$15/20 half-/full day for up to five people) are now mandatory if you want to venture inside the canyon. In addition to having expert knowledge of river conditions – which can become dangerous during the wet season – guides also blend local insight with adventure and create a richer experience.

Guides from the local community of Sonis, at the entrance to the reserve, have formed a fantastic community tourism organization called Somoto Canyon Tours and work on a rotation basis. They offer a fantastic package, including transportation from Somoto, life vest and water shoes, a dry bag, entrance fee, guide, lunch and a boat trip for US$25 per visitor for the standard loop and US$30 for the longer version. They also offer **horseback-riding tours** to the surrounding mountains to get a bird's-eye view of the area, and organize homestays in the community so you can spend more time exploring. You can identify their guides by their neat, green uniforms. If you reserve in advance they'll wait for you at the bus station in Somoto.

Another option is to visit with one of the guides from local tour operator Namancambre Tours (found in Somoto town).

To visit the canyon take any El Espino–bound bus (US$0.40, 30 minutes) from the bus terminal to the trailhead at Km 231 near the community of Sonis (look out for the sign). A taxi will cost around US$8. From here it's a 3km hike to the canyon, including a river crossing that may be over a meter deep. The last bus back to Somoto passes through at around 5:30pm.

If you're coming from Honduras via El Espino – the Del Sol bus line has an authorized stop right at the entrance – there's no need to go into Somoto.

The canyon often closes in October, when the water is too high. Call the guides to check on conditions.

🏃 Activities

★ **Somoto Canyon Tours**   ADVENTURE TOUR
(☑ 8610-7642; www.somotocanyontours.org; Carretera Somoto–El Espino Km 229.5) 🖉 A well-run community tourism organization based in the village of Sonis, right by the entrance to the Cañon de Somoto. They specialize in natural adventures in the canyon, including an overnight option where you'll sleep in tents under the stars, but also organize **horseback riding** and other **hikes** in the region. Highly recommended.

Namancambre Tours   ADVENTURE TOUR
(☑ 2722-0889; http://namancambretours.nicaragua-info.com; reloj, ½c sur) A well-regarded local tour operator with good equipment offering a range of trips into the Somoto Canyon. The standard four-hour tour costs US$17 per visitor (not including transport) and it will run a trip even with just one client. Also offers overnight canyon trips and other outdoor activities in the region.

🛏️ Sleeping

Sonis Homestay   HOMESTAY $
(☑ 8610-7642; www.somotocanyontours.org; Carretera El Espino Km 229.5, Sonis; dm/r US$7/15) 🖉 If you are in Somoto only to see the canyon, consider staying with one of the local families in the village of Sonis (right at the canyon entrance) as part of their community tourism project. Accommodations are in purpose-built *cabañas* right next to family homes.

Sleeping right next to the canyon will give you plenty of time to get out and explore, and also provide the chance to experience life in a rural community. You can eat excellent, inexpensive meals with your hosts. Contact Somoto Canyon Tours coordinator Henry Soriano to reserve a room.

Quinta San Rafael   LODGE $$$
(☑ 8449-1766; info.canondesomoto@gmail.com; entrada Cañon de Somoto; house for up to 12 visitors US$250, cabaña for 6-8 visitors US$120) With a privileged location down in the valley just before the entrance to the canyon, this spacious rural property offers the most comfortable accommodations for kilometers around. The main house has two floors, with

an open fireplace in the lounge and kitchen area and a wonderful deck with panoramic views of the mountains. There are also several smaller *cabañas*.

✕ Eating & Drinking

Carne Asada El Buen Gusto NICARAGUAN $
(frente Intae; mains US$3; ⊙7am-10pm, closed Sun) Pull up a handcrafted wooden stool and dine under the traditional pottery hanging from the ceiling in this popular grill restaurant west of Parque Central. There are your standard *fritanga* (grill) options as well as a variety of typical regional plates and great *refrescos naturales* (cold drinks made from local fruits and herbs blended with water and sugar).

Aroma CAFE
(Parque Central; drinks US$0.50-2; ⊙7:30am-8pm Tue-Sun) Pull up a chair on the deck of this tranquil, open-air cafe within the leafy central park and enjoy a variety of coffees made from quality local beans. Also prepares light meals.

🛍 Shopping

Rosquillas Vilchez FOOD
(⟲2722-2002; Enitel, 8c S, 1c E; rosquillas US$0.70-1.50; ⊙4am-6pm) Prepares the best traditional *rosquillas* in town. This local institution still prepares them the traditional way, baking each batch in one of three massive, wood-fired ovens. The ovens are lit at 2am in order to be hot enough to begin baking at 4am – come before 11am and you can watch the process.

ℹ Information

BanPro (reloj, 1c E) Reliable dual-currency ATM.
Hospital (⟲2722-2247; Panamericana) On the highway near the El Espino exit.
Marena (Ministry of the Environment & Natural Resources; ⟲2722-2431; INSS ½c N; ⊙8am-2pm Mon-Fri) It has limited information on Cañon de Somoto and Reserva Natural Tepesomoto-Pataste, and can source guides (though not as efficiently as your hotel or local tour operators can).

ℹ Getting There & Away

The bus terminal is on the Panamericana, six blocks from the town center.

Destination	Cost (US$)	Duration (hr)	Frequency (daily)
El Espino (Honduran border)	0.50	40min	5:15am-5:15pm, hourly
Estelí	1.15	1¾	5:20am-5pm, every 40min
Managua (expreso)	4	4	5am, 6:15am, 7:30am, 2pm, 3:15pm
Managua (ordinario)	3	4½	4am-5pm, almost hourly
Ocotal	0.60	1	5:15am-4:30pm, every 45min

Ocotal

Sunken into a boulder-strewn valley sprinkled with Ocote pines and wildflowers and ringed with gorgeous Segovias, Ocotal is the commercial center of the mythic Segovias.

These mountains once baited gold-hungry pirates up the Río Coco from the Caribbean Sea. Then, in 1927, Sandino and his 'Crazy Little Army' seized control of Ocotal from federal forces for his first big victory. This action won him some extra attention from the White House, and the US soon made humble Ocotal the first city in history to be bombed by fighter planes.

Today, Ocotal is just a peaceful market town that serves farmers and families who live in the dozens of surrounding *pueblos* (villages).

◎ Sights

Parque Central PLAZA
The undisputed star of the town center is Nicaragua's finest Parque Central. Former mayor Fausto Sánchez was a botanist, and he planted hundreds of tropical plants here, including magnolias, roses, orchids and birds of paradise – all set among soaring mature cypress and pine trees.

🎊 Festivals & Events

Festival de La Virgen de la Asunción PARADE
(⊙Aug) The Festival de La Virgen de la Asunción is held in mid-August, when area ranchers parade through Ocotal showing off their riding skills.

🛌 Sleeping

Despite being the closest city to the border at Las Manos, accommodations options in Ocotal are limited. There is one good mid-range hotel but budget options are fairly average.

Hotel Frontera HOTEL **$$**
(☑ 2732-2668; hofrosa@turbonett.com.ni; Panamericana, contiguo a Shell Ramos; s/d with fan US$23/34, with air-con US$50/67; P ❄ 🖥 🏊) It's a little removed from the center of town but this place on the highway is easily the most comfortable option in Ocotal. The rooms are huge and come with creature comforts like hot water, air-con and a pool.

🍴 Eating & Drinking

While there's not a lot of variety, Ocotal has a handful of good restaurants serving Nicaraguan plates, as well as one fantastic buffet.

Llamarada Cafetín del Bosque NICARAGUAN **$**
(Parque Central; meals US$2-3; ⏾ 6am-4pm) This steam-table buffet deluxe is your best breakfast and lunch destination, where trays of fluffy pancakes, *gallo pinto* (rice and beans) and scrambled eggs rotate with great barbecued chicken wings, beef in onion sauce and plantains. Unfortunately, the new location lacks the leafy courtyard of the original spot, but the food is still outstanding value.

La Yunta NICARAGUAN **$$**
(☑ 2732-2180; Parque Central, 2c O, 1c S; mains US$7.50-10; ⏾ noon-11pm Tue-Thu, to 1am Fri-Sun) Recently refurbished, Ocotal's succulent staple still serves up the same big portions of top-quality meals. Being an agricultural town, the menu is focused on the grill. The bar is also a decent place to down a few cold beers. It draws a bar crowd on weekends.

★ **Casa Vieja** BAR
(Supermercado San Juan, ½c N; ⏾ 6pm-midnight) Step through the majestic wooden doors of this lovely old adobe house and enjoy cold beer and typical snacks in a wonderful social atmosphere, accompanied by a *trova* (Latin folk music) soundtrack that complements, rather than dominates, the conversation.

ℹ️ Information

BanPro (frente mercado) Has a Visa/Plus ATM.
Hospital (☑ 2732-2491; Panamericana) The biggest hospital in the region.
Intur (☑ 2732-3429; intur_ocotal@yahoo.com; Parque Central, 3c S, 1c O; ⏾ 8am-2pm Mon-Fri) Helpful tourist office that offers advice on visiting coffee farms in the region and arranges guides to climb Cerro Mogotón. It is also able to help book accommodations.

ℹ️ Getting There & Away

Buses depart from the main bus terminal, 1km south of the Parque Central. Border-bound buses stop to pick up passengers by the Shell station at the northern end of town.

Minivan services that get packed go to Ciudad Antigua (US$0.50, 45 minutes, 5am and noon). Alternatively, take any Jalapa- or Jicaro-bound service to the junction and pick up a shared taxi.
Bus Terminal (☑ 2732-3304) On the highway on the southern edge of town. All buses leave from and arrive here.

Dipilto

It would be hard to dream up a sweeter setting than what you'll find in this tiny mountain *pueblo* 20km north of Ocotal, and just a 30-minute drive from Honduras.

BUSES FROM OCOTAL

DESTINATION	COST (US$)	DURATION (HR)	FREQUENCY (DAILY)
Estelí	1.80	2¼	4:45am-6pm, hourly
Jalapa	1.85	2½	5:45am-4:30pm, every 1¼hr
Jícaro (Ciudad Sandino)	1.40	2½	6:15am, 10:45am, 3:20pm, 5pm
Las Manos (Honduran border)	0.60	1	5am-4:40pm, half-hourly
Managua	3.85	3½	4am-3:30pm, every 90min
Murra	2.10	3½	5:15am, 7am, 8:45am, 12:30pm, 1:25pm
Somoto	0.50	1¼	5:45am-6:30pm, every 45min

Think narrow, cobbled streets, surrounded by the pine-studded, coffee-shaded Segovias, carved by a rushing, cascading river. The principal site is the Santuario de la Virgen de la Piedra, where the radiant Virgin of Guadalupe blesses a kneeling pilgrim surrounded by fragrant gardens that attract butterflies. Her faithful arrive on Saturday and Sunday to light candles and voice their prayers. And if you land here on December 12, the Día del Virgen de Guadalupe, you can be a part of the festive love mob, which descends from all corners of the Northern Highlands.

The majestic mountains around Dipilto are known for producing some of the best coffee in Nicaragua. Staff in the alcaldía (Mayor's office; ☎ 8429-3489) can help organize hikes through some of Dipilto's stunning shade-grown plantations with specially trained local guides. Several of the farms offer rustic accommodations, including Finca San Isidro (☎ 2732-2392; r per person US$20), a charming old hacienda (estate) with great views. Also ask about guided treks to quetzal nesting grounds in the cloud forest on the 1867m El Volcán.

❶ Getting There & Away

Dipilto is divided into two communities, Dipilto Nuevo and Dipilto Viejo, which is a further 3km along the highway toward the Honduran border. The alcaldía and access to the santuario is from Dipilto Nuevo. Take any bus bound for the Las Manos border crossing and ask the driver to let you out in Dipilto Nuevo (US$0.45, 30 minutes). Buses run south to Ocotal and beyond every 30 minutes or so until around 5pm.

Ocotal to Jalapa

North of Ocotal a sinuous, 65km (mostly) brick road branches into the Segovian pine forests and leads to mountainous Jalapa, Nicaragua's wild north. From ceramic factories to ancient cities with ties to Captain Morgan, there's a lot to see here. It helps to have your own vehicle, though Ocotal buses serve most of these locations several times daily. Remember, when it rains, some of the dirt spur roads get messy, so if you're planning deep off-road adventures make sure to rent a 4WD.

The town of Mozonte, just 5km from Ocotal, is located on the site of a pre-Hispanic Chorotega community and still retains strong indigenous roots. There are numerous ceramics workshops, where you can watch artisans work a variety of ceramic materials and techniques. It's a fascinating spectacle and you can buy your vases, candleholders, wind chimes and wall ornaments here on the cheap.

Looming above town is Hermita de la Virgen de Guadalupe, a rock-top shrine with spectacular views. Take a stroll up the forested hill overlooking town to Capilla Los Pozos, where locals gather in the afternoon to play music. Along the way, keep an eye out for the golden warbler, an endangered bird species that migrates between here and Texas.

There's a well-signed turnoff at the beginning of the 4.5km brick road to Ciudad Antigua (Segovia), a cute old Spanish town famous for its ties to an ambitious Brit. Founded in 1536 and under almost constant attack from local indigenous groups for the next century, it was sacked in 1654 by pirate Henry Morgan, who had come up the nearby Río Coco in a canoe, thirsty for gold. Calling it a 'city' is a bit of a stretch – the main movements around the leafy central park are the slow paces of old donkeys. The city's jewel is the sensational Santuario de los Milagros (Parque Central), with its gorgeous brick arches and enormous wooden doors and a Christ figure brought from Austria. Local legend says that whenever pirates entered the sanctuary, the sculpture grew to enormous proportions and could not be taken out the doors. Across the road, the small but fun Museo Segoviano (frente iglesia; admission US$0.30; ⏰8am-4pm Mon-Fri) has a few pre-Columbian ceramics, some ancient wine goblets and the original stone altar from the church.

Back on the main road, continue to the speed bumps of San Fernando, which has a great Parque Central and is famous for its cheles (individuals with white skin), which many trace to the presence of US marines in the area from 1927 to 1931. Cerro Mogotón, Nicaragua's highest peak, is less than 20km from town.

About 10km past San Fernando, you can make a right onto the sketchy dirt road to El Jícaro (Ciudad Sandino), where Sandino's military mined for gold at Las Minas San Albino. It's possible to visit the ruins of the mine and check out what remains of

Sandino's rusted old mining gear. The town itself is attractive and friendly, and makes a good base from which to explore the attractions in the surrounding countryside – on foot or on horseback – or just soak up the rural mountain vibe.

If you have a 4WD, stay on this road and you'll eventually come to the community of Murra, where the surrounding countryside undulates between 820m and 1300m and hides Salto El Rosario, one of the highest – and quite possibly the most spectacular – waterfalls in the country. The water falls for nearly 200m in three sections close to gorgeous Finca Santa Rita, which sits on 200 hectares of land outside Murra.

Returning to the main highway, about 30km south of Jalapa you'll reach the newly developed Termales Don Alfonso. Another 12km further on is the turnoff to El Limón, where sulfuric thermal springs seep out of the mountains, forming small caves alongside a river. Somoza once had private thermal baths here, but the pools were destroyed by Hurricane Mitch. There are no pools for swimming here.

To the north of El Limón, there are two sustainable farms in the Las Nubarrones area. Finca Ecológica Sonzapote (☑8644-0830; El Limón) grows organic, shade-grown coffee and is in the transition zone between the pines and cloud forest. It has a *tobogán* – a butt-bruising but fun concrete slide – and large swimming pool. Finca Ecológica La Reforma (☑8653-3082; Los Nubarrones, El Limón) is set in the pines, laced with trails and split by a crystalline river flush with swimming holes. It offers accommodations in a pair of rustic *cabañas*.

🏃 Activities

Nicaragua's highest peak, Cerro Mogotón (2107m) towers over the coffee fields of Nueva Segovia, close to the Honduran border. Once off-limits due to land mines, it is now safe to climb with a local guide. The easiest access is from the Ocotal–Jalapa road near the village of Achuapa. It's a seven-hour round-trip hike to the peak, which is covered in dense cloud forest. Independent guide Mayerlin Ruiz runs trips to Mogotón (US$65 per person, minimum two people), departing from Ocotal.

Termales Don Alfonso
Nueva Segovia   HOT SPRING
(Termales Aranjuez; Aranjuez; admission US$5; ⊙8:30am-4:30pm, closed Mon) Around 30km south of Jalapa, these newly developed thermal baths are constructed over mineral-rich waters, which are reputed to have medicinal properties and gush out of the ground. The waters are so hot at their source that you can boil an egg (there are even dedicated cooking holes for this). Fortunately the relaxation pools are not quite so hot; there is a large, round pool included in the admission price and three smaller rectangular baths for private soaks, one of which is wheelchair-accessible.

The whole complex is surrounded by nature and there are huts with picnic tables and hooks for hanging hammocks dotted around the property.

Any bus between Jalapa and Ocotal will drop you at the entrance by the river, from where it's about a 1.5km hike to the springs. A taxi from Jalapa costs around US$25.

Mayerlin Ruiz   HIKING
(☑8234-9784; mayerlinruiz89@yahoo.com) An enthusiastic local guide specializing in hikes to the summit of Mogotón.

🛏 Sleeping & Eating

El Segoviano   GUESTHOUSE $
(☑2735-2293; salida a Murra; s/d US$7/11; 🐕) On the road out of town leading to Murra, this is one of the better places to crash if you need to spend the night in El Jícaro.

Comedor Kenia   NICARAGUAN $
(Petronic Station, 1c S; meals from US$2; ⊙11am-9pm) This friendly diner set in a large, bamboo-walled hut offers delicious typical meals cooked to perfection – which is fortunate, as it may very well be the only place open when you pass through town.

❶ Getting There & Away

Buses run on the main highway between Ocotal and Jalapa almost hourly and can drop you anywhere along the route. El Jícaro has services to both Ocotal and Jalapa and you can also use Ocotal–El Murra buses.

For Ciudad Antigua, minibuses leave from Ocotal at 5am and noon, but they can get very crowded. It's often more convenient to take a Jalapa- or Jícaro-bound bus and get off at the junction, from where *colectivo* taxis (US$0.50) run into town.

Jalapa

In a region freckled with remote mountain towns, Jalapa is one where the emerald hills are so close you can see their dips and grooves, their texture and shadows.

While the town itself is not likely to win any beauty contests, the surrounding countryside boasts such dramatic natural beauty and so many adventure opportunities that the utter lack of tourism here is difficult to fathom.

◉ Sights & Activities

Cerro de Jesús   MOUNTAIN, FARM
(☑2737-2474; www.jesusmountaincoffee.com) Just outside Jalapa you'll find Cerro de Jesús (1885m) the largest mountain in the area. It is dominated by the Jesus Mountain **coffee plantation**, which boasts 400 hectares of organic coffee. But on the flanks of the mountain you'll also find a small local community, intact primary forest and a gushing 8m waterfall. If you're up to it, you can hike to the peak.

Hotel El Pantano   TOUR
(☑2737-2231; www.hotelelpantano.com; Parque Central, 6c O; ⊘8am-4pm) This is by far the best resource for tourists in the area. It hosts and/or arranges many guided treks and trips, spanning from one to four days. If you wish to organize your own adventure yourself, the helpful English-, Dutch- and Spanish-speaking owner, Wim Van der Donk, can suggest local guides and offer directions.

⭐ Festivals & Events

Feria del Maíz   FERIA
(⊘Sep) The Feria de Maíz (Corn Festival) blooms around the September harvest, when farmers converge in corn clothing to erect corn altars, enjoy a week of corn contests, and take part in theater and dances that shed a local light on corn history.

🛏 Sleeping & Eating

There are a couple of hotels in the center of town, but it's more pleasant to stay among the natural beauty found on the outskirts.

There's not a lot of diversity in Jalapa's dining scene, although a new pizza place at least provides an alternative to more *gallo pinto*.

Hotel El Pantano   HOTEL **$$**
(☑2737-2031; www.hotelelpantano.com; Parque Central, 6c O; s/d/tr US$20/25/30, all incl breakfast; ☏) Easily your best bet in Jalapa, this welcoming hotel is set on lovely, lush grounds by a creek a short walk from town. The comfy brick rooms have cable TV and hot water and you'll be serenaded by birdsong in the mornings. Campers are welcome to pitch their tent (per night US$3.50) and warm up in the morning over amazing coffee at the **restaurant** (meals US$3.50 to US$8).

Comedor Sandra   NICARAGUAN **$**
(costado sur mercado; meals US$2.50; ⊘7am-3pm) This humble *comedor* by the market serves cheap, filling Nica meals from a steam-table buffet.

🛍 Shopping

Flor de Pino   HANDICRAFTS
(☑8704-0532; frente Plazoleta, Champigny; ⊘9am-6pm) 🌿 Members of this small women's cooperative weave elegant baskets from pine needles. The products are absolutely charming, as are the women who make them. Don't rush your visit here: take some time to learn a little about the craft and local village life. The workshop is in the community of Champigny, 4km north of town.

ℹ Information

Cyber Mavicenter (Enacal, 1c Sur; per hr US$0.30; ⊘8:30am-9pm) The best internet connection in town.

ℹ Getting There & Away

The bus terminal is just south of town, near the cemetery. The taxi drivers who hang out here are sharks, so if your bags aren't too heavy, walk a couple of blocks and hail a cab to pay half the price.

Bus services include the following:

El Jícaro (Ciudad Sandino) (US$1.75, 1½ hours, noon and 4pm) Meets buses to Murra.

El Porvenir (US$1.50, 30 minutes, hourly until 6pm)

Estelí (US$4, four hours, 4am and 10:50am)

Managua (US$6.50, 5½ hours, 3am, 4am, 5:30am, 9am, 9:40am and 1:45pm)

Ocotal (US$1.85, 2½ hours, 5am to 4pm, hourly)

Estelí–Jinotega Road

The coffee-country hinterland between Estelí and Jinotega contains tiny farming villages, gorgeous farms clinging to steep mountainsides and tracts of lush forest. It's an accessible yet rarely visited area that offers fascinating insights into authentic rural Nicaraguan culture.

The gorgeous back-country drive between Estelí and Jinotega – two hubs of the expanded Ruta de Café – has multiple personalities depending on your chosen path.

The most direct route is a smooth drive over new paving stones and recently tarred roads through oak-studded rangeland and spectacular mountain vistas. Leaving from Estelí, take the 'La Pelota' exit from the Pan-American Hwy, from where it's a straight shot to La Concordia (899m), almost exactly 33km from both Jinotega and Estelí.

Once you arrive in sleepy La Concordia, you can stroll through the lovely, peach-tinted Iglesia Nuestra Señora de Lourdes, built in 1851 and crowned with Gothic crosses on its white-domed facade. From La Concordia it's a steep climb up a narrow but good mountain road to San Rafael del Norte.

The alternative (and much longer) route is reserved for those who fancy themselves rally drivers and have taken out the no-excess policy on their rental. Don't even think about attempting it without 4WD. Take the road to Miraflor out of Estelí and keep to the left, climbing through the heart of Miraflor along a rough dirt track before reaching the small town of San Sebastián de Yalí which has petroglyphs in the Parque Central. Consider taking a detour 10km further north to La Pavona, where you'll find a huge petroglyph storyboard carved into the rocks near Cerro la Cruz.

The road from Yalí to San Rafael del Norte skirts the edge of the Reserva Natural Volcan Yalí; it has recently been refurbished with paving stones and is now a straightforward drive. The reward for taking this out-of-the-way route is fresh mountain air and splendid landscapes known to few travelers.

From San Rafael it's a pleasant 30-minute drive along the shores of Lago de Apanás past tiny fishing villages to Jinotega. If you're feeling hungry, make a short detour down to the lake edge at Sisle for a plate of fresh fried fish.

❶ Getting There & Away

It's possible to travel these roads on the cheap with public transport. There are half a dozen buses a day from Estelí via Concordia and San Rafael (US$1.80, two hours).

Alternatively, there are four buses a day from Estelí to Yalí (US$2, 2½ hours) along the rough road through Miraflor. From Yalí there are regular connections to Jinotega (US$2, 2½ hours).

San Rafael del Norte

One of the highest towns in Nicaragua, charming San Rafael del Norte is surrounded by soaring, fissured peaks with coffee *fincas* on their shoulders. Founded in the 1660s, it is rich in culture and a great jumping-off point for hikes and outdoor activities high in the mountains.

◉ Sights & Activities

★ Templo Parroquial de San Rafael Arcángel   CHURCH

Beginning in 1955, the revered Father Odorico D'Andrea turned this antiquated cathedral into a labor of divine love. It's impeccably restored, with a soaring interior flooded with light streaming through stained-glass skylights that illuminate a wonderful altar and a series of inspiring murals, which were painted by Austrian artist Juan Fuchs Holl in 1967 and 1968. It's no wonder it was made a National Artistic Monument in 2000.

El Jaguar   PARK

(☑8886-1016, 2279-9219; www.jaguarreserve. org; costs vary by activity) ✐ Both coffee enthusiasts and nature lovers will be enamored with this fantastic private reserve with comfortable cabañas (dorm/ room per person including three meals US$35/75) and family-friendly trails (read: nothing too long or too steep) as well as strenuous ones through primary cloud forest and past coffee stands to spectacular *miradores* (viewpoints). It's just outside town on the road to Lago de Apanás. Advance reservations are essential.

La Brellera Canopy Tour   ADVENTURE TOUR

(☑2784-2356; labrelleranatural@yahoo.es; per person US$20; ☉8am-4:30pm) Tired of coffee? Head just 4km from San Rafael to La Brellera to traverse 1500m through pine forest via nine platforms, eight cables and two hanging bridges. For an extra US$7 you can make the return trip on horseback. There is an on-site restaurant serving barbecue dishes and typical Nica meals.

Finca Kilimanjaro OUTDOORS
(☑2782-2113, 8838-9418; fincakilimanjaro@hotmail.com) This working farm at 1300m near San Rafael offers a wide variety of activities, including horseback riding, hiking, cow milking, swimming, and harvesting during coffee season. Day trips (US$35 per person) include lunch, transportation from Jinotega and a short tour of San Rafael. If you want to stay longer, overnight packages (per person including all meals US$50) are also available. Reserve at least two days in advance and bring warm clothes.

If you don't have a vehicle, the owners can arrange transport from Jinotega.

🛌 Sleeping

San Rafael is very doable as a day trip from either Jinotega or Estelí, but if you want to stick around there is one fine hotel in town and two top rural lodges just outside.

Casita San Payo GUESTHOUSE $
(☑2784-2327; casitasanpayo@gmail.com; Parque Central, 2½c N; s/d/tr US$13.50/17/21.50) This is a terrific budget hotel with sunny upstairs rooms wired for cable TV, and it has an even better restaurant (mains US$4 to US$6). The fabulous owner, Naraya Zelaya, is beyond helpful – she rents out a pick-up and a minibus, complete with driver, to explore the region and can also arrange guides (per half-/full day US$10/20).

Among the destinations the hotel arranges trips to are the Cascadas Verdes and Salto Santa María waterfalls, the Cuevas del Hermitanio caves and pine-blanketed Volcán Yalí (1542m).

❶ Getting There & Away

Buses (US$0.80, 45 minutes) and minibuses (US$1, 30 minutes) to Jinotega leave at regular intervals from a small bus terminal on the north side of town. Buses for Estelí (US$1.50, 90 minutes, every two hours) travel via La Concordia.

Jinotega

Hidden in a cat's eye of a valley, Jinotega, the 'City of Mists,' is enclosed on all sides by mountains dappled in cloud forests,

crowned with granite ridges and pocked with deep gorges.

While coffee tourism percolates in Matagalpa, Jinotega, which brims with adventure and promise, still sees far more foreign-aid workers than tourists. So walk these cobbled streets, visit nearby Lago de Apanás and hike into the misty mountains, where you can harvest coffee with locals and stroll through primary forest. Just make sure to get to Cerro La Cruz on a clear day to glimpse the cat's eye in all her jade glory.

And that City of Mists moniker is no joke. The average temperature is just 20°C (68°F) and the town can get 2600mm of rain annually. Bring rain gear and a fleece for the cool evenings.

◉ Sights

★Cerro La Cruz RELIGIOUS SITE
A steep yet worthwhile hour's hike from the cemetery and embedded in a boulder-crusted ridge is the town cross, originally placed here in 1703 by Franciscan Fray Margíl de Jesús. The view of Jinotega and the layered Cordillera Isabelía from up here is unreal. Take the center path through the cemetery and begin the sweaty climb. When you emerge from the trees and come to a plateau, hug the ridge tightly and keep climbing.

If you land here during Jinotega's biggest party, the Fiestas de la Cruz (p188; April 30 to May 16), which peaks on May 3, you can follow the *abuelas* (grandmothers) as they ascend, ever so gingerly, en masse.

Catedral San Juan CHURCH
The beauty of Jinotega's cathedral (c 1805) is in the sanctuary, where you'll marvel at the chestnut and gold-leaf altar and pristine white arches and rows of heavenly saints, sculpted with so much life and light they make spiritual peace contagious. Opposite the church is a terrific, split-level Parque Central shaded by palms and towering laurel trees.

🎉 Festivals & Events

Fiestas de la Cruz RELIGIOUS
(☺Apr 30-May 16) One of Nicaragua's most athletic *fiestas* – since 1703 visitors have been shamed into climbing to the cross by area octogenarians (at the festival's peak on May 3). Don't forget to breathe…

Jinotega

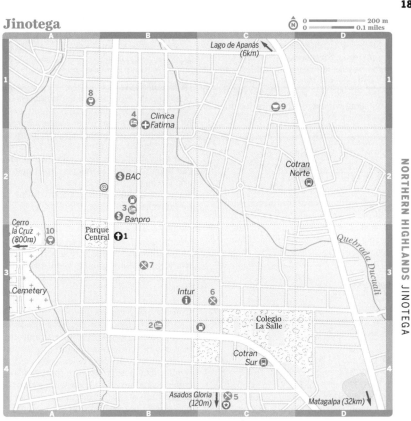

| 0 | 200 m |
| 0 | 0.1 miles |

San Isidro Laborador RELIGIOUS
(☉ May 15) Locals honor the patron saint of farmers by building altars out of fruits and veggies.

Fiestas Patronales RELIGIOUS
(☉ Jun 24) Solemn processions, rodeos, beauty queens and more celebrate the feast day of San Juan Bautista.

🛏 Sleeping

Jinotega has a good range of accommodations with more and more opening on a regular basis. Supply far outstrips demand so you should be able to negotiate a good deal.

Hotel Sollentuna Hem HOTEL **$**
(☎ 2782-2334; solentunahem@gmail.com; Parque Central, 4c N; s/d US$13.50/16; P 🛜) A favorite among travelers, this small, welcoming hotel has a variety of good-value rooms with cable

Jinotega

TV and hot water. Ask to take a look around, as some are better than others.

Hotel Central HOTEL $
(☑ 2782-2063; Parque Central, 1c E, ½c N; s/d/tr US$14.40/18/32; P 🏠) A reliable budget bet in the center, this place rents plain but comfy rooms with hot water and cable, although the walls are somewhat thin. The rooms on the north side are brighter as they have outside-facing windows (albeit overlooking the gas station).

★ **Hotel Café** HOTEL $$$
(☑ 2782-2710; www.cafehoteljinotega.com; Gasolinera Uno, 1c O, ½c N; s/d incl breakfast US$50/60; P ❄ 🏠) The most comfy sleep in Jinotega is located at this three-star property. Most (but not all) of the rooms are flooded with natural light, which reflects pastel paint jobs. Service is professional and courteous. The marble baths and hyper-speed laundry service are nice, too.

✖ Eating

Eating in Jinotega is very budget-friendly – even the best restaurants in town won't break the bank.

★ **La Casa de Don Colocho** BAKERY $
(☑ 2782-2584; Parque Central, 3c E, 3c S; pastries US$0.60-1.10, coffee US$1.50; ⊙ 8am-6pm Mon-Sat; 🖶) A bakery every town would love. The cinnamon rolls are dense and sugary and the pineapple triangles are addictive – and those are just two of the dozens of items this place turns out daily. The ovens begin to open at around 1pm, except on weekends. Plan your visit accordingly.

Comedor Chevy NICARAGUAN $
(Hospital, ½c E; mains US$2.90; ⊙ 8am-10pm, closed Tue) Jinotega's favorite cheap eats are found at this unpretentious steam-table buffet. Pounce on a vacant table and take your pick from beef, chicken and pork mains and all the usual sides. Tasty and filling.

Soda El Tico NICARAGUAN $
(☑ 2782-2059; Parque Central, 1c E, ½c S; buffet meals US$4, mains US$6; ⊙ 7:30am-10pm) By far the most appetizing restaurant in town, Soda El Tico is a classic steam-table buffet with steak, pork loin and grilled chicken served with a tasty salad bar. You can also order a variety of snacks and specialties from the menu.

🍷 Drinking & Nightlife

There are a couple of surprisingly hip bars in town. No surprise is the presence of cafes serving excellent coffee.

★ **Bar Jinocuba** BAR
(Alcaldía, 5c N; ⊙ 3-11pm Mon-Thu, to midnight Fri-Sun; 🏠) A groovy bohemian bar (and guaranteed *ranchero*-free zone) with occasional, hip live-music performances and cultural events. The young owners are very knowledgeable about tourism in the region and can hook you up with independent English- and German-speaking guides to explore the surrounding mountains. Also serves Cuban and international meals.

La Taverna BAR
(Parque Central, 2c O; ⊙ noon-midnight) The coolest dive bar in the Northern Highlands has timber tables, a dark wood interior, a lively late-night crowd and tasty beef fajitas (US$5).

Café Flor de Jinotega CAFE
(☑ 2782-2617; Cotran Norte, 1½c N; espresso drinks US$0.50-0.75; ⊙ 8am-6pm) Quite simply the best cup of coffee in town, and possibly on all of the Ruta de Café. Relax at one of the see-through tables filled with three kinds of coffee beans and get to know what good java is. Staff can also arrange guides and transport to visit nearby coffee farms.

ℹ Information

BanPro (Catedral San Juan, ½c N) and **BAC** (Parque Central, 1½c N) both have ATMs that accept Visa and MasterCard credit and debit cards.

Clinica Fatima (☑ 2782-6577; Esso Central, 2½c N; ⊙ 8:30am-5pm Mon-Fri, to noon Sat) Private clinic with a range of specialists.

Cyberzone (catedral, 1c N; per hr US$0.50; ⊙ 8am-10pm) Central internet facility with plenty of machines.

Intur (☑ 2782-4552; Parque Central, 2c S, 3c E; ⊙ 8am-4pm) Stop in to pick up the latest brochures.

Police (☑ 2782-2398, emergency 118; costado este del hospital)

ℹ Getting There & Away

BUS

There are two bus terminals. Cotran Norte, on the edge of the market, is little more than a chaotic parking lot. A wonderful contrast,

WORTH A TRIP

LA RUTA DE CAFÉ

Formed to promote rural tourism in the north, **La Ruta de Café** is a loose association of coffee *fincas* (farms) that welcome tourists to their fields (which range from *colectivos* of small subsistence growers to 100-year-old plantations). While promotion and funding of the project seems to have dried up, most properties involved still welcome visitors.

You can spend the night, hike through neighboring cloud forests, join in harvests (October to March) and sip plenty of local joe. There are four branches to Ruta de Café, which spans the entirety of the Northern Highlands.

Estelí & Nueva Segovia

Near Estelí, the **Área Protegida Miraflor** is a tapestry of family coffee *fincas* that formed in the wake of the Sandinista revolution. Further north, the lush, layered and shady coffee fields of **Dipilto** produce some of the most acclaimed beans in Nicaragua, while **Finca Cerro de Jesús** (p186) grows terrific coffee among large tracts of cloud forest in the rocky peaks surrounding Jalapa.

San Rafael del Norte

Accessed from San Rafael del Norte, **El Jaguar** (p187) is a family farm and model of sustainability, with 14 hectares of organic coffee parcels surrounded by 53 hectares of tropical cloud forest. Nearby **Finca Kilimanjaro** (p188) also arranges tours and overnight stays. In addition to joining the harvest, you can ride trails to glorious *miradores* (lookout points), plunge into swimming holes and milk the family cows.

Jinotega

When German coffee growers and their families first arrived in Nicaragua in the early 20th century, they came to the mountains that soar above Jinotega. It is here that you'll find **La Bastilla Ecolodge** (p192), a nonprofit initiative within a nature reserve that offers full coffee tours that include tasting sessions.

Also in the reserve are **Finca La Estrella**, where you can harvest berries with family farmers, and **Cooperativa Lina Herrera**, a shade-grown cooperative surrounded by thick forest. Check in at **Café Flor de Jinotega** (p190) for information on touring coffee farms here.

Matagalpa

The big draws here are two very different coffee-farm experiences. **Selva Negra** (p199), an 850-hectare estate, was founded by German immigrants in the 1880s and is still managed by their heirs. It offers sustainable coffee and wildlife tours.

For a more rustic experience, head to the communities surrounding **San Ramón**, where you can join the locals in the harvest and follow the beans to a community roasting plant.

the brand-new Cotran Sur sits near the town's southern entrance and is the best terminal in the region: it has shops, departure announcements and even a waiting lounge with wi-fi.

Buses departing from Cotran Norte:

Estelí (US$1.80, two hours, 5:15am, 7am, 9am, 1pm, 2:45pm and 3:30pm)

Pantasma (Asturias) (US$2, 1½ hours, 4am to 4:30pm, hourly)

Pantasma (San Gabriel) (US$1.80, 1½ hours, 5:30am to 4:30pm, hourly)

San Rafael del Norte (*ordinario* US$0.80, 40 minutes; *expreso* US$1, 30 minutes, both 6am to 6pm, half-hourly)

Yalí (US$2, two hours, 6am, 8:30am, 10am, noon and 2:30pm)

Buses departing from Cotran Sur:

Managua (US$3.40, 3½ hours, 4am to 4pm, 10 daily) Goes via a new road and does not enter Matagalpa.

Matagalpa (US$1, 1¼ hours, 5am to 6pm, half-hourly)

Reserva Natural Cerro Datanlí-El Diablo

The mountains towering over and buffering the eastern end of Jinotega are part of this stunning 10,000-hectare reserve, which climbs well into the quetzal zone at 1650m. It's a magical place, with butterflies dancing around coffee bushes that cling to impossibly steep mountainsides in the shade of lush cloud forest. A network of trails connects communities within the reserve and makes for great hiking.

◉ Sights

The main southern entrance to the reserve is 12.5km down a lousy dirt road from the signed turnoff 'Km 146' on the Matagalpa–Jinotega road. Continue on straight until you reach the village of La Fundadora, located on the site of an expansive former Somoza hacienda.

From La Fundadora, it's another rough 30-minute drive to the impressive La Bujona waterfall in the community of La Esmeralda.

La Bujona   WATERFALL
(La Esmerelda; admission $1) Surrounded by ethereal cloud forest, La Bujona is a wide wall of water that crashes over the rock face in various streams. It feels far from civilization and receives very few visitors. The path begins by two small posts just before the wooden bridge. You can trek the 12km from La Fundadore on your own, but it's more fun with a local guide: the Eco-Albergue will organize one for US$10 per group.

🛏 Sleeping

Eco-Albergue La Fundadora   LODGE $$
(☑ 8855-2573, 7747-7805; www.fundadora.org; La Fundadora; r per person US$10) An incredibly peaceful, community-run rural lodge consisting of half a dozen cute brick huts with tiled roofs overlooking farmland, found about 1km outside the village. The savvy young management arranges a variety of activities for visitors, including a truly authentic coffee tour (US$10 per visitor) with a local farming family and horseback riding.

Tasty typical meals (US$2.50 to US$3.50) are served onsite.

★ La Bastilla Ecolodge   LODGE $$$
(☑ 2782-4335, 8654-6235; www.bastillaecolodge.com; Reserva Natural Datanlí–El Diablo; dm/s/d/tr incl breakfast US$20/45/70/100; P 🛜) Set on a dramatic, forested mountainside at 1200m with views all the way down to Lago de Apanás, La Bastilla Ecolodge has easily the most comfortable accommodations in the reserve. The spacious, solar-powered brick *cabañas* have red floor tiles, sparkling bathrooms with solar hot water, and sensational views over coffee plantations full of birds from the wide wooden balconies.

There are also comfy tents set up on wooden platforms with private bathrooms and panoramic views (US$15 per guest) and a comfortable dormitory.

But first-class comfort and service is only half the story here. The ecolodge is an entirely nonprofit initiative that funds the nearby technical training center. Many students from the center work as guides and can take you along the 300-hectare farm's three hiking trails. You can even try your hand picking your own coffee.

ℹ Getting There & Away

One daily bus leaves Cotran Norte in Matagalpa at 1:45pm for Las Nubes, passing through La Fundadora and La Esmeralda, returning at 6am. It gets full, so arrive early or you may be riding on the roof. During the coffee harvest buses also run to the area from Jinotega, but the schedule is irregular and they are usually packed.

If you miss the direct bus, it's also possible to hike into La Fundadora from Las Latas on the old Matagalpa–Jinotega highway; it's a much shorter trek than walking along the main Fundadora road but there's also less traffic, so your chances of hitching a ride are minimal.

For La Bastilla, take any Pantasma (via Asturias) bus from Jinotega and jump out at the 'empalme La Bastilla,' from where it's a tough 5km hike uphill. If you call in advance, staff will pick you up at the turnoff (US$5). The same Pantasma bus can drop you at the village of Venencia, a short distance further down the road from La Bastilla, from where it's a 3km, one-hour walk down a rough spur road to El Gobiado. If you phone ahead it's possible to organize horses to save you the walk.

Lago de Apanás

The third-largest body of water in Nicaragua came into being in 1964 when the Mancotal dam was built on the Río El Tuma, just 6km north of Jinotega. It's actually two lakes – the much larger Lago de Apanás (54 sq km) to the south, and Lago Asturias (3 sq km) to the north.

🏃 Activities

If you like freshwater bass, you can try the *guapote,* on sale at lots of rickety-looking *ranchos* (small houses) lining the lakeshore in the town of Asturias – or if you'd prefer to catch your own, fishers will take you out on the lake for around US$5 per hour in a rowboat, or US$10 per hour with a small outboard.

On the western lakeshore in the village of **Sisle**, local fisherfolk will take you out on boat tours to nearby islands, including Isla Ave (US$2) and Isla Conejo (US$5); departures are from the Malecón Turistica de Sisle (Sisle Tourist Dock) overlooking the water.

About a 20-minute drive further north along the road that hugs the lakeshore, near the community of **Yanque**, you'll find the **Comedor Norita** (☑8924-9487; Yanque No 1; meals from US$2), where you can ride horses, learn about local agriculture and visit a viewpoint with panoramic vistas of the lake and surrounding countryside.

✖ Eating

In both Sisle and Yanque you can get healthy plates of fried lake fish at a bargain price.

ⓘ Getting There & Away

There are two bus routes to Pantasma from the Cotran Norte in Jinotega: via Asturias on the eastern shore of the lake and via San Gabriel on the western side. To get to Sisle, take any San Gabriel bus and ask to be let off at the Pulpería Emilio Gomez, from where it's a 800m walk downhill to the dock. For Yanque stay on the bus and ask to be let off at Pulpería Adrian Granados.

Matagalpa

If you love coffee, mountains and urbanity, then have your cake and eat it in Matagalpa, a town where for decades an ever-increasing number of Liberal coffee patriarchs and subsistence Sandinista farmers have rubbed shoulders during city festivals and at market. Growth has sent Matagalpa sprawling into the foothills, up crumbling streets lined with shacks and onto graded plateaus laid out in tony subdivisions. Just glance skyward from nearly every city street and you'll see pristine boulder-strewn peaks.

When you've sipped your last cup of city, head for the hills, where you can hike through primary forest to gushing waterfalls, pick coffee, explore mineshafts and listen to *ranchero* troubadours jam under a harvest moon.

If you're looking for a base from which to explore the best the region has to offer or just want to hang around in an accessible, authentic city, it's hard to beat Matagalpa.

◉ Sights

★Casa Museo Comandante Carlos Fonseca
MUSEUM

(Parque Rubén Darío, 1c E; admission by donation; ⊙9am-5pm Mon-Fri, to noon Sat) FREE Commander Carlos Fonseca, the Sandinista equivalent of Malcolm X (read: bespectacled, goateed, intense, highly intelligent and charismatic), grew up desperately poor in this humble abode with his single mother and four siblings, despite the fact that his father was a coffee magnate. Now it's a tiny but enthralling museum that follows his evolution as a leader from childhood until his death.

Museo de Café
MUSEUM

(Av José Beníto Escobar, Parque Morazán, 1c S; ⊙8am-12:30pm & 2-5pm Mon-Fri, to noon Sat) FREE Recently overhauled, this absorbing museum features large, glossy, printed displays in Spanish and English on the roots of regional *café* and modern coffee production in the region, as well as old coffee processing machinery. Particularly interesting are the panels on the hardy immigrants who set up the first plantations in the region. Well worth a visit before any trip into the surrounding countryside.

🏃 Activities

Local hiking opportunities abound. The gorgeous boulder fields and red-rock faces of **El Ocote** are sensational. You can access the trail from behind El Castillo del Cacao and hike two to three hours before rejoining the highway to San Ramón at Finca La Praya. It's just a US$0.50 bus ride back to town.

For more hiking options, pop into nonprofit **Café Girasol** (☑2772-6030; www.familiasespeciales.org; contiguo Puente Salida Managua; ⊙7am-6pm) 🖉 for detailed leaflets (US$1) explaining a number of self-guided walks in the Matagalpa area that vary in length from four to eight hours. While you're there, make sure to sample the excellent coffee and homemade yogurt – profits support projects for children with disabilities. The cafe is located by the main bridge, a couple of blocks southwest of the market.

Reserva Natural Cerro Apante
PARK

(admission US$1.50) Matagalpa's most popular hiking trail leads from Finca San Luis, a 20-minute walk (or US$1 taxi ride) south of Parque Rubén Dario, into this reserve. It's

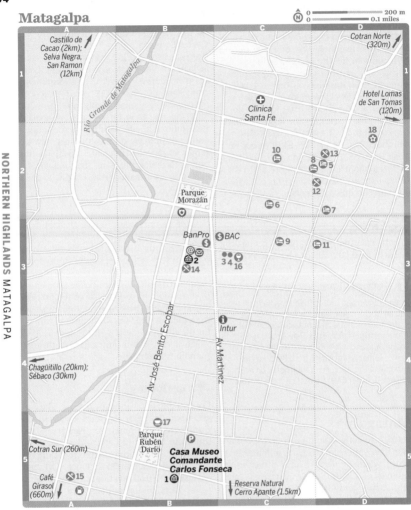

a two-hour round-trip hike to the *mirador*. If you're aiming for the misty, 1442m-high peak, it's best to hire a guide.

There is an alternative trail up to the new cross atop the mountain, which leaves from near the monastery in the south of town. It's an easier hike but the nature is less impressive. There are two other entrances to different sectors of the park: one is just north of town on the road to El Tuma; the other is on the road to Guadalupe-Samulali, off the Matagalpa–Muy Muy road.

Courses

Escuela de Español Colibrí　LANGUAGE COURSE
(www.colibrispanishschool.com; Parque Morazán, 1c S, ½c E; tuition per hr US$11-12) This popular school inside Matagalpa Tours offers one-on-one Spanish classes, plenty of cultural activities and volunteer placements for students. Packages that include 20 hours of classes per week plus a homestay with a local family and all meals cost US$344.

Matagalpa

👁 Top Sights
1 Casa Museo Comandante Carlos
  Fonseca...B5

👁 Sights
2 Museo de Café B3

🎯 Activities, Courses & Tours
3 Escuela de Español Colibri C3
4 Matagalpa Tours....................................C3

🛏 Sleeping
5 Buongiorno Principessa........................D2
6 Hostal Don Guillermo C2
7 Hotel El Castillo D2
8 La Buena Onda.......................................D2
9 Maria's B&B C3
10 Martina's Place.......................................C2

11 Montebrisa..D3

🍴 Eating
12 El Mexicano D2
13 La Vita é Bella..D2
14 Rincón Don Chaco..................................B3
15 Taquero A5

🍷 Drinking & Nightlife
16 Artesanos C3
17 Selección Nicaraguense........................B5

🎭 Entertainment
18 Centro Cultural Guanuca D2

🛍 Shopping
Telares de Nicaragua....................(see 4)

🧭 Tours

⭐ **Matagalpa Tours**   ADVENTURE TOUR
(☑ 8647-4680, 2772-0108; www.matagalpatours.
com; tours from US$15; ⊘ 8am-12:30pm & 2-6pm
Mon-Fri, 8am-4pm Sat) Matagalpa Tours offers
nearly a dozen interesting and enriching
ways to get into this city and the surrounding
countryside. In Matagalpa proper it offers
urban walking tours and rents out bicycles,
but its best work is done around the local
mountains, where it offers both day trips
and multiday excursions, including an informative tour of local coffee farms.

It also offers a wide range of adventure
activities, including white-water rafting on
the Río Tuma and excellent, nature-focused
adventures that get visitors well off the beat-
en path.

El Castillo del Cacao   FOOD
(☑ 2772-2002; www.elcastillodelcacao.com; Carretera La Dalia; admission US$6; ⊘ 9am-noon
Tue-Sat) On the road to San Ramón is Matagalpa's sweetest site. You've seen the chocolate bars by now, and if you know what's
good(-tasting) for you, you've also tasted
Castillo de Cacao. Now tour the 'castle'
where they mix the cacao with sugar, cash-
ews and coffee beans. Make sure to call first
to make sure they're working.

The tour is given by ordinary staff who
speak only Spanish. Matagalpa tour operators also offer a visit here with bilingual
guides. A taxi from town costs US$1 per
person.

🎉 Festivals & Events

Anniversary Party   CULTURAL
(⊘ Feb 14) Matagalpa's big bash is a fire-
works-splashed extravaganza with live music, horse shows, parades, beauty contests
and lots of *chicha bruja* (fermented corn
liquor).

🛏 Sleeping

Matagalpa has the best accommodations in
the Northern Highlands, with quality options for all budgets.

Hotel El Castillo   HOTEL $
(☑ 2772-0034; hotelelcastillomt@gmail.com; Parque Morazán, 3c E; s/d/tr US$15/17/24; 🖥) Set on
a hillside with great views, this family-run
hotel is only three blocks from the cathedral. Rooms at the front of the building
have small private balconies overlooking
the city and are outstanding value; the view-
less rooms at the back feel too enclosed and
are not particularly inviting. Add US$2 for
breakfast.

La Buena Onda   HOSTEL $$
(☑ 2772-2135; www.labuenaonda.com.ni; Can-
cha Brigadista, 2½c E; dm/s/d US$9/25/30; 🖥)
Clean, centrally located and with a chilled
vibe, this fine hostel ticks all the boxes. It's
located in a cozy, converted house with
well-furnished rooms, spacious dorms with
private bathrooms and big lockers) and a
balcony overlooking the street. There is a
kitchen for guest use and the helpful man-
agement provide plenty of information on
attractions in town and beyond. There is

another, slightly cheaper branch on the corner half a block west.

Buongiorno Principessa   GUESTHOUSE $$

(✆2772-2721; buongiornoprincipessa35@gmail.com; Colonia Lainez; dm/r US$12/30 incl breakfast; 🛜) This laid-back guesthouse in a narrow lane is an excellent-value base for exploring town. Dorms feature good mattresses and are not overcrowded, while private rooms are bright and welcoming. The included breakfast is top quality but the highlight is the fine rooftop terrace offering 360-degree views around town.

Martina's Place   HOSTEL $$

(✆2772-3918; www.martinasplace-hostal.com; Cancha El Brigadista, 1½c E; dm/s/d with shared bathroom US$8/14/28, s/d US$15/30; 🛜) A homey new hostel offering neat and comfortable private rooms and a massive dorm in a convenient location. The mattresses are comfortable and the owners extremely helpful, but the best reason to set up here is the spacious garden area – complete with barbecue and outdoor kitchen. That and the pet rabbit, George.

Maria's B&B   HOTEL $$

(✆2772-3097; www.mariasbnb.com; BanPro 1c E, ½c N; r US$46-66; P✳🛜) A fantastic addition to the local hotel scene, this intimate place right in the center of town has just half a dozen bright, spotless and comfortable rooms surrounding inviting common areas. Guests can access the open-plan kitchen. Service is warm and welcoming, particularly from Doña Chepa, who will cook your breakfast to order each morning.

Hostal Don Guillermo   HOTEL $$

(✆2772-3182; www.hoteldonguillermomatagalpa.com; Claro, 1/2c E; s/d US$30/35; 🛜) With a great location, elegant furnishings and a relaxed atmosphere, this small hotel offers some of the best value in town. The rooms are bright and spacious and the ample bathrooms have piping-hot water and good pressure. Breakfast is served in the small, plant-filled courtyard. A top choice.

Montebrisa   BOUTIQUE HOTEL $$$

(Parque Morazán, 3c E; r US$90-120; P✳🛜) Finally, Matagalpa has a high-end hotel with character. This beautifully renovated art deco house is a modern classic set in lush gardens on a hill just three blocks from Parque Morazán. The eight rooms are spacious and light-filled, with elegant cedar furniture;

some boast small private balconies that offer glimpses of Cerro Apante through the trees.

🍴 Eating

Matagalpa has a few good restaurants, but you'll need to look to the smoky booths that set up at sunset just north of Palí supermarket and the cathedral for the regional specialty, *güirílas*. Made with a fresh corn *masa,* they are sweeter and thicker than your average tortilla; a *servicio* includes a hunk of crumbly, salty *cuajada* cheese and *crema,* and costs about US$0.50.

Taquero   NICARAGUAN, MEXICAN $

(Parque Darío, 1c S, 1½c O; meals US$3-7; ⏱5:30pm-midnight) Part *fritanga* (grill), part Mexican diner, this hugely popular hybrid serves up surprisingly good grub until late. Ignore the tasteless stuffed iguanas on the wall and pick between impossibly tender barbecue beef, tangy chicken and ribs from the grill, or hit the menu for quality tacos, burritos and quesadillas.

Rincón Don Chaco   NICARAGUAN $

(Av José Beníto Escobar, Parque Morazán, 2c S; batidos US$1-1.80, burgers US$1-2, mains US$4.30-4.80; ⏱7:30am-5pm Mon-Fri, to 3pm Sun) A fresh-pressed, Formica diner with amazing *batidos* (fruit shakes made with milk or water). The pineapple and celery in orange juice is an instant classic, while the coconut in milk is also worth a try. There are also tasty veggie burgers and other snacks as well as a small selection of main meals available.

Follow it with the rather indulgent pound cake that's dripping with simple syrup.

El Mexicano   MEXICAN $

(Parque Morazán, 1c N, 2½c E; mains US$3-4; ⏱11am-9pm Mon-Sat; ✎) Enjoy cheap, authentic Mexican food prepared by the owner/chef from Guadalajara and served in a casual dining area. It comes out fairly tame but hot sauce is always available.

⭐La Vita é Bella   ITALIAN $$

(✆2772-5476; Parque Morazán, 2½c E, 1½c N; pastas US$3-4, mains US$5-8; ⏱noon-10pm, closed Tue; ✎) This local institution serves up flavorful authentic Italian dishes at low prices in a relaxed bistro atmosphere. The thin-crust pizza is some of the best in Nicaragua and the pasta dishes are also full of flavor. Vegetarians can take their pick from a wide selection of menu items. The only downer: canned mushrooms. Come early for a table.

El Pullaso STEAK $$
(Carretera Managua; dishes US$5.75-14.40; ⊙10am-10pm) Matagalpinos love beef and it's no surprise that their steakhouse of choice is El Pullaso, which serves big portions of tender cuts of meat at bargain prices. It's so popular they've constructed a 2nd floor. Come with an appetite. It's a US$1.50 to US$2 taxi ride from town.

🍷 Drinking & Nightlife

For events around town, check out the website Aguali (www.aguali.net).

Artesanos BAR
(☑2772-2444; Parque Morazán, 1c S, ½c E; ⊙9am-midnight) Hands down the grooviest bar-cafe in town. There's an all-dark-wood dining room, a large patio, great coffee, and a young, hipster crowd who drink and groove to electronica and Latin rhythms till closing time.

Selección Nicaragüense CAFE
(www.sn.com.ni; Parque Darío; ⊙8am-10pm) Pretty slick for the Northern Highlands, this modern cafe serves up good hot and cold coffee-based drinks using single-origin beans from around the region. Enjoy a cup in the fancy air-con lounge space or in the large patio out the back. Also sells bags of coffee to go – whole or ground.

It's fairly high-end; don't expect to see too many of the small plot growers themselves in here. If it feels a bit like a chain, it's because it is: there's another branch just north of the cathedral and one in Estelí.

☆ Entertainment

Centro Cultural Guanuca CULTURAL CENTER
(☑2772-3562; Guadalupe, 1½c S; ⊙10am-10pm) 🖋 Run by a nonprofit women's organization, this great venue shows art-house movies and hosts concerts and live events ranging from theater to dance competitions.

🛍 Shopping

Telares de Nicaragua HANDICRAFTS
(☑2772-0108; Parque Morazán, 1c S, ½c E; ⊙8am-5pm Mon-Fri, to 2pm Sat) 🖋 In the Matagalpa Tours building, this fair-trade outlet sells brightly colored fiber arts from indigenous artisans in El Chile, corn-husk dolls, beaded jewelry, baskets and a selection of the smooth, black local pottery, which is mixed with volcanic ash and fired at extreme temperatures.

ⓘ Information

Most banks are located on Av Martínez, a block south of Parque Morazán.

BAC (Parque Morazán, ½c S) ATM serves Visa and MasterCard networks.

BanPro (Parque Morazán, 1c Sur) Reliable Visa/MasterCard ATM.

Clinica Santa Fe (☑2772-5113, emergency 8419-6283; catedral, 3c N, ½c E; ⊙24hr) Professional private hospital with emergency services.

Copymat Cyber (Parque Morazán, 1c S; per hr US$0.40; ⊙7am-9pm) Cheap and speedy internet access.

Correos de Nicaragua (Parque Morazán, 1c S, 20m E; ⊙8am-4pm)

Intur (☑2772-7060; inturmatagalpa@gmail.com; Av Martínez, Parque Morazán, 3c S; ⊙8am-noon & 1-5pm Mon-Fri) Friendly office with good information on attractions around town.

Lavandería Cuenta Conmigo (☑2772-6713; Parque Morazán, 2c E, 3½c N; per load small/large US$2.90/4.30; ⊙8am-5pm Mon-Fri) Wash your clothes and support mental-health programs at this pioneering nonprofit laundry service.

Police (☑2772-3870, emergency 118; Parque Morazán)

ⓘ Getting There & Away

BUS

There are two main bus terminals in Matagalpa. Clean and fairly well-organized **Cotran Sur** (☑2772-4659), about 800m west of Parque Rubén Darío, generally serves Managua, Jinotega and most points south.

Disorienting by comparison, **Cotran Norte** (Cotramusun) is next to the northern market and goes to mostly rural destinations in the north.

San Ramón

Only 12km from Matagalpa, the small town of San Ramón feels a world away, with small-town pleasantries and a relaxed vibe. But the real reason to come here is to get an authentic taste for rural life among the hardworking farmers in the surrounding hills.

Unfortunately, like many areas in Northern Nicaragua, San Ramón's coffee crops were hit hard by the outbreak of coffee rust disease – some local farmers lost 60% to 80% of their crops. But at the time of research new varieties had been planted and farmers were hopeful of a rapid return to full production.

🏃 Activities

Finca Esperanza Verde HIKING, VOLUNTEERING
(www.fincaesperanzaverde.com; Yucul, San Ramón) Hikers will love the five well-marked **nature trails** weaving through coffee plantations and forest from this plantation lodge. **Birdwatching** is fantastic, with more than 250 species recorded here, but you might also spot sloths and monkeys near the paths. Other activities include a butterfly enclosure, Nicaraguan **cooking workshops** and specialized **coffee tours**.

Day-trippers can come and enjoy the trails or just relax at the **restaurant** (meals US$10 to $12). **Volunteer opportunities** are also available. Advance reservations are essential.

The *finca* is located 3.5km up a rough dirt road from the village of Yucul, 15km from San Ramón. You'll need a 4x4 vehicle if you plan on driving. If you don't have heavy luggage it's possible to walk, otherwise the hotel can arrange transportation from the Yucul junction or from Matagalpa.

👉 Tours

La Reina CULTURAL TOUR
🪧 La Reina was once one of Nicaragua's main mining communities; local guides can take you deep into an **abandoned mine**. Other activities include spotting howler monkeys and toucans in the forest and learning to make handicrafts with local artisans. It's a 45-minute walk (or a US$4 taxi) from San Ramón, or take the Matiguas bus (hourly departures) from Cotran Norte in Matagalpa.

🛏 Sleeping

⭐ **Finca Esperanza Verde** LODGE $$$
(www.fincaesperanzaverde.com; Yucul, San Ramón; group r per person US$23-46, cabaña s/d US$75/95; [P][🛜]) 🪧 With lush gardens full of hummingbirds, spectacular mountain views and enchanting nature trails, this

BUSES FROM SAN RAMÓN (COTRAN SUR)

DESTINATION	COST (US$)	DURATION (HR)	FREQUENCY (DAILY)
Chinandega	3.40	3½	5am and 2pm
Ciudad Darío	0.85	1	5:30am, 7:30am, 10:25am, 11am, 11:25am, 12:55pm
Estelí	1.20	2¼	5:20am-5:40pm, half-hourly
Jinotega	0.80	1	5am-6pm, half-hourly
León	3	2½	6am, 9:30am, 3pm, 4pm
Managua (expreso)	3	2¼	5:20am-5:20pm, hourly
Managua (ordinario)	2.10	2¾	3:35am-6:05pm, half-hourly
Masaya	3	3	2pm and 3:30pm (no buses Thu or Sun)

BUSES FROM SAN RAMÓN (COTRAN NORTE)

DESTINATION	COST (US$)	DURATION (HR)	FREQUENCY (DAILY)
Cerro Colorado (via Yucul)	2	2	5:30am-4pm, hourly
El Cuá	2.30	4	6am, 7am, 9am, 10:30am, noon, 1:30pm
Esquipulas	1.50	1½	5:40am, 7am, 8am, 9am, noon, 1:30pm, 3pm, 4:30pm, 5:30pm
San Ramón	0.40	30min	5am-7pm, half-hourly

large organic farm is a fantastic place to stay whether you want to get active or just relax with a good book. The three new wooden *cabañas* are simple in design but well constructed and very comfortable, offering top vistas right from your bed.

There are also even simpler (but still very comfortable) group *cabañas* with their own private porches. All room showers are cold but there's a communal wood-fired hot shower block. There's also a superb, open-air pavilion with sofa hammocks that offers panoramic views of the valley framed by jungle-covered mountains. During harvest, it's a great spot to watch the buzz of activity in the small coffee *fincas* below.

ℹ Information

UCA San Ramón (☑5777-0998; www.tourism. ucasanramon.com; frente Parque Municipal, San Ramón; ⊙8am-5pm Mon-Fri) Organizes visits and homestays in rural villages surrounding San Ramón.

ℹ Getting There & Away

Buses between Matagalpa and San Ramón (US$0.40, 30 minutes) run every half-hour between 5am and 7pm, leaving from Cotran Norte in Matagalpa and the park in San Ramón.

Colectivo taxis (US$0.80, 20 minutes) run on the same route from 5am to 7pm, leaving from the Parada San Ramón in Matagalpa.

Reserva Natural Cerro El Arenal

A short drive from Matagalpa on the old highway north to Jinotega, this 1430-hectare nature reserve is home to cloud forest interspersed with shade-grown coffee plantations. Despite being one of the smallest nature reserves in the country, it boasts varied landscapes and a wide variety of flora and fauna. It has a pleasant, cool climate – making it an attractive destination for great hikes through ethereal forest landscapes sprinkled with orchids.

◉ Sights & Activities

Selva Negra   NATURE RESERVE
(☑2770-1894; www.selvanegra.com; admission US$1.80; ⊙7am-9pm) If you're looking for comfort with your virgin cloud forest experience,

then Selva Negra – part family resort, part coffee farm and part rainforest preserve – could be for you. The 850-hectare estate blooms with bromeliads and rare orchids year-round and is home to nesting quetzals in April and May. Founded in the 1880s by German immigrants – who were a part of the original German coffee invasion that created the industry – it's named after Germany's Black Forest.

Their descendants still manage the reserve, which is webbed with several kilometers of lush **jungle trails**. Visitors can go on **nature tours** (US$15 per hour, at 7am), **coffee tours** (US$20, at 9:30am and 2pm), sustainable **agriculture tours** (US$12 per person, at 10am and 1:30pm) and **night walks** (US$10, at 6pm), and enjoy **horseback riding** (US$5 per hour). Or you can simply hike the 20km of trails at your leisure or relax at the **restaurant**, which overlooks a swan lake backed by cloud forest. Given the setting and abundance of activities, it's no surprise that North American families and package tourists flock here.

If you want to stay, there's a variety of accommodations options. The cute brick *cabañas* (US$95), with fireplaces and roofs sprouting bromeliads, are sprinkled in a magical fern gully, while the superior rooms (US$55) have lovely lake views. There are also perfectly comfortable budget rooms (US$15 per person) available on the other side of the lake.

🛏 Sleeping

Aguas de Arenal   LODGE **$$**
(☑8886-3234;   aguasdelarenal@gmail.com; Carretera Matagalpa–Jinotega Km 142.5; r s/d US$25/35, cabañas s/d US$40/55, all incl breakfast; 🅿) 🏊 In the heart of the Reserva Natural Cerro El Arenal, this secluded and intimate lodge is perfect for those looking for a more laid-back coffee country experience. The 10-*manzana* (7-hectare) coffee farm has five spacious and comfortable *cabañas* as well as four rooms in the main house, where you'll also find the cozy common area, complete with a fireplace.

The farm is powered by its own hydroelectric plant and the gregarious owner roasts his own coffee. There are five trails on the farm and accommodations include an informative tour. The bus from Matagalpa to Aranjuez passes close by the entrance to the farm but it gets very crowded. Alternatively, the farm is about a 30-minute walk from the Matagalpa–Jinotega road; the owner will pick you up at the turnoff for US$5, or in Matagalpa for US$15.

ℹ️ Getting There & Away

The reserve can be accessed via a number of dirt spur roads leading off the old Matagalpa–Jinotega highway. The most used entrance is the road to Aranjuez.

One bus a day leaves from Cotran Sur in Matagalpa (US$0.75, one hour, noon) to Aranjuez, traveling into the reserve. You can also take any Matagalpa–Jinotega bus to the Aranjuez junction and hike in.

For Selva Negra, take the Matagalpa–Jinotega bus and get off 12km north of town at the signed turnoff, which is marked by an old tank from the revolution. From there it's a pleasant 1.5km walk to the lodge.

It's also possible to access the reserve from the Matagalpa–La Dalia highway, near San Antonio de Upas.

La Dalia & Peñas Blancas

Easily accessible from both Matagalpa and Jinotega, the area around the hardworking rural town of La Dalia is dotted with thundering waterfalls, coffee farms and the north's most impressive tracts of virgin forest. The undoubted star of the show is the Reserva Natural Macizos de Peñas Blancas, a series of spectacular stone bluffs topped by cloud forest that is inhabited by scores of monkeys as well as jaguars and other felines.

⊙ Sights

Heading east from Matagalpa, no sooner than you have left the city, you will begin driving through gorgeous green hills typical of the hinterland of the department.

Take a break at the **Cascada Blanca** (Carretera La Dalia Km 147; admission US$1.80; ⊙ 8am-5pm), also known as Salto Santa Emilia, a gushing 15m waterfall surrounded by forest that fills a large, deep swimming hole. When its quiet it's absolutely lovely but it loses its appeal when it gets rammed with sightseers; come early. A path leads behind the falls to the cave on the other side. There is also around 2km of trails through coffee, banana and cacao plantations along the river that passes several other swimming holes. The waterfall is a short walk from the highway near Puente Las Cañas (Km 147), about 25 minutes out of Matagalpa.

Continuing along the highway, turn off at the community of La Empresa to visit the **Cascada La Luna**, a towering 40m-high waterfall that splits into twin streams. A new high-adrenaline, three-stage **zip line** (☑ 8825-5653; Comunidad La Empresa; ⊙ 8am-5pm) crosses the falls.

Shortly after La Empresa you'll arrive at the town of **La Dalia**, a busy agricultural center surrounded mostly by cleared farmland but with some tracts of cloud forest to the northwest. If you keep heading north, eventually you'll spot the breathtaking sheer white cliffs draped in forest of the **Reserva Natural Macizos de Peñas Blancas**, one of the six nuclear areas of the Reserva Natural Bosawás and possibly the most enchanting nature reserve in Northern Nicaragua.

Here you'll find the mossy, misty, life-altering primary cloud-forest scenery you've been waiting for. In addition to the massive cathedral trees draped in orchids and bromeliads, you'll find as many as 48 waterfalls, some of which pour into crystalline swimming holes; at least one of them is over 120m tall. And we haven't even got to the wildlife – the 116-sq-km reserve is home to an incredible array of fauna, including pumas, jaguars, large troops of monkeys and many rare bird species.

☞ Tours

★ **Centro Entiendemiento con la Naturaleza**   ECOTOUR
(CEN; ☑ 7671-9186; www.cenaturaleza.org; empalme la Manzana, 800m E, Peñas Blancas) ✈ To delve deep into the reserve, pay a visit to this grassroots environmental education and conservation project. Besides reforesting and managing vast swaths of the reserve, it also serves as a scientific research post and even produces its own honey. It organizes guides for the trek to the magnificent **Arco Iris waterfall** (US$10) and wildlife zones high in the mountains.

Guardianes del Bosque   ECOTOUR
(☑ 8471-8380; empalme la Manzana, 400m E, Peñas Blancas) ✈ This environmentally focused farming cooperative offers a variety of activities around the reserve, including **treks** with local Spanish-speaking guides (US$15 to US$20) to many waterfalls and lookouts. It also offers **coffee tours** (US$10) and can organize accommodations in its own basic lodge or in homestays in the village.

🛏 Sleeping

La Dalia has a comfortable ecolodge just outside town and a couple of cheaper hotels in the center.

Apart from a couple of good *cabañas*, Peñas Blancas has mostly rustic accommodations, but don't even consider not spending the night – you won't want to miss out on gazing in awe at those cliffs in the late evening and early morning light.

Centro Entiendemiento
con la Naturaleza   LODGE $$
(CEN; 📞 Matagalpa 8940-0891, Peñas Blancas 7671-9186; www.cennaturaleza.org; empalme la Manzana, 800m E, Peñas Blancas; dm US$13-20, s/d US$30/50, all incl breakfast) On the grounds of this environmental education center you'll find one lovely wooden *cabaña* split into two private rooms. The upstairs room is open to the elements – a wire wall at the far side lets in the sounds of the jungle – while downstairs has a small porch and more conventional walls with windows (for those who fear creepie-crawlies).

There are also cheaper, dormitory-style accommodations. Note that the water here is icy cold. Meals are available in the charming open-air dining area – go for the table on the 2nd-floor bamboo hut overlooking the treetops. Package deals that include three meals, accommodations and a guided trek run at US$35 per visitor in dorms or US$50 in the *cabaña*.

La Sombra Ecolodge   LODGE $$$
(📞 2770-1278, 8468-6281; www.lasombraecolodge.com; Carretera Waslal, La Dalia; r per person incl 3 meals US$45-55; 🅿) Just north of La Dalia, this 220-*manzana* (153-hectare) coffee *finca* set among tracts of cloud forest has wonderful views and plenty of activities for guests. In addition to tours of the coffee plantations, there is excellent birdwatching, scenic nature trails, waterfalls, a fine *mariposario* (butterfly enclosure), a zip line and a *ranario* (frog enclosure).

The day-trip package (US$15 including lunch and activities) is a great deal if the rooms are out of your budget. Advance reservations are recommended.

❶ Getting There & Away

If traveling in a private vehicle note that the road north from La Dalia is paved until the turnoff to El Cua, after which it is dirt and often features muddy puddles. A 4x4 vehicle is highly recommended if visiting Peñas Blancas.

Buses leave Matagalpa for La Dalia (US$1.25, 1½ hours) almost hourly from 6am to 6pm. To get to Peñas Blancas, take any bus leaving Matagalpa for El Cuá and get off at 'Empalme la Manzana' – the Peñas Blancas turnoff (US$2.25, three hours). There are also two buses a day from Jinotega to Peñas Blancas. The village is 600m off the main road.

South of Matagalpa

The smooth, paved road from Matagalpa to Managua slithers down the shoulders of stunning peaks into prairies framed by distant volcanoes. Most travelers zip right through on their way to or from Managua, but the road passes an excellent museum and some other interesting diversions.

Chagüitillo

You may miss the right turn into tiny Chagüitillo, just 20km south of Matagalpa and 4km north of Sébaco. There's no Spanish grid or Parque Central, just a single brick road where all *pueblo* life blooms. The main reason to visit is to check out the pre-Columbian museum and petroglyphs around town.

◉ Sights

Santuario Salto
Apa Mico   ARCHAEOLOGICAL SITE
Don't miss this fine petroglyph site just outside town. It features a swirl of moons, snakes and dancers 3m long and 2m high carved into rocks alongside a river. The site is well signposted and a guide is not necessary – although it's well worth hiring one in order to learn more about the site. Ask for directions at the **museum** (📞 8659-7567, 5755-9148; Puente, 1c N, 2c O, 1c S; admission US$1; ☺ 8am-5pm Mon-Fri, to noon Sat).

❶ Getting There & Away

Any *ordinario* (non-express) bus between Matagalpa and Managua can drop you at the entrance to town, from where you can walk in to the museum.

Ciudad Darío

About 5km down a paved turnoff from the highway, and tucked back into the chaparral-speckled Cordillera Dariense, is cute, hilly Ciudad Darío. Follow the spur all the way and you'll wind up at the leafy Parque Central.

◉ Sights

Casa Natal Rubén Darío   MUSEUM
(☑2776-3846; Parque Central, 2c E; admission US$4; ⊙8am-4:30pm Tue-Fri, 9am-4pm Sat & Sun) Two blocks east of the Parque Central you'll find the town's primary roadside attraction, where Rubén Darío was born. Although the baby poet didn't spend more than a few weeks in this sweet 19th-century adobe (this was his aunt's house), the museum is quite cool, with a mid-1880s kitchen, a Rubén Darío timeline and a wonderful amphitheater on the grounds, where the museum hosts the rare poetry reading or theater production.

❶ Getting There & Away

Buses leave for Managua (US$1.60, two hours) and Matagalpa (US$0.85, one hour) every half-hour.

Caribbean Coast

Best Places to Eat

➜ Habana Libre (p238)

➜ Casa Ulrich (p227)

➜ Desideri (p239)

➜ Sea Side Grill (p234)

➜ Restaurante Faramhi (p209)

Best Beaches

➜ Long Bay (p231)

➜ Grape Key (p229)

➜ Monkey Point (p225)

➜ Otto Beach (p236)

➜ Maroon Key (p229)

Why Go?

An overland ramble to Nicaragua's Caribbean coast would be the perfect terrain for an epic novel. Your settings would include wide, muddy rivers surrounded by thick jungle, a fascinating tropical port town and an expanse of mangrove-shrouded black water, home to more than a dozen ethnic fishing enclaves. And we haven't even got to the pristine offshore islands ringed by white sand with a turquoise trim.

Your cast will feature tough and insightful characters from English-speaking Creole towns and indigenous Miskito, Mayangna, Rama and Garifuna communities. And there will be plenty of action too, with scuba diving, epic treks through dense rainforest, beachcombing, and fishing in the mangroves.

But even the most skilled author would struggle to capture the essence of the region, a vibrant mix of indigenous, African and European cultures that you'll only really get a feel for if you check it out for yourself.

When to Go

➜ From February to April visitors are greeted by clear skies and perfect beach weather, although you may be sharing your patch of paradise and accommodations prices tend to increase.

➜ The region's strong winds drop off significantly from March to April, bringing the best conditions for diving around the Corn Islands and snorkeling in the Pearl Keys.

➜ While technically in the middle of the wet season, during September and October the heavy rains ease off, prices are low and beaches are empty.

➜ For a high-energy full-color carnival experience, head to Maypole in Bluefields in May for a full month of partying, culminating in the colorful Carnival and Tulululu.

HONDURAS

Atlántico Norte

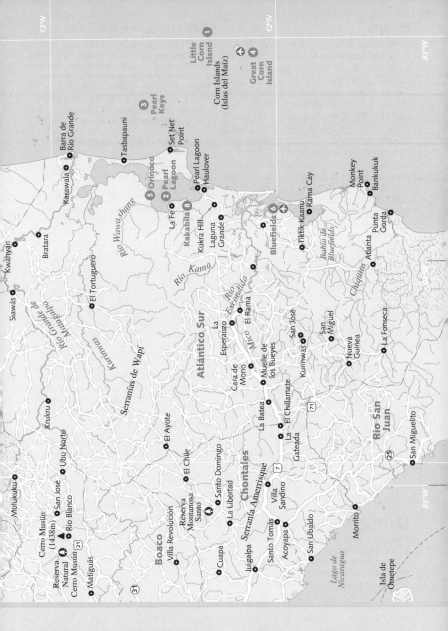

⑤ Orinoco (p228)
Eating fresh fish and listening to talented Garífuna drummers during National Garífuna Week.

⑥ Bluefields
(p221) Dancing through the streets then partying all night in Maypole madness.

⑦ Bilwi (p206)
Exploring the vast Miskito hinterland of tiny villages and waterways bursting with wildlife.

⑧ Kakabila
(p227) Hiring an indigenous guide to trek deep into the dense jungle.

History

Christopher Columbus landed on Nicaragua's Caribbean coast in 1502, during his fourth voyage, but with the Spanish focused on settling the Pacific coast, their hold on the Caribbean was tenuous. Portuguese, Dutch and British pirates patrolled these seas (Bluefields was named for the Dutch pirate Blewfeldt), attacking and robbing Spanish vessels full of South American gold. Meanwhile, the British crown cultivated relations with the indigenous Miskito people, who had battled Mayangna and Rama communities for regional supremacy long before Columbus came calling. In 1687 they created the puppet kingdom of Mosquitia, which ruled until the mid-19th century.

During this period, British colonists moved with their African slaves from Jamaica to the Corn Islands, which until then had belonged to the Kukra and Sumu people. They also arrived in Bluefields, where slaves worked banana groves and mingled with free West Indian laborers of mixed ethnicity to form English-speaking Creole communities that are still thriving.

English-speaking Nicaraguans have never fully bought into Spanish-speaking rule. During the Contra war, many took up arms against the Frente Sandinista de Liberación Nacional (Sandinista National Liberation Front; FSLN), while many more fled to neighboring Costa Rica to avoid the conflict, emptying villages that have still not recovered. Although the region was eventually granted special autonomy status by the Sandinistas with the rights to have a say in the exploitation of its natural resources, it remains the poorest and least developed part of the country.

ℹ Dangers & Annoyances

Nicaragua's Atlantic coast is as poor and underserved as Nicaragua gets. Expect dodgy infrastructure, bring a flashlight (torch) and enjoy those occasional bucket showers.

Local agents for Colombian coke impresarios keep a fairly low profile, but the cocaine traffic in Región Autónoma Atlántico Norte (North Atlantic Autonomous Region; RAAN) and Región Autónoma Atlántico Sur (South Atlantic Autonomous Region; RAAS) isn't bloodless. However, tourists won't have any problems as long as they refrain from purchasing and partaking.

But, given the poverty, even in seemingly innocuous small towns, sober travelers should stick to big-city rules: stay alert, don't wander alone, take taxis at night and watch your valuables.

ℹ Getting There & Away

You can travel overland from Managua to the Caribbean coast, but most visitors take the frequent inexpensive La Costeña flights. There are active commercial airstrips in Bilwi, Waspám, Bluefields, Great Corn Island and two of the three Las Minas towns. Still, if you have more time than cash and enjoy the (really) slow lane, there are two overland routes into the region.

BILWI (PUERTO CABEZAS)–WASPÁM & RÍO COCO

We won't sugar coat this. You're in for a grueling ride on a beat-up old school bus packed to the gills. It begins with a 10- to 12-hour bus ride from Managua to Siuna in Las Minas, where you can access the Reserva de Biosfera Bosawás (Bosawás Biosphere Reserve). From Siuna, it's another 10 to 12 hours on a horrendous road to Bilwi. Waspám and the Río Coco are a smoothish six hours north from there.

JUIGALPA–EL RAMA–BLUEFIELDS–CORN ISLANDS

The (much!) preferred trip to the crystalline Caribbean Sea unfurls on the smooth, paved road to El Rama, with rejuvenating side trips to the mountain towns of Boaco and Juigalpa. From El Rama, you can hop on a testing five-hour bus along the rutted dirt road to Pearl Lagoon or take a convenient two-hour fast boat ride down the Río Escondido to Bluefields, from where there are twice-weekly boat services to the Corn Islands and daily speedboats to Pearl Lagoon.

ℹ Getting Around

Most local travel within the region is by *panga* – an open speedboat with outboard motor. Tickets are much more expensive than a comparable distance by bus.

Bilwi (Puerto Cabezas)

This impoverished Caribbean port town and ethnic melting pot sprawls along the coast and back into the scrubby pines on wide brick streets and red-earth roads, full of people and music, smiles and sideways glances. Old wooden churches, antique craftsman homes and ramshackle slums are knitted together with rusted sheet-metal fencing, coconut palms and mango trees. In a single stroll you'll eavesdrop on loud jagged Miskito banter, rapid-fire *español* and lovely, lilting Caribbean English. Sure, this city has systemic problems (poverty, decay, crime), and its ramshackle infrastructure lags behind the rest of the country. But with tasty

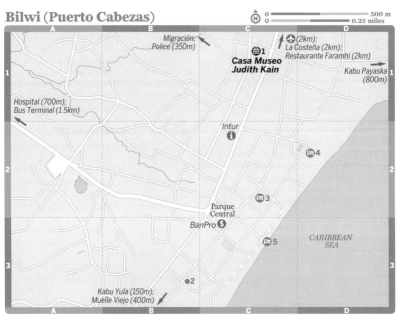

Bilwi (Puerto Cabezas)

seafood, great-value historic lodging options, and seaside indigenous communities a boat ride away, it can also be as alluring as a sweet, yet slightly sketchy, new friend.

History

Founded in 1690 by three English pirates who called it Bragman's Bluff, the port was always referred to by indigenous Miskito and Mayangna people as Bilwi (Mayangna for 'Snake Leaf'). Then, in 1894, General Rigoberto Cabezas invaded and flew the Nicaraguan flag over an area ruled by an English-indigenous alliance for two centuries. In 1925 the Nicaraguan government honored Cabezas by naming the port after him. Spanish-speaking locals still refer to the capital of Nicaragua's enormous RAAN as Puerto Cabezas, or just Puerto.

Yet even after the English were forced out, English-speaking companies like the banana giant Standard Fruit, which built the dock, helped keep federal interference in the region minimal as it siphoned fruit, fish and timber from the Caribbean coast. It wasn't all bad for the locals. Old-timers still reminisce about the good old days of high-paying jobs and a thriving middle class. Which is why it was such a tragedy when Standard Fruit pulled out just before its dock was used in the 1960s to launch Kennedy's Bay of Pigs invasion of Cuba. There are still plenty of international pirates and profiteers. They hail from Colombia and trade in a certain ego-boosting powdery substance, some of which is off-loaded in the area and heads north to Mexico and the US.

Mother Nature has roughed up Bilwi too. Her most recent assault came in the form of Hurricane Felix in 2007, which decimated the Miskito Keys and wreaked havoc in local communities. In fact, emergency relief efforts sparked a new wave of

CARIBBEAN COAST BILWI (PUERTO CABEZAS)

NGO involvement, and aid workers and missionaries still far outnumber tourists.

◉ Sights

There is next to no tourism in Bilwi and local beaches are nobody's idea of the Caribbean dream. La Bocana, an old pirate hangout at the river mouth north of town, has a stretch of decent beach, but crooks still dig it here. Come with a local.

★ **Casa Museo Judith Kain** MUSEUM
(✆ 2792-2225; Parque Central, 4c N, 1c O; ⊙ 8am-5pm Mon-Fri) FREE Set in the former home of a prolific local painter, this museum provides a window into what it was like to live in Bilwi in the good old days. There are B&W photos, old dugout canoes, terrific local handicrafts and an antique collection (the sewing machines are especially cool); dozens of Kain's paintings are also on display. It's attached to one of the best hotels in town.

Muelle Viejo PORT
Take a stroll along the wooden boards of the historic Muelle Viejo (Old Pier), where both Sandino and the Contras received arms smuggled in from abroad, the former with the assistance of the town's prostitutes. But the 420m-long pier's biggest moment in the spotlight was in 1961, when Somoza lent the facility to US-funded Cuban exiles to launch the failed Bay of Pigs invasion.

It's a hive of activity, especially in lobster season, when gallant divers line up outside with their wooden paddles waiting their turn to get onto deep-sea boats – motherships from which they'll launch their small wooden canoes before diving down in search of the crustaceans.

There is a security gate halfway down the pier, but if you ask permission it's possible to walk all the way to the end. As you walk back, check out the *panga* graveyard in front of the military base on your right where large fiberglass skiffs seized from narcotics traffickers lie half-buried in the sand – a testament to the not-so-legal shipping lanes that pass in front of the town.

🏃 Activities

Amica CULTURAL TOUR
(Association of Indigenous Women on the Atlantic Coast; ✆ 2792-2219; asociacionamica@yahoo.es; Parque Central, 3c S; ⊙ 8am-noon Mon, 2-5:30pm Mon-Fri, 8am-noon Sat) 🖉 Your ticket into the area's natural reserves and indigenous communities is through Amica. In addition to working to stop domestic violence and promote family planning and indigenous rights, it can arrange forest treks, canoe tours and fishing trips in the mangroves. It also offers overnight visits to the Miskito Keys (US$600, eight visitors) and guides (US$6) to visit communities around town.

🎎 Festivals & Events

Dance of King Pulanka CULTURAL, DANCE
(⊙ Jan 6–mid-Feb) First performed in the late 1800s, the dance of El Rey and La Reina is still performed throughout the Mosquitia. Two groups of dancers wearing 18th-century costumes represent the king's allies and enemies, and stage a mock battle using arrows, machetes and *triki trakas* (firearms). The good guys win and there's traditional food and drink to keep the party going.

The event moves around the many local communities on a turn basis and is also hosted in some of the outer lying barrios (districts) of Bilwi.

🛏 Sleeping

Casa Museo Judith Kain HOTEL $
(✆ 2792-2225; www.casamuseojudithkain.com; Parque Central, 4c N, 1c O; r/tw with fan US$13/16, r/tw ti air-con US$24/28/32; P ❋ 🛜) In a town with an abundance of great-value lodging, this may be the best of the bunch. Rooms set in two superb old craftsman gems are super clean and charming with high, beamed ceilings, hot water, porches and balconies sprinkled with wooden rockers overlooking gardens full of birds. No wonder it's always booked up.

Hotel Liwa Mairin HOTEL $
(✆ 2792-2315; Parque Central, 2c E, 1c S; s/d US$12/25, with air-con US$23/27; P ❋ 🛜) This centrally located hotel right by the Caribbean Sea offers spacious air-con rooms with firm mattresses, wooden furnishings and high ceilings. It's a fantastic deal, even if rooms are equipped with temperamental electric-shock showers.

El Cortijo II GUESTHOUSE $$
(✆ 2792-2340; cortijoarguello@yahoo.com; Parque Central, 3c N, 1c E; s/d US$18/21.50, with balcony US$21.50/25; ❋ 🛜) This 60-year-old craftsman gem is your Caribbean grandma's house. Rooms are spotless with worn wooden floors and high ceilings. The common living room is filled with gorgeous antiques –

including old hand-blown glass buoys – and if you reserve ahead, you may snag a room with a private sea-view balcony, steps from a creaky wooden walk that leads to the rolling sea. Nice!

El Cortijo   GUESTHOUSE **$$**
(📞2792-2340; cortijoarguello@yahoo.com; Parque Central, 1½c N; s/d downstairs US$18/21.50, upstairs US$19.50/23; ❄ 📶) This beautiful wooden home is so nice the Sandinistas once used it as their east-coast base. Grab one of the more attractively furnished rooms upstairs in the original house; they have the wooden fixtures and high ceilings. Downstairs rooms are less charming, but cheaper. Fabulous breakfasts (US$3) with terrific coffee are served on the wide deck overlooking a rambling garden.

Rooms have hot water, although you rarely need it in Bilwi.

🍴 Eating & Drinking

Most local lobster is exported, but when it's in season you'll find it at around US$7.50 a plate – often the same price as chicken or fish! If you're pinching pennies, head to the market, where you'll find some stalls selling tasty fried fish.

Comedor Amica   NICARAGUAN **$**
(Parque Central, 3c S) Next to the Amica office, this great second-floor *comedor* (basic eatery) specializes in regional seafood dishes. Come and work your way through the menu. It is also a fine place for breakfast.

★Restaurante Faramhi   SEAFOOD **$$**
(📞2792-1611; frente Aeropuerto; mains US$7.50; ⏱11am-10pm) Close to the airport, this popular restaurant serves easily the best food in town. It's a very Bilwi kind of place: the open-air dining area features sea shell light shades, a random disco light and a country music soundtrack. The menu reflects the town's multi-ethnic roots with typical seafood plates starring alongside an ensemble of good Chinese dishes.

Wachi's Pizza   PIZZA **$$**
(Parque Central, 2c E; pizzas US$4.50-13; ⏱noon-9pm) Being the only real pizzeria within a 200km radius, this place would run a brisk trade even if it wasn't up to scratch – fortunately it is, with generous-sized pies sporting good thick crusts and tasty toppings

served on a pleasant porch overlooking the Caribbean.

Kabu Yula   BAR
(Parque Central, 5c S; ⏱2pm-2am) A two-story open-air bar with unbroken sea views; the 'sea dog' is the perfect place for an afternoon tipple.

ℹ Information

BanPro Changes dollars and has a Visa/MasterCard ATM.
Hospital (📞2792-2259, 2792-2243)
Intur (📞2792-1564; puertocabezas@intur.gob.ni; Parque Central, 2c N; ⏱8am-4pm Mon-Fri) Friendly and dedicated staff know the area in detail and are able to facilitate trips to local communities.
Migración (Immigration Office; 📞2792-2258; contiguo a la Policia; ⏱8am-4pm Mon-Fri) Visa extensions and entry/exit stamps for the Honduran border.

ℹ Getting There & Away

AIR
Although you can hop on a super-long-distance (and rather painful) bus from Managua or (occasionally) catch a boat from Corn Island, most people come by plane. **La Costeña** (📞2792-2282; Aeropuerto; ⏱8am-noon & 3-6pm) offers regular flights to Managua and Bluefields. Book tickets in advance. Departure tax is US$2. Flights include:
➡ **Bluefields** (one way/return US$96/148, 50 minutes, 11:20am Monday, Wednesday and Friday)
➡ **Managua** (one way/return US$97/149, 1½ hours, 7:40am, noon and 3:40pm Monday to Saturday, 7:40am and noon Sunday)

BOAT
The only regular boat service to/from Bilwi is the **Captain D** (📞8850-2767), which runs between Corn Island and Bilwi (US$22, 10 to 12 hours) about once a month depending on demand. Call to check the schedule.

BUS
Buses depart from the bus terminal, 2km west of town.
Managua (US$25.20, 20 to 24 hours, 10am and 1pm)
Rosita (US$7.50, six to 10 hours, 6am and 7pm)
Siuna (US$10, 10 to 12 hours, 7am)
Waspám (US$6, six hours, 5:30am and 7pm)

Around Bilwi

The shores of the Caribbean to the north and south of Bilwi are dotted with ultra laid-back Miskito villages rich in culture and surrounded by nature.

Haulover

The first Moravian missionaries arrived here, 30km south of Bilwi, in 1860, and named it in honor of the sandbar that boats had to cross to enter the lagoon. Protected by Reserva Natural Laguna Kukalaya and Reserva Natural Layasiksa, it's a peaceful town of colorful wooden houses where horses roam free on soft grass studded with coconut palms. There is no electricity here – the only sounds are the crashing of the sea and the occasional Miskito hit emanating from small radios.

❶ Getting There & Away

Collective *pangas* leave from the dock at Lamlaya around noon (US$9), and return at 5am daily. A private charter will set you back around US$150.

Wawa & Karatá

Wawa is a scenic Miskito village 17km south of Bilwi, at the mouth of the Río Wawa. There's a beautiful lagoon packed with migratory birds and alligators, plus a sandy oceanfront beach. Further upriver is Karatá, which is perched on the edge of the lagoon and surrounded by mangrove forests.

Hiking, fishing and canoeing options abound in both villages.

❶ Getting There & Away

Transportation is by collective *panga* (Wawa/Karatá US$2.20/3.30), which leave from Lamlaya, 5km south of Bilwi.

---

❶ DRINKING WATER

Tap water on the Atlantic coast generally comes from wells or rainwater collection tanks and is usually untreated. Often it is potable, but it may also contain bacteria; bring water purification tablets if you don't want to take the risk. Bottled water is widely available and some hotels offer filtered water refills.

Krukira

About 20km north of Bilwi, this is the gateway to the Reserva Natural Laguna Pahara, with lots of wildlife, including huge tarpon. It's a tranquil yet well-developed town with a Moravian church and a neat central park.

It's possible to organize canoe tours and fishing trips in the lagoon, as well as visits to Trakislandia, a freshwater swimming hole.

❶ Getting There & Away

Buses leave Bilwi for Krukira daily at 1pm (US$1.50, one hour), returning early in the morning.

Miskito Keys

Sitting 50km offshore, the Miskito Keys are a group of rocky Caribbean isles rimmed with stilted Miskito fishing villages. Their thatched over-water bungalows loom above crystalline turquoise coves that double as ideal lobster habitats. The historic first meeting between the British pirate Captain Sussex Camock and his future Miskito allies took place here in 1633. It's still a haven for sea-faring bad guys, so if you see any boats with Colombian plates, look the other way.

Unlike the Pearl Keys further south, this is a cultural rather than beach destination – very few of the islands have any sand at all. Most are pure rock with the odd bit of scrubbish vegetation. Nevertheless, a visit to this isolated community sticking out of the ocean is a fascinating experience, although it doesn't come cheap.

It's possible to rent traditional wooden canoes from the fishers to explore the area, although the sea can get rough so it's better to get a local to paddle.

Bring plenty of insect repellent.

⌂ Sleeping

There are no hotels in the keys, but having spent a fortune to get out here you are going to want to spend the night. Fortunately, it's possible to arrange a bed or hammock in the stilted homes of locals. Make reservations at Amica (p208) in Bilwi.

❶ Getting There & Away

Amica (p208) arranges overnight visits for US$600 for up to six visitors, a large chunk of which goes toward transportation costs. Transport in a large, fast *panga* for up to 12 will cost you around US$800 round-trip; Intur (p209)

THE MOSQUITIA

Some legends say that the Miskito nation originated in the Miskito Keys, then took control of the Miskito Coast of Nicaragua and Honduras, more properly known as the Mosquitia. The keys first appeared on a European map in 1630, labeled the Musquitu Islands, '14 leagues from Cabo de Gracias,' where the Miskitos first made contact with pirate captain Sussex Camock in 1633.

The Miskitos quickly grasped the potential of firearms and, in return for the new technology, aided in the sacking of Spanish strongholds up and down the Río San Juan and Río Coco. In 1687, the English monarchy was pleased enough to help found the Miskito monarchy, and by the mid-1800s most of the Caribbean territory between central Honduras and Limón, Costa Rica, was under Miskito and British control. When the crown hosted King Jeremy in England, his tutors were surprised that he looked more African than Indian.

Miskito culture has historically embraced outsiders, and not always figuratively. Many trace their African roots to a Portuguese slave ship that was wrecked on the keys in 1640, though waves of escaped slaves and West Indian banana workers are part of the mix.

The Miskitos did not submit willingly to Nicaraguan rule in 1894, and their discontent at domination by the 'Spaniards' in Managua was brought to a head by one of the most horrific chapters of Sandinista rule. President Somoza had been somewhat popular in the region, mainly because he left the Miskito to get along with their business. However, being off the radar meant the region was also seriously neglected and did not share in the profits from the exploitation of Nicaragua's natural resources.

Thus the Miskitos' loyalty was split, and when the revolution triumphed, some joined the Frente Sandinista de Liberación Nacional (Sandinista National Liberation Front; FSLN)-backed group Misurasata (MIskito, SUmo, RAma, SAndinista & AslaTAlanka), hoping to help with the literacy campaign. Volunteers were soon informed, however, that the Sandinista-led government had decreed Spanish the official language, which few people spoke, much less read. The FSLN then declared the Mosquitia's natural resources to be public property, 'to be exploited efficiently and reasonably.' Tensions simmered.

At the same time, Somoza's Guardia Nacional regrouped in the Mosquitia. The Sandinistas got intelligence that they would be meeting in San Carlos on December 23, 1981, and sent 7000 troops to evacuate the people, burn the houses, kill the animals and destroy the wells. Every single town on the Río Coco was burned to the ground, and no one knows how many civilians died. It is remembered as Red Christmas.

Some 20,000 people became refugees, moving to Honduras, Bilwi, San José de Bocay and what's now known as Tasba Pri ('Free Land'), the impoverished string of roadside towns that stretches from Rosita to Bilwi.

The Sandinistas backpedaled and apologies were issued, but it was too late. In 1987, the National Autonomy Law granted the RAAN and RAAS official independence in response to local pressure. The major international gold mine in Las Minas is not part of the autonomous zone, however, even though it is in the center of the region. Anomalies such as this have led some locals to believe that the central government legislated provisions so it could continue to exploit the region's natural resources, and not be held responsible for providing much-needed infrastructure.

After the war, former Contras and Misurasata members formed Yapti Tasba Masraka Nanih Asla takanka (Yatama; 'Descendants of Mother Earth'), a political party that gets the vast majority of the indigenous vote in every election. With the return of the FSLN to power, Yatama leaders, many of whom are former Contras, divided their supporters by aligning themselves with the Sandinistas before withdrawing from the government, citing electoral fraud in the region.

In 2015, violence broke out in the region with Miskito villagers claiming their lands were being usurped by mestizo farmers and that the agricultural frontier was advancing deep into their ancestral lands. Regular battles between mestizo *colonos* (colonizers) and Miskito villagers near Waspám led to deaths on both sides.

To add fuel to the fire, Yatama leader Brooklyn Rivera was stripped of his place in parliament by the Sandinista government, which claims that he was personally involved in illegal land sales. Rivera claims the decision is political payback for withdrawing from the government.

is able to recommend responsible captains. To make the journey on the cheap, you'll need to make arrangements with a lobster fisher who is already going: do-able, but your return could take days. It's two hours to the keys on a fast boat, up to five on a lobster vessel, and the ride is often rough.

Waspám & the Río Coco

Waspám feels different from the rest of RAAN. Yes, it's just as poor and has the same development issues and jagged-edge feel as Bilwi and Las Minas, but there's also a simple beauty: children at play, twittering flocks of parakeets in the trees, and dugout canoes plying the edges of Waspám's biggest attraction, the lazy, mocha Río Coco.

Known as Wangki in Miskito, the Río Coco, the longest river in Central America, links 116 Miskito communities that run from the rainforested interior to the Atlantic coastal marshlands. This makes Waspám, its epicenter, the cultural, geographic and economic heart of the Mosquitia. It also forms a natural border with Honduras, a fact most Miskitos prefer to ignore. You shouldn't. If you plan on crossing into Honduras, get your passport stamped at Bilwi Migración (p209).

But even if you remain on the Nica side of things, you will probably spend plenty of time on the river. Upstream lies the Reserva de Biosfera Bosawás. Access isn't cheap and will require boat charters, but trips are easily organized and your memories will be well worth the investment.

◉ Sights

★ **Museo Auka Tangki**   MUSEUM
(✆8417-8128; brownmelgara@hotmail.com; Planta Electrica, 150m E; donations accepted; ⊘by appointment) Don't miss Dr Dionisio Melgara Brown's museum, a 10-minute walk along dirt roads curving away from the river. Brown, a retired teacher, built this museum

---

GOLD FEVER

If you've arrived in Waspám and are wondering where all the people are, you've probably come during the gold rush. Every dry season, hordes of locals travel up the Río Coco to the rapids near Carizal to pan for gold, leaving the place feeling like a ghost town.

---

on the ground floor of his home with his own savings in order to preserve Miskito language, history and tradition.

Inside you'll peruse photos and artifacts including hammocks and a fishing net handwoven from natural materials, cow-skin drums, shakers made from horse clavicles, wooden bowls, turtle shells, and huge mortar-and-pestle sets used for making *wabul,* a traditional Miskito power shake consisting of plantains mashed with coconut or cow's milk. Brown also sells the world's only Miskito-Spanish and Miskito-English dictionaries (US$25), which he wrote and published himself.

🛏 Sleeping

Hotel Casa de la Rose   HOTEL $
(✆5729-9380; frente la pista; s/d with fan US$10.50/14.50, with air-con US$17/21; ❄) One of Waspám's two really good hotels. Rooms are clean with fresh tiles, cable TV and a lovely wooden porch nestled in the banana palms. It has a terrific restaurant set in a sweet wooden *cabaña* patrolled by parrots.

★ **Hotel El Piloto**   HOTEL $$
(✆8642-4405, 8331-1312; hotelitoelpiloto@live.com; Muelle, 20m S; r/tw US$25/35; ❄🖥) Waspám's best all-round choice. Rooms have fresh paint and bathroom tiles, and a terrific location steps from the river. The friendly owners are a wealth of information and will happily arrange all manner of local excursions. Also serves quality meals.

ℹ Information

Hospital A small public hospital is located near the entrance to town.

Marena (detras Mercado; ⊘8am-4pm) In the little green house behind the market, staff can show you maps of the Bosawás, but won't recommend guides or arrange boat charters.

Western Union (✆8416-9999; Muelle, 20m S; ⊘9am-5pm) Receive wire transfers

ℹ Getting There & Away

AIR

La Costeña (✆8415-8210; Aeropuerto; ⊘9am-noon) planes only seat 12, so it's best to book in advance. Flights depart from Managua to Waspám (one way/return US$104/160, 90 minutes) at 11am and return at 12:40am, though they are frequently late.

BUS

Buses leave for Bilwi (US$6, six hours) at 6am and 7am daily. Come early if you want a seat.

ALAMIKANGBAN & PRINZAPOLKA

The isolated towns of Alamikangban, about 70km southeast of Rosita, and Prinzapolka, another two hours by boat along the Río Prinzapolka on the Caribbean coast, don't get many visitors, but nature lovers might want to consider making the trip.

The main reason to go is the Río Prinzapolka, which marks the southern boundary of natural pine forest that phases into tropical rainforest, with wetlands that are a haven for all sorts of birds. The fishing is also top-notch.

The towns themselves are traditional Miskito settlements: think board houses with rusted tinned roofs and no fences between neighbors.

Both towns, as well as the smaller communities lining the river, have indigenous government structures, so ask for the *wihta* (judge) or *síndico* (resource manager) when trying to find guides or lodging.

The entire region is susceptible to flooding; during rains, check on conditions before heading out.

Buses leave Rosita (US$4, four hours) twice daily for Alamikangban, where you can hire a private boat to Prinzapolka.

There are also several direct buses a week to Managua (US$25, 25 hours), usually departing on Monday, Wednesday, Thursday and Saturday at around 8am.

Río Coco

Waspám's prime attractions are out of town and accessible by the Río Coco, which upriver from town forms the northern boundary of the Bosawás reserve and downriver flows leisurely to Cabo Gracias a Dios. Access is pricey but easily organized.

🏃 Activities

Salto Yaho   TOUR

The classic river trip from Waspám (US$450 per boat) takes you 135km upriver to this spectacular waterfall on the Río Waspuk. After swimming in the falls, you'll spend the night in the small village downriver before returning home in the morning.

Cabo Gracias a Dios   FISHING

There's excellent tarpon-fishing in Cabo Gracias a Dios, where the river mouth meanders into a lagoon dotted with colorful wooden homes. A two-day trip will cost around US$500. One problem: if there's no wind, you will feel like you're starring in a horror movie called 'Attack of the Killer Sand Fleas'.

❶ Information

The Río Coco is no stranger to bloodshed and, unfortunately, it has once again become a hot bed of violence with land disputes between indigenous communities and mestizo farmers spawning armed conflict between the two sides.

The troubles have even made it to the center of Waspám, where in 2015 a shootout left one Miskito leader dead and many wounded.

With no solution in sight, it's important to check the latest before planning a trip to the Río Coco. While foreign visitors are unlikely to be targets, there is always the chance of getting caught up in the crossfire and at present tourism is the last thing on the minds of locals in many communities.

❶ Getting There & Away

Expect to pay US$60 per day for boat hire plus fuel, which will make up most of the cost.

Transporte Castillo (☑ 8421-0826; Barrio Santa Ines; ⊘ 6am-8pm) has honest and experienced navigators who will take you wherever you want to go at the drop of a hat. You can also arrange trips through Hotel El Piloto, where owner Barry Watson speaks terrific English.

Managua–El Rama Road

If you plan on heading to and from the Costa Atlantica overland (and don't fancy the grueling 24-hour journey to Bilwi), then you can take the smooth paved roads from Managua to El Rama, a river-port town that is just a two-hour boat ride from Bluefields.

You can make the trip in six hours on a reasonably comfortable (but usually overcrowded) bus, but then you'll miss the rugged Serranía Amerrisque. In and around these muscular granite peaks are a number of cute ranching *pueblos* (villages), and one worthwhile city (that would be Juigalpa), linked by twisting, rutted back roads that also connect to Matagalpa and the Northern Highlands. So, embrace that whole 'journey is the destination' cliché, take the slow road and enjoy a welcome blast of earthy Nicaraguan culture before or after diving into the Caribbean.

Boaco

'The City with Two Floors' was once two separate ranching communities separated by a steep 400m slope. They've grown together from the hill and valley, and now this *ranchero* market town, a couple of hours' drive from Managua, is a bustling agricultural hub. Being off the main highway, Boaco receives few visitors, but its good hotels and restaurants make it a decent overnight stop for those looking to explore the region's petroglyph-studded mountain hinterland.

◉ Sights & Activities

Sitio Arqueologico
La Laguna   ARCHAEOLOGICAL SITE
(Comarca La Laguna) Around 10km from Boaco, this archaeological site is only just beginning to be investigated and features a number of petroglyphs in stones scattered around local farms. One bus a day leaves from the Boaco market around noon to the La Laguna community, where it's possible to find a guide to show you around.

Parroquia de Nuestra Señora
del Perpetuo Socorro   CHURCH
(salida, 1c N, 2c E) This intriguing church on the lower level of town has brightly painted onion domes that hint at a Russian heritage, but it's Catholic and always has been.

Aguas Claras   THERMAL BATHS
(☑2244-2916; admission US$1.25; ☺Tue-Sun) On Hwy 9, 15 minutes west of town, you'll find this ageing mid-level hot-springs resort. Water is mineral rich, if not steaming, and funneled into concrete pools. Midweek it's mostly deserted and feels like a good place to hide out after a bank heist, but according to management it pulls a big local crowd on weekends.

If you want to stay, there is an L-shaped concrete accommodations block housing fairly uninspiring air-con rooms, although the leafy grounds attract plenty of birds and there are two private pools for hotel guests. Simple, typical meals cost US$4, while menu options are US$7 to US$9.

Any Managua-bound bus from Boaco (or Juigalpa) will drop you here. A taxi from Boaco runs about US$8.

🛏 Sleeping

Hotel Sobalvarro   HOTEL **$**
(☑2542-2515; frente Parque Central; r with/without bathroom US$16/11; ❄) You'll sacrifice some comfort and space here, but the clean, wooden-floored budget rooms have a fresh coat of paint and come with access to the deck, offering fine mountain views. The shared bathrooms are downstairs, next to the more expensive rooms with newly tiled floors and private bathrooms.

★Tijerino's Hotel   HOTEL **$$**
(☑2542-2798; hoteltijerinos@gmail.com; Parque Central; r with/without air-con US$30/40; ❄) Way ahead of everything else in town, this fancy new hotel on the park seems almost too chic for rural Boaco. The bright, modern rooms boast elegant furniture, top appliances and ultra-comfortable bedding and are the finest for kilometers around. But the biggest draw here is the two ample terraces with majestic mountain panoramas. Outstanding value.

🍴 Eating & Drinking

Restaurante Alpino   NICARAGUAN **$$**
(Banpro, 40m N; mains US$6-9; ☺9am-9pm Mon-Thu, to 10pm Fri-Sun) A spotless tiled-floor restaurant with pressed yellow tablecloths serving up tasty Nica cuisine. The menu is pretty much the same as every other restaurant around here but the plates are well prepared with fresh ingredients, and service is prompt. Also prepares good burgers and other snacks.

Restaurante Maraita   BAR
(Parque Central, 1c N, 1c E; meals US$4-6; ☺9am-midnight) Locals descend on this sociable watering hole after work to knock back cold beers to a classic rock soundtrack. Also serves up fairly decent meals.

❶ Information

Banpro (Iglesia Santiago, 1c N) Visa/Master-Card ATM.

Cyber Space (frente Casa Pellas; per hr US$0.40; ☺8am-9pm) The town's swiftest connection; international calls are available as well.

Hospital (☑2542-2542) This new hospital is one of the most modern in Nicaragua.

Intur (☑2542-4760; Alcaldia, 20m E; ☺8am-noon & 1-5pm) This welcoming tourism office

LAS MINAS (THE MINING TRIANGLE)

During their heyday early last century, the towns of Las Minas bustled with immigrants from China, Europe, North America and the Caribbean looking to strike the mother lode. These days very few outsiders visit this wild and remote part of the country, and its main towns, **Siuna**, **Rosita** and **Bonanza**, are most notable for their shocking infrastructure and abundance of armed, inebriated men.

While gold panning is still popular among villagers, the gold rush is well and truly over and the only real money being made here is in Bonanza, where a large foreign-owned mine continues to operate despite criticism from environmentalists. But Las Minas still has one jewel more valuable than any that has been dug out of these red soils, a place so remote and untouched that only the most dedicated tourist ever sets foot in it: the Reserva de Biosfera Bosawás (p217).

The easiest access to the Reserva de Biosfera Bosawás is from Siuna via the **Parque Nacional Saslaya**. Head to the ranger station, 3.5km from the community of Rosa Grande, where you'll register and contract a guide for the trek to **Piedra Colorada**. You'll overnight by a pine-shaded lagoon and in the morning begin the three-day climb to **Cerro El Toro** (1652m), the park's highest point, or an overnight trip up **El Revenido**. A rolling trail circumnavigates both peaks, and can be done in one day. **Hormiguero** is another national-park gateway. From the ranger station at the trailhead it's a five-hour hike to Camp Salto Labú, with a stunning swimming hole that has a cave, canyons and petroglyphs. From here you can also begin a four-day trek to the top of **Cerro Saslaya** (1651m). Bring a sleeping bag, tent and water purification for both treks.

Siuna has a number of other worthwhile attractions. Locals love the nearby, crystalline **aguas calientes** (hot springs). Take a taxi to La Bomba, then follow the trail for about an hour across private Finca Dorado to the springs. Also popular are the rocky beaches of the lazy **Río Wani**, a slow-motion, sinuous beast carving rocky sand bars and encroaching jungle with lazy grace about 11km from town.

Bonanza is the jumping-off point for **Reserva Natural Cerro Cola Blanca** and the Mayangna indigenous communities downriver on the **Río Waspuk** and **Río Pispis**. There are also a couple of great swimming holes and waterfalls around town.

If you plan to visit the mines, local tour operator **Wiwi Tours** (☑2794-2097; wiwitour. raan@gmail.com; Miskito Town, Siuna) is a good first port of call. Run by an energetic young team, Wiwi specializes in Las Minas and offers a number of overnight packages to local attractions as well as trips into the Bosawás reserve and a rugged six-day adventure into Parque Nacional Saslaya. **Intur** (☑8665-9534; adentro Alcaldía, Bonanza; ⊘8am-4pm) in Bonanza is also able to recommend guides for hikes and activities throughout the region.

All three towns have airports, but at the time of writing only Bonanza and Siuna had daily flights to and from Managua on 12-seat prop planes. Make reservations in advance, as flights fill up. Flights leave Managua International Airport at 8am for Bonanza (one way/return US$96/148, 1½ hours) and at 9am for Siuna (one way/return US$82/127, one hour). Return flights leave from both destinations at 10:30am.

The road here from Managua is scenic but terrible. It's a long, hard slog in a bus from Managua to Siuna (12 hours) and an even more challenging journey to Bonanza (14 to 17 hours). The Río Blanco–Siuna stretch of the 12-hour hump from Managua is considered one of the country's worst. Rosita is a slightly more manageable eight-hour ride from Bilwi. It involves a river crossing by cable barge and lots of ceiba trees.

If you're eager to see the region, the best plan is to fly into either Bilwi or Las Minas and take buses from there.

hardly receives any visitors so you'll be warmly welcomed upon arrival. It provides tips on visiting sites around the region and accurate transport schedules. Also a good place to organize local guides.

⊙ Getting There & Away

Boaco is 12km from the Empalme de Boaco, on the main Managua–El Rama Hwy. Local buses leave from the market. Managua-bound buses leave from the station, another 200m uphill.

Matagalpa-bound folks need to take the bus to Muy Muy, from where there are frequent departures for Matagalpa. Bus services include:

➜ **Managua** (US$1.20, two hours, 3:45am to 5:25pm, half-hourly) Express minivans (US$1.90, 1½ hours) depart when full from the market area until around noon.

➜ **Muy Muy** (US$1.25, one hour, 5am to 5:30pm, every three hours)

➜ **Río Blanco** (US$2.20, 2½ hours, 7am and 1pm)

➜ **San José de los Remates** (US$1.25, 1½ hours, noon)

➜ **Santa Lucia** (US$0.80, 30 minutes, noon and 3pm)

Santa Lucia

Just 12km north of Boaco off a newly paved road, the picturesque, crumbling Spanish-colonial town of Santa Lucia is nestled in the heart of a 1000-year-old volcanic crater surrounded by rainforested peaks that are part of **Reserva Natural Cerro Cumaica-Cerro Alegre**.

◉ Sights & Activities

Cueva Santo Domingo   CAVE
A tough 4km hike from town, this cave is an old Sandinista stronghold with many petroglyphs left by the previous indigenous residents.

Helman Rene Luna   WALKING TOUR
(☑ 5813-9908) A registered tour guide based in Santa Lucia who offers guided treks in the local region.

❶ Getting There & Away

Irregular buses connect Santa Lucia with Boaco (US$0.80, 30 minutes). If you're in a hurry, consider taking a taxi.

Back Road to Matagalpa

If you're heading north from Boaco and not in any hurry, consider taking the scenic backcountry route to Matagalpa through peaceful pastoral lands at the foot of rugged and rarely visited mountains.

The first stop is the quiet farming town of **San José de los Remates**, an hour north of the turnoff at Teustepe on the Boaco–Managua road. San José has relatively easy access to **Reserva Natural Cerro Cumaica-Cerro Alegre**, and it flaunts it through a municipal tourism program launched to help preserve its own clean water supply.

Several years ago, a Boaco-based cattle-ranching operation had polluted the watershed to the point that municipal ground water was threatened. The townspeople mobilized, convinced the rancher to grow sustainable organic coffee instead, and reforested much of the property themselves. The land is now protected as a municipal park, **Reserva Hídrica Municipal La Chorrera**, adjacent to the national reserve. Local tourism helps foot the bill.

Within the reserve, the four-hour Ruta de los Chorros trail takes you past three 50m waterfalls (one of which you can see from town) to a *mirador* (lookout point) with views clear to the Pacific Ocean. You can organize a local guide at the **Gabinete de Turismo** (☑ 8364-4057; Alcaldía).

From San José de los Remates, the road continues north past a string of rural communities with strong Chorotega roots to scenic **Esquipulas**, where you can hike through the cloud forest to Cerro Santa Maria, which offers terrific views of Boaco; or head for the orchid show on El Cerro del Padre.

From Esquipulas, it's a long and rutted road past family *fincas* (farms) and forested volcanoes. **San Dionisio**, which has some basic *hospedajes* (guesthouses), is the biggest town on this stretch of road. Continue onward to **El Chile**, an indigenous community which is known for its colorful textiles, handbags and dolls. You can visit any of the family workshops before navigating the final 12km to Matagalpa.

Public transport on this route is very limited and it's best explored in a private 4WD vehicle. There are buses from Teustepe (US$1, one hour) to San José de los Remates at 7am and 5pm, the latter of which continues on to Esquipulas. Alternatively, once in San José, try to track down the town's only taxi driver to arrange a private transfer for the 8km trip. From Esquipulas, there are frequent onward bus services to Matagalpa.

Juigalpa

Blessed with a wonderful setting, Juigalpa is nestled on a high plateau peering into a golden valley quilted with rangeland carved by a crystalline river, and enclosed on all sides by the looming Serranía Amerrisque, the sheer granite faces and layered peaks of

RESERVA DE BIOSFERA BOSAWÁS

Supported by three neighboring reserves in Honduras (Río Patuca National Park, Tawhaka Anthropological Reserve and Río Plátano Biosphere Reserve), Reserva de Biosfera Bosawás is the largest protected expanse of rainforest north of the Amazon, clocking in at 20,000 sq km (more than 14% of Nicaragua's national territory).

Named for three geographical features that delineate the reserve – the Río Bocay, Cerro Saslaya and Río Waspuk – enormous Bosawás is also home to more than 200,000 people, including 30,000 Mayangna and Miskito, who have some claim to this land. Tragically, the reserve loses up to a staggering 30,000 hectares of forest per year to slash and burn farmers and illegal lumber operations. A 1.2-million-hectare, multi-use 'amortization area' aims to protect Bosawás by promoting sustainable economic development, such as collecting wild plants to sell, organic cacao and coffee *fincas*, and, of course, tourism.

That's the trick. Access to the reserve's 800,000-hectare wild and undeveloped nucleus ranges from challenging to almost impossible, and is never cheap or risk-free. Come prepared: someone in your group (don't do this alone) should speak a fair amount of Spanish, and consider taking malaria pills for longer adventures. Water-purification technology is necessary for most of the reserve. But the real key to access is persistence – you can get in, just don't count on it happening on your timetable, and expect to be following leads like: 'find Jaguar José at the *pulpería* near the *empalme* of (something unpronounceable); he's got a truck that can get through.'

During the reserve's February to April dry season, rivers (read: the freeway system) may be too low to travel, unless you help carry the canoe around the rapids.

Luckily, it's usually raining, and some spots (for instance, the Río Waspuk region) get 3200mm of rain per year – regular roads may be impassable most of the year. Temperatures average a sweaty 26.5°C (80°F), but bring a fleece for Cerro Kilambé (1750m).

You can begin inquiries at the Bosawás office at **Marena Central** (p57) in Managua, or any of the satellite offices located in most large towns bordering the reserve, where they can arrange guides and transportation, or at least point you in the right direction. It's often easiest to access the reserve through lodges on the periphery or private organizations, however, so ask around. Following are some points of entry:

➡ **Peñas Blancas** Take guided trips to waterfalls and the stunning cliff-top mesa.

➡ **Siuna** Park rangers guide you to campsites in Parque Nacional Saslaya.

➡ **Waspám & the Río Coco** Take a riverboat ride into the waterfall-strewn wilderness, spending the night in a jungle paradise.

➡ **Musuwas** Head from Bonanza into the heart of the Mayangna nation.

➡ **Reserva Natural Cerro Cola Blanca** These waterfall-strewn highlands were named for the white-tailed deer teeming on its forested slopes. The Bonanza **Intur** (p215) office can get you there.

which are ripe for contemplation and adventure. To the west is a series of smaller hills and dry valleys that crumble into marsh, which melts into Lago de Nicaragua. The town itself, sprinkled with well-preserved colonial buildings and peopled by ranchers, rambles along both sides of the Managua Hwy. Apart from a fascinating archaeological museum, there are not a lot of attractions here and the pulse of tourism is quite faint, which makes Juigalpa a particularly authentic destination.

◉ Sights

★**Museo Arqueológico**
Gregorio Aguilar Barea   MUSEUM
(☎2512-0784; Parque Central, 2½c E; admission US$0.40; ◷8am-noon & 1-5pm Tue-Fri, 8am-noon & 1-4pm Sat, 9am-noon & 1-3pm Sun) Mystical stone statues rise like ancient totems in the courtyard entrance here. It houses the most important collection of stelae in the country, with more than 120 basalt statues, carved betwe en AD 800 and 1500, including *La Chinita,* known as 'The Mona Lisa of Chontales.' She too has appeared at the Louvre.

Inside the museum are hundreds of pre-Columbian pots, incense burners, funeral jars, art objects and the largest *metate* (corn grinder) ever found.

Pozo el Salto WATERFALL
This lovely partially dammed swimming hole, 4km north of town on the road to Managua, is framed in cascades of water and has been popular with picnickers for generations; unfortunately, it's often polluted so ask around before diving in. It's about a five-minute walk down the path from the highway. Any nonexpress bus from Juigalpa to Managua will drop you at the entrance, otherwise it's a US$2 ride from town.

✯ Festivals & Events

Fiestas Patronales CULTURAL
(☉Aug 11-18) Internationally known for their *hípicas* (horse parades and rodeos), the party's beating heart is Juigalpa's **Plaza Taurina Chontales** (Carretera La Libertad; admission US$2.50-4), a rodeo venue that hosts events and shows throughout the year.

🛏 Sleeping

Hotel El Regreso HOTEL $
(☑2512-2068; Catedral, 1c E; r US$11-18; 🛜) In the center of town, this excellent-value small hotel offers bright freshly painted rooms with wi-fi, flat TVs and private bathrooms.

Hotel Nuevo Milenio GUESTHOUSE $
(☑2512-0646; Iglesia, 1c E; s/d US$7/11, r with air-con US$12.50-14.50; ❄) The best of the cheapies, this homey place has a sweet family atmosphere, and clean and basic rooms.

★**Hotel Los Arcangeles** HOTEL $$
(☑2512-0847; detras Iglesia; d US$46; ❄) This large ranch-style hotel has a variety of spotless rooms set around plant-filled corridors in a top location directly behind the cathedral. Some are too enclosed while others are spacious with high ceilings, so ask to see a few – they're all the same price. All have flatscreen TVs and modern bathrooms.

✗ Eating & Drinking

The Chontales region is known for its beef and dairy products, both of which figure heavily on local menus.

Palo Solo NICARAGUAN $$
(☑2512-2735; Parque Palo Solo; dishes US$7-12.50; ☉noon-10pm) Set on a shady patio at the western edge of Parque Palo Solo, this restaurant serves up tasty Nicaraguan mixed grill plates. It's not exactly fine dining, but it's lively, the food is good and the view is fantastic.

El Parrillero NICARAGUAN $$
(Gasolinera Esso, 1c N, 3c E, frente Plaza de Tauros; mains US$6.50-12.50; ☉11am-midnight) Upstairs on an open balcony, this busy bar-restaurant serves up a variety of Nicaraguan steak and artery-busting mixed platters. Once the plates are cleared away it's a good spot to linger over some cold beers.

Coffee Break COFFEE
(frente Petronic; coffee US$1-2.50; ☉6am-9:30pm) This traveler-friendly place on the highway serves up a good variety of hot and cold caffeinated beverages in a modern and bright air-con space decked out with comfy booths. The food is not too inspiring but will do the trick if you're hankering for a panini, quesadillas or other gringo fare.

ℹ Information

BanPro (frente Parque Central) Reliable Visa/MasterCard ATM.
Cyber Palo Alto (Parque Palo Alto, 1½c O; per hr US$0.60; ☉10:30am-9pm) New machines and cheap calls.
Hospital (Barrio Hector Ugarte)
Intur (☑2512-2445; Parque Central, 1c O, ½c N; ☉8am-noon & 1-5pm Mon-Fri) Friendly tourist office that is able to arrange guides to surrounding attractions.

ℹ Getting There & Away

Buses to Managua, El Rama and San Carlos all leave from the Cotran bus terminal across Hwy 7 from downtown, 500m south of the hospital (taxis US$0.60). Minivans for Managua (US$3.30) leave the Cotran when full. Passing *expreso* buses between Managua and San Carlos or El Rama do not enter the Cotran – hail them on the highway. Buses to Cuapa, La Libertad and Puerto Díaz leave from the Mercado.

➡ **El Rama** (US$3, five hours, almost hourly, 4:30am to 2:45pm)

➡ **Managua** (*expreso* US$2.50, two hours, 5:45am & 1:15pm; *ordinario* US$2, three hours, 4am to 6pm, half-hourly)

➡ **Puerto Díaz** (US$1, one hour, 5:30am, 9:30am, 11:30am and 1pm) The latter buses do not always run – check at the market.

➡ **San Carlos** (US$4, four hours, 3am to 1:30pm, every two hours)

Puerto Díaz

Just 28km west of Juigalpa, the lakefront village of Puerto Díaz defines the term *tranquilo*. Aside from visiting some of the least-visited islets in the lake, eating fresh fish and contemplating the vast expanse of water that is Lago de Nicaragua, there's not a whole lot to do here.

It's possible to arrange boat trips with local fishermen (per day US$50, six to seven passengers) to the archipelago in front of town, where you can visit each of the three rocky islands with their array of birdlife and swimming beaches. There's a house on Isla Redonda where you may be able to sling your hammock for the night, but you'll need to bring food and water with you from the mainland. Isla Grande is home to a tiny farming community and Isla El Muerte is owned by an absent foreigner, but the guard will probably let you poke around.

In a breezy ranch by the water, El Pescadito (☑ 8732-6774; meals US$3-5; ⊙ 6am-10pm) serves a terrific fried fish (so fresh the meat really does fall off the bones) with panoramic lake views. Bar y Restaurant Lizayel (☑ 8840-3629; meals US$3.50-4.20; ⊙ 6am-10pm), right across the road, has a similar menu but less ambience. It also organizes boat trips to the islands.

For a refreshing swim, head up to the cement pools and thatched bar of Mirador Vista Linda (☑ 8360-5508; adult/child US$0.80/0.40; ⊙ 8am-7pm Sat & Sun), on the hill just above town. Even if you don't plan to jump in, it's worth walking up here for the view, which is magnificent. It takes in the three islands and a stunning back view of Isla de Ometepe's smoldering crater. Order a cold beer and let the view work on you a while.

❶ Getting There & Away

Buses and trucks (US$1, one hour) run to Juigalpa at 4am, 5:30am, 7am, 3:40pm and 4:30pm. These schedules change often and the return buses don't always run – so check in Juigalpa before setting out. Taxis from Juigalpa cost around US$25.

If you're feeling adventurous, it's also possible to travel from here to Isla de Ometepe (US$4, six hours) on one of the sailing boats that bring plantains to the mainland. Departures depend on cargo but they leave around four times a week, usually setting sail around 7pm.

Cuapa

This small, picturesque mountain town became a famous pilgrimage-worthy destination thanks to the Virgin of Cuapa, the porcelain goddess holding flowers in her angelic hands at the entrance to town. On April 15, 1980, when tailor Bernardo Martínez was walking home, the statue began to glow. The Virgin then appeared to him five times, three times as apparitions and twice in his dreams, over the next five months. Her message was that all Nicaragua would suffer without peace.

This, of course, turned out to be true, which is why pilgrims descend on the Virgen de Cuapa Santuario (www.cuapa.com; Parque Central, 2km N; ⊙ 8am-5:30pm) for a week each May. The grounds, surrounded by magnolias, mango trees and boulder-strewn rangeland, include two shrines, a replica statue and a small amphitheater. Pilgrims are welcome to sleep here on May 8 to commemorate the first apparition. Sunday services are held at 11am weekly.

The leafy *parque central* is set on a hill just above downtown, across from the Catholic church, where Martínez is now laid to rest beneath a marble stone in the chapel floor.

Cuapa's other big draw is El Monolito de Cuapa, a massive stone dome that rises from a hillside savanna. If you walk from town, it will take about two hours to reach the peak. Or you could drive to the base and scramble up the back until you reach the top (10 to 20 minutes).

❶ Getting There & Away

Buses run regularly during the day between Juigalpa's market terminal and Cuapa (US$0.50, 30 minutes).

Villa Sandino

It doesn't get many visitors, but the tiny rural town of Villa Sandino on the Juigalpa–El Rama Hwy is the gateway to two of Nicaragua's most important archaeological sites.

The main attraction here is Parque Arqueológico Piedras Pintadas (US$1; ⊙ 8am-4pm), 8km north of town on a firm dirt road, where you'll find hundreds of petroglyphs carved into the mossy boulders, including deer, snakes, turtles, crocodiles and spirals, set among rolling green hills. There are also large stones with carved channels that are said to have been used for ritual sacrifice and an impressive bathing pool carved out of a single massive boulder. The park is overgrown with thick scrub and high grass – bring sturdy footwear. There are no explanation panels, so it's best to go with a guide (US$12 per group). Buy your entrance ticket and organize guides at the Alcaldía (☑ 2516-0058; www.villasandino.gob.ni; Iglesia Catolica, 1c O; ☺ 8am-4pm) before leaving town. A round-trip taxi from town is around US$12.

If you are feeling particularly Dr Jonesish, consider the three-hour horseback ride to the **pre-Columbian pyramids**, the largest ruins of their kind in Nicaragua. What you see are the partially buried bases of larger pyramids that once stood on the site. It's no Tikal, but it's interesting to sit and contemplate how the area looked when the pyramids were complete and the area was full of indigenous worshippers.

🛏 Sleeping

Hotel Santa Clara HOTEL $
(☑ 2516-0055; maisalar@hotmail.com; frente Alcaldía; r with/without air-con US$20/15; 🞱) Has comfortable air-con rooms and also serves meals. Best option in town.

⊙ Getting There & Away

Any Juigalpa–El Rama bus will drop you here. The town center is just a couple of blocks from the highway.

El Rama

The Río Rama and Río Escondido converge at El Rama, turning an otherwise lazy tropical river into an international thoroughfare that empties into Bahía de Bluefields. Roads between El Rama and Managua are some of the best in the country thanks to the commerce of Rama International Port, Nicaragua's only heavyweight Atlantic harbor.

While you are still 60km from the Caribbean sea, take a walk around town and you'll notice plenty of Creole influence with booming reggae, braided hair and a plethora of Bob Marley T-shirts. But in reality Rama is neither here nor there and remains at heart a scruffy port town that does not generally inspire travelers to extend their layover on the way between Managua and Bluefields.

⊙ Sights

La Loma HILL
(Cerro de Rama) It's possible to climb this hill on the edge of town for good views of the local rivers but you'll need to navigate the poor neighborhoods on the periphery.

🛏 Sleeping & Eating

Being a transit hub at the end of the highway, El Rama is chock-full of hotels. Unfortunately, most are pretty dire flophouses and there are only a few comfortable accommodations options.

Hotel Rio Escondido HOTEL $
(☑ 2517-0287; rioescondidohotel@yahoo.es; Enitel, 1c E, 30m S; r with/without air-con US$14.40/11, tr with fan US$16; 🞱 🞱) This reliable hotel has spacious rooms with high ceilings, spotless, tiled bathrooms, small flat-screen TVs and wooden beds with firm sprung mattresses. It's not in that good shape any more but is about as good as it gets in Rama.

Hotel Doña Luisa HOTEL $
(☑ 2517-0073; frente Muelle; r with/without TV US$9/7) If you've got an early boat (or express bus) this is where you want to be. It's right by the dock and offers clean rooms with fans and cable TV. Don't worry about missing your connection – the hustle outside should get you out of bed.

Comedor Siu NICARAGUAN $
(Muelle 4c E, 1c Sur; ☺ 8am-8pm) One of Rama's best steam-table buffets, Comedor Siu serves a mean *bistek en salsa jalapeño* (beef in jalapeño sauce) and good breakfasts too. Be punctual at meal times or it might all be gone.

Casa Blanca NICARAGUAN $$
(☑ 2517-0320; Bancentro, 1c Sur, 1c Este; mains US$4-8.50; ☺ 8am-midnight) A popular open-air restaurant perched on the banks of the Río Escondido on the south side of town that serves solid portions of Nicaraguan favorites. It's also a fine place to kick back with a drink and watch the comings and goings on the river, complete with a *ranchero* soundtrack.

El Expresso STEAKHOUSE, SEAFOOD $$
(Muelle, 4c E; meals US$6.50-10.50; ☺ noon-10pm) This modern, spacious dining room is known for its generous cuts of export-quality beef and seafood dishes, including lobster prepared in nine different ways.

ℹ Information

BanPro (Muelle, 4c E, 3c Sur) Has an ATM that usually works, and changes US dollars.

Cyber Central (Muelle 1c N, 4c Sur; per hr US$0.60; ⊘7am-8pm, to noon Sun) Fast internet access.

ℹ Getting There & Away

El Rama is walkable, but you may choose to take a pedicab (US$0.30) the 1.5km to **Rama International Port** (⌨2517-0315) for large, slow boats to Bluefields. The *Río Escondido* (US$8, five hours), the most punctual service, leaves at 9pm on Tuesday and spends the night in Bluefields before continuing to Corn Island. The *Captain D* (US$4, seven hours) departs at 9pm on Tuesday, with continuing service to El Bluff and Corn Island (US$16).

At the Muelle Municipal, close to the *expreso* buses, **Transporte Vargas** (⌨2517-0073; ⊘24hr) and **Transporte Jipe** (⌨8622-2937, 8937-2913; ⊘24hr) have a faster, more convenient collective *panga* service to Bluefields (US$10.50, two hours). Boats leave at first light and then 'when full' throughout the day. There is usually always service around noon and another around 3pm if there is demand.

Transporte Vargas also runs private *expreso* buses to Managua that are timed to leave once the morning *pangas* arrive from Bluefields, with a further service leaving around noon.

Other *expreso* buses, which actually stop along the way, depart from outside the *muelle* throughout the day. Even slower *ordinarios* park at the small square one block east and one block south.

Bus services include:

➡ **Juigalpa** (US$4, four hours, 4:40am to 2:55pm, hourly)

➡ **Managua** (*expreso* US$6, six hours, 2am, 3am, 9am, 10:30am, noon, 5pm and 7pm; *ordinario* US$5, eight hours, 4:40am to 9:40am, hourly)

➡ **Pearl Lagoon** (US$6.50, five hours, 4:20pm)

Bluefields

With brick streets etched into a series of jade peninsulas, Bluefields (the city) stretches into Bluefields (the bay) like many fingers. In between is a series of docks, floating restaurants, shipwrecks, and fish and produce markets. The city was once full of old wood Victorian charm before Category IV Hurricane Juana wiped it off the map in 1988. Today's Bluefields is rather overindulgent in new concrete boxes, especially in the loud knot of streets downtown that eventually give way to poor tin-roof neighborhoods that ramble over nearby hillsides and inland along polluted brackish creeks.

Named after the Dutch pirate Blewfeldt, who made his base here in the 1700s, the capital of the RAAS is the beating heart of Creole culture, famed for its distinctive music, colorful dances and delicious cuisine, considered by many as the best in the country. And while it is not your typical Caribbean dream destination, if you give it a chance and get to know some of the town's colorful locals, Bluefields' decaying tropical charm will definitely grow on you. Still, you probably won't linger too long. After all, you are just a boat ride away from the intriguing Pearl Lagoon basin, the spectacular Pearl Keys, and those luscious Corn Islands.

◎ Sights

★ **Museo Histórico Cultural de la Costa Caribe**   MUSEUM
(CIDCA; Iglesia Morava, 2c S; admission US$2; ⊘9am-noon & 2-5pm Mon-Fri) Learn about the Caribbean region's diverse cultures with a visit to this fascinating museum that contains an interesting mix of historical items from the pre-Columbian era and British rule, including a sword belonging to the last Miskito king and artifacts left by the Kukra indigenous group.

Moravian Church   CHURCH
This large concrete church is Bluefield's most iconic building and was constructed to the exact specifications of the 1849 wooden original, destroyed in Hurricane Juana. Like all churches of the order it has a red tin roof and all-white exterior.

Rama Cay   ISLAND
Located inside Bluefields' bay, this barbell-shaped island is home to around 800 people – around half of all remaining Rama Indians. Isolated by the dominant Miskito culture, they still speak their own language and use their traditional government structures. It's a crowded place and a trip here is a cultural experience rather than a relaxing Caribbean island excursion.

Visits can be organized through the GTRK office (p224) in Bluefields, which can arrange transport and also lodging.

Malecón de Santa Rosa   WATERFRONT
(Barrio Santa Rosa) A new waterfront area on the way to the airport offering views across

Bluefields Bay that is a popular gathering place for families. It also pulls a crowd for social drinks in the evening.

🏃 Activities

Rumble in the Jungle   FISHING
(☑ 8832-4269; www.rumbleinthejungle.net; Casa Rosa, Loma Fresca; packages per day from US$375) The only sportfishing outfitter in the area, Rumble in the Jungle is run out of hotel Casa Rosa. Owner Randy Poteet knows all the best fishing spots and offers lagoon, river and blue-water options around Bluefields, Pearl Lagoon and beyond.

🎊 Festivals & Events

⭐ Palo de Mayo   CULTURAL
(Maypole Festival; ☉ May) Nicaragua's best street party simmers along throughout May with a series of neighborhood parties and cultural events, but the highlights are the energetic Carnival on the last Saturday of the month and the closing Tulululu march on the 31st.

🛏 Sleeping

Bluefields Bay Hotel   GUESTHOUSE $
(Tia Irene; ☑ 2572-2143; Barrio Pointeen, frente Nicafish; r with/without air-con US$20/15; ❄) Run in conjunction with a local university, this laid-back guesthouse by the bay has a variety of recently renovated rooms offering excellent value and a great walk-anywhere location. The attached open-air restaurant is built right over the water; the food is hit or miss, but it's a fine place for a drink while watching the *pangas* come and go.

Hostal Doña Vero   GUESTHOUSE $
(☑ 2572-2166; hostaldvero@yahoo.com; Galileo, ½c N; s/d US$12.50/14.50, with air-con US$20/21.50, without bathroom US$9.50/11; ❄ 🛜 🏊) A great centrally located budget option with clean, comfortable rooms including private bathroom, unlimited coffee and filtered water. There is a small pool area out the back that feels far removed from the downtown bustle.

Hotel Jackani   GUESTHOUSE $$
(☑ 2572-0440; hoteljackani@gmail.com; frente Policia, Barrio Punta Fria; s/d/tw/tr incl breakfast US$30/40/50/60; ❄ 🛜) This new family-run hotel in front of the police station is already very popular with travelers thanks to its spotless rooms and warm welcome. Guests also appreciate the included breakfast, thefast internet and the large balcony out front with views over to the bay.

Couples should go for room 18, which has a small, private balcony.

Hotel Caribbean Dream   HOTEL $$
(☑ 2572-0107; Mercado, 1c O, ½c S; r US$27-32; ❄ 🛜) A reliable downtown hotel that strikes a good balance between price and amenities. Rooms are not particularly inspiring but feature air-con and hot water, and there is a great balcony with rockers overlooking the street – perfect for getting to know some of Bluefields' colorful characters.

Casa Rosa   LODGE $$$
(☑ 8832-4269; Loma Fresca; r/ste US$55/75; ❄ 🛜) Perched on a tributary of the Río Escondido in the breezy Loma Fresca neighborhood, this Nica-American sportfishing resort is a 10-minute taxi ride from the commercial heart of town, but looks and feels a million miles away. Most guests come to fish, but the clean and comfortable wooden rooms with air-con, wi-fi, cable TV and a river serenade would work for anyone.

The owners have plans to build some economic waterside bungalows so call to check on accommodations options.

Hotel Oasis   HOTEL $$$
(☑ 2572-2812; reservations@oasiscasinohotel.com; Muelle Municipal, 1c O; s/d US$50/60, ste US$72, presidential ste US$150, all incl breakfast; 🅿 ❄ 🛜) Easily the best hotel downtown, as long as you avoid the dark rooms downstairs. Up top there are ample modern rooms, some with bay views, boasting bright tiled floors, big comfortable beds and powerful air-con. The service is courteous and professional, and there is a free pickup service from the airport.

🍴 Eating

Bluefields' favourite snack is the *paty* – a savory spiced meat pastry sold for US$0.30 by roaming vendors all over town.

⭐ Cevicheria El Chino   SEAFOOD $
(frente Colegio Bautista; ceviche US$2; ☉ 7am-9pm) Don't leave Bluefields without trying El Chino's marvelous ceviche prepared fresh everyday and served in small polystyrene cups, alongside an array of auto parts at this unremarkable grocery shop. Choose from shrimp, fish, oyster or mixed and watch out

Bluefields

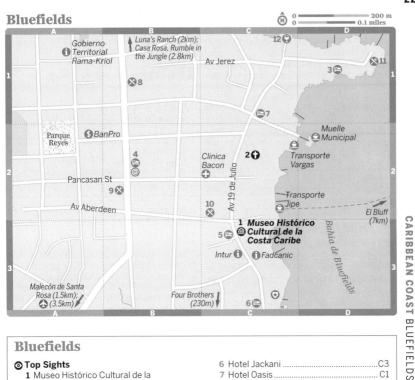

N 0 ————————— 200 m
   0 ————————— 0.1 miles

Bluefields

◎ Top Sights
1 Museo Histórico Cultural de la
Costa Caribe C3

◎ Sights
2 Moravian Church C2

◎ Sleeping
3 Bluefields Bay Hotel D1
4 Hostal Doña Vero B2
5 Hotel Caribbean Dream C3

6 Hotel Jackani C3
7 Hotel Oasis C1

◎ Eating
8 Cevicheria El Chino B1
9 Comedor de Las Platas B2
10 Galeria Aberdeen C2
11 Pelican Bay D1

◎ Drinking & Nightlife
12 Midnight Dream (LaLa's) C1

for the outrageously spicy homemade 'Ass in Space' chili sauce – made with pounds of habanero chilies.

There's no sign and El Chino tells us plenty of readers walk right by with their heads in the guidebooks. It's the only store on the block in front of the Baptist School.

Comedor de Las Platas   NICARAGUAN $
(contiguo Galileo; meals incl drink US$3; ◎ noon-8pm) A quiet *comedor* serving budget lunches during the day, this local institution transforms into the best *fritanga* (grill) in town in the evenings, serving up delicious *fritos* – greasy fried chicken on piles of plantain chips with pickles. Come early.

★ **Galeria Aberdeen**   CAFE $$
(Los Pipitos; ☎ 2572-2605; Mercado, 1½c O; light meals US$4-7) Feeling just a tad too chic for grimy Bluefields, this light-filled, split-level cafe serves real coffee (US$1 to US$2.50) in addition to panini, pasta dishes, salads and other meals you won't find anywhere else. Also has a great selection of desserts and a fridge full of imported beers. The walls are covered with works by local artists and it hosts regular cultural events.

Luna's Ranch   NICARAGUAN $$
(Loma Fresca, frente Urracan; mains US$5-9; ◎ 11am-10pm) There are many reasons to visit this impressive thatched restaurant on

the Loma Fresca hill, such as occasional live concerts and the interesting collection of images of the old Bluefields, including many of the devastation wrought by the hurricane. But the biggest attraction is the generous portions of seafood. It's a 10-minute taxi ride (US$0.50) from downtown.

Pelican Bay NICARAGUAN **$$**
(☑2572-2089; Barrio Pointeen; mains US$7-12.50; ☺noon-10pm) At the end of the Pointeen peninsula, this flash restaurant has an elevated balcony with fantastic views across the bay to El Bluff. The house specialty is seafood and the mixed plate (US$12.50) featuring shrimp, fish and lobster sautéed with herbs is outstanding.

🍷 Drinking & Nightlife

★**Four Brothers** CLUB
(Parque Reyes, 6c S; ☺8pm-4am Thu-Sun) Dance up a storm to dancehall, country and reggae on the wooden dance floor at this legendary disco ranch, comfortable in the knowledge that your dignity is protected by the extremely low-wattage lighting. It doesn't get going until after midnight. Go in a group as it sometimes gets a little rough later on.

Midnight Dream (LaLa's) BAR
(Iglesia, 2c N; ☺11am-midnight) With an open-air deck that feels like it is floating on the bay and ridiculously loud reggae numbers, this atmospheric spot is where cool cats go to drink and get their groove on.

ⓘ Information

BanPro (frente Iglesia) Reliable Visa/Master-Card ATM.

Clínica Bacon (☑2572-2384; Iglesia, 1c S, ½c O) Private clinic with a range of specialists and a laboratory.

Cyberzone (Galileo 20m N; per hr US$0.35; ☺8am-7pm Mon-Sat) Fast internet connection.

Gobierno Territorial Rama-Kriol (GTRK; ☑8622-8407, 2572-1765; www.rama-territory. com; Parque Reyes, 2c N; ☺8am-5pm) The official representatives of the vast territory south of Bluefields belonging to the indigenous Rama and Creole populations. Staff can help arrange transport and accommodations in villages throughout the region, including Monkey Point, Rama Cay, Tik Tik Kaanu and Bang Kukuk.

Visitors can choose between staying in cultural centers or homestays in each village. Conditions are often very basic with pit latrines and bucket showers the norm in some destinations.

Intur (☑2572-0221; Iglesia, 2c S, Punta Fria; ☺8am-5pm Mon-Fri) Tourist office with some basic information about traveling in the region. There is also a small kiosk at the airport to orientate new arrivals.

Police (☑2572-2448; Barrio Punta Fria)

ⓘ Getting There & Away

AIR
Take a taxi (US$0.50) to the Bluefields Airport, where **La Costeña** (☑2572-2500, 2572-2750; Aeropuerto; ☺6am-5pm) has daily flights to Managua and Great Corn Island, and flies to Bilwi three days a week.

➡ **Bilwi** (one way/return US$96/148, 50 minutes, 11:10am Monday, Wednesday and Friday)

➡ **Corn Island** (one way/return US$64/99, 20 minutes, 7:25am and 3:05pm)

➡ **Managua** (one way/return US$82/127, 70 minutes, 8:45am, 1:10pm and 4:15pm)

BOAT
There are a couple of scheduled boat services to Corn Island departing on Wednesday. The government-run **Río Escondido** (US$10, five hours) has the most reliable schedule, departing from the **Muelle Municipal** (Municipal Dock) at 9am on the dot. Larger and more comfortable but slightly slower, the **Captain D** (☑8850-2767; seat/bunk US$10/12) leaves around noon. If it arrives fully loaded from Rama it may depart from Bluff as it is unable to enter Bluefields. Its schedule often changes, so call to check.

There are also a number of cargo boats making the trip on irregular schedules.

Transporte Vargas (☑2572-0724, 2572-1510; contiguo Muelle Municipal; ☺5am-4pm) at the Muelle Municipal has collective *pangas* to El Rama (US$9.50, two hours) with guaranteed departures at 5:30am and then further services when boats fill up. There are usually departures at around noon and 3pm. Transporte Vargas also runs boats to Tasbapauni and Orinoco in the greater Pearl Lagoon area.

Transporte Jipe (☑2572-1879; contiguo Mercado; ☺5am-4pm) next to the market also runs *pangas* to El Rama (US$9.50, two hours, 5:30am and 3pm).

For Pearl Lagoon (US$6, one hour) *pangas* leave from the dock next to the Muelle Municipal at 8:30am, 11am, 2pm and 3:30pm. Note that schedules are flexible – if a boat fills up, it will leave early. *Pangas* crossing the bay to El Bluff (US$2, 30 minutes) leave from behind the market when full.

Pearl Lagoon

At last, you've arrived in the real Caribbean. Here are dirt roads and palm trees, reggae music, and an English-speaking Creole

TERRITORIO RAMA-KRIOL

If you really want to get away from the crowds and discover the best the Caribbean coast has to offer, plan a trip into the little visited Territorio Rama-Kriol. Jointly administered by the indigenous Rama and Creole peoples of the region, it stretches from the southern half of Bahía de Bluefields all the way to the Costa Rican border, and includes stunning solitary beaches, mysterious ruins cloaked in virgin rainforest and lazy mocha-colored rivers teeming with wildlife.

It's possible to visit the territory on a loop from Bluefields or continue all the way down to San Juan de Nicaragua near the mouth of the Río San Juan. Begin with a visit to **Rama Cay**, a tiny, rocky, barbell-shaped island in Bahía de Bluefields, 15km southeast of the city and de facto capital of the Rama nation. The island is dotted with coconut and banana palms and mango and breadfruit trees and is laced with earthen trails that link clusters of stilted thatched bungalows, home to over 1000 people, which accounts for over half of all remaining Rama. Check out the Moravian Church or head up to the breezy point on the north side of the island to chill out under coconut trees. If you're feeling more active, learn to sail a traditional *dory* (dugout canoe) on the bay and head across to wild **Mission Cay** for a picnic.

Across the bay and up the Kukra River you'll find **Tiktik Kaanu**, a remote Rama community that's a great place to spend the night surrounded by the sounds of the jungle.

Heading out of Bahía de Bluefields through the Hone Sound passage (a turbulent gathering of breaking waves that is a true test of your captain's skills) you'll come to **Monkey Point**, a Rasta-influenced Creole community spread out on hillsides by the sea and surrounded by thick jungle. Here you'll find some of the best beaches on the Caribbean mainland and a fascinating yet unexplored indigenous burial site shrouded in thick foliage, which is said to be one of the oldest archaeological sites in the country.

A short boat ride further south is **Bankukuk**, a small Rama community with fine beaches and jungle-covered headlands jutting out into the calm Caribbean Sea.

Continuing south past Punta Gorda, you'll arrive at **Corn River**, one of the most important waterways of the magnificent Reserva Natural Indio Maíz. At the river mouth you'll find a tiny Creole community, but the real attraction here is upriver, where you'll be treated to some of the best wildlife-viewing in the country. The towering trees are awash with birds and monkeys and you may spot sloths or even a tapir.

Visit the **Gobierno Territorial Rama-Kriol** (GTR) in Bluefields to arrange your trip.

Getting There & Away

The GTRK's planned regular *panga* service to the communities is still not up and running. Until it gets off the ground, you'll either have to charter a boat or hitch a ride with a traveling local – you'll be expected to contribute to fuel costs.

It may also be possible to get to some of the communities using the regular Bluefields–San Juan de Nicaragua express *panga* but you'll have to negotiate with the driver as most villages require a deviation from the normal journey.

community that fishes the local waters for shrimp, fish and lobster, and still refers to Spanish-speaking Nicaraguans as 'the Spaniards.' You can feel the stress roll off your shoulders as soon as you get off the boat from Bluefields. And the best part is that despite its obvious charms, this town still sees very few tourists – which means you may well be the only foreigner buzzing through the mangroves and jungle that surround Pearl Lagoon (the bay). The bay is a timeless expanse of black water and home to more than a dozen ethnic fishing villages.

If your Caribbean dream is tinted turquoise, you can easily arrange a tour of the nearby Pearl Keys, where you'll find sugar-white beaches that double as turtle hatcheries, and swaying coconut palms that lull you into inner peace. Of course, nothing tops off a day on the water like cold beer, lobster with coconut sauce and heavy doses of reggae music, all of which are available among Pearl Lagoon's collection of restaurants and bars sprinkled along traffic-free roads patrolled by fishers, their families and free-roaming horses.

◉ Sights

The town is laid out along two main north–south roads: Front Rd, on the water, and another road a block inland.

At the southern end of the inland road you'll find the **Moravian Church**, with its characteristic red tin roof. Take the path opposite the church due west and walk through town until you reach the savanna, a striking flat ecosystem with several freshwater creeks and interesting birdlife. Keep on the concrete path and after around 2km (30 minutes) you will reach the humble Miskito fishing communities of **Awas and Raiti Pura**, where the grassy shore is perfect for a picnic. The water here is shallow and great for swimming.

You can also make the journey by bike; Queen Lobster Tours rents bikes for US$1 per hour.

☞ Tours

Fuel costs make up the lion's share of any boat charter. Plan on paying around US$60 to US$80 per day for the boat and captain plus fuel. If you're on a budget, look for a boat with a small engine; it will take longer but you'll save plenty. Note that small engines are only an option when the weather is calm.

While fluctuations in fuel prices affect prices dramatically, a ball park price for a one-day trip to the keys is around US$180 to US$200 for a small group. For larger groups, budget around US$45 per visitor. All tours include transport and lunch on one of the islands.

★**Captain Sodlan McCoy**   BOAT TOUR
(☑8410-5197, 8368-6766; Up Point) Anyone can take you to the Pearl Keys, but few know the area even half as well as Captain Sodlan McCoy, a colorful, no-nonsense fisherman who has been visiting the islands since he was a boy. A trip with Sodlan is much more than sightseeing, it's a cultural experience. He also offers birdwatching, fishing and community trips.

To find him turn right out of the dock and head to the end of the path.

Kabu Tours   ECOTOUR
(☑8714-5196; www.kabutours.com) Kabu Tours is a community-run venture set up by the Wildlife Conservation Society to offer an alternative source of income to turtle fishers from the community of Kakabila. It offers overnight and multiday trips to the Pearl Keys, including turtle spotting and snorkeling. It also runs fascinating cultural tours to communities in the Pearl Lagoon basin. See the website for a list of packages.

Queen Lobster Tours   BOAT TOUR
(☑8662-3393, 8499-4403; www.queenlobster.com; Muelle, 200m N) Professionally run eco-tourism outfit specializing in overnight trips to the Pearl Keys, as well as inventive activities around town such as traditional cooking classes.

George Fox Tours   BOAT TOUR
(☑8648-3489; Front Rd, Muelle, 150m N) A true Pearl Lagoon gentleman, George not only provides transport to the Keys and communities, he walks and talks you through the area's culture, history and cuisine.

🛏 Sleeping

Comfort Zone   GUESTHOUSE $
(☑8829-7113; Muelle, 2c S, ½c E; r with air-con US$35, s/d/tr with fan US$11/14.50/18; ❊) Next to the family store, these tiled rooms with flat-screen TV, small desks, fans and private bathroom are a good deal, and the owners couldn't be more accommodating.

Slilma Guesthouse   GUESTHOUSE $
(☑2572-0523; slilma_gh1@yahoo.com; Enitel, 1c S, 1c E; r with air-con US$30-35, r with fan US$15-20, r without bathroom US$10; ❊) Take the first left after the cell tower to find this budget guesthouse offering small but very clean rooms with small TVs and the cleanest shared bathrooms in the Atlantic region. There are also more spacious rooms with air-con and private bathrooms upstairs.

Queen Lobster   BUNGALOW $$
(☑8662-3393; Front Rd, Muelle 200m N; s/d/tr US$25/35/45; 🐾) An innovative small hotel offering two beautifully crafted bamboo and thatch huts (single/double/triple US$30/40/50) on stilts over the water with private bathrooms and hammocks on the porch. The attached restaurant is one of the best in town, serving fantastic seafood dishes, but the owners plan to close it down to make space for more rooms.

Best View Hotel   HOTEL $$
(☑2572-5099, 8824-3962; Up Point, Barrio Ivan Dixon; s/d/tr US$35/40/50; ❊@🐾) Jutting out into the water at the end of the footpath, this modern hotel catches plenty of breeze and is a good place from which to observe

Miskito sailing canoes and local fishing boats out on the lagoon. Rooms are small but modern and come with cable TV, air-con and reliable wi-fi.

Casa Blanca HOTEL $$
(8362-6946; Enitel, 250m O; r with air-con US$35, s/d/tr without bathroom US$10/20/30; ❄🌐) This lovely white house has wooden floors and furnishings made in the attached workshop. The small rooms upstairs have very low ceilings but those out the back are spacious and full of natural light. These ladies can cook too. Try the shrimp in coconut sauce.

Green Lodge HOTEL $$
(2572-0507; Front Rd, Muelle 75m S; s/d with air-con US$30/35, r without bathroom US$7-14; ❄❄🌐) Half a block from the dock, this long-running hotel is a fine choice. The cheaper rooms upstairs in the family home are a little cramped, but those in the new wing are clean, spacious and comfortable. Owner Wesley Williams is a knowledgeable source of information on local history and culture.

Eating

Coconut Delight BAKERY $
(Miss Betty's; Muelle, 30m S; bakery items US$0.25-US$1; ⊙8am-8pm Mon-Sat) Follow the sweet smells to this pink wooden hut to discover Caribbean baking at its finest. Tear into hot coconut bread, *toto* (sticky ginger bread), journey cakes, fluffy soda cakes and even vegetarian *paty* served with a smile by jolly giant and all-round-nice-guy Mr Byron.

★Casa Ulrich INTERNATIONAL $$
(8603-5173; Up Point, Muelle 350m N; mains US$5.50-12.50; ⊙7am-10pm; 🌐) Local boy and Swiss-trained chef Fred Ulrich has returned to Pearl Lagoon after a long absence working in resorts all over the Americas and has invested in his own hotel and restaurant right by the water. Everything on the menu is top-notch, but make sure you try the tender fillet steaks that arrive at your table on a sizzling platter or the delicate shrimp pasta.

They accept credit and debit cards for meals.

Information

Western Union (frente Muelle, Tienda Miss Isabel; ⊙9am-5pm Mon-Fri) Receive international transfers here. It will also give a cash advance on a credit card for a percentage fee.

Wildlife Conservation Society (WCS; 2572-0506; www.wcs.org; Muelle, 20m S, Pearl Lagoon; ⊙9am-5pm Mon-Fri) A conservation organization working to protect endangered marine turtles on the Pearl Keys. Swing by the office to find out more about their programs.

Getting There & Away

Boats run to Bluefields (US$6, one hour) at 6:30am and 1pm. Sign up the day before for the early boat.

Every Monday, Wednesday, Thursday and Saturday, a *panga* makes the run to Orinoco and Marshall Point from Bluefields via Pearl Lagoon (US$12, two hours, 9am); it returns to Pearl Lagoon and Bluefields the following day. This boat can also drop travelers at the communities of Kakabila, Brown Bank and La Fe. There are *pangas* from Bluefields to Tasbapauni (US$12, 2½ hours) that pass Pearl Lagoon every day at 11am. Times are liable to shift depending upon the season, so you'll need to ask about departure times at the dock.

One bus (US$6.30, five hours) a day leaves Pearl Lagoon at 5am for El Rama from where you can connect to services to Managua and San Carlos.

Around Pearl Lagoon

With a dozen villages belonging to three distinct ethnic groups clinging to its shores and a similar number of jungle-lined rivers feeding it, a boat trip on Pearl Lagoon can make you feel like an 18th-century explorer venturing into an intriguing new world. This is authentic, off-the-beaten-track cultural tourism at its best, and there is nothing like it anywhere else in the country.

Kakabila

Crossing the lagoon to the northwest from Pearl Lagoon town, you'll come to Kakabila, a welcoming Miskito village carpeted with soft grass and studded with mango, pear and breadfruit trees and coconut palms. There's definitely some tropical country romance happening here. To the south of town is Tuba Creek, a narrow, jungle-lined river that is great for wildlife spotting.

Getting There & Away

A private transfer from Pearl Lagoon to Kakabila will cost around US$50 for a large boat or US$20 to US$30 in a motorized canoe.

Alternatively, the public *panga* from Bluefields to Orinoco (US$11) will drop you here on request.

Río Wawashang

This lazy, wide, mocha-colored river surrounded by jungle flows into Pearl Lagoon just west of Orinoco. Its banks are home to two fascinating projects run by the **Fadcanic** (☑ 2572-2386; wawashang@fadcanic.org.ni; Barrio Punta Fria, oficinas del PNUD; ⊙ 9am-5pm Mon-Fri, 9am-noon Sat) 🌐 organization. Call or visit its office in Bluefields to arrange a trip.

Wawashang Education Center (☑ 8930-0248; Río Wawashang) 🌐 is a vocational training school where youth from all over the Región Autónoma Atlántico Sur (RAAS: South Atlantic Autonomous Region) learn about sustainable agriculture. You can tour the greenhouses, check out the cool coconut farm or sample artisanal chocolate made from locally grown cacao.

Continue upriver to Pueblo Nuevo, the jumping-off point for the **Reserva Natural Kahka Creek** (☑ 2570-0962, 8725-0766; Pueblo Nuevo), a reforestation and ecotourism project set in lush gardens surrounded by jungle. There are a number of hiking trails and a lookout tower above the forest canopy. Visitors can also get involved in the reforestation process by planting trees. Accommodations (dorm/room US$7/13) are available in a solar-powered wooden lodge and cheap meals are served.

ℹ️ Getting There & Away

Pangas depart Bluefields to Pueblo Nuevo (US$10, 2½ hours) at 7:30am on Sunday and Wednesday and 2pm on Thursday via Pearl Lagoon and the Río Wawashang. They can drop visitors directly at the Wawashang Education Center.

Reserva Natural Kahka Creek is a 30-minute walk from the town of Pueblo Nuevo. It's possible to make the journey on horseback with advance notice.

Orinoco

When you can hear the call of the *djimbe* (wood and animal skin drum) spilling out across the rippling water from the red-earth streets of Orinoco, you know you're approaching Garifuna country.

Orinoco is home to 2000 of Nicaragua's approximately 5000 Garifuna. Here you can learn to paddle dugout canoes, try artisanal fishing or take the 30-minute stroll northeast along the water to Marshall Point, a neighboring Creole village.

🛏️ Sleeping

Hostal Garifuna   GUESTHOUSE $
(☑ 8504-5724; www.hostalgarifuna.net; Muelle, 50m inland; s/d/tr US$7.50/10/15) Owned by local anthropologist, activist and entrepreneur, Kensy Sambola, this very comfortable budget hotel has spotless tiled rooms with shared bathrooms. At the time of research a new room with private bathroom was under construction upstairs. The restaurant serves tremendous seafood meals (US$6).

Kensy and her staff can organize a range of cultural activities, including boat transport to La Fe, yet another Garifuna village, famous for its acoustic troubadours.

ℹ️ Information

Note that a number of robberies targeting tourists, including serious assault, have been reported in and around Orinoco. All visitors, but particularly female travelers, should exercise caution and not walk through remote areas without a trusted local guide. Ask at your hotel for a recommendation.

ℹ️ Getting There & Away

Daily public boats run from Bluefields to Orinoco (US$11, two hours) via Pearl Lagoon, leaving from next to the municipal dock in Bluefields between 9am and 10am and passing Pearl Lagoon one hour later.

A private round-trip boat transfer from Pearl Lagoon to Orinoco costs around US$120.

Pearl Keys

You would be hard-pressed to imagine a more beautiful and romantic tropical island chain than the snow-white, palm-shaded, turquoise-fringed Pearl Keys. Located in the Caribbean Sea 30km from Pearl Lagoon town, there were once 18 pearls, but rising tides have trimmed the number to 12.

Once communally owned by Miskito and Creole villagers, some of the keys have been bought – illegally according to locals – by foreign investors with dreams of tropical island isolation.

You can certainly understand the appeal. Larger islands include lagoons and shady palm groves in the interior, while smaller islands seem to exist purely for their cotton-white sand beaches. Sheltered by reefs, and channeled into crystalline coves, the sea gets bathtub warm here.

Endangered hawksbill turtles nest from May to November in the Pearl Keys, peaking in August and September. Traditionally hunted by the locals for their shells, as opposed to the meat of the tastier green turtles, hawksbills are now also under pressure because of island development that has compromised their nesting grounds. The Wildlife Conservation Society (WCS; p227) has helped by hiring fishers to watch turtle nests and by educating them about the damaging effects of artificial light and egg poaching on the ecosystem. Before WCS arrived, 97% of hawksbill eggs were poached by fishers. Now they lose only 10% a year. The WCS also manages an extensive turtle-tagging program that has enabled international scientists to learn how vast the turtles' range actually is. It's worth dropping by the WCS office in Pearl Lagoon to learn more.

The only way to visit the keys is on a private boat tour. Arrange trips in Pearl Lagoon town. A day trip will set you back around US$180 to US$280, depending on the size of your group and how many islands you want to visit. There are no longer any hotels operating on the keys, but it's possible to stay in tents on one of the several islands that remain in community hands. Expect to pay an additional US$35 per visitor for each night on top of transport costs to cover meals and tents.

In calm weather, it's just another hour (and another US$200) by *panga* from the keys to the Corn Islands. Considering the adventure quotient, the price and the time involved, it actually makes good sense to travel to the Corn Islands from Pearl Lagoon via the Pearl Keys rather than doubling back to Bluefields and flying to Great Corn from there.

◉ Sights

Grape Key ISLAND
Home to an abandoned hotel, this lovely round island has probably the best swimming in the archipelago with pure white sand beaches sloping down to deep crystalline water. The caretaker may charge visitors to land on the island, which is why many local operators don't dock here.

Maroon Key ISLAND
The closest key to the mainland, this tiny football-field-sized patch of white sand and coconut trees is completely uninhabited and the perfect place to indulge in your shipwreck fantasies. Unfortunately, its isolation leaves it unprotected from the force of increasingly powerful waves and the island is rapidly disappearing.

Crawl Key ISLAND
This is a slender crescent of white sand bunched with soaring coconut palms. It's also home to an unfinished three-story concrete monstrosity that was destined to be a private pad for a wealthy American until the community called in the authorities because the beach is a prime hawksbill-nesting ground.

Wild Cane Key ISLAND
(☑2572-1644) This large island with a spectacular long beach was once the family

PEARL KEYS: PRIVATIZING PARADISE

For the fishers of the Pearl Lagoon basin, the Pearl Keys are like a second home, a place to rest and gather fresh water while out at sea for days. So when in 1997 a foreign land speculator, Peter Tsokas, purchased some old deeds to the islands – the legality of which are disputed – and proceeded to sell them off at huge profits to wealthy expat dreamers, things took a turn for the worse.

Soon the new 'owners' began raising foreign flags, constructing large houses and hotels and ordering the locals to keep off the islands, despite Nicaraguan laws guaranteeing public access to beaches.

In response, the local community hired a lawyer to take up the case. In addition to claiming to be the legitimate owners of the keys, the community also expressed concerns that the unregulated construction was destroying the sensitive ecosystem.

A combination of community pressure, the harsh realities of life on a remote island, and the failure of an expected tourism boom to materialize has seen many of the original buyers abandon their island dream and move out. However, a couple of hardcore buyers remain.

The Nicaraguan government has publicly stated its commitment to returning the islands to the community, but there has yet to be a definitive resolution.

THE GARIFUNA

The Garifuna people trace their origins to the Caribbean island of San Vicente where the survivors of a wrecked slave ship intermarried with the indigenous population. The resulting ethnic group was referred to as the Black Caribs by the British, who, following repeated indigenous rebellions, forcibly moved them from San Vicente to the island Roatan in Honduras.

From Roatan, the Garifuna spread throughout Central America, founding their own free communities such as Orinoco, where they practiced their Yoruba religion in relative peace. Christianity eventually came calling in the 19th century, but traditional shamanic healing ceremonies, such as the three-day *walágayo* ritual, persist.

The best way to get a taste of Garifuna music, ritual, history and cuisine – such as *hudutu* or *fu fú* (a mash of plantains and fish flooded with coconut sauce and paired with home-distilled, clove-spiced rum), is to attend November's **National Garifuna Week**. Events include live music and dance performances, and historical and cultural symposiums that climax on November 19.

paradise of a young New Zealand millionaire. However, after the watchman up and left following a pay dispute, local fishers moved in, and like an army of leafcutter ants each taking what they could carry, stripped the once-opulent resort bare.

Visiting the island now is an eerie experience: the whole place looks like it was hit by a devastating hurricane

Corn Islands

The Caribbean coast's biggest tourist draw is actually 70km offshore on a pair of enchanting islands with horseshoe bays, crystalline coves and underwater caves. Great Corn is larger and peopled by a Creole population that lives in colorful wooden houses, many of which are sprinkled along the main road that encircles the island. And though tourism is the second-largest industry, behind lobster fishing, you won't see mega-developments here. Little Corn, a tiny, jungled, car-less jewel, actually attracts more tourists, with most visitors heading for funky, creative beachside *cabañas* that are the perfect setting for Robinson Crusoe 2.0. The dive sites are more diverse on Little Corn, the jungle is thick and the food is outrageously good, which explains why so many ignore the larger island and indulge in car-free tranquillity. But there is a catch. During high season there can be more foreigners than locals.

History

Christopher Columbus breezed through the Corn Islands in 1502, but it wasn't until 1660, when a French pirate by the name of Jean-David Nau arrived, that relations with the indigenous Kukras were cultivated. In the 1700s, European pirates patrolled these waters and British residents of the island brought in African slaves to work the fields. Both groups mingled with the Kukras. Although the British were asked to leave the islands in 1786, as part of their treaty with the Spanish, they returned in 1841 after Nicaragua's independence from Spain, which signified the end of slavery. The Crab Soup Festival (p233) celebrates freedom every August 27 with music, dance and, of course, crab soup.

🏃 Activities

Both islands have excellent diving and snorkeling, with over 40 species of coral and migrating hammerhead sharks. While Little Corn probably edges its larger rival for diversity and quantity of marine life, you are more likely to have the dive sites to yourself on Great Corn (known locally as Big Corn or Big Island).

Most dive sites are within 10 minutes of the shore and fairly shallow (9m to 18m), with 30m visibility on the best days. Dive sites can be inaccessible during high winds. Dive shops monitor long-term forecasts; call ahead to check on conditions. Popular dive sites:

➡ **Blowing Rock** (10m to 30m) This pinnacle is accessible from both islands and is arguably the best of the local dive sites. It attracts large pelagics year-round.

➡ **The Caves** (9m) A swim-through flooded with light on Little Corn's east coast. Geographical set-piece diving at its finest.

➡ **Nautilus House Reef** (9m to 19m) Just off the northwest shore of Great Corn is a patch of reef teeming with colorful fish and large fan corals.

➡ **Tarpon Channel** (9m to 22m) When the water cools off, hammerheads cruise this channel regularly.

➡ **White Holes** (9m) A favorite site on the northern side of Little Corn, thanks to the resident nurse sharks, eagle rays and barracuda.

➡ **Yellowtail** (9m to 15m) Dolphins are sometimes seen here, at the southern corner of Little Corn.

🛈 Getting There & Away

By far the fastest and easiest way to reach the islands is by air. La Costena links Great Corn Island with Bluefields and Managua with three daily flights.

Alternatively, there are also at least a couple of boats a week carrying passengers between Bluefields and Great Corn.

Great Corn Island

Large enough to get lost in humble hillside and beachfront neighborhoods that are poor but still full of spirit, and small enough to find your way home again, Great Corn is on the shortlist for most authentic Caribbean island. Here are barefoot bars, commercial fishing wharfs, pick-up baseball games on the beach, smiling young lobster divers catch-in-hand, an ever-present armada of elders sitting in rocking chairs on creaky front porches, and elegant virgin beaches backed by picturesque headlands. It's a place where reggae and country music can coexist without irony. Where fresh lobster is a staple ingredient rather than a luxury. And the longer you stay, the less you want to leave.

◎ Sights

Great Corn measures about 6 sq km and is looped by one main road – which has several spur roads that lead to various beaches and neighborhoods. **Long Bay** is where you'll find the island's best stretch of golden sand. It arcs from a pile-up of local fishing *pangas* and lobster traps to a wild, jungle-covered headland. If you're looking for a place to snooze and swim in absolute tranquillity, this is your destination. **Southwest Bay** beckons with another outstanding wide beach. The water here is calmer but the area is more developed and less rustic.

Walk up the dirt trail behind the Sunrise Hotel in South End past the banana groves and you will be rewarded with panoramic views from **Mt Pleasant** as the sun plunges beneath the Caribbean Sea. Or make your way to **Quinn Hill**, where Spanish artist Rafael Trénor has installed a cube (the lower half is buried to make it look like a pyramid) symbolizing one of the earth's eight vortex points as part of his Soul of the World Project (www.souloftheworld.com).

Next to the stadium, the **Culture House** (Mt Pleasant, contiguo Alcaldía; ◷ 8am-8pm Mon-Fri) museum won't hold your attention very long with its pictures of old beauty queens, preserved lobsters and collection of John

---

SAFE & RESPONSIBLE DIVING

Exploring the coral reefs and underwater caves is one of the Corn Islands' main attractions, but the scuba diving industry is far more low-key here than in many other destinations in the region.

Most dives around the Corn Islands are in fairly shallow waters, which alleviates many safety concerns, but it's still vitally important that you choose a responsible dive center that you feel comfortable with.

When choosing an operator, find out the instructor-to-student ratio and ask to see the equipment before you dive to make sure it is well maintained. You may also want to test the air in the tanks (it should be taste and odor free) and make sure that the boats have sufficient life vests.

Sustainable practices have come a long way on both islands and local dive operators now run pretty tight ships, but visitors still play an important role in protecting the fragile ecosystem. Follow the instructions of your divemaster closely, fasten all your equipment tightly so nothing is flapping about, and resist the temptation to reach out and touch, no matter how insignificant it may seem – small organisms are often the most fragile.

Great Corn Island

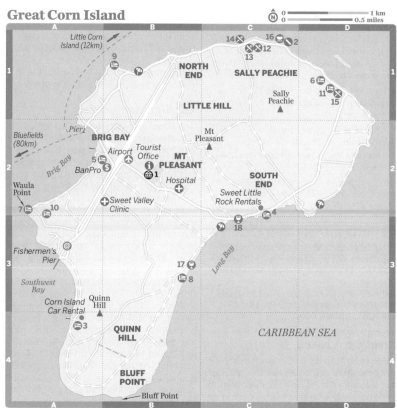

Grisham novels. But there are a couple of pre-Columbian pots and, if you come in the evening, you can watch the local youth band jam in the music room.

🏃 Activities

The tourist office (p235) is able to organize guides (US$15 to US$30 per person) for hikes all over the island, including to the wild **Bluff Point**.

There's terrific snorkeling along the reef off the **Sally Peachie** coast. Among the other highlights for snorkelers are the remains of a Spanish galleon off Waula Point – there's not much left, you'll mostly just be checking out some old cannons and an anchor but it's still neat – and a more complete wreck of a steamship full of fish in shallow water off Sally Peachie. Mr Dorsey at **Yellow Tail** (☑ 8909-8050; Sally Peachie; r US$25) offers highly recommended guided snorkeling

tours. **Paraiso Club** (☑ 2575-5111; www.paraisoclub.com; Waula Point; cabañas s/d US$54/70, bungalow s/d US$66/84, all incl breakfast; ❄ 🛜) rents snorkel gear as well as arranging chartered snorkeling tours (US$25 per person) and fishing trips (US$40 per person).

There are two new dive shops on the island and this has helped put Big Island firmly back on the dive map. New dive sites are being discovered all the time, leading to an ever-expanding list of attractions for divers of all skill levels.

Dos Tiburones   DIVING
(☑ 2575-5167; www.divecornisland.com; Sally Peachie; ⊙ 7am-5pm) On the north side of the island, this well-run dive shop is very popular among visitors for its friendly staff, professional approach and quality equipment. In addition to local dive sites, it also offers one-day dive trips to Little Island and snorkeling. The onsite cafe is a great place to chill between dive sessions.

Great Corn Island

🎉 Festivals & Events

Crab Soup   CULTURAL

(⊙ Aug) Corn Island's big party celebrates the emancipation of the island's slave population on August 27 with parades, concerts, beauty contests and lots of delicious crab soup. Most events are focused around the baseball field in South End. If you're in the region, make sure you're there.

🛏 Sleeping

G&G   HOTEL **$**

(☑2575-5017; martinez-downs69@hotmail.com; contiguo Pasenic, Brig Bay; r with/without air-con US$25/15; ❄) If you don't need to be right by the water's edge, save your cash for lobster and beers and check into this modern hotel in town that offers outstanding value on clean and spacious rooms. It's within walking distance to a fairly inviting stretch of beach and the main dock.

Mi Mundo   HOSTEL **$$**

(☑8526-6379; www.mimundocornislandhostel.com; Brig Bay; dm US$10-12, r US$30-40; ❄🛜) A budget traveler's dream, this welcoming new hostel is literally built over the water. It offers a range of comfortable rooms and dormitories and has a breezy common area and communal kitchen upstairs with fantastic views over the brilliant turquoise Caribbean. Management offer great local advice and rent snorkel gear in order to explore the reef, which is right on the doorstep.

Hospedaje Los Escapados   GUESTHOUSE **$$**

(www.losescapadosecocabanas.com; Sally Peachie; s/d/tr from US$36/49/71.50; 🛜) Perched up on the hillside in Sally Peachie, this small guesthouse offers something different with four large luxury tents with polished wooden floors and fantastic private bathrooms set among lush tropical gardens. The tents can be totally opened out at the front to catch the fresh breeze and each has its own wooden deck with sea views.

⭐ Arenas Beach Resort   HOTEL **$$$**

(☑2575-5223; www.arenasbeachhotel.com; Southwest Bay; s/d bungalow US$67/84, s/d US$87/109; ❄) Corn Island's most professionally managed resort. Choose from colorful wooden bungalows with sea views from the hammocks on the balconies, or modern rooms with fantastic bathrooms (and hairdryers!) in the main building. The white-sand beach comes raked and dotted with cushy lounge chairs surrounding a bar in a wooden boat.

Lodge at Long Bay   GUESTHOUSE **$$$**

(☑8660-6785, 8853-2197; lodgeatlongbay@gmail.com; Long Bay; r US$50-55; 🛜) You won't find better value than these two small, comfortably furnished apartments alongside the wild and beautiful beach at Long Bay. Both have bright tiled floors, wooden walls and ceilings, and are equipped with comfortable beds, a sofa and a kitchenette, which can really bring down the costs around here.

It's a great choice even without the new dipping pool and barbecue area for guests that are in the pipeline.

Casa Canada   HOTEL **$$$**

(☑2575-5878, 8644-0925; www.casa-canada.com; South End; s/d US$92/99, cabaña s/d/tr US$121/133/139, all incl breakfast; ❄🛜🏊) The resort unfurls amid tropical flower gardens on the rocks just above the sea. Long Bay glows to the south, palms sway above and waves crash endlessly. The rooms are just OK, but the large, dark-wood *cabañas* with

...ings, Spanish-tiled floor, ceiling ...ner sofa and queen-sized bed are ...ous.

La Princesa de la Isla   HOTEL **$$$**
(☑ 8854-2403; www.laprincesadelaisla.com; Waula Point; r/bungalows US$55/70) Set behind thick coral walls are a handful of large wooden bungalows and cheaper, but spacious and attractive, wooden rooms. All come with indoor-outdoor bathrooms, hammocks and sea views. There is also a large communal lounge area with a great sun deck up top.

The Italian owners make tremendous coffee and outstanding pastas (US$9 to US$15) and three-course meals (US$19 to US$26). Nonguests can eat here if they call in advance to make a reservation.

✕ Eating

Island Bakery and Sweets   BAKERY **$**
(Sally Peachie; ⊘ 7am-6pm Mon-Sat) Head to this good old-style Caribbean bakery and indulge in all kinds of delicious sweet snacks including fantastic cinnamon rolls, coconut pies and cakes. There's also a good variety of natural drinks – try the ginger and pineapple.

Victoria's   NICARAGUAN **$**
(Sally Peachie; dishes US$1.35-5; ⊘ 6:30am-9pm) Pull up a plastic chair on the roadside porch at this friendly shop/bar/restaurant hybrid in Sally Peachie and enjoy delicious local-style fast food and ice-cold beers. Among the options are *fritos* (fried chicken or pork and cabbage salad on heaps of fried green plantain chips) and Nica-style tacos. A very local experience.

Sea Side Grill   SEAFOOD **$$**
(North End; mains US$7-14; ⊘ 7am-9pm) A friendly waterside restaurant that serves up consistently excellent seafood dishes with a choice of three sides as well as lobster burgers and other light meals. The open-air dining area catches a good breeze and is inviting enough to keep you there for a few beers after you've finished your meal. With two hours' notice they'll cook *rundown* to order.

Comedor Mari   SEAFOOD **$$**
(☑ 2575-5135; Sally Peachie; mains US$7-11; ⊘ 8am-9pm) Eat at your Corn Island mom's house. You will sit right outside the mother chef's home, under the palms with a cricket serenade, and taste king fish braised in tomato sauce, shrimp sautéed in garlic and lobster *al gusto* (to your liking). She makes *rundown* (seasoned fish cooked in coconut milk with root vegetables) upon request. Order it a day in advance.

🍷 Drinking & Nightlife

Island Style   BAR
(Arturito's; Long Bay; ⊘ 10am-10pm) The only bar and restaurant on Long Bay is of the barefoot, palm-thatched variety. It's not as popular as it once was, but draws its biggest crowds on Sunday afternoons for a soulful reggae jam after the baseball games. During the week you'll probably have the place to yourself.

ⓘ STAYING SAFE ON & BETWEEN THE CORN ISLANDS

Bare-bones law enforcement and a growing tourist industry has seen theft become a problem on the Corn Islands, especially from hotel rooms.

While muggings are uncommon, Little Corn has seen its paradisaical reputation sullied recently by a number of attacks, including serious assaults, on foreign visitors on remote jungle paths. Always travel in groups when heading into the interior of the island – especially after dark. Ask the latest in the village before heading out on your adventure.

Tourists on Great Corn are discouraged from walking around Bluff Point without a local chaperone.

The *panga* crossing between Great and Little Corn can get extremely rough, especially during the windy season (November to January). Squalls are common and swells can grow as high as 3m. It makes for a white-knuckle, and sometimes bruising, roller-coaster ride. The back seats bounce less, but you are more likely to get wet.

The dangers of the crossing were illustrated tragically in early 2016 when a *panga* carrying tourists between the islands flipped over about 4km offshore from Little Corn, claiming the lives of 13 Costa Rican visitors. All passengers should make sure they have a well-fitting life vest securely fitted before departure, even when the conditions are apparently calm.

Spekito's Place   BAR

(South End; ⊙11am-midnight) At the far side of South End, this laid-back local watering hole has several tables out the back overlooking rock pools full of fish and across the sea to windswept Long Bay.

Dive Cafe   CAFE

(🖉2575-5167; inside Dos Tiburones; breakfast US$4-9, dishes US$8-12.50; ⊙7am-10pm) Sit on stools overlooking the multi-hued sea out on the grass foreshore and enjoy quality coffee prepared on the island's only espresso machine. Also serves a variety of breakfasts and light meals.

ℹ Information

There is only one ATM on Great Corn Island and it does run out of money occasionally, so you should still plan ahead and carry ample cash. Few businesses on the islands accept credit cards (although more expensive hotels do accept plastic).

BanPro (Brig Bay) ATM and currency conversion available on the main road, just southwest of the airport.

Cyber Comisariato (🖉2575-5268; entrada Picnic Center; per hr US$0.70; ⊙7am-8pm) Most reliable internet access.

Hospital (🖉2575-5236; Alcaldía, 500m E) This 24-hour public clinic offers emergency services.

Police (🖉2570-1440; contiguo Aeropuerto) Up on the hill between the airport and the stadium.

Sweet Valley Clinic (Doctor Somarriba; 🖉2575-5852, 8355-3140; osomarriba@yahoo. com; Costado Derecho Estadio; ⊙8am-noon & 3-6pm Mon-Fri) Corn Island's only private clinic offers a full range of medical services and also makes house calls to hotels.

Tourist Office (🖉ext 29, 2575-5091; lgarcia@ intur.gob.ni; contiguo Estadio; ⊙8am-noon & 1:30-5pm Mon-Fri) Inside the alcaldía (town hall), this friendly office can recommend guides for treks around the island.

ℹ Getting There & Away

Great Corn's small airport is served by La Costeña, which runs flights to Bluefields (one way/return US$64/99, 20 minutes), with continuing service to Managua (one way/return US$107/164, 70 minutes) at 8:10am, 12:45pm and 4:10pm.

Several regular boats make the five- to six-hour trip to Bluefields via El Bluff. The government-run Rio Escondido (US$10) leaves on Thursday at 9am and is the most punctual service. More comfortable but slightly less reliable is the Captain D (seat/bunk US$10/12), a large

cargo ship that leaves at 11pm on Saturday. It also runs once a month from Corn Island to Bilwi (US$22, 10 hours), usually leaving Thursday in the evening.

There are a number of other less comfortable fishing and cargo boats that make the Bluefields run and there is usually always at least one departure on Sunday nights. Bring a hammock or you will be trying to get comfortable on the cold steel deck.

ℹ Getting Around

Taxis cost US$0.70 per person (US$1 at night) to anywhere on the island. During the day, there is one bus (US$0.35) that continuously runs a clockwise circuit, but you might wait a while until it passes.

Rentals are a great way to explore the island. **Corn Island Car Rental** (🖉2575-5222, 8644-8357; cornislandcarentals@hotmail.com; Southwest Bay; golf cart per 2hr US$25-39, per day US$50-89, motorcycle per day US$35-40) offers motorbike and golf-cart (US$50 to US$89 per day) rentals. Both **Sweet Little Rock Rentals** (🖉8942-1605; South End; ⊙7am-6pm) and **Franky's Rentals** (🖉8299-8000, 8848-1315; Brig Bay; per day bicycle/scooter US$12/40) rent bicycles and scooters.

Little Corn Island

This jade isleta is a dreamy escape with imaginative bungalow properties encamped on otherwise virgin beaches. Even if cars were allowed (which they aren't), they wouldn't be able to maneuver the thin concrete and muddy jungle paths that wind beneath the mango, coconut and breadfruit trees, and into the thick forest that buffers the northern and eastern coasts. The northern end of the island is the most secluded, has the best beaches and is the perfect setting for your Crusoe homage. Locals live, drink, dine, shoot pool and dance in the Village, which is set on a serene harbor sheltered from the north winds. The rugged, windy eastern coast makes for a transcendent afternoon of beachcombing: gorgeous white-sand beaches are framed by boulders, driftwood, headlands and coconut groves.

⊙ Sights

The island's best and most picturesque beaches are on opposite ends of the island. Unfortunately, at the time of research, many of the beaches on the windward side had lost a fair bit of their sand to erosion, although

Great Corn Island

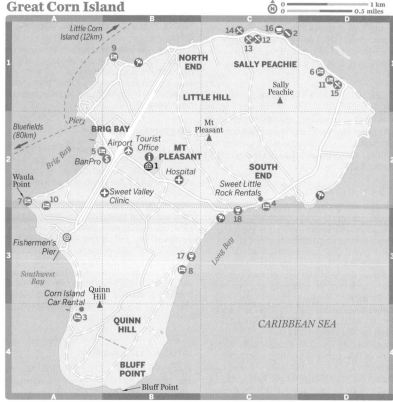

locals say that with an extended set of good north winds the sand should pile up again.

From Casa Iguana you can stroll south along the windward shore, scramble over the rocks and arrive on **Big Fowl House Beach** FREE, then **Jimmy Lever Beach**. Or walk 2km (20 minutes) north from the Village through the jungle to **Otto Beach**. Then navigate the rugged northern shore until you find the spectacular Goat Beach, framed by two headlands.

On the way back, don't forget to head up to the **lighthouse**, a steel tower jutting 6m above the mango trees, where you can glimpse the island's curves and coves, and catch an outrageous sunset.

Cocal Beach
BEACH

A long stretch of white sand fronted by brilliant turquoise waters. It has lost a lot of its mass through erosion but is still a fine place for a stroll.

Iguana Beach
BEACH

Situated below the hill of Casa Iguana, this is really just the southern extension of Cocal beach. There is a solid stretch of sand here as it is protected by the headland.

Goat Beach
BEACH

A secluded bay surrounded by jungle on the north side of the island that gets very few visitors.

🏃 Activities

There is great snorkeling on the east and north sides of the island. Many hotels in these areas rent snorkeling gear, as do the dive shops. If you want a guide, ask in the Village for Aqua Boy (p237) or on the windward side for **Schweizer** (☑ 8367-0939; snorkeling US$20).

Up the hill from the school, **Alfonso** (☑ 8732-6398; School, 300m N; fishing per person

Little Corn Island

US$60) organizes fishing trips (US$60 per person) in his boat.

Kite Little Corn   KITESURFING
(www.kitelittlecorn.com; Steadman's Hotel; ⊙8am-6pm) Soar over the turquoise waters of Little Island with this new kitesurfing school run by Nacho, an affable Spaniard who is passionate about the sport. Located on the windy side of the island inside Steadman's Place, it offers two-day intensive courses (US$300) and group tuition (US$35 per hour).

Dolphin Dive   DIVING
(☑8917-9717; www.dolphindivelittlecorn.com; 1/10 dives US$35/280; ⊙8am-6pm) Professional yet laid-back, this locally owned dive shop has good equipment and experienced instructors who really know their reefs. They visit over 20 different sites, and offer open water (US$330) and advanced open water (US$260) courses.

Dive Little Corn
(☑8856-5888; dlcshopstaff@
lage; 1/10 dives US$35/280; ⊙
Corn's original dive shop is
aged by Casa Iguana and pr
el of service. It offers oper
and advanced open water d

Aqua Boy   SNORKELING
(☑8422-4500, 8573-2875; Front Rd, Village; snorkeling US$20) The best organized of the many local guides offering snorkeling adventures, Aqua Boy has two daily departures at 9am and 1pm as well as a night snorkeling tour. Also offers fishing trips for US$50 per angler.

🛏 Sleeping

You can stay either in the Village, which is convenient and offers the most restaurant and nightlife options, or in one of the more secluded slices of paradise. Most businesses have signs in the Village telling you which path to take.

Steadman's Place   CABAÑAS $
(☑8504-9113; r US$15) The cheapest place to crash on the beach, Steadman's is ultra basic with rickety wooden huts without electricity, saggy mattresses and rustic shared bathrooms, but it's cheap and well located and if it's not raining you wont be spending much time in your room anyway.

Lighthouse Hotel   HOSTEL $$
(☑5723-2477; www.thelighthouselci.com; dm/cabaña US$17/50; ☎) On the highest point of the island, this welcoming new hotel has cute wooden *cabañas* with fantastic views over the windward side waters. Both the private *cabañas* and dorms are simple but comfortable and the onsite bar/restaurant serves great food and has become something of a hot spot for drinks. A fine choice if you don't need to be right on the sand.

Casa Iguana   LODGE $$
(www.casaiguana.net; cabañas s/d US$30/35, casitas US$65-75) This gathering of freshly painted wooden *cabañas* (smaller, with shared bathrooms) and *casitas* (larger, with private bathrooms) arranged on a rocky cliff just above the beach is hugely popular. The location and views are tremendous and the restaurant serves first-class fare; however, the constant stream of expat staff means it doesn't have much local flavor.

BUNGALOW $$

suenos-littlecornisland.com; cabañas US$30, casas US$70-100) Surrounded by forest and fruit orchards, and perched on a golden crescent of sand and a sheltered turquoise cove, this enchanting hotel features a variety of different rustic candelit *cabañas* by the waterside and three delightful solar-powered *casas* with small kitchens a bit further back.

It is run by Ramón, a Spanish artist/naturalist/bohemian madman (and we mean that in the best way) and his family. Excellent gourmet meals are prepared on demand.

Elsa's Place BEACH HUT **$$**
(☑ 2575-5014, 8848-8136; elsasplace@yahoo.com; cabañas US$30-60, r without bathroom US$15-25) Miss Elsa sticks to a winning formula: cheap, comfortable rooms right by the water. There are a variety of simple but neat wooden bungalows with private bathrooms and some basic cheapies out the back. Probably the best deal on this stretch.

★ Yemaya HOTEL **$$$**
(☑ 8239-5330; www.littlecornhotel.com; r incl breakfast US$400) Leagues ahead in terms of luxury, Yemaya is an exclusive holistic retreat on the northern tip of the island offering luxurious accommodations and professional service to match. The fan-cooled rooms feature all the modern conveniences and offer fantastic sea views through the large glass sliding doors, which open onto porches with comfy bamboo chairs.

The restaurant is set on a big wide deck with waves crashing on the rocks below and offers excellent cuisine that makes use of many ingredients grown in the hotel's own organic gardens. Yoga classes are offered in a fan-cooled pavilion surrounded by trees and on a sea-side platform, while there are three massage studios in the banana groves.

Guests have access to free kayaks and yoga classes and can sign up for a variety of activities, including a snorkeling trip on a Miskito sailing boat (US$15 including beverages).

Derek's Place BUNGALOW **$$$**
(www.dereksplacelittlecorn.com; cabañas US$60-100) The dreamiest beach bungalows on the island are found spread out over a lovely grassy promontory covered with coconut palms that feels far from the crowds. The *cabañas* are thatched, geometrically inspired and fashioned from bamboo, wood, old bottles, recycled shipping line and other natural materials. There's dedicated hammock space, snorkel gear for rent and a small, friendly dive shop onsite.

Tasty meals are served communal style in the small dining area.

Little Corn Beach & Bungalow BUNGALOW **$$$**
(☑ 8333-0956; www.littlecornbb.com; r US$79-209; ☎) The most upmarket place on Cocal Beach has elegantly furnished bungalows with big doors opening onto a hammock-strewn beach with plenty of coconut palms. The downside: it's pricey for what you get and the rooms are fairly close together, detracting from any castaway fantasies. Even if you don't stay, make sure to eat at the restaurant (mains US$9.50 to US$18.50).

Farm Peace & Love FARMSTAY **$$$**
(www.farmpeacelove.com; apt US$85-100) Set back from a gorgeous sheltered cove and nestled in the palms is this farm with just two accommodations options. The smaller one is joined to the main farmhouse and has one bedroom and a kitchenette, while the larger is a traditional white house with a kitchen and rockers on the front porch. It's not flash but it's quiet and private.

✗ Eating & Drinking

El Bosque NICARAGUAN **$**
(breakfast US$3.50, mains US$4.30-7) A simple sand-floored *comedor* surrounded by greenery, El Bosque serves up good breakfasts and filling portions of local specialties to hungry travelers.

Rosa's NICARAGUAN, VEGETARIAN **$**
(breakfast US$3.50, meals US$4.30-7; ☺ 6:30am-9:30pm) This humble *comedor* on the trail between the Village and Iguana Beach is a fine spot for breakfast and also has vegetarian pastas and coconut curries, as well as other typical local dishes.

★ Habana Libre CUBAN **$$**
(☑ 2572-9086; mains US$8-12; ☺noon-10pm) Long considered the Corn Islands' best restaurant, this Cuban-run kitchen serves up outstanding plates of fish, shrimp, roast pork and *ropa vieja* (a Cuban shredded-beef delicacy) in a swank dining patio. But the absolute star of the show is the lobster in jalapeño sauce – don't leave the island without trying it. There's also Cohiba cigars and Cuban rum if you really want to live it up.

Comedor Bridget NICARAGUAN **$$**

(☑8437-7295; meals US$7-9.50; ☺7am-10pm)
Pull up a chair on the porch of this converted family home and order the superb salt-dusted, lightly fried fish and a cold beer. It also serves great-value lobster, shrimp and fried-chicken dishes. It's your number one choice for no-nonsense authentic local dining.

Mango's Pizza PIZZA **$$**

(pizzas US$4.50-8.50; ☺11am-8:30pm) Sit in a pair of small huts on a bluff overlooking the sea and tuck into surprisingly tasty pies at this small, family-run pizzeria. The shrimp version is good when they have it. It's up on the hill near the health center; look for the house made from bottles.

Desideri ITALIAN, INTERNATIONAL **$$$**

(☑8412-6341; Front Rd, Village; mains US$8-22; ☺8am-9pm) Boasting the most interesting menu in the Village, this popular restaurant overlooking the water tempts hungry travelers with authentic Italian pastas, tasty burritos and the house specialty, lobster thermidor. There's also a good selection of desserts and excellent coffee. The spacious deck is a fine place for a drink after the plates have been cleared away.

Tranquilo Cafe CAFE

(☺8am-late; ☎) Feeling homesick? Head to this hip open-air cafe for great burgers, buffalo wings and bruschetta with an indie-rock soundtrack. It's the most popular haunt among travelers for an evening drink and hosts regular bonfire parties and other events. It might feel a bit too gringo for some.

Aguila's BAR

(☺11am-1am) Little Corn Island's most popular after-hours hangout. The sweaty pool hall is a hotbed of hustling and competition, and the music thumps in the open-air dancehall just above the beach. It's not the slightest bit classy, but it's good fun.

❶ Getting There & Away

Collective *pangas* to Little Corn (US$5.20, 40 minutes) leave from the pier on Great Corn at 10am and 4:30pm; if you're staying on the northern end of Little Corn, you should take the morning boat. Boats leave Little Corn at 7am and 1:30pm from the main pier. If you're taking the morning flight to Managua, it's best to travel the day before. It can be very rough and you may get soaked. Bring garbage bags to cover your luggage. For a smoother ride, it's possible to ride on the large cargo ships (US$2 to US$3, 1¼ hours) that supply the *islita*, but there are only a handful of departures each week.

San Carlos, Islas Solentiname & the Río San Juan

Best Wildlife Spotting

➡ Río Papaturro (p251)

➡ Reserva El Quebracho (p252)

➡ Islas Solentiname (p247)

➡ Río Indio (p255)

➡ Aguas Frescas (p256)

Best Places to Sleep

➡ Sábalos Lodge (p253)

➡ Hotel La Comunidad (p248)

➡ Río Indio Lodge (p258)

➡ Refugio Bartola (p256)

➡ Hotel Sábalos (p253)

Why Go?

You could roam the globe for decades and it would be tough to top what you are about to experience here. This is a place where an enlightened priest once mingled with transcendent artists on forgotten island utopias. Where the beautiful teenage daughter of a Spanish conquistador stared down an on-rushing armada of British pirates. It's a haven for migratory birds, ranchers and fishermen where the monkeys howl, alligators cruise the black water, and enormous 500-year-old trees bangled in delicate orchids shelter fluorescent fingernail-sized tree frogs and carnivorous jaguars under one canopy.

It's also a place thousands of travelers simply pass through on their way to Costa Rica, ignoring the sweet Archipiélago de Solentiname, mythic Río San Juan and spectacular Reserva Biológica Indio-Maíz. Huge mistake. Spend some time and money. Explore. Take it all in. These are the places you imagined when you booked your ticket. This is why you travel.

When to Go

➡ Dry season in the Río San Juan runs from February to April, with more sunshine and shrinking pools of water concentrating migratory waterfowl in Los Guatuzos.

➡ In June, you'll find the best bird watching in the jungles around Boca de Sábalos.

➡ Around mid-September, top anglers descend on the Río San Juan for the Torneo Internacional de Pesca and it becomes possible to hook huge tarpon in the Caribbean Sea at the mouth of the Río Indio.

➡ In October, there is the best bird watching in San Miguelito, and dancers and artists from all over the country descend on San Carlos for Río San Juan's biggest party – the Carnaval Acuático.

History

Almost as soon as Columbus happened upon Nicaragua in 1502, the search was on for a passage that would link the Atlantic to the Pacific Ocean. In 1529, the Spanish finally navigated the rapids and reached the mouth of the river at the Caribbean Sea, where they established San Juan de las Perlas in 1539.

In the 17th and 18th centuries, Granada was growing wealthier by the year, which attracted unwanted attention from English, French and Dutch pirates, who sacked the city three times in five years. A series of forts, including one in San Carlos and another in El Castillo, were built along the river and lake to ward them off.

When the gold fever took hold in North America in the 1800s, the Río San Juan became part of the fastest route between New York and San Francisco. American Cornelius Vanderbilt's ships sailed from New York to New Orleans and then steamed down to Greytown before continuing upriver to Lago de Nicaragua, where voyagers traveled overland to an awaiting steamship on the Pacific.

After the Panama Canal was built in 1914, dashing hopes for a local version, Greytown (by then reincorporated into Nicaragua as San Juan del Norte) reverted to a sleepy outpost at the end of a rarely transited jungle river.

ℹ Getting There & Away

The Río San Juan is an international entry point to Nicaragua with both boats and buses linking San Carlos with Los Chiles in Costa Rica.

La Costeña operates twice weekly flights between San Carlos and Managua via Ometepe. You can also arrive in San Carlos and San Miguelito by bus from Managua, Juigalpa and El Rama.

All other destinations in this section are only accessible by boat from San Carlos. Things can get cramped, damp and cold. Layer accordingly.

San Carlos

The capital of the isolated Río San Juan department is the gateway to some of Nicaragua's most compelling countryside, but is itself a curious place with a bit of an identity crisis. During the day it is a busy international port filled with herds of travelers in transit, which explains the bustling and festive *malecón* (waterfront) lined with restaurants. But when night falls, and the

magnificent views disappear with the setting sun, it reverts to a rather lackluster small town where gossiping is the main form of entertainment.

Most travelers burn their San Carlos hours by exploring the old Spanish fortress, planning river and island adventures, stocking up on córdobas and checking emails one last time before they drop off-grid for a while.

⊙ Sights

San Carlos is less a tourist destination and more a place to wait for your ship, or *panga* (small motorboat), to come in, but there is beauty here – particularly on the grounds of **Centro Cultural José Coronel Urtecho**, which is set within the crumbling walls of **Fortaleza de San Carlos** (⊙9am-5pm) `FREE`. It's no El Castillo, but it was built in 1724 and has amazing lake and Río San Juan views from several lookout points linked by garden trails. The cultural center has some interesting displays on local culture, biology and history. It even has a map of the Nicaraguan canal that never was, c 1791. There's another old **Spanish observation post**, with cannons, at Restaurant Mirador.

Mirador   VIEWPOINT
(contiguo Restaurante Mirador) A charming old Spanish observation post complete with cannons and panoramic views. To reach it, head up the staircase at the far end of the *malecón*.

Malecón   WATERFRONT
The social heart of the town, this waterfront promenade overlooks both the lake and river and is always busy with children playing and couples taking a stroll.

🏃 Activities

Fundación del Río   ECOTOUR
(☑2583-0035; www.fundaciondelrio.org; El Proyecto) 🏵 A non-profit organization staffed by an enthusiastic young crew that arranges visits to Mancarroncito in the Archipiélago de Solentiname and La Quebracha nature reserve near Boca de Sábalos. In dry weather it also organizes an excellent multiday trip for bird enthusiasts into the forests around Boca de Sábalos to spot the rare *lapa verde* when it is nesting.

The organization accepts volunteers with skills in developing social and environmental projects.

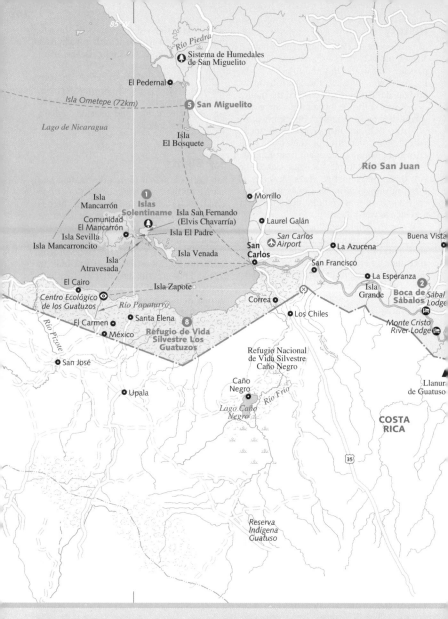

San Carlos, Islas Solentiname & Río San Juan Highlights

1 Islas Solentiname
(p247) Hiking, swimming
and stargazing.

2 Boca de Sábalos
(p252) Catching up with
your reading while swinging in

a hammock or from a riverside
balcony.

3 El Castillo (p253)
Scaling an imposing Spanish
fortress with river views.

**4 Reserva Biológica
Indio-Maíz** (p255) Trekking
beneath the canopy of
500-year-old orchid-jewelled
giants.

La Fonseca

N

0 ____ 40 km
0 ____ 20 miles

Punta Gorda

Pijibaye

Región Autónoma
Atlántico Sur

Caribbean
Sea

Río Indio

Che Guevara

4 🧍
Reserva Biológica
Indio-Maíz

Fish Creek

11°N

El Castillo
3 🏛 La Fortaleza

Aguas Frescas

6
San Juan
de Nicaragua

Bahía de San
Juan del Norte

Laguna Azul

Refugio
Bartola

Río Bartola

Río Indio Adventure Lodge

Greytown

Laguna
la Barca

Río San Juan 7

Laguna
Silica

Boca de
San Carlos

Barra del
Colorado
Airport

Caño Bravo

Llanura de
San Carlos

La Laguna del
Lagarto Lodge

La Trinidad

Río San Juan

Boca
Tapada

Isla Nelson
(Mico)

Río Chirripó

Río Colorado

Río Sarapuquí

---

⑤ **San Miguelito** (p246)
Spotting migratory birds on a
tour through humid forests.

⑥ **San Juan de Nicaragua**
(p257) Taking a boat ride
through hidden, jungled

lagoons inhabited by
manatees.

⑦ **Río San Juan** (p251)
Trolling for tarpon along
isolated stretches of a mighty
river.

⑧ **Refugio de Vida
Silvestre Los Guatuzos**
(p251) Spotting alligators
at night on cruise through the
wetlands.

Agua Trails
BOAT TOUR

(☑8859-1481; www.aguatrails.com) Reliable tour group organizing day trips around San Carlos as well as longer kayak adventures in the Río San Juan. Also offers a regular cross-border shuttle service between the Río San Juan and La Fortuna in Costa Rica.

⭐ Festivals & Events

Carnaval Acuático
DANCE, FOOD

(☺Oct) The Río San Juan's biggest party features a colorful river parade, concerts and a food festival on the *malecón*.

🛌 Sleeping

For a town that receives a lot of passing visitors, the San Carlos hotel scene is fairly disappointing. Don't expect much more than a place to lay your head.

Hotel Ocaso
HOTEL $$

(☑2583-0340; moacruf@hotmail.com; iglesia católica, 1½c Sur; s/d US$30/40; ❄🛜) On the path to the *mirador*, this modern hotel has small but tidy rooms with good amenities and an open-air restaurant upstairs with fine views. The interior rooms are a little dark but those on the end of the corridor overlooking the street are a good deal.

Gran Lago Hotel
HOTEL $$

(☑2583-0075; www.grandhotelsnicaragua.com; Parque Central, 1c O, 1c S; s/d/tr incl breakfast US$36/40/60; ❄🛜) Right on the edge of the lake with views over to the Archipiélago de Solentiname, this small hotel has a variety of rooms split over two levels. Those downstairs are a bit closed in and dark but the bigger upper floor rooms get plenty of light and views of the lake. The small rear deck is a lovely place to hang out with a book.

Hotel-Cabinas Leyko
HOTEL $$

(☑8699-6841, 2583-0354; leykou7@yahoo.es; Parque Central, 2c O; d with/without air-con incl breakfast US$50/30; 🅿❄🛜) The comfy wooden air-con rooms overlooking the wetlands at the rear of the hotel are a little pricey but they are the most peaceful accommodations in San Carlos. Avoid the dingy cheaper rooms above reception. The friendly owners speak English and arrange tours.

🍴 Eating

The cheapest eats in town are at the cluster of bus-terminal *comedores* (basic eateries),

the best of which is **Comedor Alondra** (terminal de buses; meals incl beverage US$3).

Soda La Fortaleza
CAFE $

(malecón; dishes US$1.75-3; ☺6am-10pm Mon-Sat) This lively spot on the lakefront serves up filling breakfasts and cheap, tasty Nica dishes. In the evening it's a fantastic place from which to observe the frenetic football games, canoodling couples and dedicated drinkers on the *malecón*.

Restaurante Kaoma
NICARAGUAN $$

(☑2583-0293; Parque Central, 1½c S; mains US$7-11; ☺8am-midnight) A beautiful terrace restaurant with old wooden floors, beamed ceilings and massive lake views. The extensive menu includes tender beef dishes and fish which comes sautéed in a buttery garlic sauce or stuffed with shrimp.

Restaurant Mirador
NICARAGUAN $$

(☑8716-3701; Parque Central, 1½c S; mains US$4.50-7; ☺7:30am-8pm) This sweet dining spot on the lake bluffs has a stone wall fringed with antique Spanish cannons. Tasty seafood is served on the breezy patio.

ℹ Information

Banpro (malecón) ATM inside the second pavilion on the *malecón*.

Correos de Nicaragua (Post Office; frente Tribunal; ☺8am-4pm)

Hospital Felipe Moncada (☑2583-0244) About 1km north of town.

Intur (☑2583-0301; riosanjuan@intur.gob.ni; contiguo a Migración; ☺8am-4pm) Not visitor focused but offers some basic travel advice.

Marena (☑2583-0296; ☺8am-4pm) Processes fishing licenses, technically required for all fishing on the Río San Juan, but unless you are in your own boat your captain/tour operator should organize these.

Migración (☑2583-0263; malecón; ☺8am-5pm) Processes entry/exit formalities for those traveling along the Río Frio to Costa Rica.

Police (☑2583-0397)

Telecentro (Parque Central; per hr US$0.70; ☺8am-5:30pm Mon-Fri) Internet by the park.

ℹ Getting There & Away

San Carlos is no longer the isolated corner of Nicaragua it once was, thanks to the construction of a new smooth tarred road to Juigalpa. The highway still receives little traffic, but that has begun to change with the opening of the new bridge over the Río San Juan at Santa Fe which links the region by road with Las Tablillas in Costa Rica.

San Carlos

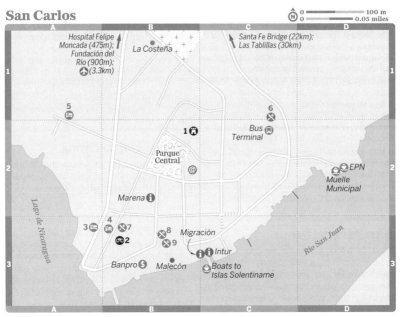

San Carlos

N 0 —————— 100 m
0 —————— 0.05 miles

AIR

With the completion of the new paved road linking San Carlos and Managua, flights to and from the region are now infrequent and often sell out, so book in advance.

The San Carlos airport is a 3km, US$1 cab ride from downtown San Carlos. **La Costeña** (☎2583-0048; frente cementerio; ☺8am-noon & 3-5pm) operates compact, 12-seat planes on Thursday and Sunday leaving San Carlos for San Juan de Nicaragua (one way/return US$55/85, 30 minutes) at 12:55pm. Going in the other direction, flights for Ometepe (one way/return US$55/85, 20 minutes) and Managua (one way/return US$76/116, 50 minutes) depart at 2:15pm – although the schedule is flexible and you may be sent on a scenic flight down the river to San Juan before heading to Managua directly from there; make sure to check in early.

BOAT

Collective riverboat services to Boca de Sábalos (US$2.85, two hours) and El Castillo (US$3, three hours) leave from the **Muelle Municipal** (Municipal Dock), half a block west of the *mercado* (market), at 8am, noon, 2:30pm and 3:30pm Monday through Saturday; 8am and 1:30pm on Sunday. Express boats to Sábalos (US$4.15, 1½ hours) and El Castillo (US$5.20, two hours) leave at 6:30am, 10am and 4pm.

At the time of research, the government-run ferry linking San Carlos with San Miguelito, Alta-

San Carlos

◎ Sights
1 Fortaleza de San Carlos	B2
2 Mirador	B3

🛏 Sleeping
3 Gran Lago Hotel	A3
4 Hotel Ocaso	B3
5 Hotel-Cabinas Leyko	A1

🍴 Eating
6 Comedor Alondra	C1
7 Restaurant Mirador	B3
8 Restaurante Kaoma	B3
9 Soda La Fortaleza	B3

gracia (Isla de Ometepe) and Granada was out of service due to low water levels on the approach to San Carlos. There were no immediate plans to reactivate the service. If it returns to operation it is likely to run on the same schedule, leaving San Carlos from the Muelle Municipal at 2pm Tuesday and Friday. Check the latest with the **EPN** (Empresa Portuaria Nacional; ☎2583-0256; Muelle Municipal) in San Carlos.

Boats to the **Islas Solentiname** leave from the public dock next to Migracíon.

BUS

Buses leave from the **bus terminal** in San Carlos for the following destinations:

➡ **Boca de Sábalos** (US$2.20, two hours, 7am, 9am, 11am, 2pm, 4:30pm and 7pm)

➡ **El Rama** (US$5.50, seven hours, 9am)

➡ **Juigalpa** (US$4, four hours, 10am, 11:10am, 12:40pm and 1:30pm) Managua-bound buses will also drop passengers in Juigalpa.

➡ **Managua** (US$5.50, six hours, 2am, 6:30am, noon, 2:30pm, 6pm, 9pm and 10:30pm)

➡ **San Miguelito** (US$2, two hours) Direct buses leave at 12:20pm and 1pm, but you can hop on any Managua- or Juigalpa-bound bus and get off at the San Miguelito turnoff.

Minivans for the border crossing at Las Tablillas (US$2.20, 30 minutes) depart when full from the terminal from 3am to 5:30pm.

Alternatively **Agua Trails** (p244) runs a shuttle service to La Fortuna in Costa Rica.

San Miguelito

Most travelers miss this mellow lakeside fishing community and gateway to the region's newest and least-visited reserve, the **Sistema de Humedales de San Miguelito** (San Miguelito Wetlands). A handful of rivers meander through the reserve, including the Río Tepenaguazapa, the Río Camastro, the Río Tule and the gorgeous Río Piedra, a glassy slice of black water framed by a dense tangle of jungle. Trees, hip-deep in water and sprouting with orchids and bromeliads in the canopy, stretch back as far as you can see. Occasionally the grasslands and lotus fields teeming with birds and butterflies intervene. The best time for birdwatching is at daybreak or dusk in September and October, when the migration peaks. If you're lucky, you may even see some alligators.

🛏 Sleeping & Eating

There are a couple of restaurants in town serving typical Nicaraguan plates by day and turning into popular bars in the evening.

Hotel Cocibolca HOTEL **$**
(☎ 8845-5029; hotelcocibolca@yahoo.com; frente muelle; s/d/tr without bathroom US$5.50/11/16) 🏊 A fantastic budget choice with wooden rooms boasting high-beamed ceilings and French doors that open onto private balconies overlooking the lake. The 24-hour management will let you in late at night after the ferry arrives and arrange fishing and birdwatching trips (US$20 for a two-hour tour).

BORDER CROSSING: TO LOS CHILES, COSTA RICA

With the completion of the first bridge over the Río San Juan at Santa Fe downstream from San Carlos, there are now two ways to cross into Costa Rica: the cheap route or the traditional scenic route.

The cheapest way to make the crossing involves taking a local minivan from the bus station in San Carlos across the bridge and to the border at San Pancho (US$2.30, 30 minutes). Vans run from 3am to around 5:30pm, but at the time of research the border was only open from 8am to 4pm – although there are plans to extend its operation if traffic warrants it. Once stamped out of Nicaragua, walk over to the Costa Rican immigration office and get your entry stamp before taking another bus to Los Chiles (US$1, 15 minutes) from where there are continuing services to Ciudad Quesada and San José. There is also one direct bus a day from Las Tablillas to San José at 2:30pm.

A slightly slower but far more relaxing way to get from San Carlos to Los Chiles involves a boat (US$8.50, two hours) ride along the Río Frío through the Refugio de Vida Silvestre Los Guatuzos – a delightful cruise through stunning wetlands. There is only one boat a day on this route, leaving San Carlos at 9:30am and returning from Los Chiles at 1:30pm.

Begin at friendly San Carlos **Migración** (p244), 1½ blocks from the Muelle Municipal (Municipal Dock), where you'll have your passport stamped, before being ushered onto the boat which leaves from the dock behind Immigration. Come at least half-an-hour before your departure to complete immigration formalities. When you arrive in Los Chiles, go to customs, opposite the dock, to have your bags searched, then another building about two blocks away to have your passport stamped.

At both border crossings you'll be required to pay US$12 to enter Nicaragua and US$2 upon departure. If you are leaving Costa Rica by road you will be required to pay US$7 exit fee by debit or credit card only – no cash.

For further information, head to shop.lonelyplanet.com to purchase a downloadable PDF of the Northwestern Costa Rica chapter from Lonely Planet's *Costa Rica* guide.

Getting There & Away

Never particularly well connected to the main tourist trail, San Miguelito has been further isolated by the cessation of the boat link with Ometepe and San Carlos.

Until the service gets up an running again, the only practical way in is via bus. Direct buses to San Miguelito (US$2, two hours) leave San Carlos at 12:20pm and 1pm, but any San Carlos–Managua bus will drop you at the Empalme de San Miguelito, from where *colectivos* (shared taxis; US$1) make the 8km trip into town.

Islas Solentiname

If you're the type who likes islands draped in jungle, surrounded by crystalline waters that reflect the forest, sun and sky, and populated by farmers and fishers who share their wealth and also happen to be terrific artists and craftsmen, you do not want to miss this oft-overlooked archipelago. And we haven't even mentioned the gators, monkeys, orchids and migratory waterfowl, the sensational offshore fishing, the mind-blowing sunsets and the spectacular starlight. Almost forgotten for 500 years, and nearly destroyed in a single day, the Archipiélago de Solentiname does not seem entirely of this world.

Getting There & Away

Transol (p249) runs a daily fast boat service (US$10, 90 minutes) between San Carlos and the islands, leaving from the dock next to Migración in San Carlos at 3pm and returning at 9am. This is by far the fastest and most comfortable way to get to the archipelago.

If you're on a tight budget and have a flexible itinerary, slow public boats (US$4, two to three hours) run on Tuesday and Friday leaving Mancarrón at 5am and stopping about 30 minutes later at San Fernando before continuing on to San Carlos. They return to Solentiname from the dock next to Migración in San Carlos at 1pm.

If that doesn't work with your schedule, you can hire a private boat (seating at least six) between San Carlos and the islands for US$120 to US$150.

Isla Mancarrón

This island feels small because residents, guests and commerce converge on a rather slender slice of land that includes the harbor and the village. But hike the muddy trails, which traverse these jungled hills, and you'll quickly notice that the island is deceptively large, sprawling into the azure lake and forming a succession of sheltered coves. The extreme western end seeps into an 800m-long stretch of wetlands that nurture fish and turtle hatcheries and are teeming with migratory waterfowl.

Sights

⭐Nuestra Señora de Solentiname   CHURCH

(US$1) Mancarrón's greatest human-made gift is Nuestra Señora de Solentiname, where populist priest Ernesto Cardenal ran a rather enlightened parish. Constructed by the community in 1979, it features a beautiful whitewashed nave from within which you can still hear the lake, and feel the trees. The altar spares the usual golden idolatry and instead is graced with a colorful yet humble mural depicting life in the archipelago. If there's no-one around, ask for access up the hill at the museum.

El Refugio   VILLAGE

(Comunidad El Mancarrón) The highest concentration of craft workshops on the islands are just inland from the dock in Comunidad El Mancarrón (also called El Refugio). Feel free to wander and watch as families carve balsa-wood figures in their homes and front yards. Children sand the pieces smooth, and the most talented adult paints. Wooden animals cost US$1.20 to US$50; prices rise with size and quality.

Activities

Familia Pedro Rivas   KAYAKING

(☑8983-7289; detrás museo; ☺8am-5pm) Local family that rents out kayaks and canoes for US$11 per day. To find the house, walk past the museum and take the path to the left that passes through the jungle and down to the waterside.

Conoce Solentiname   TOUR

(☑8869-6619, 8963-2845; hostalbuenamigo@gmail.com; inside Hospedaje Buen Amigo; tours US$20-100; ☺6am-8pm) Energetic tour operator that offers a great variety of natural and cultural activities, including fishing, bird watching in the wetlands, hikes to petroglyphs and trips to Los Guatuzos. Call ahead.

Sleeping & Eating

Mancarrón has the widest selection of accommodations in the archipelago, ranging from simple huts with shared bathrooms to a couple of fine hotels. There are no restaurants here, but all hotels offer meals and welcome non-guests with advance notice.

Hotel Sueño Feliz GUESTHOUSE $
(☎8478-5243; esperanzosales.29@gmail.com; El Refugio; r per person with/without breakfast US$10/8) A simple guesthouse set in the home of a friendly local artisan family. It offers three simple rooms with peach paint jobs in the main house, as well as a log and concrete *cabaña* out the back that sleeps up to six. Affordable meals are available and it offers a full range of tours.

Guests can sign up for the 'artisan for a day' tour (US$10) where you'll try your hand at carving and painting your own Solentiname-style animals, after which you get to take home your masterpiece.

★**Hotel La Comunidad** GUESTHOUSE $$
(☎8966-7056, 2277-3495; contiguo muelle; r per person with/without meals US$40/20) 🖋 This pair of charming solar-powered wooden houses overlooking the bay is easily the best deal on Mancarrón, with breezy hammock-strung balconies, spacious rooms and huge bathrooms with outdoor showers. Some even have bidets (no joke!). Guests can use the wi-fi at the library and hotel profits support the local school. If there is no-one around, ask for Ernesto at the library.

Good meals can be enjoyed up by the museum or in the private dining area of each house. Management also organizes very reasonably priced tours of the archipelago.

🛈 Information

Biblioteca Ernesto Cardenal (internet per hr US$0.60; ⊙8am-noon & 1-5pm Mon-Sat) A working library with the only internet service on the islands. Book donations are appreciated.

🛈 Getting There & Away

Both the Transol express service and the slow local boat call at Mancarrión as their final stop on arrival from San Carlos. Morning boat services to San Carlos originate from here.

ERNESTO CARDENAL & REVOLUTIONARY CULTURE

As a poet, his subject matter ranges from theoretical physics to Marilyn Monroe; as a sculptor, from the creatures of the jungle to the life of Christ. A Trappist monk originally committed to nonviolence, Ernesto Cardenal came to fully support the Sandinista-led revolution, by any means necessary. He was Nicaragua's original liberation theologian, the revolutionary government's Minister of Culture, but has since fallen out with his former bosses.

When Cardenal arrived in Solentiname in 1966, he found a community all but forgotten by the modern world, impoverished and poorly educated, but where a special wisdom had been born. Cardenal helped erect the islands' first simple adobe church, where he gave Mass. Here, the people of Solentiname interpreted the scripture through their own eyes and lives, a living word of Christ, which Cardenal recorded and published as *El Evangelio de Solentiname* (Gospel of Solentiname). It would later be rendered in song by legendary artist Carlos Mejía Godoy as *La Misa Campesina* (Peasants' Mass).

One day, a grateful islander named Eduardo Arana presented Cardenal with an elaborately decorated jícara shell, which impressed the priest into giving the young man paints and a canvas. Those first few paintings launched Nicaragua's Primitivist art movement, internationally recognized for the vibrant colors and expert lines that capture this tropical paradise. One artist, Ufredo Argüello, began applying the same saturation of color to balsa-wood carvings, which also caught on.

Throughout the late 1960s and early 1970s, families worked together painting and sculpting, sending their work to market in Managua. There, trouble was brewing, and even this peaceful haven could not isolate itself. In October 1977, inspired by Cardenal, the islands rebelled; retribution by the Guardia Nacional was swift and complete. Solentiname was abandoned and Cardenal was denounced as an outlaw.

When the Sandinistas took power in 1979, however, they appointed Cardenal Minister of Culture, a position he used for almost a decade to successfully preserve and enrich Nicaraguan arts and folklore. Since then he's fallen out of favor with the Sandinistas, after he criticized front man Daniel Ortega's 'Stalinist' control of the party. And even at 91, he remains a thorn in the government's side, rallying opposition to the proposed canal which he says would destroy the Solentiname Archipelago he holds so dear.

Isla San Fernando

With even fewer people, tranquil San Fernando has comfortable accommodations, delicious meals, and the islands' only gallery and museum. But the biggest attraction is the San Fernando sunset. First the lake loses its color before reflecting the deep jungle green of the surrounding forests. Then the sky pales, streaks pink and burns gold behind the neighboring islands. When it gets dark, expect a black dome sky full of stars.

⊙ Sights

Unión de Pintores y Artesanos de Solentiname 'Elvis Chavarría'　　GALLERY
(☑7250-8882;　upassolentiname@yahoo.com; ⊙8am-noon & 1-4pm) Set in an old mahogany house uphill from the sheltered dock, this cooperative features the work of about 50 of the islands' top artists and artisans. Affordable balsa sculptures are in one room, and higher-end paintings (US$40 to US$1200) are in the other. The view from here is incredible. If it's closed, ask at the tourist office.

✗ Activities

Located at the main dock, the **Oficina de Turismo** (Tourist Office; ☑7250-8882; solentinamecantur@yahoo.com; ⊙9am-5pm) is able to provide guides (US$15 per group) and recommend captains for boat tours. The **Sendero El Trogón** is a 45-minute walking trail that passes some impressive petroglyphs and a lookout point. At the time of research the trail was overgrown and rarely used, but plans are afoot to clean it up and charge a US$5 admission fee to hikers for maintenance. Pay at your hotel or the tourist office. Albergue Celentiname rents two-person canoes (US$4 per hour) to explore the surroundings, while **Hostal Vanessa** (☑8740-8409; jose.sequeirapineda@gmail.com; muelle, 10m O; r per person with/without bathroom US$12/10) organizes sportfishing trips (US$100 per day for up to three participants).

🛏 Sleeping & Eating

All hotels are located to the west of the dock, along the path that runs along the southern edge of the island. Most larger hotels offer rates with and without meals.

There are no dedicated restaurants on San Fernando, although the local shop will prepare meals for travelers with advanced notice. Otherwise you'll need to take meals at one of the hotels.

Albergue Celentiname　　GUESTHOUSE $$
(☑8465-2426, in Costa Rica 506-7096-8676; http://hotelcelentiname.blogspot.com; r per person incl full board US$40) Tucked into a flowering garden that feels like something out of a tropical utopia is this secluded guesthouse, a gorgeous 10-minute walk from the main dock on the extreme northern end of the west-coast trail. Basic but neat wooden *cabañas* (cabins) come with two beds and a terrace with lake and garden views.

Some rooms are better than others, so ask to look around – the larger *cabaña familiar* is the one you want. Guests get free access to kayaks and canoes. It also offers packages for backpackers including accommodation and two simple Nica-style meals for US$30.

Hospedaje Mire Estrellas　　GUESTHOUSE $$
(☑7255-6293; r per person with/without bathroom US$10/8) With tidy wooden rooms right by the water's edge, this simple *hospedaje* is a fine budget choice. The laid-back owner offers cheap tours in his small boat.

Pulpería Doña Juanita　　NICARAGUAN $
(muelle 200m O; ⊙7am-7pm) With just one table on the porch outside the family shop, this is the only eating option not attached to a hotel. The menu is limited to simple Nica *comida corriente* but it's cheap and filling. Swing by to order in advance.

❶ Getting There & Away

Transol (☑8828-3243, 8555-4739; www.transol.com.ni; ⊙24hr) Runs a daily express service (US$10, 90 minutes) between San Carlos and the Solentiname Archipelago. Boats leave from the dock next to Migración in San Carlos at 3pm, and return from Solentiname at 9am. They will drop you on Mancarrón, San Fernando or Isla Venada depending on where you plan to stay – make sure to advise the captain.

Isla Mancarroncito

Across a narrow strait from Mancarrón's western shore is this small, rocky jewel thick with the last stands of primary forest in the archipelago. **Loma San Antonio**, a 15m boulder, protrudes from a hill on the eastern shore. Local legend has it that *brujas* (witches – not the good kind) once lived in the caves at the top of the cliff, which may explain why the island is still so wild. There are exploratory trails on the island (admission US$5) which are maintained by the local biological station and guides can be arranged for US$18 per group.

🛏 Sleeping

Most visitors come for the day to explore the trails but if you really want to experience nature in all its glory, it's possible to stay the night at the Estación Biológica, a biological research station that offers basic lodging in its wooden cabin (room per person US$10).

Call Fundación del Rio (p241) in San Carlos in advance to arrange your stay.

ℹ Getting There & Away

Full-day motorboat tours around the archipelago will make a stop at Mancarroncito on request. Kayakers can reach the island by paddling across the narrow channel on the west side of Mancarrón.

Overnight guests should arrange transportation directly with the Fundación del Río (p241) in San Carlos.

Isla Venada

Meet the Aurellanos. Three generations of the archipelago's most renowned artists come from the jumble of wooden homes overlooking a gorgeous, glassy strait on the northwestern shore of this wooded island.

Rodolfo Aurellano was the trailblazer. His works are dreamy, colorful reflections of Isla Venada and the surrounding islands, Islas Rosita, Carolina and El Padre. Take some time to talk with the elderly, barefoot artist and he might tell you about how he used to have to hide deep in the bush to paint, to avoid being identified as a revolutionary by Somoza's forces. Despite being in his late 70s, Rodolfo still paints regularly and maintains a small collection of works for sale (US$30 to US$1000).

Rodolfo's daughter and granddaughter, Clarissa and Jeyselle Aurellano, have followed his example and also have works on display in the family home.

🏃 Activities

A system of caves at the waterline honeycombs the island's northern shore and are only visible in the dry season. You'll need a boat to explore them and see the many petrolgyphs carved into their walls. Guides are available (US$7 per day) at the Aurellano residence.

🛏 Sleeping

In addition to selling truly remarkable work, some of which tours art galleries internationally, the Aurellanos (☑ 8815-1761) also rent out simple rooms in the family home (US$8 per person). Typical meals are also available (US$2.50) and guides (US$7 per day) can be arranged to explore the island on foot. Call in advance to let them know you are coming; they don't get many visitors.

ℹ Getting There & Away

Both the express and regular boats from San Carlos will drop you on Isla Venada on request. From other islands, private round-trip transport costs around US$35.

Isla Atravesada

Named because it's the only island oriented north–south, rather than east–west like the rest of the archipelago, Atravesada (meaning 'to cross') is famed for its enormous 5m alligators and rich bird life. Flocks of ives, with their crab-cracking beaks, congregate in the north-shore canopy alongside trees full of the dangling nests of the resident black cormorants. Look for tiny colondrines in the marsh at sunset.

ℹ Getting There & Away

Most visitors get to Isla Atravesada on a package tour of various islands in the archipelago. It's also close enough to paddle a kayak or canoe from either Mancarrón or San Fernando.

Other Islands

There are at least 36 islands in the archipelago, many privately owned and most without much to interest the casual visitor.

You will hear the residents of Isla El Padre before you see them. Set between Mancarrón and San Fernando and named for yet another priest who long ago sought solitude in these tranquil waters, it's inhabited by a troupe of howler monkeys.

Isla Sevilla, just west of Mancarroncito, is a haven for bird watchers, with thousands of cormorants, tiger herons and pelicans here to enjoy some excellent fishing.

Avid birders won't want to miss tiny Islas Zapote and Zapotillo, with Nicaragua's highest concentration of birds, most famously flocks of roseate spoonbills that nest in February and March. Migratory birds of all kinds converge here between December and April – where more than 30,000 nests have been counted by visiting biologists.

🛏 Sleeping & Eating

There are no accommodations on any of the minor islands.

Outside the main islands of the archipelago, there are no places to purchase food so make sure to bring snacks or a picnic plus plenty of water if heading out to explore.

ℹ Getting There & Away

The closer islands can easily be explored by kayak or canoe. Isla Zapote and Zapotillo are in a remote location, 12km from the rest of the archipelago, but can be visited on a chartered motor boat trip from the main islands or San Carlos. They also make an interesting stop on the way to or from Los Guatuzos.

Refugio De Vida Silvestre Los Guatuzos

Like so many national treasures, Los Guatuzos wildlife reserve, a 44,000-hectare band of rich, river-streaked wilderness wedged between the Costa Rican border and Lago de Nicaragua, was conserved by accident. The earliest inhabitants, the Guatuzos, were sold into slavery, their lands co-opted by farmers whose crops (rubber and cacao) demanded shade. Just as foreign timber companies were poised to buy out the subsistence farmers, revolution and war hit hard along the border, leaving this region as pristine as only a minefield can be. (It was declared mine-free in 2001.)

◉ Sights

The Río Pizote (Long-Tailed Raccoon River) and Río Medio Queso (Half Cheese River) form the eastern and western boundaries of the preserve, home to 18 rivers, 2000 people, 81 amphibians, 42 mammals and almost 400 bird species. The wetlands are a paradise for mosquitoes – bring plenty of repellent.

🛏 Sleeping & Eating

The local village in Papaturro has three *comedores* that serve up cheap and filling typical plates that taste just delicious after a tough day trekking or kayaking. In Río Frío, you'll need to arrange meals with your hosts.

★**Cabañas Caiman**   GUESTHOUSE **$$**
(📷8676-2958, 506-8704-3880;   aillenm@hotmail.com; Río Papaturro; per person incl breakfast US$18) Papaturro's original crocodile man and former Centro Ecológico manager Armando Gómez has opened his own guesthouse on the opposite bank of the river. The two wooden rooms are charming and comfortable and tasty meals are served, but where this place really excels are in the fantastic tours with one of the region's most energetic and knowledgeable ecologists.

It also rents bicycles (US$5 per day) to explore the village and surrounding area.

**Centro Ecológico de
Los Guatuzos**   LODGE **$$**
(📷 2270-3561, 8877-5096; www.losguatuzos.com; Río Papaturro; r per person US$13) 🛶 This professionally run research station in the Río Papaturro community is primarily geared to scientists and students. However, tourists are welcome to bunk down in the basic but comfortable wooden *cabañas*. Typical meals (US$5) are available at local homes.

The center offers several tours, including a two-hour guided hike (US$8 per person) with visits to an alligator hatchery and a short detour through the jungle canopy on a hanging bridge, and a moonlight alligator tour (US$45 for one to three visitors). Kayaks are also available to rent.

ℹ Getting There & Away

There are slow collective boats from San Carlos to Río Papaturro (US$4, five hours) on Monday, Tuesday, Wednesday and Friday at 9am and on Saturday at 10am; returning at 8am on Monday, Tuesday, Thursday and Sunday and at 9am on Friday from the Papaturro dock. They make painfully slow progress at times, especially when water levels are low in the river, but are a social affair with what seems like half of the local village accommodating themselves in the big wooden hull and shooting the breeze.

It costs around US$130/240 one way/round-trip from San Carlos for a transfer in a private *panga*. It's cheaper to rent a boat (round-trip boat/*panga* US$70/100) in Solentiname.

Río San Juan

You simply must see this river. It surges purposefully through rolling green hills, thick jungle and wetlands on its irrepressible march to the Caribbean.

Not that you'll be sitting around all day admiring its beauty. This river demands action. After all, it was once the domain of indigenous traders, Spanish conquistadors, British pirates, gold-hunting travelers and even Mark Twain. Follow their example and penetrate the vine-hung wilderness of jaguars and macaws that is the Reserva Biológica Indio-Maíz, troll for tarpon, search for alligators in the moonlight and then make a toast to your adventures while overlooking the remains of a 16th-century Spanish fort. All of which will cost you. But it's worth it to fully experience this spectacular and unforgettable waterway.

Heading downriver from San Carlos there are several lodges lining the banks of the river, as well as hotels in the towns of Boca de Sábalos and El Castillo. After the Río Bartola, the Reserve Biológica Indio-Maíz begins and there are no more accommodations until San Juan de Nicaragua. El Castillo has some tasty places to eat, while options are more limited in Boca de Sábalos and fairly poor in San Juan de Nicaragua. All riverside lodges serve meals for their guests.

La Esperanza

The first major settlement after passing under the La Fe bridge, La Esperanza is a typical Río San Juan rural community, surrounded mostly by pasture but with some pockets of jungle and plenty of birdlife.

🛏 Sleeping

Grand River Lodge   HOSTEL
(📞7892-8374, 8375-7248, 7628-6500; www.hotelgrandriverlodge.com; La Esperanza; tents or hammock US$3, dm/s/d US$7/10/20) Up on a hill overlooking the Río San Juan you'll find Grand River Lodge, one of the few backpacker-orientated places on the river and a great place to experience Nicaraguan rural life. It is run by affable local and veteran cruise-ship employee, Marvin, who has converted his family farm into a rural lodge with 11 simple thatched-roof huts with private bathrooms.

Prices include free use of kayaks and canoes, and the friendly staff organize plenty of activities to keep clients occupied including treks to see resident monkeys, horseback riding and artisanal cheese-making workshops. It also runs a cacao tour (US$5) beginning in the plantation beside the lodge and a massive swimming pool is in the works. Tasty and filling meals (including beverage US$4.50 to US$6.50) are served in the rustic bar-restaurant.

It also offers cheap secure parking for those heading down river by boat. The lodge is 2km from the village and can be reached by boat or bus just let the driver know where to drop you.

🛈 Getting There & Away

Any San Carlos–El Castillo (US$3, one hour) boat will drop you at the Grand River dock, from where its a five-minute walk along a boardwalk through the swamp and up to the hotel. It's also possible to arrive by bus – take any Sábalos-bound bus from San Carlos (US$2, 1½ hours) and asked to be let off at the entrance from where it's a short walk down to the lodge.

Boca de Sábalos

It feels like that thick jungle looming on its edges is about to reclaim this muddy, dusty town set at the confluence of the Río San Juan and Río Sábalos (Tarpon River). And therein lies its appeal. When you lounge on the terrace of your hotel, lodge or guesthouse at sunset, you'll watch birds fish and ride end-of-the-day thermals as you hear that familiar, primordial roar of the howler monkeys.

Río Sábalos effectively splits the town in half, with the inexpensive *hospedajes* and main road on one side, and a smaller community, threaded by a slender footpath past rustic homes and gardens, on the other. It's two córdobas (US$0.10) to cross the canal in a dugout canoe.

⊙ Sights

Reserva Privada
El Quebracho   NATURE RESERVE
(📞2583-0035; www.fundaciondelrio.org; US$5) 🌿 Administered by the Fundación del Rio, this 90-hectare property borders the Reserva Biológica Indio-Maíz, and offers a peek at the region's very big trees, very small frogs, beautiful rivers and wealth of wildlife. Take a bus or taxi to Buena Vista, and walk the last hour to the reserve, where you can hike and horseback ride along two trails through primary forest dangling with orchids. If it inspires you to stick around, accommodations are available in simple rooms with shared bathrooms.

If you are visiting for the day, take the *colectivo* from the dock in Sábalos to Buenavista at 7am (US$2.50, one hour), and make sure you are back in Buena Vista by 1pm for the bus back to town.

🛏 Sleeping & Eating

Basic budget lodging is located in town while two comfortable mid-range hotels are just across the Río Sábalos from the dock. A fine pair of more comfortable ecolodges are further downstream on the Río San Juan; tell the riverboat driver where you're staying and you'll be dropped in the right spot.

There are a couple of cheap *comedores* near the dock. Apart from those inside hotels, there are no real sit-down restaurants in Boca de Sábalos.

Hospedaje Kateana GUESTHOUSE $
([✑]2583-3838; muelle, ½c N; s/d US$11/16, without bathroom US$9/14.50; [✳]) The best of the cheapies, Kateana is far from luxurious but is a decent choice in town with small but clean wood rooms, a nice porch overlooking the main street and – absolutely essential for vegetarians in Sábalos – kitchen access. They'll also lend you the washing machine to clean that bag of stinking clothes you've been hauling through the jungle.

★ Sábalos Lodge LODGE $$
([✑]8823-5514, 8823-5555; www.sabaloslodge.com; muelle, 1km E; bungalows US$35-75) This collection of stilted bungalows set in one meandering riverside row achieves the *Robinson Crusoe* ideal. Each one has an indoor-outdoor living room with hammocks, a bed swathed in mosquito netting, and an outdoor shower. The best part: each bungalow has its own personalized view of the river and offshore island, which is alive with birds at sunset. Meals run US$9 to US$12.

The best deal is the family *cabaña* (US$75) which can fit four to five guests.

Tarpon River Lodge HOTEL $$
([✑]8944-1898; alojamientoriosabalo@hotmail.com; Río Sabalos; s/d US$25/30) A fine choice a bit upstream from the dock on the other side of the Río Sabalos, Tarpon River has spacious polished wood rooms with sparkling tile floors. There is a fine riverside restaurant area but the best reason to stay here is the onsite thermal waters, which you an enjoy in your bathroom or the Jacuzzi out the back.

Hotel Sábalos HOTEL $$
([✑]8659-0252; www.hotelsabalos.com.ni; frente muelle; s/d US$22/38, with river view US$27/42, all incl breakfast; [☎]) Perched on stilts over the water at the mouth of the Río Sábalos, this charming hotel has comfortable wooden rooms with hot water, and rocking chairs on the wide veranda. It also has the only real restaurant in Sábalos (mains US$6 to US$7) serving quality meals with a river view. They'll run across the river from the dock in their boat.

❶ Getting There & Away

Boca de Sábalos is pretty much the last town on the river accessible by road, and has fairly frequent bus services. This makes it a convenient place to spend the night if you miss the last boat downstream from San Carlos.

Boat services from Boca de Sábalos:
➡ **El Castillo** (US$0.55, one hour, 10am, 2pm, 4:30pm and 5:30pm Monday to Saturday, 10am and 2:30pm Sunday; express US$1, 30 minutes, 7:30am and 11am)
➡ **San Carlos** (US$3.50, 2½ hours, 6am, 7am, 8am and 3pm Monday to Saturday, 6am and 3pm Sunday; express US$4.75, one hour, 6am and noon)

Buses from San Carlos cross the Río Sábalos on a sketchy looking barge (you want to get off before it drives on!) and continue right on into town.

Bus departures from Sábalos:
➡ **San Carlos** (US$2.50, two hours, 4am, 6am, 7am, 1pm, 3pm and 4pm)
➡ **Buena Vista** (US$1.50, one hour, 11am and 4pm) Returning at 6am and 1pm.

❶ Getting Around

Public transportation by road to communities surrounding Boca de Sábalos consists of 'taxis' – beat-up old 4WD vehicles that are filled to bursting point and make collective runs (US$2.50) to local communities. They have no fixed schedule, departing from the dock when full, usually coinciding with the arrival of river transport to the port.

It's also possible to hire a vehicle (up to eight passengers) for an express trip – expect to pay around US$50 to US$60 to Buena Vista.

El Castillo

Cute, compact and crowned with its stunning 17th-century Spanish fortress, it's no surprise that diminutive El Castillo is the Río San Juan's showpiece destination. It's laced with pebbled-concrete walking paths that wind up, down and around the hill, shaded by mango, coconut, orange and almond trees, and cradled by the Río San Juan – wide and foaming with two sets of rapids that proved to be the bane of British pirates for centuries. A town this civilized means that the jungle has been tamed here, so don't expect the howlers to sing you to sleep. The good news is that you are just 15 minutes by boat from Nicaragua's best-preserved lowland rainforest, the Reserva Biológica Indio-Maíz.

⊙ Sights

La Fortaleza
FORT

(US$2, camera fee US$1; ⊙8am-5pm Mon-Fri, 8am-4pm Sat & Sun) Properly known as La Fortaleza de la Limpia, Pura e Inmaculada Concepción, this photogenic fortress was constructed between 1673 and 1675, commissioned after Granada was sacked three times in five years. The Raudal El Diablo rapids were key – they slowed the pirates down just long enough to aim enormous cannons their way. Still, it was attacked, rebuilt and fortified every other decade for 200 years.

The fort's cinematic moment arrived when proto-feminist folk hero Rafaela Herrera was only 19 years old. Her father, the fortress commander, was critically wounded in a 1762 battle with an on-rushing British fleet. Herrera, still the region's favorite heroine, stepped into command (evidently wearing a nightgown) and successfully repelled the pirates. In some versions of the story she fired the cannon that sank the lead ship.

Then, in 1780, 22-year-old Brit Horatio Nelson conquered the edifice. However, British control was short-lived, malarial mosquitoes ravaged the battle-depleted party and within a few months, the Spanish were able to walk back into the abandoned fort. Today the fortress houses a terrific museum, with informative Spanish-language displays. Your entry fee includes a tour by the enthusiastic staff.

⌖ Tours

Conveniently located at the dock, El Castillo's **tourist office** (⌨ 8526-9267; frente muelle; ⊙8am-6pm) sources local guides for a variety of tours. It helps to make reservations a day in advance. Some menus of guided hikes and *panga* trips:

➡ **Reserva Biológica Indio-Maíz, Río Bartola** (US$75 for up to five people, four hours) Take a private *panga* to the Río Bartola entrance of the Indio-Maíz reserve, then hike 3km though primary forest, where you'll be dwarfed by 500-year-old giants, taste medicinal plants, and spot tree frogs, green iguanas and three types of monkey (spider, white-faced and howler). After the hike you'll motor up Río Bartola, where you'll swim in a crystal-clear river surrounded by jungle.

➡ **Reserva Biológica Indio-Maíz, Aguas Frescas** (US$85 for up to five people, five hours) Virtually identical to the Bartola trip in terms of scenery but the Aguas Frescas trail is a slightly longer and more challenging hike.

➡ **Reserva Biológica Indio-Maíz, Caño Sarnoso** (US$120 for up to five people, five hours) This boat trip travels further down the Río San Juan to observe the ruins of the old steamboats and abundant wildlife around the El Diamante rapids, including crocodiles and birdlife. It can also be combined with one of the trails within the reserve. The tourist office also organizes a night caiman-watching tour (US$45 for up to four visitors).

You don't have to go through the tourist office, which can seem less than helpful at times. There are several private operators with signs up around town offering similar tour rosters.

★**Nena Tour**
ADVENTURE TOUR

(⌨ 2583-3010; www.nenalodge.com) A fantastic tour operator based at Nena Lodge offering the full range of hikes in the Reserva Indio-Maíz plus canoe tours on the nearby Río Juana (three hours, US$15 per person) and a night alligator tour (US$45 for up to four passengers). Also rents an inflatable raft to run the rapids in front of town (US$20 for up to three participants).

The attached guesthouse on the second floor has small but clean and functional rooms (US$10 to US$25) set around a large balcony.

Basiliscus Tour
RIVER TOUR

(⌨ 5798-9313; darwing86@gmail.com; muelle, 110m E) Specialists in canoe trips down the river, including a four-day, 160km trip all the way to San Juan de Nicaragua (US$350 per person, minimum two people). You'll sleep in tents on the river bank and prices include all meals. The same trip in kayaks costs US$550, while a five-day kayak version is US$600. Prices include all meals.

Also offers overnight camping trips to the Río Bartola (US$75 per person, minimum two people).

Coodeprosa
FOOD

(frente colegio; US$5; ⊙8am-4pm) This well-run cooperative on a small path behind the baseball field organizes a fascinating cacao tour that explains the chocolate-making process. It sells a variety of locally made chocolate in the small shop.

🛏 Sleeping & Eating

There are a handful of very basic but pleasant *hospedajes* lining the waterfront close to the dock.

Some establishments offer 'internet access' via a USB modem but it is frustratingly slow even when it works.

Casa de Huesped
Chinandegano   GUESTHOUSE $

(📞2583-3011; muelle, 240m E; s/d US$12/18, without bathroom US$8/15; 🛜) This creaky wooden house done up with potted tropical plants and a shabby-chic dining area is built right over the river and is the best cheapie in town. The wooden and bamboo rooms are breezy and have high ceilings. Get the corner room if you can. Or just come for lunch or dinner.

Hotel Tropical   HOTEL $$

(📞5772-5283; muelle 130m E; r incl breakfast US$25; ❄) Lie back and listen to the rushing water of El Castillo outside your window at this small hotel above Restaurant Vanessa. While the wooden rooms with air-con, cable TV and tiled bathrooms are a fine deal, the best thing is the breezy wooden porch perched right above the rapids.

Lara's Planet   HOTEL $$$

(📞8367-1440, 8743-9351; www.hotellarasplanet.com; muelle 200m O, 80m N; r US$75-90) Pushing the high-end bar a little higher in El Castillo, this stylish new hotel is beautifully crafted from polished wood and bamboo. Rooms are huge with high ceilings, quality fittings, bar fridges and private balconies high over the river below. The open-air restaurant mains (US$9 to US$10) serves dishes you won't find elsewhere, and is a fine place for a drink.

Luna del Rio   HOTEL $$$

(📞8842-0429, 8624-6263; riosanjuannicaragua@yahoo.es; frente raudal; s/d incl breakfast US$30/60) A comfy new hotel right by the rapids offering a handful of charming and well appointed wooden rooms, complete with hot water bathrooms that open onto private balconies with swinging chairs. There is not a lot of space but the place exudes a welcoming, homely vibe.

Hotel Victoria   HOTEL $$$

(📞2583-0188, 8697-2509; hotelvictoria01@yahoo.es; Muelle, 250m E; s/d incl breakfast US$35/60; ❄) On the eastern edge of town, the rooms in this professionally run hotel are spread over two buildings. Some single rooms are a little small, but the spacious doubles are easily the best in town with split-system aircon, shiny wooden floors, stylish modern bathrooms and private balconies.

The attached restaurant is as close as you'll get to fine dining in El Castillo.

★ Borders Coffee   CAFE $$

(📞8408-7688; detrás Base Militar; meals US$5.50-9; ⏰8am-10pm; 🛜) A block back from the river at the eastern edge of town, this fun open-air cafe is a traveler's favorite and is a great place to chill out between activities. The menu is a pleasant change from typical Nica grub with plenty of pasta dishes and veg options. It's also a great place for breakfast.

The food is delicious, and the coffee (US$1 to $2.50) wins the unofficial title of 'best in region'.

Casa de Huesped
Chinandegano   NICARAGUAN $$

(📞2583-3011; muelle, 240m E; meals US$5.50-7; ⏰7am-10pm) Locals come for tasty chicken plates, but they do a good trade in fish, too – it comes perfectly grilled and glazed with garlic butter, garnished with a tomato salad dressed in vinegar and plated with golden *tostones* (fried green plantains) and a carved heart of lime. Service is just as good as the food.

ℹ Getting There & Away

From El Castillo, collective boats leave for San Carlos (US$3, three hours) via Boca de Sábalos (US$0.50, 30 minutes) at 5am, 6am, 7am, and 2pm. On Sunday there are only two services at 5am and 2pm. Fast *pangas* to San Carlos (US$5, two hours) via Boca de Sábalos (US$1, 15 minutes) leave at 5:30am, 9am and 11am.

Slow boats to San Juan de Nicaragua (US$10, seven to eight hours) pass El Castillo around 9am on Tuesday, Thursday and Friday. Express services (US$20, four to five hours) pull into the dock at around 8:15am on Tuesday and Friday.

Reserva Biológica Indio-Maíz & the River Eastward

About 15 minutes downriver from El Castillo, after Costa Rica's border tumbles down to the edge of the river's southern bank, you'll notice a smaller river flow into the jungle to the north. That's the Río Bartola, which marks the boundary of Nicaragua's second-largest tract of intact primary forest, the 2606-sq-km Reserva Biológica Indio-Maíz. For years 85% of the reserve's landmass belonged to Somoza. Thanks to geographic isolation and inaccessibility, followed by more than a decade of war, it was spared the chainsaw. Once the Sandinistas took power, it was legislated as a reserve and for the next several years it was the domain of scientists and remained off-limits to tourists.

While the vast majority of the reserve remains restricted, it is now possible to visit some small designated sections where you can hike among 50m-tall, 500-year-old cathedral trees, search for fingernail-sized tree frogs and watch monkeys perform death-defying leaps through the canopy.

🏃 Activities

At the confluence of Río Bartola and Río San Juan, the park ranger's office administers a 3km walking trail that winds through the reserve's towering trees. A local guide is obligatory to enter this amazing rainforest ecosystem and most visitors come on a package from El Castillo. Another 20 minutes downriver by boat is the reserve entrance at **Aguas Frescas**, where the scenery is similar but there is a slightly longer and more challenging trail. While Aguas Frescas was once less visited and hence attracted more wildlife than the Bartola section, both trails are now very popular and choosing a section depends mainly on how far you want to walk. Note that despite the collection of entrance fees to use the facilities, both trails are in very poor shape, with deep mud the norm in many parts.

About an hour further along from the mouth of the Río Sarapiquí, the San Juan Delta begins to weave through the wetlands, meeting up with the almost-as-enormous Río Colorado. Birding becomes increasingly interesting, and fishing even better – but note that you have officially entered the bull sharks' territory, so no swimming.

When you finally enter the expansive Bahía de San Juan del Norte, you'll notice the rusted old dredger owned by Cornelius Vanderbilt's Transit Company, which kept the shipping lanes open for would-be gold prospectors en route to San Francisco. The dilapidated dock to the south marks the entrance to what's left of Greytown, founded on what was then the mouth of the Río San Juan, now a sandy extension of dry land. After you cross the bay to the mouth of the remarkable Río Indio, you'll reach San Juan de Nicaragua, where you can explore black-water creeks, hidden lagoons and thick jungle within the wide reach of the Indio-Maíz.

🛌 Sleeping

The Indio-Maíz is a restricted area and there are no accommodations within the reserve; however, there are a couple of excellent options just outside its boundaries on the other side of the Río Bartola. The next beds are all the way down in San Juan de Nicaragua.

Basecamp Bartola   COMMUNITY LODGE **$$$**
(☑8919-6320, 8433-4664; indio.maiz@gmail.com; Comunidad Bartola; per person incl meals, transport & activities US$54-154) 🚣 Run by the tiny community of Bartola, 6km up the Río Bartola, this groundbreaking new project is the future of sustainable tourism in the region. Visitors sleep in tents (complete with mattresses and towels folded into swans) on wooden platforms overlooking the thick canopy of the Indio-Maíz across the river.

Activities include fantastic guided treks through nearby virgin forest full of monkeys, horseback riding, night hikes and trips in traditional boats. Prices vary depending on number of visitors.

Refugio Bartola   NATURE RESERVE **$$$**
(☑8376-6979, 8885-7386; www.refugiobartola.com; s/d/tr incl meals US$70/110/153) 🚣 Set at the confluence of Ríos San Juan and Bartola, opposite the ranger post, this rustic wooden lodge and private reserve is the superlative option in the region for true nature lovers. Accommodations are in simple, breezy wooden rooms with high ceilings set around a lovely garden overlooking the river where agoutis rummage around oblivious to your presence.

The large tract of virgin forest is identical to the vegetation inside the reserve and the animals don't know the location of the boundaries; the only difference is here you are free to walk deep into the jungle along a network of trails. Kayaks are available to explore the Río Bartola at your own pace.

Unfortunately management here are unreliable and reservations are not always honored. Best make a backup plan.

ⓘ Getting There & Away

Most visitors to the Indio-Maíz explore its eastern reaches on a day trip form El Castillo. While riverboats heading to San Juan de Nicaragua from San Carlos and El Castillo can drop you at either Bartola or Aguas Frescas, you'll need to bring a local guide with you if you want to enter the reserve.

The hotels on the far bank of the Río Bartola offer transport from El Castillo.

San Juan de Nicaragua

Dripping wet and laid-back, one of the Americas' oldest European cities feels like it's on the edge of the world. There are wide streets but no cars; and few businesses have signs. But it's certainly not lazy or joyless. Fishers and boat builders work from morning to night, and they do not want for food, shelter or activity. How could they, in a town surrounded by rivers teeming with fish, virgin rainforest and jungle-fringed lagoons? They are cash poor, however, which leads to spotty electricity (carry a flashlight) and water service (shower when you can), and the locals dream of a tourism gold rush. Considering the number of knowledgeable local guides and the nearby adventure-soaked terrain, a future ecotourism boom is definitely plausible. Today, however, it remains a dream destination for those comfortable on the edge.

Note that there is not a lot to do in town itself and when the rains come in, it's not the most entertaining place to be stuck. Plan your trip around transport schedules.

◉ Sights & Activities

There's little to keep you occupied in town, so plan to spend your days exploring the surrounding jungle.

San Juan de Nicaragua's traditional tourist attraction is the swampy remains of **Greytown**, a short boat ride (up to four people US$80 to US$100, three to four hours) across the bay. Here you'll find a few solid building foundations and four very interesting cemeteries: one for the British (including those members of Horatio Nelson's doomed campaign who were not fed to the sharks), another for Catholics, a third for North Americans, and the last allegedly for Freemasons from St John's Lodge. Unfortunately, the new airport has been constructed bang in the middle of the ruins, which torpedoes the atmosphere somewhat. Most tours also include a visit to some of the jungle lagoons and make a stop at the beach at the mouth of the Río Indio.

More and more visitors are coming to San Juan de Nicaragua to explore deeper into the mystical Reserva Biológica Indio-Maíz. There are few hiking trails – you will spend most of your time exploring the spectacular jungle in your boat.

You can spend a glorious six hours cruising between enormous yet hidden **Laguna Silica**, **Laguna de San Juanillo** and **Laguna La Barca** (up to four people US$200, six hours), which are surrounded by primary rainforest. You will occasionally hack through humid forests with machetes just to get from place to place and may spot manatees.

Or dedicate a day or two to the jungle and its original Rama inhabitants along the Río Indio, which runs parallel to the Caribbean Sea before turning inland and winding deep into the heart of the reserve.

On a typical one-day trip (up to six visitors, US$200) you'll cruise upriver through **Laguna Manatee** to **El Encanto**, where

---

THE RAMA: GUARDIANS OF THE FOREST

For the indigenous Rama people, the low jungle of the eastern Reserva Biológica Indio-Maíz is sacred. Rama ownership of these lands has been recognized by the Nicaraguan government and they are the only group permitted to live within the reserve.

Traditionally, tours into the magnificent forests of the Rama ancestral homeland have been run by *mestizo* tour operators based in San Juan de Nicaragua; however, many Rama have begun organizing jungle tours themselves. Whether it proves to be a positive thing or not for the community depends on the attitude of their visitors.

You will probably have a more polished, professional experience going with the tour operators in town. The Rama are new to tourism and still learning the ropes. However, they know this vast jungle better than any tour operators and spending some time traversing the area with them is an immensely cultural experience.

Whoever you choose to go with, once you reach the traditional lands you'll have Rama company, as local regulations require that all tour groups hire an assistant from the local community to explore the area.

To find out more and get details of recommended Rama guides get in touch with the **Gobierno Rama-Kriol** (☎ 8711-6898, 8622-8407; gobiernocomunalgreytown@gmail.com) or ask in the **tourist information office** (p258) in San Juan.

there is a hiking trail in the forest. On the way back you'll stop on the beach at El Cocal, where you'll sip fresh coconut water on the sand.

The two-day version (US$400 per group) continues upriver to **Makenge**, a Rama community where you'll spend the night in the solar-powered communal house or in a homestay with a Rama family. The next morning hike four hours through primary forest to **Canta Gallo (Piedras Basálticas)**, a basalt outcrop that local Rama say is the foundation of an ancient pyramid. Others say the formation is geological in nature. Whatever. It's stunning, and the hike is tremendous. It's also possible to extend this trip to three or four days in the jungle in order to fully explore the area.

Prices listed are those charged by experienced tour guides with well equipped boats and include transport, guides, meals, accommodation and refreshments. It's possible to find cheaper deals if you're prepared to go in a smaller boat with a less powerful engine and to bring your own food.

Hotelito Evo   FISHING, KAYAKING
(☑ 8624-6401, 8350-5145; evohotel@yahoo.es) In addition to being top jungle guides, the Gutiérrez family at Hotelito Evo offer kayaking trips (US$25 per person, minimum two people) and nocturnal alligator-spotting tours (US$25 per person, minimum two people) in the waters around town. They also offer half-day sportfishing trips (US$180 per boat).

🛏 Sleeping & Eating

There are just a couple of places to eat in town. There's usually fish on the menu alongside standard Nica fare of *gallo pinto* with pork, chicken or beef.

★ Hostal Familiar   GUESTHOUSE **$$**
(☑ 8660-6377, 8446-2096; muelle, 300m S; r with river view US$25, s/d US$15/20) A fantastic choice offering two big, breezy wooden rooms right on the river and a couple of cheaper options upstairs. The attached restaurant serves outstanding fresh seafood (imagine shrimp and snook steaks braised in coconut-tomato sauce).

Río Indio Lodge   LUXURY HOTEL **$$$**
(☑ in Costa Rica 506-2231-4299, in the US 866-593-3168; www.therioindiolodge.com; s/d incl all meals & drinks US$231/370, sportfishing packages US$2650; ❄ 🛜) This enormous, and at times deserted, sportfishing lodge has an epic perch on the Río Indio, surrounded by rainforest with views of Vanderbilt's dredge ruins. It offers opulence in the middle of the jungle with fine wooden rooms linked by elevated walkways through the jungle. Prices include some local tours. Don't expect to drop in, you'll need to reserve well in advance.

ℹ Information

Intur (☑ 8665-9560; meyjimenezobregon20@gmail.com; inside Alcaldía) A helpful local tourism office that can connect visitors with recommend guides. It should be your first port of call when arranging local activities.

ℹ Getting There & Away

San Juan de Nicaragua's airport is located across the bay, next to the Greytown ruins. La Costeña flies from Managua to San Juan (one way/return US$110/165) via San Carlos at noon on Thursday and Sunday, returning at 1:30pm. The airline has no office in San Juan town, so you'll need to purchase your return ticket online or before you arrive. There is also no public transport from the airport to San Juan, but Hotelito Evo offers a water taxi service for US$10 per person (minimum two people) – call before you arrive.

Slow boats leave from San Carlos for San Juan de Nicaragua (US$12, nine to 12 hours) at 6am on Tuesday, Thursday and Friday stopping in Boca de Sábalos at 8:15am and El Castillo around 9am. Fast boats leave San Carlos for San Juan de Nicaragua (US$23, seven to eight hours) at 6:15am Tuesday and Friday and 8am on Sunday and Wednesday, stopping in Boca de Sábalos and El Castillo one hour or 90 minutes later respectively.

Slow boats return from San Juan de Nicaragua at 5am Thursday, Saturday and Sunday. Fast boats return at 5am Thursday and Sunday and at 6am Monday and Friday.

There is a fairly regular *panga* service between San Juan and Bluefields (US$35, three hours) leaving on Wednesday mornings and returning on Fridays. Note that this is a long trip in a small boat on the open ocean that oscillates between uncomfortable and spine shattering depending on the swell. You'll probably also get soaked; bring plastic bags for your luggage. When the sea gets high, the boat is sometimes unable to depart so don't count on this service if you have a tight schedule.

Otherwise, it is occasionally possible to pay for a ride on a local boat that is making the trip but these journeys often involve delayed departures, breakdowns, fuel shortages and a really rough ride.

Understand Nicaragua

Nicaragua Today

Like him or loathe him, President Daniel Ortega's reelection in 2011 delivered something that Nicaragua had lacked for a long time: a sense of stability. After years of devastation from civil war, the country's infrastructure slowly started rebuilding. Gone were the transport strikes, debilitating power rationing and unpredictable rallies. But as he prepares to run for a third consecutive term in 2016, Ortega's anti-poverty platform has raised questions – behind Haiti, Nicaragua remains the second-poorest country in the Western hemisphere.

Best on Film

La Yuma Portrays the challenges facing a female boxer from Managua.
Palabras Mágicas The making of modern Nicaragua through the lens of a young filmmaker.
Walker Biopic of a megalomaniac with music by the late, great Joe Strummer.
Carla's Song British bus driver falls for Nicaraguan dancer in exile in romantic drama with a political edge.
Pictures from a Revolution The story behind the famous war images of Susan Meiselas.

Best in Print

Blood of Brothers (1991; Stephen Kinzer) Fascinating account of revolution and war.
The Country Beneath My Skin (2002; Gioconda Belli) Autobiography by revolutionary poet.
Selected Poems of Rubén Darío (2001; translated by Lysander Kemp) Bilingual anthology of the master poet's best work.
The Jaguar Smile (1987; Salman Rushdie) Accessible insider's look at the Sandinistas during the revolution.
Tycoon's War (2008; Stephen Dando-Collins) Documents the epic battle between imperialists Vanderbilt and Walker.

2011 Election Controversy

Prior to reclaiming the top job, President Daniel Ortega had appeared on the ballot paper in every one of the previous four Nicaraguan elections, so it was not a huge surprise when, as his return term was nearing its end, reports surfaced that the FSLN leader was not too hot on the idea of handing over the reins to a successor.

Confirmation that Ortega was not yet ready to relinquish power surfaced in 2009 when the Supreme Court – dominated by the Frente Sandinista de Liberación Nacional (Sandinista National Liberation Front; FSLN) – overturned a constitutional ban on consecutive presidential terms. The opposition launched unsuccessful legal challenges in an attempt to overturn the ruling.

Despite the controversy, the lead-up to the November 2011 election was somewhat subdued. Ortega's return to the presidency had not turned out to be the disaster that many on the right had predicted. During his five years in office, the economy had performed strongly with exports doubling and foreign direct investment increasing fivefold.

Polls leading up to the election showed Ortega well in front, confirming the suspicion that many in the once-rabidly anti-FSLN private sector had gotten over its distrust of the former rebel.

In the end, Ortega cruised to victory with 62.7% of the vote, more than twice that of his closest rival, conservative radio personality Fabio Gadea, who claimed fraud. Observers from the Organization of American States reported significant irregularities, but not sufficient to change the outcome.

Ortega's democratic credentials were further challenged in local elections in 2012, in which the FSLN won 127 of the 153 municipalities. Monitoring organization, Ética y Transparencia (Ethics and Transparency), identified irregularities in 70 municipalities it surveyed.

The End of Term Limits

Traditionally, Nicaraguan presidents have only been permitted to serve two five-year terms. But 2014 saw a landmark moment in Congress: the decision to abolish term limits, as well as to dispense of a long-time rule requiring a presidential candidate to garner at least 35% of the vote. Riots and protests in opposition to the policy change prompted violent conflicts between police and the public.

The implications for Daniel Ortega, of course, are significant – at the time of writing, he was preparing for a third run in November 2016. Third *official* run, that is: Ortega also served as president from 1985–1990, but Nicaragua's Supreme Court, in a controversial ruling, decided that the term didn't count toward his term limit.

The Nicaragua Canal

It's not the first time that an interoceanic canal through Nicaragua has been proposed, but it's the first time that the project has seemed halfway feasible. The Hong Kong Nicaragua Development (HKND) Group, in agreement with Nicaraguan president Daniel Ortega, put up the original investment for the 286km canal. The proposed waterway would be significantly wider than the Panama Canal, allowing the passage of larger boats. But initial excitement, mostly about job creation and an expected uptick in the economy, has been tempered by practical concerns.

There's the environmental impact – conservationists point to the inevitable harm to Lago de Nicaragua, and to the violation of protected indigenous territories – and then there's the financing. Though work on the canal commenced in late 2014, progress has faltered and even halted several times, hinging on the fluctuating fortunes of HKND frontman, the Chinese billionaire Wang Jing. At the time of writing, developers promised that construction would continue at the end of 2016. But whether plans for the canal move forward, and how its success or failure affects Ortega's political future, remains to be seen.

POPULATION: **6.1 MILLION**

AREA: **129,494 SQ KM**

GDP: **US$12.32 BILLION**

GDP GROWTH: **4%**

INFLATION: **4.2%**

UNEMPLOYMENT: **6.1%**

if Nicaragua were 100 people

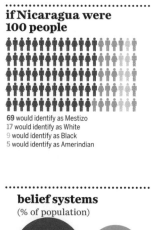

69 would identify as Mestizo
17 would identify as White
9 would identify as Black
5 would identify as Amerindian

belief systems
(% of population)

47 — Catholic
37 — Protestant
12 — Atheist/Agnostic
4 — Other

population per sq km

USA   NICARAGUA

👤 ≈ 10 people

History

For such a small country, Nicaragua has played a disproportionate role in modern history. In the midst of cold-war tensions, the young Sandinista revolutionaries' reforms captured the attention of the most powerful governments on earth and unleashed scandals in the corridors of power. But when the bullets stopped flying, the world lost interest, making the clean-up, reconstruction and return to power of the Sandinistas like a captivating sequel that never made it to the big screen.

Indigenous Nicaragua

Pre-Hispanic Nicaragua was home to several indigenous groups, including the ancestors of today's Rama, who live on the Caribbean coast, and the Chorotegas and Nicaraos, on the Pacific side. The latter spoke a form of Náhuatl, the language of the Aztecs. Many Nicaraguan places retain their Náhuatl names.

By 1500 BC Nicaragua was broadly settled, and though much of this history has been lost, at least one ancient treaty between the Nicarao capital of Jinotepe and its rival Chorotegan neighbor, Diriamba, is still celebrated as the Toro Guaco.

In Situ Petro-glyphs

....
Isla Ometepe

Chagüitillo
....
Islas Solentiname

Villa Sandino

European Arrival

Although Columbus stopped briefly on the Caribbean coast in 1502, it was Gil González de Ávila, sailing north from Panama in 1522, who would really make his mark here. He found a chieftain, Cacique Nicarao, governing the southern shores of Lago de Nicaragua and the tribe of the same name. The Spaniards thus named the region Nicaragua.

Nicarao subjected González to hours of inquiry about science, technology and history. González famously gave Nicarao an ultimatum: convert to Christianity, or else. Nicarao's people complied, a move that in the end only delayed their massacre at the hands of the Spanish; other native groups were thus warned.

Six months later González made Cacique Diriangén the same offer; Diriangén went with 'or else.' His troops were outgunned and eventually destroyed but inspired further resistance. After conquering four Pacific

TIMELINE	6000 BC	450 BC	AD 800
	Indigenous groups construct elaborate burial sites out of clam shells at Monkey Point on the Caribbean coast.	The agricultural revolution arrives in the region, with the introduction of domesticated corn, yucca and beans. Soon after, trade links with modern-day Colombia and the USA are established.	Petroglyph and statue fever sweeps across Nicaragua. Many designs, including an Aztec calendar and representations of the deity Quetzalcóatl, herald the arrival of one of Nicaragua's most important migrations.

tribes – 700,000 Chorotega, Nicarao, Maribios and Chontal were reduced to 35,000 in 25 years – the nations of the central highlands halted Spanish expansion at the mountains, with grim losses.

Colonial Settlement

The main Spanish colonizing force arrived in 1524, founding the cities of León and Granada. Both were established near indigenous settlements, whose inhabitants were put to work.

The gold that had attracted the Spaniards soon gave out, but Granada and León remained. Granada became a comparatively rich colonial city, with wealth due to surrounding agriculture and its importance as a trading center. It was also a center for the Conservative Party, favoring traditional values of monarchy and ecclesiastical authority. Originally founded on Lago de Managua, León was destroyed by volcanic eruptions in 1610 and a new city established some 30km northwest. León in time became the center for radical clerics and intellectuals, who formed the Liberal Party and supported the unification of Central America and reforms based on the French and American Revolutions.

The difference in wealth between the two cities, and the political supremacy of León, led to conflicts that raged into the 1850s, at times erupting into civil war. The animosity stopped only when the capital was moved to the neutral location of Managua.

Enter the USA

In 1893 a Liberal general named José Santos Zelaya deposed the Conservative president and became dictator. Zelaya soon antagonized the US by seeking a canal deal with Germany and Japan. Encouraged by Washington, which sought to monopolize a transisthmian canal in Panama, the Conservatives rebelled in 1909.

After Zelaya ordered the execution of two US mercenaries accused of aiding the Conservatives, the American government forced his resignation, sending marines as a coercive measure. Thus began a period of two decades of US political intervention in Nicaragua. In 1925 a new cycle of violence began with a Conservative coup.

The Conservative regime was opposed by a group of Liberal rebels including Augusto C Sandino, who recruited local peasants in the north of the country and eventually became leader of a long-term rebel campaign resisting US involvement.

Somoza Era

When the US marines headed home in 1933, the enemy became the new US-trained Guardia Nacional, whose aim was to put down resistance by Sandino's guerrillas, as is documented in Richard Millett's

CACAO FORGERIES

There were forgers even before coins were invented and the currency was cacao – they'd scoop the cacao out of the seed and replace it with mud.

1502	1523	1635	1821
Christopher Columbus sails down the Caribbean coastline looking for a sailing route to the Pacific Ocean, landing briefly in the north. First recorded contact between indigenous inhabitants and Europeans.	The main colonizing force arrives, led by Francisco Fernández de Córdoba. Cities of León (later moved after being buried by Volcán Momotombo) and Granada are founded soon after.	The first European settlement on the Atlantic coast is founded near Cabo Gracias a Dios by the grandly named British Providence Company.	Nicaragua, along with the rest of Central America, becomes independent from Spain and briefly joins the Mexican Empire and then the United Provinces of Central America.

comprehensive study *Guardians of the Dynasty: A History of the US-Created Guardia Nacional de Nicaragua and the Somoza Family*. This military force was led by Anastasio Somoza García.

Somoza engineered the assassination of Sandino after the rebel leader was invited to Managua for a peace conference. National guardsmen

WILLIAM WALKER: SCOUNDREL, VAGABOND, PRESIDENT

In a country long accustomed to land grabs and mysterious foreigners with hidden agendas, none has managed to shine quite like Tennessee-born William Walker.

While Walker's name is pretty much unheard of outside Central America, you can bet that every Nicaraguan you meet will know exactly who he was.

A quiet, poetry-reading youth who had mastered several languages and earned various degrees by early adulthood, Walker first found work as a newspaper editor, publishing outspoken pieces condemning slavery and the interventionist policies of the US at the time (warning: irony approaching).

A different type of opportunity presented itself in 1848 when the Treaty of Guadalupe was signed, ceding half of Mexico to the US and leaving the other half dangling temptingly. Walker quickly jettisoned his liberal ideals, got a posse of thugs and crooks together, and embarked on a career that would etch his name into history books forever – filibustering.

Taken from a Dutch word meaning pirate, filibustering came to mean invading a country as a private citizen with unofficial aid from your home government.

Walker's foray into Mexico was as successful (he managed to take the Mexicans completely by surprise, raise his flag and name himself president before getting chased back over the border) as it was short-lived.

Word of Walker's derring-do spread, though, and it wasn't long before the city of León offered him the job of taking care of their pesky rivals in Granada.

With another rag-tag group of mercenaries at his command, Walker arrived in San Juan del Sur in September of 1855 and, aided by the element of surprise and the latest in US weaponry, easily took Granada.

Walker's Liberal Leónese employers must have felt a bit put out when he decided not to hand over Granada after all, but instead stayed around, got himself elected president, reinstituted slavery, confiscated huge tracts of land and led an ill-fated invasion attempt on Costa Rica.

These audacious actions, supported by then US president Franklin Pierce, inspired something that has been sadly lacking ever since – Central American unity. But even getting chased back to the US by every Central American army in existence (stopping long enough to burn Granada to the ground) didn't dampen Walker's imperial ambitions. He returned to Nicaragua once more (and was sent briskly packing) before trying his luck in Honduras, where the locals were much less lenient, and put him before a firing squad in September 1860.

1838	1848	1853	1857
In abandoning the regional union, Nicaragua becomes the first modern Central American nation to declare independence.	The British seize the Caribbean port of San Juan del Norte, renaming it Greytown.	Filibuster William Walker arrives in San Juan del Sur, taking Granada quickly and installing himself as president soon after.	In an effort to quell continued fighting between León and Granada, the small fishing village of Managua is named capital. The fighting stops, but the rivalry continues to this day.

gunned Sandino down on his way home. Somoza, with his main enemy out of the way, set his sights on supreme power.

Overthrowing Liberal president Sacasa a couple of years later, he established himself as president, founding a family dynasty that would rule for four decades.

After creating a new constitution to grant himself more power, Somoza García ruled Nicaragua for the next 20 years, sometimes as president, at other times as a puppet president, amassing huge personal wealth in the process (the Somoza landholdings attained were the size of El Salvador).

After his assassination in León, Somoza was succeeded by his elder son, Luis Somoza Debayle. In 1967 Luis died, and his younger brother, Anastasio Somoza Debayle, assumed control, following in his father's footsteps by expanding economic interests throughout Nicaragua.

Rising Opposition

In 1961 Carlos Fonseca Amador, a prominent figure in the student movement that had opposed the Somoza regime in the 1950s, joined forces with Colonel Santos López (an old fighting partner of Sandino) and other activists to form the Frente Sandinista de Liberación Nacional (Sandinista National Liberation Front; FSLN). The FSLN's early guerrilla efforts against Somoza's forces ended in disaster for the fledgling group, but over the years it gained support and experience, turning into a formidable opponent.

On December 23, 1972, at around midnight, an earthquake devastated Managua, leveling more than 250 city blocks. The *Guardian* newspaper reported that, as international aid poured in, the money was diverted to Anastasio Somoza and his associates, while the people who needed it suffered and died. This dramatically increased opposition to Somoza among all classes of society.

By 1974 opposition was widespread. Two groups were widely recognized – the FSLN (Sandinistas) and the Unión Democrática de Liberación, led by Pedro Joaquín Chamorro, popular owner and editor of the Managua newspaper *La Prensa,* which had long printed articles critical of the Somozas.

In December 1974, the FSLN kidnapped several leading members of the Somoza regime. The government responded with a brutal crackdown in which Carlos Fonseca was killed in 1976.

Revolution & the FSLN

For a Nicaraguan public tired of constant violence, the last straw was the assassination of Chamorro in 1978. As street violence erupted and a general strike was called, business interests and moderate factions in the

Hyperinflation played havoc with Nicaragua's currency during the war. Immediately prior to Somoza's fall, one US dollar would buy you 10 córdobas but it eventually peaked at 3.2 million to the dollar. The Sandinistas were unable to print money fast enough and resorted to stamping existing bills with new values.

1912	1914	1934	1937
The USA, in response to a rebellion against the corrupt Conservative administration, sends 2500 marines to Nicaragua, thus beginning two decades of US-dominated politics in Nicaragua.	The Bryan-Chamorro Treaty is signed, granting the US exclusive canal rights in Nicaragua. It has no intention of building such a canal, but wants to ensure that no one else does.	Guerrilla leader Augusto Sandino is killed by troops loyal to military strongman Anastasio Somoza García after being invited to Managua to discuss peace.	Somoza overthrows Liberal President Juan Sacasa, thus beginning the Somoza dictatorship – 42 years in which the old man, then his sons, Luís and Anastasio, would rule the country.

Frente Amplio Opositor (Broad Opposition Front; FAO) unsuccessfully attempted to negotiate an end to the Somoza dictatorship.

By mid-1978 many major towns were rising up against government forces. The Guardia Nacional's violent reprisals garnered further support for the Sandinistas.

The FAO threw in its lot with the Sandinistas, whom they now perceived as the only viable means by which to oust the dictatorship. This broad alliance formed a revolutionary government provisionally based in San José, Costa Rica, which gained recognition and arms from some Latin American and European governments.

Thus the FSLN was well prepared to launch its final offensive in June 1979. The revolutionary forces took city after city, supported by thousands of civilians. On July 17, as the Sandinistas were preparing to enter Managua, Somoza fled the country. He was assassinated by Sandinista agents a year later in Asunción, Paraguay. The Sandinistas marched victorious into Managua on July 19, 1979.

They inherited a shambles. Poverty, homelessness, illiteracy and inadequate health care were just some of the problems. An estimated 50,000 people had been killed in the revolutionary struggle, and perhaps 150,000 more were left homeless.

Trying to salvage what it could of its influence over the country, the USA (under President Jimmy Carter) authorized US$75 million in emergency aid to the Sandinista-led government.

However, by late 1980 it was becoming concerned about the increasing numbers of Soviet and Cuban advisers in Nicaragua and allegations that the Sandinistas were supplying arms to leftist rebels in El Salvador.

BEN LINDER

The Death of Ben Linder by Joan Kruckewitt is a painstaking investigation (incorporating declassified CIA documents) into the assassination of Linder, the first US citizen to die at the hands of the Contras.

Contra War

After Ronald Reagan became US president in January 1981, relations between Nicaragua and the US began to sour. Reagan suspended all aid to Nicaragua and, according to the Report of the Congressional Committees Investigating the Iran-Contra Affair, by the end of the year had begun funding the counterrevolutionary military groups known as Contras, operating out of Honduras and Costa Rica, despite the US maintaining formal diplomatic relations with Managua.

Most of the original Contras were ex-soldiers of Somoza's Guardia Nacional, but as time passed, their ranks filled with disaffected local people. Honduras was heavily militarized, with large-scale US-Honduran maneuvers threatening an invasion of Nicaragua. The Sandinistas responded by instituting conscription and building an army that eventually numbered 95,000. Soviet and Cuban military and economic aid poured in, reaching US$700 million in 1987.

1956	1961	1967	1972
Somoza is assassinated in León by Rigoberto López Pérez, a poet disguised as a waiter. López Pérez is shot at the scene but becomes a national hero.	Diverse guerrilla groups, inspired by the Cuban revolution and united by their opposition to the Somozas, combine to become the Frente Sandinista de Liberación Nacional (FSLN).	Luis Somoza Debayle dies, and his younger brother, Anastasio Somoza Debayle, assumes control of the country.	A devastating earthquake hits Managua, killing more than 6000 people and leaving 300,000 homeless. Somoza embezzles international relief funds, fomenting support for the FSLN.

A CIA scheme to mine Nicaragua's harbors in 1984 resulted in a judgment against the US by the International Court of Justice. The court found that the US was in breach of its obligation under customary international law not to use force against another State and ordered it to pay repatriations to the Nicaraguan government; the Reagan administration rejected the findings and no payments were ever made.

Shortly afterward, the *New York Times* and *Washington Post* reported the existence of a CIA-drafted Contra training manual promoting the assassination of Nicaraguan officials and other strategies illegal under US law, causing further embarrassment for the Reagan administration.

TEN WHO SHAPED NICARAGUA

President Violeta Barrios de Chamorro (president 1990–96) The first female president in the hemisphere pulled together a fractured nation.

Cacique Nicarao Along with Cacique Nagrandano (for whom the Llanura Nagrandano, or northwestern plains, are named) and Cacique Diriangén (still remembered on La Meseta), wise Nicarao gave the nation his name.

President Daniel Ortega (president 1984–90, 2007–present) Love him or hate him, you've got to admire the man's tenacity (and patience), waiting 17 years for another bite at the presidential apple.

Rubén Darío Began busting rhymes at age 12 and went on to become the favorite poet of a poetry-obsessed nation.

Carlos Fonseca Cofounder of the Frente Sandinista de Liberación Nacional (Sandinista National Liberation Front; FSLN). The martyred, intellectual hero of the Sandinista revolution, felt by many to represent its true ideals.

US President Ronald Reagan (president 1981–88) Together with political philosopher Jeanne Kirkpatrick, Secretary of State Alexander Haig Jr and Colonel Oliver North, Reagan masterminded the Iran-Contra debacle.

Augusto C Sandino His somber silhouette still dominates the Managua skyline, and his refusal to back down dominates the Nicaraguan collective consciousness.

Costa Rican President Oscar Arías Sánchez (president 1986–90, 2006–10) Architect of the 1987 peace accords that finally brought peace to Central America. Picked up a Nobel Prize for his efforts.

The Somozas A dynasty of Nicaraguan dictators, the first installed by the US military, and the last deposed more than four decades later by popular revolution.

William Walker The Tennessean who thought he could take on Central America but ended up in front of a Honduran firing squad.

1976	Jan 1978	Aug 1978	1979
The government responds to FSLN kidnappings and attacks with a brutal crackdown in which FSLN co-founder Carlos Fonseca is killed.	A general strike is declared following the assassination of newspaper editor and Somoza critic Pedro Joaquín Chamorro. Moderates unsuccessfully attempt to negotiate an end to the Somoza dictatorship.	FSLN occupies the Palacio Nacional, taking more than 2000 hostages and securing release for 60 imprisoned Sandinistas. There are uprisings in many towns. Guardia Nacional responds by shelling cities.	At the end of seven years of guerrilla warfare and 52 days of all-out battles, Sandinistas march on Managua. Anastasio Somoza flees the country on July 17 – the revolution is victorious.

Nicaraguan elections in November 1984 were boycotted by leading non-Sandinistas, who complained of sweeping FSLN control of the nation's media. The Sandinistas rejected the claims, announcing that the media was being manipulated by Contra supporters (*La Prensa* eventually acknowledged receiving CIA funding for publishing anti-Sandinista views). Daniel Ortega was elected president with 63% of the vote, and the FSLN controlled the National Assembly by a similar margin.

In May 1985 the USA initiated a trade embargo of Nicaragua and pressured other countries to do the same. The embargo lasted for five years, helping to strangle Nicaragua's economy.

With public opinion in the US growing wary of the war, the US Congress rejected further military aid for the Contras in 1985. According to the congressional report into the affair, the Reagan administration responded by continuing to fund the war through a scheme in which the CIA illegally sold weapons to Iran and diverted the proceeds to the Contras. When the details were leaked, the infamous Iran-Contra affair blew up.

After many failed peace initiatives, the Costa Rican president, Oscar Arías Sánchez, finally came up with an accord aimed at ending the war. It was signed in Guatemala City in August 1987 by the leaders of Costa Rica, El Salvador, Nicaragua, Guatemala and Honduras. Less than a year later, the first ceasefire of the war was signed by representatives of the Contras and the Nicaraguan government at Sapoa, near the Costa Rican border.

Oliver North, coarchitect of the Iran-Contra scheme and the man whom Ronald Reagan called 'an American hero,' is now a TV host and video-game consultant.

Polls & Peace

By the late 1980s the Nicaraguan economy was again desperate. Civil war, the US trade embargo and the inefficiencies of a centralized economy had produced hyperinflation, falling production and rising unemployment. As it became clear that the US Congress was preparing to grant the Contras further aid, Daniel Ortega called elections that he expected would give the Sandinistas a popular mandate to govern.

The FSLN, however, underestimated the disillusionment and fatigue of the Nicaraguan people. Economic problems had eclipsed the dramatic accomplishments of the Sandinistas' early years: redistributing Somoza lands to small farming cooperatives, reducing illiteracy from 50% to 13%, eliminating polio through a massive immunization program and reducing the rate of infant mortality by a third.

The Unión Nacional Opositora (UNO), a broad coalition of 14 political parties opposing the Sandinistas, was formed in 1989. UNO presidential candidate Violeta Barrios de Chamorro had the backing and financing of the USA, which had promised to lift the embargo and give hundreds of millions of dollars in economic aid to Nicaragua if UNO won. The UNO took the elections of February 25, 1990, gaining 55% of the presidential

1980	1980s	1985	1987
Ousted dictator Anastasio Somoza Debayle is assassinated by Sandinista agents in Asunción, Paraguay.	Opposition fighters known as the Contras carry out nationwide attacks. With US funding, the Contras grow in number to 15,000; the FSLN responds by implementing compulsory military service.	Daniel Ortega takes power in his first five-year term – a term that Nicaragua's Supreme Court will later rule doesn't count toward his term limits.	Central American Peace Accords are signed. Ortega promises to lift press censorship, enforce a ceasefire and hold free elections as a sign of the Sandinistas' commitment to democracy.

votes and 51 of the 110 seats in the National Assembly, compared with the FSLN's 39. Ortega had plenty of grounds for complaint, but in the end he went quietly, avoiding further conflict.

Politics in the 1990s

Chamorro took office in April 1990. The Contras called a heavily publicized ceasefire at the end of June. The US trade embargo was lifted, and foreign aid began to pour in.

Chamorro faced a tricky balancing act in trying to reunify the country and satisfy all interests. Economic recovery was slow; growth was sluggish and unemployment remained stubbornly high. Nevertheless, in 1996, when Nicaragua went to the polls again, the people rejected the FSLN's Ortega and opted for former Managua mayor Arnoldo Alemán of the PLC, a center-right liberal alliance.

Alemán invested heavily in infrastructure and reduced the size of the army by a factor of 10, but his administration was plagued by scandal, as corruption soared and Alemán amassed a personal fortune from the state's coffers, earning himself a place on Transparency International's list of the top 10 corrupt public officials of all time. Meanwhile, however, the Sandinistas had their own image problems, as the ever-present Ortega was accused by his stepdaughter of sexual abuse. In a gesture of mutual self-preservation, Ortega and Alemán struck a deal, popularly known as *el pacto* (the pact), which *Time* magazine reported was designed to nullify the threat of the opposition, pull the teeth of anti-corruption watchdogs and guarantee Alemán immunity from further investigation.

Sandinista diehards felt betrayed by Ortega's underhanded dealings, but many still believed in their party, and Ortega remained an important figure.

Sandinista 2.0

After losing three successive elections, FSLN leader Ortega returned to power in the November 2006 elections, capitalizing on disillusionment with neoliberal policies that had failed to jump-start the country's economy and an *el pacto*–sponsored law that lowered the threshold for a first-round victory to 35% of the votes (Ortega received 38%).

Taking office in January 2007, Ortega proclaimed a new era of leftist Latin American unity, leaving the USA and some international investors a little jumpy. The early days of Ortega's presidency were a flurry of activity, with Nicaragua's energy crisis seemingly solved via a deal with Venezuela's Hugo Chávez, and Ortega pledging to maintain good relations with the USA while at the same time courting closer ties with US archrival Iran.

Sandino's Daughters by Margaret Randall is a series of interviews that takes a look at the way feminism was incorporated into the Sandinista revolution.

HISTORY POLITICS IN THE 1990S

1990	1996	2001	2006
Violeta Barrios de Chamorro beats Daniel Ortega in presidential elections. Ortega cedes power graciously. The process of national reconciliation begins as the Contra War and US-led economic embargo end.	Voters go to the polls again, once more rejecting the FSLN's Ortega, opting instead for former Managua mayor Arnoldo Alemán of the PLC, a center-right liberal alliance.	Enrique Bolaños is elected president by a small margin. After 11 years of trying to make a comeback, it is Ortega's third defeat.	After three failed bids, Ortega regains the presidency with 38% of the vote. He seeks closer ties with left-wing governments in Venezuela, Bolivia and Cuba.

But as the Ortega government found its feet, there was no sign of the radical land reforms or wave of nationalizations that the business sector had dreaded and some die-hard FSLN supporters had hoped for. Ortega for the most part followed the economic course set by the previous government and continued to honor Nicaragua's international financial obligations.

The first test for Nicaraguan democracy under the new Ortega government surfaced in 2008, with countrywide municipal elections. The FSLN claimed victory in over 70% of municipalities, when it had come to power with only 38% of the vote. Opposition forces claimed widespread voter fraud and *La Prensa* labeled the election 'the most fraudulent elections in Nicaraguan history.'

Nevertheless Ortega weathered the storm and by the end of his return term was able to point to solid economic growth alongside the reintroduction of free health care and education among the achievements of his government.

ORTEGA'S THEME

Daniel Ortega's 2006 presidential comeback featured its very own theme song – a Sandinista version of the John Lennon classic 'Give Peace a Chance'.

2010	2011	2014	2016
Tensions flare at Harbour Head in the Río San Juan with Costa Rica responding to Nicaraguan dredging operations by sending heavily armed police to the border.	After the FSLN-dominated Supreme Court overturns a constitutional ban on successive terms, Ortega wins reelection with an increased majority.	Nicaragua's Congress abolishes presidential term limits and a long-held rule that victorious presidential candidates must win 35% of the vote, sparking public protests.	Current president Daniel Ortega prepares to run for what would be his third consecutive presidential term, with elections in November 2016.

Nicaraguan Way of Life

Nicaraguans strike a wonderful balance of pride and humility. While many live in poverty and even the middle classes struggle to make ends meet, when asked about their country, most prefer to highlight its rich culture and natural beauty than dwell on the difficulties. And while the nation's distinct ethnic groups have their own cultures, all Nicaraguans are united by their laid-back style, great sense of humor and an openness that manifests itself in their love of socializing.

The National Psyche

Nicaragua has a fierce cultural streak and prides itself on homegrown literature, dance, art, music and cuisine. This spiritual independence is a holdover not only from the revolution and Contra War, but back to Spanish colonization, when indigenous nations won limited autonomy at enormous personal cost.

Nicaragua also still suffers from a bit of post-traumatic stress disorder. Spanish-speakers will hear plenty of stories involving tanks, explosions and aerial bombings, not to mention 'the day the family cow wandered into the minefield' stories. Former Sandinistas and Contras work, play and take Communion together, however, and any tensions you might expect seem to have been addressed and worked through. Opinions differ about the Sandinista years, but both sides will always agree to a good debate. Jump in and you'll learn more about the political scene than you ever would by reading a newspaper or guidebook.

Of course, attitudes differ from place to place. Residents of the English- and Miskito-speaking Atlantic coast rarely consider themselves part of Nicaragua proper, and many would prefer to be returned to the British Empire than suffer further oppression by the 'Spaniards' on the other side of the country. The cattle ranchers of the central highlands resist interference from the federal government, while coffee pickers in Matagalpa or students in León are willing to walk to Managua to complain to the government if they perceive that an injustice has been done.

Many of Managua's retired old school buses have been converted into *bus pelones* (bald buses) – open-air party buses that give residents without vehicles the chance to cruise the streets of the city in the evening.

Lifestyle

Nicaragua is a country in motion. One in five Nicas live outside the country, most in the USA, Costa Rica and Honduras. Waves of migration to the cities, which began in the 1950s, have left more than 55% of the population urban. Most internal immigrants are young women, and most go to Managua; men tend to follow the harvest into rural areas and the surrounding countries. Regular jobs are difficult to find, and more than half of employed Nicaraguans are in the 'informal sector' – street vendors, maids, artisans – without benefits or job security.

Despite the country's Catholic background, couples often live together and have children without being married, especially in larger cities. Nicaraguans are generally fairly accepting of the GLBT community, although the community is still fighting for full legal recognition.

Wealth is distributed unequally, with the moneyed elite living much as they would in Miami or elsewhere. For the vast majority of Nicaraguans, however, just putting food on the table is a daily struggle, with 46% living below the poverty line and perhaps a third of the country subsisting on two meals or fewer per day; almost one-fifth of Nicaragua's children are at risk of problems relating to malnutrition, while in the Atlantic regions it is more than 30%.

However, when hitting the streets, even the poorest Nicaraguans will generally always appear in clean, freshly pressed clothes, which is why they find 'wealthy' backpackers in smelly rags so amusing.

Economy

Nicaragua's solid grounding as an agricultural nation is a blessing and a curse. While the average *campesino* (farmer) will generally have something to eat, the sector as a whole is vulnerable to a range of threats. Plunging world commodity prices, natural disasters and environmental factors such as soil degradation and water shortages are all problems that Nicaraguan farmers face regularly. Coffee remains Nicaragua's main agricultural export, followed by beef, shrimp, dairy products and tobacco.

Industrial production, encouraged under the last of the Somozas, was all but destroyed by the war and is only now beginning to slowly pick up again. By far the biggest industry is textile and apparel production, but the cigar industry is growing rapidly. Gold mining is another important industry. Tourism plays an increasingly important role in the economy, and it is here more than anywhere else that many see a bright future for Nicaragua.

By the end of the war, Nicaragua was a heavily indebted nation. In 1979 the departing dictator Somoza emptied the country's coffers. The incoming Sandinista government engaged in some shaky economic policies (including massive public spending financed by foreign lending), while the economy was being slowly strangled by the US trade embargo. In 2000 Nicaragua was included on the Highly Indebted Poor Countries list, meaning that a large chunk of its massive foreign debt was canceled after it complied with a series of conditions set down by the World Bank

It's not uncommon for Nica shopkeepers to engage in unbridled flattery and even declarations of love when trying to sell you something, especially in markets.

FREE TRADE VS FAIR TRADE

In March 2006, Nicaragua ratified the Dominican Republic–Central America Free Trade Agreement (DR-CAFTA). An agreement between an economic superpower like the US and various struggling nations was always going to be controversial, and plenty of political mileage was made, but it's worth remembering that, in the end, the agreement was approved by liberals and Sandinistas alike.

The central question to any such agreement is this: who benefits? The US stood to gain from cheaper imports, wider markets, investment opportunities and access to cheap foreign labor, but what was in it for Nicaragua?

The short answer was exports, foreign investment and jobs. What *kinds* of exports, investment and jobs? Well, there's been a little spike in the export of primary products such as beef and sugar, but the biggest change to Nicaragua's economic landscape has been the spread of the *maquiladoras* (clothing assembly factories) across the country. These factories provide much-needed work (Nicaragua's underemployment rate runs at around 46%), but critics say the *maquiladoras* are no real solution – they set up in Free Trade Zones (Nicaragua has four), which aren't bound by Nicaraguan law, so they don't pay minimum wage or respect workers' rights. When exported, goods don't incur export duty, so Nicaragua ends up earning very little. It's a process that workers' rights and environmental activist Ralph Nader calls 'the race to the bottom,' where poor countries end up competing to see who can offer the most favorable deal to investor nations.

and IMF. These measures – which included privatizing public assets and opening the economy to foreign markets – are highly controversial and it remains to be seen whether Nicaragua's participation in the program will produce long-term gains for its ordinary residents.

Population

With 6.1 million people spread across 130,000 sq km, Nicaragua is the second-least densely populated country in Central America after Belize. The CIA World Factbook estimates that 69% of the population is *mestizo* (of mixed ancestry, usually Spanish and indigenous people), 17% white, 9% black and 5% indigenous. The most recent census reports that just over 440,000 people describe themselves as indigenous: the Miskito (121,000), Mayangna/Sumo (9800) and Garifuna (3300), all with some African heritage, occupy the Caribbean coast alongside the Rama (4200). In the central and northern highlands, the Cacaopoeras and Matagalpas (15,200) may be Maya in origin, while the Chorotegas (46,000), the Subtiavas (20,000) and the Nahoas (11,100) have similarities to the Aztecs.

European heritage is just as diverse. The Spanish settled the Pacific coast, while a wave of German immigrants in the 1800s has left the northern highlands surprisingly *chele* (white, from *leche*, or milk). And many of those blue eyes you see on the Atlantic coast can be traced back to British, French and Dutch pirates.

The original African immigrants were shipwrecked, escaped or freed slaves who began arriving soon after the Spanish. Another wave of Creoles and West Indians arrived in the late 1800s to work on banana and cacao plantations in the east. Mix all that together, simmer for a few hundred years and you get an uncommonly good-looking people who consider racism a bit silly.

Sports

It's just not a weekend in Nicaragua without the crack of a baseball bat, but there really are other sports in the country – you just have to look.

Football (soccer) is growing in popularity and is especially big in the north of the country. The National Fútbol League has a website (www.fenifut.org.ni) with schedules and stats. Boxing is also extremely popular and Nicaragua produces some champion pugilists, especially in the lower weight divisions.

Many towns have pickup soccer, baseball, volleyball and basketball games, and foreigners are usually more than welcome to join in. It's a fine opportunity to interact with the locals without worrying about the subjunctive tenses.

Cockfighting and bullfights, while considered barbaric by many people, are still some of Nicaragua's most popular spectator sports, especially in rural areas. Beautiful alpha roosters with knives strapped to their feet slash each other apart in miniature bullrings while the crowd place bets and drinks copious amounts of moonshine. It can be a gloomy affair if you're even moderately concerned about animal welfare, as can rodeos and bullfights, which generally take place during *fiestas patronales* (saints' days). Though considerably less gory than their Spanish counterparts – it's illegal to use any weapons or kill the bull – they're still pretty lowbrow affairs, and there's no doubt in the world that the bull does not enjoy the spectacle.

Media

International media-monitoring bodies have reported that freedom of the press in Nicaragua has deteriorated significantly under the Frente Sandinista de Liberación Nacional (Sandinista National Liberation

Stunning Pearl Lagoon's handful of ethnic fishing villages are home to Miskito, Creole and Garifuna people who have lived and traded with one another for more than 300 years.

In Caribbean Nicaragua, domino tournaments are serious events with neighborhood clubs decked out in team T-shirts slamming down tiles in front of noisy spectators.

Front; FSLN) government, although an independent media still operates in the country.

The current FSLN leadership are particularly media savvy and have made controlling the airwaves a priority. According to the *New York Times,* since returning to power, Daniel Ortega has invested heavily in media operations, while at the same time cutting government advertising in non-Sandinista outlets. The newspaper goes on to report that Ortega's children run television networks Multinoticias, Channel 8 and Channel 13, and that the FSLN leader now controls nearly half of Nicaragua's television outlets.

According to the Committee to Protect Journalists (CPJ), Ortega uses these media outlets to launch character attacks against his critics as part of an effort to marginalize independent media.

CPJ stated that one such example was directed at television journalist Carlos Fernando Chamorro, son of former *La Prensa* editor Pedro Joaquín Chamorro whose assassination by Somoza was one of the sparks of the revolution. Following the airing of reports on an extortion scheme involving the Sandinista party, Chamorro was formally investigated for money laundering. After a wave of domestic and international criticism, the charges were later dropped.

Despite Nicaraguan law stating that officials must supply accurate information to the media upon request, local journalists have reported restrictions in accessing government press conferences and officials, while those working for government-linked news outlets are given free rein. According to CPJ, First Lady Rosario Murillo is like a virtual prime minister, managing all government communications; officials in the executive branch are permitted to talk to the press only with her authorization.

While the government controls many of the radio and TV stations, Nicaragua's two national daily newspapers – *La Prensa* and *El Nuevo Diario* – remain critical of the Ortega government (a fact the FSLN

> Most Nicaraguan TV stations have two types of news: a sensationalist ambulance-chasing edition featuring graphic portrayals of fights and accidents – usually displayed on the big screen at dinner time – followed by a far less popular political edition.

TAKE ME OUT TO THE BÉISBOL GAME

Every Sunday, all over the country, from abandoned lots to the national stadium, there's one game that's got Nicaraguans obsessed, and if you think it's football, you're dead wrong.

Despite popular belief, baseball was big here even before the marines arrived in 1909 – their presence just gave the sport a shot in the arm. The first recorded series was played in 1887, when two Bluefields teams – Four Roses and Southern – battled it out over seven games. Four years later, baseball fever hit the Pacific coast and by 1915 there was a national championship.

While major-league Nica players are generally treated like royalty here, very few of them don't dream of going to the US to play, joining a long list of their countrymen, including Tony Chevez, Albert Williams, David Green, Porfirio Altamirano, Vincent Padilla, Marvin Bernard and, of course, Hall of Famer Denis 'El Presidente' Martínez, who pitched more winning major-league games than any Latino and who had Nicaragua's national stadium, Estadio Denis Martínez, named after him.

Every town has some sort of baseball ground, from a dusty lot on the outskirts to some fairly fancy affairs in Managua, León, Granada and Chinandega (among others). These four towns, incidentally, compete in Nicaragua's major league.

Games are played on Sunday in villages, towns and cities all over the country, but if you'd like to catch some major-league action, log on to www.lnbp.com.ni (in Spanish) for schedules. For even better atmosphere, check out the biennial Atlantic Series, which features teams from all over the Caribbean region playing off for a cup. The tournament takes place in different cities and towns throughout the region, but is always a great party.

repeatedly alludes to when confronted with claims of censorship and media control). The former is your classic conservative rag – understandably railing against all things Sandinista. The latter (more classically a blue-collar publication) seems to draw a distinction between the old-school Sandinistas (whom it still vaguely supports) and the new-breed Danielistas (for whom it has very little patience).

It remains to be seen if, as it consolidates its power and media empire, the Ortega government will continue to tolerate independent opinion.

Religion

Although Nicaragua's majority religion is Catholicism, Nicaraguan Catholicism retains many indigenous elements, as the decor and ceremonies of churches such as San Juan Bautista de Subtiava and Masaya's María Magdelena make clear. Liberation theology also made its mark on Nicaraguan Catholicism, influencing priest and poet Ernesto Cardenal to advocate armed resistance to the Somoza dictatorship. Publicly chastised and later defrocked by Pope John Paul II, Cardenal remains a beloved religious leader. Nicaragua's incredible selection of Catholic churches and fascinating *fiestas patronales* remain highlights of the country.

On the Atlantic coast, Moravian missionaries from Germany began arriving in the early 1800s, and today their red-and-white wooden churches are the centerpieces of many Creole and Miskito towns. More recently, more than 100 Protestant sects, most US-based and collectively referred to as *evangelistas,* have converted at least 21% of the population; in fact, many of the foreigners you'll meet in rural Nicaragua are missionaries, who may try to convert you too.

Perhaps most interesting, around 12% of Nicaraguans say they are atheist or agnostic, an unusual proportion in Latin America.

Women in Nicaragua

Women, especially in rural sectors, are likely to work outside the home and do half of all agricultural labor. This stems in part from ideals espoused by the (original) Sandinistas, who considered women equal players in the remolding of the country, but also from necessity, as many men died or were maimed during the wars, or later emigrated to find work; after the Contra War, the country was more than 55% female. The strong women's movement is fascinating; check out Boletina at www.puntos.org.ni to learn more.

Despite loud protests by many organizations, in 2006 Nicaragua passed a controversial law declaring abortion illegal even when the life of the mother is at risk. Women's groups say the law has led to the deaths of dozens of women and mostly affects the poor as the wealthy (including the daughters of politicians) are able to travel to other countries for medical attention without restrictions.

In traditional Miskito societies – mostly concentrated on Nicaragua's Caribbean coast – women own the farmland and plant crops.

Arts & Architecture

Nicaragua, as any book will tell you, celebrates literature, and particularly poetry, with appropriate passion, revering its writers with a fervor reserved, in more developed countries, for Hollywood stars. But it's not all about printed prose, Nicaragua also boasts a variety of homegrown musical genres, energetic dances and renowned painters all shaped by the nation's dominant themes of romance and rebellion.

Nation of Poets

Poetry lies at the very heart of Nicaragua's cultural identity. Both major daily newspapers run a literary supplement in their Friday editions, high-school kids form poetry clubs, and any *campesino* (farmer) picking coffee in the isolated mountains can tell you who the greatest poet in history is: Rubén Darío, voice of the nation. They will then recite a poem by Darío, quite possibly followed by a few of their own.

Nicaragua is also home to the peculiar cultural archetype of 'warrior poets,' folks who choose to go with both the pen and the sword. Among the most famous are Leonel Rugama, who held off the Guardia Nacional while hero Carlos Fonseca escaped; Rigoberto López Pérez, who assassinated the original Somoza in León; liberation theologian Ernesto Cardenal; and former Sandinista undercover agent, Gioconda Belli.

The nation's original epic composition, the Nica equivalent to *Beowulf* or *La Chanson de Roland,* is *El Güegüense,* a burlesque dating from the 1600s. A morality play of sorts, it pits an indigenous Nicaraguan businessman against corrupt and inept Spanish authorities; using only his sly wit and a few multilingual double entendres, the Nica ends up on top.

León has been home to the nation's greatest poets, including Darío, Azarias H Pallais, Salomón de la Selva and Alfonso Cortés, the last of whom did his best work while going insane in Darío's childhood home. A Rubén Darío tribute site (www.dariana.com, in Spanish) has biographies and bibliographies of major Nicaraguan writers. The most important modern writers include Pablo Antonio Cuadra, a former editor of *La Prensa,* and Ernesto Cardenal.

One of the few Nicaraguan writers regularly translated into English is Gioconda Belli (www.giocondabelli.org), who was working undercover with the Sandinistas when she won the prestigious Casa de las Américas international poetry prize. Her internationally acclaimed work is both sexual and revolutionary, and is the best way to get a woman's-eye view of Nicaragua in the 1970s.

Selected Poems by Rubén Darío (translated by Lysander Kemp) has verses from Nicaragua's most famous poet in the original on one page and in English translation on the facing page.

Music

Folkloric music and dance received a huge boost from the revolution, which sought to mine Nicaraguan culture for cultural resources rather than import more popular options, quite possibly at great cost. As a result, you'll probably be able to see a musical or dance performance during even a short visit, the most convenient being *Noches Verbenas,* held every Thursday evening at the Mercado de Artesanías (National Artisans Market) in Masaya. Also check out cultural centers, close to the Parque

Central in most larger towns, or at the municipal theaters in Granada, León and Managua, to see what's on. *Fiestas patronales* (patron saint parties) are a good time to catch a performance, which in the northern highlands will likely have a polka component.

Perhaps the most important musical form is marimba, usually played on xylophones made of precious wood with names such as 'The Lovers,' 'Dance of the Black Woman,' and 'Fat Honey,' which you'll enjoy over a cold glass of *chicha* (mildly alcoholic corn beverage) at some shady Parque Central. The guardians of this and other traditional forms of Nicaraguan music are the Mejía Godoy brothers (see www.losmejiagodoy.com, in Spanish), whom you can (and should) catch live in Managua.

Marimba music was given a new sense of cool with the arrival on the scene of La Cuneta Son Machín (www.lacunetasonmachin.com), a cumbia-rock fusion group heavily influenced by traditional Nicaraguan sounds. If you get the chance, check out their energetic live performances.

On the Atlantic coast reggae and country are king but there are also homegrown sounds including upbeat Maypole music, which is often accompanied by spicy dance moves, and Miskito pop, heavily influenced by the electronic-keyboard music of rural churches, where many of the musicians learned to play.

Considering how few venues there are available for them to play, new talents are plentiful in Nicaragua. If you're looking for laid-back electronica, try Momotobo. Quirky bossa-pop fans should hunt down anything by Belén, while División Urbana is probably the best of many groups doing the hard-rock thing. Manu Chao fans will probably like Perrozompopo, and for sheer lyrical beauty, floating melodies and electro-pop crossover, keep an eye out for discs by Clara Grun.

Famous Nicaraguan musician Carlos Mejía Godoy, who wrote theme songs for the Sandinista revolution, went on to sue the FSLN for improper use of those very songs.

RUBÉN DARÍO

To say that Rubén Darío is a famous poet is an outrageous understatement. The man is a national hero – his birthplace (Ciudad Darío), the national theater and the entire Cordillera Dariense mountain range are named after him.

Something of a child prodigy, Darío could read by age four (he'd polished off *Don Quixote* and various other classics by age 10) and had his first poetry published in León newspapers at age 12.

Deemed too 'antireligious' to be awarded a scholarship to Europe, Darío was sent to El Salvador at the age of 15. There he met and befriended Salvadorian poet Francisco Gavidia, whose work and teachings would have a profound influence on Darío's style.

Darío traveled extensively – to Chile, where he worked as a journalist and wrote his breakthrough piece, *Azul*; Argentina, where he became a leading member of the Modernist literary movement; and, last, to Europe, where he continued to write some of what Chilean poet Pablo Neruda called some of the most creative poetry in the Spanish language.

Darío was appointed Nicaragua's ambassador to France, then Spain, but such officialdom never slowed him down. His hard-drinking, womanizing lifestyle was by now legendary (and somewhat requisite for poets of the era), but it took its toll in 1914 when Darío contracted pneumonia. He recovered, but was left weak and bankrupt. Friends banded together and raised the money for him to return to Nicaragua. He died in León two years later, at the age of 49.

Poesía en Español (www.luis.salas.net/indexrd.htm) has most of Rubén Darío's poems available online, while English-language Dariana (www.dariana.com), a Rubén Darío tribute site, has 11 of his poems translated into English by fellow legendary Leónese poet Salomón de la Selva.

GIOCONDA
BELLI

Gioconda Belli's
*The Inhabited
Woman* is well
worth tracking
down. It's a
loosely political
tale based partly
on true events,
but the magic
here is in Belli's
sensual, poetic
prose.

Painting & Sculpture

The oldest artistic tradition in Nicaragua is ceramics, dating from about 2000 BC with simple, functional vessels, developing into more sculptural representations by around AD 300. By the time the Spanish arrived, Nicaraguan ceramics were complex, artistic and often ceremonial, and indicate a pronounced Aztec influence in both design and decoration. Remember that it's illegal (and lame) to remove pre-Columbian ceramics from Nicaragua.

Today, top-quality ceramics are most famously produced in San Juan de Oriente, which is known for colorfully painted fine white clays and heavier, carved pots; in Mozonte, near Ocotal; and at Matagalpa and Jinotega, which are renowned for their black ceramics.

Almost as ancient an art, stone carving probably became popular around AD 800, when someone realized that the soft volcanic basalt could be shaped with obsidian tools imported from Mexico and Guatemala. Petroglyphs, usually fairly simple, linear drawings carved into the surface of a stone, are all over the country, and it's easy to arrange tours from Isla de Ometepe, Granada and Matagalpa.

Stone statues, expressive and figurative, not to mention tall (one tops 5m) are rarer but also worth seeing; the best museums are in Granada and Juigalpa. Much finer stone statues are being produced today, using polished, translucent soapstone worked in the backyard workshops of San Juan de Limay, near Estelí.

Painting apparently arrived with the Spanish (though there's evidence that both statues and petroglyphs were once more vividly colored), the earliest works being mostly religious in nature; the best places to see paintings are in León, at the Museo de Arte Sacre and the Museo de Arte Fundación Ortiz-Guardián. The latter also traces Nicaraguan painting through to the present, including the Romantic and Impressionistic work of Rodrigo Peñalba, who founded the School of Beaux Arts, and the Praxis Group of the 1960s, led by Alejandro Arostegui and possessed of a heavy-handed social realism, depicting hunger, poverty and torture.

In the 1970s Ernesto Cardenal founded an art colony on the Islas Solentiname, an isolated group of islands in the southeast corner of Lago de Nicaragua, today internationally renowned for the gem-toned paintings and balsa-wood sculptures that so colorfully (and accurately)

THE PAINTING ON THE WALL

Nothing quite captures Nicaraguans' spirit, creativity and political sentiment like their love for murals. Often strikingly beautiful pieces of art in their own right, murals served a practical and political end in the days before the Sandinistas' Literacy Crusade of broadcasting a message to an audience that was largely illiterate.

There are murals in all major cities, but the Sandinista strongholds of León and Estelí are standouts, where at one stage nearly every blank wall in the downtown was covered with colorful revolutionary messages. The area around the UCA university in Managua has some fine examples, too.

However, with the modernization of the cities, some of the best examples have been painted over, often with propaganda from multinational cell-phone networks.

Estelí has its own NGO teaching mural painting to children and teenagers, and is also home to a new movement of muralistas, who use more recognizable graffiti techniques but continue to paint the walls of the city with images of a social slant.

For a look at murals from around the country, check out the gorgeous coffee-table book *The Murals of Revolutionary Nicaragua* by David Kunzle.

CHURCHES OF NICARAGUA

Nicaragua hasn't always been this poor – in the 1960s Costa Ricans were sneaking across the border to work here. From the first days of the Spanish conquest through to the late 1800s, when Nicaragua controlled the only warm-water route between the world's two great oceans, this little country was a major power broker.

With cash to spare and a Catholic population to impress, the authorities constructed churches even devout atheists will enjoy. León may be the nation's pinnacle of religious architecture, but here are a few other must-sees.

➡ **Cathedrals of Managua** The interior of the poignant, burnt-out husk of Managua's original cathedral is off-limits, but you're welcome to ponder the new cathedral's ultramodern domes: cooling towers for a divine nuclear reactor? Homage to Islam? Eggs hatching into a peaceful tomorrow?

➡ **Basílica de Nuestra Señora de la Inmaculada Concepción de la Virgen María** Even Pope John Paul II visited the beautiful Virgen del Trono, patron saint of Nicaragua and mistress of La Gritería, the nation's most important religious event.

➡ **Templo de El Sauce** Quite literally a pilgrimage-worthy destination; every January thousands come to see El Señor de Esquipulas, the Black Christ.

➡ **Moravian Church in Bluefields** Faithfully rebuilt to its Victorian-era specs after Bluefields' utter destruction during Hurricane Juana; it's not just lovely, it's a symbol of hope and perseverance.

➡ **Iglesia Catedral San Pedro** This baroque 1874 beauty, known for its twin bell towers, remains one of the country's most elegant churches despite a desperate need for renovation.

➡ **Templo Parroquial de San Rafael Arcángel** This is religion as sensory overload, with beautiful architecture and truly amazing murals.

➡ **Nuestra Señora de Solentiname** Ernesto Cardenal and the Solentiname community built this heartfelt and humble adobe church, its murals designed by children.

capture the tropical landscape. If you can't get to the islands yourself, try the Masaya markets, or any of the art galleries in Managua or Granada.

A more venerable form of the art is on display every Semana Santa in the Subtiava neighborhood of León, when 'sawdust carpets,' scenes painstakingly rendered in colored sawdust, are created throughout the neighborhood, and then swirled together as religious processions go by.

Theater & Dance

Traditional music, dance and theater are difficult to separate; all are mixed together with wild costumes to create spectacles that generally also have a religious component, plus plenty of fireworks. Pieces you'll see performed by street-side beggars and professional troupes include *La Gigantona,* with an enormous Spanish woman and teeny tiny Nicaraguan guy. Another common piece is *The Dance of the Old People,* in which an older gentleman woos a sexy grandma, but once she gives in, he starts chasing younger women in the audience.

Modern theater is not well developed in Nicaragua, and only major towns have performance spaces. There's a growing independent film scene, and you can catch very low-budget, usually documentary films, often with overtly feminist or progressive themes, at cultural centers – but never movie theaters, which show mostly Hollywood blockbusters.

Architecture

The success of the Spanish conquest let the motherland finally break free of French architectural forms, such as Gothic architecture, and experiment with homegrown styles both at home and in the Americas.

Some of the earliest New World churches are a Moorish-Spanish hybrid called *mudéjar*, with squat silhouettes, wooden roofs and geometric configurations. Influenced by Islam as well as the Italian Renaissance are *plateresque* (elaborate silver filigree) on altars such as in El Viejo.

Baroque hit big in the mid-1600s, and was the most popular choice for major buildings over the next century. Primitivist Baroque, featuring graceful but unadorned adobe and wood columns, and common in smaller colonial towns, was followed by full Spanish Baroque style, with extravagant design (stone grapevines wending up massive pillars, for example), sometimes called *churriguera.*

The most famous examples of Spanish colonial architecture can be found in Granada and León, but colonial gems are scattered throughout the country.

To Bury Our Fathers by Sergio Ramírez – one of Nicaragua's most respected writers (and former Sandinista Vice President) – is possibly the best fiction-based portrait of the Somoza years in print.

Land & Wildlife

With more than a million hectares of virgin forest, 19 active volcanoes and vibrant coral reefs, and thriving populations of birds, butterflies, tropical fish, and various species of turtles, Nicaragua has been endowed with more than its share of natural beauty. Combine that with a low population density and very little industrialization and you'll discover that in Nicaragua, wilderness is never far away – and you'll have it mostly to yourself when you get there.

The Land

The formation of the Central American Isthmus began about 60 million years ago, connecting the two massive American continents for the first time three million years ago. Marking the volcanic crush of the Cocos and Caribbean tectonic plates, the Maribios Volcanic Chain is one of the most volcanic places in the world.

There are 40 major volcanic formations, including 28 volcanoes and eight crater lakes, among them Reserva Natural Laguna de Apoyo, with hotels and private homes, Laguna Tiscapa in downtown Managua, and Laguna Asososca, with no development at all.

The region's appeal to early colonists increased as they realized that the soil was further enriched by this striking geological feature. Earthquakes and volcanoes are a part of life along the borders of the Caribbean and Cocos plates, and you'll find very few authentic colonial buildings that haven't been touched up since the 1500s.

Nicaragua's highest mountains, however, are metamorphic, not volcanic. Running down the center of Nicaragua like an opening zipper, they rise to their greatest heights as a granite chain contiguous with the Rocky Mountains and the Andes. They go by several names, including Cordillera Dariense (after Rubén Darío). Topped with cool cloud forests above 1200m, these refreshing regions are home to some of the best national parks and protected areas. Two of the most accessible reserves up north are Área Protegida Miraflor, close to Estelí, and Reserva Natural Cerro Apante, a hike from Matagalpa. Or go deeper, to Reserva Natural Macizos de Peñas Blancas, actually part of Bosawás, the largest protected swath of rainforest north of the Amazon. It's 730,000 hectares of humid tropical and subtropical forest, also accessible by the largest river in Central America, the Río Coco (560km).

Nicaragua also has the two largest lakes in Central America, Lago de Managua (1064 sq km) and Lago de Nicaragua (8264 sq km), with more than 500 islands, some protected, as well as wonderful wetlands, such as Refugio de Vida Silvestre los Guatuzos.

The Atlantic coast is worlds apart, geologically as well as culturally, from the drier, more developed Pacific side. A vast eroding plain of rolling hills and ancient volcanic plugs, here's where around 90% of the country's rainfall ends up. This is the region with the wildest protected reserves and worst access – with very few exceptions, it's difficult and relatively expensive to travel here, as most transportation is by boat. The

You can learn all you ever wanted to know (and probably a fair bit more) about Nicaragua's stunning biodiversity at www.bio-nica.info.

lowlands are remarkable for their dry pine savannas and countless wetlands and have four major river systems. The easiest way in is along the Río San Juan, a Unesco biosphere reserve.

Flora & Fauna

Nicaragua is home to about 1800 vertebrate species, including 250 mammals, and 30,000 species in total, including 688 bird species (around 500 resident and 150 migratory).

Animals are slowly working their way northward, a migration of densities that will one day be facilitated by the Mesoamerican Corridor, a proposed aisle of shady protected rainforest stretching from Panama to Mexico. Other countries in on the agreement are just getting started on the project, but Nicaragua's two enormous Unesco biosphere reserves, Bosawás and Southeast Nicaragua (Río San Juan), make a significant chunk.

The Naturalist in Nicaragua by Thomas Belt was published in 1874 but is still available in reprints. As much about human life as the insects it studies, Charles Darwin called it 'the best of all natural history journals.'

Animals

Most people are looking for monkeys, and there are three natives: big howler monkeys, smaller spider monkeys and sneaky capuchins. Pizotes, elsewhere called coatis, are the long-tailed, toothy-smiled rodents that are particularly bold on the Rivas peninsula – feed them at your own risk. Several cats (pumas, jaguars and others) survive, but you probably won't see them. Baird's tapirs, 250kg herbivores, are another rare treat. At night you'll see hundreds of bats, including, maybe, vampire bats – which usually stick to livestock when feeding.

Birders are discovering Nicaragua, in particular the estuaries of the wild east coast, where migratory birds flock, starting in August and packing places like the Río San Juan and Islas Solentiname by September and October.

While Nicaragua has no endemic bird species of its own, 19 of Central America's 21 endemics are represented here. Nicaragua's spectacular national bird, the turquoise-browed mot mot (*guardabarranco* in Spanish), has a distinctive notched tail.

DID THE EARTH MOVE FOR YOU?

Straddling two tectonic plates has had mixed results for Nicaragua. On the one hand, it's produced the spectacular Maribios chain and the rest of the 40 volcanoes that make up western Nicaragua's dramatic skyline, providing geothermal energy, poetic inspiration and hiking opportunities galore.

On the down side, volcanoes have, over the years, blackened skies, changed landscapes and buried entire villages, not to mention the entire original city of León.

Nicaragua's position between the stationary Caribbean plate and the eastward-moving Cocos plate (the two are colliding at a rate of about 10cm per year) has produced some other geologic excitement as well – most of it spelling bad news for the locals.

Tension builds between colliding plates and is released in the form of earthquakes. Nicaragua gets rocked on a regular basis – the 1972 quake all but flattened Managua, which had already been hit hard in 1931. In 2000, two major quakes in two days leveled villages in the southwest.

When earthquakes happen at sea they cause tsunamis. Tsunamis were registered in 1854 and 1902, but the biggest one in recent history was in 1992, when waves of up to 10m pummeled the Pacific coastline, killing 170 people and leaving 130,000 homeless.

Slower (but no less dramatic) plate movement produced the Lago de Nicaragua – the theory being that the Pacific and Atlantic were once joined, but the upward thrust of earth caused by plate collision cut them off. Volcanic sedimentation and erosion then created the Pacific and Atlantic coastlines.

Kingfishers, swallows, scarlet tanagers and Tennessee warblers are just a few of the birds that make their winter homes here. Local birds are even more spectacular, including the red macaw, the yellow-chested oropendola (which hangs its ball-shaped nests from trees), the three-wattled bellbird of the cloud forests, with its distinctive call, and of course the resplendent quetzal.

Other winged attractions are the uracas (huge blue jays) of Isla de Ometepe, the canaries living inside the fuming crater of Volcán Masaya and the waterfall of Reserva Natural Chocoyero–El Brujo, and the beautiful waterfowl of the Río San Juan.

Other visitors are more interested in the undersea wildlife, which on the Pacific side includes tuna, rooster fish and snook. Lago de Nicaragua and the Río San Juan have their own scaly menagerie, including sawfish, the toothy gaspar, mojarra, guapote and, most importantly, tarpon, as well as the extraordinary freshwater bull shark.

There are lots of reptiles, including five kinds of sea turtle, two kinds of iguana and several snakes. When walking in rainforests, keep your eyes peeled for the feared tercipelo (fer-de-lance, or venomous pit viper), the most dangerous snake in Central America. Unlike many snakes found in the region, it is aggressive and often chooses to attack rather than flee danger. It's common in the jungles of the Río San Juan. Other poisonous snakes to look out for include the coral snake and the cascabel (rattlesnake), a danger mostly to cattle.

Nicaragua also has plenty of scorpions, you'll find them living in dark corners (they love those atmospheric old houses), under rocks, in wood piles and on the beach. But while they look mean, their sting is not lethal and is more like a hardcore bee sting.

Insects, of course, make up the vast majority of species, including more than 1000 species of butterflies. Tarantulas are common, but not deadly, and be on the lookout for leaf-cutter ants, which raise fungus for snacks beneath massive anthills the size of VW Beetles. Acacia ants are hidden inside the hollow thorns of acacia trees – and the weird-looking woody balls in the trees? Termites.

Endangered Species

Nicaragua has about 200 species on the endangered list, including sea turtles and iguanas, both traditional food sources, as well as boa constrictors and alligators. Golden frogs and blood frogs, like amphibians across the globe, are also dwindling. Endangered birds include quetzals, peregrine falcons and macaws, with two of Central America's last viable populations in Reserva Natural Volcán Cosigüina and Reserva Biológica Indio-Maíz. Several endangered or threatened mammals also make their homes here, including howler, white-face and spider monkeys; several kinds of cats, including jaguars and mountain lions; as well as aquatic species such as manatees and dolphins. Offshore fisheries are being, or have been, depleted of oysters, lobsters, green turtles and all manner of fish.

Plants

Nicaragua has four major environment zones, each with very different ecosystems and plants. Dry tropical forests are the rarest, as their location – below 500m, often right by the beach – and seven-month dry season make them perfect places to plant crops and build resort hotels. These forests are home to more than 30 species of hardwood, including precious mahogany.

Some dramatic species found in the ecosystem include strangler figs, which start out as slender vines and end up entombing the host tree in

BIRD BOOKS

Wildlife-watchers migrating to Central America should read L Irby Davis' *Field Guide to the Birds of Mexico & Central America* or Adrian Forsyth's *Tropical Nature: Life & Death in the Rainforests of Central & South America.*

About 18.2% of Nicaragua's land is federally protected as part of 76 wildlife areas. The system isn't even close to perfect, and problems with poaching and deforestation are rife. But the government has deemed it worth fighting for and is stepping up patrols in and around parks.

Nicaragua's national parks and reserves are unlike those in many other countries in that the majority have next to no facilities for visitors. Accommodations within park boundaries are rare, dedicated zones to pitch a tent even more so. There are very few marked trails, and reliable maps of the reserves are also hard to come by, which makes hiring local guides even more important.

Marena administers most wildlife areas, often through other public and private organizations. There's a Marena office in most major towns, and while tourism is not its main job, staff may be able to find guides, transportation and lodging for more-difficult-to-access parks. They can at least point you toward folks who can help; it could be, for example, a women's organic coffee collective. Have fun! Following are Nicaragua's main parks and reserves.

MAJOR PARK OR NATURAL AREA	FEATURES	ACTIVITIES
Parque Nacional Volcán Masaya	most heavily venting volcano in Central America, possible gateway to hell; lava tunnels; parakeets	driving to the edge of an active crater, birdwatching, hiking
Reserva Natural Volcán Concepción & Parque Nacional Volcán Maderas	1 island, 2 volcanoes: gently smoking Concepción & dormant Maderas, crowned in cloud forest	hiking, petroglyph hunting, swimming, kayaking
Reserva Biológica Indio-Maíz	epic riverboat rides, macaws, walking trees, frogs	canoeing, kayaking, hiking
Reserva de Biosfera Bosawás	largest reserve in Central America, indigenous villages	testing your limits on trail-free hikes
Reserva Natural Cerro Musún	quetzals, cloud forests, huge waterfalls, real trails	hiking, birdwatching, swimming
Área Protegida Miraflor	cloud-forest reserve innovatively managed by agricultural cooperative: it's nature & culture!	milking cows, hiking, swimming in waterfalls, admiring orchids
Área Protegida Cerro Tisey-Estanzuela	cloud forests, views across the Maribios Volcanic Chain, goat's cheese	hiking, swimming, eating cheese
Monumento Nacional Cañón de Somoto	the Río Coco is born – in the 'Grand Canyon' of Nicaragua	hiking, rock scrambles, swimming in freezing-cold water
Reserva Natural Isla Juan Venado	sandy Pacific barrier island; mangroves, sea turtles, lagoons	boating, surfing, camping, swimming
Parque Nacional Archipiélago Zapatera	isolated islands covered with petroglyphs, ancient statues, small volcano, rustic accommodations	climbing, hiking, boating, pretending you're an archaeologist
Refugio de Vida Silvestre La Flor	leatherback & olive ridley turtles, primary dry tropical forest, beaches	surfing, camping, sea-turtle ogling
Reserva Natural Volcán Mombacho	volcanic views of Granada & Cocibolca, dwarf cloud forest, 100 species of orchid, fumeroles, butterfly garden	hiking, camping, riding in military transport
Reserva Natural Volcán Cosigüina	volcanoes, hot springs, crater lakes, macaws, archaeological sites	hiking, camping, swimming, thermal baths

a dramatically buttressed encasement; the wide-spreading guanacaste of the endless savannas; and the pithaya, a branch-dwelling cactus with delicious edible fruit. Most plants lose their leaves by January, except in the largest remaining mangrove stand in Central America, partially preserved as Reserva Natural Isla Juan Venado and Reserva Natural Estero Padre Ramos, and crossing borders into El Salvador and Honduras.

Subtropical dry forests have sandy acidic soils and four species of pine tree (this is their southernmost natural border); they can be seen in the Región Autónoma Atlántico Norte (Northern Atlantic Autonomous Region; RAAN) and the Segovias.

Humid tropical forests are home to the multistory green canopies most people think of as classic rainforest. Conditions here are perfect for all plant life; almost no nutrients are stored in the soil, but there is

SEE SEA TURTLES

At least five of the world's sea-turtle species nest on the shores of Nicaragua, all (theoretically) protected except for green turtles, present only on the Atlantic coast and legal to catch July to April.

The most common Pacific turtles, the olive ridley (Paslama), are only 45kg and at their most impressive when invading a nesting beach (July to December, peaking in September and August) in flotillas of 3000 or more that storm ashore at the same time to lay. Often using the same beaches from November to February, leatherbacks (*tora* or *baula)* are the largest (450kg) and rarest of the turtles; because they eat jellyfish they often accidentally consume plastic bags and bottles, which kill them. Both species have edible, and widely available eggs, illegal to harvest but considered by locals to be an aphrodisiac. In this book we do not list establishments that serve them, but if you see them on the menu, make your distaste known to the proprietors.

Hawksbill (carey) turtles – which nest May to November, peaking in October and September – are inedible and have lousy-tasting eggs; they're generally caught only for their shells, which are made into graceful, beautiful jewelry that we hope you won't buy. Loggerhead (caguama) turtles are also inedible, but their 160kg bulk often gets caught in the green-turtle nets.

Most tours only take you to see the eggs being laid, usually between 9pm and 2am, except during olive ridley *arribadas* (arrivals), when the beaches are packed day and night. Babies usually hatch about 60 days later, just before sunrise, then make their run to the sea; it's worth camping to see this. If you want to get more involved, you can hook up with grassroots turtle-conservation initiatives once you arrive, or contact the Cocibolca Foundation (www.mombacho.org) or the **Wildlife Conservation Society** (p227).

Places to see the turtles:

Refugio de Vida Silvestre La Flor (p133) Easily accessible from San Juan del Sur, La Flor's wildlife reserve has the best infrastructure, access and protection for its collection of olive ridley and leatherback turtles – plus camping!

Refugio de Vida Silvestre Río Escalante-Chacocente (p124) Access to this wildlife reserve is limited, but it's within walking distance of rapidly developing Playa El Astillero, so guided tours are just a matter of time.

Reserva Natural Isla Juan Venado Conveniently close to León, and olive ridleys show up right on time.

Reserva Natural Estero Padre Ramos Not much infrastructure, but there's a grassroots turtle-conservation program where you can volunteer.

Pearl Keys This group of expensive-to-access Caribbean islands hosts hawksbill turtles, while green turtles feed on the seagrass just offshore.

Other nesting sites on the Atlantic coast include the Miskito Keys, even more difficult to get to, and Río San Juan Wildlife Preserve, where green, hawksbill and leatherback turtles nest, and which can only be reached via San Juan de Nicaragua, a challenge in itself.

RAINFOREST

a vast web just beneath the fallen leaves of enormous ceibas, formed of tiny roots, fungus and other assorted symbiotes that devour every stray nutrient as soon as it hits the ground.

Cloud forests are found above 1200m and are easily the most impressive (and rarest) biome, with epiphytes, bromeliads (a variety of high-humidity plant that grows in the branches of other trees), mosses, lichens and lots of orchids, which you can see at Reserva Natural Cerro Datanlí–El Diablo, among many other places.

The central subtropical forests of Boaco and Chontales have been largely devoured by cattle ranches, and while there are a few reserves, including Reserva Natural Sierra Amerisque, access to these areas is limited. Just to the east are the Caribbean lowlands, where there are swamps and thick, dense foliage that you can see on the riverboat ride from El Rama.

Environmental Issues

With a developing economy, poor infrastructure and limited resources, Nicaragua faces a tough task in protecting the environment at the same time as lifting its citizens out of poverty.

While there has certainly been progress in recent times, the country still faces a variety of pressing environmental issues.

Deforestation

The Reserva Biologica Indio-Maíz, arguably Nicaragua's best-preserved rainforest, is home to more than 400 bird species, 200 reptile species and four species of wildcats (including puma and jaguar).

One of the biggest environmental issues facing Nicaragua is deforestation – the country has lost about 85% of its virgin forest cover since the colonial period. Since the end of the war, overall forest cover has fallen from 63% to 42%, although the rate of deforestation has slowed somewhat since 2000.

Deforestation is a major issue because it affects the entire biosystem. Root systems prevent erosion, thus keeping water supplies clean of soil runoff. Foliage supplies habitat for wildlife. Trees also help maintain climatic conditions. With climate change, scientists are noticing that pollinating insects are migrating to more favorable environments, leaving plants unpollinated.

Part of the problem is commercial logging. With the national economy struggling after the war, environmental issues took a back seat and liberal governments granted a number of forest concessions that contributed significantly to deforestation.

NICARAGUA'S ECO-WARRIORS

If you see a large bunch of heavily armed men making their way through the canopy while you are in one of the country's nature reserves, don't be alarmed – it's probably just the national army's new Batallón Ecológico (Ecological Batallion).

And if you think Nicaragua is not serious about environmental protection, try telling these guys. Made up of 580 soldiers, the batallion was created in late 2011 to combat deforestation and the illegal lumber trade, and has an annual budget of 6.2 million dollars. It sounds like a reality TV show, but these guys take their job very seriously.

And they've already had some success. Only months after their inception, they seized 112,000 cubic meters of illegally felled lumber in the Wawashang reserve on the Atlantic coast.

But the soldiers don't just carry guns, they also carry shovels so they are able to plant trees in their downtime. Together with the national forestry institute, they have created a network of 28 tree nurseries that will supply saplings for an ambitious reforestation plan in natural reserves affected by illegal logging.

NOT FOR SALE: NICARAGUA'S NATURAL RESOURCES

It's not ecologists or politicians but Nicaragua's indigenous communities that are the most fundamental players in the conservation of the disappearing forests of the Caribbean lowlands.

In 2001 the indigenous Mayangna of Awas-Tingni won a landmark battle when the Inter-American Court ruled that the Nicaraguan government had violated the rights of the community by signing a deal with an Asian company for lumber extraction on 62,000 hectares of the community's land.

Shortly afterward, the national government passed a new autonomy law giving the indigenous communities of the Atlantic autonomous regions free determination of the use of their territories and the management of all natural resources found on their land. Nicaragua has since issued land titles to Awas-Tingni and to many other indigenous groups in both the Región Autónoma Atlántico Sur (South Atlantic Autonomous Region; RAAS) and Región Autónoma Atlántico Norte (North Atlantic Autonomous Region; RAAN).

However, the issuing of titles without providing support to reclaim the lands has created problems for some of the communities. Many indigenous groups don't have the resources to patrol and protect their lands, which are subject to land invasions by *mestizo* farmers. Particularly affected are the indigenous Rama, who number less than 5000, but administer a large territory stretching from the Río San Juan to Bluefields Bay. Many Rama have been displaced by armed farmers who refuse to respect the titles.

Sustainable tourism is one way these communities are able to exercise ownership and derive profits from their lands without destroying precious natural resources.

Illegal logging is another contributing factor, particularly on the Caribbean coast, where the environment ministry has limited resources to patrol and manage vast reserves with difficult access.

Another major concern is the advance of the 'agricultural frontier' – the eastward migration of small farmers slashing and burning forest in the hope of carving out a subsistence livelihood. As the land often occupied is usually humid tropical forest, the soil generally only has enough oomph for two or three harvests, when the would-be farmer has to carve another farm from the jungle. Even more alarming are the wealthy land speculators who illegally clear large tracts of forest, then sell the land and move on.

The traditional dependence on firewood as a means of cooking and heating is another contributor to deforestation, especially affecting the dry tropical forests that surround densely populated regions.

The pine forests of Nueva Segovia took a huge hit from their natural enemy the pine bark beetle in late 1999, with an estimated 6000 hectares of forest destroyed by the time it had finished its rampage. Recent hurricanes, particularly Hurricane Felix in 2007, have felled large numbers of trees in the Caribbean region and caused erosion and landslides in areas that have been deforested.

The tiny strawberry poison dart frog (*Dendrobates pumilio*) is famous for its color morphs, with around 30 different color combinations identified.

Agricultural Chemicals

Another pressing issue is the use of agricultural chemicals, which is widespread in Nicaragua, although nowhere near the levels of its famously 'green' neighbour Costa Rica. Any time you travel in rural areas you'll see farmers decked out with their pump backpacks ready to spray herbicides, fungicides, pesticides or fertilizers on their crops. Chemical use is poorly regulated and many of these products end up in the local river systems.

In 2010 there was a major fish kill in Pearl Lagoon that was unlike any that even older members of the community had seen. Many locals blamed agricultural run-off, either from the local palm-oil plantations or farmlands up the Río Grande de Matagalpa, although a government-sponsored investigation found no evidence of this.

Whether or not it was connected to the fish kill, environmentalists maintain that large-scale African Palm plantations destroy critical habitat for endangered species and contribute to soil erosion.

Mining

While mining companies provide well-paid employment (even if profits do go straight out of the country), conservation groups maintain that cyanide, mercury and other industrial pollutants flow into the water table. The mines in Las Minas are of particular concern to environmentalists because they are located on the edge of the Reserva de Biosfera Bosawás, the largest nature reserve on the Central American isthmus. Small-scale mining in rural Chontales has lead to mercury contamination in local water supplies around La Libertad.

The Mesoamerican Biological Corridor was established in 2008 to protect 106 critically endangered species. It stretches from Panama to Mexico.

Climate Change

Global warming is taking its toll in Nicaragua. Of the 18 original Pearl Keys, six have been swallowed by rising sea levels. A few are visible seasonally, but they are no longer the full islands they used to be. The smaller keys remain at risk.

Nicaragua is also particularly at risk to both flooding and drought. The extended dry period is often followed by heavy downpours. Flooding is made worse by deforestation in catchment areas.

Erratic rains have severely effected small-scale farmers, many of whom have no access to irrigation systems. However, a new water harvesting project in the north of the country is dramatically increasing yields among farmers in that region.

Positive Developments

It's not all ecological doom and gloom. Environmental consciousness is growing within Nicaragua and there have recently been a variety of victories, on small and large scales.

The government has declared the environment a national priority and has made a measurable commitment to fighting deforestation and other pressing environmental issues.

Each municipality now has a department devoted to natural resources and, in general, respect for conservation laws has grown, while practices such as wildlife hunting and trafficking are on the downturn.

The government has also mobilized the army to protect endangered sea turtles and created a special ecological battalion to fight the illegal lumber trade.

Nicaraguans are starting to organize on a community level. Restaurant owners in San Juan del Sur have agreed not to offer menu items made from turtle eggs, and the communities in the Cordillera Volcánica act as volunteer firefighters when wildfires threaten the endangered dry tropical forest. There has also been a significant move toward growing organic coffee and vegetables in the north of the country, with many farming cooperatives adopting chemical-free methods.

Sustainable Harvest International works with indigenous communities to help them move away from slash-and-burn agriculture and toward more sustainable methods. For more info go to www.sustainableharvest.org.

More Information

For an overview of Nicaragua's protected areas, the issues they are facing and some of the efforts being made to save them, start with the official Ministry of the Environmment & Natural Resources website, www.marena.gob.ni (in Spanish). For general activism (some of it related to the environment), check www.nicanet.org.

Survival Guide

Directory A-Z

Accommodations

Ranging from five-star resorts to windowless shacks with shared latrines, you really have your choice of accommodations in developed A-list destinations such as Managua, Granada, León, San Juan del Sur and the Corn Islands. Top-end places start to thin out a bit as you head for the interior.

We divide hotels into categories according to price, then order by author preference. The majority of hotel rooms in Nicaragua have their own bathroom, and in our listings we stipulate when the bathroom is shared, except of course in dorms where the bathroom is always shared.

Absolute peak season in Nicaragua is really only two weeks or so – Christmas and Easter, when entire towns book out and prices skyrocket. Outside that time, many hotels maintain prices year-round. If there is a high season, it's somewhere between November and March – outside the rainy months. We list prices for normal high season, not absolute peak.

BOOK YOUR STAY ONLINE

For more accommodations reviews by Lonely Planet authors, check out http://lonelyplanet.com/hotels/. You'll find independent reviews, as well as recommendations on the best places to stay. Best of all, you can book online.

ADDRESSES IN NICARAGUA

As few streets are named and fewer houses are numbered, Nicaraguans use a unique system for addresses. They take a landmark, then give the distance from it in blocks, using cardinal points for directions.

N	*norte*	north
E	*este*	east
S	*sur*	south
O	*oeste*	west
C	*cuadra*	block

For example, 'de la universidad, 2c S, 1c E' would be two blocks south, then one block east from the university. Some locals use *arriba* (up) and *abajo* (down) to refer to east and west respectively, terminology derived from the rising and setting of the sun.

We sometimes provide other landmark-based addresses such as '*frente catedral*' (in front of the cathedral) in Spanish, so that locals can point you in the right direction.

Budget

Budget hotels, sometimes called *hospedajes*, are inexpensive compared to the rest of Central America. You can almost always get your own clean wooden room, with a window and a shared bathroom, for under US$6 per person per night. Double that and you get a bigger room and a private bathroom. Prices are higher in A-list destinations, where there are always cheap dorm beds (US$8 to US$10) if you're traveling on a shoestring. In less-developed regions, you may be using bucket-flush toilets and bucket showers in this price range. Budget travelers should always bring candles and a flashlight (torch), just in case. If there's no mosquito net, just ask.

Midrange

There's a good midrange option, with clean, modern rooms, private bathroom,

Climate

Bluefields

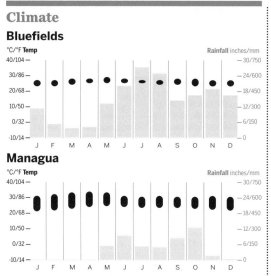

Managua

24-hour electricity, running water and a nice setting or neighborhood, in every major town. It tends to cost US$20 to US$35 for a double; tack on US$10 to US$15 for an A-list destination. Solo travelers usually get, at most, a 20% discount in this category. Also note that hotels in the midrange and top-end categories have a 15% tax added to the rate.

Top End

Luxury accommodations, where they exist, can be a good deal – the most expensive resort in the country clocks in at around US$250 per person, which certainly isn't for everyone, but is a steal compared to Costa Rica. Boutique hotels (with doubles going for US$80 to US$120), are concentrated in Managua, generally have fewer than 10 rooms, and are creatively decorated with lots of little luxuries.

Other Accommodations

In rural areas, there may not be signed guesthouses, but almost all small towns have families who rent rooms. Ask at the *alcaldía* (mayor's office) for leads on weekdays, or any open business on weekends. Some communities have formalized homestays through Spanish schools (you don't need to be a student – just ask at the school) or as part of community-based alternative tourism, such as at Área Protegida Miraflor. Camping

is available in a few private and natural reserves, and is also allowed for free on most less-developed beaches.

Children

Nicaragua, like all Latin American countries, is relatively easy to travel around with children, despite the lack of infrastructure. Parents rarely pay extra for hotels, transportation or other services for youngsters small enough to fit in a lap comfortably, and even complete strangers will make an effort to accommodate and entertain children.

Practicalities

➡ Some top-end (and very few midrange) hotels will be able arrange a cot if you ask ahead.

➡ Major car-rental companies can organize car seats if given enough notice, but don't count on it or expect one at the last minute. Car seats for Nicaraguan toddlers tend to be mom's lap.

➡ Breastfeeding in public is very common and should only really be avoided in places of worship.

➡ Baby formula is widely available, while disposable diapers are available in every *pulpería* (corner store) around the country.

➡ Baby-changing tables are almost nonexistent.

Customs Regulations

When you leave Nicaragua, among the regular list of things that shouldn't be in your backpack are pre-Columbian or early colonial artifacts – you could end up in prison for trying to take these out of the country. On arrival, you can bring pretty much anything legal as long as it's obviously for personal use and not for resale within the country.

SLEEPING PRICE RANGES

Price indicators for sleeping options in our listings denote the cost of a standard double room with private bathroom.

Category	Cost
$	less than US$20
$$	US$20–US$50
$$$	more than US$50

Electricity

120V/60Hz

120V/60Hz

Embassies & Consulates

Most embassies and consulates are located in Managua.

Canadian Embassy (Map p44; ☏2268-0433; http://travel.gc.ca/assistance/embassies-consulates/nicaragua; Los Pipitos, 2c abajo, Bolonia)

Costa Rican Consulate (Map p48; ☏2251-0429; www.rree.go.cr; Rotonda Rubén Darío, 2c E, 500m N; ☺8am-3pm)

Danish Embassy (☏2276-8630; http://nicaragua.um.dk; Plaza España, 2c N, 1½c O)

Dutch Embassy (Map p48; ☏2276-8643; https://netherlands.visahq.com/embassy/nicaragua; Colegio Teresiano, 1c S, 1c O)

French Embassy (Map p44; ☏2228-1056; www.ambafrance-ni.org; Iglesia El Carmen, 1½c O)

German Embassy (Map p44; ☏2266-7500; www.managua.diplo.de; Rotonda El Güegüense, 1½c N)

Guatemalan Embassy (☏2279-9606; Carretera a Masaya Km 11.5)

Honduran Embassy (☏2276-2406; Av del Campo 298, Las Colinas; ☺9am-5pm Mon-Fri)

Mexican Embassy (Map p48; ☏2278-1859; http://embamex.sre.gob.mx/nicaragua; Altamira d'Este, frente Claro)

Panamanian Embassy (Map p44; ☏2266-8633; https://panama.visahq.com/embassy/nicaragua; Cuartel General de Bomberos, 1c E)

Salvadoran Embassy (☏2276-2132; https://el-salvador.visahq.com/embassy/nicaragua; Av del Campo 142, Las Colinas)

US Embassy (☏2266-6010; http://nicaragua.usembassy.gov; Carretera Sur, Km 5.5)

Food

Many Nicaraguans eat lunch on the go, but the majority eat dinner at home, so outside tourist areas you may find eating options are reduced in the evening. Budget eateries including *comedores* (basic eateries), where you choose from a variety of ready-prepared dishes, and market stalls serve a limited range of filling dishes and set meals from US$2 to US$5. Also in this price range are *fritangas* (grills), which serve grilled meats and fried sides.

Midrange eateries will have a decent-sized menu charging US$5 to US$10 per plate. Top-end establishments (mostly found in Granada, Managua and San Juan del Sur) will have an even better range, including dishes from around the world, costing more than US$10.

While both breakfast and dinner are often served with a big scoop of *gallo pinto* (a common meal of blended rice and beans), at lunch the rice and beans are usually separate – it's said to be more filling that way. Be sure to keep an eye out for local specialties including *nacatamales* (banana-leaf-wrapped bundles of cornmeal, meat, vegetables and herbs), *baho* (plantain and beef stew) and *rundown* (seasoned fish or meat cooked in coconut milk with root vegetables).

Nicaragua has a wonderful array of fresh fruits which are often sold cut up in small bags on the side of the road or as *refrescos naturales* (juices in water with sugar).

Gay & Lesbian Travelers

While consensual gay sex was recently decriminalized in Nicaragua, attitudes may take a bit longer to change. As in most of Latin America, gay and lesbian travelers

---

EATING PRICE RANGES

Price indicators for eating options in our listings denote the cost of a typical main course.

Category	Cost
$	less than US$5
$$	US$5–US$10
$$$	more than US$10

will run into fewer problems if they avoid public displays of affection, and ask for two beds and then push them together. That said, lots of Nicaraguan gays and lesbians flaunt their sexuality, so you probably won't have much difficulty figuring out the scene.

There are a small selection of gay and lesbian bars and clubs in Managua and a vaguely tolerant scene in Granada, but apart from that, it's a pretty straight (acting) country.

Health

Most visitors to Nicaragua travel without incident. However, it is a developing nation with poor infrastructure and a tropical climate, and so there are certain things you should be aware of to avoid an unnecessary visit to the doctor.

Stomach problems and diarrhea are the result of bacteria, viruses and parasites which may be present in contaminated food and water. Many other illnesses affecting travelers, such as infected bug bites, rashes and heat exhaustion, are the result of Nicaragua's tropical climate.

Other more serious diseases are carried by infected mosquitoes; bring clothes that provide protection against bites, and repellent.

Particular attention should be paid to the Zika virus which poses serious risks for pregnant women. Travelers who are pregnant should seek medical advice before making plans.

Availability & Cost of Health Care

Medical attention in Nicaragua is cheap; however, apart from in the best clinics in the capital, it is probably not up to the standards you are used to at home.

In rural areas and small towns, English-speaking doctors are hard to find.

Local clinics are fine for dealing with minor illnesses, cuts and sprains, but for anything more serious you should make your way to Managua, where there are several competent private hospitals. If you develop a life-threatening medical problem, you may want to be evacuated to a country with more advanced medical facilities.

Drinking Water

Tap water is potable in cities and larger towns but should be avoided in rural areas and throughout the Región Autónoma Atlántico Sur (South Atlantic Autonomous Region; RAAS) and Región Autónoma Atlántico Norte (North Atlantic Autonomous Region; RAAN). In cheaper restaurants, ice and juices are usually made with untreated water.

Health Insurance

Most health care is cheap in Nicaragua and short-term health insurance is not widely available. Ensure that your travel insurance covers medical bills, hospitalization and evacuation.

For long-term visitors, the Hospital Metropolitano (www.metropolitano.com) in Managua offers a variety of monthly packages that include emergency coverage and discounts on appointments with specialists.

Infectious Diseases

➡ **Dengue fever** is a mosquito-born viral infection transmitted by Aedes mosquitoes. It's most commonly transmitted during the day and usually close to human habitations, often indoors.

➡ **Malaria** Transmitted by mosquitoes, although those that carry the disease prefer to bite in the evening. It's more common in rural areas.

➡ **Leptospirosis** A rare but serious bacterial infection transmitted through water contaminated with animal urine.

➡ **Zika virus** The Zika virus is a mosquito-borne disease that is spreading rapidly through tropical and sub-tropical areas of Latin America. The illness usually causes only mild symptoms including fever, rash, joint pain and red eyes, and most cases don't require hospitalization. However, Zika poses a serious threat to pregnant women, as it is suspected of traveling through the placenta and causing birth defects. Pregnant women should consider postponing travel to areas affected by Zika until the virus has been controlled and more is known about its effects on fetal development. The virus is mainly spread by the Aedes mosquito, which is most active during the day, although can also bite at night. It's often found indoors or close to buildings. The virus can also be spread sexually, so it's important to use condoms while traveling and for three weeks upon returning from a Zika-infected area to avoid affecting partners. For the latest details on the virus and the risks in the region consult the US Center for Disease Control's dedicated web page (www.cdc.gov/zika).

Mosquito Bites

As a number of illnesses are primarily spread by mosquitoes, it is essential that travelers to areas all over Nicaragua take all precautions to avoid bites:

➡ Cover up exposed skin and use liberal amounts of insect repellent containing DEET, picaridin or oil of lemon (OLE).

➡ Treat your clothing and shoes with permethrin solution before arriving in Nicaragua.

➡ When booking accommodations, choose air-conditioned rooms, which offer some protection from bites. If this is not available, look for a room with good screens on the windows.

MEDICAL CHECKLIST

Travelers should consider packing the following items:

➡ antidiarrheal drugs (eg loperamide)

➡ acetaminophen/paracetamol (Tylenol) or aspirin

➡ anti-inflammatory drugs (eg ibuprofen)

➡ antihistamines (for hay fever and allergic reactions)

➡ antibacterial ointment (eg Bactroban) for cuts and abrasions

➡ steroid cream or cortisone (for poison ivy and other allergic rashes)

➡ bandages, gauze, gauze rolls

➡ adhesive or paper tape

➡ scissors, safety pins, tweezers

➡ thermometer

➡ pocket knife

➡ DEET-containing insect repellent for the skin

➡ permethrin-containing insect spray for clothing, tents and bed nets

➡ sunblock

➡ oral rehydration salts

➡ iodine tablets (for water purification)

➡ syringes and sterile needles

➡ tampons

➡ contraceptive pills

Recommended Vaccinations

There are no obligatory vaccinations for Nicaragua, with the exception of yellow fever for travelers arriving from affected areas. However, you may consider getting typhoid and hepatitis shots before you set out. Some travelers also choose to take anti-malaria medications.

Insurance

Nicaragua is an unpredictable kind of place and infrastructure is poor, so travel insurance is always a good idea. Health care is generally cheap but in many places well below acceptable standards. Insurance is essential in the case of a big emergency, so that you can get transport to and treatment at the best private hospitals in Managua.

Make sure your policy covers emergency helicopter evacuation, full coverage for lost luggage and, if you're into it, extreme sports.

Worldwide travel insurance is available at www.lonely-planet.com/travel-insurance. You can buy, extend and claim online any time, even if you're on the road.

Internet Access

Internet access on the Pacific coast is fast (US$0.50 to US$0.70 per hour), cheap and widely available, even in small towns. The Caribbean coast has slightly slower, more expensive internet service, which is not widely available. Top-end hotels mostly have 'business centers' and often connections for laptops and wi-fi in rooms. The computer icon used in our hotel listings signifies that the hotel has a computer with free internet access available to guests.

Public wi-fi in restaurants and cafes is becoming more common, but is still rare outside big cities. Consider purchasing a USB modem, which works well in larger cities but is often very slow in rural areas.

Nicaragua's mobile data network is continually improving and works fairly well in big cities but can be painfully slow in rural towns, where everyone is trying to get online through one tower. SIM cards are cheap and prepaid internet packets are also very affordable.

Legal Matters

Nicaragua's police force is professional and visible, and very approachable by Central American standards.

For minor traffic violations your driver's license will normally be confiscated, and you will need to go to the bank to pay your fine and then to the nearest police station to retrieve your document. This can be a pain if you are only driving through. Some people advocate slipping traffic cops a 100-córdoba (US$4) bill with your ID to smooth out minor traffic violations, but that could always backfire. It's best to play it cool and hope they let you off with just a warning.

If you get caught with drugs or committing a more serious crime, it won't be that easy to get away from the law.

Maps

Detailed maps are hard to find inside Nicaragua, so consider purchasing one before you arrive if you plan to get off the beaten track.

Intur (www.intur.gob.ni) Offices have a tourist-oriented regional and city map.

Ineter (Nicaragua Institute for Territorial Studies; ☎2249-3890; www.ineter.gob.ni; frente Dirección de Migración y Extranjería, Managua) Has the best selection of detailed maps in the country. Many are out of print, but bring a flash drive and they'll upload the files.

International Travel Maps & Books (www.itmb.ca) Publishes a detailed road map (US$12.95), but don't trust it completely for secondary roads.

Mapas Naturismo (www. mapas-naturismo.com) Has a detailed road map but it hasn't been reprinted in a while and lacks new developments, especially in the north of the country (US$9).

Money

Nicaragua's currency is the córdoba (C$), sometimes called a *peso* or *real* by locals. Córdobas come in coins of C$0.50, C$1, C$5 and plastic bills of C$10, C$20, C$50, C$100, C$200 and C$500. Older plastic bills are flimsy and tear easily and some paper bills remain in circulation. Bills of C$200 and larger can be difficult to change; try the gas station.

US dollars are accepted almost everywhere, but they will be rejected if they are even slightly marked, ripped or damaged. Córdobas are usually easier to use, particularly at smaller businesses and anywhere off the beaten track – always keep at least 200 córdobas on you, preferably in smaller bills.

The córdoba is devalued according to a fixed plan against the US dollar. Our listings give prices in US dollars (US$), as the costs in córdoba are more likely to fluctuate.

ATMs & Banks

ATMs (*cajeros automáticos*) are the easiest way to access cash in Nicaragua. They are available in most major towns and tourist regions.

Visa is the most widely accepted card followed by MasterCard. Amex is not generally accepted. Most Nicaraguan ATMs charge a fee (around US$3) on top of what your bank charges.

It's possible to organize a cash advance over the counter in many banks. Traveler's checks are inconvenient and no longer widely accepted in the country.

Branches of the following banks have reliable ATMs:

BAC Visa/Plus and MasterCard/Cirrus

Bancentro La Fise Visa/Plus and MasterCard/Cirrus

BanPro Visa/Plus and MasterCard/Cirrus

Banco ProCredit Visa/Plus

Credit Cards

Visa and MasterCard are accepted throughout Nicaragua, and you can almost always count on midrange hotels and restaurants to accept them. In places where electricity is unreliable – for instance, most of the Caribbean coast – credit cards may not be widely accepted, so be prepared.

Moneychangers

Moneychangers (*coyotes*) are regularly used by locals to change córdobas for US dollars at about the same rates as the banks. *Coyotes* in cities and towns are generally honest, but you should know the exchange rate and how much to expect in the exchange. *Coyotes* may also exchange other currencies, including euros, UK pounds, Canadian dollars, Honduran lempira and Costa Rican colones, for a much larger fee.

Coyotes at border crossings are much less reputable. Stay on your toes and avoid changing large amounts.

Tipping

Tipping is not widespread in Nicaragua except with guides and at restaurants.

➡ **Guides** Tipping guides is recommended as this often makes up the lion's share of their salary.

➡ **Restaurants** A tip of around 10% is expected for table service. Some high-end restaurants automatically add this to the bill. Small and/or rural eateries may not include the tip, so leave behind a few coins.

Opening Hours

Opening hours vary wildly in Nicaragua as there are many informal and family-run establishments. General office hours are from 9am to 5pm. Some offices and shops, especially in rural areas, close for lunch from noon to 2pm. Government departments usually close slightly earlier and also take a meal break.

Comedores (cheap eateries) usually open for breakfast and lunch while more formal restaurants serve lunch and dinner.

Banks 8:30am–4:30pm Monday to Friday, to noon Saturday

Comedores 6am–4pm

Government Offices 8am–noon & 1–4pm Monday to Friday, 8am to noon Saturday

Museums 9am–noon & 2–5pm

Restaurants noon–10pm

Bars noon–midnight

Clubs 9pm–3am

Shops 9am–6pm Monday to Saturday

Post

Considering that there are no real addresses in Nicaragua, the mail service is surprisingly effective. It costs about US$0.80 to send a standard letter or postcard to the US, about US$1 to Europe. You can receive mail at any post office by having it addressed as follows:

(*your name*)
Lista de Correo
Correo Central
(*town name*)
Nicaragua

Make sure you bring your passport when you go to check your mail, and don't leave mail sitting there for more than two weeks.

Public Holidays

New Year's Day (January 1) Shops and offices start closing at noon on December 31.

Semana Santa (Holy Week; Thursday, Friday and Saturday before Easter Sunday) Beaches are packed, hotel rates skyrocket and everything is closed – make sure you have a place to be.

Labor Day (May 1)

Mother's Day (May 30) No one gets away with just a card – more places close than at Christmas.

Anniversary of the Revolution (July 19) No longer an official holiday, but many shops and government offices close anyway.

Battle of San Jacinto (September 14)

Independence Day (September 15)

Día de los Difuntos (November 2) All Souls' Day.

La Purísima (December 8) Immaculate Conception.

Navidad (December 25) Christmas.

Safe Travel

Despite the fact that Nicaragua has one of the lowest crime rates in Central America, as a 'wealthy' foreigner you will at least be considered a potential target by scam artists and thieves.

➡ Pay extra attention to personal safety in Managua, the Caribbean region, around remote southern beaches and in undeveloped nature reserves.

➡ In larger cities, ask your hotel to call a trusted taxi.

➡ Backcountry hikers should note there may be unexploded ordnance in very remote areas, especially

around the Honduran border. If in doubt, take a local guide.

Telephone

Nicaragua's calling code is 505. There are no area codes within Nicaragua. While less common with the wide adoption of mobile (cell) phones, some homes and businesses 'rent' their phone for a fee (usually around US$0.25 per minute) for national calls to landlines and cell phones. Direct calls abroad using the phone network or cell phones are expensive – any internet cafe will offer much cheaper rates.

Cell Phones

Many travelers simply buy a phone upon arrival – prices start at around US$15, and there are phone shops at the airport. You can also buy a SIM card (around US$3.50) and insert it into any unlocked GSM phone. The two phone companies are Claro and Movistar, which now have similar levels of coverage. Electronic top-ups are available at *pulperías* and gas stations all over the country.

Time

Local time in Nicaragua is GMT-6, equivalent to CST in the US.

Toilets

➡ In cities and towns, toilets are your regular sit-down flush variety.

➡ Public toilets are not common but most businesses will let you use their facilities.

➡ As you venture into rural areas you will come across dry latrines, little more than a hole in the ground covered by a wooden box.

➡ There is often no toilet paper in public bathrooms. Always carry a spare roll. And when you've finished,

throw it in the trash basket, don't flush it – the pipes get blocked easily.

Tourist Information

Intur (Nicaraguan Institute of Tourism; ☎ 2222-3333; www. visitanicaragua.com/ingles), the government tourism office, has branches in most major cities. It can always recommend hotels and activities (but not make reservations) and point you toward guides. The *alcaldía* (mayor's office) is your best bet in small towns without a real tourist office. Although tourism is not the mayor's primary function, most will help you find food, lodging, guides and whatever you might need. In indigenous communities, there may not be a mayor, as many still have councils of elders. Instead, ask for the president (or *wihta* in Miskito communities), who probably speaks Spanish and can help you out.

Travelers with Disabilities

While Nicaraguans are generally accommodating toward people with mobility issues, and will gladly give you a hand getting around, the combination of cobbled streets, cracked sidewalks and stairs in pretty much every building can make life tough.

There are few regular services for disabled travelers and because of difficulties in finding suitable transport, it's easiest to go through a tour company. Vapues Tours (www.vapues.com) is an experienced local operator, specializing in accessible travel. There are very few wheelchair-accessible toilets and bathrooms in Nicaragua, so bringing toilet-seat extensions and wall-mountable mobility aids are highly recommended.

Visas

Visitors from most countries can stay in Nicaragua for up to 90 days without a visa, as long as they have a passport valid for six months, proof of sufficient funds (US$200 cash or a credit card) and an onward ticket (rarely checked).

Citizens of some parts of Eastern Europe and Latin America, and many African and Asian nations, need visas to enter Nicaragua, while others can apply for a visa on arrival. Check the Nicaraguan Foreign Ministry website (http://oaip.cancilleria.gob.ni) for the full lists.

Nicaragua is part of the CA-4, a regional agreement covering Nicaragua, Honduras, El Salvador and Guatemala. Officially, you can only stay for 90 days maximum in the *entire* CA-4, at which point you can get one extension of 90 days from the **Migración (Immigration) office** (Dirección de Migración y Extranjería; ☎2244-3989; www.migob.gob.ni/dgme; Semaf Tenderí, 200m N) in Managua for around US$10 per month. After those 90 days, you must leave the region (this means going to Costa Rica, basically) for 72 hours, which automatically renews your visa.

Don't bet on it, but flying between CA-4 countries may get you another 90 days on landing, especially if you transit a nation outside the agreement. Land border officials are stricter in adhering to the regulations.

Volunteering

Nicaragua has a very developed volunteer culture, traceable to the influx of 'Sandalistas' (young foreign volunteers) during the revolution. Many hostels and Spanish schools maintain lists of organizations. Also check out Volunteer South America (www.volunteer-southamerica.net) and Go Abroad (www.goabroad.com).

Local Organizations

Fundación del Río (www.fundaciondelrio.org) Runs environmental and social projects in the Río San Juan.

UCA San Ramón (www.ucasanramon.com) Works with rural coffee-growing communities near Matagalpa.

International Organizations

Habitat for Humanity (www.habitatnicaragua.org) Construction brigades work on new housing in impoverished communities.

Seeds of Learning (www.seedsoflearning.org) Sends work brigades with an educational focus to Nicaragua.

Techo (www.techo.org) Operates poverty-reduction projects in impoverished urban areas.

Women Travelers

The biggest problems that many solo female travelers encounter in Nicaragua are the *piropos* (catcalls) and general unwanted attention from men. Nicaragua is not particularly dangerous for women, but you know the drill: dress conservatively (knees should be covered, though shoulders are OK), especially when in transit; avoid drinking alone at night; and – this is the hard one – reconsider telling off the catcalling guy, as he might become violent. Sigh. The Caribbean coast is more dangerous in general, so all this goes double there.

Work

Nicaragua is one of the poorest countries in the hemisphere, with almost 50% of its adults unemployed or underemployed. Thus, finding a job in Nicaragua is difficult and taking one that a Nicaraguan could be doing is probably just plain wrong. Backpacker-oriented businesses may offer you under-the-table employment, usually in exchange for room and board, but this is mostly about extending your vacation. If you're a serious, qualified English teacher, you may be able to find a job in an international school or private-language center.

To legally work in Nicaragua you are required to apply for a work permit through the immigration office.

Transportation

GETTING THERE & AWAY

Nicaragua is accessible by air via the international airport in Managua, by road using five major border crossings with Honduras and Costa Rica, and by boat between El Salvador and Potosí, and Costa Rica and San Carlos.

Flights, cars and tours can be booked online at lonelyplanet.com/bookings.

Entering the Country

All visitors entering Nicaragua are required to purchase a Tourist Card for US$10.

Those entering by land also pay a US$2 migration processing fee. Upon departure by land or boat there is another US$2 migration fee while a small municipal charge – usually around US$1 – may also be levied

by the local government depending on the border crossing.

Air

Upon arrival in Nicaragua by air, visitors are required to purchase a tourist card for US$10; make sure to have US currency handy.

It's worth checking fares to neighboring Costa Rica, which is an air-conditioned bus ride away and may be significantly cheaper.

Airports & Airlines

Nicaragua's main international hub is Managua International Airport, a small, manageable airport that doesn't receive many flights but does have connecting services to Miami, Fort Lauderdale, Atlanta and Houston in the US, and several major cities within Central America.

Nicaragua has no national airline, but is served by the following carriers.

American Airlines www.aa.com
Avianca www.avianca.com
Copa www.copaair.com
Delta www.delta.com
Spirit www.spirit.com
United www.united.com

Land

Border Crossings

Nicaragua shares borders with Costa Rica and Honduras. Generally, Nicaraguan border crossings are chaotic (there are no signs anywhere), but the procedure is fairly straightforward provided you have your documents in order.

Ocotal to Tegucigalpa, Honduras See the sunny Segovias and the Honduran capital at this major, business-like border. The Las Manos crossing point is efficient, although sometimes crowded.

Somoto to Choluteca, Honduras A high-altitude crossing that

CLIMATE CHANGE & TRAVEL

Every form of transport that relies on carbon-based fuel generates CO_2, the main cause of human-induced climate change. Modern travel is dependent on airplanes, which might use less fuel per kilometer per person than most cars but travel much greater distances. The altitude at which aircraft emit gases (including CO_2) and particles also contributes to their climate change impact. Many websites offer 'carbon calculators' that allow people to estimate the carbon emissions generated by their journey and, for those who wish to do so, to offset the impact of the greenhouse gases emitted with contributions to portfolios of climate-friendly initiatives throughout the world. Lonely Planet offsets the carbon footprint of all staff and author travel.

comes with an amazing granite canyon. Crossing point El Espino is laid-back and easy.

El Guasaule to Choluteca, Honduras The fastest route from Nicaragua, an easy cruise north from lovely León. The El Guasaule crossing is hot, hectic and disorganized.

Sapoá to Peñas Blancas, Costa Rica The main border crossing is generally easy unless your arrival coincides with an international bus or two, in which case it could take hours. The local municipality charges an additional US$1 fee at this crossing.

Bus

International buses have reclining seats, air-conditioning, TVs, bathrooms and sometimes even food service, and are definitely safer for travelers with luggage. Crossing borders on international buses is generally hassle free. At many borders the helper will take your passport, collect your border fees, get your stamp and return your passport to you as you get back on the bus. At the Costa Rican border post at Peñas Blancas you must complete the formalities in person.

There are direct bus services (without changing buses) to Costa Rica, Honduras, El Salvador and Guatemala, and connecting services to Panama and Mexico.

King Quality (www.king-quality ca.com) Luxury buses to Costa Rica, Honduras, El Salvador and Guatemala.

Nica Expreso (www.nicaexpreso. com) Runs from Chinandega (via León) to San José, Costa Rica.

Tica Bus (Map p44; ☏8739-5505; www.ticabus.com) Travels to Costa Rica, Honduras and El Salvador with connecting services to Guatemala, Mexico and Panama.

Transnica (Map p48; ☏2270-3133; www.transnica.com) Serves Costa Rica, Honduras and El Salvador.

Transporte del Sol (Map p44; ☏2422-5000;

www.busesdelsol.com) Same-day service to Guatemala and San Salvador.

COSTA RICA

There are several bus companies running direct services between San José and Managua. The journey usually takes around nine to 10 hours and costs around US$29.

EL SALVADOR

Although there is no common border, there are several direct buses a day to San Salvador passing through Choluteca in Honduras. The journey costs US$35 to US$50 and takes around 11 hours, but may be significantly longer if there are delays at any of the two border crossings.

HONDURAS

There are two main bus routes between Honduras and Nicaragua. From Tegucigalpa it's around seven to 10 hours and costs US$23 to US$30, while from San Pedro Sula it's 11 hours and costs US$37.

Car & Motorcycle

To bring a vehicle into Nicaragua, you'll need the originals and several copies of the ownership papers (in your name), your passport and a driver's license.

You'll get a free 30-day permit (lose it and you'll be fined) and you will need to purchase obligatory accident insurance for US$12. You may also be required to pay US$3 to US$4 for the fumigation of your vehicle. Your passport will be stamped saying you brought a vehicle into the country; if you try to leave without it, you'll have to pay import duty. It's possible to extend the vehicle permit twice at the DGA office in Managua before you have to leave the country.

You can now drive across two border crossings to Costa Rica. The most popular is at Sapoá–Peñas Blancas

near Rivas; the new crossing at San Pancho-Las Tablillas in the Río San Juan still sees few vehicles.

It's possible to drive across the Nicaragua–Honduras border at El Guasaule, Somoto–El Espino and Ocotal–Las Manos.

River

The river crossing between San Carlos and Los Chiles, Costa Rica is a breeze – a gorgeous boat ride down an egret-lined river. From Los Chiles there are regular bus services onto Ciudad Quesada and San José.

You can also cross into Honduras from Waspám to Puerto Lempira, but it's a serious jungle adventure.

Sea

It's now possible to travel directly between Nicaragua and El Salvador by boat through the Golfo de Fonseca. Ruta del Golfo (www.rutadelgolfo.com) runs a boat from Potosí on the Cosigüina peninsula to La Unión (two hours, US$65) every Tuesday and Friday. It also runs connecting minibus shuttles to León (US$35), and San Salvador and Suchitoto (US$35). Prices do not include *migración* (immigration) fees.

GETTING AROUND

Air

The hub for domestic flights is Managua International Airport. Other airports are simple affairs and some are little more than dirt strips outside town (or in Siuna and Waspám, in the middle of town). The airport in San Juan de Nicaragua is located across the bay in Greytown and is one of the few airports in the Americas where you need to take a boat to get on your flight.

There is one domestic carrier, **La Costeña** (✆2263-2142; www.lacostena.com.ni; Managua International Airport), which services Bluefields, the Corn Islands, Las Minas, Ometepe, Tola, San Carlos, San Juan de Nicaragua (Greytown), Bilwi and Waspám. Many domestic flights use tiny single-prop planes where weight is important and bags necessarily get left behind, so keep all necessities in your carry-on luggage.

Note that La Costeña is one of the few airlines that actually charges more to book online – a US$18 surcharge.

Bicycle

Nicaragua gets praise from long-distance cyclists for its smooth, paved roads and wide shoulders. Apart from in the mountainous northern region, the main highways through the country are also fairly flat, which gives cyclists plenty of opportunities to enjoy the spectacular scenery.

Bicycles are the most common form of private transport in the country and most drivers are used to seeing them everywhere from main highways to country roads. However, while the infrastructure is designed to accommodate bicycles, the extremely limited enforcement of speed limits and drink-driving legislation is an issue, and the hazards of riding on Nicaraguan roads are not negligible.

Rental

Renting bicycles is difficult outside Granada, San Juan del Sur, Ometepe and León, but your hotel can probably arrange it for you. Bikes rent for around US$5 per day – weekly discounts are easily arranged. Bike-rental places may require a few hundred córdobas or your passport as deposit.

Purchase

Buying a bike is easily done; even the smallest towns will have somewhere selling them. The price-to-quality ratio is not great – expect to pay a little under US$100 for a bottom-of-the-line model. Something fancy will probably cost more than it would back home. Selling your bike when you leave is a matter of luck; places such as Granada, León and San Juan del Sur all have notice boards in travelers' cafes, which would be your best bet. As a last shot, try selling it to a bike-rental place, but don't expect to recoup much of your investment.

Boat

Many destinations are accessible only, or most easily, by boat. Public *pangas* (small open motorboats) with outboard motors are much more expensive than road transport – in general it costs around US$6 to US$8 per hour of travel. In places without regular service, you will need to hire your own private *panga*. Prices vary widely, but you'll spend about US$50 to US$100 per hour for four to six people; tour operators can usually find a better deal. It's easy, if not cheap, to hire boat transport up and down the Pacific coast. On the Atlantic side, it's much more difficult. While it's not common, boats *do* sink here and tourists

have drowned – please wear your life jacket.

River boats on the Río San Juan tend to be slow and fairly cheap. There are often express and regular services – it's worth paying a bit extra for the quicker version.

Following are the major departure points with regular boat service.

Bluefields To Pearl Lagoon, El Rama and Corn Islands.

Corn Islands Regular boats run between Great Corn and Little Corn Islands.

El Rama To Bluefields.

San Carlos To the Islas Solentiname, the Río San Juan, the scenic border crossing to Costa Rica and several natural reserves.

Waspám The gateway to the Río Coco.

Bus

Bus coverage in Nicaragua is extensive although services are often uncomfortable and overcrowded. Public transport is usually on old Bluebird school buses, which means no luggage compartments. Try to avoid putting your backpack on top of the bus, and instead sit toward the back and put it with the sacks of rice and beans.

Pay your fare after the bus starts moving. You may be issued a paper 'ticket' on long-distance buses – don't lose it, or you may be charged again. Some bus terminals allow you to purchase tickets ahead of time, which should in theory guarantee you a seat. While buses sometimes cruise around town before hitting the highway, you're more likely to get a seat by boarding the bus at the station or terminal.

Bus terminals, often huge, chaotic lots next to markets, may seem difficult to navigate, particularly if you don't speak much Spanish. Fear not! If you can pronounce your destination, the guys yelling will help you find your bus – just make sure they put you on an *expreso* (express) and not an *ordinario* (ordinary bus) or you'll be spending more time on the road than you planned.

Costs & Classes

Buses generally cost around US$1 per hour/50km, a bit more for *expreso* (express) buses, which supposedly only stop in designated bus bays. *Ordinarios* or *ruteados* (ordinary buses) stop everywhere and for everyone, and will turn off the highway to enter towns along the way.

Faster microbuses cost about 25% more, and service most major routes, with vans leaving when full. Some very remote rural destinations accessed only by bad roads will use covered military trucks with bench seats. These cost about the same as a regular bus but are way less comfortable.

Shuttle buses are privately owned minibuses that zip between major tourist destinations. They're OK value if you're traveling alone and can't handle another public bus, but if there are two (or more) of you, a taxi often works out to be cheaper and more convenient.

Car & Motorcycle

Driving is a wonderful way to see Pacific and central Nicaragua, but it's best to use public transport on the Caribbean side as roads are, for the most part, terrible.

Driver's Licence

Your home driver's license is valid for driving in Nicaragua for the duration of the entry stamp in your passport.

Fuel & Spare Parts

Gas stations are generally located on the outskirts of major towns and cities and can be rare in rural locations. The availability of spare parts depends on the make of your car. Toyota, Nissan and Hyundai are the most common,

and parts are widely available. For other makes you may have a frustrating wait while parts arrive from Miami.

Hire

To hire a car, you'll need a driver's license and major credit card. Most rental companies want you to be at least 25 years old. Renting a car at Managua International Airport costs 15% extra, so consider taking a taxi to an off-site office.

Following are some of the better car-rental agencies:

Budget (www.budget.com.ni)

Dollar (www.dollar.com.ni) Also rents vehicles with drivers in the Managua area.

Hertz (☑airport 2233-1237; www.hertz.com.ni; Managua International Airport)

Lugo (Map p44;☑2266-4477; www.lugorentacar.com.ni; Canal 2, 2c N, 3c O, Managua)

Insurance

Whether renting or driving your own vehicle you must purchase obligatory third-party insurance. If arriving in Nicaragua in your own vehicle, you'll purchase

it at the border. For rentals it costs around US$12 per day.

When renting, you'll also be recommended supplemental insurance, ranging from US$10 to US$30 per day depending on the coverage and excess. Your credit card may already cover it; call to make sure.

Road Conditions

Road conditions vary wildly throughout the country, although there has been some progress with continuing projects to improve them.

The Panamericana (Pan-American Hwy) is paved all the way from Honduras to Costa Rica while the roads from Managua to both El Rama and San Carlos are also wide, paved highways.

Some secondary roads are very good, particularly in the north, while others are suspension breakers. Access to Pacific beaches is generally poor, as is the majority of the road network on the Atlantic side.

There are no up-to-date maps showing real road conditions, which change every rainy season. Ask locals if you're not sure. Older paved roads are often horribly

---

NICARAGUA'S TRAVELING TRADERS

Who said traveling by bus is boring? In Nicaragua not only are there awe-inspiring volcanic landscapes to gaze at through the windows, but inside the bus is a whole world of entertainment.

And we're not talking about the soft-rock soundtrack or classic Steven Seagal marathon on the tiny TV. The real entertainment on Nicaragua's battle-scarred school buses comes from the traveling salesmen, particularly those hawking cut-priced medicines and ointments.

Need to get smarter before arriving in Rivas? No problem. Hair-loss issues? There's an elixir to cure both of these. And you probably didn't even know that in addition to your backpack, you were carrying around all those parasites on the unnecessarily graphic images on the salesman's full-color poster.

While they are not doctors, nor even pharmacists, these 'medicine men' must be on to something as they always do a brisk trade. Although they haven't yet cracked the traveler market – perhaps the lack of a hangover cure has something to do with it.

pockmarked with axle-cracking potholes. One tactic is to get behind a local driver and follow them swerve for swerve. It can be helpful to keep an eye on older tire tracks.

You'll often see people with shovels pointing to a dirt-filled pothole, which they just fixed for free. They're asking for a couple of córdobas (US$0.10) from you for their efforts.

During rainy season, roads flood, wash away and close. Some roads are never recommended for casual drivers, including the Río Blanco–Bilwi road, easily the worst in the country.

Road Hazards

The biggest danger on Nicaragua's highways isn't other cars (although gas stations selling liquor is a worry), but rather everything else that uses the roads: from bicycle rickshaws to drunk, staggering pedestrians and wandering wildlife. It's best to have an eagle eye and keep speeding to a minimum. Driving after dark is best avoided if possible, as it is difficult to spot the many potential hazards on unlit roads.

Road Rules

Nicaragua's traffic laws are pretty standard and universally ignored, although driving on the right, giving way to anything bigger than you, wearing a seat belt at all times and keeping speeds well below 50km/h in cities should keep you out of trouble.

Many towns are mazes of unsigned one-way streets that prove a boon to traffic cops.

There have been reports that traffic cops target foreigners, looking for a quick shakedown. Officers may wave drivers over and accuse them of something as vague

as 'poor driving.' Drivers should never initiate a bribe – it may be an honest officer who just wants to give a warning. If a bribe is requested, prudent drivers pay it.

If a real ticket is issued, you'll need to surrender your license and then pay the fine at the bank, before picking up your documents at the departmental police station closest to the infraction (which may be a fair distance from your final destination). The procedure may take several days and is more than a little inconvenient.

Hitchhiking & Ride-Sharing

Hitching is never entirely safe, and we don't recommend it. Travelers who hitch should understand that they are taking a small but potentially serious risk.

Nevertheless hitchhiking is very common in Nicaragua, even by solo women – to find a ride, just stick out your thumb. Foreign women, particularly those carrying all their bags, should think twice before hitchhiking solo. Never hitchhike into or out of Managua.

In rural areas where bus service is rare, anyone driving a pick up truck will almost certainly stop for you. Climb into the back tray (unless specifically invited up front) and when you want to get off, tap on the cabin roof a couple of times.

You should always offer to pay the driver, which will almost always be refused.

Local Transportation

Bus

The only city really big enough to warrant catching local buses is Managua,

where pickpockets and bag slashers may make you think twice. If you can keep your wits (and belongings) about you, there are some handy cross-town routes that could save you some coins on taxi fares.

Rickshaw & tuk-tuk

In smaller towns there are fewer taxis and more *tuk-tuks* (motorized three wheelers) and *triciclos* (bicycle rickshaws). They're inexpensive – around US$0.50 per person to go anywhere in town – and kind of fun (although the *triciclo* driver pedaling around Rivas wearing the 'I love my job' T-shirt was probably overstating the case slightly).

Taxi

Almost all taxis in Nicaragua are *colectivos* (shared taxi or minibus), which stop and pick up other clients en route to your destination, however it is always possible to pay a bit extra for an express service.

Managua taxis are unmetered and notorious for ripping off tourists. Always negotiate the fare before getting in. Taxis at major border crossings may also overcharge, given the chance.

Most other city taxis have set in-town fares, usually around US$0.50 to US$0.70, rising slightly at night. Ask a local how much a fare should cost before getting into the cab.

Hiring taxis between cities is a comfortable and reasonable option for midrange travelers. Prices vary widely, but expect to pay around US$10 for every 20km.

Language

Spanish is the national language of Nicaragua. Latin American Spanish pronunciation is easy, as there's a clear and consistent relationship between what you see written and how it's pronounced. Also, most sounds have equivalents in English.

Note that kh is a throaty sound (like the 'ch' in the Scottish *loch*), v and b are like a soft English 'v' (between a 'v' and a 'b'), and r is strongly rolled. There are some variations in spoken Spanish across Latin America, the most notable being the pronunciation of the letters *ll* and *y*. In our pronunciation guides they are represented with y because they are pronounced as the 'y' in 'yes' in most of Latin America. Note, however, that in some parts of the continent they sound like the 'lli' in 'million'. Read our colored pronunciation guides as if they were English, and you'll be understood. The stressed syllables are indicated with italics in our pronunciation guides.

The polite form is used in this chapter; where both polite and informal options are given, they are indicated by the abbreviations 'pol' and 'inf'. Where necessary, both masculine and feminine forms of words are included, separated by a slash and with the masculine form first, eg *perdido/a* (m/f).

BASICS

Hello.	*Hola.*	o·la
Goodbye.	*Adiós.*	a·dyos
How are you?	*¿Qué tal?*	ke tal

Fine, thanks.	*Bien, gracias.*	byen gra·syas
Excuse me.	*Perdón.*	per·don
Sorry.	*Lo siento.*	lo syen·to
Please.	*Por favor.*	por fa·vor
Thank you.	*Gracias.*	gra·syas
You are welcome.	*De nada.*	de na·da
Yes./No.	*Sí./No.*	see/no

My name is ...
Me llamo ...   me ya·mo ...

What's your name?
¿Cómo se llama Usted? ko·mo se ya·ma oo·ste (pol)
¿Cómo te llamas?   ko·mo te ya·mas (inf)

Do you speak English?
¿Habla inglés?   a·bla een·gles (pol)
¿Hablas inglés?   a·blas een·gles (inf)

I don't understand.
Yo no entiendo.   yo no en·tyen·do

ACCOMMODATIONS

I'd like a single/double room.
Quisiera una	kee·sye·ra oo·na
habitación	a·bee·ta·syon
individual/doble.	een·dee·vee·dwal/do·ble

How much is it per night/person?
| *¿Cuánto cuesta por* | kwan·to kwes·ta por |
| *noche/persona?* | no·che/per·so·na |

Does it include breakfast?
¿Incluye el desayuno? een·kloo·ye el de·sa·yoo·no

campsite	*terreno de cámping*	te·re·no de kam·peeng
guesthouse	*pensión*	pen·syon
hotel	*hotel*	o·tel
youth hostel	*albergue juvenil*	al·ber·ge khoo·ve·neel
air-con	*aire acondicionado*	ai·re a·kon·dee·syo·na·do

EL VOSEO

Nicaragua differs from much of Latin America in its use of the informal 'you' form. Instead of *tuteo* (the use of *tú*), Nicaraguans commonly speak with *voseo* (the use of *vos*), a relic from 16th-century Spanish requiring a slightly different form of verbs. Examples of *-ar*, *-er* and *-ir* verbs are given below – the pronoun *tú* is only given for contrast. Imperative forms (commands) also differ, but negative imperatives are identical in *tuteo* and *voseo*.

The most common irregular verb you'll hear is *ser* (to be). In much of the Spanish-speaking world, you may be asked *¿De dónde eres?* (Where are you from?), but in Nicaragua, be prepared for *¿De dónde sos?*

This chapter uses the *tú* form in relevant phrases, as it's more useful throughout Latin America – Nicaraguans will have no trouble understanding if you only use the *tú* form.

A Nicaraguan inviting a foreigner to address him or her informally will say *Me podés tutear* (literally, 'you can address me with *tú*') even though they'll use the *vos* form in subsequent conversation.

Verb	Tuteo	Voseo
hablar (to speak): You speak./Speak!	*Tú hablas./¡Habla!*	*Vos hablás./¡Hablá!*
soñar (to dream): You dream./Dream!	*Tú sueñas./¡Sueña!*	*Vos soñás./¡Soñá!*
comer (to eat): You eat./Eat!	*Tú comes./¡Come!*	*Vos comés./¡Comé!*
poner (to put): You put./Put!	*Tú pones./¡Pon!*	*Vos ponés./¡Poné!*
admitir (to admit): You admit./Admit!	*Tú admites./¡Admite!*	*Vos admitís./¡Admití!*
venir (to come): You come./Come!	*Tú vienes./¡Ven!*	*Vos venís./¡Vení!*

bathroom	*baño*	ba·nyo
bed	*cama*	ka·ma
window	*ventana*	ven·ta·na

DIRECTIONS

Where's ...?
¿Dónde está ...? — don·de es·ta ...

What's the address?
¿Cuál es la dirección? — kwal es la dee·rek·syon

Could you please write it down?
¿Puede escribirlo, por favor? — pwe·de es·kree·beer·lo por fa·vor

Can you show me (on the map)?
¿Me lo puede indicar (en el mapa)? — me lo pwe·de een·dee·kar (en el ma·pa)

at the corner	*en la esquina*	en la es·kee·na
at the traffic lights	*en el semáforo*	en el se·ma·fo·ro
behind ...	*detrás de ...*	de·tras de ...
in front of ...	*enfrente de ...*	en·fren·te de ...
left	*izquierda*	ees·kyer·da
next to ...	*al lado de ...*	al la·do de ...
opposite ...	*frente a ...*	fren·te a ...
right	*derecha*	de·re·cha
straight ahead	*todo recto*	to·do rek·to

EATING & DRINKING

Can I see the menu, please?
¿Puedo ver el menú, por favor? — pwe·do ver el me·noo por fa·vor

What would you recommend?
¿Qué recomienda? — ke re·ko·myen·da

Do you have vegetarian food?
¿Tienen comida vegetariana? — tye·nen ko·mee·da ve·khe·ta·rya·na

I don't eat (red meat).
No como (carne roja). — no ko·mo (kar·ne ro·kha)

That was delicious!
¡Estaba buenísimo! — es·ta·ba bwe·nee·see·mo

Cheers!
¡Salud! — sa·loo

The bill, please.
La cuenta, por favor. — la kwen·ta por fa·vor

I'd like a table for ...	*Quisiera una mesa para ...*	kee·sye·ra oo·na me·sa pa·ra ...
(eight) o'clock	*las (ocho)*	las (o·cho)
(two) people	*(dos) personas*	(dos) per·so·nas

Key Words

bottle	*botella*	bo·te·ya
breakfast	*desayuno*	de·sa·yoo·no
(too) cold	*(muy) frío*	(mooy) free·o
dinner	*cena*	se·na

LANGUAGE EATING & DRINKING

fork	tenedor	te·ne·dor
glass	vaso	va·so
hot (warm)	caliente	kal·yen·te
knife	cuchillo	koo·chee·yo
lunch	comida	ko·mee·da
plate	plato	pla·to
restaurant	restaurante	res·tow·ran·te
spoon	cuchara	koo·cha·ra
appetisers	aperitivos	a·pe·ree·tee·vos
main course	segundo plato	se·goon·do pla·to
salad	ensalada	en·sa·la·da
soup	sopa	so·pa
fish	pescado	pes·ka·do
with/without	con/sin	kon/seen
fruit	fruta	froo·ta
vegetable	verdura	ver·doo·ra

Signs

Abierto	Open
Cerrado	Closed
Entrada	Entrance
Hombres/Varones	Men
Mujeres/Damas	Women
Prohibido	Prohibited
Salida	Exit
Servicios/Baños	Toilets

Meat & Fish

beef	carne de vaca	kar·ne de va·ka
chicken	pollo	po·yo
duck	pato	pa·to
lamb	cordero	kor·de·ro
pork	cerdo	ser·do
prawn	langostino	lan·gos·tee·no
salmon	salmón	sal·mon
tuna	atún	a·toon
turkey	pavo	pa·vo
veal	ternera	ter·ne·ra

Fruit & Vegetables

apple	manzana	man·sa·na
apricot	albaricoque	al·ba·ree·ko·ke
banana	plátano	pla·ta·no
beans	judías	khoo·dee·as
cabbage	col	kol
capsicum	pimiento	pee·myen·to
carrot	zanahoria	sa·na·o·rya
cherry	cereza	se·re·sa
corn	maíz	ma·ees
cucumber	pepino	pe·pee·no
grape	uvas	oo·vas
lemon	limón	lee·mon
lettuce	lechuga	le·choo·ga
mushroom	champiñón	cham·pee·nyon
nuts	nueces	nwe·ses

onion	cebolla	se·bo·ya
orange	naranja	na·ran·kha
peach	melocotón	me·lo·ko·ton
peas	guisantes	gee·san·tes
pineapple	piña	pee·nya
plum	ciruela	seer·we·la
potato	patata	pa·ta·ta
spinach	espinacas	es·pee·na·kas
strawberry	fresa	fre·sa
tomato	tomate	to·ma·te
watermelon	sandía	san·dee·a

Other

bread	pan	pan
cheese	queso	ke·so
egg	huevo	we·vo
honey	miel	myel
jam	mermelada	mer·me·la·da
oil	aceite	a·sey·te
pepper	pimienta	pee·myen·ta
rice	arroz	a·ros
salt	sal	sal
sugar	azúcar	a·soo·kar

Drinks

| beer | cerveza | ser·ve·sa |
| coffee | café | ka·fe |

Question Words

How?	¿Cómo?	ko·mo
What?	¿Qué?	ke
When?	¿Cuándo?	kwan·do
Where?	¿Dónde?	don·de
Who?	¿Quién?	kyen
Why?	¿Por qué?	por ke

(orange) juice	zumo (de naranja)	soo·mo (de na·ran·kha)
milk	leche	le·che
red wine	vino tinto	vee·no teen·to
tea	té	te
(mineral) water	agua (mineral)	a·gwa (mee·ne·ral)
white wine	vino blanco	vee·no blan·ko

EMERGENCIES

Help!	¡Socorro!	so·ko·ro
Go away!	¡Vete!	ve·te
Call ...!	¡Llame a ...!	ya·me a ...
a doctor	un médico	oon me·dee·ko
the police	la policía	la po·lee·see·a

I'm lost.
Estoy perdido/a. es·toy per·dee·do/a (m/f)
I'm ill.
Estoy enfermo/a. es·toy en·fer·mo/a (m/f)
I'm allergic to (antibiotics).
Soy alérgico/a a soy a·ler·khee·ko/a a
(los antibióticos). (los an·tee·byo·tee·kos) (m/f)
Where are the toilets?
¿Dónde están los don·de es·tan los
baños? ba·nyos t

SHOPPING & SERVICES

I'd like to buy ...
Quisiera comprar ... kee·sye·ra kom·prar ...
I'm just looking.
Sólo estoy mirando. so·lo es·toy mee·ran·do
Can I look at it?
¿Puedo verlo? pwe·do ver·lo

NICA SLANG

Here's a small selection of the huge array of Nicaraguan slang.

¡Chocho!	Wow!
¡Tuani!	Good!/Relaxed!/Cool!
bochinche	an all-in brawl
chele	white person
chunche	a small object
dominguear	to dress up
estar hasta el tronco	to be very drunk
palmado	broke, penniless
pateperro	aimless wanderer

I don't like it.
No me gusta. no me goos·ta
How much is it?
¿Cuánto cuesta? kwan·to kwes·ta
That's too expensive.
Es muy caro. es mooy ka·ro
There's a mistake in the bill.
Hay un error ai oon e·ror
en la cuenta. en la kwen·ta

ATM	cajero automático	ka·khe·ro ow·to·ma·tee·ko
internet cafe	cibercafé	see·ber·ka·fe
post office	correos	ko·re·os
tourist office	oficina de turismo	o·fee·see·na de too·rees·mo

TIME & DATES

What time is it?	¿Qué hora es?	ke o·ra es
It's (10) o'clock.	Son (las diez).	son (las dyes)
It's half past (one).	Es (la una) y media.	es (la oo·na) ee me·dya
morning	mañana	ma·nya·na
afternoon	tarde	tar·de
evening	noche	no·che
yesterday	ayer	a·yer
today	hoy	oy
tomorrow	mañana	ma·nya·na
Monday	lunes	loo·nes
Tuesday	martes	mar·tes
Wednesday	miércoles	myer·ko·les
Thursday	jueves	khwe·ves
Friday	viernes	vyer·nes
Saturday	sábado	sa·ba·do
Sunday	domingo	do·meen·go
January	enero	e·ne·ro
February	febrero	fe·bre·ro
March	marzo	mar·so
April	abril	a·breel
May	mayo	ma·yo
June	junio	khoon·yo
July	julio	khool·yo
August	agosto	a·gos·to
September	septiembre	sep·tyem·bre
October	octubre	ok·too·bre
November	noviembre	no·vyem·bre
December	diciembre	dee·syem·bre

TRANSPORT

Public Transport

boat	*barco*	*bar*·ko
bus	*autobús*	ow·to·*boos*
plane	*avión*	a·*vyon*
taxi	*taxi*	*tak*·see
train	*tren*	tren
first	*primero*	pree·*me*·ro
last	*último*	*ool*·tee·mo
next	*próximo*	*prok*·see·mo
A ... ticket, please.	*Un billete de ..., por favor.*	oon bee·*ye*·te de ... por fa·*vor*
1st-class	*primera clase*	pree·*me*·ra *kla*·se
2nd-class	*segunda clase*	se·*goon*·da *kla*·se
one-way	*ida*	*ee*·da
return	*ida y vuelta*	*ee*·da ee *vwel*·ta
bus stop	*parada de autobuses*	pa·*ra*·da de ow·to·*boo*·ses
ticket office	*taquilla*	ta·*kee*·ya
timetable	*horario*	o·*ra*·ryo
train station	*estación de trenes*	es·ta·*syon* de *tre*·nes

Does it stop at ...?
¿Para en ...?   pa·ra en ...

What stop is this?
¿Cuál es esta parada?   kwal es es·ta pa·ra·da

What time does it arrive/leave?
¿A qué hora llega/sale?   a ke o·ra ye·ga/sa·le

Please tell me when we get to ...
¿Puede avisarme   pwe·de a·vee·sar·me
cuando lleguemos a ...?   kwan·do ye·ge·mos a ...

I want to get off here.
Quiero bajarme aquí.   kye·ro ba·khar·me a·kee

Driving and Cycling

I'd like to hire a ...	*Quisiera alquilar ...*	kee·*sye*·ra al·kee·*lar* ...
bicycle	*una bicicleta*	*oo*·na bee·see·*kle*·ta
car	*un coche*	oon *ko*·che
motorcycle	*una moto*	*oo*·na *mo*·to
helmet	*casco*	*kas*·ko
mechanic	*mecánico*	me·*ka*·nee·ko
petrol/gas	*gasolina*	ga·so·*lee*·na
service station	*gasolinera*	ga·so·lee·*ne*·ra

Is this the road to ...?
¿Se va a ... por   se va a ... por
esta carretera?   es·ta ka·re·te·ra

(How long) Can I park here?
¿(Cuánto tiempo)   (kwan·to tyem·po)
Puedo aparcar aquí?   pwe·do a·par·kar a·kee

The car has broken down.
El coche se ha averiado.   el ko·che se a a·ve·rya·do

I have a flat tyre.
Tengo un pinchazo.   ten·go oon peen·cha·so

I've run out of petrol.
Me he quedado sin   me e ke·da·do seen
gasolina.   ga·so·lee·na

MISKITO PHRASES

There are more than 150,000 native speakers of Miskito scattered along the Caribbean coast. Here are a few phrases to get you started.

Hello./Goodbye.	*Naksa./Aisabi.*
Yes./No.	*Ow./Apia.*
Please./Thank you.	*Plees./Dingki pali.*
How are you?	*Nakisma?*
Good, fine.	*Pain.*
Bad, lousy.	*Saura.*
friend	*pana*
Does anyone here speak Spanish?	*Nu apo ya Ispel aisee sapa?*
My name is ...	*Yan nini ...*
What's your name?	*An maninam dia?*
Excuse me, could you help me?	*Escyus, man sipsma ilpeimonaya?*
How do I get to ...?	*Napkei sipsna gwaiya ...?*
Is it far/near?	*Nawina lihurasa/ lamarasa?*
Could you tell me where a hotel is?	*Man ailwis hotel ansara barsa?*
Do you have a bathroom?	*Baño brisma?*
Where is the bus station?	*Ansarasa buskaba takaskisa?*
What time does the bus/boat leave?	*Man nu apo dia teim bustaki/duritaki sapa?*
May I cross your property?	*Sipsna man prizcamku nueewaiya?*
Are there landmines?	*Danomite barsakei?*
Where can I change dollars?	*Ansara dalas sismonaya sipsna?*
How much is it?	*Naki preis?*
I'm a vegetarian.	*Yan wal wina kalila pias.*
I feel sick.	*Yan siknes.*

GLOSSARY

See p304 for more useful words and phrases dealing with food and dining.

alcaldía – mayor's office
arroyo – stream or gully
ave – bird

banco – bank
baño – bathroom
barco – boat
barrio – district, neighborhood
bicicleta – bicycle
bomba – gas station; short funny verse; bomb
bosque – forest

caballo – horse
cabinas – cabins
cacique – chief
calle – street
cama – bed
campesino/a – peasant; person who works in agriculture
campo – field or countryside
carretas – wooden ox carts
carretera – road or highway
cascada – waterfall
catedral – cathedral
caverna – cave
cerro – hill or mountain
chele/a – White/European, from *leche* (milk)
ciudad – city
cocina – kitchen; cooking
colectivo – buses, minivans or cars operating as shared taxis; see also *normal* and *directo*
colibrí – hummingbird
colina – hill
cooperativa – cooperative
cordillera – mountain range
córdoba – Nicaraguan unit of currency
correo – mail service
coyote – moneychanger; people smuggler
cruce – crossing
cueva – cave

dios – god
directo – direct; long-distance bus that has only a few stops

emergencia – emergency
empalme – three-way intersection
estación – station (as in ranger station or bus station); season
estero – estuary

farmacia – pharmacy
fiesta – party or festival
finca – farm or plantation
flor – flower
frontera – border

gringo/a – male/female North American or European visitor (can be affectionate or insulting, depending on the tone used)
guapote – large fish caught for sport, equivalent to rainbow bass
hacienda – a rural estate

iglesia – church
Ineter – Nicaragua Institute for Territorial Studies
Interamericana – Pan-American Hwy
Intur – Nicaraguan Institute of Tourism
isla – island

jardín – garden

laguna – lagoon
lancha – boat (usually small); see also *panga*
lapa – parrot
lavandería – laundry facility, usually offering dry-cleaning services

malecón – pier; sea wall; waterfront promenade
Marena – Nicaragua's Ministry of the Environment & Natural Resources
marimba – xylophone
mercado – market
mesa – table
mestizo – person of mixed descent, usually Spanish and Indian
migración – immigration
mirador – lookout point
mono – monkey
moto – motorcycle
muelle – dock

museo – museum

Nica – Nicaraguan, male or female
normal – long-distance bus with many stops

panga – light boat; *ruteado;* see also *lancha*
pántano – swamp or wetland
parque – park
parque central – central town square or plaza
parque nacional – national park
piropos – catcalls
piso – floor (as in 2nd floor)
pista – airstrip
playa – beach
posada – guesthouse
pueblo – village
puerto – port
pulpería – corner grocery store

rancho – thatched-roof hut
refresco – soda or bottled refreshment
refugio nacional de vida silvestre – national wildlife refuge
río – river

salto – waterfall (literally, jump)
sendero – trail; path
sierra – mountain range
soda – very Costa Rican term for a simple cafe; they're all over southern Nicaragua
supermercado – supermarket

tienda – store
típica/o – typical; particularly used to describe food (*comida típica* means 'typical cooking')
tope – dead end or T-intersection
tortuga – turtle
tucán – toucan

Unesco – UN Educational, Scientific and Cultural Organization

viajero – traveler
vivero – plant nursery
volcán – volcano

zona – zone

FOOD GLOSSARY

arroz – rice

baho – dry plantain, yucca and beef stew

camarones – shrimp
chicharrón – fried pork rinds
chile – vinegar with chilli peppers
cuajada – fresh, salty, crumbly cheese

ensalada – salad

frijoles – beans

gallo pinto – rice and beans

hamburguesa – hamburger
huevos del toro – bull testicles
huevos de paslama – turtle eggs
huevos fritos/revueltos – fried/scrambled eggs

maduros – ripe plantains served boiled or fried
mondongo – tripe soup

nacatamales – cornmeal with spices and meat

postre – dessert

raspados – shaved ice flavored with fruit juice

rundown – also *rondon;* thick Caribbean soup with coconut

quesillo – soft cheese with cream wrapped in a *tortilla*
queso – cheese

salchicha – sausage
salsa de ajillo – garlic sauce

tajadas – thin sliced green plantain fries
tortilla – cornmeal pancake
tostones – green plantains cut thick, mashed then fried

ADDRESSES

Following are some terms and abbreviations commonly used in Nicaraguan addresses.

abajo	down
arriba	up
costado	beside
entre	between
esq (esquina)	at the corner of
frente	in front of
int	inside
salida	exit
semaf semáforo	traffic lights

Behind the Scenes

SEND US YOUR FEEDBACK

We love to hear from travelers – your comments keep us on our toes and help make our books better. Our well-traveled team reads every word on what you loved or loathed about this book. Although we cannot reply individually to your submissions, we always guarantee that your feedback goes straight to the appropriate authors, in time for the next edition. Each person who sends us information is thanked in the next edition – the most useful submissions are rewarded with a selection of digital PDF chapters.

Visit **lonelyplanet.com/contact** to submit your updates and suggestions or to ask for help. Our award-winning website also features inspirational travel stories, news and discussions.

Note: We may edit, reproduce and incorporate your comments in Lonely Planet products such as guidebooks, websites and digital products, so let us know if you don't want your comments reproduced or your name acknowledged. For a copy of our privacy policy visit lonelyplanet.com/privacy.

OUR READERS

Adam Straight, Aimee Spriggs, Anna Bonven, Brooke Gallagher, Cameron Kirsch, Charles Ferrer, Charles Sullivan, Chiara Subhas, Dario Rucco, David Baril, Deni Cooperrider, Diego Moreno, Greg Kondrak, Helen Hawes, Hope Loudon, Jahaira Valle, Jane Toubin, Jean Berube, Jean-Francois Gourgues, Jeff Butler, Joelle Gaultier, John Bettinger, Joris van Empel, Juliette Giannesini, Karen Jose, Katrin Riegelnegg, Kay Harrison, Kory Marchisotto, Lexie Woodward, Liane Hartmann, Mark Dodd, Martine de Zoeten, Miranda Essink, Patti Gorman, Rich Jenkins, Rouli Plelli-Tsaltaki, Simon Walters, Wolfgang Blum, Ylva Hellerud, Zenon Lewycky

AUTHOR THANKS

Bridget Gleeson

Thank you to La Esperanza Granada for providing such a positive first impression of Nicaragua, and to all the local families I worked with there, years ago, for their kindness and patience as I learned Spanish. Thanks to the staff at Rosita's in San Juan del Sur for helping me out of a jam, and to all the travelers and Lonely Planet readers I met on the road – your advice and perspective helped me, and your enthusiasm for Nicaragua inspired me.

Alex Egerton

On the ground in Nicaragua, thanks go out to Juan Lasso, Rafi, Z, Edwin, Stijn, Floris Weebers, Rupert Allen, Marjiory, Juana Boyd, all the staff at Cuculmeca and Arjen; on the homefront, big thanks to Nicholas and Olga.

ACKNOWLEDGEMENTS

Climate map data adapted from Peel MC, Finlayson BL & McMahon TA (2007) 'Updated World Map of the Köppen-Geiger Climate Classification', *Hydrology and Earth System Sciences*, 11, 163344.

Cover photograph: Boats on San Juan harbour, San Juan del Sur. Matthew Micah Wright/Getty Images©

THIS BOOK

This 4th edition of *Nicaragua* was researched and written by Bridget Gleeson and Alex Egerton. The previous edition was written by Alex Egerton and Greg Benchwick, while the second edition was by Lucas Vidgen and Adam Skolnick. This guidebook was produced by the following:

Destination Editor Bailey Johnson

Product Editors Kate Chapman, Paul Harding, Saralinda Turner

Senior Cartographer Mark Griffiths

Assisting Cartographers Rachel Imeson, Julie Sheridan

Book Designer Mazzy Prinsep

Assisting Editors
Carly Hall, Victoria Harrison, Kellie Langdon, Ali Lemer, Jodie Martire, Anne Mulvaney

Cover Researcher Naomi Parker

Thanks to Joel Cotterell, Andi Jones, Catherine Naghten, Ellie Simpson, Tony Wheeler

Index

NOTES

Map Legend

Sights

- Beach
- Bird Sanctuary
- Buddhist
- Castle/Palace
- Christian
- Confucian
- Hindu
- Islamic
- Jain
- Jewish
- Monument
- Museum/Gallery/Historic Building
- Ruin
- Shinto
- Sikh
- Taoist
- Winery/Vineyard
- Zoo/Wildlife Sanctuary
- Other Sight

Activities, Courses & Tours

- Bodysurfing
- Diving
- Canoeing/Kayaking
- Course/Tour
- Sento Hot Baths/Onsen
- Skiing
- Snorkelling
- Surfing
- Swimming/Pool
- Walking
- Windsurfing
- Other Activity

Sleeping

- Sleeping
- Camping

Eating

- Eating

Drinking & Nightlife

- Drinking & Nightlife
- Cafe

Entertainment

- Entertainment

Shopping

- Shopping

Information

- Bank
- Embassy/Consulate
- Hospital/Medical
- Internet
- Police
- Post Office
- Telephone
- Toilet
- Tourist Information
- Other Information

Geographic

- Beach
- Gate
- Hut/Shelter
- Lighthouse
- Lookout
- Mountain/Volcano
- Oasis
- Park
- Pass
- Picnic Area
- Waterfall

Population

- Capital (National)
- Capital (State/Province)
- City/Large Town
- Town/Village

Transport

- Airport
- Border crossing
- Bus
- Cable car/Funicular
- Cycling
- Ferry
- Metro station
- Monorail
- Parking
- Petrol station
- Subway station
- Taxi
- Train station/Railway
- Tram
- Underground station
- Other Transport

Note: Not all symbols displayed above appear on the maps in this book

Routes

- Tollway
- Freeway
- Primary
- Secondary
- Tertiary
- Lane
- Unsealed road
- Road under construction
- Plaza/Mall
- Steps
- Tunnel
- Pedestrian overpass
- Walking Tour
- Walking Tour detour
- Path/Walking Trail

Boundaries

- International
- State/Province
- Disputed
- Regional/Suburb
- Marine Park
- Cliff
- Wall

Hydrography

- River, Creek
- Intermittent River
- Canal
- Water
- Dry/Salt/Intermittent Lake
- Reef

Areas

- Airport/Runway
- Beach/Desert
- Cemetery (Christian)
- Cemetery (Other)
- Glacier
- Mudflat
- Park/Forest
- Sight (Building)
- Sportsground
- Swamp/Mangrove

OUR STORY

A beat-up old car, a few dollars in the pocket and a sense of adventure. In 1972 that's all Tony and Maureen Wheeler needed for the trip of a lifetime – across Europe and Asia overland to Australia. It took several months, and at the end – broke but inspired – they sat at their kitchen table writing and stapling together their first travel guide, *Across Asia on the Cheap*. Within a week they'd sold 1500 copies. Lonely Planet was born.

Today, Lonely Planet has offices in Franklin, London, Melbourne, Oakland, Beijing and Delhi, with more than 600 staff and writers. We share Tony's belief that 'a great guidebook should do three things: inform, educate and amuse'.

OUR WRITERS

Bridget Gleeson

Managua, Masaya & Los Pueblos Blancos, Granada, Southwestern Nicaragua, León & Northwestern Nicaragua Based in Buenos Aires, Bridget is a travel writer and occasional photographer. Her first experiences in Latin America were in Nicaragua. She lived, worked, and learned to speak Spanish in Granada before moving on to South America; this assignment was a welcome opportunity to return to the place where the great adventure started. Bridget also researched the Plan Your Trip and Understand chapters.

Alex Egerton

Northern Highlands, Caribbean Coast, San Carlos, Islas Solentiname & the Río San Juan A journalist by trade, Alex has been visiting Nicaragua for more than a decade and has spent many periods based in the country while working as a travel writer in Latin America. He has explored villages from Nueva Segovia to Río San Juan, paddled through the remote rivers in the Bosawás, eaten tons of *gallo pinto* and ridden on the roof of countless chicken buses. Alex still visits Nicaragua regularly, especially the Caribbean Coast, which keeps luring him back with the simple pleasures of cold beers, warm soup and hot dancehall tunes. Alex also researched the Survival Guide chapters.

Published by Lonely Planet Global Ltd
CRN 554153
4th edition – October 2016
ISBN 978 1 78657 116 8
© Lonely Planet 2016   Photographs © as indicated 2016
10 9 8 7 6 5 4 3 2 1
Printed in China